best of
the times
magazine

*stories and imagery
from the archives of*

The TIMES Magazine
(a.k.a The Walkerville Times)
1999 – 2005

Chris Edwards   Elaine Weeks
publisher   *managing editor*

graphic designers

Vanda O'Keefe
Chuck Rees
Stephan Rohatyn

Revised Edition © *2006*

SECOND EDITION NOTES
This 2006 edition of *Best of The Times Magazine* contains several revisions and updates of stories from the first edition. There are also 11 new stories from our last ten issues (#47 - #56) and dozens of new photos and readers' letters.

On the cover
Walkerville Publishing graphic designer Chuck Rees combined selected imagery found in this book as described below:

Clockwise from Top: *British American Brewery beer truck (National Archives of Canada); Boxer Harry Marshall (courtesy Tom Marshall); Bathing beauties at the Ford City Beach docks (photo Sid Lloyd, courtesy Walter Lloyd); the Bob-Lo steamer Ste-Claire (courtesy David L. Newman); Bozo the Clown (courtesy CBC TV); Gordon McGregor, founder of Ford Canada in Walkerville (Ford Canada Archives).*

Inside front cover
Rite of summer: boys diving off the Walkerville Ferry Wayne in 1930s.
both inside cover photos Sid Lloyd, courtesy Walter Lloyd

Inside back cover
Back in the day, kids would play on the sewer pipes and swim in the Detroit River.

© Chris Edwards and Elaine Weeks, 2006

Second printing – 2006

all rights reserved

No part of this book may be reproduced in any manner without the prior written permission
of The Walkerville Publishing Company, except in the case of excerpts used in reviews and articles.

The information in this book is as accurate as possible, given that a portion of it was provided by our readers,
who were relying on their memories. We have made every effort to ensure all facts have been checked and verified.

Unit 201- 420 Devonshire Rd.
Windsor ON Canada N8Y 4T6
www.walkerville.com • www.thetimesmagazine.com • www.walkervilletimes.com
e.mail: sales@walkerville.com
519-255-9898

Printed in China

Library and Archives Canada Cataloguing in Publication

Edwards, Chris, 1956 – Best of the Times Magazine: stories and imagery from the archives
of The Times Magazine (a.k.a. the Walkerville Times) / Chris Edwards, publisher;
Elaine Weeks, managing editor. — Rev. ed. 2006

Includes bibliographical references.
ISBN 0-9781290-0-8

1. Walkerville (Windsor, Ont.) — History.
2. Windsor (Ont.) — History.
3. Essex (Ont.: County) — History. I. Weeks, Elaine, 1956 - II. Title.

FC3099.W295E49 2006   971.3'32   C2006-903883-X

Dedicated to:

Jon and Rosalie

Ange and Jack Edwards

the memory of Bert and Sheila Weeks

and the people of the Border Cities

(wherever they may be)

Chris Edwards ~ Elaine Weeks
2006

A View From South of the Border, 1929

The Detroit skyline, looking remarkably similar in 1929 as it does today, beckons with billboards and signs promoting businesses that have faded from our collective memories with the passage of time: Vernor's Sodas, Hudson's Department Store, steamer trips to Bob-Lo and Tashmoo Park. At least six passenger lake steamers are docked at the port of Detroit, including the City of Cleveland, the ill-fated Noronic, and the Tashmoo. A barge supports equipment for the construction of the Windsor-Detroit Tunnel. Most of the buildings on the Windsor side of the river are gone.

photo courtesy Windsor's Community Museum P6614

"It was the best of times...

it was the worst of times."

A Tale of Two Cities
Charles Dickens

Unemployed men of all ages gather on the steps of Old City Hall
in Windsor during the Great Depression.
photo City of Windsor archives

From an 8-page tabloid to a 408-page book

It's all a bit of a blur. One minute we're moving back to Windsor after an eight-year absence and then, before we know it, we're publishing the second edition of a book, comprised of a healthy portion of stories and photos from a magazine we developed to celebrate local history.

My head is still spinning.

Flashback to Christmas, 1998. My brother Howard suggests Chris and I start a community newspaper for the Walkerville area where we have resettled, to kick-start our publishing and advertising business.

We thought Howard's idea was sound as we were no strangers to publication design. We decided to include stories about Hiram Walker in our first issue, Walker being the founder of both Canadian Club and the town of Walkerville. When we discovered its launch would coincide with the 100th anniversary of Walker's death, the timing seemed significant.

Chris and I took turns developing story ideas and designing the paper's layout on our lone computer set up on the dining room table. I also sold 22 ads to Walkerville business owners to pay for printing and delivery of 7,500 copies to every home and business in Old and South Walkerville.

When Issue #1 of *The Walkerville Times* hit the streets in mid-March, 1999, it was an instant hit. People absolutely loved the local history aspect and immediately began suggesting ideas about other facets of Walkerville's amazing past. Plus, they began sending us stories about their own unique family histories.

The paper grew from an 8-page tabloid to a 24-page magazine format in two years. We had moved out of the dining room and into a real office just a block away and had hired staff. In mid-2002, we dropped "Walkerville" from the masthead as, due to popular demand, we had begun featuring stories about all the Border Cities: Windsor, Sandwich, Ford City, and even Detroit.

By our fifth anniversary the magazine had nearly five times the number of pages of our first issue and was regularly quenching a thirst for area history for locals, or for those who had moved away. Our subscription list now included Windsorites transplanted across North America, in England, Australia and Israel.

From the start, we held back several copies of each issue; people just discovering *The Times* were interested in purchasing back issues. When we started running out of early issues we decided to cull the best of the thousands of stories and photos published thus far and organize them into a book. And we'd call it, *Best of The Times Magazine* (naturally).

In the winter of 2004, we hired graphic designer Stephan Rohatyn on a four-month contract primarily to help with the basic layout of the book, while Chris and I, along with our other graphic designers, Vanda O'Keefe and Chuck Rees, remained busy with various other projects.

Then, for the last two months before our August 31st press deadline, the four of us devoted as much time to the book as possible as we raced toward completion. (If I hadn't been working with Chris, I would have hardly seen him for two months since he never got home before 9 p.m.!)

As the mother of two wonderful kids, (who were great during this whole process, even providing feedback on stories and photos), I've often compared producing each issue of the magazine to giving birth: painful but gratifying. Producing a 400-page book was a definite labour of love.

By early December 2005, we had sold out of the first edition of the book; we were certainly surprised and pleased with the response. Upon completion of Issue #56 of *The Times* that same month we decided to put the magazine on hiatus due to the demands of our growing publishing business. During 2005, we had published several other books; including *"Postcards From the Past"* (see page 406) and by the end of the year, we had four other book projects on the go.

Requests for *"Best of..."* kept on coming so in early 2006 we decided to release a second edition. We truly hope you enjoy our latest "baby!"

Elaine Weeks

managing editor

photo: Chris, Elaine, Jon and Rosalie return to Walkerville, 1998
H. Weeks

Editor Elaine Weeks looks over the "Crime in the City" and "Sports Heritage" sections of the first "Best of The Times" edition in Hong Kong, September 2004.
photo C. Edwards

A Big Thank You

To everyone who purchased every copy of our first edition of "Best of The Times Magazine" in one year, we will be eternally grateful. At certain times during its creation, we doubted we would ever get such a massive project into the printer's hands. Knowing our labour was worth it is extremely gratifying.

We have so many others to thank. During its seven year run, *The Times Magazine* was a magnet for people fascinated with our region's colourful past. For the first two years, Elaine and I ran the entire show. Little did we know we would become the unofficial keepers of local artifacts donated by our readers. Our filing cabinets became stuffed with clippings and photos, our shelves crammed with local history books, old newspapers and magazines. We just didn't have the time to properly track material as it came in – first as a trickle, then as a steady stream. We were very thankful when Wendy Carol Fraser, author of *Hiram Walker Remembered* and a former librarian, volunteered to help us put things into some kind of order.

Vanda O'Keefe joined us in August 2001 shortly after graduating from St. Clair College. She was responsible for the bulk of page layout duties in the magazine. Vanda also made our readers feel welcome, whether walking into the office to pick up the latest issue, or calling to correct a name or date that was misprinted. She managed subscriptions and sold items in *The Times* bookstore. Vanda's knowledge of past issues of the magazine brought many of the story layouts in the book up to snuff and she added her touch to the design and layout.

Chuck Rees, also a St. Clair grad, was hired in December 2001. Chuck works on print, Web and multimedia projects for a variety of Walkerville Publishing clients. While designing every *Times* cover from February 2002 on, he became expert at old photo restoration as well as at creating montages and graphics elements for feature stories and special sections in the magazine. Chuck designed this book's cover, the chapter sections, aided in layout, and brought new life to faded and damaged photographs.

For four months during the making of the original edition of *"Best of The Times,"* St. Clair College graduate and graphic designer Stephan Rohatyn was involved in scanning, layout and design of the book.

At Hiram Walker & Sons, archivist Art Jahns provided us with useful Walker information and images on transparency; we convinced him to write some pieces for us. Dan Tullio and Tish Harcus of Walker's were also big supporters.

David L. Newman's collection of local memorabilia is astonishing, particularly, his devotion to all things related to the Ambassador Bridge and Bob-Lo Amusement Park. David's postcard collection may be the most in-depth set of local images in existence and with his permission, we've reproduced several in this book. (Following the printing of the first *"Best of The Times,"* David partnered with us in the creation of the engaging *Postcards from the Past: The Border Cities. (see page 407)*

Tim Baxter's huge postcard collection may be the second best set in the region. Tim's cards helped us fill in some gaps.

Ralph Howling, a pilot and a big fan of local aviation history, kindly provided us with access to his collection of photos and he was the first to share the book, *Walkerville-1898* with us.

Windsor's Community Museum also supplied us with historical images and its staff helped us corroborate or find information. Special thanks to Madelyn Della Valle.

Two brothers, Terry and Bill Marentette, were big fans of *The Times* from the start; Bill's collection of local, regional and national beer memorabilia is legendary. He also supplied us with numerous images, and eventually, he too penned some stories for us. Terry is never without news concerning goings-on in Walkerville – some of it is even true!

Local authors who have written books on this region's history should also take a bow. Marty Gervais' legendary work, "The Rumrunners," (we love its narrative style), may be back in print some day. Carl Morgan and Herb Colling wrote the definitive tome of Windsor's glorious automotive history, *Pioneering the Auto Age*. No local book collection should be without either of these two fine publications. Several of their stories appear here.

Walkervillian Al Roach wrote two books, *"All Our Memories, Volume 1 and 2."* His musings about the early days of Walkerville are fun to read and we have reprinted several pieces here. Sadly, Al passed away before the first edition was released, but he was well represented at the first book launch by members of his large family.

Other regular contributors whose work appears in these pages include local author Stan Scislowski (whose antics could not possibly be made up), Tom Paré, Richard Lindell, local historians Trevor Price and Larry Kulisek, writers Bonnie Hazen-Nelson, Walt McCall, Mickey Moulder, Andrew Lochhead, Shelley Divinich Haggert, Hester Curtis, and illustrator Pat Kelly.

Jeff Mingay co-authored *100 Hundred Years – A History of Essex Golf and Country Club: 1902-2002* with Dick Carr, a book we also published, and two pieces from that work appear here. Jeff helped proofread the massive *It All Began in Walkerville* section.

Sherrill Tucker knows the "westend" and has been a big supporter since Day 1. Some of her articles, penned as *The Westender*, appear on the following pages.

Renka Gesing has written numerous pieces for us, and her work can be found in the *My Old House* section. She has also been "co-mom" for Elaine, helping her juggle child care after school and on P.A. days.

Laryssa Landale spent many hours proofing and correcting copy for us; her work in this regard has been much appreciated. She also authored some of the stories that appear in this book.

Bob Jones was one the first to knock on our door with his scrapbook of Walker memorabilia. His notes helped us in our early efforts to "connect the dots" in order to make sense of a place called Walkerville.

Phil and Mickey Chauvin's grandfather, Francis X. Chauvin, was commissioned in 1927 to research a book on the history of Walkerville and the Walker family that remains unpublished. The Chauvins loaned us a copy of his manuscript, *Hiram Walker – His Life, His Work and The Development of Walker Institutions in Walkerville, Ontario*. Someday we'd like to publish this work, as it is fascinating read.

Supported by readers, friends, family, advertisers, and various high-tech gadgets.

Charlie Fox knows Walkerville; being from the "old school" he was able to provide us with many photos and tidbits about this model town on the banks of the Detroit River. I don't think he has forgiven us for removing "Walkerville" from our masthead! (In fact, for many of our readers, we will forever remain *The Walkerville Times*).

We'd also like to acknowledge support from historical groups, including the Essex Historical Society, HEIRS and WACAC.

There are many others to thank: Walter Lloyd, Walter McGregor, Dick Carr, Peter Rindlisbacher, Nancy Morand, Ed Agnew, Jim Scorgie, George White, Neil McPhee, Lowell Boileau, Andrew Foot, Larry Burchell at the Old Vic, Charlotte Watkins, Dr. Tom Robson, David Wharton, Phil Hernandez, George Brooks, Lowell Boileau, Cathy Nantais, and of course, Camilla Stodgell Wigle, (who turned 104 years young in 2005, and is a font of information on the early days of Walkerville and Ford City).

And a big thank you to all the people from the Border Cities, and points beyond, who sent us letters (yes, some folks still know how to write letters – we have hundreds on file to prove it!), e.mails, photos, memorabilia and memories of life and times in this region. We couldn't possibly re-publish them all, but we have included a fine cross-section of correspondences throughout this book.

Our subscribers were our most devoted readers and we are eternally grateful for their tremendous interest and support. To our advertisers, thanks for coming along for the ride. We couldn't possibly have done all this without you! (Wayne Strong, owner of Ye Olde Walkerville Bed & Breakfast, advertised in all 56 issues.) We also must thank the numerous Legacy Sponsors (whose stories appear in the back of the book) who helped make this book possible through their generous financial support.

I'd also like to acknowledge our families. Elaine and I both come from rather large clans, and family members, including in-laws, were always available to lend an ear. This list includes my parents, Jack and Ange, brother Mike and his wife Jaquie, sister Jan and husband Wayne Dean, sister Maggie and husband Larry Hugg, sister Paulah and husband Ralf Dauns, and sister Maureen Paul.

The Weeks clan has also been strong supporters of The TIMES. We feel that Albert "Bert" Weeks is looking down on us, providing spiritual guidance (and fiscal responsibility!) to the business. Interestingly, Bert made a valiant attempt to launch his own publication in the mid-1960s. Other Weeks family members who provided support include Barb and Harry Moluchi, Carol and Bill Chedour, Howard Weeks, who suggested the idea for *The Walkerville Times*, Brenda and Chris Clarke, and Douglas Weeks.

A few words about the role technology has played in this business are in order. I began working with Apple Macintosh computers in 1985, at the dawn of what was then called "desktop publishing." I realized this new technology would de-centralize publishing and free it from the hands of the information "power brokers" – giant media conglomerates. Today, almost anyone with a computer, scanner, digital camera and a printer can be a "publisher." Thank you Steve Jobs, founder of Apple Computer, for having the vision to break the mold.

The next technological wave that impacted our business was the advent of the Internet and digital photography. When we launched *The Walkerville Times* we'd shoot photos with our trusty 35mm camera, then run to a 1-hour photo processing lab and wait for the results – very nervewracking at deadline. I'll never forget when our film was trapped inside a processor that had broken down – at the 11th hour! Our first digital camera cost over $1,000, but saved so much time and money it quickly paid for itself; similar cameras now cost under $50!

The Internet provided the opportunity to work until the last possible moment. We built pages on our computer and when they were done, we popped them over to our printer via the Internet; no more couriers or discs to worry about. This completely changed the way we did our business, not to mention how we conducted research.

Our main website, *walkervilletimes.com* continues to evolve. From April 2002 to August 2006, it measured over half a million page views and connected former Walkervillians from all corners of the planet. It now serves as a repository for our archives and receives more than 1,000 visitors a day.

E.mail has also been a great benefit to our business; photos and letters (already typed – what a time saver!) arrive from all over the world and it certainly is a handy way to send ad proofs to clients.

We have certainly come a long way from the days of moveable type. (The irony of using the latest technology to produce a publication that celebrates the past is definitely not lost on us!)

No doubt we have forgotten people. We apologize; consider this not an error of omission, but of commission. There have, quite frankly, been so many of you crossing our paths in the past seven years, we couldn't possibly keep track of you all!

And for those of you who don't see your contribution in this book, we really wanted to include it, we just ran out space – and time!

publisher

Windsor at the Crossroads of History

Windsor, from its earliest days, has been a crossroads where land and water routes joined, linking people and trade from across North America and beyond. Through canoes and footpaths, sailing ships and wagons... to the rail corridors, shipping, air travel, trucking and superhighways of today, transport has made Windsor the busiest border crossing in the country. It is a community that thrives on reaching out to the world to trade ideas and skills, raw materials and manufactured goods. Transport led to trading, and trading laid the basis for manufacturing. Windsor's geographic advantages have made it an ideal place to bring in raw materials, apply skilled labour and export fine goods to the world.

From the beginning, our community has attracted entrepreneurs and skilled workers. First Nations people came here to meet and trade. French and British colonists sought furs and lumber, and established farms and mills to supply their growing empires. As our Canadian nation matured, entrepreneurs established salt mines, a major distillery and automobile plants, attracting people who built new lives and a dynamic, colourful city.

Windsor's growth has never been problem-free. Our people have endured wars, economic recessions, fierce competition and obstructions to trade. We have felt the political, economic and personal impacts of grave international crises, and yet we persist in finding better ways to live together and prosper as a community.

Today, Windsor offers a diversity of people, skills, activities and cultures far beyond most communities of its size. Windsorites are engaged not only in long-standing occupations but in high-tech manufacture, communications and information, research and development, tourism, and many different trades and professions. We speak many languages and follow various customs. We have developed public art, theatres, museums, an art gallery and libraries, and have fostered many other forms of cultural expression. Our parks and public spaces are the envy of our neighbours. Our restaurants, nightclubs, casino, racetrack and sports facilities attract large numbers of visitors. We remain diverse and yet we have in common a strong pride in our community and a determination to reach out to the world.

I am very pleased that *Walkerville Publishing* chose to tell the story of our strong, persistent and ingenious community. The first printing of this book was sold out within a year – testament to the fact that so many people find our story as fascinating and inspiring as I do.

Sincerely,

Eddie Francis
Mayor of Windsor

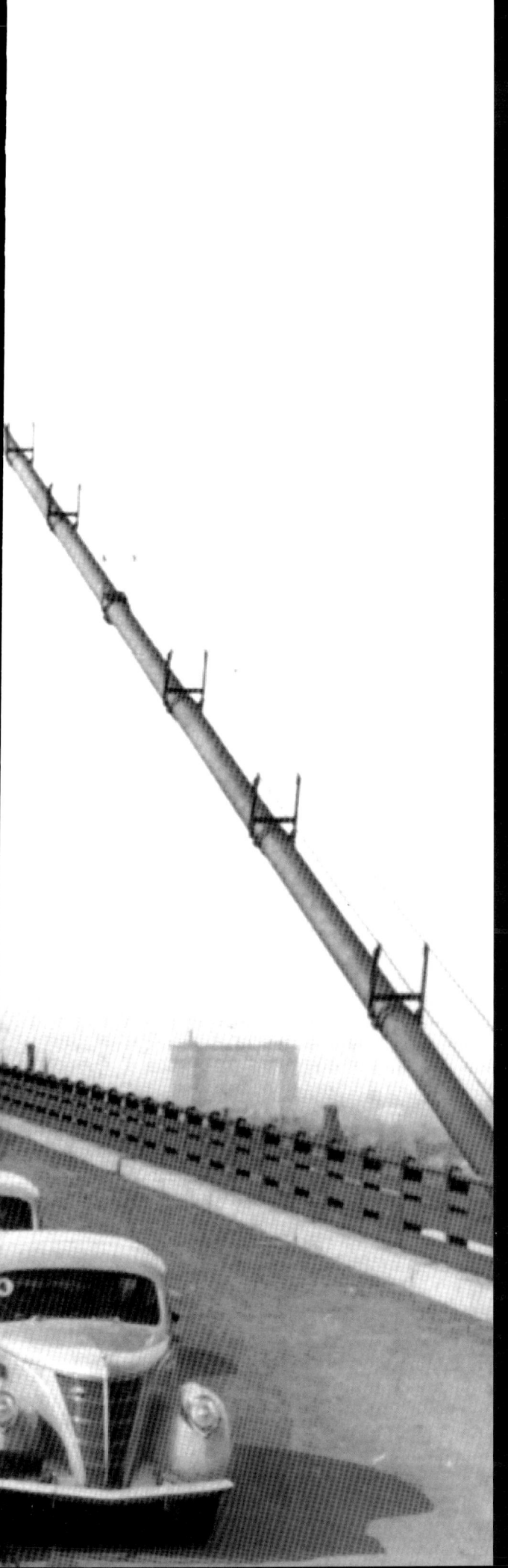

contents

19   It All Began in Walkerville

84   On the Border

130 Birth of the Auto

168 Crime in the City

206 The Mysterious and Disastrous

226 My Old House

246 Places We Remember

288 Black History

302 Sports Heritage

320 School Daze

338 Why We Must Remember

369 Paintings and Postcards from the Past

385 Cover Story

394 Legacy Profiles

contents

1 It All Began in Walkerville
Hiram Who?	20
Walkerville: 1700-1882	22
Boom Town: Walkerville 1882- 1898	24
Walkerville Snapshot: 1913	25
How Walker's Club Became Canadian	27
Hiram Walker's Whisky Palace	31
The Legend of Albert Kahn	33
Albert Kahn's Crown Jewel: Willistead Manor	36
The Walkerville Theatre: Design by C. Howard Crane	37
St. Mary's Church: Hiram Walker's Spiritual Legacy	38
Queen Victoria Jubilee Fountain	39
The Walker Farms : "The Finest in Canada"	40
Walker Airport: When Windsor Got Its Wings	43
NEW: Saving The Lanc	48
Monmouth Road Row Houses	49
Walkerville's First Apartment House	52
The Crown Inn	52
The Walkerville Exchange a.k.a "The Vic"	53
The Walkerville and Detroit Ferry Co.	54
The L.E.E. & D.R.R.: Walker's Train Station	56
Hiram Walker's Influence on Harrow and Area	57
Give Me a Dollar To Spend	58
The Alleys of Our Youth	59
Of Boys and a Bridge	60
A Remarkable Life	61
Dish Nights at the Tivoli	63
Letters from Margaret	64
The View From Grandma's Window	66
FLASHBACKS Readers' Memories of Walkerville	68
Walkerville Photo Gallery	73

2 On the Border
A City is Born: Windsor: May 24, 1892	85
NEW: Lost Beaches of the Border Cities	88
NEW: Let's Go to the Drive-In	91
Well Hung: A Brief History of the Art Gallery of Windsor	94
The Dawn of Local TV	97
Windsor's Community Museum: The François Baby Residence	101
The Eight Day Mayor	103
Once Upon a Brewery	106
And they're off!	111
So You Think This Is Cold?	113
Saving Patti	114
Breaking the Ice	115
Sunday in Detroit	116
A Christmas Story: 1942	117

A Christmas Quite Unlike All Others: 1932	119
NEW: Wednesday Was Mending Day	120
Remembering Sid Lloyd – Photographer Extraordinaire	122
On The Border Photo Gallery	124

3 Birth of the Auto
Henry & The McGregors	131
Portrait of Ford City	133
Trolley Clang, Clang Rings No More	136
Ford Strike of '45	137
Racing Into History	141
The Dodge Brothers	147
The First "Modern" Automobile	149
The Chrysler-Windsor Connection	150
From Cows to Cars: General Motors in Walkerville	152
Birthplace of the Modern Firetruck	154
The Ghost of Seagrave	155
The Lincoln Toy Factory	157
For Many Upstarts, the Road was Short, Rough and....	159
In Good Company: A Salute to Windsor's Tool & Die Industry	161
15 Minutes of Fame: The Ford Family of Riverside	165

4 Crime in the City
Detroit – Prohibition Trial Run	169
Windsor Went Wild in the Roaring Twenties	170
The Roadhouses	173
Mobsters, Mayhem & Murder	175
Kidnapped by Rumrunners	178
King Canada	186
Breakfast with Marty	188
The End of this Story?	191
The Legacy of the 1943 Detroit Riots	192
Recollections: Life During the 1967 Detroit Riots	194
NEW: Portrait of a Scandal	198
The Great Bank Robbery of '59	202
NEW: The Slasher	204

5 Mysterious and Disastrous
The Curse of Peche Isle	207
Explosion Shattered Essex in 1907	211
Executions in Sandwich: 1809-1909	214
Tornado! 1946	216
NEW: Windsor Twice Engulfed in Flames	217
Last One Over!	218
Local Bed & Breakfast Serves Up the Occasional Ghost	220
Ghosts of Our Highways	222
The Ghost of Colonel Bishop School	224
Does Elizabeth Haunt the Duff-Baby House?	225

6 My Old House

The Crassweller Home	227
Treble-Large House	228
Charles McLerie House	230
Solomon Wigle House	232
The Yellow Brick Question	234
NEW: The John Wesley McConnell House	237
The Amedee Marentette House	238
The Griggs House	240
The Cobbles	241
1136 Devonshire Road	241
NEW: The Davis H. McCay House	242
NEW: Foxley	244

7 Places We Remember

Long Live Bob-Lo!	247
To the Mettawas!	250
The Old CPR Station	253
The Chilver Family of Walkerville	254
Angus Mackintosh: Ruler of Moy Hall	256
Memories of St. Joe's	258
Cleary's First Auditorium	260
Dominion House (Tavern), c. 1878	261
Aboard The Aquarama	263
The Lansdowne: Last Paddle Wheeler on the Great Lakes	265
The Junction: Birthplace of Windsor & Area's Transit System	266
Hudson's North Pole	268
Last Roar at "The Corner"	270
Places Photo Gallery	272
The Lost Resort	287

8 Black History

The Underground Railroad	289
The Legacy of John Freeman Walls	290
The Real McCoy – Born in Colchester, Ont.	291
First Black Lawyer in Canada	293
Street Named for Slave Descendant	294
Still a Watkins on Watkins Street	295
Sandwich First Baptist Church	296
Local Racism in the 1950s	298
NEW: Black Cemeteries a Mystery	300
Mary Ann Shadd: Founder of Provincial Freeman	301

9 Sports Heritage

Reno Bertoia: Tiger by Day, Student by Night	303
The Walkerville Chicks: Baseball in the 20s	304
Olympian Ian Allison: The "Major"	305
Harry Marshall: Windsor Boxer	306
Don Parsons: One Man Basketball Team	307
Ernestine Russell: Canada's First Female Olympic Gymnast	308
Roseland Park Country Club	309
100 Years of Golf at Essex	313
Sports Photo Gallery	318

10 School Daze

School Days - 1907	321
Walkerville Collegiate Institute: Home of the Tartans	322
NEW: The Bare Naked Truth	324
Edith Cavell School: From Learning to Living	328
The Sock Hop - October 1960	330
The Mad Chemist	331
Lowe Tech: Knuckle Sandwiches and Scoffed Textbooks	332
School Photo Gallery	333

11 Why We Must Remember

Forever Young	339
I Crash Landed on Sable Island	340
The Taking of Xanten: Turning Point of WWII	342
A Family Affair	344
The War Bride	346
From Windsor to Korea	347
Searching for Subs on the Detroit River	351
Too Young To Die	352
When The Sky Was Falling	353
We Took Our Harbours With Us	354
Ross Mingay: M.I.A. – Presumed Dead	356
Churchill to Mackenzie King: "What About Your Women?"	357
Safe Haven	359
Reflections of a Blitzkrieg Kid	360
A British Child Guest Remembers	363
Saviours of Ceylon	364
Turning in My Tin Helmet	366
Walkerville Landmark Bombed!	368

12 Paintings and Postcards from the Past   369

13 Cover Story   385

14 Legacy Profiles   394

Resources

A Walking Tour of Historic Sandwich, 2002
A Walking Tour of Victoria Avenue, 2000
A Walking Tour of Walkerville Ontario, 1997
Windsor Architectural Conservation Advisory Committee

AIA Detroit: The American Institute of Architects Guide to
Detroit Architecture, by Eric J. Hill, FAIA and John Gallagher,
Wayne State University Press, 2003

Albert Kahn: Builder of Detroit,
by Roger Matuz, Wayne State University Press, 2002

All Our Memories 1 & II,
by Al Roach, Herald Press Limited 1981-1982

A Mansion on the Detroit Frontier: The Duff Baby Story – a bicentennial
celebration, by Elizabeth Burrell & Evelyn G. McLean, Les Amis Duff - 1998

Bob-Lo: A Tiny Canadian Island,
edited by Jack Creed, B.A., F.R.O.B., Herald Press Limited, 1987

Border City Sketches: A Walk Through the Thirties,
by Corky Deir Rawson, 1991

Central High School – 1930, The Crier Yearbook, Herald Press Limited, 1930

Detroit in Its World Setting: A Three Hundred Year Chronology, 1701-2001,
edited by David Lee Poremba, Wayne State University Press, 2001

Detroit Then and Now, by Cheri Y. Gay, PRC Publishing Ltd., 2001

Dreamland: America at the Dawn of the Twentieth Century,
by Michael Lesy, The New Press, 1997

Duty Nobly Done – The Official History of the Essex and Kent Scottish
Regiment, by Sandy Antal and Kevin R. Shackleton, Walkerville Publishing
Inc., 2006.

Essex County Sketches, Essex County (Ontario) Tourist Association, Herald
Press Limited, first printing 1947, 2nd, 1974 and 3rd, 1985

Ford City Mural Guide,
Ford City Greater Drouillard Revitalization and City of Windsor

Garden Gateway to Canada: One Hundred Years of Windsor and Essex
County 1854-1954, by Neil F. Morrison, M.A., PH.D., Herald Press Limited,
reprint 1982

Harrow and Colchester South 1792-1992, Harrow Early Immigrant Research
Society (HEIRS), Harrow History Book Committee, 1993

Hiram Walker Remembered,
Wendy Carol Fraser. Forest Press, 1992

Images of America Detroit's Michigan Central Station,
Kelli B. Kavanaugh, Arcadia Publishing, 2001-2002

Into the New Millennium – All Saints' Anglican Church, 1852-2002,
Joanne & Conrad Reitz, All Saints' Anglican Church, 2002

Kingsville 1790-2000: A Stroll Through Time, Volume 1 & 2,
Kingsville-Gosfield Heritage Society, 2003

Lake Erie: A Pictorial History,
Julie Macfie Sobol & Ken Sobol, Boston Mills Press, 2004

Mansion to Museum: The François Baby House and its Times,
R. Alan Douglas, Occasional Paper No. 5, Essex County Historical Society, 1989

Not All of Us Were Brave,
Stanley Scislowski, Dundurn Press, 1997

One Hundred Years, A History of Essex Golf & Country Club: 1902-2002,
Jeff Mingay with Richard H. Carr, Walkerville Publishing, 2002

Picture Windsor: A Photo Essay
Spike Bell M.P.A., Profile Publishing Corp., 1989

Pioneering The Auto Age,
Herb Colling with Carl Morgan, TraveLife Publishing Enterprises, 1993

Postcard History Series: Detroit A Postcard History,
Richard Bak, Arcadia Publishing, 1999-2002

Postcards from the Past – Windsor & The Border Cities, David L. Newman,
with Chris Edwards and Elaine Weeks, Walkerville Publishing, 2005.

Rum Running and the Roaring Twenties: Prohibition on the Michigan-
Ontario Waterways, Philip P. Mason, Wayne State University Press, 1995

Sketching Rambles in Ontario Volume two,
George P. Rickard, George Rickard Studio, 1981

Sixty Golden Years: 1915-1975 The Story of Motoring in Ontario,
Ontario Motor League - Nickel Belt Club, 1975

Souvenir Programme: Official Opening Walker Airport,
The Border Cities Star, Sims Publications, 2003

The American Auto Factory,
Byron Olsen and Joseph Cabadas, MBI Publishing Company, 2002

The Blue & White, Walkerville Collegiate 1928, 129, 1946, 1972 & 1973
Yearbooks, Herald Press Limited

The Last of the Magic: Short Stories, Poems and Essays Then and Now,
Corky Deir Rawson, 1992

The Olympians Among Us: Celebrating a Century of Excellence,
Tony Techko and Carl Morgan, TraveLife Publishing Enterprises, 1995

The Purple Gang: Organized Crime in Detroit 1910-1945,
Paul R. Kavieff, Barricade Books Inc., 2001

The Ford Century: Ford Motor Company and the Innovations that Shaped
the World, Russ Banham, Artisan Press, 2002

The Rumrunners: A Prohibition Scrapbook,
G.H. (Marty) Gervais, Firefly Books Ltd., 1980 (reprint 2005)

The Story of Canadian Whisky,
Lorraine Brown, The Seagram Museum, 1994

The Three Rs of Essex: Riches, Rags, Recovery,
Evelyn Couch Burns, 1979

The Township of Sandwich Past and Present,
Fredrick Neal, The Essex County Historical Association and The Windsor
Public Library Board, reprint 1979

The Violent Years: Prohibition and the Detroit Mobs,
Paul R. Kavieff, Barricade Books Inc., 2001

The Western District; Papers from the Western District Conference,
edited by K.G. Pryke and L.L. Kulisek, Essex County Historical Society and
The Western District Council, 1983

The Windsor Border Region: Canada's Southernmost Frontier, edited by Ernest
J. Lajeunesse, C.S.B., The Essex County Historical Association, 1971-1972

This Is Detroit: 1701-2001,
M. Woodford, Wayne State University Press, 2001

Turning Points: The Detroit Riot of 1967, A Canadian Perspective,
Herb Colling, Natural Heritage/ Natural History Inc., 2003

We are the Champions: Canadian Championships Sports Teams Windsor,
Ontario, Windsor Essex County Sports Hall of Fame, Great Lakes Printing

Windsor 1892-1992 A Centennial Celebration,
Trevor Price and Larry Kulisek, Chamber Publications, 1992

Windsor: 1913, including Walkerville, Ford, Sandwich and Ojibway
The Evening Record, The Record Printing Co. Limited, 1913

Windsor: Photographic Art. Spike Bell M.P.A., 1998

On the Web

Note: Websites come and go, but these sites hopefully will stand the test of time.

Windsor Public Library – online history
www.windsorpubliclibrary.com

Photographs from the Detroit Publishing Company: 1880-1920
(U.S. Library of Congress)
lcweb2.loc.gov/ammem/detroit/dethome.html

Detroit Publishing Company at The Henry Ford Museum
www.hfmgv.org/exhibits/dpc/default.asp

Detroit News: Rearview Mirror (Yesterday's news from its archives)
info.detnews.com/history

The Fabulous Ruins of Detroit
detroityes.com/home.htm

The Bob-Lo Boats
www.bobloboat.com

Pere Marquette Historical Society
www.pmhistsoc.org/index.html

Rusted Chrome: A Tribute to Detroit Rock and Roll
home.att.net/~s.m.geer/home.htm

International Metropolis
www.internationalmetropolis.com

The Purple Gang
www.crimelibrary.com/gangsters/purple/purplemain.htm

The Coaster Enthusiasts of Canada
www.CEC.chebucto.org/ClosPark//Lagoon.html

1
It All Began in Walkerville

Hiram Walker: Portrait of a Visionary
photo from the Walker Family Collection, Boston MA

Walkerville Timeline

Founding Father, Patriarch, Benevolent Dictator. Hiram Walker was a fascinating man whose vision shaped an industry and a model town. Born in East Douglas, Massachusetts in 1816, Walker moved to Detroit, Michigan in the 1830's.

1856

Hiram Walker purchased 468 acres of land east of Windsor, Ontario, Canada, (pop: 1,000), across the river from Detroit and relocates his Detroit whisky operation. He favoured its the lax liquor laws and easy access to an expanding Victorian British Empire on the Canadian side of the border.

1858

Walker's invested $40,000 to build a flour mill, a distillery and a hog farm opposite the bustling city of Detroit on lands once settled by the Ottawa Indians and the great chief Pontiac.

the visionary

Walker's empire in 1880, as sketched from a hot air balloon, includes a feed mill and drying elevator, a ferry operation, a grain elevator, several warehouses, and a growing community, Walkerville. The unincorporated village consists of four streets extending north and south, and five running east and west. From Fifth Street (Walker Road) west to east are Fourth, Third, Second and First Streets (Monmouth, Argyle, Devonshire, Kildare). photo: Hiram Walker & Sons archives

Hiram Who?   by Elaine Weeks, Issue #1, March 1999

"Perhaps some would like to know something of my childhood? I was born a pauper. I was taken in by friends, kind and generous friends. Later, I was sent to schools and I worked on the farm. I was also taught the value of a penny, not to cast it to the wind. The young men of the present do not know the value of money. I hardly had time, as a young man, to go fishing, for I was always working. My habit, in my younger days of saving the pennies, has placed me where I am today."
Hiram Walker, speaking on his 74th birthday

In 1899, the man who put the club into Canadian and the Walker into ville, lapsed into a coma and died. Other than driving past his former enterprise, still going strong on Riverside Drive, or sniffing that unmistakable aroma of fermenting hops and yeast as we open our front doors and windows, few of us in the border cities think much about Hiram Walker. Which is a shame since there was much more to the man than just whisky.

Born in New England on the fourth of July in 1816, Hiram Walker headed "west" to Michigan in the 1830's to seek his fortune. After a few false starts, he launched a successful grocery business in Detroit, then learned how to distil his own cider vinegar instead of selling someone else's for a minuscule profit. Walker then decided to branch out into whisky. His first barrels were produced in 1854 and were popular due to their fine quality and purity.

Finally reaping some rewards after years of hard work, Walker naturally became concerned by Michigan's strong puritanical temperance atmosphere. Aware of the good farmland being opened up by the Great Western Railway on the Canadian side of the river, he trained his eye across the water to the fledgling community recently named Windsor.

In 1856, Walker purchased a French farm lot one and a half miles upriver from Windsor in East Sandwich from Eugene Hall for 300 pounds. Soon thereafter, he purchased another track of land, giving him ownership of land between what is now Kildare and Walker Roads and inland to Wyandotte Street.

Walker cleared trees for his operation and in addition to building a whisky distillery along the waterfront, he grew and bought grain, milled flour and raised hogs and cattle fattened with left over mash from his distillery. And, he began building houses to lease to his employees.

20 • it all began in walkerville

In his day, distillers sold their products in unmarked barrels, but Hiram Walker set a precedent by putting his product in bottles that bore his name: Walker's Club Whisky. This product was a hit and became the first Canadian brand of whisky to be marketed around the world. According to legend, success in the States prompted U.S. competitors to lobby Congress to force Hiram Walker to add the word "Canadian" to the name.

Walker envisioned a "model town" that would be the envy of not only the region, but of the continent. As he grew more successful, Walker purchased more land, built more homes for his employees, and even established and provided free public utilities. He built the first St. Mary's Anglican Church on Sandwich Street in memory of his wife, Mary Abigail, who died in 1870. And, he campaigned for good schools, which he supported generously.

Tired of the long journey between his offices in Walkerville and his home in Detroit, Walker had his own ferry system built in 1881. Then, the next year, he built a short railway to connect his new farm in the interior of Essex County. By 1898, the railway went as far as Kingsville, transforming Walkerville from a small village adjacent to Windsor into an important town.

By 1895, Walker nearly employed his town's entire population of 600 souls in some capacity. Workmen were offered a lease to a Walker cottage. If they declined, they would likely be denied employment!

Hiram Walker bottling line: 1890s. photo: Hiram Walker & Sons archives

Walker refused to sell the land or the company-built cottages. Consequently, he was able to control the type of individual that would live in the village. Ronald Hoskins, in his Master's Thesis for the University of Windsor on the *Life and Times of Hiram Walker,* (1964) wrote:

"As town patriarch, (Walker) always envisioned Walkerville as a progressive, self-sustaining, model town, a separate, exclusive entity whose well being would rest on a strong industrial basis. He endeavoured to foster a strong civic spirit, efficiency, and a unique relationship between himself and the townspeople, that of working together toward a common end – a flourishing Walkerville."

The town of Walkerville was incorporated in 1890, partly to prevent amalgamation with Windsor – something Walker was dead set against. Walker provided fire and police protection, street lighting, well-paved and drained streets, and running water. Walkerville was a model community unparalleled in Ontario, with a high standard of urban planning, designed by the finest architects of the day.

When Walker decided to expand his railway to transport produce from his farms in South Essex directly to the distillery and cattle barns at what is now the junction of Tecumseh and Walker Roads, he didn't take no for an answer.

Hoskins wrote: "Walker reigned undisputed monarch of all under his surveillance. If he cherished a railway, he would have it, if humanly possible. As in his other endeavours, he would tolerate no interference from other sources, but would accept nothing less than complete control over the enterprise."

Hiram Walker's enterprises were so profitable, he was able to provide capital for the development and growth of many other new firms, including the Walkerville Wagon Works, which later became the Ford Automotive Plant.

1865

Walker's operation continues to expand; he announces he will "brand" his whisky. In his day, distillers sold their products in unmarked barrels, but Hiram Walker set a precedent by putting his product in bottles that bore his name: Walker's Club Whisky. "We will make a fine whisky and we do not wish it to be confused with inferior products. We will also brand each barrel, so that discriminating patrons... can trust its quality."

1870

In only 12 years, Hiram Walker's becomes the biggest operation of its kind in the new Confederation of Canada.

1875

Hiram Walker provides amenities – lacking in many larger urban centres – for the people of Walkerville, including street lights, well-paved and drained streets, a water pumping station, running water, a police force and a fire department – all at his expense.

best of the times • 21

1880

For twenty-one years, Hiram Walker commuted from his home in Detroit through Windsor to Walkerville. Tired of this often arduous and time consuming journey, he leased the ferry Essex, built docking facilities at the distillery and on his property at the foot of Walker Street in Detroit. Thus began the Walkerville and Detroit Ferry Company, which continued to operate until 1942.

1880

According to Walker archivist Art Jahns, a myth was perpetuated that U.S. distillers feared "Walker's Club" whisky's growing popularity, and petitioned Washington for legislation requiring imports to designate their country of origin, hoping to limit Club's growth; Walker complies and "Canadian Club" is born.

1890

Hoping to expand his model community, Hiram Walker strives to keep Walkerville a separate entity and succeeds in incorporating it as a town, partly to prevent amalgamation with Windsor. Walkerville soon becomes the envy of the Border Cities, and widely regarded as one of the finest communities in North America.

Riverside Drive at Devonshire Road, 1890. photo: Hiram Walker & Sons archives

Walkerville: 1700-1882

by Elaine Weeks, Issue #3, May/June 1999

A small village, situated on the riverside, about a mile above Windsor. It contains a distillery, carried on by Hiram Walker and Company, a hotel store, etc... and several tenements built by Walker and Co. for the convenience of their employees, which number from eighty to one hundred.
From the County of Essex Gazetteer and General and Business Directory for 1866 – 67 (Woddstock: Sutherland and Company, 1867)

Long before Hiram Walker made the first of his many land purchases, the inhabitants of the area that became Walkerville were Indians of the Ottawa tribe under Pontiac. In 1763, after failing to dislodge the British from Fort Detroit, Pontiac, the Chief of all the Ottawas, apportioned several land grants on the southern shore of the Detroit River to the French and English.

Pontiac transferred land to Lieutenant Edward Abbott of the Royal Artillery Regiment in 1765, and to Alexis Maisonville. This constituted the entire territory of the future town of Walkerville. In 1769, Abbott transferred this land to Antoine Louis Labadie who deeded his land to his wife and nine surviving heirs. One daughter, Phyllis, married John Hall, and their son Eugene Hall received his mother's ninth share after her death.

On December 22nd, 1856, Hall sold this portion of land to future whisky baron Hiram Walker, who was based in Detroit but was ready to establish himself on the Canadian side of the border. Walker favoured this location, with its close proximity to the Great Western Railway, which increased market access into the British Empire.

In 1857, Walker obtained additional parcels of land from C.F. Labadie and from grantors John Montreuil and Alexander Chapoton, bringing his land holdings in Canada to 468 acres.

Hiram Walker began clearing land along the riverfront to make room for his distillery, a flour mill, and areas to hold hogs, which he sold to France and England after fattening them up with mash left over from the distillery. Walker began building homes for his employees and, in 1858, "Walkerton" was born. In the 1860s, the names

Walkerville and Walker's Town were both used by the inhabitants of this hamlet. On March 1st, 1869, the name Walkerville was officially sanctioned by Ottawa and the settlement was recognized as a post office village.

In 1870, Walker established a church with a day-school in the basement for his employees. By the winter of 1875, Walkerville was illuminated by street lights erected at Walker's expense; he also built a water system, a pumping station and a fire department.

By 1884, the unincorporated village of Walkerville consisted of four streets extending north and south, and five running east and west. Presumably the first street to be laid out was Walker Road, or Fifth Street, about 1860. Running west of Walker Road were Fourth, Third and Second Streets (Monmouth, Argyle, and Devonshire). The east-west streets were Sandwich (Riverside), on the riverfront, with Assumption, Brant, Wyandotte and Tuscarora Streets running parallel, south of Sandwich Street.

The distillery buildings were situated on the riverbank between the main street (Sandwich) and the river. These buildings included the feed mill and drying elevator, a ferry house (1884), barber shop, the grain elevator and malthouse, the Walker residence and driving shed, various warehouses, waterworks, mill and distillery, boiler house and rectifying still house, and large number of coal yards.

On the south side of Sandwich was a three-storey structure built in 1882 known as the "flat-iron building." The first floor housed several stores. The second floor was the location of the Walkerville Music Hall, which served as a type of community centre and could accommodate nearly 600 people.

Also located in this triangular area, bound by railways tracks, Sandwich Street, and Walker Road: a brick stable, several bonded warehouses, a wooden firemen's hall and reading room, a little brick church, a butcher shop, the fire engine house, a paint shop, a cooper shop that manufactured all of Walker barrels, a carpenter's shop, and the Walker planing mill and stave factory.

Almost the entire populace, which numbered approximately six hundred in 1882, were employed in some capacity by the Walker family in their numerous enterprises. Only three industries existed in the settlement, the dominant one being the Walker distillery and its associated components, the Kerr Brothers Engine and Foundry Company, and the Dominion Syrup and Sugar Refining company.

The little village of Walkerville was about to experience a huge building boom, and Walker wanted it to be a carefully planned community.

Walker employed the entire population of 600 souls in some capacity. Workmen were offered a lease to a Walker cottage and if they declined, they would likely be denied employment!

Walker never sold the land or the company-built cottages. Consequently, he was able to control the type of person who would live in the village.

Walkerville is unparalleled as a Canadian community due to its high standard of urban design and architectural standards. The quality of life inspires in its residents a sense of fierce loyalty and pride.

Who's the best man in this town?
Hiram Walker, Hiram Walker.
What's the best brand in this town?
Old Club Whisky, Old Club Whisky.
Favourite Drinking Song in the 1880s

1888

Walker opens The Lake Erie and Detroit River Railway. Six years earlier, he had built a short run to connect with his new farm in the interior of Essex County.

By 1894, the railway links up with Leamington, then St-Thomas and Port Stanley. It offers local service to Walkerville Junction, Pelton, Oldcastle, McGregor, Marshfield, Harrow, Arner, Kingsville and Ruthven.

The line has a reputation as the best local railway in the country.

Lawn bowling at the CC headquarters, early 1900s photo: Hiram Walker & Sons archives

best of the times • 23

Aerial view of Walkerville, 1906 – note fledgling Ford of Canada facility at left. photo: Hiram Walker & Sons archives

Boom Town: Walkerville 1882-1898

Issue #3, July/August 1999

"The Queerest, quaintest place in all Christendom."
(from "The Detroit Journal" on the occasion of Walkerville's incorporation as a town, 1890)

1892

Hiram Walker declares war on "frauds" who counterfeit his brand of whisky. He warns the public with a series of daring advertisements describing the crime and the list of offending brands. He publicizes the fakers by name and invites them to file a libel suit to prove he is wrong. "It is only the good things which are imitated," says one sign.

1894

At a cost of $100,000, Hiram Walker erects a beautiful new main office on the riverfront. Designed by Mason-Rice and modelled after the Pandolfini Palace in Florence, Italy, the dominant architectural style of the structure is Italian Renaissance. The building remains in operation today as part of Hiram Walker Distillers, in Windsor, Ontario.

Walkerville's origin and growth clearly illustrate the skill and entrepreneurial abilities of Hiram Walker and reflect the changing nature of Ontario and its development as an urban industrial province to which men such as Walker greatly contributed.

In terms of its physical development, Walkerville was very much a small town in the years leading up to incorporation. In 1884, the village consisted of four streets extending north and south and five running east and west.

Parallel to the Detroit River was Sandwich Street, the village's business centre. Most of the Walker interests were located along this riverfront street, but such centres as the Walkerville Music Hall, large enough to accommodate six hundred persons for lectures, dances and other entertainments, were found there too; the remainder of the village was residential.

After twenty-five years of existence, the village of Walkerville had a population of 600 people. Most of the inhabitants of the village were Walker employees. They were offered a lease to a Walker-owned cottage in the village, none of which were privately owned by the workers. In this way, Walker could control the type of individual who lived in his village.

The inhabitants used and drank water pumped through pipes laid by the Walkers. They received police and fire protection at Walker's expense. They attended St. Mary's Church constructed by Hiram Walker and named after his late wife. The children of the village attended school on a site donated by Hiram Walker.

In the absence of a commercial bank, the Walker employees could deposit their savings in the Walker bank. Walkerville in the 1880's was a wholly owned family principality and it had been developed with great care.

Although a company town, it was never of the type intended to survive no longer than it takes the loggers to cut the timber or the miners to raise the ore, its foundations were well and truly laid and it was built to endure.

Until 1890, Walkerville retained its lowly position as an unincorporated post-office village. On the 29th day of January, 1890, a petition was forwarded to the Ontario Legislature, requesting the incorporation of Walkerville as a town, citing the significant contributions of the Walker family to the development of the settlement.

Since the founding of the village, it had been under the immediate jurisdiction of the Township of Sandwich East. However, as Walkerville became more populous and active industrially, this relationship began to prove unsatisfactory.

The village needed additional territory for future industrial development and homesites for the workers who were expected to follow the various industries to Walkerville. These problems required extensive planning, and the delineation of definite municipal boundaries through incorporation as a town would permit the formulation of a more extensive long-term program.

Incorporation as a town released the Walkers from the continued maintenance of a police force and fire department. As a town, Walkerville would enjoy increased stature, and as owners of extensive real estate handsome profits would accrue to the Walkers. At the same time, the family could expand its municipal lighting and waterworks system to serve a large community as an additional source of profits.

From 1890 to 1910, Walkerville witnessed a fantastic metamorphosis during which the distillery town became a flourishing industrial centre of considerable importance. The transition probably began in 1880 with the establishment of ferry service between Walkerville and Detroit.

Cruise ship docked at Walkerville. photo: Hiram Walker & Sons archives

In 1888, Walker turned his talents to the art of railway building. A railway to the Walker holdings in south Essex enabled him to ship farm produce directly to the distillery and cattlebarns with a minimum of handling. Also, the presence of a railway with connections to eastern rail lines enhanced the value of the Walker real estate in south Essex.

By 1901, two years after his death, the railway was completed with its eastern terminus at St. Thomas. Until 1888, the Walker distillery and its affiliated enterprises dominated the Walkerville scene. The railway, however, attracted numerous industrial enterprises into the village, including the drug firm Parke Davis, the Globe Furniture Company, the Walkerville Malleable Iron Company, the Ontario Basket Company, and the Milner-Walker Wagon Works, the forerunner of the Ford Motor Company of Canada. The latter began production in January 1898, with a daily output of twenty-five wagons.

Additional industries moved into the village before the turn of the century, creating an impressive industrial complex along Walker Road, the street running parallel to the Lake Erie, Essex and Detroit River Railway.

In 1890 the Walkerville Land and Building Company was incorporated and the Walker real estate holdings in Walkerville were placed under the management of that firm. Walker's son, Edward C. Walker, served as president for many years until his death in 1915, while his brothers were directors in the company.

After 1890, the firm gradually disposed of the Walker real estate holdings to private persons, and in the process of this task, the firm continued to influence the planning of the town in significant ways.

Just as Hiram Walker had done during the earliest years of town development, every effort was made to instill pride with contests for the finest flower-bed, the most attractive vine-covered home and for general household appearance.

Although many of the earliest Walkerville buildings have disappeared, the concept of a garden community in the midst of the city remains intact.

Walkerville Snapshot: 1913

Issue #4, September/October, 1999

Publisher's Note: *This text is reprinted from "Walkerville, 1913 – including Windsor, Ford, Sandwich and Ojibway – an authentic compilation embracing in word and pictorial representation the growth and expansion of these municipalities," published by The Evening Record (The Record Printing Company), Windsor, Ontario. Compiled by H.W. Gardner.*

Marked by rapid manufacturing, mercantile and residential development and coupled with a coherent conception of its further possibilities, Walkerville truly approaches the stimulating standards of a model town. In fact, the town is unique in its brief history. It did not pass through an uncouth and primitive childhood such as did its sister municipalities, but may be said to have sprung into being fully formed and comely.

Its founders, the Messrs. Hiram Walker & Sons, had certain well-defined ideals, and from the first council elected to the present, successive bodies of representatives have been imbued with the spirit of progress that was instilled in the founders, whose conceptions have been faithfully worked out. Walkerville, because of its generous encouragement of industrial settlement and civic adornment, is not only for its size and age the busiest, but probably the most attractive and orderly town in the whole Dominion.

1899

Hiram Walker dies at the age of 84. Canadian Club whisky, the brand he built into a worldwide success and Walkerville, the town he built into the pride of the Great Lakes, remain as his legacy.

In his lifetime, Walker reigned undisputed monarch of all under his surveillance. If he cherished a railway, he would have it, if humanly possible. As in his other endeavours, he would tolerate no interference from other sources, but would accept nothing less than complete control over the enterprise.

1900

Hiram Walker & Sons erect the world's biggest electrical sign, designed by the eminent architect Albert Kahn (one of many Kahn Walkerville creations). The sign measured 150 feet across, stood 60 feet tall, and required 4,300 light bulbs – an astounding accomplishment for the times!

1903

Hiram Walker's heirs hire Boston architect Ralph Adams Cram to design St. Mary's Anglican Church in memory of their parents, Hiram and Mary. Architect Albert Kahn, a Jew, declined the commission; the church was consecrated in 1904.

1904

Construction begins on Albert Kahn's Walkerville masterpiece, Willistead Manor, home of E. Chandler Walker, one of Walker's 8 children. Named for Willis, an elder brother who died in 1877, Willistead is completed in 1906.

1921

Mary E. Walker, widow of E.C. Walker who died in 1915, returns to the United States and donates the mansion to the Town of Walkerville. The park includes a tennis court that is flooded in the winter for a public skating rink. It serves as the council chambers, an art gallery, a library and is currently operated by the City of Windsor as a conference centre and reception facility.

Hiram Walker & Sons employees, c. 1930 photo: Hiram Walker & Sons' archives

Walkerville early realized the value of pavements and other public improvements. While neighbouring places were floundering in the mud, the youthful but ambitious Walkerville was in the enjoyment of advanced civic conditions, with its cool boulevards, well-kept pavements, adequate sewers, street lighting, gas, waterworks, and all the other comforts that pertain to metropolitan existence.

And rather strange to say, one of the chief inducements of locating in Walkerville, either for residential or manufacturing purposes, is the uncommonly low tax rate. Added to this are the liberal encouragements given by the Messrs. Walker to the establishment of manufacturing concerns and the splendid shipping facilities.

The town is situated on the Detroit River, the busiest waterway on the continent, if not the world.

The town is traversed by the Pere Marquette (formerly L.E.E. & D.R.R.), Grand Trunk and Wabash Railroads, while the recently constructed Essex Terminal Railway brings it into touch with the Michigan Central and C.P.R. Railroads. Thus, Walkerville is really in close touch with six railway lines.

In any mention of the chief manufacturing concern the distillery ranks first. Walkerville, in fact, owes its existence to the indomitable pluck of its founder, the late Mr. Hiram Walker, who, in the early days of his business career, encountered discouragements that would have dampened the ardour of most men. But although Mr. Walker in those strenuous days was, at times, short on the means to "lubricate" the wheels of his business, he was long on faith, which never was known to falter. The distillery, the second largest in the Dominion, stands as a monument to his phenomenal business qualities and superb courage and energy.

Walkerville is, par excellence, a place of beautiful homes, and probably no town of its size in the Dominion will rank with it in this important respect. First in order comes "Willistead," the home of Mr. E. Chandler Walker. With its sixteen acres of park this splendid residence in its architecture and surroundings reminds the travelled visitor of some of the fine old demesnes in the old land. This lies to the southwest of St. Mary's church and makes a part of that charming section of which the church may be regarded as the centre.

There are many other beautiful homes in the vicinity. In all respects Walkerville appeals to home lovers and the stranger within its gates because of unexcelled conditions conducive to comfort, pleasure and convenience.

An attractive spot in Walkerville is the Riverside Park, near the ferry dock, a favourite spot for young people during the summer months. It is one of the most popular and flourishing organizations that Walkerville people are identified with. Social enjoyment is also found at the Walkerville Lawn Bowling Club, while the Walkerville Country Club is an attraction for tennis players and golf lovers.

In all particulars, Walkerville makes an appeal to the esthetic sense and also makes progress along utilitarian lines. The effect has been a settled conviction with the individual householder that civic adornment is of immeasurable value. He takes pride in the appearance of his home, more especially since the Messrs. Walker inaugurated their annual garden competition, which has been a gratifying success.

How Walker's Club Became Canadian

by Art Jahns, Hiram Walker & Sons archivist, Issue #14, March, 2001

At its peak, Canadian Club was among the most recognized products in the world. Queen Victoria drank Canadian Club at the end of the nineteenth century, as did fictitious British secret agent James Bond, seventy-five years later. Canadian Club whisky was the brand that established the Hiram Walker distillery and the town of Walkerville, and made them famous throughout the world.

Canadian Club whisky was an ambassador not only for Walkerville but for Canada.

When Hiram Walker founded his distillery in the wilds of East Sandwich in 1858, most whisky was sold in barrels. Brand names, however, were beginning to make an impact on the industry. Brands such as "Monongahela" from Pennsylvania had already become well known in the eastern United States.

Walker was brand conscious from the outset. His first brand of whisky was called "Magnolia," most likely named after a town in Massachusetts, not far from his hometown. Although not very successful, the brand was available from the distillery from 1858 until around 1900.

Incredibly, by 1882, the distillery offered twenty-seven different whisky products for sale. Brands such as "Walker's Old Rye," "Toddy," "Family Proof," "Superior," and "Excelsior" were just a few. Although these brands achieved moderate success, Walker knew he needed one key brand to ensure lasting success in the distilling field.

Above: Transforming a Brand – From Club Whisky in 1882 to Canada Club and the ultimate brand, Canadian Club in 1883, including a rare Canadian Club bottle on right. photo: Hiram Walker & Sons' archives

1926
The Walker Era Ends – three Walker sons and a grandson who have operated the distillery since Hiram's death, sell it to Harry C. Hatch of Toronto for $14 million.

1934
In a plebiscite in December 1934, Walkervillites vote 2,535 to 641 against amalgamating with the City of Windsor. Despite the vote, Walkerville, with 10,000 residents, is forced into amalgamation the following year.

The citizens never forgot the pride of this great community, which grew and flourished as a distinct element for almost 80 years. A large sign was painted on the side of a barn 5 km outside of Walkerville in protest.

Over one hundred years after his death, the site where Hiram Walker built his mill and distillery in 1858 remains the home of Canadian Club. It is the #1 whisky sold in Canada, and the leading premium whisky sold in over 150 countries – all based on Walker's simple premise: "Put quality first."

Today, the region is still lovingly referred to as "Walkerville."

best of the times • 27

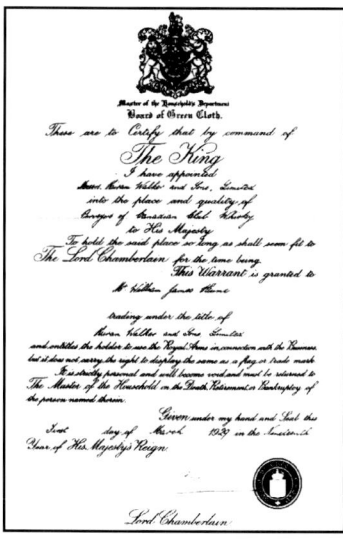

Getting The Royal Treatment

A Royal Warrant is the coat of arms of the reigning monarch of England. It is granted by the Sovereign and gives the holder the privilege of using the Royal Arms in connection with his or her trade or business.

In order to receive the Warrant, firms must have supplied goods direct to the Royal Household Departments for a minimum of three years. Warrants were void on the death of the reigning monarch and were re-petitioned with each new monarch.

Hiram Walker & Sons Ltd. was granted the Warrant of Queen Victoria on September 17th, 1898. Queen Victoria's coat of arms appeared on Canadian Club labels soon after.

On the Queen's death, Hiram Walker applied for and received the Warrants of subsequent Monarchs, Edwards VII, George V, George VI and Queen Elizabeth II.

During the later years of Queen Victoria's life, Hiram Walker also held the Warrant for the Prince of Wales. Canadian Club labels, with both the Arms of Queen Victoria and the Prince of Wales, are quite rare.

After holding the Royal Warrant for Queen Elizabeth for 10 years, the Warrant was reviewed and withdrawn. The action was probably political – the Queen no doubt wished to endorse whiskies made in Great Britain rather than a "foreign" country.

Hiram Walker & Sons was the only North American distiller to have been granted a Royal Warrant.

Cover Issue #14 – The very rare "pumpkin" bottle (centre) was first used by Hiram Walker & Sons as a branding tool. Starting clockwise in this collage, the pumpkin bottle is framed by the village of Walkerville in 1884, scenes from Walkerville at the turn of the 20th century, and Hiram Walker, founder of Walkerville and Canadian Club whisky. Hiram Walkers' archives

One brand that appeared at this time was called "Three Star." By the end of 1881, the brand was known as "Three Star Club." Within a year, the "Three Star" was dropped, and by 1882, the brand was changed to "Club" whisky.

In April 1882, Walker registered "Club" as a trademark for the customary fee of $25. Walker hoped this would be the name that would secure his fame and fortune for himself, the distillery and his fledgling town of Walkerville.

Walker positioned his Club as a premium brand, promoted not only for its purity, but also for the time it was aged: a full seven years in oak barrels, an unheard length of time in that era (U.S. bourbons were aged for less than a year, if at all). Early price lists show Club was considerably more expensive than other brands offered by the company. Club was not an instant success – like the barrels it was aged in, it took time for the market to catch up to Walker's genius. In 1882, only 43 barrels were sold, compared to 15,000 barrels of Walker's Old Rye.

Surprisingly, a government intervention cleared a path for Club's success. In 1883, the Canadian government passed the "Bottled in Bond Law." Distillers were able to bottle whisky with a Canadian government excise or strip stamp, so in effect the Canadian Government was guaranteeing the age of the bottled whisky.

No other country in the world employed such a system – the U.S. did not follow suit for another 13 years. This simple process gave consumers confidence in whisky products and made Canadian whisky famous throughout the world.

With a new method of packaging and marketing whisky, Canadian distillers delegated their best or most innovative brands for bottling. Hiram Walker's first bottled and bonded whiskies were Old Rye and Club.

Distilling whisky was a very competitive industry and sales of Club were less than stellar. In 1884, only 87 cases were exported to the U.S. By 1890, this figure had climbed to only 4,817 cases. But heavy advertising and hard work led to steady growth; by 1915, the number of U.S. exported cases was a respectable 137,353.

Hiram Walker branded his bottles with a "Canadian Club" seal.

Hiram Walker's Bottling Department, c. 1895. photo Larry Burchell

Hiram Walker and Sons arhives

In 1889, a significant and pivotal change occurred to the "Club" package. The word "Canadian" was added to the top of the label, set in block letters. Canadian referred to a type of whisky (as opposed to Scotch, Irish or Kentucky). Canadian whisky, as pioneered by Walker, was a blend of neutral corn spirits and rye flavouring spirits blended together before storage in the barrels. Bills for mash, (the leftover matter from distilling), from the early 1860s confirm that this method was employed by Walker from the earliest days of his operation. Walker was now using his methods as a way to promote his products in the U.S.

A common myth is that the U.S. government forced Walker to insert the word "Canadian" at the insistence of American bourbon distillers; research done to date finds no evidence to support this notion. In 1882, sales of Canadian whisky were so small that Washington hardly needed to take action. No matter, as it makes for a great story and secured the legend of Hiram Walker as an astute businessman. What is known is that Walker always printed the words "Canada" or "Canadian" from the beginning of bottling operations.

In 1890, Club whisky changed again. The distillery fully incorporated Canada into the product's name and the brand was then called "Canada Club." The brand was bottled in a pumpkin seed flask. This unique bottle was on the market for a very short time, and is exceedingly rare and seldom seen.

In 1893, another label change led to "Canadian" as the prefix to Club, with both words in what would become the company's famous script face. With that humble begin-

Bill of Sale, 1864: Hiram Walker & Sons was first known as "The Windsor Flouring Mill & Distillery." Magnolia whisky was the principal brand promoted by Hiram Walker.

ning, one of the best known brands in the world was born. This last change may seem obvious with the passing of time, but in fact, it was a mental exercise that took several years. The Canadian Club label, based on this simple format, has been used by Hiram Walker & Sons for over 110 years.

With the dawning of the 20th century, Canadian Club gained a solid foothold in the coveted U.S. market. But the new century would bring new challenges to Hiram Walker's sons, who inherited the business after Walker's death in 1899.

The looming Great World War led to the closing of the U.S. border to Canadian whisky in 1917, dealing a blow to the Walkers. But this was minor compared to the passing of the Vollstead Act in 1920, and the gathering clouds of Prohibition – the complete banning of all manner of drink throughout North America.

Walkerville would soon be ground zero for smugglers and rumrunners – and that, as they say, is another story!

Queen Victoria Goes Canadian

The events leading up to Queen Victoria drinking Canadian Club and Hiram Walker receiving the Royal Warrant are rather interesting. Queen Victoria's physician, Sir William Jenner, ordered her to cease drinking claret and champagne; he prescribed as a digestive, Canadian Club Whisky and mineral water, in the proportions of four parts of water to one of whisky. The Prince of Wales tried the prescription, liked it, and it was soon adopted as the favourite tipple in the Prince's 'set.'

"The drink now in vogue in the clubs of the metropolis of the Empire is Walker's Canadian Club Rye... Sir William Jenner's prescription has the endorsement of physicians as well as the pleasant tingle of aerated waters."

"The enormous increase in the consumption of Walker's Canadian Club has been largely due to the desire of the public for a mild spirit, which makes a most beneficial beverage with cool mineral waters."

The Counterfeiters

As Hiram Walker's Canadian Club whisky grew in popularity, it was inevitable that his brand would be copied. The collection of bottles at right demonstrate the extent to which whisky makers cloned the CC brand – even employing CC's label design and typeface and then liberally adding the word "Club."

In the U.S., Hiram Walker commissioned a series of billboards to challenge counterfeiters, like the one posted in Chicago, below. He published the counterfeiters' names and employed strong language: "FRAUD FRAUD FRAUD. We have given the parties fair warning but they continue to sell fraudulent goods.

We expose the swindlers in public...This is plain language and we intend to stand by it. If the accused wish to sue us for libel they will not have to look for us. We will gladly meet with them in their own courts. Let them give us the word and our local attorney will accommodate them."

They say imitation is the best form of flattery but apparently Hiram Walker wasn't amused.

photos: Hiram Walker & Sons archives

30 • it all began in walkerville

Hiram Walker's Whisky Palace

by Art Jahns, Hiram Walker & Sons archivist, Issue #17, September 2001

It would be difficult to imagine traveling along the Olde Walkerville section of Riverside Drive without noticing the Hiram Walker main office building. Since 1894, it has remained a constant in an ever-changing landscape. The building is one of the last remaining fragments of the old Hiram Walker Empire.

The cliché "if walls could talk" certainly applies to this grand old building. Hiram Walker himself worked here, as did his sons and grandsons. The building witnessed the transfer of the company from the Walker family to the Hatch syndicate in 1927, and again in 1989 when Allied Domecq purchased the company. Employees and world dignitaries walked through its doors. It was decorated for King George VI and Queen Mary when they passed through in 1939.

The giant elm trees, which stood in front of the office for almost 100 years are gone. Traffic, which evolved from horse and buggy to a few automobiles, is now a steady stream of cars.

The office was constructed to house the many interests of the Walker empire, including the distilling business, farming, real estate, the Lake Erie and Detroit River Railroad, the Mettawas Hotel in Kingsville, and other small enterprises.

For a building of this era, it had the usual features – a kitchen and dining room with a side entrance for staff, but it also boasted a barbershop and an exercise room.

When the west wing was added in 1920, a swimming pool was constructed in the basement and living quarters were built on the second floor. Harry Hatch, who purchased the Company from the Walkers in 1926, was still headquartered in Toronto and on his frequent trips to the distillery, was able to use the accommodations available in the building rather than stay in hotels. The pool was available to employees and their families until about 1945, when it was closed and floored over to create much needed file space.

The building is an outstanding example of Italian Renaissance architecture. The street façade was modeled after the Pandolfini Palace in Florence, Italy, and other features — external and internal — were copied from a variety of European palaces and grand houses.

Contrary to conventional wisdom, the building was not designed by Albert Kahn, but by the firm of Mason & Rice, who were one of the top architects in Detroit. The designs of the internal office and some of the exterior features were, however, detailed by Albert Kahn, who was

Above: Grand Opening Reception of Hiram Walker's new headquarters, 1894; "an outstanding example of Italian Renaissance architecture"
photo: Hiram Walker & Sons archives

Scenes from the Whisky Palace

Guest bedroom

Rare photo of basement swimming pool

Original boardroom, 1905

Opening Ceremonies in 1894 featured the full regiment of the 48th Highlanders

Book keeping offices, 1915

Reception room in 1899 – little has changed over time.
all photos this page: Hiram Walker & Sons' archives

an apprentice in the Mason and Rice office. Kahn was to become one of the greats in American architecture. He continued to design buildings in the Walkerville area for many years after he completed the Walker office buildings.

The office is constructed of a sandstone base, with Roman brick and terra cotta trim. The building has a partial steel frame, which was imported from Germany. Construction took two years mainly because the Ontario Terra Cotta and Brick Company, suppliers of the brick, were unable to deliver their goods on time. This was no doubt difficult for the contractor, N. Reaume, who eventually, in frustration, substituted carved stone pieces in place of the terra cotta that was never shipped. The street elevation, which most of us see, boasts a pair of ornate hammered bronze gates, now black with age, and a pair of lamps copied from the Strozzi Palace in Florence.

Contrary to popular belief, Mason and Rice (above) designed Hiram Walker's world headquarters, not Albert Kahn.

The interior remains a delight, basically untouched since construction. Dark red Vermont marble steps, Numidian marble columns with capitals copied from the Zorzi Palace in Venice, marble from Egypt and yellow Mexican onyx, are just some of the interior features that greet the eye.

Most of the wood is oak, with individual offices finished in mahogany, walnut or gumwood. The Globe Furniture Company of Walkerville was responsible for the interior. All interior woodwork cost a grand total of $16,000. The architect made a special trip to the Chicago World's Fair in 1894 to purchase furniture and accessories to be used in some offices.

A German who had immigrated to Detroit, Julius Melchers, did the intricate carving found throughout the interior of the building. Melchers was considered one of the best woodcarvers of his era. Before construction began, Melchers had also created a model of the building, featuring details that the architect had designed.

The office was officially opened on September 1894 with a gala party. More than 600 guests were invited; a caterer from Chicago provided the music. Festivities went on into the night, with employees taking part after the day's work was done.

When the building was completed it received a considerable amount of media attention. An article in the Amherstburg Echo compared the building to the Bank of England. The Empire, a Toronto newspaper, dedicated a four-page section to the office, calling it a "Commercial Palace." The Detroit Free Press had an equally impressive write up with artist's sketches of office interiors.

In 1990, the building underwent an extensive $1.2 million restoration. It was washed to remove almost a century of dirt, clinging vines were removed, and terra cotta was brought in from England to replace pieces that had deteriorated over time. In 2001, Hiram Walker's main office was converted into a Brand Heritage Centre and for the first time, was open to the public.

The Legend of Albert Kahn

by Chris Edwards, Issue #3, July/August 1999

Albert Kahn (1869-1942) has been hailed as *the* architect of the modern industrial era. His portfolio is phenomenal: Kahn built more than 1,000 buildings for Ford Motor, including the River Rouge complex and the Model T factory, and hundreds for General Motors. The entire automotive industry used his services. Kahn also designed and built numerous office spaces, including the dazzling Fisher Building, and General Motors Building in Detroit's New Centre district. A massive 1,320,000 square foot structure, the GM building was the largest office building in the world at the time.

Kahn was responsible for almost all of the major industrial plants of the Big Three and other auto manufacturers in the U.S., and also for aviation industry plants, hospitals, banks, commercial buildings, public buildings, temples, libraries, clubs and over one hundred spectacular mansions.

What is lesser known about Albert Kahn is the role he played in the design and construction of many of Walkerville's finest buildings. In Walkerville, as a young man, Kahn made his mark that lead to a shining career as one of the greatest architects of the 20th century.

Much of Walkerville's urban design flowed out of Hiram Walker's desire to emulate Britain's Garden Cities. The "Garden Plan," as it has become known, separated industry from residential areas by streetscape design.

Initially, Detroit architects Mason & Rice, who were heavily influenced by the style known as "Richardson Romanesque," delivered much of the work. Created and popularized by Boston architect Henry Hobson Richardson (1838-1886), this style is characterized by low-slung arched entrances, dark masonry and detailed brickwork. Examples of this architectural style can be seen on Devonshire Road north of Wyandotte toward the river, (once considered main street in Walkerville), and throughout Detroit.

At the tender age of 15, Kahn abandoned his formal education to apprentice with Mason & Rice, where he learned to draft and sketch. The novice soon won a scholarship to study in Europe. Kahn's experiences in Europe proved valuable to Mason & Rice, and the young draftsman was assigned to help design the interior of the new Hiram Walker & Sons Main Office Building – a masterpiece that still stands on Riverside Drive in Walkerville. Kahn's touch is evident throughout the interior, particularly in the lavish fireplaces and paneling in the offices. The dark, cozy Sample Room – the inner sanctum in the building – was inspired by sketches he had done in Nuremberg.

Kahn Does Walkerville

The Bank of Commerce
415 Devonshire Road, built in 1907
A classic bank design of the era, its Roman pillars impart a sense of strength and stability.

The C.C. Ambery-Isaacs House: "Foxley"
811 Devonshire Road, built in 1906-07
National attention focused on Walkerville in 1910 when Foxley was featured in The American Architect & Building News. The name Foxley is carved over the entrance. *(See page 244 for story)*

Harrington Walker House
1948 St. Mary's Gate, built in 1911
Two prime lots opposite St. Mary's Church were reserved for Hiram Walker's grandsons, Harrington E. Walker and Hiram H. Walker. Both privileged men had Albert Kahn design their residences (the Hiram H. Walker house has been razed).

A detached garage with chauffeur's apartment stands on Kildare Road's curve. The windows were originally enhanced with louvered wooden shutters. The house appears to have been patterned on Kahn's design for the larger Packard auto magnate Henry B. Joy's mansion in Detroit.

Willistead Manor, designed by Kahn in 1904 for Edward Chandler Walker. photo: Chris Edwards

Upon completion of the new headquarters, the young architect's career was meteoric. In 1896, he joined forces with George Nettleton and Alexander Trowbride. In 1899, he founded his own firm, Kahn & Associates, with his brother Julius. This company recently celebrated its 100th anniversary and is still considered a leader in industrial plant design, with more than 300 architects on staff.

Upon Hiram Walker's death in 1899, Walker's heirs continued their patriarch's hands-on tradition, and Kahn played a pivotal role. Edward Chandler Walker and his wife Mary Griffen directed the Garden Plan. To fund the development of lands between Wyandotte and Richmond Streets, they sold Walker's Lake Erie and Detroit River Railway to Pere Marquette Railways for $2,870,000.

The interrupted street pattern design reduced traffic, creating a park-like setting, especially heading south on Devonshire to St-Mary's Church – a landscaped "island." The Walkers employed this feature to promote as fine a neighbourhood as existed in North America. Since lots near the church were sold only to those who could build homes of at least 3,500 square feet, the character of the neighbourhood was assured.

In Walkerville and Detroit's Indian Village (across the river in Detroit's near east side), Kahn embraced the Arts and Crafts Movement, a philosophy of design founded around 1850. Emphasizing handmade architecture in an era when factory mass-production was taking hold, every Kahn designed home expressed the movement's influence. Kahn believed that historic period styles were best suited to homes and public institutions, while factories should be utilitarian, brightly illuminated and devoid of ornament.

Kahn's most unique Detroit home may be the Edsel Ford estate on Lake Shore Drive in Grosse Pointe Shores. The palatial English cottage-style mansion overlooking Lake St. Clair currently acts as a show house for local events, and as a public museum. The gardens include an exquisite walk-in playhouse made for Josephine Ford.

Under the direction of Edward Chandler Walker, Kahn's commissions in Walkerville flourished, and his influence can be seen in many buildings. Kahn is responsible for many of the finer structures that remain in Walkerville, including King Edward School (the ornate entranceway was saved from the wrecker's ball), the Town Hall (which now houses an art gallery), the Bank of Commerce, the Strathcona Block, many of the grander private residences and possibly the row houses on Monmouth Road.

But it is Willistead Manor that showcases Kahn's architectural genius. Built in 1906, Willistead Manor is the epitome of Edwardian elegance, combining stone walls and half-timbered wall areas under a grouping of picturesque medieval roofs and chimneys.

While Kahn's influence in Walkerville is evident, it is also possible to tour many of his works across the river in Detroit. Readers may be familiar with many of Kahn's buildings, including The Fisher Building (dubbed "the

Most Beautiful Building in the World"), the Conservatory and Police Station on Belle Isle, the Cranbrook House in Bloomfield Hills, (originally a private home for the Scripps family of newspaper fame), Temple Beth-El, the Detroit Free Press Building, the Detroit Athletic Club, the Detroit Golf Club, Hill Auditorium in Ann Arbor, and many fine homes in Indian Village and Grosse Pointe.

Kahn supervised the construction of every building he designed. Much of his legacy can easily be toured and appreciated by fortunate residents of the border cities.

Kahn designed Ford's Highland Park plant, once the world's largest automotive factory

Albert Kahn and The Automotive Industry

For the automotive industry to succeed, factories had to be re-designed to suit the critical needs of emerging assembly modes of production. At the dawn of automotive manufacturing, auto factories were primitive – often no more than mere garages or large buildings.

Albert Kahn developed several modern architectural practices at the beginning of the 20th century. His first project was to design a factory for Henry Joy and the Packard Motor Car Company – the Packard Plant #10 in Detroit. Upon examining conventional factories, Kahn realized that wooden floors were poorly suited for the job, as they soaked up oil and could easily become fire hazards (many early auto manufacturing facilities actually did burn to the ground). Support beams and walls of early factories were ill-equipped to handle the load of heavy machinery, limiting the facilities' abilities to allow for windows and ventilation.

Kahn determined that concrete was an ideal material for the construction of automotive factories; it was fireproof, could absorb the vibration of heavy machinery (if it was reinforced with steel bars), and permitted larger window openings in their designs.

Kahn beccame the first architect to utilize reinforced concrete in factory construction when he built Packard's #10 plant. This design completely and irrevocably altered the method for building factories around the world. Kahn championed functional, useful buildings, and in this respect was a forerunner to the Bauhaus school of design popularized in the 20s and 30s.

Kahn's career was closely tied to Henry Ford. He completed over 1,000 projects for him, including many of Ford Canada's Windsor facilities; Ford's Highland Park plant (above), the world's largest automotive factory of its time; and River Rouge – a complex that revolutionized factory design by allowing the assembly of automobiles on one level remains a marvel of modern architecture.

Lesser-known facilities designed early in Kahn's career include factories for Chalmers Motors, which became the foundation for Chrysler Corporation. He designed the Dodge Brothers Hamtramck plant, the DeSoto pressing shop, and the famed Willow Run plant in Ypsilanti. During the Great Depression, as business faltered in North America, he designed over 500 plants in an expansion-minded Soviet Union.

At the time of his death in 1942, Kahn's firm had designed more than 2,000 factories. From humble beginnings as an apprentice in Walkerville, his legacy remains as one of the greatest architects of the modern era.

Walkerville Town Hall

350 Devonshire Road, built in 1904. This building features the stone foundation from the original St-Mary's Church built in 1870. The design is Classical Revival, featuring a dark tile roof and low-arched dormers specified by Albert Kahn. The building was moved from its original site by a group of determined volunteers, and currently houses commercial tenants.

"The Most Beautiful Building in the World"

It may be the most famous Albert Kahn structure in the border cities, and many would argue that it is the most magnificent.

When the seven Fisher Brothers of Fisher Body fame hired architect Albert Kahn in 1927 to design a building that would bear their name, they gave him a blank check and the instructions to build "the most beautiful building in the world."

Plans for a $35 million three-phase project were announced by the brothers in January, 1927. The original plans called for three units to be built over a period of several years (above), but due to the onset of the Great Depression in 1929, only phase one, the Fisher Building, was completed at a cost of $10 million.

The seven brothers – Frederick, Charles, William, Lawrence, Edward, Alfred and Howard – were the sons of Lawrence Fisher Sr., an Ohio carriage maker. On arrival in Detroit in 1908 they founded the Fisher Body Company with a capital of $50,000. Less than 20 years later, they sold out to General Motors for $208 million.

In 1929, Albert Kahn's Fisher Building was honoured by the Architectural League of New York as the world's most beautiful commercial structure. In 1930, Kahn was awarded first place in commercial structures by the Detroit chapter of the American Institute of Architects.

Albert Kahn's Crown Jewel
Willistead Manor

by Elaine Weeks, Issue #11, November, 2000

photo: Chris Edwards

Many locals have a soft spot in their hearts for the grand Edwardian Manor called Willistead. Thought by many to be the residence of Walkerville and Canadian Club founder Hiram Walker (Willistead would certainly have been a fitting home), but Walker had in fact been dead for five years when construction of the Manor began in 1904.

Willistead was built by Hiram Walker's second son, Edward Chandler Walker, and named for his deceased older brother Willis.

Completed in 1906, Willistead was designed by renowned American architect Albert Kahn in the 16th Century Tudor-Jacobean style of an English Manor house. No expense was spared in constructing the manor. The exterior gray limestone was quarried in Amherstburg and hand cut at the Willistead worksite by Scottish stonemasons, specifically imported for the project.

Inside, marble fireplaces, rich wood paneling and exquisitely detailed hand carving throughout the many rooms were fitting backdrops for the Walker's elegant furnishings and extensive art collection. Even an elevator was included in the design.

In 1914, architects Stahl, Kinsey and Chapman designed the stone and iron fence, which surrounds the property.

photo: E. Weeks

Chandler Walker's love for his father Hiram is evident by the positioning of the stone portico which graced the front door of Hiram's Detroit home directly in line with a small window in Chandler's dressing room on the second floor. As he prepared for his day, Chandler would gaze out this window and be reminded of his father.

Chandler and his wife Mary married later in life and did not produce any heirs. After Chandler's death in 1915, Mary lived alone in the huge estate with her servants. After failing to convince her sister and spouse, Col. and Mrs. Brewster, to move to Walkerville from their U.S. home, (Edgewood, at 1857 Richmond, was built for them), Mary donated the 16-acre estate to the town of Walkerville in 1921 and moved to the U.S.

Willistead served as Walkerville Town Council chambers, then as the Walkerville Public Library (changed to Windsor Public Library after amalgamation in 1935), and the original Art Gallery of Windsor. Having fallen into a state of disrepair by the mid-seventies, the manor was threatened with demolition. Fortunately, the manor was spared and major restoration work began in 1978. Owned by the people of Windsor and operated and maintained by the Windsor Department of Parks and Recreation, the manor reopened in 1981 in its present capacity as a meeting and special event facility as well as a historical site available for tours.

Kids Say the Darndest Things!

For the premiere edition of "The Walkerville Times," (March 1999) managing editor Elaine Weeks visited Ms. Arya's Gr. 3 Class at King Edward School and quizzed the students about local history.

She asked: Who was Hiram Walker? And, who lived in Willistead Manor? Here are some of their amusing responses:

Hiram Walker is the captain of Detroit, or he is a pilot. I think that a lady lives in the Willistead Mansion. She is old, with white hair, with blue eyes. She wears a pink dress. Her name is Rose from the Titanic. She is very pretty. *Chantel*

Hiram Walker is a man that made wine and Hiram Walker opened a wine store. I think the Prime Minister lived in Willistead. *Nathanial*

I think Hiram Walker was the principal of Walkerville High School. I think the person that lived in Willistead was Henry Ford. *Dustin*

Hiram Walker was a Prime Minister who died 100 years ago. He is nice. I wish he were still alive so I could figure out who he is. An old lady lived in Willistead. I don't know who she is. *Jonathan*

I think Hiram Walker invented beer and he died 100 years ago. *Troy*

Hiram Walker is the person that created Walkerville High School. And then when he died the people that helped him named it after his last name. His last name is Walker. *Caitlin*

Hiram Walker is a very, very important man because HE IS RICH! He is the KING of Windsor and Kingsville. *Devon*

Boom Town

Aerial View of Walkerville, taken from hot air balloon, circa 1906. Dominant buildings include the Canadian Club whisky storage warehouses; a burgeoning Ford Motor Company is obscured by a clump of trees on the river. photo: Hiram Walker & Sons' archives

Design by C. Howard Crane
The Walkerville Theatre

A fixture on Wyandotte Street East for over three-quarters of a century, The Walkerville Theatre has undergone many changes since its grand opening in 1918.

Designed by renowned architect C. Howard Crane, who later gained fame by designing Detroit's Fox Theatre (which holds the distinction of being the largest continually operating theater in the country) and Earl's Court in London. The Walkerville Theatre has lost most of its former charm and beauty over the last fifty years.

When the theatre first opened, it was illegal to show movies on Sunday. The Tivoli, as it became known in 1930, enjoyed great success by offering both silent movies and vaudeville acts, guaranteeing it an audience every day of the week. Early theatre-goers could choose to watch the shows from either Windsor or Walkerville, as the town border ran right down the middle of the theatre!

photo courtesy Andrew Foot

Vaudeville gradually faded away after the introduction of sound motion pictures in the late 1920s, but live theatre made a short-lived comeback in 1959 when the Windsor Light Opera Association staged a musical and briefly considered buying the acoustically exquisite building for its permanent home.

The Tivoli was instead converted back into a movie house and was known as "The Tiv" until closing in 1965. In later years it was briefly resuscitated as a bingo hall, then as a community music/dance studio and even a gay nightclub.

Recently, the building was converted into a venue for small local theatre companies and special events.

Hiram Walker's Spiritual Legacy
St. Mary's Church

by Elaine Weeks, Issue #4, September/October, 1999

This church, with its pretty sylvan setting, and well-kept cemetery attached, is full of reposeful charm. Looking at this building, with its ivy-mantled tower, one might easily imagine himself... in England, and that when darkness descends on the scene, the "solemn stillness" might be broken by the voice of the "moping owl," complaining to the moon. (compiled by H.W. Gardner)

The first organized congregation in Walkerville was the village church, built by town founder Hiram Walker at his own expense. His wife Mary Abigail, who died in 1872, shared his great interest in the community. She was an earnest and devoted churchwoman and it was largely through her that Walker's interest in the social and religious welfare of his people was awakened. Walker erected the church in 1874 on Sandwich Street (Riverside Drive), the site of what later become the Walkerville post office and civic offices.

The church was originally Methodist because Walker had surveyed his workers as to their preferences of services. Each minister appointed to the church by the Canadian Methodist Conference was "distinctly given to understand that no reference was to be made to the liquor traffic during his stay."

The first two ministers observed this stricture but the third, the Rev. Alex. Hardie evidently did not for Walker discontinued Methodist services in the church and closed it for two years. It is thought that Walker's actions were also motivated by business concerns, as his firm was feeling the effects of a general depression in Canadian trade and business.

The distillery was on the verge of collapse several times and was saved only by the tenacity of its founder, and the patience of its employees. Walker offered the church to the Anglicans but they were reluctant to undertake the expense of a new church in such a small community, only a mile and a half from All Saints in Windsor. However, Walker undertook to make up any deficit. On this arrangement, Church of England services commenced, and the church was named St. Mary's (the East Window, a memorial to his wife, was given to St. Paul's Church, Essex in 1904).

By 1902, it became apparent that St. Mary's, lacking both chancel and vestry, was not large enough for the congregation. And, the Sunday school rooms were inadequate. Passing trains also disturbed services.

Walker died in 1899, and three of his surviving sons, Edward Chandler, Franklin Hiram, and James Harrington, offered to provide a new church, Sunday school and rectory, in memory of both their parents. A new building was erected at the centre of Devonshire Road, immediately north of Niagara Street. The cornerstone was laid on May 25th, 1903, and the building was consecrated on April 10th, 1904.

The visitor to Walkerville will find in St. Mary's Church a bit of 16th century England transplanted to North America. Here is reproduced an English scene of church, churchyard and rectory. Nearby is Willistead taking the place of the English manor house. Combined, these buildings create a picture of peace and beauty rarely found in North America, which will endure and grow with the passing years.

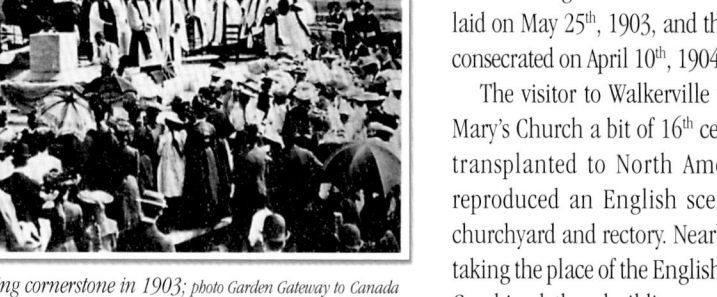

In architectural terms, St. Mary's belongs to the Perpendicular period of 16th century Gothic, when most of the smaller English churches were built. The joy of St. Mary's is found in the creative work of the artists, who added their own personalities to what otherwise would have been at best a faithful reproduction of a bygone age.

Laying cornerstone in 1903; photo Garden Gateway to Canada

Walkervillians did not want to miss the laying of the fountain's cornerstone in 1897; a model of it is at centre. At right, the fountain today.

Queen Victoria Jubilee Fountain

Issue #37, September, 2003

In his radio sketch of June 22, 1957, N.F. Morrison, Ph.D., provides a contemporary account of Walkerville Diamond Jubilee proceedings as reported in the Evening Record (Windsor), June 23, 1897 (Radio Sketches 1945-1962 Essex County Historical Assoc.)

Processions are proverbially unpunctual and Walkerville experienced the usual difficulty in getting a large body in motion. Ten was the hour set for the opening ceremony to lay the foundation stone of the memorial fountain, but it was after this hour before the procession began to move.

The formation of the column was made at Sandwich Street [now Riverside Drive], the rear resting at the Grand Trunk, while the head reached Fifth Street [now Walker Road]. At 10:15 am the order was given to move by the chief marshal Alex Leavitt. The march began.

The procession was in the following order: the mayor, councilors, Windsor visitors in carriages, the Walkerville band, Nos. 1, 2, 4 and 5 of the Essex Fusiliers, the celebration committee, the school children, teachers and trustees, the bicycle club, and the fire department. The bicycle club was a very conspicuous feature, as each wheel was gaily decorated, a prize of $5 having been offered by the club for the best and most original decoration.

The route observed was east on Sandwich, south on Walker Road, east on Tuscarora and north on Second (now Devonshire Road) to the site of the memorial fountain, which was reached at 10:40 am. Preparations were made for the ceremony of laying the corner stone. The school children were seated on benches provided at hand for them, and Mayor Reid (of Walkerville) surrounded by his colleagues, opened the proceedings by reading the following telegram from the Queen at Buckingham Palace, addressed to the governor General at Rideau Hall, Ottawa: "From my heart I thank my beloved people; may God bless them all."

Mr. Reid, on behalf of the town, thanked Mr. Walker for the princely gift from the firm and asked Mrs. E.C. Walker in the name of the Queen to lay the corner stone, presenting her with the beautiful silver trowel for the occasion.

That lady stepped forward and gracefully performed the function assigned her, while a photograph was taken of the assembly in the position it then occupied. Rev. Dr. Cook fittingly closed this part of the proceeding with prayer. After the children led by Mr. Woolatt had sung the national anthem, the councilor and visitors (prominent citizens of the area), were invited to a platform, which had been erected under the shade of the trees for the speech making.

The children sang "Rule Britannia" under the baton of Mr. Woolatt and the company dispersed for luncheon. The rank and file of the volunteers going to the Farmers' Rest Hotel [later known as the Metropole], and the officers to the Crown Inn.

After dinner the people retired to the Walker Grove, which was located in the vicinity of the present Willistead Park. There, a lengthy programme of military evolutions and games occupied the whole of the afternoon, the last closing with a baseball game between the Walkerville and Harrow clubs.

painting by Nicholas Hornyansky

The Walker Farms
"The Finest In Canada!"

by Elaine Weeks, Issue #8, April/May, 2000

It's hard to imagine that one of the finest dairy farms in North America was situated on the outskirts of the town of Walkerville. The Walker Farm, founded in 1904 by Hiram Walker & Sons, (later operated by Walkerside Limited), was the source of about one-quarter of the milk and cream sold throughout the Border Cities by the Walkerside Dairy.

The Essex Stock Yards, situated on the present-day site of the GM Transmission plant, was developed over 120 years ago and was used to breed various farm animals to stock Hiram Walker's county farms. Walker pumped mash from his distillery through a pipeline to fatten the cattle.

A farm which apparently was the predecessor of The Walker Farm, was established around 1893 – its exact location is not clear although it's likely that it was on the site of the expanded Walker Farms. This farm was regarded as a model of scientific experiment and innovation. A steam engine and a special cable plow were brought from England, and soil and culture experts were contacted from the United States and Great Britain.

Walkerside Farms, also known as Walker Farms, was developed by Hiram Walker's sons in the area now bounded by Walker, Central, E.C. Row and lands south that eventually formed Windsor Airport. It is said that 3rd Concession, which became part of E.C. Row in 1971, was the first cement road in Canada. Reportedly built by Hiram Walker, it was one car wide and featured one foot thick concrete.

An early *Border Daily Star* newspaper report describes the farm as "a revelation of modern methods in agriculture. Its spacious barns, its administration offices and its semi-circle of homes for the farm employees are evidences of the new era in farming. The milk from the farm ranks so high that it brings nineteen cents a quart as against fifteen cents for the other milk sold in the Border Cities."

There were 600 head of cattle at the farm and some 300 were milking cows; many of these animals were prize winners. Two thousand acres of land supported corn, alfalfa, barley, oats, wheat, etc. to feed the cattle, and eight hundred men did the work of looking after the needs of the animals and getting the milk to market. There was also a fine orchard with some 6,000 apple trees and an apiary of 35 colonies.

To many Windsor and area people, the farm still holds a special place in their hearts. For Joanne McMurren of Woodslee, the earliest incarnation of Walker Farms was where her maternal grandparents met and fell in love. "My grandmother Susan Diem worked at the farm in the early 1890s as a housekeeper, cook and maid. She used a lantern to go to the barn to milk the cows in the morning before light – she also made the butter and bread. Her future husband, Fred Dahl, and his father lived in the

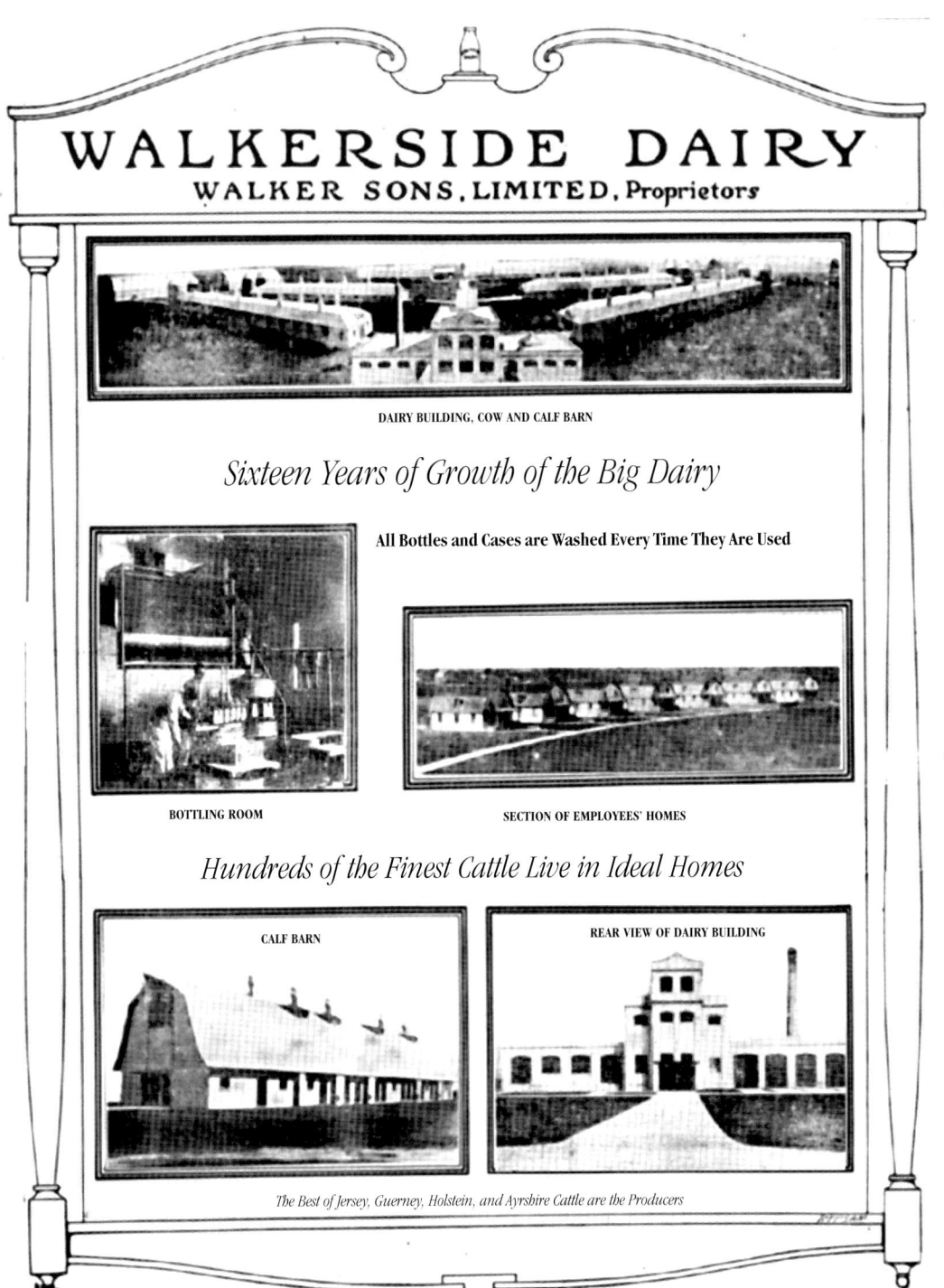

WALKERSIDE DAIRY
WALKER SONS, LIMITED, Proprietors

DAIRY BUILDING, COW AND CALF BARN

Sixteen Years of Growth of the Big Dairy

All Bottles and Cases are Washed Every Time They Are Used

BOTTLING ROOM   **SECTION OF EMPLOYEES' HOMES**

Hundreds of the Finest Cattle Live in Ideal Homes

CALF BARN   **REAR VIEW OF DAIRY BUILDING**

The Best of Jersey, Guerney, Holstein, and Ayrshire Cattle are the Producers

The Evening Record
May 23rd, 1917

In 2000, this illustration was reproduced by Windsor Print & Litho for The Times, from an original newspaper provided by Walkerville resident Niki Byng. In a feature article in The Evening Record from the early 1900s, writer Wilfred Southwood notes: "The Walkerside Dairy... is a model institution that is the finest of its kind in Canada."

Woodslee area but worked at the farm as bricklayers. They probably took their horses and wagon and boarded the train to go to work and returned home late. My grandparents married in Woodslee in 1895 and had 12 children."

Before Midge Kristinovich was born, her family lived on Walker Farms. Her dad moved the family from Pelee Island in 1928 so he could work in the horse barn. The family lived on the farm until 1949 when they returned to Pelee Island. An older sister of Midge's recalls that Hiram Walker's horse and carriage were stored in a building attached to the horse barn. "Mr. Walker (who had died in 1899) had one particular horse that his sons kept on the farm – it lived for 32 years."

Midge's family made their home in one of the dwellings on Walker Circle. "These were grey cement duplexes with identical small trees in front – there was a boarding house on each end of the circle. There was a lavatory at the back of each duplex. My sister remembers that when you put the lid down to sit, the water would start running!"

Midge's sister also recalls the Great Hall at Walker Farms – one room with a stage. It was the site of meetings and Christmas concerts. For school, she walked one mile to the Walker Road School, which had four rooms and went up to Grade 8. The high school, which she also walked to, was Mayfair High near Chrysler.

At 99, Camilla Stodgell Wigle of Windsor still remembers afternoon excursions in the family carriage to Walker Farms for fresh produce. "We would head up Walker Road, past all the houses and factories – and at last – we'd arrive at the farm; it was wonderful!"

rendering: Hiram Walker & Sons archives

By the 1940s, the farm's future was in jeopardy, plagued by several fires, including one in 1937, when a large storage barn and implement shed in the orchard burned. According to the *Windsor Daily Star*, "a crowd came to watch the fire and many took advantage of the opportunity to sample Walker Farm apples and picked them off the trees."

By February 1946, the remaining Walkers, now living in the U.S., closed the dairy business and put up a complete herd of dairy cows for auction — over 1,200 buyers came to the sale. Walker Farms would carry on strictly as a produce farm.

In January 1949, the Walker Farms barn, empty for two years, was destroyed by fire; this was the seventh case of arson on the farm. The Walker brothers had severed several hundred acres of land to form Walker Airport (now Windsor Airport) in the 1920s and as the airport grew, more land from Walker Farms was gobbled up (see following story). As the city of Windsor pushed its boundaries south and east, it was only a matter of time before the remaining animals and implements were sold and the Farm was shut down for good.

The circle of homes remained and for many years served as housing for area residents on a budget. Eventually, the buildings fell into disrepair, and as more and more of the Farm was bought up for light industrial use, the homes disappeared. Except one, which was moved further east to serve as the club house for the Shriners.

Today, all that remains of this once enormous state-of-the-art farm and dairy is a small neglected lot sandwiched between two light industrial buildings on Deziel Road. A walk through the lot reveals nothing but some scraggly trees and shrubs and what appears to be remnants of the narrow cement road that linked some of the dairy buildings. How soon before this disappears too and everyone says, "Walker Farms — never heard of it!"

Main road on the farm

From The Evening Record, Windsor, 1907

There is almost every trade represented among (the Farm's) employees; most of the work is done on the place. Sixty horses, most of them working, call for the constant services of a blacksmith. The farm is like a village in itself. Sixty men regularly live on the farm, all a part of the busy thriving village, its pulsating efficiency being shown at every hour with products of the dairy. A home is provided for each of the married regular employees. There are 36 of these homes, and they are a picturesque addition to the general landscape of the vicinity by their uniformity of neatness. The splendid co-operative community spirit among the employees and the diffusion of the distinction of capital and labour would furnish food for thought for a sociologist. There is a good open brand of the democratic spirit engendered by an understanding of the Walkers by their employees which is kept alive on the employer's part by due appreciation of their workmen. Free houses and public utilities service, such as telephones, gas, water and light are provided.

Two former residents in front of the Great Hall

Walker Airport

When Windsor Got Its Wings

by Elaine Weeks, Issue #37, September, 2003

On December 17th, 1903, two young bicycle mechanics from South Carolina built and successfully flew a plane at Kitty Hawk, North Carolina. The flight wasn't long – 12 seconds, 120 feet – but it was the first controlled, sustained flight in a heavier-than-air craft. Orville and Wilbur Wright had changed the world forever. Twenty-five years later, the collective dream of several Windsor WWI vets to build an airport became a reality. Many Times readers contributed memories of the airport, planes and flying as well as wonderful photographs for this story.

When the Wright brothers finally proved that flight was possible, people flew planes purely for sport. But soon after the outbreak of World War I in 1914, military planners realized that airplanes could be useful in warfare and even influence the outcome of the war.

In 1915, soldiers witnessed the first effective use of new weapons of war, including the airplane, the tank, and the submarine. Soon the skies over battlefields were filled with blimps, planes, and tethered balloons. The rapid evolution of aircraft during World War I was profound, unmatched by any other advancement at the time. From reconnaissance to bombing, the use of airplanes in the war became a necessity and by the end of the war, airplanes and pilots earned the respect they deserved. By 1918, planes had become a symbol of fear, and victory.

Clockwise from top left: A 1930s mailplane; a 1930s Border City Aero Club pin awarded to flyers who passed their flying test ; BCAC president Norman Reynolds and Evelyn Elmquist of Detroit at the annual "Pilots' Prom," February, 1939; Walker Airport hangar (courtesy Walter Ritchie); local pilot Ruth St. Louis (née Gooby) (courtesy Ruth St. Louis); group photo taken with comedian/actor Bob Hope during his visit to Windsor's No. 7 Early Flying Training School in 1943. Bob Hope (centre) stands with Flight Sgt. Haddon (possibly on wing behind him) and three employees of the airport, Earl, Gorno and Scotty.
Courtesy Hester Curtis

Grand Opening: Walker Airport 1928 postcard David L. Newman Collection

Sprouting Wings

In 1920, two years after the end of the "war to end all wars," a local group of Royal Air Force veterans formed the Border Cities Aero Club in remembrance of their wartime service. This association was the first group in Canada to be granted a charter as a member of the Royal Canadian Flying Clubs Association.

Flying drew the interest of many in the border cities. In 1919, a crowd gathered near a large field at the corner of Howard Avenue and Tecumseh Road to go on flying trips in Universal Company planes, piloted by Lieut. Charles Stocking, a famous U.S. military aviator.

An Aviation Committee of the Border Cities (Windsor, Sandwich, Walkerville, Ford City and East Windsor) Chamber of Commerce was organized in 1924 to explore the construction of a landing field and the development of an aircraft industry. Far-sighted committee members believed that when commercial flying became practical in Canada, an established local business organization should exist to promote aviation in this community.

The successful New York to Paris flight of Colonel Charles A. Lindbergh (May 20 – 21, 1927) electrified the entire world. His solo non-stop flight across the Atlantic took him 33 hours and 19 minutes. No other event in aero history had captured the imagination and admiration of so many. Lindberg's flight served to inspire eager flyers ready to follow him into the skies.

In Windsor, local aviation enthusiasts decided to promote their own non-stop, trans-Atlantic flight – from Windsor, Canada to Windsor, England. In September 1927, American Phil Wood and Duke Schiller, a pilot in the Ontario Provincial Air Service, began their flight from a field near Walker Road. The pair flew the "Royal Windsor," a Stinson-Detroiter monoplane for about a week before bad weather and mechanical breakdowns forced them to give up their attempt.

Despite its failure to reach England, the Royal Windsor expedition sparked considerable interest in local aviation. The unique geographical position of the Border Cities stirred the belief that this community could rapidly become the airplane manufacturing and aviation centre of Canada, especially as it was already at the epicentre of the booming auto industry.

A branch of the Aviation League of Canada soon formed, and the Chamber Aviation Committee was enlarged to include Aero Club workers and officers with a mandate to establish an aerodrome (airport) in the community.

Walker Airport

Their efforts were greatly assisted by the generosity of Harrington Walker and Hiram H. Walker (offspring of Hiram Walker who had died in 1899) who managed the Walkerville Land and Building Company (a wholly owned company of Hiram Walker's & Sons Distillery).

The company was petitioned by local aviation enthusiasts for permission to rent a field in their Walker Farms holdings for flying activities. The Walker's responded by providing a tract of land ideally located at the edge of town for a period of five years, free of rent, in addition to a gift of $10,000 to be used in assisting with the building of the hangar. The township of Sandwich East exempted the property from taxes with the exception of local improvement and school taxes.

The dream of a local airport became a reality when Walker Airport officially opened on September 8th, 1928. White-painted planks, two feet wide and 24 feet long, marked the perimeter of the field.

A rotating beacon was installed, and the roof of the hangar was painted in large squares of alternating colour. Barrels of oil were set up for lighting to illuminate the runway during poor weather and night landings. In the centre of the field, a square enclosed in a circle painted white designated it as a port of entry for Canada Customs during daylight hours.

The grand opening ceremonies featured parachute drops, exhibition flying, and an

Aerial view of Walker Farms, May, 1947; Walker Airport began in one of its fields. photo Benoit Marier

44 • it all began in walkerville

Essex County air derby – Canada's first air competition. The Puritan, a Goodrich blimp, arrived amid much excitement. It was the first such craft to land at the airport.

The following day marked the start of Canada's first international air race. Five planes flew out of Walker Airport bound for Los Angeles, competing for more than $10,000. A pilot from London, Ontario was declared the technical winner when his plane was the only one to reach Omaha, Nebraska before the 4-day deadline.

The early years of the Depression, and a disastrous fire in 1930 – which destroyed aircraft and equipment – created much hardship for the Border Cities Aero Club. The legality of its agreement with the Walker estate, to whom they paid a dollar a year for the land, was challenged by Sandwich East Township, since the club was exempt from paying taxes to the township. When the flying club could not pay up, the township seized the property. In 1931, the Walker estate redeemed the land.

The flying club managed to keep operating with the help of Roy Patterson, who continued to lease the land. Things greatly improved in 1933 when John Canfield rented the airport and became its manager. Canfield and his wife, Mary, both flying instructors, were a colourful pair and attracted many new fliers to the airport. Known to many as "Windsor's Father of Aviation," Canfield developed an ambitious plan to expand the airport in 1936.

Despite several years of success in flight training, the financial impact of the Depression was staggering. Like so many other businesses in the area, the club became insolvent, and in late 1938, Leavens Bros. of Toronto leased the airport. The new company moved in personnel, aircraft, and established its own flight training school. The Border Cities Aero Club continued to exist only as a social organization.

WWII and Expansion
Canfield's plans for the airport's expansion were realized in 1940 when the city of Windsor bought the airport for $54,000 and turned it over to the Department of Transport for $1. The government in turn paid the city $176,000 to begin the airport's expansion. Surrounding lands were purchased, and construction began on three permanent runways, administration buildings, and a control tower. Transport Minister C. D.

Paving the runway during the Windsor airport east expansion of 1944.
photo courtesy Harry Patterson

Howe officially opened the expanded Windsor airport in October 1940.

The No. 7 Elementary Flying Training School was established at the field and kept the airport busy during WWII. Part of the Commonwealth Air Training program, the school taught more than 1,600 Royal Canadian Air Force pilots to fly between July, 1940 and November 15th, 1944, when the school was disbanded.

In 1941, all civilian flying was banned. Only Trans Canada Airlines and military aircraft were allowed into the airport. Civilian aviation did return to Windsor early in 1945 and expanded rapidly. The Chamber of Commerce's aviation committee and a group of Americans from Detroit entered into discussions to build the world's first international airport in Windsor. The Canadian government offered farmland west of Huron Church Road for the project, but the plan fizzled.

In 1948, the Department of Transport extended two runways. Four years later, a new $1 million air terminal building was completed. In 1950, the city of Windsor decided against an option to resume operation of the airport and control remained with the federal Department of Transportation.

In the 1960s, Windsor Airport entered the Jet Age. Canadian Pacific Airlines became the second major airline to operate at the airport when two Douglas DC-8 Superjets took off in 1964. Several hundred people watched as the jets departed for Rome and Mexico City.

Air Canada soon added jets to their business. In 1969, DC-9 jet service began after a runway was extended 300 metres and intercontinental jet cargo routes started a year later. In 1973, the federal Department of Transport announced its intention to expand the airport and create a new runway, but plans sparked debate over the location of the airport; alternative sites in the county were discussed. The airport remained at its site near Walker Road but concerns about its environmental impact led to the formation of a Citizen's Advisory Committee in 1974, which began long-range planning for the airport. With help from the federal government, runways, taxiways, aprons and parking areas were resurfaced and other improvements were made through 1985.

The Concorde made its first visit to Windsor in the summer of 1987. A crowd of about 10,000 people jammed the airport and surrounding highways to see the British Airways plane land.

Aerial View of Windsor Airport, 1959 photo courtesy Harry Patterson

Fifteen Minutes Over Windsor:

Over 55 years ago, when I moved with my family from Montreal, Quebec to Windsor, I noticed a small ad in the newspaper advertising a 15-minute ride at Windsor Airport for $3. A day's earning for me then, but I went anyway. The picture at left shows me as I got off the plane; I was 19 years old at the time.

I flew over my home at Walker Farms, [just north of the airport] which had been recently re-opened after the East Windsor tornado hit in 1946. I was living at the Farms with my family. We only paid $20 a month for rent.

Benoit Marier, Windsor

Flying Fleet Finches

At right three Fleet16B Finch trainers fly over south Windsor in the early days of World War II, when R.C.A.F. training planes were based at Windsor Airport. These planes had a top speed of 104 MPH with a 'normal' cruising speed of 85 MPH. Over 15 years ago this photo was part of the descriptive paraphernalia for the restored Fleet Finch on display at the national air museum in Ottawa.

In the lower left of the photo, the former Devonshire Race Track and a portion of Kenilworth Race Track can be seen. The Detroit River and Belle Isle in the background are barely visible through the haze.

John F. Garswood, born in Walkerville

Fleet trainers were made in Canada from 1930 to 1941 in models 2, 7, 10, and 16 for the RCAF and civil operators, and were exported to nine countries. The models differed in their engines and in the minor changes made to the undercarriage and control surfaces. The model 16 was designed especially for primary pilot training in the RCAF. From 1943 on, the Finch was gradually replaced by the Fairchild Cornell. After the war, many were sold as war surplus for civilian use and a few were still flying in the 1990s.
Source: Canada Aviation Museum (Canada)

First Air Show Over Windsor

At right is a picture of two DeHavilland Vampires. One was flown by Hal Knight, the other by Jerry Billing. The picture was taken in 1950 by my husband, Ray East, with his Voightlander Bessa II camera at the Windsor Airport. This is the first time that Windsor had an air show with jet planes. At that time the commercial airport was off Walker Road. Hal Knight, who lived in Chatham, died a few years ago. Jerry Billing (Spitfire Ace) still flies his own plane from his property in Essex County.

Ray's first airplane ride was in the 1930s. It was a bi-plane with two open cockpits, owned and piloted by Cyril Cooper at Walker Airport. Ray's family moved from Oshawa to Windsor in 1928 and lived in the Norton Palmer Hotel for a year while his dad had a house built at 638 Lincoln Road, Walkerville – after being "crucified" (a term used at the time to stop Windsor from taking over Walkerville), it became 2240 Lincoln.

Irene East, Windsor

Fleet Finch bi-planes were lined up every day at Windsor Airport for WWII pilots-in-training; photo courtesy Hester Curtis

46 • it all began in walkerville

postcards from David L. Newman Collection

**Pictoral timeline:
the changing face of flying at
Windsor Airport.**

1940s

1950s

1960s

Windsor Airport, 1940s.
photo courtesy Harry Patterson

The Goodyear blimp at Walker Airport's grand opening in 1928. photo courtesy Audrey McArthur

Captain Bebe, flight instructor, 1930s.
photo courtesy Walter Ritchie

Sid Lloyd took this photo of a collision between student airforce pilots at Windsor Airport in 1943. photo courtesy Bev Marshall

Mail plane, 1930s. photo courtesy Walter Ritchie

best of the times • 47

Saving the Lanc

Condensed from "Lancaster Bomber Recollections" by Harry O. Brumpton, Issue #53, May/June, 2005

Early in the 1960s, a great deal of public interest was generated locally in the disbandment of the RCAF's remaining Lancaster Squadrons. Following the preparation of a favourable study, City Council approved the purchase of a Bomber for the sum of $1,250.

Following negotiations with War Assets of Canada, our initial task was to fly up to Dunnville, Ontario and select a Lancaster from the many that were stored at that abandoned airfield. The selection presented no problem due to the fact that, unlike all the other Lancasters, which were stored on the open tarmac, FM212 was housed indoors in a mothballed condition. In actuality, FM212 was airworthy and could have been readied for flight at an estimated cost of $10,000.

Yard owner Capt. George Dilts was a true entrepreneur of the old school. When pressed for a price to move the bomber from Dunnville to Windsor, Capt. Dilts dropped to the shop floor and there with a piece of chalk quickly computed a price for all to see of $3000, which was acceptable to everyone present.

Captain Dilts' trip to Windsor on August 29th, 1964 was memorable. He had removed the wings of the aircraft and stored them alongside the fuselage of the aircraft which had been pushed aboard the barge. The four motors were put aboard in their heavy tank-like containers. The whole entourage of tugs and barge then began a challenging voyage across Lake Erie and up the Detroit River to Windsor. Dilts nearly lost his load twice due to rough seas.

FM212 was partially re-assembled at the riverfront site primarily for the purpose of generating public interest in the fundraising programme. A single wing, along with one motor, were mounted on the aircraft by Parks mechanics. It was a debilitating sight to see our once proud Lancaster perched on the river's edge minus a wing and three motors – sort of like a plucked turkey.

Once ashore, the Lancaster was readied for public inspection at 25 cents per head. A fixed stairway was constructed leading into the cockpit through the forward escape hatch. Eventually, funds in the amount of $20,000 were raised for the construction of the plinth in Jackson Park.

Once the plinth was completed, it became necessary to move the bomber from its location on the riverfront in downtown Windsor to Jackson Park, some two miles distant. The move was accomplished at night under the direction of a local house mover. Fortunately, the route led straight from the river up our main street, Ouellette Avenue, directly to Jackson Park. Mid-winter was chosen as the time for the move so that the heavy bomber could be towed across the frozen park without causing damage to the turf. With the aircraft finally home, it was then locked down and the engines and props were reinstalled.

Over time, the Lancaster began looking wear for wear. The Canadian Historical Aircraft Association was formed in Windsor in 1992 and officially incorporated as a non-profit organization in 1995. Arrangements for a cooperative work program with the City of Windsor were made and volunteers began working on basic maintenance and modest restoration efforts in September of 1993. Volunteers replaced many missing components of the aircraft including a new cockpit canopy and bomb aimers nose blister. The engines were inhibited against corrosion yearly to prevent them from seizing.

Unfortunately, due to furthur deterioration of the aircraft, it was removed from its pedestal on May 26th, 2005, and replaced with two full scale replica WWII memorial aircrafts, the Spitfire and the Hurricane. FM212 is to be restored for future viewing in a yet-to-be determined controlled environment.

Above: Windsor's own Lancaster Bomber FM 212 as she looked while still in service.

Left: Aerial photo of Lancaster in Jackson Park by Spike Bell. Right: Future Windsor Mayor, Bert Weeks with children Elaine and Doug visiting the Lancaster at the Windsor riverfront in Dieppe Park, 1964.

Monmouth Road, 1917 postcard David L. Newman Collection

Classic British Design
Monmouth Road Row Houses

by Elaine Weeks, Issue #38, October, 2003

The rowhouse, townhouse, party-wall house or whatever you choose to call it, is most frequently found in older North American cities. This remarkably versatile concept can embrace virtually any vertical treatment and any type of establishment: you can find rowhouses with tiny stoops or ample porches, with flat surfaces of the Federal period or the towers and bays of the Romanesque.

Whatever the style, the distinguishing characteristic of the row house is the presence of at least one party, or common wall that's shared with a neighbour on one or both sides. The idea was (and still is) to fit as many building lots on a block as possible – to the obvious benefit of the developer. The building spreads backwards and upwards rather than sideways as a result. Most often the narrow, streetfront façade has a front door at one side and two windows at the other. The grand townhouses of the wealthy may have four bay windows in front.

The typical row house has two or three storeys rising above a high basement, but some (particularly in Boston, New York and Philadelphia), may stretch to four or even five. The single-storey rowhouse is largely a 20th century phenomenon.

Clues to the age of the house are provided by rooflines, dormers, and windows. The high-pitched gable and gambrel roofs of the 18th century gave way to lower pitches in the second quarter of the 19th century. Flat roofs with a rearward slope became common around the time of the Civil War, only to be replaced in the 20th century by the gable once again. Dormers moved from the simple, shed roofed projections of the early 18th century to more ornate, gabled and pedimented structures, often with round-arch heads and pilasters, in the latter part of the century.

The age of the house is also suggested by building projections, which became bigger and higher with each passing decade. Construction methods and materials are other clues: row houses of frame construction, although built well into the 19th century in later and smaller cities, are usually found

Monmouth Road occupants in the early 1900s
photo courtesy Charlie Fox

only in the earliest sections of major older cities where fire codes were in place by the late 18th century. Fire walls (now also a computer term for a system designed to prevent unauthorized computer access) were built of masonry, erected between row houses and projected above the roofline to prevent sparks from traveling from one roof to another.

Brick became stylish, as did smooth-faced brownstone (sandstone) from the mid-19th century until about 1900. It was laid in even, rectangular, "ashlar" patterns. Hand-cast, 18th century bricks tend to be rougher than the smooth, hard, mechanically formed pressed brick of the late 19th century.

The interior configuration of most late 19th and early 20th century, urban, three-bay rowhouses is so standardized that a visitor from Philadelphia would have no trouble finding his or her way to the bathroom in a Washington, D.C. counterpart.

The rear yard may have access to the street by means of a covered side passage carved out either from one or both houses, or through an alley along one side. Rear alleys facilitated "back-door" services.

Born on Monmouth

I was born in a Walker townhouse at the north end of Monmouth road in 1926. It was the same house my mother and dad moved into after they were married in 1910. Dad was a volunteer fireman so an alarm system was set up to ring in our house. Dad would pull on his boots and gear, and run to either Wyandotte Street or Walker Road to jump onto the rig as it passed by.
Ray Pillon, Mississauga

The 900 block of Monmouth Road, 2002 photo E. Weeks

Hiram Walker's Rowhouses

Monmouth Road (originally 4th Street) from the 700 block to Ottawa Street in the Olde Walkerville area of Windsor is lined with dark red brick rowhouses, built for Hiram Walker distillery workers and other Walker-supported satellite industries. The apparent sameness of these row houses is misleading.

The 800 block has twelve row houses with four units each. The presumed designer of this block, built in 1904, is Detroit architect Albert Kahn. At the middle of the block are two semi-detached houses intended for the foremen of the Hiram Walker's distillery and their families. They were built for the Walkerville Land & Building Company, which collected the rent. All are now privately owned.

Some have flat parapets, end gables, or have paired frontal gables. All terraces have central open passageways leading to the backyards. Decorative brickwork provides interesting texture to the houses and to the streetscape. While the plain shutters are not original to the buildings, residents find them attractive and serve to distinguish one unit from another.

To the north, along the 700 block of Monmouth are found some of the early (c. 1890) frame semi-detached cottages with shared Tudoresque dormers along the west side of the block. On the east side is a block of red brick semi-detached houses built c. 1893-94, and believed to be designed by Mason & Rice.

During the past 20 years, this area has experienced significant re-gentrification. The value of these homes has risen dramatically from the $20,000 range in the early 1980s to over $150,000 today.

the 700 block

photo C. Edwards

Life Lessons on Monmouth Road

Our house on Monmouth Road was the sort of row housing unit the privileged class provided for their workers. We're familiar with them from scenes of old England and coal mining communities. They were close to the work site in order to maximize available work hours for the Company and usually symbolized row-on-row poverty.

Monmouth Road looked the same as Argyle Road – the 1200 block mirrored the 900 block. But things had changed by the time I was growing up. The row housing in Walkerville was not the drab scene of old England but a vibrant community with strong family and neighborhood values. Today, it would be difficult to find a more equitable social structure than the housing units of Monmouth and Argyle Roads.

During my childhood the units were sold by the original owners (Hiram Walker & Son's Walkerville Land and Building Company) to the bank; the bank demanded that renters either buy or move out. My Dad, through some magical financial wizardry, was able to come up with financing to buy our unit at 1279 Monmouth Road for about $1600.

This was an exciting time on the block, as decisions had to be made; it wasn't so much whether to buy or not, but could one come up with the money for the down payment? Most fathers worked at Ford or Chrysler, all had large families and none of the mothers worked – except for "pin money," altering elderly widows' baggy printed dresses.

Almost everyone purchased their home and stayed. It was a good deal and tenants could be proud house owners in just ten to twelve years. The Telliers, Lefavres, Kennons and Soumis' settled on the 1200 block.

In those days people didn't often move; they stayed until their kids grew up and left home for a house usually not too far from their homestead, which is what happened at our house. You could tell which house had kids and how many by the condition of the front yard. Absolutely no grass meant four or more. Patches of crab grass and some plantain, less than four. All grass, usually a widow or a childless old couple, but there weren't many of these. All the houses had three bedrooms and a bathroom upstairs, plus a "hall closet."

The hall closet became significant in my life when I was around five. Before that time, it was a place where I would use as a unique hiding place during a game of hide-and-seek. I could just squeeze into the 24-inch deep bottom ▸

50 • it all began in walkerville

recess and almost close the door. Of course, everyone knew where I was, but my older sisters always let me think I was fooling them.

The "linen" closet was the official name of our hall closet, but it never held much linen – unless those big heavy army greatcoats were made of linen. We used to keep them on our bed in the winter to keep ourselves from freezing. Those coats sure could absorb a lot of pee; I think I got the connection between a WWI greatcoat and a latrine from a Gary Cooper movie – I imagined that's how a latrine must have smelled in the trenches on the front lines.

Then came the day when I would never go in that closet again. One evening Mom and Dad were out, most likely at the "Farmer's Roost" (Metropole Hotel on Walker Road) – probably a Friday payday since Dad would often call Mom to join him for a couple of beers. The girls put my brother Gord to bed. He slept in Mom and Dad's room in a crib even though he could walk, run, jump and climb.

He wasn't a very active kid and usually stayed put – unlike myself. When Mom and Dad were out, I had the habit of waiting until Gord was asleep and then I'd sneak into his room and slide under his crib. I would lay on my back, place a foot on the bottom side of the mattress and start a violent kicking rhythm, while making strange monster sounds. He would wake terrified and, not being able to see anything, would go into a complete panic attack.

I thought this was hilarious and would slip out the door before the girls came to his rescue. After many successful months of this, I was eventually caught and received my just reward – although nobody knew it but me.

One night my sister Bev told if I got out of bed again that night the Bogeyman would come and get me. She knew he lived in the hall closet and was watching me. He'd take me away and I would never see home again.

I don't know why this scared me that night. Maybe it was because I was so tired or maybe it was the guilt for being caught scaring my brother, but whatever it was, I couldn't shake the fear that the Bogeyman was in the closet and was out to get me.

Every sound that night was the sound of the Bogeyman approaching my bed to spirit me away for my dastardly past deeds; and every hint of light was the glint from the demon's eyes as he gloated about his newfound disciple. Surely he would take me to join the underworld and I would live in hell forever. From then on, my brother rested peacefully with no more late night volcanic eruptions.

Sonny Batstone, Anchim Lake, BC

Milkman, Keep Those Bottles Quiet!

October 1929. My parents moved with five kids to Monmouth Road, in the block between Ontario Street and Richmond (Huron Street at that time).

When the milkman rattled his bottles at 5 a.m., delivering milk to an insulated container on the porch, it gave birth to a popular song of the era, "Milkman, Keep Those Bottles Quiet!" The clippety clop of horses' hooves was also a warning that it was time to rise. Then there was the breadman serving his customers via horse and wagon. As he went from house to house with his basket of bread and goodies, his horse would follow, occasionally chewing the leaves on low-hanging boughs.

I can still smell the lilacs filling the spring air, as almost every home had a lilac bush. In summer, there was the aroma of fresh bread and pies coming from Canada Bread on Walker Road and Bennett's Bakery on Ontario Street. If the smell was too much to take, for 35 cents you could have a pie straight from the oven and for another 35 cents, a brick of ice cream from Wilson's Drug Store on the corner of Ontario and Monmouth. Now that was a drugstore, complete with a soda fountain – a place to "hang out."

The Great Depression was in full swing (1929-1934) and for 5 cents you could enjoy a "cherry coke;" ten cents bought an ice cream soda. If finances were low, for a penny you got a real licorice root. Or you could check out the magazines and comic books, all presided over by Claremont Wilson, who cut quite a figure as he walked back and forth from his home on Windermere, often jauntily swinging his walking stick.

Close by was the small Red & White store run by Tom and Lily Wilkinson. They provided Saturday work for two boys, George Haworth and my brother Orville Zavitz, who were lucky to have a Saturday job as a clerk in the store and delivered orders by bicycle.

During the Depression, the Wilkinsons carried many family accounts. When payments were made on the accounts, customers would receive a bag of candy, usually creams and chocolate mounds. The Wilkinsons had children and were very kind to the little ones coming for penny candy. We could purchase four caramels for a cent, or two honeymoons, or a licorice pipe or whistle. If you had 5 cents, the candy world was yours – what joy!

Next to the Drug Store was Charlie Winter's barbershop where news was dispensed and discussed; a hairdresser shared the front of the building. St. Anne's School, a fixture on Monmouth Road was demolished in 1954-55 and replaced by a modern structure; the school's belfry school was a haven for pigeons. The "Sisters" taught music after school; in warm weather, when windows were open, nearby residents were treated to the warbling of singers. I believe Paul Martin Jr. attended St. Anne's in his early years.

All of those early residents knew each other if not personally, by names and faces. A few of the families come to mind: Leishman, Stewart, Allison, Dixon, Toal, Zavitz, McCall, Walker, Winters, Winterburn, McKee, Bowbeer, DuFour, Courtemanche, Soumis, Desmarais, McCloskey, Brown, McLaughlin, Montrose, Cork, Glassford, Meek, Hemingway, LaVallee, Okeefe, Riddick, Sharp, Murphy, Kenyon, Fitch, Hall, Baker, Kelton, North, Wigle, Kirkup, Boussey, Tate, Stauth, Kerr, Mills.

How many streets can boast Olympic Basketball participants? Jim Stewart, Archie Stewart, Ian Allison went to Germany with the Ford team. Walkerville Collegiate's Girls' Basketball team included Monmouth residents Mamie Thomson, Betty Thomson, Audry LaVallee, Jean Fredenburgh, Molly Stewart, Ether Dixon and Betty Stewart. Our street claimed the Kerr girls as Canadian swimming champions. The "Huron" softball team included Monmouth's "Red" McCall, "Smitty" Smith, Crawford Stewart and Hugh Steel.

Monmouth Road was not many blocks in length, but it was alive. I can close my eyes and travel up and down the street envisioning the homes, faces, and scenes; these are fond memories. A previous contributor, Mark Kulbacki, wrote, "The soul rests where it finds home." How true!

Evelyn (Zavitz) Linney, Windsor

Walkerville's First Apartment House

by Chris Edwards, Issue #8, April/May, 2000

Realizing the need for an apartment house in Walkerville, land developer Charles Chilver (Chilver Road is named for him) erected the Grier Apartments on the corner of Chilver (then known as Victoria Road) and Riverside Drive (Sandwich Street) in 1918.

Considered to be "the most modern and up-to-date structure of its kind in this vicinity," the two-story brick building was erected for $18,000 and housed a doctor's office in addition to 14 apartments containing 5 to 6 large rooms. The interior finish is of Georgia pine on the Chilver side and oak in the apartments facing Riverside. Smith & Walker were the architects of the building.

The Grier apartment has been very well preserved. The units are in excellent condition. Craftsmanship is evident in the construction of the building, such as the front entrance door. When the Peabody Bridge was torn down, drivers and pedestrians were able to get a proper view of the building, and tenants were once again able to enjoy the magnificent Detroit skyline and traffic on the river.

The Crown Inn

A visit to the Crown Inn on Devonshire Road is like opening a window into the past. Construction of this three-storey brick structure began in 1892, to accommodate visitors to Hiram & Walker & Sons.

Of late Victorian design, the building was the first public hotel facility opened in Walkerville, which was expanding with the development of Walker's distillery. It was in keeping with this development that Hiram Walker decided to construct the Crown Inn on Devonshire Road, adjoining his expanding empire.

From its location on the northeast corner of Devonshire and Assumption, the inn provided a clear view of the Detroit River. This

The Crown Inn, painted by Nicholas Hornyansky.

view was possible at the time because Hiram Walker had yet to expand to the west, taking over a popular park called Riverside.

At the time of the Crown Inn's opening, Devonshire Road was the main street in Walkerville. The inn was one of two built by Walker, the other being the Mettawas, located in Kingsville. During its heyday, the Crown featured all the modern conveniences of the era under one roof. In addition to the hotel rooms, there were dining and beverage rooms along with a barbershop for patrons.

While the hotel operation vanished in 1921, when the building was converted to a combination apartment building-store facility, the structure has changed little in its exterior appearance over 100 years. Among other businesses, it housed a motor vehicle license bureau. Currently, a gracious cafe and two other businesses are located on the ground floor, with apartments above.

The Crown Inn in the sixties. photo courtesy Charlie Fox

The Walkerville Exchange a.k.a "The Vic"

by Chris Edwards, Issue #7, February/March, 2000

In 1904, Henry Ford dreamed of selling his cars in the British Empire. This would require a production facility in Canada, preferably close to his Detroit production facility. Walkerville was a natural location for the new facility, given its superb infrastructure of railroad, ferry boats, electricity and water, all designed by entrepreneur extraordinaire Hiram Walker.

Henry Ford agreed to enter into an agreement with the Walkerville Wagon Works, after a series of meetings with owners Gordon MacGregor and investors Charles and John Stodgell. The documents to seal the deal of what is arguably one of the most important Canadian business transactions in the 20th century were signed at The Exchange (the Old Vic).

The Old Vic owes its existence to Charles Chilver, a Walker supporter, building and road commissioner, and developer. In May 1897, he converted his house at the corner of Chilver and Assumption into a tavern, and after much deliberation, christened it "The Walkerville Exchange."

In August 1900, the business was sold to Frank Laforet, reputedly one of the first door-to-door milkmen in the region. Then, in April 1903, Laforet announced that he would build a $10,000 two-story brick hotel on the site. Rather than tear down the house however, he moved it one lot south, and it was rented out as a rooming house (now 438-442 Chilver).

The hotel served as an overnight facility catering to passengers in horse-drawn carriages headed to the nearby Walkerville train station. Business boomed and in 1906, a third floor was added, featuring a balcony, awnings and stylish brackets. Lodging, meals, and entertainment were available, and coal fired heating units at the end of the hallways kept the rooms warm in the winter.

The name was changed to The Victoria Hotel sometime around 1930. The business stayed in the hands of the Laforet family until 1982. Old regulars remember the spinster Ida Laforet, a colourful and eccentric descendant of Frank who lived upstairs. Ida reportedly never came down from her room to the tavern for 14 years!

A major fire in 1968 led to a complete remodelling of the interior and some exterior brickwork. Then in 1982, an investment group led by Larry Burchell purchased the Old Victoria Tavern. One partner was killed in a motorcycle accident; another died during surgery. Burchell stayed on as the sole proprietor.

Top: Frank Laforet's Exchange; Above: The original Vic gang, c. 1898. photos courtesy Larry Burchell

According to current proprietor Aaron Edwards (no relation to publisher Chris Edwards), "The Old Vic is a comfortable and safe environment, where one can enjoy quality draft and home-cooked meals. Our U-shaped bar is very conducive to conversation and camaraderie, and our 'stand ups' are extremely popular during our special event parties."

"The Old Vic remains one of Walkerville's best kept secrets. Our clientele comes from all walks of life. You may have a bus driver sitting next to a CEO of a large corporation," says Edwards.

1888 - 1942
The Walkerville and Detroit Ferry Co.

by Al Roach, Issue #7, February/March 2000

In 1942, a sign was posted at the foot of Devonshire Road, which read: "On May 15th, 1942, this ferry service will be discontinued." It was signed by the Detroit-Walkerville Ferry Company. Thus ended the familiar Detroit-Walkerville ferry service, which had carried on for 61 years.

Outmoded and shoved into the transportation background by the tunnel and bridge, the Walkerville ferries had, nevertheless, continued to ply back and forth between Devonshire Road and the foot of Joseph Campeau in Detroit for four years after the Windsor Ferry Company had given up the ghost (1938).

But even in that late time, commuters recalled when the Wayne and Halcyon, built for the ferry service in 1923 and 1925 respectively, were the latest thing in river transport.

Old-timers recalled when the Essex was launched and put into service back in 1913. And real old-timers talked of the Ariel, first of the ferries, which was born with the company in 1881.

The handwriting had been on the wall, of course, for several years. But in their heyday in the 1920s, the reliable little gray smoke-belchers had ferried as many as 611,283 vehicles and 568,374 pedestrians in a single year.

If you were a boy living in the north end of Walkerville during the '20s and '30's, the ferries provided a daily service for you in the summertime but it had nothing to do with crossing the river.

You would slip under the Peabody Bridge and cross over the CNR track. Then, grabbing the wire mesh fence for support, work your way along the narrow wooden ledge that ran alongside the river until you reached the ferry.

Then, when no one was looking, you jumped from the spiles – the partially submerged poles that helped protect the dock – onto the foot-wide ledge running round the ferry. If you managed to make it around to the back of the boat before a deckhand saw you and turned a hose on you, you had only to wait until the ferry started for a wonderful dive into the foaming, propeller-churned water six or eight feet below.

If you were a novice at the game, you swam or drifted with the strong current a few hundred feet downstream to the storm sewers just east of Beard's Boathouse.

But if you were one of the older and more daring of the breed, you rode well out into the river before leaping in, and perhaps you "swam down" – which in reality meant you carried on with the current to the twin boathouses at the foot of Moy avenue, a half-dozen blocks downstream.

You weren't deterred by the stories of a boy – real or fancied – who had jumped off the ferry, not knowing it was backing away from the dock, and had been sucked into the swirling propeller blades and slashed to death.

Nor were you more than scarcely conscious of the weeds between you and the safety of the shore – weeds where at least one boy you actually knew had been entangled and dragged to his watery grave.

It was all part of the game. And you looked with the proper amount of disdain upon any "sissy" who swam in a pool, or even at a supervised beach.

No one worried about water pollution. And no one called you a delinquent for "snitching" a ride on the ferry.

It was a grand and glorious way of wiling away the lazy summer days until the long, shrill scream of the Parke-Davis whistle, accompanied by the short, deep-throated blasts of the Hiram Walker horn, beckoned you home for 5 p.m. dinner.

photo: Sid Lloyd

Roach Reminisces

Al Roach, teacher, journalist and raconteur, published two books about life in Walkerville and the Border Cities entitled "All Our Memories I & II." The TIMES has published many of his stories. Readers will find them throughout this book. "I was born in Toronto but realized at the age of one that this was a mistake and moved to Walkerville. I have lived on the shores of the Detroit River (the centre of my universe) most of my life." Al passed away in the fall of 2004.

photo: Larry Burchell

photo: Hiram Walker & Sons archives

photo: Tim Baxter Collection

photo: Tim Baxter Collection

Top left: The Ariel, docked at the Walkerville pier, built in 1881, was the first boat built specifically for the Walkerville-Detroit Ferry Company. This 100-foot wooden boat, served passengers and horse-drawn vehicles in the days before the automobile; note the Tecumseh Boat Club in the background, floated over from Detroit in 1890, to pay a debt owed to Hiram Walker. On April 6, 1908, the structure was engulfed by fire and completely destroyed.

Above: The Halcyon stuck in the ice. The steamer Wayne (left) leaves the dock at Walkerville. At 140 feet long with a capacity for 45 cars, it was pressed into service in 1926.

Bottom: The old ferry docks at the foot of Devonshire with The Essex, launched in 1913.

best of the times • 55

The L.E.E. & D.R.R.
Walker's Train Station

by Al Roach, June 7, 1958 (unpublished)

Six months ago, wreckers' hammers destroyed an old fortress – like building near the foot of Devonshire Road. In doing so they destroyed another of Walkerville's links with its quaint Victorian past.

The beautifully designed red brick structure, with its dormers, gables, large square turret, and peigions had been a landmark of this district for almost 70 years.

Back in 1888, two years before Walkerville became incorporated as a town, Hiram Walker built the station as the Detroit River terminus of his Lake Erie, Essex & Detroit River Railway.

From it thundered the old wood-burning engines of a bygone era. With sparks flying from their great funnel-like smoke stacks, they chugged across the countryside linking Walkerville with Harrow, Kingsville and Leamington, and later pushed through to St. Thomas and Port Stanley.

As the years rolled away, the line was absorbed into the Pere Marquette system (1903) and, still later, in the 1940s, became part of the Chesapeake and Ohio. Over the decades, the aging station became involved in one way or another with the lives of most residents of Walkerville. Many farewells and joyful reunions were witnessed there.

In the 1920s, business began to fall off, and in 1926, some passenger trains were replaced with a strange conglomeration of passenger, mail and freight cars known, for obvious reasons, as the "mixed."

By the 1930s, all the trains were "mixed." One left Walkerville and one left St. Thomas each day. The crews lived in St. Thomas and one night out of town they were away from home, staying in Walkerville.

No longer financially successful, the "mixed" came to an inglorious end about 1947. Only freight trains ran until 1955.

Had you been a boy living in the district a quarter of a century ago, however, you would have had little concern for the failing revenues of the Pere Marquette. For the station and its ground provided a veritable treasure-house of places to play in and things to do.

You could play, for instance, "French and English" on the hedged and grassy area beside the station. You could race for house back and forth in usually futile attempts to capture the enemy's flag. And – once in a long, long while – you could burst with exhilaration as you raced to victory with the enemy's banner tucked firmly under your arm.

Or you could race home-made soap-box cars around the smooth gravel track surrounding the field. And you could complain vociferously when some railway express truck interrupted the race. It never occurred to you that you were playing on his territory.

Or you could have water fights at the old Victoria Fountain at the Devonshire Road end of the grounds, a beautiful monument which in that day had not yet fallen prey to the ravages of time.

Right: Train schedule from Walkerville to St. Thomas, and points beyond, c. 1905

postcard Tim Baxter Collection

Hiram Walker's Influence on
Harrow and Area

compiled by Chris Edwards, Issue #17, September 2001

*excerpts from "Harrow and Colchester South: 1792-1992,"
Harrow Early Immigrant Research Society, (HEIRS) 1993*

Not only did Canadian Club founder Hiram Walker create his town called Walkerville, he also stimulated the development of South Essex and the towns of Harrow, Kingsville, and Leamington. Walker initially purchased land at Marshfield and hauled marsh hay for his livestock via land to Amherstburg, and then by water to Walkerville.

As roads improved, he used steam-powered locomotive tractors, but they damaged the roads and bridges, so he decided to build a rail line – the Lake Erie, Essex and Detroit Railroad (LEEDR). "Essex" was later dropped and it became the LEDR. Just the mere mention of the plans for this line resulted in Harrow's growth.

In August 1888, track was laid south from Walkerville to Harrow by nearly 170 Italian immigrant workers, who put down nearly a mile a day. On September 21st, the local paper announced: "The rails will reach Harrow tomorrow – the engine whistle was heard in Harrow from Walker's marsh."

The Amherstburg Echo's September 28th, 1888 edition reported that: "The rails crossed the road at Harrow on Tuesday, and are now rapidly approaching Kingsville, which they will reach by Monday next if the bridges are completed on time." Then, on October 12th: "Bridges on the railway between Harrow and Kingsville are completed except the one across Cedar Creek, which is well under way."

The line was extended to Ruthven by November 1888. As 1889 dawned, the Lake Shore stage connected with the morning train. Passengers going to Windsor could connect with the Windsor Electric Street Railway at a nearby station at the Walkerville Bridge (Peabody Bridge), paying a five cent fare to go to Windsor. Four passenger trains made regular trips to Harrow.

In 1890, track was re-laid at Marshfield in anticipation of the cultivation of Walker's cranberry crop. Although Walker spent $250,000 developing his cranberry farm at Marshfield, and hired an expert from Massachusetts to oversee the operation, the crop was an abysmal failure – a rare misstep for a man who seldom made poor business decisions in his later years (he did manage to extract crude oil of superior quality from Marshfield, however!)

Excursions to Harrow from Windsor were popular. In 1892, over 300 people travelled in fourteen cars for May 24th celebrations. By 1893, Walker extended the railroad east to St.Thomas, and the movement of goods from Essex County to Detroit and Ontario was in full force. The quantity of grain, livestock and produce shipped from Harrow and environs steadily increased. The railway boom enjoyed by Harrow became a source of amazement for locals.

In 1904, the LEDR was sold to Pere Marquette. The personal attention Hiram Walker had given to his railroad was sorely missed – people were soon complaining of old engines and delayed services. In 1910, the Marshfield Station burned to the ground and was not rebuilt.

In 1991, the last train came through Harrow and the old rail line built by Hiram Walker was abandoned. Recently, it was converted into a Greenway, with support from Chrysler Canada. It is now possible to bicycle or walk from Oldcastle to Leamington along Walker's old railway line.

From Top: Harrow Railway Station; Pere Marquette steam engine pulls into Harrow; crowd gathers outside Clark & Company Fine Groceries. photos courtesy HEIRS

Give Me a Dollar To Spend

On Wyandotte Street in the 1930s

by Al Roach, Issue #6, December 1999

When my daughter Cathy came back from Mexico, she brought quite a collection of jewellery with her. To add to the leather coat she had purchased in Spain – to add to the outfits she bought in Vancouver.

In the early 1930s my world of stores (apart from the occasional visit to Detroit) was confined to five blocks along Wyandotte Street East in the Town of Walkerville. Come along for a little tour with me, Gentle Reader, and we'll look in on some of the honest merchants, who are no longer with us, to listen to the tinkle of the little spring-held brass bells above their front doors.

Leaving my boyhood home on the northeast corner of Wyandotte and Devonshire Road, walking west along the north side of Wyandotte, past Lanspearys Drug Store #1 and the CP telegraph office (Mr. A. C. Donaldson, manager) into the John A. Jones grocery store. Mr. Jones, with his white cotton apron tied in back (before World War II shortages put him out of business), reaches into the bins in front of his counter and brings out handfuls of cookies, which cost 15 cents per dozen. And the free aromas – fresh ground coffee, spices and tea in large open tin foil-lined boxes.

Proceeding past the offices of the Walkerville Land and Building Company (where my mother pays her $35 per month rent) and the Walker Insurance Agency Ltd., we come to A. H. Black's Jewellery Store, where Mr. Black will one day sell me my first watch – one of the best in his exclusive store – for $39.

Past A. J. Stevens and Son Bicycle Shop (where I will buy .22 ammunition during my brief and fruitless hunting career as an 18-year-old, skipping classes at Walkerville Collegiate Institute on magnificent October mornings to walk country lanes in search of elusive crows).

Into Cole's Book and Stationery Store at the corner of Kildare Road. The proprietor, Mr. Charles F. Cole and his assistant, Mr. Jacobs, exude the dignity befitting genteel merchants and tell us of the window display of impressive (and expensive) toys planned for next Christmas. *The Border Cities Star* will carry a photograph of the display – a battlefield scene with tin soldiers attacking, real barbed wire, tanks, field guns, and exploding shells (little white lights flashing on and off within cotton puffballs).

Across Kildare, past the barber shop in the old brown frame house where Mr. Snowden cuts my hair for 15 cents. Past lean and grey Nate K. Cornwall (the area's first curler), standing in shirt sleeves and bowler hat in the April sunshine in front of his real estate office.

Past the Chinese restaurant, the Victoria Café, and on to the tiny B.A. service station (always looking and smelling of oil and grease), where the proprietor tries once again to lure us into the large leather armchair he had wired to give neighbourhood boys a mild shock.

Across Victoria Road (Chilver), to the vacant house where we defy ghosts on our nocturnal visits and into Nessel's Department Store – old Mr. Nessel with his head of steel wool sells me a new pair of $1.98 Sisman scampers every spring. Scampers conveniently left at home throughout most of the long hot barefoot summer.

Drop in to see Mr. G. W. Dickie standing on the sawdust-covered floor of his butcher shop, hoping he will offer us a raw wiener. On to visit Mr. Zakoor

Above: Dr. Ken James, whose office was located on Wyandotte near Gladstone, supplied this photo of his father's store, James Meat Market (formerly near the northwest corner of Windermere).

at the Sunshine Fruit Land on the corner of Windermere Road. Where my mother is shocked to see large cabbages offered for sale for five cents and wonders how much of even that minuscule sum reaches the farmer.

Across Windermere, past the familiar red United Cigar Store and James Meat Market to the Walkerville Flower Shop where I buy my annual Mothers' Day plant for 35 cents and dream of the day I will be able to walk in with a dollar and order the best in the house from the proprietor, Miss Lucretia J. Bamford.

Past Gascoyne Soda Fountain (with its mouth-watering display of Easter chocolate bunnies and chickens). Past the Morris Funeral Home and the old grey frame house at the corner of Lincoln. Across Lincoln. Past the Imperial Bank of Canada. Past Loblaw's, with not its name but a huge sign reading "We Sell for Less" across the front of the store. Past the Tivoli Barber Shop.

On to the Tivoli Theatre (formerly the Walkerville) managed by a young man named J. J. Lefaive (of future Cleary Auditorium fame). Who once caught us trying to sneak in to see Jackie Cooper and Wallace Beery in "The Champ," but changed his mind about sending us to jail for ninety-nine years and let us go with a warning.

This is the west boundary of Walkerville and the end of my world. And so across to the south side of the street, keeping a wary eye out for crawling streetcars. Across from the Tivoli we glance at the Dandy Bar-B-Q and Economy Lunch.

And so east along the south side of Wyandotte Street. Crossing Lincoln again we pass Paterson's #4 Drug Store. And come to the M&P (for Mailloux and Parent) where I will one day deliver groceries for 15 hours on Saturdays for $1.25 (that's right, it works out to about eight cents per hour).

Past Bernhardt's Furniture Store (where all of the rich people buy their furniture), across Windermere, past Pleasance Jewellery Store and into the old red and gold decorated F. W. Woolworth's emporium, where I bought my first school bag for 25 cents. Past the Walkerville Bakery and Tea Room (in the Bates Building-1914) where my mother buys Saturday donuts for 20 cents a dozen on Monday mornings.

Past the Bank of Montreal ("Established 1799"), across Victoria [Chilver], past Lanspeary's #12 and so on to the southwest corner of Devonshire and Wyandotte, where the large, screen-porched home houses the office of Dr. G. Gordon Little. On the second floor Dr. L. D. Hogan tries, with limited success, to straighten my crooked teeth. Across Devonshire to the Royal Bank of Canada's Walkerville Branch and north across Wyandotte. And so home.

Spain? Mexico? Vancouver? As shopping centres, they're all right, I guess. But give me a dollar to spend. On Wyandotte Street. In the 1930s...

The Alleys of Our Youth

by Al Roach, Issue #3, July/August 1999

I had a disadvantaged childhood. What's the use of trying to conceal it? I admit it frankly. And every one of my friends was similarly deprived. We attended no antiseptic daycare centres, we were not driven to school on rainy days, we swam in no ceramic-tiled swimming pools, we flew to no vacations in Switzerland, we did not live in air-conditioned homes, we had no manicured lawns to keep off of.

We had no organized little leagues and no expensive tax supported playgrounds, we rode no $2,000 ten-speed Peugeots, we owned no record collections of Led Zeppelin, we ate no store-bought cookies.

We were deprived. We spent long leisurely summer days building rafts on the Detroit River's bank and sailing them down the weed-infested shoreline. We spent innumerable hours riding shunting boxcars in railway yards. We built tree houses in the old oak tree on the spare lot down the street.

And we played in the alleys of Walkerville.

The term "suburbia" was not yet, thank God, even an aberration in a developer's mind; everyone lived downtown. We lived on elm and maple-lined streets. Never far away were streetcars, factories, empty warehouses, abandoned frame homes of the Depression, and dairies with stables filled with magnificent Percherons and the pungent odour of manure.

And never far away were the alleys.

At the foot of every backyard was a high unpainted board fence. And behind the fence was the alley: the centre of all of our social activities. The streets were for the adults. For our parents, for the policeman, the school teacher, the neighbourhood banker and the corner druggist.

The alleys were for us.

They were dirty. They contained garbage and branches and ashes. They

Alley between Niagara Street and Willistead Crescent looking east; Howard Weeks photo

were invariably sprinkled with broken glass. They were inhabited by scrawny alley cats and lean mongrels gnawing on fly-covered bones.

And rats. Big, bold, voracious, flea-infected rats. In short, one brief glance at our alleys would have brought an instant attack of apoplexy to any social worker (had there been any).

But our alleys were an integral part of our lives. In them, on long summer evenings, we played hide-and-go-seek, run-my-sheepy-run, red light, tag and hop-scotch. We rollerskated there and we raced our second-hand C.C.M.'s wildly from alley to alley in hectic, rip-roaring contests of fox and hounds.

Our alleys led to large garbage bins behind the factories where we scrounged for stamps, broken tools, almost empty paint cans ("Hey, this red will be jim-dandy for my soap-box racer!"), pieces of rope, broom handles, rusty razor blades, empty jars, almost straight nails and pop bottles worth two cents each. The treasure trove of youth.

And down our Walkerville alleys rode the neighbourhood ragman blowing his squeaky tin horn. On his rickety grey wagon pulled by a starving bag of bones, listlessly clip-clopping along. A wagon filled with orange boxes, piles of newspapers and nondescript rags. A guy who haggled us down to four cents for the Model-T tire we had previously used as a yard swing. *(cont...)*

Of Boys and a Bridge

by Al Roach, Issue #5, November/December, 1999

illustration by Robert F. Rudkin

Two thunderous blasts reverberate off the Detroit skyline through the crisp November air. Passing to port. The 633-foot Canada Steamship Lines bulk carrier Lemoyne, biggest on the Great Lakes, is butting her way majestically upstream on the choppy, white-capped river.

Watching from the top of Peabody Bridge, four pairs of boy's eyes follow the vessel's progress downstream.

The boys are sitting on the rivet-covered grey metal wall on the north side of the bridge, oblivious to the ear-piercing squeals of steel wheels from the east bound S.W. and A streetcar executing the sharp curve at the top of the bridge just a few feet behind them.

Heavy corduroy trousers insulate the boys' butts from the cold of the steel wall. Rough woolen jackets (with snaps instead of buttons) fend off November blasts. The kid with the big nose fastens his aviator cap under his chin. It will keep his ears warm on this late fall Saturday afternoon of 1934.

Bored with the river, the boys swing their legs over the wall and face the Walker Power Building. While three of them are wearing boots, one retains his annual pair of Sisman scampers from the summer holidays. Going barefoot most of the summer, he has kept them in good shape.

The red-headed boy jumps down onto the streetcar tracks. A heavy grey woollen sock sags to his ankle. He yanks it back up just under the knee and pulls it over the buttoned bottom of his navy blue course serge knickers.

The clip-clop of a horse's hooves on pavement and the rumbling of solid rubber wheels attracts their attention. Head lowered, snorting warm steam onto his frosted velvet snout, a weary roan comes labouring up the bridge, pulling a tall and narrow brown wooden wagon.

The driver sits on a worn black leather seat, over which the curved roof of the wagon extends to protect him from the elements. His wicker basket rests on the seat beside him.

The boys gaze impassively at the black letters reading "Soble Tea and Coffee" on the side of the wagon.

"My Old Lady buys from them," says the chubby one.

The other boys hop down from the wall. They look to the east where the streetcar has now stopped to drop a passenger in front of the tall craneway of Ford's Plant #1 on the north side of Sandwich Street near Drouillard Road.

A sudden rush of a gaggle of boys across the bridge roadway, over a second steel wall and down a sidewalk to the foot of Victoria Road (Susan Avenue to very old-timers, the Chilver Road of the future).

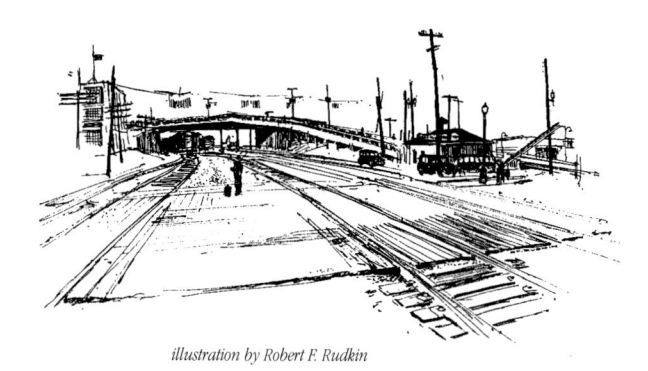

An impulsive challenge to walk across the concrete railing between the sidewalk of the bridge and tracks of the Canadian National Railways 30 feet below. Boys with arms outstretched, airplane style. Wobbling precariously high above the cold steel of the tracks. Gusts of wind rumpling their chunky hair.

The safety of the far bank approaches slowly – ever so slowly.

Four thumps. On the sidewalk at the foot of Devonshire Road. Safe for another day. Until the next challenge of boyhood is accepted.

The boys hang around the traffic gates operated by the corpulent Mr. Jones from his perch, a grey wooden gatehouse stuck on four steel posts 15 feet above the tracks.

The railroader hoists one of the greasy wooden windows of his oversized birdhouse, sticks his head and sings one stanza of his ribald version of "It's a Long Way to Tickle Mary," bringing appropriate replies from the boys.

The chubby kid leans against one of the gateposts, which is still lettered "G.T.R.R." (for Grand Trunk Railroad, which owned these tracks before selling to the CNR in 1923). The boys remember their wagon at the top of the bridge. There is a mad dash for possession and the right to "ride down" first.

A howling mob rolls downward (three on the wagon and one "outrider" pounding along behind) around the blind corner at the foot of Victoria Road onto Sandwich Street (Riverside Drive). Narrowly missing two outraged ladies who give them a "Well, I never" purse of the lips as the wagon roars past.

Darkness comes early on a November afternoon; streetlights come on, and the boys go their separate ways. The skinny dark-haired kid adjusts his red earmuffs, pulls his wagon wearily over the bridge, and heads east towards his mother's boarding house at 111 Sandwich Street. She rents the 10-room brick home from Hiram Walker and Sons Limited for $25 per month.

The streetlights blink three times. Walkerville Chief Constable James Smith wants the town police cruiser to report back to the station in the coach house at Willistead Park.

It is after dark now. And the town has a curfew. "Maybe they've seen me," thinks the skinny dark-haired kid. And he hurries homeward.

(continued from previous page)

True, we had none of the amenities, none of the luxuries, none of the opulence of the 1990s. But then we had none of the consequent frustrations, neuroses, and vandalism which bedevil our society today. Just the odd overturned garbage can or raid on a pear tree. You know.

If I were a city planner today I know what I'd do for the children. I'd plan housing developments which include rivers and railway tracks and factories and old oak trees and street cars and abandoned frame homes and empty warehouses and dairies with magnificent Percherons and the pungent odor of manure. And alleys.

Walkerville's Huckleberry Finn?

Ah HA! This morning I was reading "Life on the Mississippi" by Mark Twain, then picked up *The Times* and found myself reading "Spring Time on the Detroit River" by Al Roach, and suddenly it hit me... Al Roach is Walkerville's Huckleberry Finn!
Charlie Fox, Walkerville

A Remarkable Life

by Elaine Weeks, Issue #2, May/June 1999

The life of Camilla Stodgell Wigle has been long and extremely interesting. Born on Lincoln Road in Walkerville in 1901, Camilla is the youngest of the three children of John and Emma Stodgell. Aside from being a surviving resident of the Walkerville area in the years just after the death of Walkerville's founder Hiram Walker, the fact that Camilla has lived through ten decades of incredible technological change is mind boggling.

When I conveyed a sense of this to Camilla at her home in Riverside, she agreed. "Yes, I've lived in a wonderful era. I have been so lucky to have seen so much and to have done so much, and I'm happy I can remember so much of it."

Camilla's parents operated three businesses in the Flat Iron Building (torn down in 1995), located across from the main office of Hiram Walker's & Sons on Riverside Drive at Devonshire Road. The Flat Iron Building, named because its shape resembled a clothing iron, was large enough to accommodate a 600-seat auditorium and reading room on the second floor, as well as a variety of other shops on the main.

"Next door to my father's set of shops was the Canadian Telegraph Office" recalls Camilla. "People were fascinated to see the operator tapping his messages; they would peer through the window for ages. Next to him was Johnson's Butcher Shop. Children loved him because he was so kind and he gave them frankfurters. Charlie McFarlane's Grocery Store was next and on the end was a shop that manufactured parts for the first 'Reo' automobile."

Camilla (small girl below welcome sign) her mother Emma (standing in doorway), her brother Simeon (leaning against wall to right of mother), and father stands by the curb in the straw hat. They are pictured in front of her parents' business, Stodgell's Confectionery, located in the "Flat Iron Building," Camilla was seven or eight at the time, which dates this postcard to 1908 or 1909. She stands to the right of her cousin, Katie Symes from New York, who lived with the family for four years. Postcard courtesy David L. Newman

The family's popular tea room, confectionery, and china shop kept her parents extremely busy. Young Camilla and her two brothers helped out wherever they could.

Camilla was often responsible for preparing dinner in "The Big House" – the large family home, built by her father, which still stands on Riverside at Strabane across from Central Park Lodge (though vastly changed).

Stodgell's Store in the "Flat Iron building" photo: Hiram Walker & Sons archives

Every Friday afternoon, beginning when she was just ten years old, Camilla would operate the family car for her dad, a non-driver. She would steer it on to the Walkerville Ferry and the two would head to Detroit. There, they would pick up ingredients required for the delicious confections and ice creams he made later at his store.

"The police officer on the corner of Woodward and Jefferson called me 'the little girl with the curls.'" Camilla remembers. "When he saw me coming, he would hold up his white gloved hands to stop the traffic and I would carefully drive around the corner."

As for whether she needed a driver's license, Camilla explains, "Driver's licenses weren't required then since there were so few cars! My dad owned the first car that came off the assembly line in Ford City. It wasn't until cars began to be more common that the need for licenses was recognized."

Camilla's uncle Charlie Stodgell, mayor of Walkerville for three years, owned and operated a wine & spirits shop, also located in the Flat Iron Building. In addition, he was involved in labeling Hiram Walker products. Camilla remembers, as a little girl of 5 or 6, helping to label the bottles.

Camilla's brother Simeon was one of the first stockbrokers in Windsor. He continued to work at his brokerage, Midland Walwyn, until shortly before his death in 1998, at the age of 103. Her other brother Charles, more commonly known as "Chick," had died several years earlier. He was well known as the only compass adjuster and boat surveyor in the Detroit River and Great Lakes region.

Camilla attended both St. Mary's Academy's (the original school

best of the times • 61

was located where the tunnel is now situated, and the second school, also was torn down, in South Windsor) and graduated from Havergal College in Toronto in 1921. She was a trained singer and an accomplished harpist. At seventeen, Camilla played for the Prince of Wales when he was the honoured guest of the City of Windsor.

Camilla drove with her father to many of her performances: "My dad would carefully set the harp on the running board of the Ford," she says. "I would drive of course. He would hang onto the harp through the open window!"

Camilla met her husband John Wigle at the dance school organized by the mothers of Walkerville. Annie Ward Foster had been teaching the offspring of the Fishers, Fords and Dodges in Detroit and agreed to instruct the young ladies and gentlemen of Walkerville in ballroom dancing. The dance school was set up on the second floor of a building at the corner of Wyandotte and Windermere, but soon moved to Wyandotte and Ouellette. At the end of the dance season, a final performance was held in Detroit. One year, Camilla led the Grand March with Edsel Ford.

Camilla's husband was elected the first mayor of Ford City (just east of Walkerville) at the age of 29. He was the youngest mayor in Ontario at the time. Camilla, who was 25, was known as the First Lady of Ford City. They had two children, Elizabeth Camilla and John Whitcombe.

Unfortunately, like so many, they lost nearly everything during the Great Depression. "For ten years we struggled," recalls Camilla. "I don't know how we got through it, but I guess we just kept thinking that one day, things would get better."

Things finally began to improve when John was presented with the opportunity to launch a business called Wigle Propane. At 57, he met an untimely and tragic death. Suddenly, Camilla was in charge of the enterprise, which she ran successfully for many years.

Camilla has been actively involved in many Windsor organizations over the years. The Windsor Symphony has long benefited from her enthusiastic support, and she is a life member of Canterbury College. Camilla did eventually receive her driver's license, and up until 96, continued to drive.

As for words of to live by, Camilla advises: "Never give up! I know there is still a lot to do in the world for me!"

Walker's Whistle: Memories Blowing in the Wind

Born in Walkerville in 1912, Bill Spears has fond memories of his childhood. Though his family 'left town,' moving to Riverside in 1922, Bill never really abandoned Walkerville. Working at Hiram Walkers Ltd. for nearly 40 years may have had something to do with it.

"Life revolved around Walker's whistle," recalls Bill. "When the whistle blew in the morning, you knew it was time to start the day. At noon, the whistle told you how long you had before it was time to go back to school. No one needed to call their children in for supper, the whistle did it for them. And at nine at night, you'd better be home when that whistle blew."

Bill attended St. Mary's Anglican Church as a child. He recalls the cards given to Sunday school children each week, with Bible verses to memorize. Once a youngster had memorized 50 weeks' worth of cards, they were rewarded with a ticket to Bob-Lo Island, location of a popular amusement park. Most children were successful.

Bill and his buddies hung around Walkerville Lumber after school, waiting for the foreman to notice them. Eventually, the foreman gave them each a pile of sticks, which they happily turned into kite frames, adding paper donated by the butcher, and glue made by Bill's mother. By pooling their pocket change, they could purchase a roll of string, and enjoy their efforts for hours.

Bill Spears and his handmade clock featuring a painting of the Walkerville ferry "Ariel" on a saw blade.

According to Bill, the fence around Willistead was erected after Mrs. Chandler Walker discovered people engaging in "inappropriate activity" on the grounds. The gates were locked every night at nine, and proved to be irresistible to adventurous climbers. Scottish Masons were imported to build the fence by the Walkers in 1914.

When his family moved to the wilds of Riverside, Bill and his siblings hated it. Compared to Walkerville, and their house on Monmouth Road, conditions were primitive. No electricity, no toilet, no bathtub – all things they had taken for granted in Walkerville.

After the war, Bill, a boat-builder by trade, applied for a vat-building job at Hiram Walker Ltd. He convinced the boss to hire him by arguing that if he could keep water out of a boat, he could probably keep whisky in a barrel. Hired for a temporary position, he retired from Walker's forty years later as a general foreman.

Bill saw many changes in his four decades at Walker's. He worked on several construction and renovation efforts. During one of these, Bill discovered a set of Christmas cards by artist Nicholas Hornyansky commissioned by Hiram himself, featuring scenes of Walkerville. The cards now hang proudly in Bill's home, carefully mounted and framed.

Technology changed the employment landscape at Hiram Walker's. Barrels were once raised by hand, using pulleys and block-and-tackle. Today, everything is automated. Where 150 men once worked in the racks with Bill, there were six when he retired in the early 1980's. The face of Walker's employees changed too. Initially, most employees were of English, Irish or Scottish descent. Today, the workforce is much more culturally diverse.

What does he miss the most from his days at Hiram Walker? "The drive along the river," asserts Bill, "gazing at the water and all those boats."

Dish Nights at the Tivoli

by Stan Scislowski, Issue #15, May 2001

If you happen to be one of that dwindling segment of the local society that grew up during the "hungry thirties," then you'll probably remember when they held "Dish Nights" at a couple of the local movie houses: the Tivoli and the Palace.

To get people into the movie theatres on the slower weekdays, the managers dreamed up the idea of giving a dish to all adult ticket holders, with a different dish being given each week. It turned out to be one good way to get the mothers out of the house for a spell, and at the same time stock the family cupboard with a set of good dishes.

And they were good dishes too... so I've been told.

photo courtesy Bill Marentette

And then there were those zany Auction Nights held at the Palace Theatre when people flocked to the show carrying all kinds of junk, bric-a-brac, and household items in brown paper bags, in burlap bags, in their pockets and purses, hoping the emcee or auctioneer would call for them.

The auction went as follows: at the intermission between the feature movie and the 'B' movie, the auctioneer on stage would call out something like this: "I'll pay fifty cents for a corkscrew. Anybody in the audience have a corkscrew?"

If you happened to have one, you hollered out: "Okay, Palace!." The first one to do so, ran up the aisle to exchange the item for a shiny fifty-cent piece (we called them half bucks). And then he might offer a whole dollar for a bottle of ink, or a chisel, or a "Big Little Book."

Some of the stuff he asked for you wouldn't think anybody'd have the presence of mind to bring along. But darned if they didn't. Unbelievable! Hilarious too!

What pains some people took to make a buck or two. But you couldn't really blame them. After all, a buck went a long way in those lean days.

photo: David L. Newman Collection

Here's a few of the items I remember people bringing in: a hot-water bottle, a thimble, a spool of thread, a soup ladle, a darning-needle, a cork, a bottle-opener — yes, and even a coat-hanger. You name it, someone had it.

We might not have had TV in those days, and a lot of people didn't even have radios, but there were all kinds of other ways to have fun, to push back the cares and concerns of those hard-scrabble days. To tell you the truth, more so than there are today. Or so I like to think.

Auction Night was just one of the many.

Stan's World

Stanley Scislowski is the author of "Not All of Us Were Brave." Stan, who still resides in Windsor, regularly provides us with fascinating accounts about growing up in the Border Cities during the 1930s and 1940s, as well as his WWII experiences.

~ Margaret Myers Stokes 1915-2002 ~
Letters from Margaret

by Elaine Weeks, Issue #22, March 2002

Margaret Myers Stokes was born in Walkerville in 1915 above Petch's Drug Store (now Peerless Ice Cream) on the corner of Chilver and Wyandotte. She moved to Hamilton over 60 years ago but her memories of Walkerville remained sharp.

Margaret began writing to The *Walkerville Times* in 1999 after someone sent her a copy of the first issue. We received so many letters from Margaret, (sometimes two a day), we decided to create a column called "Letters from Margaret."

From Margaret, we learned about the bats that flew into the Walkerville Bell Telephone office one hot night, and how the operators were so embarrassed when police arrived in response to their screams because they were in their slips due to the heat.

She also described in the "Lipstick Caper" how a thief was brought into court for making off with her Elizabeth Arden lipstick in 1937. And she told us about her beloved younger brother, Cameron, a WWII hero who was shot down at the age of 20.

In our September 2001 issue, Margaret wrote: "I turned 86 on July 19. I didn't know whether to go outside, raise my arms and yell 'Hurrah' or sit down on the curb and cry because I'll turn 90 in four years!"

That was the last letter we received from Margaret. We learned from friends that she was not doing very well. Then on the morning of Tuesday, February 26th, 2001, we received a call informing us that Margaret had passed away.

We never met Margaret but we will miss her, and her letters.

May she rest in peace.

Above: Times editor Elaine Weeks with Margaret's letters. photo Vanda O'Keefe

Moose on a Noose

Issue #3, July/August 1999

The stables (now the Coach House) at Willistead Manor served as the Walkerville Jail and Police Station. There was a giant Englishman who was the Police Chief in those days. He had a huge mustache, and each year he hung a big moose, which he shot while hunting who knows where, from one of the beams in front of the station. People and kids flocked to see the moose hung upright.

Editor's Note: Margaret sent us a photocopy of a photo depicting this amazing sight and we were able to track down an actual photo with the help of staff at Windsor's Community Museum. The photo is undated but is probably from the early 1920s. According to Margaret, the man in the fedora was Police Chief Smith, who shot the moose. The man in the cape was possibly the Mayor. The constable with bare hands was Carl Foster who patrolled Walkerville for many years. This picture was taken at Willistead's Coach House along Chilver Road, showing the moose hanging from the 2nd storey of the jail.

64 • it all began in walkerville

My Walkerville Roots

Issue #8, April/May 2000

I was born in Walkerville, July 19, 1915. My father was a barber, a friend of Bert Snowden who was mentioned in one of your earlier papers. My dad's name was Harry Myers (wife Mable Dickson). I was born above Petch's Drug Store (corner of Victoria – now Chilver and Wyandotte).

When I was born, my father was barbering above Black's Bakery which was owned by Mr. and Mrs. Blackmore who had a daughter nicknamed Bubbles. Then my dad moved around the corner and down a little ways from Ed Keith's gas station. There was a pool hall behind my father's shop and next to it, on Chilver, a Chinese laundry.

When we moved to a flat on the corner of Windermere and Cataraqui, my father liked to go to Bert Graham's Pool Hall for card games on Sunday afternoons. It was across from the Victoria Hotel. My big brother Malcolm and I would be sent by my mother to tell dad to come home for supper. She would say, "Malcolm, you go in – Margaret, you wait outside!!" We were probably 7 and 6 years old.

Later, my father moved his shop to the Crown Inn Building, owned by the Walkerville Land and Building Company. He faced the railway tracks and next door to him was the Telegraph Office. Later, the Walkerville Land & Bldg. Co. added a small storefront to it and we also sold ice creams, tobacco and cigarettes.

In 1927, my family moved to what is now 666 Devonshire Road, one of the houses owned by W.L. & Bldg. Co. across from the Pentilly Manor. At that time, a Colonel Robinson (either an M.P. or M.P.P.) owned Pentilly Manor with his wife and six grown children: Cecil, Sydney, Edward, Florence, Edith and Louisa. Whenever we got too noisy, my mother would say, "Shish! The Robinsons will hear you!"

My mother's dad, William Dickson, worked as a boy at the "Scotten Farm," I think at what is now Moy and Hall Avenue, formerly Moy Hall, on the Detroit River around 1878. William bought a spyglass so he could read the names of the sailing ships up and down the river.

The Pentilly Manor photo courtesy: Charlie Fox

Missing Margaret

My cousin Anne is the widow of Harry Heydon, the Windsor V8's basketball player who could not afford to go to the 1936 Olympics in Berlin. Harry and I are first cousins to Charles E. Fox, who just sent in a photo of his cat reading The TIMES (Issue 28). She and Harry were best friends of Ian and Margaret Stokes (author of The TIMES' "Letters From Margaret" until she passed away this past February). I miss Margaret so much – we spent so much time on the phone, especially after each edition of The TIMES.

Agnes Weaver, Dundas ON

The Lipstick Caper

Issue #10, Sept./Oct. 2000

In 1937, while I was engaged to Ivan (Stokes), Flora Breese (Elizabeth Arden's niece) was training to be a nurse at Grace Hospital (Salvation Army Hospital in those days). One evening, after visiting the A.K.O. frat boys in Colchester where they had a cottage, we decided to get something to eat in Windsor. We parked on Ouellette near the tunnel exit and went into a restaurant at about 10:30 pm.

Ivan had a "coupe" car and Flora and I left our purses behind the seat on the rear window shelf. When we came out, a policeman was standing by the car and told us that a lawyer working nearby had seen a young man force the door open and steal the purses. The lawyer had chased and apprehended the young man.

It turned out the man had thrown away the purses before the police arrived. We probably only had $2 or so in them – it was the depression so no ordinary kids had money – but he had also kept a lipstick.

The lipstick was one that Ivan bought me in Toronto at Simpson's department store. We had gone shopping with Mary Simpson, a childhood Walkerville friend from Windermere Road who was then secretary to Mr. Stuart Henry, head of B.C. Salmon Cannery (Toronto).

Simpson's was showing off a brand new kind of lipstick manufactured by the one and only Elizabeth Arden. What made it exclusive was that it was in a square, oblong case with a mirror that snapped open for quick and discreet lipstick repair in public. (Mother always said, "no lady ever combed her hair, cleaned her nails, applied makeup in public, or on the street.")

When the young thief appeared in court, I explained the newness of the lipstick and that it was not yet sold in the Windsor area. The judge sentenced the young man to six months in jail.

Well, the story made the paper with a caption, "Lipstick Caper." We were shocked at the identity of the thief, as he was someone Ivan had gone to Lowe Tech with. I never heard of him getting into trouble again.

P.S. We were late getting Flora back to the nurses' residence the night of the theft. I think the students had to be in by 11 p.m. and were disciplined if they were late. Flora crawled in through a window that another nurse opened for her but she wasn't caught!

best of the times • 65

The View From Grandma's Window

"It's gone – nothing – not a brick – not even a blade of grass."

by Bonnie (Hazen) Nelson, Issue #8, April, 2000

Five thirty three Windermere is no more; nothing remains. I returned after 35 years, only to find myself standing in a parking lot, feeling overwhelmingly sad. Grand Barnes' big, three story, red brick apartment building and the barn-like garage, the beautiful garden, all gone. But not really – I can still see it all, and grandma still standing at the driveway gate. Never mind. I soon found something very special – my initials and long lost friends' initials in the cement sidewalk. My fingers ran across them fondly. Yes! This is where I spent my childhood!

Mom, Dad and I lived at 580 Lincoln, in the big home that they had moved to the back of the lot to build two stores on Wyandotte. Grandma, being so close, gave me a pleasant refuge from that hectic corner of Lincoln and Wyandotte.

Grandma had so many wonderful tenants over the years. All with their own stories – Thelma Montrose, Millie Morrow, Miss Harkness and Elmer Sirs – I remember them well.

As I stood in that void, so many great times started to well up from my memory banks. The roses, oh, the roses. The whole perimeter of the yard was filled with every colour imaginable. And the fragrance was so memorable that to this day, some rose perfumes put me right back into Grandma's garden.

The garage had the most magnificent cascade of red roses, which almost hid an old weathered window and door. It was a picture to behold every spring and summer.

But the best was Grandma's big old apricot tree. A plethora of fragrant pink blossoms, her pride and joy. That stately tree supported my swing, and it shaded half the yard. The fruit – well, how can I tell you – just heavenly.

I remember the Mother's Days and the Children's Days we celebrated at Lincoln Road United Church with Rev. Sam Henderson and his wife, who always wore the most beautiful spring hats. Those days meant bouquets of lily of the valley, roses and lilacs. That garden celebrated those memorable times as much as we did.

Tulips, daffodils, and narcissus lined the driveway and offered up their blooms for our spring bouquets. Lily of the valley blanketed the ground beneath the apricot tree, and along side the garage. Hands full of this fragrant delicate flower always went to now forgotten teachers at King Edward School.

But my favourite was the trellis covered with sweet peas. Every year, they would reappear in great profusion and to this day, I grow sweet peas just because they were a part of my childhood.

Now I have what I call my own "Grandma's Garden." I have moved to St. Andrews-By-The-Sea in New Brunswick. There, my son Jeff and daughter Christie, help me operate a beautiful bed and breakfast called, "It's The Cat's Meow B & B." My garden is so much like Grandma Barnes' garden that I feel like she is gardening right along side me. The lilies, roses, lilacs, fruit trees, and on and on, have all come full circle in my life. Everything reappears every spring, much to my amazement.

Every blossom is a loving tribute to "Grandma's Garden."

The Junk Collector

Issue #14, March 2001

Grandma's apartment building housed five families and we all interacted in one way or another. One special tenant was Milly Morrow, a perky elderly widow with an eye for "stuff." Never a day passed that Milly wasn't hauling a treasure home (good "fixer-upper" she would say, proud as punch with her latest find).

At spring cleaning time Milly was in her glory. While the neighbourhood was discarding, Milly was acquiring. Her apartment was like a wondrous flea market. She was always scraping and refinishing, hammering and dragging discarded furniture up to her third floor apartment. Milly was our queen of recycling – nothing went to waste.

The old three-car barn next to Grandma's was a real catchall. Grandma discarded pieces of furniture there; well-worn stairs led to a dark attic, and as a child I discovered grandma's legacy therein. Trunks filled with old clothes from the 1800s, hatboxes concealing huge feathered hats. Old letters tied with ribbons; antique rockers and tiny wash stands.

The View From Grandma's Window

Born and raised in Walkerville, Bonnie (Hazen) Nelson lives in St. Andrews By-The-Sea in New Brunswick. We published her memories in early editions of The Walkerville Times.

There was another space in Grandma's life that was a treasure to explore. It was a room in the basement – right out of 'ma and pa kettle.'

The center of this room was occupied by a huge iron roller, a terrifying contraption when viewed through the eyes of a young child. In constant use, I think it was Grandma's most prized possession, next to her treadle sewing machine.

But it was the mountainous piles of wondrous things that attracted me. Grand and Mom both sewed and every snip of a leftover was in a heap that touched the ceiling in a few places. They made their own hats and gloves too – there was so much in this room that to find something one literally had to tunnel. I loved this room, and was allowed to create great Halloween costumes from its contents. Piles of discarded linens, blankets quilts, and best of all, feather ticks.

Here at the B & B in New Brunswick, I display an extensive thimble collection that actually originated from that room. Numerous Alka-Seltzer bottles filled with thimbles, each with a story to tell. They were from Grand's grandmother, aunts and sisters. Yes, they did come in handy in time, to be displayed lovingly in my home.

Raising the Dead

Issue #17, May 2001

Our house at 580 Lincoln had two fair sized chestnut trees in front, which were the worry of my mother's life. If the neighbour boys weren't climbing them, they were throwing sticks up into the branches to bring down those brown jewels.

We had a stained glass window above a picture window that came to a few near misses during those years. It did survive while we lived there, but was gone 45 years later when I walked by the house during my last trip back.

Other vivid memories include Morris's Funeral Home. We lived right next door. Each September, there were always four to six young male Lowe Tech students who moved into the apartment above the funeral home. Which meant there was always someone on the premises, especially during the night, to keep any eye on things.

Well, boys would be boys and their weekend parties were really something. It wasn't too long before they discovered that they could get into the casket show room and, you guessed it, they would lay each other out in a casket and take pictures and mail these photos home. Surely there was a mother or two revelling at the thought of a nice letter from her son and instead shocked to find a picture of him in a casket!

I recall one spring my dad found that the boys were raising turtles on the store roof, which always had water on it and a gravel area and at one point a turtle had laid eggs there. But the best part was the music that they had blasting out of the place every evening – loud enough to raise the dead, which was quite appropriate I'd say.

When my family moved away from Walkerville to Dunnville, Ontario, the funeral home became a night club of sorts. Boy, living next door to that would have been fun – talk about going from one extreme to the other! From dead as a doornail, to all night live entertainment! My mom would have loved that. I'm sure those chestnuts would have been the least of her worries!

Hiram Walker's great great grandson enjoying himself in Walkerville; photo E. Weeks

Finding My Walker Roots

I am awestruck at finding The Walkerville Times website, and deeply appreciate the dedication and detail you have devoted to this wonderful interactive site that answers many of my personal questions.

Let me explain. I am Hiram Walker Smith, the grandson of Hiram Holcomb Walker, grandson of Hiram Walker. My mother, Elsa Elizabeth Walker, passed away in 1986. Hiram Holcomb passed away in 1954. My sisters and I have very little in the way of family heirlooms that answer our many questions. I have spent the last few hours sojourning through this wonderful historical treasure that you have compiled. And I especially thank you.

Seeing how my great great grandfather was so concerned about the quality of life for all people living there just touched my heart deeply. My wife and I would love to come visit Walkerville to thank you in person.

Hiram & Jan (Walker) Smith, Eldersburg, Maryland

A Family We Never Knew

Few words can truly convey the gratitude we feel for the gift of roots that we have received from the gracious people of Walkerville, especially Elaine Weeks and Chris Edwards of the Walkerville Times, and Art Jahns and the people at Hiram Walker's. It is an awesome thing to find that not only were your forebears nice people, but they had earned the respect of so many people over many generations because they tried to make life better for those around them to the fullest of their ability.

Traditions that we want to hold on to are traditions that bring us warmth and meaningfulness, that touch us with compassion for family and community... And that is the true foundation of Walkerville. We thank the many fine people of Walkerville and Windsor for spending so much of their time to make sure that this rich and meaningful history is not lost, that people for generations yet to come will treasure living there because of this heritage. Thank you for embracing us, for sharing not only what you know, but yourselves. Our trip in August was like finding a family we never knew. No, it was finding family itself.

We loved all of it.

Hiram & Jan (Walker) Smith, Eldersburg, Maryland

FLASHBACKS
Readers' Memories of Walkerville

Every Nickel Counted

I was 16 when I worked at Pleasance Jewellers on the corner of Windermere and Wyandotte for the summer. A fellow employee was a petite and beautiful young blonde woman who looked like one of the Gabor sisters. I admired her elegance and classy appearance. Around the corner was a Woolworth's Five & Dime, which was a favorite of the children in the area. This is where we headed when we had a nickel in our pocket. I remember once I lost a nickel down the sewer grate, which was devastating in those days. I tried desperately to retrieve it!

Further down the block came a wonderful aroma from the Walkerville Bakery which provided delicious fresh bread. The Bank of Montreal was at the corner of Wyandotte and Chilver. Across Chilver was the Peerless Dairy, which is still there today. Gascoynes was across Wyandotte at Lincoln was a favourite of the locals, especially children, who could buy all kinds of confections, three for a penny. They could also get ice cream cones and sodas. I had my share whenever I could get five cents from my dad on a summer evening.

My mother would sometimes send me past Lincoln to Loblaw's to buy groceries. One sad day for me was when she gave five dollars for groceries and I returned home without correct change. I was sent back to have them recount the register to prove they owed me money, which they did! What an embarrassment! These were Depression days – every nickel counted!

James' Meat Store was in the same block as Loblaw's. I knew the James boys, who worked with their father. There was a Chinese laundry on Chilver near Wyandotte. I recall the tinkle of the bells when I would be sent there to collect the linen tablecloths.

A fruit market across the street on Wyandotte at Windermere sold Christmas trees every year as well. One year my dad bought a tree for one dollar at the last minute. He tied the top of the tree with a string. The tree was crooked as could be. The worst looking tree you've ever seen but we had to take what was left.

Despite lack of money in the thirties we were one of the lucky families; my dad never lost his job, although his income went down steadily. He worked at the Canadian Bridge Company on Walker Road, which is no longer there. I recall as a child going to see him and being given pennies by the men who worked there. The building has now been torn down. I've told my children how their grandfather was involved in building bridges between the United States and Canada. I believe they are monuments to him and others like him.

As you can tell, we did not lack for much. A barbershop on Wyandotte Street would put a plank across the chair and cut my hair to the tip of my ears as I remember.

Walkerville was a great place to live and grow up in. Family and friends surrounded me who all cared for me!
Patricia Scholz, Windsor

Solving the Missing Spike?

I was born in Ford City and my parents' first home in 1922 was an apartment in Olde Walkerville. Outside of my teenage years and a stint in the Armed Services overseas in the early 40s, until my retirement at age 60, I spent my whole life in Windsor. As a child in the twenties, I rode the old streetcars (fare: 3 cents for kids), the Detroit-Windsor ferries, and the old Tashmoo steamer pictured on your June-July issue, and seem to remember Houdini making an elephant disappear from the stage of the old Capitol Theatre.

I lived through the Great Depression when baloney sandwiches were a luncheon treat. I served 36 years at the Windsor Star, from Copy Boy to Advertising & Public Relations Director. I had the privilege of knowing and working with many fine Windsorites. Although my last 15 years have been spent on Vancouver Island, Windsor will always be my hometown (shared with Harrow, where I spent my teenage years).

I would like to share a Walkerville story recently related to me by the late Vic Brown of Harrow. Vic grew up as a boy in the western Drouillard Road area. In the early 1930s, along with other neighborhood kids, he often frequented Willistead, which was enclosed with the same iron fence in effect today but in those days the gates were locked at night. It seems that on this particular summer night, Vic's gang got locked in the park. The only escape route was over the fence. All the kids made it over, except for one youngster, who had his hand impaled by one of the iron spikes at the top of the fence.

The only way to save him was for the fire department to cut off the spike from the top of the fence and rush him to the hospital where the spike was removed.

I never learned who the boy was, or who the other boys present were, though Vic did say Lyle Molyneau, lifetime proprietor of Lyle's Mens Wear was one of them. Vic spent his working years as a Customs Officer in Windsor. Unfortunately, both Lyle and Vic are no longer alive to fill you in on the details.

However, on the east side of the Willistead fence about halfway down the street, one of the spikes at the top of the fence is missing, where this mishap occurred so many years ago.
Bill Viveash, Vancouver Island

Ed: Reader Frank Pengelly was there that night and remembers that the spike went through the boy's wrist. He and the gang had to hold him up until the firemen came to rescue him. Frank can't recall his name but does know his wrist healed beautifully.

Horses and Sheep on Lincoln Road

In the 1890s, some Walkervillians owned sheep, cows and other livestock. Occasionally, these animals went astray and became a nuisance to residents, especially in the Lincoln Road area, which was developed in the early 1890's. A town pound-keeper was appointed in 1893 to rid the municipality of such wandering nuisances as horses, cattle, sheep, goats, swine and geese. The pound-keeper used his own property for the retention of the various animals. At times, irate householders brought animals to the pound that had damaged their properties and the pound-keeper charged damage fees from the owner of the impounded animal before it was freed. The keeper received fifty cents per day of confinement for a horse, thirty cents for cattle, swine fifty cents, sheep and goats ten cents each. Geese were hardly worthwhile, netting him a mere five cents a day.
Henry Gordon, Walkerville

This Side Up

I have just spent some time roaming around your Virtual Walkerville site which is really excellent! I was busily perusing your article about St. Mary's Church when suddenly I was struck by a memory which has never left me over these past 70 some years.

While most of my family were not members of this parish, my mother was and often went there to attend services. At one time I was a member of a Boy Scout troop that held its meetings in St. Mary's church hall. The scoutmaster was Mr. Creed (Jack Creed's father) – a great character in many ways!

One summer day when it was particularly warm inside, Mr. Creed had us move to the outside lawn area to continue our program. While this was going on, a small gnome-like old man continuously paraded back and forth with a water sprinkling can in his hand. After a while Mr. Creed, who seemed to know this character, asked him what he was doing shuttling back and forth with the water sprinkling can in and out of the graveyard area. His reply astounded me and I have never forgotten it 'till this day!

"I'm watering my wife's grave," he said, "because I know she would rather have grass on her back than flowers on her belly."

For years I speculated as youngsters are prone to do… about why she had been buried "face down."

Army Ellis, California

Many Friends in St. Mary's Churchyard

My parents left England in 1912 to settle in Windsor. Their first home was a Hiram Walker cottage at 91 Argyle. It was a 2-bedroom house with no bathroom for which they paid ten dollars a month.

My sister, May, and I were born there. Our neighbours were Mrs. Kelly, Mrs. Stevens and Doris and Kathline Stevens. Dr. McCormick, whose office was located on Wyandotte and Windermere, was our doctor. We went swimming at Bairds Beach, a strip of sand at the side of Peabody Bridge. With a growing family we moved to 1149 Lincoln and the four of us graduated from King Edward School with O.M. Stonehouse as principal (we called him Old Man). We went to Walkerville High and then on to W.D. Lowe. My dad was on welfare and paid for our food orders by helping dig (by hand) the overpass on Walker Road and Wyandotte.

Our life was centered around St. Mary's Church where I was christened, confirmed and married. I taught Sunday school at the back of the church – our thrill was climbing the spiral stairs to the bell tower.

We moved to Walker Road and watched the Lowe Mansion (later Paul Martin's house), being built. In 1965 I bought a mink stole at Lazarre's Furs only to discover that it had once belonged to Mrs. Martin. I still wear it. At 87 I have many friends in St. Mary's churchyard. I hope my rambling has helped jog some memories!

Rosa Millis Linton Tyler, Windsor

The Merchants of Walkerville

Walkerville resident Henry Gordon, 85, remembers well what area businesses were like when he was a lad.

The Walkerville Bakery: Located between Windermere and Chilver. "You could buy all the bread and fancy cakes you wanted from the most exquisite to the most simple. They made a lemon square, no icing but a lemon butter filing – delicious!"

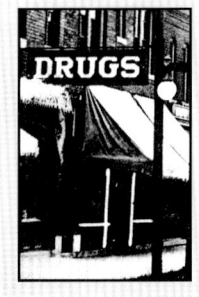

Petch's Drugstore & Soda Fountain: Corner of Windermere and Wyandotte. The Walkerville boys used to hang out here and at Bert Snowden's barber shop next door.

Arnold's Gingerale: Early 30s. Assumption Street near Walker on north side of street. Manufactured Gingerale. Had a soda fountain. Bought by Vernon's.

Walkerville's First Gas Station: Run by Ed Keith at Victoria (Chilver) and Wyandotte. He lived in Windsor and his son went to King Edward School.

Walkerville's Jewel

Willistead Manor in Olde Walkerville has meant so much to me. As a child in the 1940s, my mother often took me by bus from our home on Erie Street to visit the small but excellent public library located there. Going to Willistead was like stepping back in time to visit an old English manor house at the turn of the century. I used to wonder about the lives of the people who had lived there.

The second floor housed Windsor's first public art gallery; I would study the paintings that hung on its walls. I was especially interested in these paintings because I loved to draw and paint.

When I was about 10 years old, my class at Dougall Avenue Public School was taken on a tour of the manor. When we reached the second floor, Ken Saltmarche, the Willistead Art Gallery's first curator, greeted us. Mr. Saltmarche was a fine artist himself. In later years, I was to learn how much he had done to develop the gallery and thereby promote the love and appreciation of art in the Windsor area.

Mr. Saltmarche showed the class around, commenting on each picture and asked for our impressions. One of the pictures on display was by a local artist, Harry Zeilig. I told the curator that I was in an art class at the local "Y" taught by Mr. Zeilig.

"Are you enjoying it?" Mr. Saltmarche asked. "Very much," I replied. "Mr. Zeilig is showing us how to draw hands and feet, but I'm still not very good at it." A good-natured laugh came from my classmates. "I'm not very good at that either," said Mr. Saltmarche, which refuelled the laughter.

Later, he asked me privately what I liked to draw and if I had any samples of my work. I said I liked to draw faces, animals, country scenes, ballet dancers and sailboats. I did have a sample, but unfortunately it was in a place that it shouldn't have been – drawn in pencil in the front of a school textbook!

Mr. Saltmarche was impressed with the sketch, but advised me to rub it out before the teacher saw it. He asked if it was drawn from life. I explained that it was our sailboat and we sailed on Lake St. Clair in the summer. Then he informed me that there would soon be art classes held at Willistead and suggested I look into taking them. Later I did take some art classes there and studied art in university. I'm certain that Willistead and Mr. Saltmarche played a part in my continued love of the graphic arts.

Willistead is no longer a public art gallery, but a multi-use cultural and social facility. I still love to visit. One of Windsor's most enchanting attractions is Art in the Park, held on Willistead's grounds. This annual exhibit allows hundreds of artists and visitors to delve into the arts and crafts in a relaxed, festival atmosphere. Indeed, Willistead is a jewel in Windsor's crown.

Sylvia Berk, Windsor

In Search of Bennett's Meat Pie

Anyone remember the Bennett Pies retail and manufacturing facility located west of the Bennett Building on Ontario Street (maybe Richmond) between Monmouth and Argyle Roads?

I can vividly remember my parents visiting Bennett Pies in the 1950s & 60s to stock up on their awesome meat pies – which were unlike any other meat pies available at the time. Mom bought them in bulk and stored them in our Coldspot deep freeze. The pies that Bennett's produced were a Windsor legend; they've gone out of business.

I'm not sure if Bennett's made the filling from scratch or whether they purchased it from an outside source. Regardless, I would be deeply indebted to anyone who might know the recipe, whether from Bennett family members or former workers in their bakery. The taste was a sensation, fondly remembered, and very much appreciated. I would greatly appreciate having this outstanding recipe.

And the Recipe is...

The response to my inquiry regarding Bennett's Pies was overwhelming. I received telephone calls from twelve individuals, including former workers, friends and associates of the now defunct Bennett's Pies, and from some direct descendants of the Bennett family.

The Bennett Bakery was located on the southwest corner of Ontario Street and Monmouth Road in the back of the building. The business operated in the adjacent building west of the Bennett apartment building. To this day, the Bennett name is emblazoned on the front of the building as a lasting memorial to the Bennett family. The Bennett's were hard working and very friendly folks.

I've managed to compile a recipe of mixed sorts by using all the relayed information. The basic recipe was quite simple but add to that a wide variety of variations and a simple task became quite complex.

Remember now, this is a BASIC recipe:

> **BENNETT'S MEAT PIE FILLING**
> 1-1/2 lbs. of medium ground beef
> 1 cup onions, diced fine
> water
> 1 cup dry bread crumbs
> salt and pepper to taste

Place the ground beef in a medium saucepan and add about 3/4 cup of water. Add the onions, season with salt and pepper to taste and cook over medium-high heat until the ground beef is browned and the onions become soft and translucent. Reduce the heat, stir in the bread crumbs and add seasoning; allow to simmer uncovered, until most of the water has disappeared. Remove from heat and allow to cool until room temperature.

In some cases, sage was offered as a seasoning but in no specific quantity. One caller suggested using cold, mashed potatoes as a substitute for the bread crumbs. I experimented using the bread crumbs with very satisfactory results. The "secret" to any pie is to ensure that the filling is cold before the pie is assembled. Most callers offered that advice in mutual agreement. In addition, most advised that lard, not shortening was used by Bennett's to make the pastry. In addition, their meat pies were completely assembled before baking.

My experience has shown that a meat pie of this nature is best cooked in a 375 F. oven for 45 minutes or until the top crust is golden brown. It was also pointed out that water was used to seal the top crust to the lower one and to prevent the meat filling from escaping during baking.

I remain graciously indebted to all those who contacted me to share their ideas and advice. Every caller was sincere, friendly and so happy to be able to offer their opinions. I could not help but feel so privileged to be an attentive listener because in every case, their phone manners and sincerity were impeccable.

Richard Vargyas, Walkerville

Dairy Delights

Walkerside Dairy's plant was located at the corner of Wyandotte and Monmouth Road. During the 30s, the milk with the cream on top was delivered in bottles. Butter and eggs were also delivered. Perhaps you can remember the milk boxes, usually at the side door of the houses. The horse and wagon I am pictured with above were in the Labour Day parades. I got to ride in the wagon once.

Walkerside Dairy was also into the ice cream business. Bricks were 25 cents and came in many flavours. My Dad's pharmacy on Monmouth Road had a sign on the side wall sponsoring their ice cream. I served many ice cream cones and milk shakes while working in the store. We usually had a brick of ice cream for the family for Sunday supper.

I have seen pictures of the old Walkerville street cars that ran from the Devonshire and Wyandotte streets over and up Monmouth Road to Ottawa Street. I took pictures of the tracks being torn up for steel needed for the WWII about 1943.

Jack Willson, Oshawa

The "Toonerville Trolley"

This little street car travelled through Walkerville. It was named the Toonerville Trolley after a popular newspaper comic. It only had four wheels and you could rock it.

For six cents you could take it from Devonshire and Wyandotte, along Wyandotte for two blocks to Monmouth, up Monmouth to Ottawa Street across to Walker then up to General Motors, then along Seminole where it reversed and retraced the route back to Devonshire. This was the transportation for all the Walkerville people who worked in all the factories and businesses along Walker Road.

During the Second World War, the double tracks for the trolley along Monmouth were torn up and cut with an acetylene torch into 2 foot lengths. They were shipped to the Hamilton Iron and Steel plant for use in the war effort.

Bruce and Norah Long, Walkerville

The Captain and Me

My great grandfather was William Henry Corr, son of William Corr and Mary (Quinn) who arrived as pensioners at Fort Malden on July 4, 1851. According to his obituary, he was "master of several of the better known river ferry boats over a span of years. Captain Corr had been in marine service from the time he was 15 years old. He had been in service up to the close of the last season.

He entered the employ of the Canada Southern Railroad before it was changed to the Michigan Central, having been stationed at Amherstburg and moved to Detroit in the early 1880s advancing through the ranks in the fleet of that company to a captaincy. He tied up the last Michigan Central car ferry when the river tunnel replaced that service, altogether serving the Michigan Central 33 years.

For 11 years he was captain of the Walkerville ferry, his last command being the steamer Essex. He formerly was in charge of the steamer Ariel (right), purchased by the state of Michigan for Mackinac ferry service and later was in command of the steamer Wayne, which replaced it.

Captain Corr was a member of Detroit Harbor local No. 47, Masters, Mates and Pilots, also affiliated with the Hibernians, Holy Name Society and Catholic Men's Benevolent Association." (Detroit Free Press, February 24, 1924)

He was married in Amherstburg to Louasa Cadoret, daughter of Joachim Cadoret and Hanorah Mullen. In 1901 they were living in Windsor with their children William, Leo, Mary, Clara, Kathleen and Beatrice. So, if he had moved to Detroit in the 1880s, he must have moved more than once.
Margaret Collrin, via e.mail

postcard from David L. Newman Collection

Walker Farms... Home Sweet Home

I stumbled onto your website during my genealogical research and what a wonderful discovery it was! So much so, I've subscribed to your magazine and have also ordered a copy of *The Best of The TIMES* book.

I was born and raised in Windsor, moved to the Northwest Territories in 1974, but most of my family still resides in Windsor. My earliest recollection of life on this earth begins at Walker Farms so I was enthralled, in particular, with your article on this subject. Our family lived there from 1946 until 1950 and our house was the end boarding house located closest to the pig farms. Unlike the other houses, we did not have a functional washroom facility and had to use a "honeybucket." There was an occasion when the water froze in the taps and we went three months without running water.

My brother and I used to walk daily through the barns (above) to visit the sows and their piglets. Sometimes we would watch our next door neighbour, Mr. Eckmier, brand the piglets' ears. I can still hear their squealing. There was a padlock behind our house where the cows and bull grazed. I remember my amazement (and fear) when I looked out our front room window one afternoon to see a cow standing on our front veranda! Mr. Eckmier came to the rescue and guided the stray back to the padlock.

The old abandoned dairy was visible from our front room window, and I vividly recall the night it burned to the ground. I was in my bed (which was near the front room window) and noticed a "red glow" in the sky before I actually saw the dairy burning. All the neighbours gathered in our front yard to watch the huge spectacular fire. I've always wondered how old I was when this happened. Thanks to one of your articles, I now know that I was six at the time.

On our semi-circle lived the Eckmiers, Crowleys, Mussons amd Kehoes. When I read Midge Kristinovich's recollections of Walker Farms in the article, something tweaked about her name. I felt I knew her but the Kristinovich surname I didn't recognize. I phoned my mother in Windsor and she confirmed a Midge Lester and Neil (her brother) lived two doors away from us and that her family was from Pelee Island. I too, like Midge, walked a mile to Walker Road School. My first grade teacher was Mrs. Smith. I still have my class photo.
Carol Green (née Malec), Northwest Territories

Walkerville Love Stories

Mae Moore worked behind the counter of the Hasty Mart on Wyandotte Street East in 1946. Ron Stewart was a single father, who delivered the store's bread from Canada Bread on Walker Road. Ron's son, Jim, happened to be in Mae's Sunday school class at Emmanuel United Church on Lincoln Road.

Eighteen months later, Ron and Mae married, and went on to have three more children, one of whom being my mother. They enjoyed 35 years of marriage, raising their family in South Walkerville, before Ron's death in March 1984.

Emmanuel United was the starting point for other long-lasting romances. Hazel Connell and Ron Payne met as teens at Bible School there, and were involved in several youth groups together. Ron, who lived on Lincoln Road at the time, was just a few blocks away from Hazel's home on Moy Avenue.

The couple married six years after they met, on October 21, 1944, and had four children. Their children and grandchildren have continued to be active in scouting and guiding groups, and every Tuesday morning, the Senior Social Group at Emmanuel relies on Hazel and Ron to be there to start the coffee and tea. They've been married 56 years and counting.

Eleanor Adams, a graduate of St. Mary's Academy, ran the family-owned Adams Family Drugstore, at the corner of Windermere and Tecumseh Road. One evening in 1937 while she was standing at the counter, Paul Martin, Liberal M.P. for Essex/Kent came in to buy his cigars. According to Paul Martin Jr., his father said to another customer: "This is the girl I'm going to marry."

Eleanor (Nell) wasn't exactly impressed with the young politician at first, but they began seeing one another soon after. Paul and Nell were married September 8, 1937. They had two children, and lived in Walkerville for the rest of their lives.

Paul's son, Paul Martin Jr., (former Prime Minister of Canada), also found the girl of his dreams in Walkerville. "I literally married the girl next door," he says. Sheila Cowan lived two doors north of the Martin family on Devonshire Road; Paul and Sheila married in 1965 and have three sons.
Shelley Divinich Haggert, Windsor

ROSE OF ABERLONE

T. C. SHERWOOD, PRESIDENT OF PLYMOUTH NATIONAL BANK, CONTRACTED IN 1886 WITH HIRAM WALKER OF WALKERVILLE, ONTARIO FOR THE PURCHASE OF A COW, ROSE 2D OF ABERLONE. BOTH PARTIES BELIEVED THAT ROSE WAS BARREN AND WOULD NOT BREED, AND THAT MISTAKE LED TO ONE OF THE MOST FAMOUS CONTRACT CASES IN U.S. HISTORY.

MR. SHERWOOD TRIED TO PAY HIRAM WALKER THE AGREED-UPON PRICE, $80, BUT MR. WALKER REFUSED IT AFTER DISCOVERING THAT ROSE WAS PREGNANT. HER VALUE WAS NOW ABOUT 10 TIMES GREATER THAN THAT AGREED TO BY THE PARTIES. MR. SHERWOOD SUED TO TAKE POSSESSION OF ROSE AT THE ORIGINAL PRICE.

THE MICHIGAN SUPREME COURT IN 1887 DECLARED IN SHERWOOD V. WALKER THAT, BECAUSE A MUTUAL MISTAKE AFFECTING THE SUBSTANCE OF THE TRANSACTION HAD BEEN MADE, HIRAM WALKER HAD A RIGHT TO RESCIND THE CONTRACT, AND KEEP THE COW. LAW STUDENTS EVER SINCE HAVE STUDIED THE CASE AS A CLASSIC EXAMPLE OF THE CONTRACTS LAW DOCTRINE OF RESCISSION BASED ON MUTUAL MISTAKE.

MR. SHERWOOD WENT ON TO DISTINCTION AS MICHIGAN'S FIRST BANKING COMMISSIONER, HIRAM WALKER & SONS IS A WORLDWIDE LEADER IN THE PRODUCTION OF ALCOHOL BEVERAGES, AND ROSE ACHIEVED IMMORTALITY IN A POEM BY UCLA LAW PROFESSOR BRAINERD CURRIE, WHO CONCLUDES, "FOR STUDENTS OF LAW MUST STILL ATONE/FOR THE SHAME OF ROSE OF ABERLONE."

PLACED BY THE STATE BAR OF MICHIGAN AND THE SUBURBAN BAR ASSOCIATION OF WESTERN WAYNE COUNTY
1993

Don't Have a Cow, Man

My daughter was walking her dog in Kellogg Park in the centre of the town of Plymouth, Michigan and happened to notice and read the plaque at left. I thought your readers would enjoy this bit of history about Hiram Walker.

When I was a small child our family lived in one of the Hiram Walker cottages located at 244 Cadillac Street. It had been moved from where the Ford Power Plant now stands. The house is still located on Cadillac although it has undergone many changes.

My father helped dig under the house for the basement and also bricked up a large fireplace in the living room. For a few years my mother had a beauty shop in a small closed-in section of the front porch. I have noticed now that the front porch had been completely closed in.

My father rented the house from about 1930-48 (and my grandmother before that). What fond memories I have of that cottage.

Audrey Houle, Windsor

From the Editor: Aberlone was an area of Scotland, which may have been where the cow came from originally. The plaque was installed in Kellogg Park, as part of the Legal Milestone Marker program of the State Bar of Michigan. The case between Walker and Sherwood resulted in a landmark legal case involving contract law and is still taught in every law school to this day. This information is courtesy of Beth Stewart, the archivist of the Plymouth, Michigan Museum

No Playing on Sundays in Walkerville

I am one who can say they were born in Walkerville. I was born in 1928. When I was three months old my house was moved. Hiram Walker's needed the land our house was on in order to build a new rack warehouse. Our house, which was located at 1 Argyle opposite "The Hut" (Legion Branch 12) was moved to the southeast corner of St. Luke at Richmond towards Ford City. We moved to 178 Monmouth (now 976 Monmouth), which my dad purchased for $1200 in the late 1940s after the Walkerville Land and Building Co. made the Monmouth row houses available for sale.

Some of my memories of growing up in Walkerville include the Percheron horses that would clear the sidewalks of snow. I also remember that on Sundays we were not allowed to play. The police would go around and if they caught any kids playing baseball, they would take your bat and ball away and then you had to walk over to the station on Monday to pick it up.

After "crucifixion" (Walkerville's amalgamation with Windsor) in 1935, former Walkerville Mayor Bennet, who I think lived on Chilver, would not accept mail if it said Windsor. He would give it right back to the postman.

William (Billy) Meek, South Windsor

Editor's Note: According to William Meek, the house at 1 Argyle was moved to southeast corner of St. Luke at Richmond (bottom left). We think the house on the northeast corner looks more like the Argyle cottages (bottom right).

Knead Some Bread?

I just came across your website and thoroughly enjoyed reading the articles. My dad and grandfather worked at Canada Bread on Walker Road during the 50s. I can remember getting up at 4:30 a.m. to go to work with my dad. I was between 5 and 8 years old. He drove a delivery truck for the company and I would help him deliver bread to stores all over Windsor. I still remember the switch over from horses to trucks and that the Canada Bread bakery had horse stalls on site.

Do you know what section/location of the city Rossini Road was officially located in – Sandwich East, Walkerville? Our family lived south of the railway tracks at 1243 Rossini. My grandfather built the house in the 20's and I lived there until 1976. My mom sold the house around 1980. She went to school at Walkerville High. My mother, aunts, uncles and grandfather all worked for Hiram Walker's at one time or another.

Larry Treverton, Kingston

Editor's Note: The only thing we have at the moment concerning Canada Bread is a small sign that was put in the window for the bread man. Rossini is in Olde Riverside, just east of Ford City. Above: A family stands in front of the Canada Bread wagon during the 20s. Photo courtesy Russel Lariviere

The Cooperage around 1910; handmade oak barrels will soon put Canadian Club whisky to "sleep" for six years.
photo: Hiram Walker & Sons archives

Hiram Walker landscaped an area near his dock, called Riverside Park (foot of Devonshire Road), and built a pagoda where citizens could sit, watch the boats or lawn bowl. *photo: Hiram Walker & Sons archives*

Canada's first trolley bus was built by the St. Louis Car Co. On May 4th, 1932, number 1 is shown on the 3.5 mile Lincoln Road route at Windermere and Cataraqui Roads near King Edward School. photo courtesy Bernie Drouillard

Electric street car in Walkerville, picks up passengers at Wyandotte Street at Chilver Road, c. 1895. The Electric street car service ended altogether in 1939.
photo courtesy George White

Interesting angle of the Walkerville terminus with the Canadian Club distillery in background.
photo courtesy Charlie Fox

William Clapper pushing Charlie Fox's 1929 Ford Sports Coupe.
photo courtesy Charlie Fox

74 • it all began in walkerville

Testing the quality of CC at the distillery.
photo Hiram Walker & Sons archives

Roll out the barrel – extremely rare photo of the CC workers in the 19th century.
photo Hiram Walker & Sons archives

Setting up shop in Olde Walkerville, around 1900. photo courtesy Charlie Fox

Walker Road at the turn of the 20th century, fire station turrets in background. photo courtesy George White

best of the times • 75

Underpass construction on Wyandotte between Walker and Drouillard Road – a depression era make-work program. From top left – streetcar tracks ready for removal; filling the cracks of the old streetcar rails; construction workers; manual labour; giant excavation pit that will soon form the underpass (note Ford Factory with water tower and Walkerville Brewery; bottom – view of finished Drouillard Road underpass looking toward river, old Ford City Hall and Ford Plant #2.
photos courtesy Harry Patterson

"With three boats in commission and unequalled facilities for loading and unloading, the company is able to take care of the ever-increasing traffic, and, at the same time, maintain its regular schedules even in the hours when the traffic is the heaviest."

Hiram Walker – His Life, His Work and The Development of Walker Institutions in Walkerville, Ontario, by Francis X. Chauvin (unpublished)
courtesy Phil and Mickey Chauvin

Left: Customs House and ferry dock during prohibition, Walkerville. photo courtesey Larry Burchell

Below: Roy Clark with his brother Elmer "Boots" Clark in front of Walkerville Printing Limited, 1949. photo courtesy Marianne Bower

Victoria Hotel, Walkerville, 1940s, still stands at corner of Chilver Road and Assumption Street.
photo courtesy Larry Burchell

best of the times • 77

"When Walkerville was granted its civic rank as a town in 1890, it possessed all the elements that constitute maturity. The town had life – social, economic and industrial.

Old enough to have had a past, it nevertheless had none, because all its history was wrapped up around the masterful mind that had founded the settlement, that had shaped its destiny and that had planned it as a model town.

It has well been said that Walkerville was a civic child of fortune."

Hiram Walker – His Life, His Work and The Development of Walker Institutions in Walkerville, Ontario, by Francis X. Chauvin (unpublished)
courtesy of Phil and Mickey Chauvin

above and right:
Having a ball at the Walkerville Golf and Country Club (now Walkerville High School and Willistead Crescent) at turn of the 20th century.
photos courtesy Charlie Fox

1936
Dick's Confectionary Free Ice Cream Day,
photo courtesy Velvet Restaurant

78 • it all began in walkerville

Tree-lined Sandwich Street (Riverside Drive) facing west, view of rectifying house, c. 1920
photo Hiram Walker & Sons archives

Rare glimpse of the Walker women on the balcony, grand opening of the new world headquarters, 1894.
photo Hiram Walker & Sons archives

Above: Panorama of Walkerville showing the old Walkerville train station, the Crown Inn, Page Fence Co., and Hiram Walker's Distillery. Photographed from original wooden Peabody Bridge on Riverside Drive East looking east towards Devonshire Road. photo courtesy Florence Anderson, Belle River

Horse and buggy crosses the tracks on Devonshire facing south in 1900 showing Walkerville train station and baggage building on right, designed by Mason and Rice. photo Hiram Walker & Sons' archives

Walkerville matures as a community, aerial view, around 1950. photo Hiram Walker & Sons' archives

80 • it all began in walkerville

"The sewers in said village have all been constructed by Hiram Walker & Sons, the fire brigade of fifty-two men, the fire appliances, the police force of two men, one for day and one for night duty, the repairs of streets and the construction of repairs of sidewalks other than the sidewalk on the main street, the night service, the electric lighting of the streets, have been provided at the expense of the said firm."
from a petition by the Town of Sandwich, 1871

Walkerville firefighters, 1885

Walkerville long room employees pose outside Customs & Excise office, Walkerville, 1931

Walkerville Fire Department, 1920s.

Last town council, Walkerville, 1935, before Walkerville was annexed by the City of Windsor, despite fierce opposition by Walkerville residents. photo: Hiram Walker & Sons archives

Charlie Lee stands in front of 624 Chilver Road in 1948 (offices of The Walkerville Times from 2000-2003). photo courtesy Chuck Lee

Fred Johnson (2nd from left) with unidentified gentlemen somewhere in Walkerville. photo courtesy Fred's grandson, Neil MacPhee

Top: Johnsons Meat Market (1905-1910), once operated in the old Flat Iron Building on Riverside Drive at Devonshire Road. Roy F. Dickie, a butcher, stands at far right. photo courtesy Roy D. Dickie

Right: Roy F. Dickie (2nd from right) and friends at the Walkerville Ferry Docks, c. 1905.

Below: Walkerville street scene, c. 1910, looking east on Wyandotte Street at Windermere. The block at right still stands, while the block in the middle left, burned down in August 2003. The buildings in the fore-ground at left were consolidated into one large building several years ago.
postcard David L. Newman Collection

2
On the Border

Ferry Landing, Windsor, 1900's
photo David L. Newman Collection

A New City is Born
Windsor: May 24, 1892

by Carl Morgan, Issue #25, June 2002 (from his 1991 book, *"Birth of a City"*)

It was one of those picture-perfect spring days: A light, caressing breeze played tease-tag with cottonball clouds, bobbing and skipping in unfettered delight across the sky, clear blue as the finest Wedgwood. It was the kind of day that made heavy hearts light and forced lingering memories of bitter winter months to retreat like the last traces of a morning fog.

If you could pick any day you wanted as the day to celebrate your city's first birthday, the best would be this one – Tuesday, May 24th, 1892.

Making it doubly important, it was also the day the British Empire celebrated the 73rd birthday of Queen Victoria. She was also making her 55th year as monarch.

The city had come awake early this Tuesday morning and even now the clock on the tower overlooking the low-slung wooden army barracks in City Square, showed that it was not yet nine o'clock. There was still more than an hour to wait before the big event – the Trades and Society Procession – would begin.

People were in a party mood; streets were alive with the sights and sounds of excited celebrants; mongrel dogs added to the bedlam, running among skittish horses, yapping at the heels of little boys with hoops doing tricks for little girls who were cuddling rag dolls and pretending not to notice.

The ladies, prim in their cotton prints, scolded their men for tardiness; the men grumbled, running thick fingers inside the stiff rim of starched collars; toes were already raw from the chafing of heavy black boots normally endured only at weddings, funerals and Sabbath services.

From the distance came the spirited strains of patriotic marching music as the 21st Fusiliers and the Toronto Grenadiers, one of the country's leading military bands, tuned their instruments for the parade.

The Grenadiers had left Toronto by train at ten o'clock Saturday night and arrived in Windsor at seven o'clock Sunday morning. They were billeted on the Janisse farm just outside the city.

Hundreds poured into the city with every passing hour; they came from the surrounding countryside by wagon, by boat, and train; others crossed by ferry from Detroit to join and congratulate their Canadian cousins on this important day.

It was a day to remember, a day marked by saturation coverage of the city's two newspapers, The Windsor Record, a daily, and its sister, The Windsor Weekly Record.

Above: Opened in 1871, Windsor Central School was renovated and became City Hall from about 1903 through 1956. The present City Hall was built on the same site, and opened in 1958. All Saints Anglican Church is in the background.

Oscar E. Fleming, who was elected mayor at the age of 30, led the battle for Windsor to gain status as a city. He was the last mayor of the Town of Windsor and the first mayor of the City of Windsor.
photo from "Birth of a City"

BOOM-TE-RA-RA
Our Birthday Party a Hummer from Hummerville

In 1892, the Klondike Gold Rush was still firing the minds of fortune seekers everywhere... a woolen mill in Essex County discovered its own mother lode by providing blankets for sale to those heading northwest in search of wealth beyond imagining.

The Weekly Record, then owned by McNee and McKay and selling for $1 per annum (in advance), had recently reported the launching of a "fine ferry boat built for the Detroit, Belle Isle and Windsor Ferry Company... Electric street lighting had arrived in 1890, the same year the first patient was admitted to Hotel Dieu Hospital.

"The citizens took right hold and nearly every building in the city was gay with bunting flags. The Trades and Society Procession was simply immense and the spirits of the people present were away up..."

Windsor's first telephone exchange came in 1880 and by 1892, there were 205 subscribers. By 1888, the city had three miles of paved streets and in 1891 council voted to spend $20,000 on paving. In June 1886 the first commercial electric railway system in Canada started running between Windsor and Walkerville...

"The procession occupied over an hour in passing a given place... About 9 o'clock in the morning people began moving towards the rendezvous for the procession at the corner of Bruce Avenue and Sandwich Street. Shortly after 10 o'clock the procession got a move on..."

Cod liver oil sold at 35 cents a bottle and was said to be good for those suffering from difficulty of breathing, tightness of chest, wasting away flesh, throat troubles, bronchitis, weak lung, asthma, cough, catarrh and colds.

Pickles were selling 20 to 30 cents per hundred; potatoes, 45 cents per bushel; dressed chicken, 6 cents per pound.

"Immediately after dinner the crowd wended its way to the park and during the afternoon, from Sandwich Street to the park, Ouellette Avenue was a veritable living mass of humanity...

The crowd was immense and exceeded all expectations. Only a small portion of the number visited the park, yet that was filled to overflowing..."

Canada's population was 4,833,000 in 1891... the Canadian West was opening to settlers... the CPR advertised trains leaving Toronto every Tuesday for Manitoba and the Northwest.

At 12 o'clock the celebration committee banqueted the visitors and officers at the British American (Hotel). A large number sat down to a good spread...

"General Committee Chairman Francis Cleary proposed the toasts to the Queen and Dominion and Provincial Parliaments... Immediately after the banquet the party took hacks and proceeded to the Driving Park (Jackson Park) to see the sports and military display..."

The Evening Record is two years old... it is a pretty feisty infant... The roads between Windsor and Amherstburg have been improved so that the stage can be used again...

"Shortly after 3 o'clock the Grenadiers and Fusiliers headed by their respective bands arrived at the Driving Park and took up positions preparatory to the Grenadiers going through the movements of trooping the colours..."

The three cars on the Sandwich line cover 462 metres per day... The demand for lights is so great that the Citizens Electric Light Company will install a new 1800 candlepower dynamo...

In April, the Ontario Legislature passed, with a one-vote majority, a new bill allowing women to study and practise law in the province.

"Before the train pulled out, Col. Dawson attempted to make a speech but the noise of the assembled was too great and beyond a few in his immediate vicinity, his remarks were unheard."

Biff Bang Boom! Oh what a jag.
Take in your flags. It was a hummer.
Didn't we spread ourselves...?

The Great Western Railway

Without a railway connection with the East, any progress for the region was virtually impossible. The opening of the Michigan Central to Chicago in 1852 helped impress those responsible for building the Great Western the urgency of their task.

The big day for Windsor and Detroit was January 17, 1854, when the first passenger trains reached Windsor from Niagara Falls.

In Windsor and Detroit, it was a day of intense excitement and celebration and properly so, since for the first time these places were in railroad communication with New York and the East.

Windsor and Detroit closed up business for some hours in honour of the great occasion. The first train was due to arrive in Windsor at 2 p.m., but it was three hours late.

When the locomotive was seen, a salute of cannon in Detroit greeted the arrival. The travellers, consisting of the president, directors, and officers of the road, with invited guests, crossed to Detroit. There an immense procession was organized, which included the mayor and officials of Detroit, together with military and civic bodies. The procession moved to the long freight house of the Michigan Central Railroad in Detroit where all enjoyed a fine dinner.

One of those at the banquet was Col. John Prince of Sandwich, who proposed his toast, "The ladies of Michigan. God bless their little hearts!"

From "Garden Gateway to Canada," by Neil F. Morrison

first electric trolley in Canada  *first international vehicular tunnel*  *birthplace of the auto in Canada*

Windsor & Area Firsts

- The first battle of the War of 1812 was fought in Windsor, and the Francois Baby House (Windsor's Community Museum) served briefly as American headquarters.

- Elijah McCoy, born in 1843 in Colchester, Ontario, invented a device to oil train locomotives, Great Lakes steamships, ocean liners, and factories machinery while they were working. By 1923 his invention was used throughout the world and popularized the expression the "real McCoy."

- Delos R. Davis of Amherstburg was the first black lawyer in Canada, admitted to the Ontario bar on November 15, 1886.

- One of the first electric streetcars in the world and first in Canada, rode the rails in Windsor in 1886. J. W. Tringham, an employee for the telephone company, invented the dynamo for the 25-foot long car, which had seats on both sides.

- John and Horace Dodge first established their careers in Windsor. They were working for Canadian Typethetic Company in 1890, where Horace became plant superintendent. The two brothers invented the Evans and Dodge bicycle (E & D), and leased the plant to manufacture the two-wheelers. In the early 1900s the Dodge brothers opened a machine shop in Detroit, where they developed a ball-bearing bicycle and attracted the attention of the early automotive manufacturers.

- Windsor was the first Canadian terminal of the underground railroad. After the War of 1812 and before the Civil War, escaped slaves from the south found protection here under the British flag. John Brown brought the first black slaves to Canada, arriving in Windsor via the underground railway.

- In 1919, the first health centre in Canada was established in Windsor. Sixteen years later, in 1935, the Windsor Cancer Clinic, one of the original cancer clinics opened in the province, was sponsored by the Ontario government.

- In 1923, stop signs were posted at major intersections. Two years later, Windsor became one of the first cities to install stop lights.

- The Detroit Red Wings hockey club played their first home game in Windsor's Border City Arena (now the Windsor Arena) on November 18, 1926.

- The Ambassador Bridge, spanning the Detroit River between Detroit and Windsor, was completed in 1929. At the time, it was the largest international span in the world.

- The Detroit-Windsor tunnel, completed in 1930, was the first underwater international vehicular tunnel in the world.

- Windsor opened the first joint YMCA-YWCA in the world in 1937.

- In 1938, Windsor was the first city in Ontario to initiate safety patrols organized in the schools by the Windsor Police Department.

- In 1957, Canterbury College became the first Anglican College in the world to affiliate with a Roman Catholic University (Assumption University). The campus became the University of Windsor in 1962.

- Prescription Services Inc., begun by Bill Wilkinson in 1958, was the first prepaid voluntary medical prescription service in North America. In the early '60s the plan was copyrighted in Canada under the name Green Shield Prepaid Services Inc., and became a forerunner to OHIP.

- Windsor was one of the first cities in Canada to have a senior citizens' centre in 1962.

- Windsor Raceway pioneered winter harness racing when it opened on October 21st, 1965. The raceway's spiral-graded track was first upon its completion for opening day in 1979.

- The invention of the world's first "palm and turn" safety top was instigated by a Windsor pediatrician, the late Henri Breault.

- Windsor has been home to more car and truck manufacturers than any other city in Canada.

Lost Beaches of the Border Cities

by Richard Bonner, Coaster Enthusiasts of Canada, Issue #54, Summer 2005

photos courtesy David L. Newman Postcard Collection

East Windsor Bathing Beach, a.k.a. Alexander Park
North side of Riverside Drive East between Strabane Avenue and Rossini Boulevard

Alexander Park has changed dramatically since the early 1930s when the site was commonly known as the East Windsor Bathing Beach (pictured above in the 1920s, During the late 1920s, the Ford City (East Windsor) Planning Department initiated a major land reclamation project at the site, an undertaking that ultimately led to the establishment of a sandy, public beach with more than 200 feet of waterfront parkland.

The City then aquired the property for Alexander Park in several stages during the 1950s. Various single lots were purchased, but the majority of the land was obtained from two sources: the David Meretsky estate and the Ursuline Order of the Diocese of London, Ontario.

Named in honour of Viscount Alexander of Tunis, then Canada's Governor General, the park was officially dedicated in 1959 with a tree-planting ceremony. Alexander Park is also the site of a plaque honouring Oscar Flemming, the last mayor of the town of Windsor (1891) and the City of Windsor's first Mayor (1892). [See Oscar Flemming story October 2004, Issue #48]

Today, Alexander Park is no longer used as a beach for local swimmers but is a passive, tranquil park where one may go to simply relax. Located across from Detroit's 1000-acre Belle Isle, its natural riverfront beauty is accentuated each summer by gardens containing hundreds of colourful rose bushes, making Alexander Park an ideal setting for outdoor weddings.

Manhattan Park/Beach

This resort grew out of John Gauthier's pleasure park which had been built around The Sandwich Mineral Springs and its hotel. It occupied about four hectares and contained 10 picnic groves with walkways and a children's playground. At night the park was illuminated by 100 gas lamps. The proprietors were Stephenson & Blanchett.

1885 ads proclaimed that the area had Beautiful Shady Lawns, a cafe serving "the Delicacies of the Season," a Dairy with Milk, Creams, Ices, Fruits and Confections, and The Children's Carousal. It's not clear if this was a merry-go-round or not as it's mentioned in conjunction with Swings, so it may have been the name of a children's play area. However, given the popularity of merry-go-rounds, this likely referred to a ride. Also available were Croquet Grounds and Lawn Tennis. There was apparently no charge for the recreations.

The park had 25 baths associated with the springs and were advertised as "Unequalled in the world for medicinal properties." Another ad proclaimed "A RESORT FOR FAMILIES -- Every precaution will be taken to guard against any Disorderly, Intoxicated or Improper persons on these grounds."

The same ferries serviced both Manhattan and Brighton Beach, but the schedules advertised for Manhattan differ from those listed for Brighton. These state that ferries ran every hour from 10:30 AM until 5:30 PM, with a final boat leaving Brighton via Manhattan at 6 PM. It appears the popularity of both resorts increased and the times in the "Brighton" article are for later in July. Another ad claims conversely, that ferries ran every half hour. Unless there was more than one ferry company serving the park, perhaps the schedules changed quite a bit for these new parks until they settled on one schedule suitable for the number of patrons utilizing the service.

Celebrations for Dominion Day (now Canada Day) on July 1st and American Independence Day on July 4th in 1885 included Brass and String Music all day and evening and large fireworks displays. The July 4th show was by a Professor Holz from Detroit. Ferries for both occasions would delay last boats leaving until after the fireworks had completed. One ad of the time called the park "The Coney Island of the West."

The park must have also had a theater, or at least an outdoor performance area for travelling troupes. Some of the acts which played Manhattan Park also went on to the Toronto Industrial Exhibition, which was later renamed The "Canadian National Exhibition." One such production was 1886s The Last Days of Pompeii.

No information has surfaced on the demise of this park, but it may have failed not long after the springs lost their luster. The ferries apparently stopped in the late 1880s. However, one source claims that the park changed hands several times. This is borne out by the fact that Stephenson & Blanchett apparently had goods seized in 1885 after a bad opening season. Eventually B.H. Rothwell and Gilbert Graham became the proprietors. They changed the name to Lagoon Park (see further on). If so, this may mean the park continued to run until 1902 when it officially became Lagoon Park.

Brighton Beach

George C. Buchanan of Kentucky opened this amusement park on the riverfront just below The Sandwich Mineral Springs, south of Windsor (now within the Windsor limits). It lay directly opposite the mouth of the River Rouge. The springs were a source of sulphur water, which was believed to have medicinal benefits.

People had flocked to the area for a number of years and the local ferry companies began to run excursions to the springs starting in 1875. This likely spurred Buchanan to open a resort a decade later. It's unclear if the "Brighton Beach" name was his or one that had been used to describe the area previously.

He built The Brighton Beach Hotel which fronted right on the Detroit River. It was an Elizabethan-style building three stories high with a verandah surrounding all but one side. A wine/barroom in the basement was catered by Charles Johns, the former steward of The Detroit Club. A newly built 400-metre driveway lead from the hotel to the springs. The constable-patrolled grounds had gravelled walkways with many flowers and shrubs, and seats under the trees for relaxation. Maple trees lined the shore.

Entertainment was provided with concerts and plays including a religious performance for July 4, 1886. There was a Japanese Pavilion theater which provided plays and likely vaudeville acts. An incident happened in July of 1886 with a troupe performing Gilbert & Sullivan's "The Mikado," a light, English-language opera. It seems the promoter never secured the rights to perform the musical in Canada and he was arrested for copyright infringement. The play had been scheduled for every night at 8PM with several matinees spread through the week. Seats were 15, 25, and 50 cents. The engagement was terminated and a new play, "The Chimes of Normandy," opened the following day, succeeded by "Three Too Many."

The only ride mentioned is a roller coaster patterned after one at Coney Island, New York. The Detroit Free Press described it as, "...a roller tobogganing arrangement where a crowd can go at the rate of a mile a minute for the space of eleven seconds. This is an exact counterpart of the celebrated coasting structure at Coney Island." The "mile a minute" is an obvious exaggeration. It works out to be 96 kilometres per hour and no coasters of that era achieved such a speed.

The ride was described as being the equivalent of 137 metres around. This implies it may have been a continuous circuit. Charles Alcoke had such a ride at Coney Island in 1884 as did Philip Hinkle in 1885. As well, La Marcus Thompson had a switchback coaster at Coney Island in 1884, and this coaster may also have been that model, if it wasn't a continuous circuit. Regardless, the Brighton ride was certainly one of the earliest such rides in Canada. (See Dundurn Park for another possible Alcoke or Hinkle creation in Canada.)

There is no word on additional Brighton Beach rides yet. However a newspaper report of an accident on the coaster has surfaced. On July 4, 1886 a man was pitched from the ride. He had been drinking and may have been showing off, or simply not hanging on. Coasters of that era had no lap bars or belts. Then again, they also provided a much gentler ride. Regardless, the man dropped about 5 metres to the ground and was thrown about the same distance from the ride. He broke no bones, but was bruised and bleeding. This is the oldest report which has surfaced of a roller coaster accident in Canada.

Additional plans called for a baseball diamond but it's not known if it was built or not. However, lacrosse games were scheduled for July 1st and 4th, 1885, so there was at least a field for that. Ads declaring the teams as the "Independents of Windsor (Champions of the West) versus Six Nation Indians, (Champion Indian Team). Games called at 3 o'clock." Although these games might have been played in any open area, this probably means the fields were constructed. Additional celebration events were "Indian War Dances" on July 2, 3, 4, and 5.

Transportation to the park was via a new bus service started in 1885 and by ferry boats which stopped at the Brighton Beach pier. Boats left Woodward Avenue in Detroit on a daily basis starting at 9:30 AM. They ran hourly until 9 PM with a final boat leaving Brighton at 10 PM. Another ad proclaims half-hourly sailings starting at 10:30 AM. Note that these times don't jive with one another nor with those shown in the "Manhattan" article above, but appear to be for later in the season when business perhaps warranted more sailings. Although not mentioned, it's possible that these boats may have picked up passengers on the Canadian side, as well.

Next to the ferry pier at the park, was an enclosure meant for sea lions when the hot season was over but it's unclear what was meant by that. One would think that these would be an attraction during the warm tourist season, not after. Also available in this location was a smaller wharf from which row boats may have been used.

For July 3rd, 1886, it was reported that 2,500 attended the park to escape a heat wave.

The park operated for only a few years until the sulphur ran out at the springs. People stopped coming so the ferry service was terminated, but it's not known if the buses continued to run. Without the draw of the springs or a ferry service, and coupled with the fact that competitor Bob-Lo Island Park offered more facilities, Brighton Beach likely ceased operations at this point.

Lyttles Bakery on Ouellette

We usually went on Saturdays. Baked goods were on the right, the lunch counter was on the left and tables and booths were toward the back. The colour scheme was black and white – Art Deco perhaps?

I remember the custard filled chocolate éclairs the best. They weren't too big or too small and made a tasty delight for a young child who sat eagerly at the lunch counter, not realizing that the baked good counter was on the right!

When we bought baked goods to take home, there were many to choose from – a lovely white or brown loaf, the small but tasty Hovis, Victoria sponge which usually had a lemon filling, or chocolate cake with thick rows of marshmallows on top. Purchases would go into a white box with string tied round and round both ways. The ladies were adept and always had a smile and a few kind words.

Fond memories of a place that provided a wonderful service to the people of Windsor.
Wendy Fraser, Windsor

Hidden Gem

After reading the memories of Lyttle's Bakery in the December/January 2004 issue, I remembered I had this photo of the Palace Theatre on Ouellette Avenue when it was being renovated. There was a hidden sign between the walls for Lyttle's Bake Shop [across the street at 329 Ouellette] advertising baked goods, fine chocolates, party favors, ice cream and catering.
Steve Ouellette, Windsor

Lyttle's Went a Long Way

Although I am not old enough to remember some of the times and places that made history in and around Windsor, the letter from Wendy Fraser that appeared in the February issue of The Times, "Lyttle's Bakery on Ouellette" sparked very fond memories of growing up in the Pelissier/Victoria/Montrose area of town.

During my high school years and then some, I worked for John and Evelyn Gilchrist (owners of Lyttle's Bakery) at their second site, Gilchrist Coffee Shop at 1362 Ouellette Avenue. Seems just like yesterday.

I remember the Volkswagen delivery van parking outside the shop and the driver unloading the trays of baked goods – Scotch meat pies, sausage rolls, every kind of fruit pie anyone could imagine, scones, raisin bread, butter tarts and all those other goodies that made Lyttle's so famous! What sticks in my mind the most were the different colored specialty breads made to order for preferred customers and the delicate checkerboard pattern tea sandwiches (no crusts) that were prepared for a neighbor's afternoon social.

It was a very busy spot that favoured by many local businesses and of course, the surrounding neighbours. I even remember their slogan: Good things come in Lyttle's boxes.

I recall a gas station on the south west corner of Ouellette Avenue and Ellis called Smitty's whose owners drove a big black Cadillac. Of course, south of the Coffee Shop were the Big V Pharmacy and Ingram's Supplies. The building owned by John and Evelyn Gilchrist also served as a commercial site for Arnoff Real Estate and Moxon's Beauty Shop with four apartments upstairs.
Andrea Grimes, Windsor

Let's Go to the Drive-In!

by Beth Fowler, Issue #54, Summer 2005

What happened to the Drive-In? First appearing as symbols of optimistic postwar modernity, they eventually became denigrated into run-down remnants of the past. Many years after the last Drive-In closed in this area, these venues gained a cultural importance in people's memories that far exceeds the actual impact they made in film or business.

Drive-Ins accounted for a large portion of ticket sales in North America only between the early '50s and late '70s, but they encapsulated the age so perfectly that their presence in everything from kitschy memorabilia books to old *Happy Days* reruns has become part of cultural memory — even among those who are too young to remember them!

The Windsor area, with its distinctive automotive background, was especially receptive to movie theatres built entirely around the popularity of cars and the pleasure of driving, both thrilling pursuits for people who were often denied individual transportation during World War Two. The combination of cars and film, two of the most celebrated technologies at the time, was an almost immediate success that would ultimately lead to a host of new experiences which would define this time period in a way few others could.

The drive-in theatre was invented in the early 1930s by Richard Hollingshead, an automotive salesman who was looking for ways to sell more cars. He figured that if people could actually drive up to a screen in order to see films, they would be more likely to make what was then an exorbitant purchase. His experiments with outdoor screens and projectors led to the first drive-in theater opening in Camden, New Jersey, on June 6, 1933. Its first showing? The classic, *Wife Beware*!

The film might have been easily forgotten, but drive-ins showed a gradual upsurge in popularity throughout the decade. The outbreak of WWII slowed this growth as rationing metals and gasoline prevented people from buying new cars or driving the ones they already owned, but this sacrifice would prove to be beneficial once the war ended. The economy picked up, and people were ready to spend money on trends that used new technologies.

In Windsor, the Dydzak family recognized the opportunity in this business, and opened Windsor Drive-In, situated on Walker Road near Highway 3, in 1950. The mid- to late-'50s proved to be the peak years for drive-ins in Canada, as numbers went from 820 theaters in 1948 to approximately 4000 by 1958. By this time, the Dydzaks had purchased Skyway Theatre, on County Road 42, and one in St. Clair Beach. There was no doubt that business was booming, and this new enterprise prompted plenty of unique experiences.

One of the reasons for the success of drive-ins in general is that they catered to suburban families, a growing demographic due to the postwar Baby Boom. Judy Dydzak Klingel, the daughter of John Dydzak, owner of the three Windsor locations, notes, "What was nice was you could put pajamas on the kids, make your own popcorn, and if the kids fall asleep you were in your car. It was a real family thing."

One Drive-In patron remembers: "When our kids were little there was never a better time than getting our kids bathed and in their PJ's and taking them to see a movie (with a pizza in tow)." Another remembers being bundled up in the back seat with her sister and being "amazed at the size of the 'big screen.'"

Above: The Skyway entrance. Courtesy Judy Klingel
Right: Paul Langan at the Skyway Drive-In 1986. Courtesy Paul Langan

In order to complete the family vibe, Klingel remembers her father arranging for fireworks to be launched on holidays and for a playground to be built right below the screen. Lynn Fabick says that "it was an odd sight seeing children in their pajamas going down slides and on little merry-go-rounds."

Families were not the theatres' only target customers, however; the advent of a teenage culture and its attendant concerns of separating from parents meant that Drive-Ins, where people could be alone without *really* being alone, became especially popular hang-outs for adolescents. Fabick enjoyed "looking at other cars (because) you'd see people making out all the time, and the windows would get steamed up."

A then-teenage Drive-In enthusiast recounts that "When a lot of us were going, the first car would get there early and place paper grocery bags on the speakers next to each other and write OUT OF ORDER on them so we could all park by each other."

The Skyway snack bar in 1950. (l-r) John Dydzak Jr, Judy (Dydzak) Klingel (little girl), Constance Dydzak and Helen Dydzak (wife of John). Photo courtesy Judy Klingel

Of course, anyone who remembers going to Drive-Ins as a teenager also remembers trying to sneak people in by hiding in the trunk. Paul Langan, who worked briefly at the Leamington Drive In in the early '70s, wonders, "why it was the girls had to hide in the trunk to sneak in without paying. I am sure it was because we could get three girls in that car trunk!"

Another attendant notes that "My girlfriend and I hid in the trunk of her brother's car so we wouldn't have to pay to get in – I only did that once!"

Apparently, there were people who made a practice of doing just that. Klingel says that "We caught onto it after awhile, so we used to start checking the trunks and we found a few people out." She does concede, however, that 'Dollar Carload' nights, where entire cars received admission for a mere dollar, helped solve the problem at least one night per week.

As with every nostalgic memory, mishaps make for some of the fondest recollections. One of the most castigated parts of the experience was dealing with the individual speakers that were handed out to each car. One patron remembers, "the speakers hung on the windows, and after you aligned your car just right and got everything set, you realized that the speaker didn't work." Fabick admits that "A lot of times we'd just turn the sound down."

Sometimes the sound was so poor that people forgot that the speakers were in the car. John McTavish, for one, recounts driving away without returning them on more than one occasion. Langan, however, puts a positive spin on the experience: "The portable speakers for the cheesy sound were part of the mystique of going to the Drive-In. When the movie sound came over the car radio it was so much better, but in some ways a part of the classic Drive-In had died."

Another dubious drive-in pleasure was the food served at the concession stand. Langan notes that these snacks "Always defied explanation. The hot dogs (and fries for that matter) were not the greatest, but then again, you expected that, and enjoyed talking about the food quality. It all added to the Drive-In experience. The food was inexpensive at least."

Perhaps the price was relative, as one attendant notes, "My husband still remembers spending at least fifty dollars on all the pop and popcorn and hot dogs." Fabick recalls that "the concession stands were really sort of questionable, but it was still fun buying a bunch of junk food to have during the movie, and then you got to sit in your car and eat it. It didn't matter how messy you were."

Incidents like these lent an air of innocence and fun to the Drive-In, one that made people line up on the highway just to see popular movies like *Easy Rider* and films of big events like the Queen's Coronation in 1953. Why then did most Drive-Ins close by the middle of the 1980s?

Klingel says that the introduction of VCRs and cable TV meant, "people were staying home with their movies instead of going to

Drive-Ins. You could see it just gradually going down and down." Fabick adds, "regular movies started having bigger screens and Dolby sound. It was more advanced, and they couldn't do that with the Drive-Ins. They tried to make the speakers better, but you can't get surround sound. People were demanding better quality with prices going up." Drive-Ins were being forced to increase their prices without providing many new amenities, and so most of them were being forced to shut down.

In Windsor, Odeon Cinema took a ten-year lease with an option to buy on the theatres when they closed in 1986, but they gave it up when the contract ran out.

An era may have ended, but the memories will live on in the collective memories of those who were lucky enough to have experienced this short but unique time in 20th century history.

Tuesday June 6, 1933

Who Invented the Drive-In?

The First Drive-In Theater was invented by Richard M. Hollingshead. Hollingshead worked out the details by hanging a sheet for a screen in his backyard. Richard began to experiment in the driveway of his home at 212 Thomas Avenue, New Jersey. Richard mounted a 1928 Kodak projector on the hood of his car, he used it to project onto a screen he had nailed to trees in his backyard. He placed a radio behind the screen for sound, then started his test of his idea. Richard tested sound with the windows up, down and half way. He tested many weather conditions; using his lawn sprinkler he simulated a rainstorm. Richard liked what he saw and heard.

One main problem did arise in his test. If cars were parked behind each other, the cars at the rear would not be able to see the whole picture, due to the car in front. This did not stop Richard. He lined up cars in his driveway, spacing them at various distances, and placing blocks under their front wheels. He was able to find the correct spacing and the correct angles to build ramps for the cars front tires to park on. Thus was born the first Patent for the Drive-In Theater.

Information courtesy www.driveintheater.com

At one time there were 4,000 Drive-Ins across Canada!

Operating Theaters in Canada in 2005

- 1 in Alberta
- 7 in British Columbia
- 5 in Manitoba
- 3 in New Brunswick
- 2 in Nova Scotia
- 22 in Ontario
- 1 in Prince Edward Island
- 3 in Saskatchewan

The Sandwich East Enterprise, Thursday, May 14th, 1959

Hot Rocks Kept Car Warm

In December 1952, while stationed at HMCS NADEN (Supply Corp School), Victoria, B.C. I met John and Ann Mains and was invited to spend Christmas Day with their family. After dinner, Ann mentioned that on Sunday evenings they all went to the local Drive-In theatre since it only cost a dollar for a carload of people.

That Sunday, I came to visit, had lunch and then was surprised when John suddenly started putting large stones in the oven. I asked what he was doing and was informed that they were the heater for the car. John drove a 1939 Ford station wagon and the heater did not work.

At about 6 pm, John took the stones out of the oven and put them in a five-gallon metal pail and put the pail in the rear of the station wagon.

Then we set off for the drive-in theatre, a ten minute drive. When we arrived, we parked in the middle of the theatre. It was a real nice position to see everything.

John and Ann were in the front seat and their two boys and myself were in the back, stretched out on a comforter with the heater.

First were the previews for next week, then the Serial (Buck Rogers) I believe, then a cartoon, and then the main feature – a cowboy movie. Every Sunday night was a western.

Surprisingly, that homemade heater kept the car warm the whole evening. I attended the Sunday night movie every week until the middle of April, when I graduated from school and transferred to Halifax.

I kept in touch with John and Ann until October 1960 when I immigrated to the United States and joined the U.S. Navy.

Now that I am able to look back to those times, I realize how full my life as a seventeen-year-old kid was. I had a great family that treated me like a son.

I made quite a few trips home to Windsor between 1952 and 1960. Some of those trips were in the winter and I was real sad to see the local Drive-In movie theatre closed for the winter. If I remember right, it was used as a parking lot for new Chrysler cars.

I wonder what this generation would do if there were a Drive-In movie theatre where the whole family could go and see a movie (in the car) for an inexpensive price?

You would not need that five-gallon metal pail and the heated stones!

Robert S. Owen, Mobile, Alabama

From a Gallery in Willistead...

Well Hung
A Brief History of the Art Gallery of Windsor

by Elaine Weeks, Issue #13, February 2001

*"I believe that Willistead has a great future...
it is there that the intellectual life of the town should centre. As time
goes on, there should be built up a museum and picture gallery."*
Anne Hume, Willistead Chief Librarian, 1921

*Kenneth Saltmarche,
first Gallery Director*

In the Beginning...

It is quite possible that if Hiram Walker hadn't relocated his distillery on this side of the Detroit River in 1858, Windsor wouldn't have an art gallery. Instead, his decision to move his flouring mill and small whisky distillery from Detroit to waterfront land just east of Windsor, proved to be the catalyst not only for a world famous product but for a world class art gallery.

A few years after Walker's death in 1899, construction of an elaborate manor for his oldest son, E. Chandler Walker and his wife Mary Griffin Walker, commenced in the Town of Walkerville. Among their plans for manor's interior was a specific request regarding the positioning of wall sconces to permit the display of their extensive art collection.

Chandler was a generous art patron and personal friend to many artists, especially the Impressionists. The manor's drawing room once held priceless paintings by Monet, Renoir, Pissarro and Cassatt. At one point, Chandler loaned 49 of his paintings for an exhibit at the Detroit Museum of Art.

The heirs of Edward Chandler Walker deeded Willistead to the town of Walkerville after his death in 1921, with the stipulation that it be used as a park, a library, and for any purpose in the public interest. Mrs. Walker donated most of their paintings to the Corcoran Gallery in Washington, D.C.

A public library was created on the main floor of the Willistead manor with offices for the Corporation of the Town of Walkerville on the second and third.

A fine librarian was hired, Miss Anne Hume, and we can thank her for initiating the public exhibition of art in this area.

Hume convinced the Royal Ontario Museum to loan a selection of Egyptian, Roman and Chinese treasures to the library in 1922 and then trained her sights on the National Gallery of Canada. After months of negotiation, she arranged for the loan of ten Canadian paintings, including works by J. E. H. MacDonald (leader of the Group of Seven) and William Brymner.

These paintings hung on the walls of Willistead Library from 1923 to 1925 and cost the Walkerville Library Board exactly 80 dollars. For the next 53 years, the name Willistead would be synonymous with art in the Windsor area.

When the Depression took hold in the early 1930s, the Library Board could no longer afford shipping and insurance charges for further exhibits.

The amalgamation of the border cities (Windsor, Sandwich, Walkerville, East Windsor & Riverside) in 1935, which had met with considerable resistance from Walkerville citizens, happily resulted in renewed interest in the local art movement. The newly organized Local Council of Women underwrote the cost of a very successful major exhibition of Canadian paintings.

Upon the show's conclusion, a public meeting was held in Willistead and the Windsor Art Association formed in 1936 with a mandate to hold regular art exhibitions in the city, fostering an appreciation of the visual arts in the community, and ultimately establishing an art gallery in Windsor.

With the arrival of Kenneth Saltmarche as director in 1946, a new phase of art appreciation began. Under his guidance, the Art Gallery and the visual arts became an integral part of our community – exhibitions were more frequent and of improved quality, informative gallery talks and art classes were developed and the Picture Loan Service inaugurated.

The Women's Committee was founded in 1953 under the leadership of Mrs. W. R. Campbell – membership campaigns and fundraising projects were initiated and paintings were purchased for the permanent collection. The Annual Sale of Canadian art became a signature event every year.

By 1958, attendance at Willistead had tripled, but an increase in activity had negative repercussions. In 1959, inadequate space, insufficient financing and conflicting administration between the Art Association and Library Board, resulted in the discontinuation of the art program at Willistead and the resignation of the director.

The Windsor art movement was in danger of collapse. After negotiations with City Hall, Windsor City Council recognized Willistead Art Gallery as an independent institution with its own Board of Directors and initiated an annual grant to assist with operation costs.

The reorganization of the Gallery, which included improved facilities, proved a great stimulus – attendance figures soared to 44,000 by 1966. However, by 1967 the Gallery again faced a crisis – inadequate space motivated the Board to reassess its facility.

Art Gallery of Windsor Founders – President Dr. Tom Robson presents certificates to (l-r): Dr. Clare Sanborn, E. Harold Thistlethwaite, Mrs. W.R. Campbell and Miss Anne Hume, April 9, 1961

Growing Pains

"(Willistead) is not fireproof nor burglar-proof and there is no temperature nor humidity control. The heating, plumbing and electrical systems are ancient and inadequate. The Director of the Detroit Institute of Arts will not lend a major work... The Gallery's permanent collection (now numbering 330 pieces with a value of $176,000) is not safely housed. Renovations to correct these deficiencies would be prohibitive in cost and would completely destroy the character of this period building. The dual occupancy of Willistead is a continuing problem. Public Library and Art Gallery activities are so different in character that conflict and disturbance is inevitable."

From the report of the Future Planning Committee, Willistead Art Gallery of Windsor, May 24, 1967

The Planning Committee decreed the only solution to the crisis at Willistead was the construction of a new art museum.

"Such a Museum should be of modern design... A downtown location would place the Gallery at the transportation hub of the city and in the area of maximum population concentration... Unless an exceptional location in the downtown-riverfront area becomes available, a new Art Gallery should be constructed in Willistead Park, immediately to the east of the new residence. It should be a separate structure in order to ensure fire, burglar and environmental control, and in order to preserve the appearance of the Manor House ... joined at ground level with the Great Hall... This would be a culmination of the art movement launched by Miss Anne Hume forty-six years ago."

In 1970, after three years of searching fruitlessly for a new building and attempting to raise funds to build onto Willistead, a "miracle" occurred. Mayor Frank Wansborough suggested the abandoned Carling Brewery Warehouse on Riverside Drive, just west of downtown might be worth a consid-

Art in The Manor: Willistead c. 1955

eration. There was unanimous agreement that the well-built, 15-year old structure was large enough and suitable for an art gallery, once renovations occurred. For the princely sum of $1, it was sold to the Art Board.

After a year of ambitious fund-raising, nearly $3 million was raised to finance renovations. In September 1975, Mayor Bert Weeks officially opened the spacious new gallery.

A New Era

For almost 20 years, the converted warehouse served the needs of the gallery. A master plan completed in 1991 pointed the Gallery, also known as the AGW, in a new grander direction. With the arrival of Casino Windsor, the opportunity to acquire sufficient funds to finance the master plan was in sight.

The AGW leased their riverfront location to the Ontario Casino Corporation to serve as an interim Casino site and the gallery "temporarily" moved into the Devonshire Mall. This arrangement, while not an ideal environment for displaying art works, brought art closer to the public and gained the AGW national publicity. As well, the AGW gained over $23 million in rent for the old warehouse.

When the permanent Casino Windsor was established, the AGW board deliberated whether to relocate to its riverfront location and renovate yet again, or build a new creation in another spot entirely. The gallery was offered space in the still-to-be constructed Chrysler Centre at Riverside and Ouellette: Glengarda, a former convent on Riverside Drive East, was also briefly considered for renovation.

Finally, in July 1999, Dr. Lois Smedick, President of the AGW Board of Directors unveiled plans for a new art museum on the old warehouse location. Shortly thereafter, the old Carling warehouse was torn down, and a gleaming new gallery rose in its place.

On February 10th, 2001, the new Art Gallery of Windsor opened its doors. Impressionist Masterworks from the National Gallery of Canada was eagerly anticipated first exhibit.

Art in Windsor has come full circle – in an elegant and synchronistic way, the Impressionists, so beloved by E. Chandler Walker have returned.

Undoubtedly, Chandler, whose own Impressionist collection graced the walls of Willistead 90 years ago, must have been there in spirit.

Research materials, photos and recollections kindly provided by Dr. Tom Robson.

Above: A brewery converted into a gallery. photo David L. Newman Collection

Below: To the gleaming new... AGW. photo Chris Edwards

The Dawn of Local TV

by Chris Edwards, Issue #27, September 2002

Post World War II. The Border Cities experienced a technological boom that has reverberated through our culture ever since: the birth of TV.

In 1947, WWJ-TV began broadcasting over Channel 4 to a handful of viewers in Metro Detroit. At that time, there were fewer than 100 TV sets in Detroit, so broadcasting was definitely an act of faith. Started by The Detroit News in the 1920s as the nation's first commercial radio station, WWJ was not alone for long. In 1947, WXYZ went on the air on Channel 7 and WJBK set up shop on Channel 2.

Even though 6,400 Detroit homes had television sets by 1948, this was still a tiny audience for three local stations. Things changed dramatically when network television came to Detroit in early 1949; appliance stores could scarcely keep televisions in stock. By 1953, WXYZ was selling more advertising and making more money than any station in the ABC chain.

It took Detroit's first radio station, WWJ, a quarter century to get radio circulation to the million mark in the Border Cities. Television reached that mark in less than a decade. With rapid growth came a demand for more programming and a host of local television heroes.

An all-time favourite Border City TV celebrity was Soupy Sales, the wisecracking comic artist formerly known as Milton Hines. The house specialty for "Lunch with Soupy" at noon was shaving cream pie – a dish served up nearly every time Soupy stuck his face out the door of his set.

Between pies, Soupy's face was pawed by the meanest dog in all Detroit, White Fang, and petted by the nicest dog in the land, Black Tooth. Pookie the Lion, Hippy the Hippo, and Willie the Worm completed the menagerie. And, Peaches the girl next door (Soupy in drag) also visited the set regularly. Soupy had a kind of magic nobody had seen before.

Television was "live" in those very early days; videotape had yet to be

When CKLW-TV ruled the local airwaves.
Top: Mary Morgan, Bill Kennedy, Bozo the Clown, Bud Davies;
Above: Erecting the TV tower, 1953.

invented and film was the primary tool. But film had to be developed in a darkroom, which took time. ABC was so new and poor in those days that it offered no more than three hours a day of programming, none of it much good. So, the three ABC stations that did exist in 1948 – New York, Detroit and Chicago – were left to produce their own programs, none of which survived since live programs weren't recorded at that time.

Enter CKLW TV

It was perhaps inevitable that a TV station would be launched in Windsor, with its unique geographical position south of the border, to tap into the huge U.S. market. And Windsor television would soon emulate – and often surpass – programming being developed by competitors in Detroit.

Windsor residents were possibly the first Canadians to purchase television sets due to the pioneering Detroit shows available over the air – four years before the first broadcast in this country! We have heard of

Mary Morgan (at right): aloof glamour

Tiny Tim (left) and Bill Kennedy: "How do you expect me to know that?"

a Westinghouse factory that actually built TV sets in Windsor during TV's early years but could not confirm this as fact. One thing is certain – Windsorites were tuning into TV faster than anywhere in Canada.

The Mutual Broadcasting Company, operating CKLW Radio, was granted a TV license in 1952 due to its broadcast experience – beating out The Windsor Star. CKLW radio personalities would migrate to the new medium, including Jim Van Kuren, Bud Davies and Art Laing.

Sod was turned for the new TV and Radio broadcasting centre on Crawford and Sandwich Street (now Riverside Drive) in 1953. When a 670-foot broadcasting tower with a 60-mile radius was erected, it had the most powerful signal in the mid-west – including the United States. CKLW Radio 800 AM's signal extended all over the mid-west, as it had a "clear signal." No other radio station could have the 800 band on the dial. It would soon become a powerhouse, but that story will have to wait for another time.

On September 16, 1954 at 2:50 p.m., local TV history was made when CKLW Television signed on with Jim Van Kuren, who probably said something like, "You're watching CLKW in Windsor." The station launched before it was ready – it wasn't quite yet set for prime time.

"It wasn't the ground floor of TV broadcasting – it was the sub-basement," said Van Kuren. "We had to learn a whole new way of broadcasting. It wasn't simply radio with pictures. Radio people were not geared to thinking visually."

CBC – The Early Years

Meanwhile, across the country, Canadians also became enamoured with the new medium. On September 6, 1952, CBFT Montreal broadcast its signal for the CBC; CBLT Toronto followed suit on September 8. The first broadcast picture on CBLT was the station's call letters – upside-down and backwards! The broadcasting day was three hours long and Lorne Greene read the news.

The first character to appear on CBC-TV was the puppet Uncle Chichimus, followed by the first human – weatherman Percy Saltzman. The first breaking news story was the escape of the Boyd Gang from Toronto's Don Jail, reported by Harry Rasky.

But it would be some years before folks in the Border Cities experienced Canadian Broadcasting Corporation programming. Unique perhaps to Canada, Windsor remained an island of independent local television production until well into the 1970's.

The Movie Channel

Movies were a natural fit for the fledgling CKLW-TV. They could be broadcast over and over, and CKLW played everything from Tarzan to Ben Hur. Early movie programs were branded as "Command Performance," "Colgate Theatre" and "Million Dollar Movies" (named after the cost of a package of movies purchased by the station for almost a million dollars!) In Detroit, hosts were hired to fill time between movies, introducing the films, conducting interviews, and reading commercials.

Rita Bell was the most popular movie hostess in the Border Cities – CKLW needed someone to compete, and soon found two that perfectly fit the bill: Bill Kennedy and Mary Morgan.

Bill Kennedy – King of the Movies

The king of TV movie hosting was former B-movie actor and film trivia master Bill Kennedy. He aired films daily, and his Sunday afternoon show regularly attracted more than half of the Border Cities' viewers - even up against pro football.

His intro theme song was his trademark as he strolled into the studio with his signature fedora hat to sit at a plain desk.

"I came to Windsor because I needed a job – simple as that," said Kennedy. "I started on Friday doing a show called 'Going Our Way.' Soon I was working six days a week."

For 30 years, Kennedy wowed locals with his blinding plaid jackets and encyclopedic knowledge of movies, stars and Hollywood gossip. Viewers would call in with questions and he would answer off the cuff. "How d'ya expect me to know that?" he'd often reply in a deep gruff voice.

He also was one of the first to conduct in-studio interviews with top name entertainers stars who came to Windsor's Top Hat or The Elmwood, including Jimmy Durante and Sammy Davis Jr.

While Kennedy ruled as the king of movie hosts, the queens had their own loyal subjects.

Mary Morgan – Queen of the Airwaves

Mary Morgan, once called "the most beautiful woman on radio," hosted movies along with starring on local TV and radio programs, including the popular "Mary-Go-Round," a precursor to Martha Stewart. Morgan began her career in the Golden Era of radio during the Depression, taking a job to help her family during those difficult days.

In between hosting movies on CKLW TV, she interviewed celebrities such as Lucille Ball and President Eisenhower. She had an aloof glamour, often syrupy and breezy. Her fans loved Mary and her dachshund, Liebchen, who once licked off one of her false eyelashes and ate it on the air.

Movie hosts were not above promoting products on their shows. Commercials were read live on air, and hosts often added unscripted plugs. In fact, Kennedy became famous for his commercial ad-libs and inflections – advertisers ate it up and the station soon became successful beyond imagination.

An interesting side note to the early rules of commercial TV: in the late 40's, Detroit's WXYX TV-7 developed a program called the "House of Charm," hosted by Edythe Fern Melrose, which became a staple watched by thousands of women for the next two decades.

It was discovered that Melrose was making more money than the president of ABC, because she was getting paid for endorsing products on the air – there was no such thing as an ethics policy.

It became Melrose's form of commerce, effectively. If she wanted a particular drape, she would plug it; furniture, she would plug that. She got all the items free and was paid on top of that. In fact, she built a beautiful house on the waterfront in St. Clair Shores, paid by all the suppliers of brick, concrete, lumber, carpets. She even had them build a studio in the house from which she broadcast her show until it went off the air in the early 1960s.

The Electronic Nipple

CKLW soon became a leader in children's programming – not just in the local market – but in North America. The networks weren't providing any children's programming – it all had to be done locally. Again products were being sold to kids in a very blatant manner – regulations and rules on what could be marketed and sold to children had yet to be developed.

Children's shows produced in Windsor included Bozo the Clown, Romper Room, Mr. Whoodini, Jerry Booth's Fun House, Captain Jolly and Poopdeck Paul. Bozo competed against Clare Cummings as Milky the Clown on Channel 7. Milky worked in a plug for his sponsor every time he did a magic trick and said the magic words "Twin Pines." Bozo the Clown's famous Treasure Chest of Toys would roll across the studio floor and was eagerly sought after by kids who tuned in or participated in the live studio broadcasts.

Romper Room featured Miss Flora and live piano playing by Wally. The show was a huge hit with the younger kids.

Clowning around with Bozo

Captain Jolly, Toby David

David, who died at age 80 in 1994, started in New York radio in the 1930s. He had parts in several NBC radio shows including Bob Hope, Garry Moore, Jackie Gleason and the children's show "Let's Pretend." He came to Detroit in 1940s, where his radio work included reading Detroit Times comics on the air.

But David is most remembered for hosting the "Popeye and His Pals" cartoon show during the 1950s and 1960s, which was among the top-rated kids' shows in the nation. His pals included Whitey the Mouse, Sylvester the Seal, puppets Cecil and Stanley and an off-camera Wihelmina the Whale who plotted constantly to get Captain Jolly into the water.

"Poopdeck Paul" worked alongside Captain Jolly on Popeye and Pals between 1956 and 1966, first as a weekend host and eventually as a seven-day-a-week personality. But he became a local cultural icon for something other than Popeye cartoons – the limbo!

Between cartoons, he hosted limbo contests on the show, when limbo (with a hit record by Chubby Checker) was the rage among grade-schoolers. After the Beatles became big in 1964, he hosted a game in which contestants were judged by their ability to lipsync Beatles records. He hosted miniature golf, football throwing, bowling and table tennis competitions, as well. All of it was a hit with youngsters.

Robin Seynour: Hot commodity

Going to a Dance Party

According to Percy Hatfield, a reporter with CBC TV since 1978 and CBC radio since 1975, "CKLW programming hooked you as a child, kept you as an adolescent and then kept you coming back for more as an adult."

Local radio disc jockeys were keen to show teens the latest dances on TV. Ed Mackenzie, Robin Seymour and Bud Davies offered programs featuring local kids dancing the "Chicken," the "Stroll," the "Swim" and a whole lot more. Bud Davies "Top Ten Dance Party" was the first to launch a format that would eventually morph into music videos and MTV.

Seymour's "Swinging Time," a dance party that was a hot commodity on CKLW until 1968, predated the MTV era by almost 20 years. Entertainers performed "live," including the popular "Motown Sound" artists like Stevie Wonder and Diana Ross, and hot artists of the day, who "lip synched" their hit songs, often to comical effect as their timing could be slightly off.

Seymour's career spanned everything from the big band era to the British invasion. But he missed a beat somewhere when he predicted that Elvis Presley was a sure loser, who "wouldn't last more than a year." Seymour's television show featured 50 to 75 local kids dancing six days a week. Two were chosen for each show to give "yea" or "boo" opinions on new records.

Tom Shannon, a popular DJ on the BIG 8 CKLW, tweaked the format with a Johnny Carson-style teen talk show, but the kids just wanted to dance and the show was a flop. The program is famous for an interview with Alice Cooper, who pioneered "shock rock" with his elaborate stage shows including snakes, guillotines and pyrotechnics.

Cooper decided in the middle of an interview that he wanted to rip apart Bill Kennedy's famous interview chair – live on the air! He had to be restrained but had the stunt occurred, it would surely have gone down in TV folklore.

Big Time Wrestling

Border City wrestling fans watched the televised antics of local stars like "Dick the Bruiser," "Bobo Brazil" and "The Sheik" on "Big Time Wresting." This live broadcast was hosted by the charismatic Lord Layton, who often jumped into the ring and mauled wrestlers, a format that has been perfected to success by Vince McMahon's World Wrestling Entertainment.

The Sheik kept his real identity secret, claiming at various times to have been born in Tokyo, Saudi Arabia, Lebanon and Traverse City. He also claimed he made $10 million by making the fans love to hate him. Wrestling fans ate it up and CKLW-TV's ratings soared.

TV Grows Up

A new technology was rapidly moving TV into a new era. Colour TV sets emerged as the "new wave." Programming became more sophisticated as the networks developed elaborate sets in giant studios or in exotic locations. Local stations found it harder to produce local shows and began to rely on network shows. The development of the videotape meant that shows could be taped and replayed later with greater control than film.

CKLW tried to keep up with the changing times. Despite the fact that the station didn't own a mobile production facility, creative TV engineers and technicians were able to produce programming on-location, including "The Bill Anderson Show" live from Cleary Auditorium, and commercials shot live on location.

Dick the Bruiser

Shifting to CBC

By 1974, the governing body of TV programming, the CRTC, ruled that Canadians must own Canadian stations. RKO General sold the station to Baton Broadcasting, which soon partnered with CBC. Over the summer of 1975, the CBC acquired 100% of the station and the call letters changed to CBET-TV.

CBC promised more local programming. Due to a quirk in the CRTC rules, a "border protection rule" meant that any program aired by the CBC that was also broadcast by a U.S. competitor had to be blocked in Windsor. If the CBC was airing "Golden Girls" then the local Windsor had to substitute it with another program so as not to compete with the Detroit affiliate that was running the same show.

Local programming at CBET continued to flourish. "Reach for the Top," "Agriscope," "Sun Parlour Country," "Around Town," "Bob Monks/ Inside Outside," on-site concerts and sporting events were produced by a talented technical crew. Windsor CBC-TV earned a well-deserved reputation as one of the best production facilities in the country.

The station also focused its energy on news programming, as a complement to world-class journalism from Toronto with newly revamped The National and The Journal. Local documentaries became a staple of the expanded 90-minute news coverage – often airing nationally – up from only five minutes of news when the station began to air in 1953. Anchors Sue Presteidge and David Compton provided the station with sky-high local ratings, and the news crew was considered one of the finest in the country.

57 Channels and Nothing On

In 1984, the Federal government, under the newly elected PM Brian Mulroney, drastically cut the CBC's operating budget. In a massive blow to local programming, 63 jobs were eliminated. Year by year, the station held on with limited resources, but local programming diminished except for news.

Soon, local weekend news was eliminated and replaced with a regional report fed from Toronto. Then the 11 o'clock newscast was cut. Local CBC Radio and TV were consolidated under one roof at the Riverside location. Today the current local TV landscape continues to evolve. Moses Znaimer of CITY-TV Toronto fame launched a satellite station in Windsor in the 1990s – the "New WI" – to compete with the local CBC news, although the New WI newscast is disingenuously broadcast out of London (unknown to most viewers who think it is a "local" newscast).

Cable TV has unleashed more channels, as has satellite and digital TV. VCRs and DVDs have allowed for program shifting (pay-per-view, if you will).

But for one shining moment, at the dawn of television, local programming ruled our TV sets, or as an old station jingle used to pronounce, "The Best View in Town."

Sources: The author gratefully acknowledges the contribution of staff CBC-TV 9, who provided access to their photo and video archives for this story; History of Broadcasting in Michigan, WXYZ TV, History: Detroitnow.com; The Detroit News: Rearview Mirror; CBC Television: Celebrating 50 years.

Windsor's Community Museum
The François Baby Residence
by Elaine Weeks, Issue #11, Novemmber 2000

"By the early years of the 19th century, it must have been increasingly apparent to François Baby that he was in need of a new house. The one he had inherited (from his mother, Suzanne Reaume Baby), had been built perhaps half a century before, and it was showing its age. His family was growing rapidly, with a new child arriving every year or two (twelve in all).

But there was one more reason, possibly left unspoken: rivalry with his brother Jacques. It must have galled François that in 1807 Jacques acquired the splendid mansion that had been built in 1798 by the merchant Alexander Duff, at Mill and Russell Streets, in the new town of Sandwich, a little downstream at the bend in the River."
Mansion to Museum: the François Baby House and its Times, R. Alan Douglas, Occasional Paper No. 5, Essex County Historical Society, 1989.

Determined not to be outdone by his brother, François Baby commenced construction of his new house in the spring of 1812 but work was halted in July with the start of the War of 1812. The property was commandeered for the use of an invading American army. The position of the house was crucial: not only would it allow them a convenient location to plan for an invasion of Fort Malden downriver in Amherstburg, it was strategic to Fort Lernoult directly opposite in Detroit. Several hundred soldiers pitched their tents in the orchards and gardens around the house while senior officers occupied the house.

Damage sustained by the Baby house during its brief occupation (by summer's end Detroit was once again in the hands of the British) embittered Baby towards the Americans.

"The Americans plundered everything I had, even what was secreted five miles back of my house… For these losses, I was but poorly recompensed."

Baby managed to repair and complete his three-story house before winter. Built in the Georgian style with two rows of symmetrical windows and another row of dormer windows, the house had thick brick walls and rivaled brother's Jacques in size and elegance.

After the war (and possibly before) several ferry operations sprang up, including one owned by Baby, in the landing area to provide convenient access to Detroit. By 1831, the 'name' The Ferry had appeared to distinguish this area from Sandwich.

Coinciding with the arrival that year of Scottish businessman James Dougall who opened a store on Baby's wharf, the community began to grow. The road in front of Baby's house was straightened to become Sandwich Street (now Riverside Drive) and a village plot was laid out on Baby's frontage. On August 6th, 1832, the first sale of an urban lot occurred. This area began to be referred to as Richmond or Richmond Landing. In 1835, another plot was subdivided by Joseph McDougall at McDougall Street and was referred to as South Detroit. On September 10th, 1836 during a meeting at Hutton's Tavern, the name Windsor was agreed upon for the entire community. (Other possible names included Bellevue and even Babylon!)

The Demolition Threat

The ensuing years were not kind to the Baby House – a fire in 1850 caused considerable damage and Baby did not have the energy to do much to restore his home. After his death in 1852, the house was passed down to his son Edmond who made several major structural changes including reducing it to two stories. Further changes by future owners significantly altered the exterior of the structure – the addition of bay windows and gingerbread trim transformed it into a "Victorian" dwelling. In 1930, the house was abandoned and soon became a virtual ruin.

In 1933, George MacDonald, a Windsor merchant with a growing collection of local historical artifacts, wrote to Baby's great granddaughter in Detroit asking her if she would sell the house for museum purposes. Although he did not receive permission from her, when the house reverted to the City of Windsor for non-payment of taxes at the end of the decade MacDonald got his wish.

The sad condition of the François Baby House, 1940, before restoration was undertaken.
photo: Windsor's Community Museum

But it wasn't until 1948 that restoration of the house began. The Windsor Historic Sites Association was formed that year to help facilitate the restoration and accepted title to the property for a token one dollar. Lacking the original plans, the work was based on research of what the house may have looked like when it was built although the third floor removed by Edmond Baby was never restored.

Encroaching urban development among other things, including the proposed Cleary Auditorium, threatened it. In 1956, Hiram Walker's & Sons Ltd. stepped in with funds to save the museum. (Interesting fact: the exhibition galleries are lined with cypress permeated with Canadian Club whiskey salvaged from Hiram Walker's old fermenting vats!)

Other donations allowed for successful completion of the project and The Hiram Walker Historical Museum opened its doors in 1958. Administered by the City of Windsor Library Board, and with the entire MacDonald Historical Collection as its nucleus, the Baby House has become an important landmark in the downtown Windsor urban landscape.

Museum Curator Janet Cobban, in charge of the museum's collection for the past five years, feels that the building existence is a miracle. "It was a narrow escape," says Cobban. "The very fact that the museum was so close to being destroyed so many times, adds a great deal to its significance."

While important historical buildings in Windsor are threatened or continue to be pulled down (such as the entire Norwich Block, northeast to the Baby House, also known as Richmond Landing), the significance of what is now known as Windsor's Community Museum, can't even be measured.

Not only has a historical gem, symbolizing the very roots of Windsor, been preserved but an ever growing historical collection – at last count, 14,000 three dimensional artifacts plus extensive holdings of maps, photographs, documents etc. – has a fitting "home."

The François Baby House now serves as Windsor's Community Museum. photo C. Edwards

Museum Offerings

Two to three hundred items are added to the museum's collection each year, but most of them are small objects, photos etc. that don't take up much space.

Each year the museum mounts approximately six exhibits in the François Baby House plus additional offsite exhibits for special events, libraries, travel centres, etc.

Keep Local History Alive!

Become a Member or, donate! Membership money or other money raised by Windsor Historic Sites pays for repairs to the Baby House or is donated to the Museum for a specific exhibit or program and is separate from the Museum's operating budget.

If you would like to donate to the museum or become a member, e-mail wmuseum@city.windsor.on.ca or, call 519-253-1812, or visit the museum at 254 Pitt Street West.

The Eight Day Mayor

by Pat Brode, Issue #39, November 2003

By 1950, Arthur Reaume (above) had been mayor of Windsor for nine years and he looked as if he would remain in office indefinitely. During the war years, he had run a progressive administration with an emphasis on providing low-cost worker housing. Through his efforts, 2,500 Wartime Housing Ltd. dwellings and 114 Housing Enterprise units were constructed. Many Windsorites were homeowners largely due to Reaume's efforts.

When the Ford strike of 1945 threatened to deprive many families of support, it was Reaume who urged City Council to provide relief for strikers' families. His strong support for the fledgling UAW was highly prized by the Union and was a signal to them that they did not have to fight City Hall, as well as the company. In subsequent elections, he could rely on labour's unwavering support.

Art Reaume was a man who looked like he should be mayor. A dapper dresser, with a confident, worldly swagger, Reaume was the ideal mayor – some even compared him with New York's famous "Jimmy Walker" as both a capable administrator and man-about-town.

Beginning his career in municipal politics in 1930 at the age of 24, Reaume was elected to the town council of Sandwich. Three years later, he became the town's mayor and the youngest chief executive in Ontario. He was profoundly affected by the misery known as the Great Depression and did what he could both personally and through the municipal government to alleviate suffering.

He was challenged by a political opponent, Ed Donnelly, with ordering a work stoppage at a riverside park. Reaume replied that yes, he had gone to the park on a bitterly cold day where about 100 men on relief were working. "They will not work until they are properly clad," said Reaume, and he sent them home. This was illegal, roared Donnelly, who felt that because of it, Reaume would not get one vote. "I will not only get one vote, I will get thousands," Reaume calmly replied.

He did, and was easily re-elected.

Later, after Sandwich's amalgamation with Windsor, he sat as an alderman and in 1941 succeeded David Croll as mayor of Windsor. In the 1948 municipal election he easily defeated a challenge from a young reporter, Tom Brophey. The lack of "ballot box fever" was so apparent that the Windsor Daily Star thought that the Reaume regime was "approaching the status of a monopoly."

Yet there were cracks showing in the administration. Organized crime was so well established in Windsor that bordellos, gambling and illegal drinking establishments operated openly in many parts of the city. In early 1950, Magistrate Hanrahan tried and convicted bootlegger Joe Assef for running a number of illegal operations in the City. It was becoming apparent that crime was widespread and little was being done to control it.

Another Magistrate, Angus W. MacMillan, the chairman of the Police Commission, initiated a hearing on charges of laxity on the part of the Windsor police force. Yet, as The Windsor Daily Star reported, "even while preparations for the probe are under way, many of Windsor's vice centres continue to carry on business as usual. Virtually everything in the way of diversion for the 'tired businessman' is readily available in Windsor."

As a member of the Police Commission, Reaume sat in on the hearings, and yet when he challenged Hanrahan that some of the accusations might just be hearsay, the Magistrate was outraged that the Mayor was not taking these charges seriously."

"There is an apparent air of hostility that is amazing and certainly not justifiable by any remarks I have made," he noted. However, Ontario's Attorney General Dana Porter closely followed the investigation. Changes in law enforcement in Windsor were obviously overdue.

The mayor himself became directly embroiled in scandal when it became known that he and the administrator of the municipality-run Metropolitan Hospital had entertained a bevy of nurses at a fashionable party at the Book-Cadillac Hotel in Detroit. Miss Maybee, the superintendent of nurses quit and another public enquiry was held. This time, Reaume could not avoid being caught up directly, and Bruce MacDonald, the lawyer for one of the groups charged that "I do not think the mayor can escape censure for his part... I think that anyone with any experience in the world will doubt his story."

While his probe was less that edifying, there was no proof of wrong-doing. Art Reaume faced the municipal election of December, 1950, still relying on the support of labour and the common people.

Once again, his opponent was the reporter, Tom Brophey. Brophey had given up journalism and decided to study law. Even though he was in the middle of his studies in Toronto, he nevertheless ran a spirited campaign.

Having sold his car in order to go to law school Brophey was forced to walk the streets of Windsor. He argued that during Reaume's "decade of progress" the property tax burden had become unbearable. "I recall having been in communist halls only twice," Brophey declared, "and each time I found Arthur Reaume in the centre of attention." Had the mayor, through fast and clever footwork avoided the effects of two major investigations?

Reaume fought back that through his influence, the most recent strike at Ford of Canada had been settled in less than 12 hours. Was this communism, or just good government? As well, he had taken efforts to assimilate the ethnic groups that were coming into Windsor and for this he deserved another term in office. Interesting as the campaign had been, no one seriously expected Art Reaume to be upset.

On the morning of December 7, 1950, Windsorites woke up to find out that by a margin of 38 votes they had a new mayor. The strongest political machine in Windsor's history had been beaten by a neophyte. The razor-thin margin of victory did not seem to bother the mayor-elect who proclaimed that "38 votes is as good as 38, 000." Inevitably, Reaume demanded and got a recount. However, the count could not be held before the New Year, and on January 1st, 1951, Tom Brophey was sworn in as mayor of Windsor.

A 24-hour police guard was mounted on the ballot boxes until Acting Judge Charles Sale began the recount on January 3. On the first day, Brophey gained an additional two votes. However, as the tedious process of recounting 33,000 ballots wore on, Brophey saw his plurality slowly slipping away. By January 9, Reaume had pulled head by 16 votes and he was declared re-elected as mayor.

It was hardly a vote of confidence.

As the Toronto Daily Star warned, the paper-thin victory spoke "of an aroused electorate which nearly elected a young man like Mr. Brophey despite all that the well-established Reaume organization could do."

Art Reaume would continue to serve Windsor as mayor until 1954, and as a member of the provincial parliament until 1967. Despite several more tries for the mayor's office, Tom Brophey would never again get close to executive office.

There was one more piece of unfinished business resulting from the contested election of 1950. After serving eight days in the mayor's office, Brophey was entitled to be paid. After some discussion, the Board of Control decided that he had earned a month's pay for his eight days in office.

One of Art Reaume's first acts back in office was to sign Tom Brophey's pay cheque for the shortest term in the Mayor's office in Windsor's history.

Dad Was "The Eight Day Mayor"

I found the article, "The Eight Day Mayor" by Pat Brode in the November 2003 Issue (concerning my father's victory over Art Reaume in the 1950 mayoralty race) very interesting, and it brought back many memories of those days.

At left is a copy of his 1950 campaign poster, which reveals that he had come close to defeating Reaume in the 1948 election. My father was born and raised in Windsor. He was always very proud of having "defeated" Reaume in the 1950 race, only to lose to him in the recount 8 days later. At his swearing in speech, which I provided to the Windsor Public Library on tape, one of his main dreams was to create parklands along the Detroit River. I remember him telling me that he and his good friend on council, Bert Weeks, often discussed the idea. My father was very proud that Mr. Weeks took the steps to bring that dream to fruition when he became mayor.

Mr. Brode mentions in his article that my father sold his car in order to go to law school. I recall the incident vividly. I remember a young lady and a child coming to our house desperately looking for transportation at a reasonable price. My father was very generous in his handling of this transaction, since the woman appeared in such need. When I returned home from school several days later, I pointed out to my mother that the car in the driveway directly across the street from us looked exactly like the car my father had just sold. My mother discussed the matter with the neighbour, only to discover it was my father's former car and the neighbour had purchased it from a used car dealer. Such is life!

Tom Brophey, Windsor, Issue # 40, December/January 2003-2004

LET BROPHEY
FINISH THE JOB
HE STARTED IN 1948

1948 VOTES
BROPHEY 13,274
REAUME 15,780

Slightly over
1000 Vote
Change Needed
to get the
NEEDED
CHANGE

VOTE BROPHEY
MAYOR

British American Brewery truck in front of the C.N.E. in Toronto, 1945.
photo: National Archives of Canada

Long Live King the Horse

Everybody knew King, the horse that pulled the Purity Dairy wagon. He was the best-fed horse around. One winter day in 1952, I was on my way to school (Begley) and while walking along Wyandotte Street, I saw that King had slipped on the ice and fallen. I joined a group of people standing around him and I heard that he would have to be shot.

In school a little while later, while we were singing "God Save the King," we heard two pops and we knew that King was gone. At lunch, there was nothing left of King but a bloodstain on the road where he had fallen. I'll never forget that day.

Vicki (Affleck) Moffat, Windsor

photo: Fred Lazurek

photo Sid Lloyd

Too "Pooped" To Swim?

I can recall the scene at left from the 2nd Annual Photo Issue #35, June 2003 very well. My dad (Dr. R.J. Coyle) constantly told us children to stay away from that area as it was one of the city of Windsor's storm/sewage outlets that went directly into the Detroit River. This was prior to the city sewage system being fully implemented and in the days before antibiotics and the polio vaccine. It was literally taking your life in your hands to swim in that area. When I was a kid I would tell friends not to go there but they would laugh. Kids, you know.

Jim Coyle, email

photo Bill Marentette

Once Upon a Brewery

Researched and compiled by William L. Marentette C.B.S. #194

Issue #11, November 2000

Walkerville has always been famous for two things: Hiram Walker and Canadian Club whisky. But did you know that this community was renowned for the quality of a premium beer brewed right here from 1885-1956, and then reborn in 1998?

Hiram Walker was a man who never rested on his laurels. Having lived through two bankruptcies, the Civil War in the USA, and a depression to rival the Great Depression of 1929, he was constantly innovating his businesses and expanding his empire. In 1885, he embarked into the field of lager making.

Walker proposed to brew the finest and purest lager beer ever made in Canada from the choicest Canadian malts and hops. Like his whisky business, Walker accepted no compromise with any venture he entered into – nothing but the finest ingredients and equipment would do.

With the entire wealth of Walker's empire backing the Walkerville Brewing Company, the most modern brewing equipment of the day was obtained. A magnificent building was unveiled on Fifth Street (now Walker Road) at Wyandotte, at a cost of $180,000. Walker boasted that his brewing process, using a vacuum fermenting system pioneered by a young German named C. Pfaudler, would completely revolutionize the brewing industry. Walkerville beer would become as famous among beer drinkers of Canada as Walker's "Club" and Imperial Rye was amongst whisky drinkers in the Dominion of Canada.

The five-story brewery had quarry stone foundation and cement mortar 8 feet deep; the building's face was Detroit red brick shipped by the Walkerville ferry (one of many Walker-owned enterprises). As described in the "Walkerville Mercury" on the opening of the brewery in August, 1890, a 12 x 30 office was located on the second floor, the brew house contained a brewing kettle with a capacity of 2,300 gallons and a room where hops shipped from Hiram Walkers farms and the United States were kept at a temperature of 30 to 40 degrees Fahrenheit.

The brewery featured two 45 horse power steel boilers, along with various pumps and brine tanks, condensers for racking off beer and an ice machine that took first prize at the 1889 Paris, France World Exposition, beating over 36 other machines of its kind. The main advantage with this brewing system was that aging and storage was greatly reduced – beer could be turned out in 28 to 35 days from brew kettle to market.

A two-storey bottling plant was soon built, along with offices for the company, are two barns, each with five stalls for the company's horses that helped deliver kegs. A spur line from the Lake Erie, Essex and De-

National Archives of Canada
Collection of Bill Marentette

troit River Railroad (a Walker owned railroad) was connected to the plant, enabling the company to ship beer to all parts of Canada.

Although Hiram Walker served only two years as president of Walkerville Brewery before turning it over to his son Edward Chandler Walker in 1892, he guided the brewery with the same enthusiasm as all his ventures.

In August 1890, the Walkerville Brewing Company produced their first brew, soon to become its famous lager. The first batch consisted of 70 barrels holding 32 gallons. By October, 1890, the brewery was receiving lager orders faster than they could meet demand. In October, an Industrial and Agricultural Exhibition was held in nearby Windsor – the brewery had an impressive exhibit of their already famous lager brew both in bottles and casks.

The brewery soon established agencies in London, Sarnia, Toronto and east to Montreal, where their vacuum lager was well received. In November, the shipments began to Goderich, Kincardine, Palmerston and Wingham.

In December 1890, the company registered its trademark, which consisted of a series of crosses, procured from the Department of Agriculture in Ottawa; this was used until 1945 on all their products, buildings, trucks and advertising items. It may be that the Walkerville registration was Canada's first beer trademark!

The company soon sent out over 500 embossed signs with its trademark for use outside hotels or public houses. A common sight on the streets of the Border Cities was the dappled gray draught horse hitched to a brightly painted wagon delivering kegs of Walkerville beer and ale to the neighbourhood Inns and Hotels. Its beer was "PURITY, CLEANLINESS, SKILL AND UNEXCELLED MATERIAL," and was advertised as "Beer that is brewed in Glass."

In the spring of 1890, Walker's distillery hired a maltster by the name of John Bott, born in the Channel Islands, Great Britain, who arrived in Canada at the tender age of 18.

Bott had been engaged in the barley trade in Toronto for ten years before moving on to Chatham, Ontario. There, he worked for Howard & Northwood as a maltster for 8 years.

Botts' wine malt and stout were legendary. "BOTT'S MALT PREPARATIONS" received the highest award in its category at the Chicago World's Fair in 1893, giving considerable fame to the Walkerville Brewing company where he was now employed. Using a German brewing method, he renamed Walkerville lager Kaiser Beer. Shortly after, a "BARBAROSSA" brand was introduced named Frederick, the first of Germany (1123-1190), who sported a red beard.

In 1895, Bott was named manager of the Walkerville Brewing Company, operating on 4 acres of land with newly remodelled ale and porter cellars. By now, the brewery was one of the finest and most complete breweries in Canada.

That same year, Edward Chandler Walker hired his schoolboy friend Stephen E. Griggs as manager of the brewery's United States operations, located at 131-146 Beaubien Street, in downtown Detroit. The Walkerville Brewery purchased the Duncan Malt House and established a Detroit bottling plant with a capacity of 400,000 dozen bottles. All brewing was done in Walkerville and shipped in kegs to Detroit, thus saving on excise duties. Through this agency, ale and lager was shipped all over the United States under the Robin Hood label.

By 1897, the plant increased its capacity to 150,000 barrels annually, a far cry from the 3,000 barrels produced just 7 years prior.

Shortly after taking charge of the Detroit operation, Mr. Griggs was named managing director of the main plant in Walkerville, and by 1905, became vice president and managing director of the brewery. Griggs was doing so well at the brewery Edward Chandler Walker asked him to assist at the Canadian Club distillery; he was made a director of Hiram Walker & Sons in 1908.

By 1911, shipments of Walkerville Brewing lager, ale and porter were delivered as far west as Rainy River and Kenora. The main brands included Superior Lager, St. George's and Rob Roy Ale.

Griggs resigned as director of the CC distillery and devoted himself to making Walkerville Brewing a showplace. Located in the centre of Walkerville, it soon became a top tourist attraction, with thousands touring the bottling shop and large cellars, where barrels of the amber nectar were stored.

In 1913, E. Chandler gave Griggs $5,000 worth of Walkerville Stock. Later, Griggs purchased shares held by John Bott, the former manager of the brewery, effectively giving him control of the company. Griggs was then made president of the Walkerville Brewing Company.

That same year, the company employed over 55 employees, and the plant consumed over two million pounds of malt, thirty thousand pounds of hops, filled thousands of glass bottles and four thousand new kegs annually.

The brewery introduced Continental, marketed XXX Porter and a stout for medicinal purposes. Despite Hiram Walker's passing in 1899, the brewery was living up to his lofty standards!

Hiram Walker's son, Edward Chandler Walker, in poor health for a number of years, died on March 11, 1915, at the age of 64. Among the many legacies in his will was a large amount of money left to his schoolboy friend, Stephen E. Griggs, who became the full owner of the Walkerville Brewery.

By 1916, with the "war to end all wars" raging in Europe, the provincial government enacted the Ontario Temperance Act, banning the selling of liquor or beer; this lasted until the end of the war.

In October 1919, a referendum was held to determine whether the act should be repealed or retained on a peacetime basis. The citizens of Ontario voted with a four hundred thousand majority to establish 'prohibition' as the permanent law of the province.

By 1920, the USA also went dry when Congress passed the Volstead Act, prohibiting the manufacturing or selling of intoxicating alcohol; this remained in force until 1933.

Like many other breweries during prohibition, Walkerville produced non-intoxicating beverages containing less than 1% alcohol. The company claimed it as refreshing as full strength beer, under the labels Continental Lager and Scotch Boy Ale.

During prohibition, the brewery established "export docks" in LaSalle – boats would load Walkerville products day and night. It also had a "Night Order Only" shipping clerk at the brewery and would ship to various export docks.

Griggs continued to guide the company until the age of 74; in 1925, he disposed of his major holdings in the company to Detroit investors and retired.

After the change in ownership in 1925, the company invested $500,000 in capital improvements. A $50,000 bottling line extension was installed the most up to date in the province at the time. No human hands touched the bottle nor its contents until after the bottle had been filled, capped and sterilized.

Storage capacity was increased to 200,000 barrels, staffed by 140 men, with an additional 25 bodies during summer months, to handle increased production.

In May 1925, the Ontario Government legalized the sale of 4.4 proof spirit beers called "Fergies Foam." The Walkerville Brewery shipped approximately 4,500 cases and 750 eight gallon and 13-gallon kegs in its first day! Huge crowds paraded the streets and jammed hotel lobbies and beverage rooms in the Border Cities, anxious to quaff the new 4.4 beer.

Billboard facing Wyandotte at the Walkerville brewery
photo: Bill Marentette

Label from the collection of Bill Marentette

The Liquor Control Act of Ontario came into effect on June 1st 1927; pre-prohibition beer was made available to the public, effectively ending Prohibition in Canada.

Of the forty-four breweries that operated prior to prohibition only 15 remained; Walkerville Brewery was one of them. Full strength beer was for home consumption only, and hotels and taverns were only allowed to serve 4.4 beer or ale.

In 1927, the Brewer's Warehousing Company was granted a charter for the distribution and sale of all brewery products along with the retail outlets attached to the breweries and a government inspector at each store.

A Detroit newspaper hailed the Motor City as the wettest city in the United States, despite continuing prohibition in the USA. Though four separate government agencies were enforcing prohibition laws, Canadian breweries and distillers were able to creatively move their product across the border.

In 1928, a $75,000 office building was built next to the plant. Walkerville introduced John Bull Ale about this time. But with the collapse of the stock market in October 1929, and the beginning of the Great Depression, the market for beer also collapsed. Only the export business kept the company afloat, but with prohibition still in force in the USA, many breweries operated at less than 20 % capacity.

In 1934, the Ontario Liberal Government announced the legalization of full strength beer by the glass, allowing standard hotels to operate beverage rooms. In Windsor, the first license was issued to the Norton Palmer Hotel – by 10:30 am on July 24th; beer was flowing in most of the local hotels and clubs, to great aplomb.

To promote the sale of Walkerville beer products, the company resumed its traditional delivery system using teams of horses hauling old beer wagons, as in the early days of the brewery.

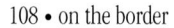

By 1939, the brewery entered foreign markets, including Trinidad, British West Indies, Jamaica and the Barbados. At the start of World War II, Walkerville's industrial centre generated machinery for the war effort. With a huge demand for labour, men and women migrated into the region, generating strong demand for beer and ale – sales of Walkerville products soared. The brewery was producing well over 100,000 barrels of their "Old Style Lager, Rob Roy Ale" along with porter and stout.

Windsor soon faced a beer shortage, due to government restrictions imposed by the War Measures Act (industrial alcohol was used to make smokeless powder, synthetic rubber and pharmaceutical products). This severely curtailed beer production by all breweries across the country – less than 10% of the 1942 total – while demand continued to grow.

Windsor Mayor Art Reaume wrote to Prime Minister W. L. MacKenzie King, proposing a beer-rationing scheme. In May 1943, a ration book was introduced for home consumption. Four coupons, each good for six bottles, were issued to those 21 years of age and over upon application; these coupons continued in use until January 1947.

For some time, Canadian Breweries, under instructions of E.P. Taylor, had been buying Walkerville Brewery shares on the open market. On March 18th, 1944, Canadian Breweries announced they had purchased the majority of all outstanding shares at a cost of $1,500,000.

When Canadian Breweries took control of the Walkerville Brewery, Charles S. King, president of the British American Brewery, stated the plant would continue to operate under the Walkerville name but could consolidate at a later date with the British American firm.

The following year a change was made – not to consolidate with British American but with another Canadian Breweries subsidiary – Carling's Breweries of Waterloo. D. Clive Bette, president of Canadian Breweries, stated all Walkerville labels would change to Carling Breweries Limited (Walkerville) and would produce both "Carling's Red Cap Ale, and "Carling's Black Label Lager."

All Walkerville brewing production came under Carling's Waterloo control. During this period, alterations to the plant were carried out. This new name change was short lived, and in 1947, a subsidiary of Canadian Breweries, O'Keefe's, took control of the Walkerville plant.

A new retail store was opened and modifications to the plant carried out. Because "O'Keefe's Old Vienna Lager" was the company's flagship beer, the name was changed from O'Keefe's Brewery to O'Keefe's Old Vienna Brewery.

On Sept. 15th 1956, an official statement from Canadian Breweries head office in Toronto announced the closing of the Walkerville Brewery (which was still producing over 100,000 barrels a year), effective November 1st, 1956.

Draught horse's hitched to a Walkerville Brewery wagon, pose in front of Memorial Park gate in South Walkerville.
photo: Bill Marentette

A. F. Fuerth, president of the Bradings Brewery in Windsor, another Canadian Breweries subsidiary, stated that sales staff and the retail store would remain in Windsor and the building would be kept intact in the event it was needed in the future.

However, the days of brewing beer in Walkerville were over. In January 1962, a permit was issued for the demolishing of the old brewery; demolition was completed by June '62. The retail store remained on site until 1965; when sales transferred to Brewers Retail in 1973, the former O'Keefe's retail store was demolished. Today, nothing remains at the site of one Canada's finest breweries, and the location is now a Credit Union and storage centre.

But some things are too good to be left to history books. In 1998, Karen Behume and her husband Michael Plunkett obtained the rights to use the name Walkerville Brewing Company. In an empty Hiram Walker warehouse, two blocks from the original brewery, Walkerville Lager is brewing once again – the region's first and only high calibre microbrewery. Thus, after fifty four years, Walkerville delivery vehicles are back on the streets of the Border Cities with their motto 'World-class beer, Made right here."

As it was in the beginning...

Bill Marentette worked at The Walkerville Brewery as a teenager.
His collection of Walkerville Brewery memorabilia is second to none.

Sources:
Amherstburg Echo; American Breweries, Donald Bull, Manfred Freidrich and Robert Gottschank; Border Cities Star; Directories of Canadian Breweries, Richard Sweet; Evening Record; Taylor E. P., Biography of Edward Plunket Taylor, Richard Rohmer; Shea, Albert A., Visions in Action, The Story of Canadian Breweries Ltd. 1935-1955 ; The Sheaf "The Canadian Breweries Employees Newspaper"; Windsor & District Telephone Directory 1927, Fall & Winter; Windsor Daily Star; Windsor Record; Windsor and Area City Directories; Windsor, Essex County Historical Scrap Books; Windsor Ontario 1931, Published by Windsor Record, Garner, H.; Windsor Public Library Main Branch, History & Literature

My Family Owned The British American Hotel

October 2003, Issue #38

Growing up in Windsor, I often sat in my grandmother's house looking through her endless collection of old tin pictures in her velvet photo album. Some photos in particular always caught my eye and she would tell me the stories behind them. One related to the British American Hotel.

My grandfather Edward Ingram and his father, Eugene Edward Ingram, owned and operated the British American Hotel from 1910 to 1925, with Eugene's wife Annie Ingram (née Hildeshime). This prestigious hotel once sat at the corner of Ouellette and Sandwich Street (Riverside Drive); many weary Canadian and American travelers and salesmen found a fine place to quaff a couple pints of their favorite brew, enjoy a good meal, and lay their heads after a long journey. Most of the patrons from the U.S. disembarked from the ferry at the foot of Ouellette and walked a short distance to the hotel.

Once inside, they would find the amiable Eugene Ingram, who made them feel right at home. My grandfather Edward Ingram was at the piano, tickling the ivories (with nary a lesson) to an appreciative crowd, taking requests while occasionally serving patrons. Scurrying about the bar/dining room was Cora Loree, serving dinners and drinks (Cora would soon marry my grandpa).

Upstairs in the private game room cards were played almost on a nightly basis. The likes of "King" Lee, a prominent member of the Chinese community, and Eliho Wigle, another upstanding member of the community, played poker into the wee hours of the morning.

It's said that my great great grandfather was so kind hearted that many guests of the hotel were relatives and friends, – many simply down on their luck.

My sister Bonnie Beaudry (née Ryan), has one of the original dining room chairs from the British American Hotel, still in immaculate condition after all these years.

After my grandfather Edward left his father's hotel, he found work at Janise's Funeral Home as an ambulance driver and embalmer, at its original location on Riverside Drive. But I think I'll save that story for another time.

Edward (Ted) Ryan, Gravenhurst, ON

Annie and Eugene Ingram

Edward and Eugene Ingram

The British American Hotel stood on the north east corner of Ouellette Avenue and Riverside Drive, was built in 1871 and demolished in 1975.

photo David L. Newman Collection

And they're off!

by Stan Scisloswki, Issue #25, June 2002

For a few glorious years in the 1930s, I was a regular at Windsor's Devonshire and Kenilworth Racetracks. I may have just been a kid with no money, but that didn't stop me.

At noon people started making their way down Parent Avenue singly, in twos and threes and in larger groups. It was a good three-mile hike to the track so any adults willing to walk that far had to have betting blood in their veins.

Canada was in the depths of the Depression and few people had money to scrape together to buy the necessities of life or a car let alone for luxuries like gambling on the ponies, yet many people still scrounged up a buck or two to bet on the nags.

Hope springs eternal in the human breast, so the saying goes, and these folks had hopes of bringing back more than they took with them to the betting windows. Most of course, made the even longer walk back home after the races somewhat lighter in the wallet.

I must have been about eight years old when I was allowed to go to the track with my brother Joe and another boy in the neighbourhood. Of course we didn't do any betting. Even had we been old enough, we didn't have any money to bet.

We didn't go just to watch the horses gallop around the mile track however. We went for the whole gamut of experiences that have been firmly rooted in my memory for over seventy years.

Without a doubt, outside the coming of the circus to town, my war experiences and a certain few events of my adult years, I'd have to say the four years or so every summer and fall when thoroughbred racing meets were held at Devonshire and Kenilworth racetracks were amongst the most exciting periods of my life.

The three of us loved hanging around the stables petting the horses. We came to know the docile ones, the ones whose foreheads you could stroke without fear of being nipped. We'd feed these favourites carrots lifted out of pails stored nearby, to the chagrin of the trainers and grooms. Most of them were amiable fellows and didn't get all riled up about it, but there were the odd, ornery types who chased us away. Of course this didn't stop us – we just made sure no one was looking when we treated our favourite nags.

On Saturday afternoons there had to be ten thousand people at the track and at least eighty percent were Americans. From scanning the license plates in the parking lot I saw that they came from practically every state in the Union.

Pari-mutuel betting was not allowed in the States, so the only place for inveterate horse bettors to satisfy their desires was to travel to Canada, either to Toronto's Thorncliffe Park, Woodbine, Fort Erie, or to Windsor's Devonshire and Kenilworth Racetracks. The latter two tracks were close neighbours, separated only by the New York Central Railway.

Every year there were two meets, the summer and fall meets, with each track holding races for two weeks. In those days only seven races were on the daily cards. After the fifth race, the gates to the grandstand were thrown wide open and everybody was let in without charge. There were always at least a hundred people hanging around the gate including the three of us. We would work our way through the press of the crowd to reach the concrete apron between the rail and the grandstand.

By the last race we were always pretty hungry, but with no money in our pockets, we resorted to picking up discarded half-eaten hotdogs or hamburgers. Of course we only picked up the ones still on a napkin. We'd break off the end where it had been bitten into and wolf the rest down.

We also picked up discarded betting slips. We must have picked up hundreds every day we went. We stuffed them into all our trouser and shirt pockets, with the overflow carried home in our hands. There my brother Peter would check them against the results marked on programs we picked up.

Winning tickets were few and far between, but when we did find one, it was a cause for celebration, even if the ticket was only worth a few dollars. One lucky day, I came up with a betting slip worth $17.75 – a veritable bonanza worth at least $200 in today's dollars. This slip certainly helped alleviate some of the money woes our family suffered back then.

I'll never forget the hawkers outside the grandstand before the races got underway shouting their spiel in that drawn-out, almost musical manner: "Racing Form and Entries, Read All About The Running Horse!" Or the guy who sold programs, shouting in his unique, clipped style, "Programs here, programs!" Again and again and again he'd shout, not changing his delivery one iota.

To add to these enchanting sounds were the sales pitches of the food vendors under the stands, especially the guy selling hot dogs, "Get 'em red hot, red hot, red hot!" Or the man selling frost bites in a mournful chant, as though he was about to break down crying, "Frost bites... get your frost bites here."

In 1937 when pari-mutuel betting was passed into law in the States, the Detroit Fair Ground Track was built shortly after and this spelled the end of thoroughbred racing in Windsor. There simply wasn't enough patronage from the people of Windsor and surrounding district to support racing.

Just before my time, horse races, band performances and other community events were held at the Driving Park, now Jackson Park.

It was a blow for me to know there would be no more racing in town, no more strolling through the barn area, no more tickets to pick up, no more tickets to cash, no more excitement of mingling with the throngs of people that came out to lay their bucks on the line.

But those sounds have stayed with me forever, to help fuel my wonderful memories of those stimulating afternoons that so influenced me as a young lad.

"Get your red hots, red hots, red hots..."

Bakery Brothers

Glad to see somebody remembers Minda Lee Pastry Shop (Issue #34, April 2003).

I went to work as a baker's helper in 1940 when it was known as Evan's Electric Bakery. I think it was late 1941 when Bill Williams, a cake baker at Little's Bakery, bought Evan's Electric Bakery and renamed it Minda Lee Pastry Shop.

In early 1942, Bill and Minda had a son Rob. My future sister-in-law Lorraine Poupard babysat for the couple. Soon she was working in the pastry shop with Minda.

In 1942, my brother Victor came to work with me. It wasn't long before Victor was called into the army. My other brother, Norman then came to work with me. In September of 1943, I also joined the army and at that time my third brother, Felix came to work with Norman.

I'm not sure exactly what year, but Bill sold Minda Lee's to Ross Miles. Ross also had a bakery on Wyandotte, east of Pillette, where my fourth brother, Paul worked.

I know of two boys born to Minda and Bill: Rob, a professor at Waterloo University, and Bruce who was working for a short time at the New WI in 2001.

Do any readers remember the Neal Baking Co.? It was between Crawford and Salter, south of London (University Avenue) Street. We went there on Saturday afternoons with a pillow case or a white flour bag, and filled them with day old bread and cakes for less than $2.

My father worked for welfare re-numbering houses. Does anybody remember what year Windsor re-numbered the houses? I know we came to Windsor in 1933 to 148 Oak, but sometime in the 1933-38 it became 458 Oak.
Orval Barrette, Windsor

Editor: Windsor renumbered houses after amalgamating the Border Cities in 1935.

l-r: Orval Barrette, Felix Barrette and Victor Barrette, 1942, brothers who worked at Minda Lee Pastry Shop

Skating party on Belle Isle, 1905

Detroit River frozen in time

So You Think This Is Cold?

by Stanley Scislowski, Issue #13, February 2001

So you think we've had cold weather lately. Big deal! Like an old-timer would say, "It's nowhere near as bad as back in the thirties!"

During one winter in 1935 or '36, it was about 15 to 20 below zero Fahrenheit for almost a whole week. And to make things even worse, we had a grandaddy of a blizzard that dropped three feet of snow overnight, stopping what little auto traffic there was in those destitute days.

The only things running were the horse-pulled milk sleighs and the streetcars. Otherwise it was the Arctic out there, a desert of snow and icy winds. Not a soul to be seen on the streets.

Man, was it ever cold! And just when our household's coal reserves were all but used up. If we didn't get some coal or wood to burn soon, it shaped up to be one God-awful cold night ahead.

With our frame house not insulated, it wouldn't take long for it to be as cold inside as it was outside, except for the wind. The main source of heat came from the lowly upright wood and coal stove set up in the dining-room; the bedrooms were all like ice-boxes.

There was no getting away from it – get some coal, whether by hook or by crook, or freeze our butts off. We were down to a half scuttleful or so of it, just enough to take us into mid-afternoon. After that, it'd be 'shiver and shake' the long day through.

With no money to buy coal, my mother had no recourse but to send me and my brother Joe to the happy hunting ground for coal'– the gondolas filled with the stuff, parked on the siding on the Essex Terminal tracks between Benjamin and Hall near Tecumseh Road. And I don't think we were the only family that depended on unlawful procurement of fuel; there had to be quite a few others in the same boat as we were – dirt poor and desperate.

So, on the coldest day of the year, with a wind-chill that had to be about 40 below, Joe and I headed out into the howling wastes with a wagon and a homemade wheelbarrow, to swipe some coal and save the family from freezing half to death.

How we made it that far through the drifts and bitter cold winds, I'll never know. But we made it and commenced loading-up, hoping to heck that old man Thompson, the railway dick didn't catch us in the act. But I guess he had more brains than I gave him credit for and didn't venture out of his heated office, wherever that happened to be. No railway cop in his right mind would patrol the tracks in the Arctic weather such as Joe and I had to brave.

With our precious load of anthracite, we made it home in the nick of time – all there was left in the stove when we got back was the last flickering glow of a few embers. Next morning we were hard at it again.

Although there were other days when things got pretty darned chilly around the house, it never got quite as bad as that particular spell of frigid weather.

The kids nowadays sure have it easy – in fact too easy. No coal to have to swipe in below-zero weather... no 3-foot snowdrifts to wade through... no forever having to feed a hungry stove with wood or coal... no sifting of ashes for the last remnants that will still burn.

A little cold? Just turn up the thermostat kids – and you'd better be happy you live now and not then!

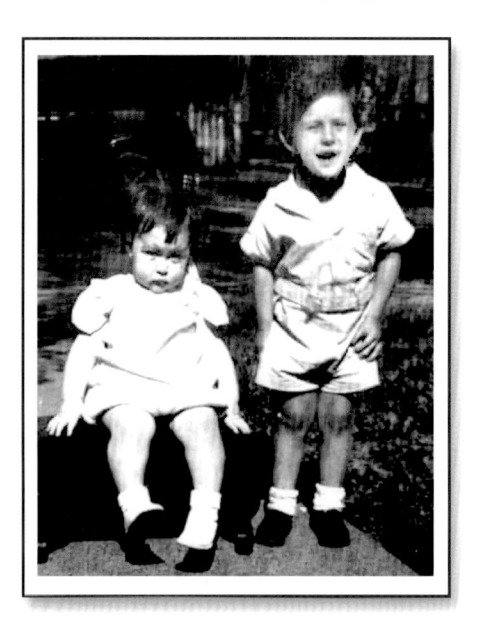

Saving Patti

By Tom Paré, Issue #21, February 2002

Usually, when a guy is about six years old and active in a neighbourhood gang, he robs trains or fights bandits and hostile Indians. But in the winter of 1939, Tommy put these things on the back burner for one day when he slipped into the new role of "hero."

Now this wasn't planned and in fact it wasn't the funniest thing to do on that cold slushy day. But as it turned out, he enjoyed the attention. Especially, the admiration from the rest of the Janette Avenue Gang.

That morning, when Tommy got ready to go out in the snow and street slush to meet Punky and throw snowballs at the milkman's horse, he tried to sneak out wearing his good shoes. Mom caught him and announced that he was going nowhere without his galoshes – the ones with the snap-up buttons.

He hated those things because none of the other guys wore them. Punky's mom had bought him a pair of high-top boots with a place for a jackknife on the side, and his dad coated them with some waterproof stuff so that he didn't have to cover them up with galoshes or rubbers.

Punky was already outside chucking snowballs at crabby old man Gormley's house when Tommy came down the porch wearing his snap-up button galoshes.

The Purity Dairy milkman would be coming down the street soon. The two boys started stockpiling snowballs at the side of the house, from where they could escape to the alley if necessary, or in case Donny Schalcraft came out and they could really "wap" him.

Tommy went out front to see if the Purity horse was coming; he heard someone calling to him.

"Tommy, Tommy, I'm coming over to play with you," called out his cousin Patti. "Mom said you would have to watch me for awhile."

The boy thought about this for a moment and then realized that she would make a perfect guard for the snowballs and could also be on the lookout for Donny Schalcraft.

"Okay, Patti. Come on over," he yelled back.

On second thought, he decided to go over and get her, since he was supposed to watch her for awhile. Tommy crossed Janette Avenue, took Patti by the hand, and started back towards his house and the snowballs.

Suddenly there was a loud noise and a car horn honking at them. A man had lost control of his car and was now coming straight toward them. At the last minute, Tommy pushed his cousin out of the way and he was run over himself.

That was the last thing he remembered until he woke up in the hospital with his mom and Patti's mom holding his hands.

Patti was there too and looked very scared, as if she had caused whatever happened. The hospital people gave him ice cream and ginger ale and the doctor showed him his bruised feet which now had the imprint of his snap-up galoshes buttons right on his insteps. There were five of them on each foot and he kinda hoped they would never go away.

Back home he was a hero to cousin Patti, his family, her family, and most of all, the Janette Avenue Gang who all came over to see his wounded feet, which were now real badges of honour.

"Wow! Tommy, doesn't it hurt a lot?' asked Eugene Bardwell.

"Nah," said Tommy. "The doctors said I hardly even cried."

Punky asked if he could just touch one of the impressions and Tommy let them all feel his feet. Patti was especially proud of his feet marks. She kinda stood there and beamed every time someone mentioned that it was her life that was saved.

After a week or so, the marks went away as did the attention, so Tommy developed a slight limp, which was easily explained to all who asked what was wrong with his legs. It was his first experience with fleeting fame.

Above: Patty, and her hero Tommy. photo courtesy Tom Paré

Breaking the Ice

by Richard Hughes Lindell
Issue #21, February 2002

We didn't go into Aunt Claudia and Uncle Jack's when we arrived in Craig's Beach, but headed directly down the cliff stairs to a frozen Lake Erie.

"Do you think it's safe?" wonders my Grade 13 buddy, Goody.

"It must be. Look at those fishermen way out there," I reply. "Let's go!"

Normally, mid-February ice on Lake Erie is at least two-feet thick. What the three of us didn't realize was that the balmy Christmas weather has made a significant difference in that year – as we were about to find out.

No sooner do we step out on the ice than we hear ominous crackling noises.

"It must just be thinner close to shore!" I shout, "Those guys must be half a mile out there."

A friendly beagle bays from outside the fishermen's ice hut and my dog Frisky is in hot pursuit. Suddenly we lose Chuck – or at least half of him as he's crashed through the ice up to his waist. He recovers quickly with Goody's help and they hurry back to shore.

I scan the horizon while shouting for Frisky and spot her in the water about half way between her beagle buddy and us. I rush to her aid. As I get closer, I notice her normally strong swimming stroke is a blur as she tries to escape her frozen trap.

Then, six feet from the broken edge, I plunge through! My feet barely touch bottom as icy water fills my boots and clothes; never have I felt this kind of cold! I manage to push Frisky out and then start breaking the ice to find a thicker area. Eventually, I slowly slide myself out.

"Let's get the hell out of here, girl!" I scream, but she has responded to Dave and Chuck's shouts and is heading for safety. She finds another soft spot and the ice caves in around her. This time I just jump in and am somewhat relieved to discover that the water is only chest high. Again I retrieve my dog and again I slowly pull myself out.

The shore is getting closer, but once more Frisky submerges into the water, barely struggling this time. Goody, the scientist of the group, shouts advice, "Lay down on the ice and increase your surface area! Slowly crawl to Frisky!"

I do as instructed, but from that moment on, I will have a more than a quiet distrust of the scientific mind. I get closer to Frisky than during the two previous episodes, but this time the ice breaks at my waist and I slide into the water face first under Frisky and past the open water.

By sheer luck (and not good management), I smash through the ice covering my "coffin," push Frisky out and then try to extricate myself – but this time, I can't move, and I don't really seem to care. I'm feeling absolutely nothing.

"Damn it Rich, get out of there!" Goody screams as he and Chuck head for me. Their shouts of encouragement somehow revive me and I heave myself out and then step onto solid ground.

The four of us climb the stairs up the hundred foot cliff to the house while the wind blows against our backs. When we reach the lawn above, we have been transformed into three snowmen and one snow dog.

Uncle Jack meets us at the back door and immediately shouts for clothes and blankets. He orders us to strip in the bathroom. After drying Frisky and bundling ourselves up, we charge to the fireplace and start to thaw. As steam rises from our hair and the shaking subsides, we finally start to feel good.

Suddenly I am aware of a major personal problem. Let's see, how should I explain this? In winter the testes of the ram ascend from their normal position in the scrotum, up the inguinal canal into the abdomen. From this position it is impossible to impregnate a ewe until the spring when the testes reverse their path...

Sorry, maybe I'm getting too technical here. How about this? Like a forgetful squirrel in winter, I have misplaced my acorns or, how about – my swallows aren't returning to Capistrano?

Eight minutes and 43 seconds later (but who's counting?) Capistrano's mission bells begin to chime, my problem reverses and I heave a huge sigh of relief. I immediately rip up my application as a perennial soprano for the Vienna Boys Choir.

Today, as a veterinarian, I will occasionally get bitten or scratched by a pet. Since I have very slow reflexes and very little pain sensation in my skin I don't tend to pull away and the damage usually is minimal, although sometimes not very pretty.

However, if I ever find myself walking on lake ice and I hear even the whisper of a cracking noise, I recall a certain day in February 1964. A charge of a primordial reflex hurls me in the direction of the shore so rapidly even Donovan Bailey would not beat me in that race to safety.

Sunday in Detroit

by Al Roach, Issue #22, March 2002

Shall we get started for Detroit? It's Sunday of course but those wicked Americans will keep their theatres open. And we've looked forward to this day for weeks. Hurry along. Get the children aboard the Wyandotte streetcar at the corner of Lincoln Road. Each of us will drop a nickel in the farebox. Three cents for the children. Give them their pennies.

Watch for the sheet metal knight on his horse in front of that shop on the north side. That's the sign that we're almost downtown. All off at Goyeau Street. Walk a block west to Dufferin, where Webster Brothers Ford dealership is located.

One short block north to the low brick building at the tunnel entrance (How many of us know that its proper name is the Fleetway Tunnel?). Quite a few Canadians going to Detroit today.

Most of them bound for the Michigan or Fox Theatres. Or the Adams or United Artists. Well, why not? To heck with the Depression. Anyway, Prosperity is just around the corner. Didn't Roosevelt say so in his fireside chat just the other day?

Board the square-cornered dark grey tunnel bus with its big exterior sun-visor across the entire windshield. Oh, my sainted aunts, how the brick roadbed of the tunnel vibrates the bus. It's like being in one of those new-fangled milk-shake machines in the Jumbo Ice-Cream Parlor on Ottawa Street.

Stay together now as we pass through the Aliens' gate at the United States Immigration. As usual, the adults are being asked: "Where do you work?" There aren't enough jobs to go around in these early 1930s and the immigration officers have their hands full trying to stop unemployed Windsorites from looking for work in the States.

Board the bus again out on seedy Woodbridge Avenue and ride up to Cadillac Square with its old brownstone Detroit City Hall. Dejected unemployed men competing with the pigeons for a place to sprawl on the imposing stone steps.

A few minutes walk on this chilly February day. Boys buttoning leather aviator caps under their chins. Goggles pulled down over their eyes. Along State Street, up prestigious Washington Boulevard to Grand River, over a few blocks to Bagley and the magnificent Michigan Theatre, one of the largest movie houses in the entire 48 states.

There's a line-up. Get your money ready. That will be a quarter for adults and ten cents for children. It's even more expensive during the week. That's why we come on Sundays.

But once inside. Incredible! Look at the rich carpeting, the statues, the painting, the grand piano over there. And look at the seven balconies!

Seated at last. There's Jesse Crawford at the organ actually rising out of the floor into the orchestra pit as he plays. Catch your breath as the soft blue spotlights sparkle on the keys.

The audience is in great voice for today's sing-song. Our voices swell with the organ to fill this vast theatre with the joyous sounds of "Wait Till the Sun Shines, Nellie." No need to worry about the words. They're all up there on the screen. And the little white ball dances along on top of them to keep us all in step.

Now it's the Movietone News ("The Eyes and Ears of the World") and a Betty Boop cartoon ("Boop-boop-a-doop") followed by the feature movie "The Champ," with Wallace Beery and Jackie Cooper.

Our eyes ache as we step out into the bright sunshine reflected on the snow. But they adjust quickly as we walk two short blocks to the White Tower Restaurant at Grand Circus Park. The hamburgers will cost five cents each but they're real doozies. Smothered in thin sliced dills – a White Tower specialty – to us they are the best hamburgers in the world.

Back down Woodward Avenue, the wind at our backs. As we approach the river, expensive shops give way to run-down tobacco stores, novelty shops and cheap cafes with their odours of chop suey.

Past the Michigan Book exchange where a fat, unkempt proprietor, cigar stub in mouth, prices second-hand books according to their size. I doubt very much that he can read.

Past the Avenue Burlesque with streetside photos of lumpy peroxide blondes draped in ostrich feathers, and a leering Scurvy, the house comedian ("Look the other way, children").

Down to the original plant of the James Vernor Company near the river where we complete our day with a five-cent glass of nose-tickling ginger ale. Or, if you could afford it, a cream Vernor's (ginger ale and real cream) for ten cents.

Now we board the Windsor-Detroit ferry "LaSalle" for the trip back. Ignore the ice floes. Fifteen minutes later we are at the Ouellette dock, disembarking via the second-deck gangplank.

Through Canadian Customs. Downstairs. Emerge behind the decrepit Ritz Hotel on the northwest corner of Ouellette Avenue and Sandwich Street. Home on the Sandwich streetcar with its breathtaking curve at the top of the Peabody Bridge.

End of a beautiful day. Total cost for a family of four: less than $3. The bad old days? Well, maybe. But not on Sunday. In Detroit.

~ 1942 ~
A Christmas Story

by Al Roach, Issue #12, December 2000

Clem bought all his presents and had exactly two dollars left. He knew just what he was going to do with that money. He asked me if I wanted to go downtown with him on Christmas Eve and make a purchase.

We decided to save the nickel bus fare each way and walk from Walkerville. It was a beautiful evening: clear, snow on the ground, temperature hovering around ten degrees Fahrenheit. Our shadows walked along with us, first behind, then overtaking us and extending out in front as we passed each yellowish street light.

We reached the corner of Wyandotte and Ouellette where, in a field on the northeast corner, a sign proclaimed that a bank would be built there as a post-war project. We found the main street alive with joyful last-minute shoppers.

We turned north and walked along the eastside of Ouellette toward the river. The wind was developing a bite and I adjusted the metal band over my brown fur earmuffs, drawing them closer to the sides of my head. My feet slipped on lumpy snow, hard-packed by hundreds of shoppers' boots.

"Where is this angel, anyway?" I asked.

"At Bartlet, Macdonald and Gow."

"It would be!"

Almost to Sandwich Street (Riverside Drive), I pulled my woolen jacket up tighter around my throat and leaned into the wind. We passed Meretsky and Gitlin Furniture, the Tea Garden Restaurant, John Webb Jewellers.

Despite wartime shortages, shop windows displayed a tempting variety of gifts "for her" and "for him," all competing for space with crossed Union Jacks, signs exhorting us to "Buy British" and purchase Dominion of Canada Victory Bonds, and others reminding us that "Loose Lips Sink Ships."

We approached the Fleetway Tunnel exit. Across the street was Liddy and Taylor Men's Wear, the store where Clem and I spent some of the dollars we earned, working Saturdays (for 40 cents per hour) at the A&P on Ottawa Street, to outfit ourselves for the return to school each fall.

We were surprised to see the newsstand at the tunnel exit open so late in the evening. The headlines were always the same in those days: success and disasters for the Allied armed forces on land, at sea and in the air, but inside, the comics were still there. War or no war, Li'l Abner was wrestling for a gun with the four-armed Mr. Armstrong, Brick Bradford was championing the weak against the strong, and Caps Stubbs remained the quintessence of boyhood.

In that festive season, all the papers, including The Windsor Daily Star and The Detroit Times were carrying Clement C. Moore's "The Night Before Christmas." And, assuring eight-year-old Virginia O'Hanlon that, yes, there is a Santa Claus, as they had done every year since the editorial first appeared in the New York Sun in 1897.

Light snow began to fall, powdering our hair and eyelashes, tickling our noses.

"What are you going to do with this angel, anyway," I asked.

"Put it on the top of the tree, of course. It's a beautiful white satin ornament with gold hair and all that. I'm going to put it up there tonight when everyone's asleep – a kind of surprise for my mother. She's been wanting one since the cat got the old one last year. Top of the tree looks bare without an angel."

We crossed Park Street, passing the Prince Edward Hotel. Through the revolving doors and down the steps came a live angel in a white satin evening gown; Persian lamb coat and dangling silver earrings. Escort in black coat with velvet collar and fringed white silk scarf. They tiptoed their way (she holding her gown up with one dainty hand) over the icy sidewalk and into the waiting checkered cab.

There was to be a New Year's Eve dance in the Prince Eddy ballroom. Matti Holli's Orchestra. Three dollars per person. Clem and I would not be there. If we could scrape up the price of admission, we'd likely take our girlfriends ice skating at the arena "to the music of Ralph Ford at the electric organ."

Moments later we passed the Canada Building where Sid Tarleton and his St. Mary's Church Boys' Choir had made their annual appearance at 9 a.m. that day, leading the building's tenants in singing Christmas carols. An old tradition.

A stubby little Sandwich, Windsor and Amherstburg Railway Ford bus crunched by, throwing dirty snow on our trouser legs. The Fords were among the first buses purchased after the streetcars were junked in 1939.

Downtown Windsor, 1942. David L. Newman Collection

Ads in this day's Star, signed by W.H. Furlong, K.C., chairman of the S.W. & A., and F. X. Chauvin, vice-chairman, thanked Windsorites for their patience. The buses were badly overloaded, what with wartime workers and Christmas shoppers vying for standing room in the aisles. Maybe they should have kept the old reliable streetcars.

We passed Honey Dew Limited, which served the best orange drink in town, and looked across Ouellette at the sparkling windows of old established retailers such as Burton the Tailor, Esquire Men's Shop and George W. Wilkinson Limited (Four decades into the future, these locations will be occupied by One Plus One Ladies' Wear, Jeanne Bruce Limited Jewellers and Chateau 333 respectively).

In front of the five-story Wilkinson's store ("Wilkinson's Shoes Wear like a Pig's Nose") stood a Salvation Army lass in her quaint bonnet with the big ribbon. Her little hand bell sounded somehow shy, matching her sad eyes.

An idea. "Why don't you give your two dollars to the Sally Ann?" I suggested. "It's Christmas Eve, you know."

"Bah! Humbug!" replied Clem in his best Dickens' manner. "Charity begins at home."

At the Palace, Cecil B. DeMille's The Sign of the Cross was playing. Starring Frederic March, Claudette Colbert and Charles Laughton.

Across London Street (University), past Stuart Stores for Men, the Singer Sewing Machine Store, C.R. Wickens and Son Tobacconist and Gift shop, across Chatham Street, Wright's Butcher Shop, Grinnell's Music Shop (piano's, sheet music, radios, records"), John A. Jackson Limited Men's Wear, the Star Restaurant, across Pitt Street, past the Canada Trust Company on the northeast corner.

As we went by the C.H. Smith Company store, we saw a small boy standing in front of Bartlet's, staring at something in the window. We recognized him; we'd seen him many times selling his magazines to the drunks coming out of The Ritz and B.A. Hotels at Ouellette and Sandwich. He must have lived over one of the stores in those old run-down, three-storey brick buildings on Sandwich. Not exactly Willistead Crescent.

Shiny black hair. Big, staring brown eyes. He was looking at a black lace shawl with a $5 ticket on it. A lot of money in those days.

Clem's pace slackened, reduced to a crawl, and came to a stop. Silence. The boy turned as if to leave.

"Nice shawl, kid," said Clem.

A pair of brown eyes looked at him innocently. A bit perplexed.

"Uh huh." A pause.

"How much money do you have?"

Again the artless eyes stared at Clem, taking him in, registering no emotion. Another pause.

"Three dollars."

Three dollars, I thought. Three dollars earned the hard way. Long hours after school on that pavement in front of the two hotels, just up short. Now that's quite a coincidence.

Clem gave me a why-don't-you-mind-your-own-damn-business look. Another pause. Clem looking at the boy. Boy looking back, wondering what was coming next. Me looking at Clem.

Finally: "Look, kid, take this two bucks and go in and buy the shawl and don't ask any questions."

A minute later we were looking into the store, watching the perfumed saleslady wrapping the shawl in a Christmassy box. A pair of brown eyes watching her every move. Five-dollar bills scrunched up in a grubby hand resting on the sparkling glass counter.

Another minute later and he was out of the store, dashing around the corner and heading west on Sandwich Street. He disappeared into a south side doorway near Fifth Brothers Tailor Shop and the Taylor Furniture Company.

I thought a certain mother was going to be very happy on Christmas morning.

We turned back down Ouellette Avenue. In silence. We stopped at the traffic light at Chatham. The snow was falling heavier now, coating the scene in fresh holiday white. I looked sideways at Clem.

"I thought charity begins at home," I grinned.

"You can just shut up," he said.

But I couldn't get over the feeling that Clem would not need his satin angel. A far more substantial one would be shining down on him on Christmas morning.

photo: C. Edwards

Manning House Hotel Still Standing

While reading The Times Magazine, I noticed in the article, "Still standing... After all these years" the statement, "... Now the oldest commercial structure remaining in the area, due to the destruction of the Norwich Block two years ago..."

I guess somebody forgot about 172 Ouellette. The Manning House Hotel was built c. 1887, so both buildings were probably built around the same time. The Manning House was part of the Royal Bank Complex until they moved across the street. As far as I can tell, it now sits vacant.

Just keeping you on your toes!
Andrew Foot, Windsor

~ 1932 ~
A Christmas
Quite Unlike All Others

by Stan Scislowski, Issue #12, December 2000

The Christmas of 1932, the year my father died, was a snowless Christmas and not as cold as one would expect at that time of year.

In mid-afternoon of Christmas Eve, my brother Joe, my sister Olga and I were sitting on the front steps of our rundown house, which was badly in need of a paint-job, doing nothing in particular except talk about Christmas.

When I mentioned I hoped Santa Claus would bring me a hockey stick and a snakes & ladders game, Olga piped up: "Santa Claus doesn't come to poor people's houses."

This shook me to the core. "How come?" I exclaimed.

"Because," Olga answered, "He just does not come to poor people's houses."

Blunt, but true. Strangely, for a lad as young as I was (9) I thought about it for awhile, and then came to terms with it. "If that's the way it is, then that's the way it has to be," was my outlook.

While we sat there in cheerless conversation, a truck drove up and stopped in front of our place; a man came up the sidewalk and thrust out a clipboard with a sheaf of papers on it for Olga to read.

He pointed a finger at a name thereon and asked if this family (ours) lived here at 1554 Parent Avenue, to which Olga nodded assent. The man turned about and hollered to the two men standing amidst a load of bushel baskets, "Okay, fellows, let's go!"

Three men carrying two bushel baskets full of groceries, candies, and other Christmas goodies, along with a large basket of meat and a plucked goose started up the sidewalk. With the excitement only kids our age could display at being handed something good and special, we followed Olga as she directed the men around to the back entrance. The largess was deposited on the kitchen floor, to the surprise and tearful enjoyment of my mother.

The Goodfellows of Windsor had come through at the last minute and delivered Christmas to the Scislowski/Hedgewick household, precisely when the prospects of a Merry Christmas appeared so bleak.

Some kind soul in the neighbourhood had submitted our names to the Goodfellows, and we were well on the way to having a Christmas celebration that would be enhanced by events in the wee small hours of the morning when we were tucked away in our feather-tick covered beds sound asleep.

Since Olga had said Santa would not be stopping at our house, I had no intention of waking up bright and early on Christmas morning. We had no tree set up and no decorations anywhere in the living or dining rooms. It would be just another day for us except for the traditional Christmas goose dinner with all the trimmings my mother could now prepare for us.

And so, on Christmas morning while I was deep in some dream long since forgotten, my brother Joe brusquely shook me awake, "Stan, Stan, come and see what Santa brought you!"

It took a few seconds to get my wits about me before I leaped out of bed, almost ran into the Quebec heater (an upright wood and coal stove) and entered the living-room or front room, as we called it. Before my dancing eyes floated balloons and multi-coloured garlands hanging from the ceiling. But best of all, a three-foot decorated Christmas tree set up on a table in the corner, with brightly wrapped gift boxes from Santa!

I literally jumped out of my skin when I spied the hockey stick standing by the table with my name on the tag, "To Stanley, from Santa." And, yes, there was also a Snakes & Ladders game. To say our household was filled with excited shouts and squeals of delight and merriment was to describe it in the mildest of terms. It was joy beyond joy and it had arisen out of adversity.

The Christmas tree, the presents and decorations had come from the hearts of my oldest sister Annie and my oldest brother Peter, both of whom somehow put enough nickels, dimes and pennies together from their meager earnings; Annie from her house-cleaning jobs and Peter from his door-to-door selling of Postian rugs and Kirby vacuum cleaners, and what he made at his caddy jobs in the summer.

And that is what they must mean when they talk about the magic of Christmas.

Story Prompted Tears

You wouldn't believe how many people, family, close friends, fringe friends and acquaintances came up to me over the holidays and complimented me on that insignificant little piece I had written about Christmas. My wife Joyce, who rarely ever reads what I write, came to me in my office crying and I was afraid she might have received some bad news over the phone. When I asked her what she was crying about, she said it was my story in your paper. I couldn't believe it. She said, "You never told me the hardship you and your family went through during the Great Depression, and so I couldn't help but cry."

Stan Scislowski, Windsor

Wednesday was Mending Day

by Hester M. Curtis, Issue #26, July/August 2002

I was born in Windsor on January 2, 1925, the fifth child of Albert and Theresa Carter. I was one of three girls and three boys. We lived at 1171 Lillian. A large family was popular then. To me, the experiences of being part of a large family are forever cherished.

My father, Albert Edward Carter, was born in London and came to Canada in his early 20s with his family. He was a very tall, dark-haired man who was always smiling. Who could ever forget his aquamarine eyes?

A grower by trade, like his father, he owned many greenhouses on Goyeau Street as well as a retail florist shop under the name of Howe and Carter. Although in poor health, he worked very hard and spent long hours growing his plants. He was always striving for the perfect blossom or richer soil.

Father was a great storyteller. Every night at bedtime, we enjoyed his concocted stories. He always stopped at an exciting part – to be continued the next day.

My mother, born in England in Rotherham, Yorkshire, was a Brumpton and came to Canada in her late teens with her parents. My parents met in Windsor and were married in All Saints Anglican Church, in Windsor City Hall Square where my sisters and I were also married. We were all baptized there as well, as were my own children.

Raising a family of six in those days was certainly no easy job, yet my mother, always smiling, was completely in charge.

Monday Was Wash Day

With six children laundry was never ending, especially since babies and young children nearly always wore white! My mother considered herself very fortunate as she had a wringer washer while many women were still using a scrub board.

Monday was wash day – rain or shine, snow or sleet – and it took all day. Mother would get up very early to prepare the soap. She shaved a bar of Fels Naptha soap and melted the shavings into a gel. After filling the washer with hot water, she added the soap along with the clothes. They swished back and forth for a while and then she would put them through the wringer, turning a crank to send the clothes into a rinse tub. After being plunged up and down, they would go back through the wringer into the clothes basket to be pegged onto the line in a very neat order: shorts all together, underwear, towels... every backyard had full clotheslines, because it was Monday.

Tuesday Was Ironing Day

After the clothes were dried and folded, some had to be sprinkled with water and rolled tightly to be ironed on Tuesday. Permapress was not yet heard of. All clothing had to be ironed and men's shirts, women's blouses, and linen table clothes were starched beforehand. As little girls we were taught first to iron handkerchiefs, then pillow cases and as we got older, blouses and dresses. It was a time-consuming chore and an unpleasant one, especially on hot summer days. Our irons were very heavy.

Wednesday was mending day. There were buttons to be replaced, knees of boy's pants to be patched and socks to be darned. This was all done in between housework and preparing meals.

Thursday was for extra chores, Friday was cleaning day

Thursday was the day for extra chores such as cleaning cupboards,

Above: Hester's cousins enjoy a picnic in their white clothes near Leamington in the 1920s – before automatic washers!

straightening dresser drawers, cleaning silver and the many other chores that come with a large home. Sometimes, my mother, an excellent seamstress, would sew on her treadle machine.

On Friday, mother cleaned as though the house hadn't been cleaned in weeks. She washed and polished the floors on her knees. The furniture was polished with paste wax and then rubbed until it shone. The windows were also cleaned. The smell of cleaning products filled the air. It was such a busy day we always had stew for supper.

This Monday-to-Friday schedule was not just mother's way; in every household, the woman of the house followed the same routine. A good housewife always had a clean and polished home.

Grocery shopping was done daily; everything was bought in the neighbourhood. The meat market, grocery store, and produce store were on Erie Street, a few blocks from our house. The owners knew all our names and knew my mother's likes and dislikes. The groceries were always put on a tab, which my mother paid off every Saturday.

On Saturday everyone had a chore and we knew no chores done meant no spending money. Going to the store to buy penny candy or an ice cream cone was the highlight of the week.

The little store where we bought our penny candy was our favourite place. Honeymoons, lollipops, caramels, black balls, fudge, and licorice awaited in glass jars and boxes. You would tell the clerk how many pennies you had and he would grab a small brown bag for them and wait patiently. After we made our choices he would give the bag a twist and away we'd go.

Sunday Was Quiet Day

We went to All Saints Church to Sunday school in our Sunday best and were home at one o'clock. Since we were to remain in our good clothes, my mother always said, "Please stay clean and play quietly."

My girlfriends and I always did our favourite thing. With our dolls in buggies, we would walk to the cemetery two blocks away. There we would meet our friends and then walk around the cemetery paths. This does seem strange to me now.

Sundays also meant company over for dinner or getting together with other families. The children were always fed after the adults. I don't know why but that was the way it was. I'm sure a psychologist today would cringe at the thought.

After the adults were finished we ate in the dining room on the fine china. The food was always good. Our manners were monitored and we always asked to be excused from the table. After eating we were allowed to play games before bed.

Then, a new week would begin: Monday was washday ...

Hester Curtis submitted several "According to Hester" articles describing what it was like to grow up in a man's world in Windsor during the 1920s, '30s and '40s as part of a large family. "There have been so many changes, some for the better and unfortunately, some for the worse. But some things never change, and I hope they never will."

Lost & Found!
The TIMES Reunites Lost Sisters

In the March/April 2005 issue we published a letter by Mary Ellen Cooper who had been searching for a lost stepsister for 40 years. Thanks to a local reader her stepsister was quickly found.

Never did I dream that my efforts to find my sister Barbara Anne Miller Baker would come true. I had searched the Internet for years and was going into phone books in every city in Ontario.

When my friend Lois Thoms told me about your magazine and that sometimes people find or reconnect with each other through your "Letters to the Editor," I thought one more try would not hurt. As a last resort, and almost giving up, I sent in a picture along with a letter about Barbara Anne and what I remembered about her while growing up.

L-R: Mary Ellen Cooper, Barbara Anne Miller (now and then)

It was a matter of a couple of days after the magazine hit the streets that word came of a gentleman who might know where she was. I made the phone call right away and Patrick put me in touch with Barbara's best friend. This lady was very apprehensive until I convinced her that I was truly Barbara's sister and that I had been looking all this time for her.

Two days later Barbara called! I think it blew her mind that I had been looking for her all this time. It was the most wonderful experience and after burning the lines with tears, we spent the next 1 1/2 hours bringing each other up to date. Barbara lives in southern Ontario, and I live in the north, but it was like we were just next door.

She sent pictures of her children and herself (middle), grey and all. Not fair. From a black-haired 15 year-old to a white-haired, well-groomed lady. I cried for the time that was lost and grateful for the days, months and years we have left. We are planning a big reunion sometime in the near future.

A really big thank you to Vanda of *The TIMES* who put me in touch with Patrick, who put me in touch with Diane, who contacted Barbara, now a part of my life. I will be forever thankful to these people.

To *The TIMES Magazine* and all the staff who so graciously gave their time and support, I thank you so very much. I will be your "Ambassador for the North." All you have to do is ask!
Mary Ellen Cooper (Beveridge)

Ed: We are very pleased and happy to have helped you in your quest to reconnect with your sister. Like you, we are amazed by how quickly it happened!

Remembering Sid Lloyd ~ Photographer Extraordinaire

To say I was surprised when the June 2003 TIMES arrived with a photo taken by my dad Sid Lloyd on the cover, is an understatement. I poured a double brandy, sat down and thought about him. He and I rarely talked about his early days but I remember one night when I found him talking about those times to Frank Wansborough who was recording his words on tape.

While I never heard the tape, I do recall Dad talking about life in Wales at the turn of the 20th century. Born in Bristol, England, in 1885, he left home in his teens to fend for himself. Bristol is on the river between South Wales and England; Dad crossed it to make a living in the Welsh valleys with his newfangled photographic equipment, travelling with two other men in separate lines of work.

He'd walk up to a house, knock on the door and say, "Good morning, I'm from the Tourist Gazette and we are photographing picturesque houses in the area. Do you mind if we photograph yours?"

With an assent, he'd suggest the housewife come out and stand beside the door, to add a little human interest to the photo. The Welsh mining towns in the valleys were all row houses – every house the same. Dad's sales pitch was: "What a beautiful window, is it yours?" (who the hell else would it belong to? It was on the front of the house!) The lady of the house would take off her apron, tie her hair back and wipe her face, while he set up for the photo. Bingo, the net was cast.

About a week later, he'd return to show the housewife the photo – now with a cardboard frame around it – and tell her that if she would like it, it was free but, there was a charge for the frame. Hence, he made a living. He knew that several weeks after the lady had lauded her prize photo to the neighbours, it was fair game to come back and hit other houses.

One time, a husband was home; he took the photo out of the frame, said thanks and gave Dad back the frame.

Think of the chore of doing this – carrying a tripod, etc. At night Dad would return to his rooming house, black out a room and develop his negatives. Printing was done with printing frames – POP (printing out paper) – in the sunlight. Also, he silvered the glass plates for the next day of taking more photos.

Photographer Sid Lloyd (top) and in Walkerville with his mobile photo gear, c. 1920.

He had only so many plate holders and that meant replacing the exposed plates with unexposed ones. Where was it done? On the sidewalk in a black light-tight bag. He put it over his head, tied it at the waist and made the changes in the dark by feel. The kids on the street would throw stones and sticks at him while he was secure in the bag. He had to rely on his assistant to keep them away.

Sadly, many of Dad's Windsor photos were discarded after his death as my mother couldn't find anyone to take them. ***Walt Lloyd, St. Louis, MO***

A Sid Lloyd Gallery

Sid Lloyd pours the jug at this camp set up as a photo shoot for Ford; he probably used a wire to trip his camera.

Windsor kids cooling off in the Detroit River in the 1930s. A couple of them stand on pipes that pumped raw sewage directly into the river.

A tyke gets a closeup of some unidentified Windsor bathing beauties at Ford Bathing Beach just east of Walkerville.

A prank photo of Windsor police officer Cec Paré giving a traffic ticket to the locals in the early 1950s.

best of the times • 123

Building an Ambassador

Before the construction of the Ambassador Bridge in 1929 (the longest international suspension bridge in North America), the only way to move people, cars and trucks across the Detroit River between Windsor and Detroit was by ferry boat (the Michigan Central Train tunnel was built in 1910). The bridge's principal builder, Joseph Bower of McClintic-Marshall Co. was responsible for its name – he thought the bridge served as an "ambassador" between Canada and the United States.

All bridge construction photos from "Ambassador Bridge – A Review of Its Construction" by McLintic- Marshall Company, from the private collection of David L. Newman

Below: Everyone knows about the Detroit-Windsor Tunnel Bus, but not everyone remembers that the Ambassador Bridge once ran a bus too. Detroit-Windsor International Coach Service buses once ran back and forth across the bridge. Photo circa, 1929. photo courtesy Bernie Drouillard

Bridge Tower Under Construction – May 26, 1928
View from Canadian shore shows erection of towers is well under way; progress on the Canadian side was faster because piers supporting barges were built sooner.

First Footwalk Cable – August 8, 1928
With the towers completed, footwalk cables were strung from anchorage to anchorage on the ground and in the bottom of the river, then raised over the towers by derricks. A huge celebration was held to mark the first physical link between Canada and the USA, as can be seen by the number of boats under the bridge, including the steamer Columbia at centre of river.

Footwalks and Cable Spinning
These wheels shuttling back and forth from anchorage to anchorage, strung 16,000 individual wires of cable.

Forming The Floor – September 27, 1929
The floor forms were begun at the centre of the span in preparation for the pouring of a concrete roadway.

Compacting Machine, December 12, 1928
The bridge cables featured 37 round strands (218 wires each) in which each cable was laid up and adjusted. This crew employed a radial jack to force the wires into a singular group. Note the lack of safety equipment on this cold winter day.

Windsor Bricklaying Crew, 1927

In this era, skilled tradesman wore ties and vests. The building in the background appears to be the present-day Hong Kong Bank at university and Victoria Avenues. Isadore Marcocchio is standing 2nd from left, Adolfo Paron is standing 4th from left.
photo courtesy Adolfo's son David Paron, Windsor

Windsor Truck and Storage, 1890, moved chattels the old-fashioned way. The business has been located at 201 Shepherd Street for more than 110 years! photo June and Fred Arthur

Above: Bernice Stoddart and friend Tilly Golding took a bike ride to Woodstock from Windsor in the 1940s. "On the way back, a guy from Keystone Contractors said 'Get off those damn bikes and I'll give you a ride to Windsor!'" Bernice Stoddart snapped Tilly's photo.
photo: Bernice Stoddart

Left: Gouin and Desjardins Cement Contractors, Tecumseh, Ontario, around 1900.
photo: Bernice Stoddart

126 • on the border

Across the Great Divide

Top: Detroit in 1890, dominated by church spires.

Middle Pictures: The ferry docks at the foot of Woodward bustle with activity around 1905. Soon, the first signs of skyscrapers and larger steamers moored at the busy port of the Detroit and Cleveland Navigation Company.

Left: Woodward Avenue facing Windsor in 1890; flags raised in remembrance of Civil War Veterans, still very much top of mind for the young Republic.

photos: The Burton Collection

Where The Action Was:
An active and thriving downtown Windsor dominated by the imposing C.H. Smith's building in late 1920s; all structures in this photo have been razed.
photo David L. Newman Collection

On Guard:
London Street (University Avenue) showing the Windsor Armouries and Curry Hall, looking west. A sentry stands on the corner while a wagon pumps water. Construction on the 21st Regiment, Essex Fusiliers Armouries began in 1900 and the building was officially opened on January 30, 1902; 7000 people attended. Postcard marked November 6, 1919.
postcard David L. Newman Collection

128 • on the border

Clockwise from top:

Old Man River: l-r: Craig, Clara, Helen, Fred and Gladys Johnson, Detroit River, 1910. photo courtesy Neil MacPhee

Al Carriere with his bread truck in front of Airport Inn, Windsor. photo courtesy Claire Carriere

The Wild Bill Hickok Show at Jackson Park pre-World War II.
photo courtesy Claire Carriere

Grace, Gerald, Gertude Carriere at Wllistead Park. photo courtesy Claire Carriere

William Hill (far right) pulls up a fresh catch at the Fishing Hatchery in Sandwich.
photo courtesy Jim Carmichael

Al Carriere tends fields near Ford City.
photo courtesy Claire Carriere

3
Birth of the Auto

Ford Canada Assembly Line, 1920s, Windsor
Ford of Canada Archives

The Walkerville Wagon Works became the Ford Motor Company in 1904

Henry & The McGregors

From the Ford Graphic, Golden Jubilee Supplement, August 17, 1954, (author unknown)
(supplied by Larry Viveash, Windsor)

Issue #46, August 2004

On a chill, late afternoon in January, 1904, three McGregor brothers sat talking in the dimly lit office of the storey-and-a-half frame building of the Walkerville Wagon Works on Sandwich Street East. Gordon, the eldest, was doing most of the talking; Walter chimed in occasionally with a question or two. Donald, barely 19, merely listened with rising excitement. They had stopped in to see Gordon on their way home from their office at the McGregor-Banwell Fence Company, across the CNR spur line.

Almost three years earlier, Gordon had left his bookkeeping post with the Photokrome Company in Detroit to take over management of the wagon works from their father, William, who had been appointed Customs Collector for the Port of Windsor, after 20 years service as MP for Essex North.

Good Steady Business

The wagon works, Gordon was saying, was a good, steady business. But he couldn't see how much future there was in making heavy farm wagons, axles and wheels.

A new era was arriving – the day of the horseless carriage. The way business people in Detroit were talking, the auto was going to make the horse and buggy a thing of the past, within a few years.

(To Donald, who knew Gordon didn't even own a horse and buggy, this sounded like very big talk, indeed, but there was no stopping his older brother's enthusiasm).

"Why, there are men in Detroit, like Henry Ford, who say every farmer will soon be using an automobile," Gordon related. "I don't see why we can't build autos right here; I think I'll have a talk with John Curry." (John Curry, who operated a private bank in Windsor, had helped finance William McGregor's purchase of the wagon works).

This is the first recollection of W. Donald McGregor, chairman of the Windsor Centennial Committee, of hearing that automobiles might soon be made in Canada for the first time – and by his own brother.

Donald, was keenly interested in autos through conversations with his fiancée's relatives. Her father was Frederick Evans, who, with Horace and John Dodge, operated the Evans and Dodge Company in the Typograph building on Medbury Lane alongside the Windsor ferry docks.

They also made the E. & D. bicycle, but sold the business to Canada Cycle and Motors, which, incidentally, made the first recorded purchases of cars produced by Ford of Canada. Later, the Dodge brothers brought out their own car in the U.S.

best of the times • 131

New Venture No Novelty
New ventures were nothing new to the McGregors. Besides the wagon works, William McGregor and John Curry had bought a large tract of land at Bruce and Elliott streets, and cultivated a big field of hops there. In addition, they acquired a cranberry marsh at Marshfield, near Harrow, Ontario.

"They poured $100,000 into that venture and never harvested a single cranberry," Donald McGregor recalls.

To most Windsorites in 1904, the horseless carriage enterprise seemed almost as risky.

Within the next few days, however, Gordon McGregor had had his talk with John Curry and whetted Curry's interest.

One day late in January, they walked down Sandwich Street from the wagon works, embarked on a ferry and took a streetcar from the Detroit dock to the Piquette plant of Henry Ford.

Later, they talked to Henry A. Leland about the possibilities of assembling Cadillac autos in Windsor. A second talk with Henry Ford proved even more encouraging but some capital would have to be raised in Canada.

Back in Windsor, Gordon McGregor began to expound the merits of the automobiles – and especially the Ford cars – to a few close friends.

Many Were Skeptical
There were many skeptics. Barely a handful shared Gordon's enthusiasm. But he was able to persuade others to give "the new fad" a chance.

And there were some surprises. Col. S. C. Robinson received a bonus from the Hiram Walker distillery, and agreed to buy shares against the advice of the Walker family. Then C. M. Walker bought shares. Miller the druggist, who operates a shop in the Crown Inn hotel at Devonshire Road and Assumption, had a cheque for $1,000 but, when Gordon didn't appear at the proper time, tore it up.

On August 17, the Ford Motor Company of Canada Limited, was chartered to make cars in Canada for the first time.

First Auto Parts
Barely a month later, Donald McGregor recalled, a horse-drawn wagon came off the Walkerville Ferry with the first auto parts to be assembled in the wagon works.

"I tried to drop in every other day or so to see how they were coming along," Donald recalls. "One of the first things they did was clear out a number of split wagon wheels which couldn't be sold. I bought the lot and they made the most beautiful firewood!"

The assembly plant was anything but orderly in those early days. The wagon painters (some of whom remained with Ford to paint cars, while others went to the West Lorne Wagon Company, which purchased the wagon works), had allowed paint drippings to accumulate on the floor, which had become extremely bumpy, while the walls, often used to clean brushes or test paint, looked camouflaged.

Supervised First Assemblies
Frank Hagen and Art Hoffmeister came across the river from the parent company to supervise the first assemblies.

The entire staff of 17 (including Miss Grace Falconer, Gordon McGregor's secretary, who remained with the company until Wallace Campbell retired as president), and a number of Walkerville and Windsor folk cheered Gordon McGregor as he drove the first car from the rear of the wagon works to Sandwich Street in October, 1904.

But for Donald McGregor, the big day came in the spring of 1905, when, at 20, he was given permission to drive Gordon's Ford for the first time.

That evening he drove down Sandwich and turned up Ouellette Avenue to stop with a flourish in front of his fiancée's home. Then, with Lillian Evans in the rear seat, he drove up Ouellette Avenue in the evening darkness.

Get a Horse
Unfortunately, the Model C had no headlights, and Donald drove right into a pile of sand in the middle of the street. The drive chain broke; Donald had to leave the Model C by the side of the road overnight, and escort his fiancée and her parents home – on foot.

But nothing could stop Gordon McGregor and the Ford cars. "I remember going to Gordon's home some years later," Donald recalls. "He said he had written to all stockholders offering to re-purchase their stock."

"Now if they don't accept, the blood is on their head," Gordon said.

By the end of 1909 shareholders had received dividends totalling $31 for every $100 invested, and in 1910, were paid a further $100.

In six years, the McGregor dream had come true.

"There are men in Detroit like Henry Ford who say every farmer will soon be using an automobile. I don't see why we can't build autos right here (in Windsor)."
Gordon McGregor

Gordon Morton McGregor

Born January 18, 1873, Gordon Morton McGregor was the founder Ford Motor Company of Canada. The son of William McGregor, a member of Parliament for twenty years, and Jessie Peden McGregor, the family resided on Riverside Drive near Crawford. On November 2, 1898, he married Harriett Dodds, of Detroit, Michigan, and moved to a residence near the corner of Victoria and Wyandotte. At the time of his death on March 11, 1922, he was both treasurer and vice-president of Ford Canada.

Portrait of Ford City

**Excerpts from "Windsor 1892-1992 –
A Centennial Celebration," by Trevor Price & Larry Kulisek, Issue #3, July/August, 1999**

The two towns of Walkerville and Ford stood side by side, but they were a complete study of contrasts, products of their origins in different historical periods and traditions. Walkerville enjoyed the solidity of measured growth and the guiding hand of one of North America's most effective business leaders (Hiram Walker).

Ford, by contrast, experienced mushroom-like growth propelled by the most dynamic industries of the age – automobiles. Its life as a municipal entity was less than a quarter of a century, and during that time it coped with difficult problems before finally succumbing to insolvency and embracing without dissent the forcible amalgamation, which its more prosperous neighbour, Walkerville, resisted to the end.

The roots of Ford go back to the late nineteenth century before it became an industrial town. The French Canadian farmers of Sandwich East Township dominated this area, and they had begun to coalesce around a small village where, in 1884, they had established a Catholic church – Notre Dame du Lac.

Prior to the building of this church, a priest from St. Alphonsus Church in Windsor had held mass in a school room on the farm of local shipbuilder Shadrack Jenking. Nearby, a number of small industries had developed: Jenking's shipyard, a small pork-processing plant, the making of staves for barrels, the manufacture of sugar from locally grown grapes, and a blacksmith's shop.

Census figures, the names of people on the assessment rolls, the importance of the Catholic Church and the significance of separate schools in this area all prove that Ford City in its origins was predominantly French.

Ford City's first four mayors were French, as were a majority of members of the first Ford City councils. The farm lots used to carve the Ford Motor Co. were almost entirely owned by French families. The main thoroughfare (Drouillard Road) was once a private lane on the Drouillard farm, which wound its way from Riverside Drive to Tecumseh Road.

François Drouillard donated the land by the river on which the church of Notre Dame du Lac (Our Lady of the Lake), later called Holy Rosary was built. Typically, Hiram Walker made a contribution to the building of the church, which was attended by some of his employees.

Above: In October 1915, 1,700 Ford factory workers crowded Riverside Drive near Drouillard to have their picture taken to raise money for the WWI war effort. According to Ford officials "All were placed in position, photographed, and returned to the factory in less than ten minutes." Photo: Ford Canada Archives.

The original Ford automobile factory site was a good location on the river to which were brought the components from the U.S. parent plant to be assembled into completed horseless carriages.

The Walkerville Wagon Works already existed, and an alert entrepreneur, Gordon McGregor, accomplished a deal with Henry Ford to bring auto parts to the Wagon Works for less duty than fully assembled cars were charged, thus getting an edge on the Canadian market. This occurred in 1904 when 17 employees produced 117 finished automobiles.

This small beginning was the springboard from which ensued the most vibrant growth of a manufacturing industry which Canada had ever seen. The Ford of Canada operation soon outgrew its original building, and after the first new building was completed in 1910, Ford continually expanded over a huge site which eventually covered hundreds of acres.

Workers poured into the area since many additional industries began making car components and other car makers began operations. By 1913 Ford of Canada employed 1,400 employees, the wages were $4 an hour and the work week was 48 hours. The wages far exceeded what was generally available in manufacturing at the time, and news of the opportunities soon spread.

The new community of Ford as well as neighbouring border communities experienced a prodigious flow of new immigrants from Europe, rural Essex County and other parts of Canada.

Neither the rural township of Sandwich East, nor the neighbouring municipality of Walkerville, had an interest in trying to organise the new community, which then experienced the results of haphazard and poorly supervised growth.

The new community was incorporated as a village in 1913 and quickly reached town status by 1915. Effective municipal organization was needed to develop housing and ensure good standards of public health.

The name Ford City was the popular choice promoted by Charles Montreuil, a local resident who became its first mayor. The irony is that the name by which it was generally known and recognized in official documents – Ford City – was a misnomer.

Ford City was always a town. In 1929, when the community actually incorporated as the City of East Windsor, it dropped the old name. The Ford Company always referred to the town of Ford without the appendage "city." However, the documents of the municipality and provincial references used the name Ford City.

By 1928 when Ford City changed its name to East Windsor, it reached its peak population of around 16,000. At this time, it covered 1,600 acres of land, had six schools and a fully developed structure of municipal services.

Along Drouillard Road could be found every kind of store and commercial facility. There were churches for every kind of religious

The 1905 Ford Model C launched a new industry, completely altering Windsor's business landscape.

Photo: Ford Canada Archives.

Walkerville's 1st Woman Driver

My daughter, Pat, thought you may be interested to know that my mother, Harriet (or Hattie as she was called) was the first woman driver in Walkerville. She is pictured in the photo at left. One day she was out cranking the car and a man said to her "that's no job for a lady" to which my mother replied, "If I want to drive the car, I have to crank it!"
Mary Kitchen, West Vancouver, B.C.
Issue #29, November 2002

Driver William J. Bradley with Msgr. John J. Blair from Toronto, sitting behind is Mrs. Hattie Bradley and John's sister, Hattie Blair, the first postmistress in Stratford, ON.

Publisher's note- see Camilla Wigle's version concerning the first woman driver in Walkerville, page 61.

Ford City Revival

When the Ford Motor Company's head office and assembly plant moved to Oakville in 1954, Ford City experienced a serious decline. Today, little is left of the town that Ford built. Drouillard Road became an eyesore with its rundown buildings and was home to motorcycle gangs and various street toughs.

In 1979, Our Lady of the Rosary Church and the East Windsor Citizens' Committee established Drouillard Place, a community centre devoted to improving the quality of life for residents. In 1996, seventeen years later, Drouillard Place and the Ford City Business Improvement Area formed the Drouillard Road Redevelopment Committee. In partnership with Human Resources Development Canada, the City of Windsor, the Canadian Auto Workers Union and Ford Motor Company Canada, the Ford City/Greater Drouillard Revitalization project began.

As part of this project, a plan was hatched to recapture some of district's rich heritage. A community mural project that depicts the boom times of the twenties, thirties and forties received the backing of the area business improvement association, Ford Canada, the federal government and the City of Windsor.

A team of artists captured the history of the area with paint and steel: Mark Williams, a Ford employee was the lead artist of the project and created a large sculpture of Ford workers, circa 1950, that graces the parkette at Drouillard and Whelpton; other project artists included Donna Jean Mayne and Ryan Pearson, airbrush specialists, Steve Johnson, cartoonist and Yong Sheng Xuan, an illustrator of children's books. They have painted 36 large, incredibly striking outdoor murals of the Prohibition era, automotive machinery, local residents, street scenes and quitting-time snapshots.

Above: "The Founders" (1999) – Gordon McGregor (seated) with Henry Ford launched the Ford Motor Company of Canada (in what was once Walkerville Wagon Works) near Drouillard and Riverside Drive.
Artists: Mark Williams, Donna Jean Mayne and Steven Johnson

Left: "Military Production" (1999) – In September 1939, Canada entered the Second World War. Recognizing conflict was possible, Ford engineers – in cooperation with the Canadian government – had already begun preparing for military production. By April 1942, civilian production had been discontinued and all Ford's resources were committed to the war effort.
Artists: Yong Sheng Xuan, Mark Williams & Donna Jean Mayne. Photos courtesy Ford City BIA

---

persuasion – Catholic, Orthodox, Anglican and United. All this, from open fields to a busy town, happened in the short space of 20 years.

By 1923, it was reported that about 85 percent of Ford residents owned their own homes, and they were able to finance the relatively large loans needed to build the infrastructure of schools, civic buildings, libraries and utility service.

The haste with which Ford was built and the fact that many of its residents were newcomers influenced the nature of the housing stock, which was largely built by owners and speculative landlords. It was not built to last.

In this creation of an instant town wedged in between industry and rail lines lay the ingredients for later urban decay. Perhaps this was inevitable because Ford grew too fast and had to borrow too much money.

By the early 1930s, the new city of East Windsor was in financial difficulty, along with most of its neighbours. High unemployment meant people lost their homes and were unable to pay their municipal taxes.

The future of East Windsor lay in the hands of the province. The idea of amalgamation with the wider metropolitan community was acceptable to the citizens of East Windsor, who expressed few of the regrets of Walkerville residents in losing their identity. The area still shows the marks of its origins as a working class, multi-ethnic community with more indications of a cosmopolitan European culture in its churches, stores and social clubs.

For a brief period at the end of the 1930s during World War II and after, Drouillard Road enjoyed a revival as a commercial and social hub, but when the main Ford assembly plant closed in the 1950s and commercial plazas opened in the suburbs, the area went into a rapid decline.

New measures for rehabilitation in the 1960s and 1970s infused new life in cooperation with the East Windsor Citizens Committee, Holy Rosary Church and various city departments.

The neighbourhood of East Windsor has survived tough times and has shown a desire to perpetuate the traditions of a feisty working town with cultures from many lands – a microcosm of what the rest of the city became.

Fond Memories Linger On
Trolley Clang, Clang Rings No More

from the Ford Graphic, Golden Jubilee Supplement, August 17, 1954, Issue #46, August 2004

"*Clang! Clang!*" went old number 101 on the Tecumseh street car line as it jangled and jumped along Sandwich Street on Thursday, August 17, 1922, taking Ford employees to work.

A placard advertising a moonlight cruise, popular with both young and old, adorned the front of the familiar green painted vehicle with its over-sized black "cow-catcher."

Slowly it crawled up Peabody Bridge, then flung itself down the other side, swaying, creaking and groaning, as the wooden body twisted around the curve past the Hiram Walker plant on the home stretch of its run.

Passengers lolled in the wicker seats, reading the Border Cities Star or just dozed.

As the street car approached Plant 1, the engineer of a yard engine put the steam to the driving wheels and started to move a string of freight cars along the siding leading to Plant 1.

Deafening Crash

At the door of the craneway in Plant 1, the two met with a deafening crash. When the dust and noise had settled, old 101 had been knocked off its trolley and lay jammed on its side in the doorway and Wabash automobile freight car NO. 19310 was tilted at a crazy angle with its rear trucks firmly embedded into the rear side of the street car.

Miracle Nobody Hurt

In just a few seconds, a crowd had gathered to rescue the passengers out of the overturned street car. Miraculously, no one was hurt, but according to M. L. Stewart of payroll department, "It caused quite a bit of excitement for a while."

This was but one incident in the life of the electric railway in Windsor, as recalled by Ford of Canada employees.

Electric railways were not new to Windsor when Ford of Canada was formed in 1904. The first electric street car in North America made its appearance in Windsor on May 24, 1886, and ran from the foot of Ouellette street to the Peabody Bridge. It was not until 1909, however, that electric street cars came into general use in Windsor.

When Albert Hall, one of the first employees in Ford of Canada customs department, was a youth, an open street car ran the length of Ouellette Avenue. It was especially busy when the Jockey Club at Jackson Park was holding a racing meet. Americans came across from Detroit in the boatloads to spend the day at the races.

A ramp ran along the sides of the street car so the conductor could collect the fares.

Unpleasant Trip in Winter

When George Dixon joined Ford of Canada in 1906, he used to ride the street car as far as the Crown Inn, which was situated opposite the Walkerville railway station. He would then walk from there to the Walkerville Wagon Works building. He recalls this was a very unpleasant trip in wintertime when the ground was covered with snow.

Quite a few of the employees preferred to walk in the "old" days rather than ride in the "jumping Lizzies," according to Patrick L. Cada, industrial relations division.

Get Out and Push

In winter, it wasn't an uncommon sight to see Ford of Canada employees leap off the street car and give it a push over Peabody bridge.

Frank Rawlings recalls the "Ford Special," a street car which was waiting every afternoon at the Ford gates to take the men home. And they were really crowded in those days. Another Ford old-timer, Jim Dark, claims that "the street cars were so crowded that men even rode the cow-catchers."

W. E. Laforet, foreman in the truck assembly, lived "away out in the country" when he first started with Ford of Canada in 1913. His house was about seven miles out along the lakefront in what is now part of Riverside.

Seven Mile Road

"I used to come to work in a street car, and believe me, that seemed like a long ride in those days."

The electric street cars were finally taken off the road in 1938 and replaced by buses. But like the memories they inspire in the minds of Ford of Canada employees, they still linger on. Dotted about the countryside there is a familiar look to the shape of chicken houses, summer cottages and even a motel. While windows have been boarded up and they are painted every colour of the rainbow, the grand old "jumping Lizzies" are enjoying their leisure years in new splendor.

136 • birth of the auto

Ford Strike of '45

by Herb Colling, Issue #27, September 2002

In 1946, residents of Walkerville were relieved and happy that the greatest upheaval in their history was finally over. It wasn't the war, but the infamous Ford strike of 1945. The 99-day strike began on September 12th, 1945, and ended on December 19th.

After WWII, people who built trucks, guns and ammunition at the Ford plants in Windsor were suddenly facing insecurity. Troops were coming home and expected to return to their jobs, as if six years of war never happened.

In my book: 99-Days, The Ford Strike In Windsor, 1945, I describe how those men fought for their democratic freedom overseas and, upon returning home, how they fought for their economic freedom at the Ford Company plants. That was over 55 years ago, a significant time in our labour history.

The seeds had already been sown by workers who remained at home during the war. They unionized the Ford plant in 1941-42 and kept strikes to a minimum to support the war. For its part, Ford treated the men better, in recognition of the work they were doing, but also because workers were scarce and the company needed to encourage production.

With the war over, the workers could see all of their labour gains disappearing. Ford was getting ready for commercial production. The job market was flooded, layoffs were threatened and Ford was clamping down, trying to return to prewar conditions in the plant. And those conditions were bad for the workers.

The boss was the boss. His word was law and if a worker didn't like it, he could quit. Foremen accepted bribes and picked favourites from "chore boys" who cut lawns, shovelled snow and painted homes to keep their jobs.

In one case, Wallace Campbell, the president of the Canadian operation of Ford, entered the plant, saw a worker dogging it and fired the man before he found out that the guy didn't even work for Ford. He was a government inspector. The company felt that workers were selling their labour like any other commodity, and had little interest in the product or the company.

Contract negotiations had been underway for 18 months, but an agreement just couldn't be reached, so the workers voted to strike. Roy England was President of UAW local 200. He complained that the company was trying to destroy the union. He declared that workers wanted a real collective bargaining agreement for the post war and he vowed that they would not go back to work until they had a new contract.

On September 12th, 1945, the history-making strike began at the Ford Motor Company in Windsor. It was a ground-breaking event, an epic battle, a struggle for the very survival of UAW Local 200. In all, Ford workers had 24 demands, including layoff pay, security for veterans,

Workers from Motors Products Corporation picket Ford of Canada in support of UAW Local 200, 1945, Public Archives of Canada, PA31232
Photo courtesy of Art Gallery of Windsor

more vacation pay, a better grievance procedure, better medical benefits and compensation for work on Sundays and holidays. First and foremost, the workers wanted union security and a check-off of dues... all union powers that many workers now take for granted.

Most workers believed in the strike, but some did not. On the first day, a worker tried to stay on the job and had to be chased around the plant before he would leave. The crane operator refused to go out, and strikers threw stones at him. Still others only served on the picket line at night, not wanting to get involved in the politics of the strike.

Picketers were nonviolent, but they did block non-union and non-striking workers from their jobs. On the second day, picketers marched four abreast across the front of the Ford buildings, preventing all access to the plant. When female office workers realized they weren't going in, they placed their lunch bags curb-side for the pickets and headed for home.

Ford officials were also refused access. They abandoned the plant and headed downtown to set up shop on the fifth floor of the Prince Edward Hotel. Later, union steward, Neil Carruthers was charged by police for 'besetting' and 'obstructing' access to the factory, which prompted debate about the legality of the union actions.

In early October and, for the first time in Ford history, the union shut down the power house, depriving the factory of light, heat and power. Company officials complained that machinery would rust in the cold, or that the plant might be destroyed by fire.

In response, Windsor police were called in to reopen the plant. They formed a 'flying wedge' around security guards to protect them from strikers, and tried to force their way in. A scuffle ensued, and strikers – by sheer force of numbers – pushed the police back. The adrenaline was flowing, but there was no violence and a black eye was the only injury. To the credit of both strikers and police, there were few reported injuries for the duration of the strike.

The most dramatic event of the strike was the blockade of vehicles around the Ford plant to prevent access by the RCMP and OPP. Strikers feared that the police would be used to open the plant and break the union and they set up the barricade to diffuse the situation. It started about six a.m. on Monday, November 5th, with union members from Ford and other auto-related companies showing up on the line. The pickets grew to the thousands as the day progressed.

Things were quite festive. There was a band, singing, and picketers marching throughout the day.

At the start of the blockade, Joe McBride, a 25-year-old millwright, hopped the Drouillard Road bus and told the driver to park it in front of the main gates at Plant One. Another bus joined them. Tommy Maclean was the first union member to drive his car across the front gates. Other member-cars followed, and then, union members seized and commandeered cars, trucks and buses, simply funnelling them into the traffic-jam.

From top: Mounties, flown from Ottawa, arrive as tensions escalated; Eastern edge of the blockage on Sandwich Street East (Riverside Drive), looking toward the Ford office building; Strikers after union officials began to clear away auto blockade; The Helen E. "picket boat" approaches the Ford plant at Drouillard.
Photos: Art Gallery of Windsor and Ford City Greater Drouillard Revitalization.

138 • birth of the auto

Parade through Ford City supporting striking Ford workers. Photo: Dave L. Newman Collection

George Burt described the blockade as a Miller Road because of its similarity to a previous action by the UAW at the River Rouge plant in Detroit. Eventually, the cars jammed Sandwich Street and up Drouillard for blocks around the plants. As one picketer suggested, it was a Model 'T' that Ford would not like. The famous blockade was known as the largest traffic jam in Windsor history!

The barricade ultimately worked. Police made no move against the strikers and the Ford plant remained closed. The strike continued. The Windsor Star called the blockade an insurrection with the mob in control and demanded that the police be used. The City of Windsor also called for order to be restored in a heated debate. Eventually, council gave the union an ultimatum: remove the barricade or the police would be called in.

Reluctantly, the rank and file agreed, if only to allow talks to resume. There was some grumbling from the men who were afraid that it would show weakness, but the barricade came down on Wednesday, November 7th.

All day, cars were returned to their rightful owners. More than a hundred insurance claims were filed, but only half were processed. They covered theft of tires, radiators, hub and gas caps and damage to paint and fenders. But most vehicles were returned in good repair, thanks to union members who kept damage to a minimum.

As a result of the barricade, meetings were held between government, union and company negotiators over the next three weeks. Progress was slow and, just when a settlement seemed imminent, all hope was dashed. A settlement was alternately helped and then

A settlement was alternately helped and then hampered, by representatives of the federal and provincial governments who couldn't agree on a solution.

hampered, by representatives of the federal and provincial governments who couldn't agree on a solution. There was a Liberal government in Ottawa and a Conservative government in Ontario and they just didn't see eye-to-eye.

Eventually, union leaders agreed to binding arbitration and held a vote of the membership to end the strike and go back to work while an agreement was worked out. There was no fanfare and no real sense of victory. The strike just ended on Wednesday, December 19th. The workers returned to their posts in the hope that Justice Ivan C. Rand would negotiate a settlement to end the bitter dispute. The membership was entirely at his mercy.

And, fortunately, they were not disappointed.

Rand recognized that there had to be a

"In 1945 Ford was paying seventy-five cents an hour. After six months you were entitled to an increase of ten cents. So they'd keep you for six months. Then they'd lay you off and rehire you again at seventy-five cents. This didn't go down very good. And none of the plants paid overtime."
George Burt, Ford Employee

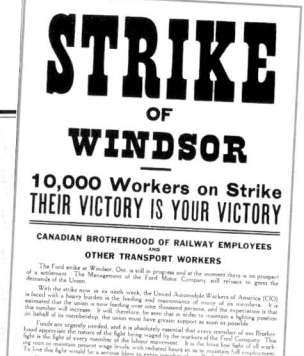

Above: Over 1,200 office workers line up across the street from their offices. They were kept from their jobs by picketers for a record 99 days.
Photo: The Art Gallery of Windsor

give and take between the union and company. He criticized both equally for their attitudes during the strike and established acceptable methods of behaviour for both the union and company. His agreement became known as the Rand Formula and represented a partial victory for the union.

Rand didn't give the union everything it wanted. He refused to allow a closed shop where every worker had to join the union. He figured that would restrict the rights of the company to hire whomever it saw fit. And, it restricted the rights of the worker. But, Rand did make it compulsory for every worker to pay dues, since every worker benefited from union activities. He required the company to collect these dues, and his decision was seen as making a big step toward union security. The union figured that most people would join the union anyway, since they were paying into it, and the agreement set the pace for union negotiations over the next 30 years. Essentially, it also established acceptable practices on the picket line.

In its day, the Rand Formula helped organized labour achieve the secure economic legal status for which it fought so fiercely since the beginning of the century. And, in that respect, militant unionism triumphed. It provided recognition by Ford that the union was there to stay. It allowed other companies to fight for similar consideration.

The Rand Formula's impact is still being felt. It was the outcome of the most important postwar strike in Canada, the crowning glory of a tumultuous time for Ford workers in Windsor.

On October 17th, members of the Women's Auxiliary rallied to support striking production workers of Ford. Headed by a brass band, and carrying placards and banners, they paraded several hundred strong in front of all pickets lines at the company gates.
photo: The Art Gallery of Windsor

No Buses Today

Received your latest edition and as usual it brought back a flood of memories. The article on the big Ford strike reminded me of the time when I worked for SW&A Bus Co. My partner and I were instructed to go down to the subway and get the buses out. Needless to say, with thousands of strikers – some real tough guys – we did not succeed.
Doug Skelding, Barrie

1901 Ford Racer, showcased at the 2002 International Detroit Auto Show. photo C. Edwards

Racing Into History

From "Ford World" (May 2001)
by Mickey Moulder, Issue #21, February 2002

At a small shop in Sterling Heights, Michigan, a group of automotive craftsmen is stepping back in time, restoring and replicating Henry Ford's 1901 racecar. While the glistening, high-tech conditions in which they work bear little resemblance to what Ford faced 100 years ago, the recreating of "SWEEPSTAKES" highlights several similarities between that racecar and modern ones.

"This is a very sophisticated car for its time" said Glenn Miller, a Ford development engineer in charge of the restoration and replica process. "Very innovative ideas went into this car. Until we started this project, people didn't realize all the technology it had in it. For the past 25 years, people at Henry Ford Museum have questioned the authenticity of this car, because it appears so advanced. But we're sure it's the original from 1901."

On October 10th, 1901, Henry Ford entered and won his one and only race. And if not for winning that race in front of some 8,000 spectators at the Detroit Driving Club in Grosse Pointe, Ford might not have created what became the Ford Motor Company.

Henry Ford entered that race to win money and get free publicity for himself and his ideas. After winning and receiving $1,000, Ford hit the front pages and his speed unofficially broke the existing land speed record of 68 miles per hour by 4 miles per hour.

Why? Because the technology used by Henry Ford was so advanced. Modern-day racing ideas included tires with no treads, non-carburettor fuel injection system (rudimentary by today's standards), distributorless ignition and variable valve timing (camshaft lift).

The racecar, called "Sweepstakes" was also lightweight and sat low to the ground compared to racecars of that era – traits that are still sought after by race teams today.

According to Miller, William Rands purchased the car from Ford early in the century, eventually donating it back so the Ford trade school could recondition it and rebuild the body. After a time at the trade school, it's believed the car went to the museum in the 1930s but was not displayed for some 50 years.

Ford Racing had the 1901 racecar replicated – in duplicate – for a wide variety of uses to celebrate 100 years of racing.

The original engine has two cylinders, measures 538 cubic inches (close to 10 litres) and creates about 26 horsepower. By comparison, today's Ford production engines range from 2.0 to 4.6 litres, while making 130 to 300 HP.

Henry's car was also lightweight. The other race cars had larger engines but heavier bodies. The body and frame are made of ash wood and the frame has steel plate reinforcement. The engine and pistons are cast iron, while numerous parts are made of brass. Iron is the component most used. The planetary transmission – a direct predecessor to today's automatic transmission – was side-mounted next to the engine with a chain drive to the rear axle.

To think that if Henry Ford had not become famous after winning this race, he would most likely not have gone on to found the Ford Motor Company.

Talk about betting the farm on one race!

Left:
Changing gears at the Windsor Train Station: horse drawn wagon and motorized truck.
photo: Ford Canada Archives

Below:
Sir Wilfred Laurier visited Windsor on September 9th, 1911. With him in the Model A were Gordon McGregor, then general manager of Ford Canada (at the wheel), W.C Kennedy, and partially hidden to the Prime Minister's right, George P. Graham.
photo: Windsor Community Museum

Bottom:
Woodward Avenue, Detroit, 1907. Delivery wagons line the west side of Woodward, but the automobile will soon render them extinct. photo: Burton Collection

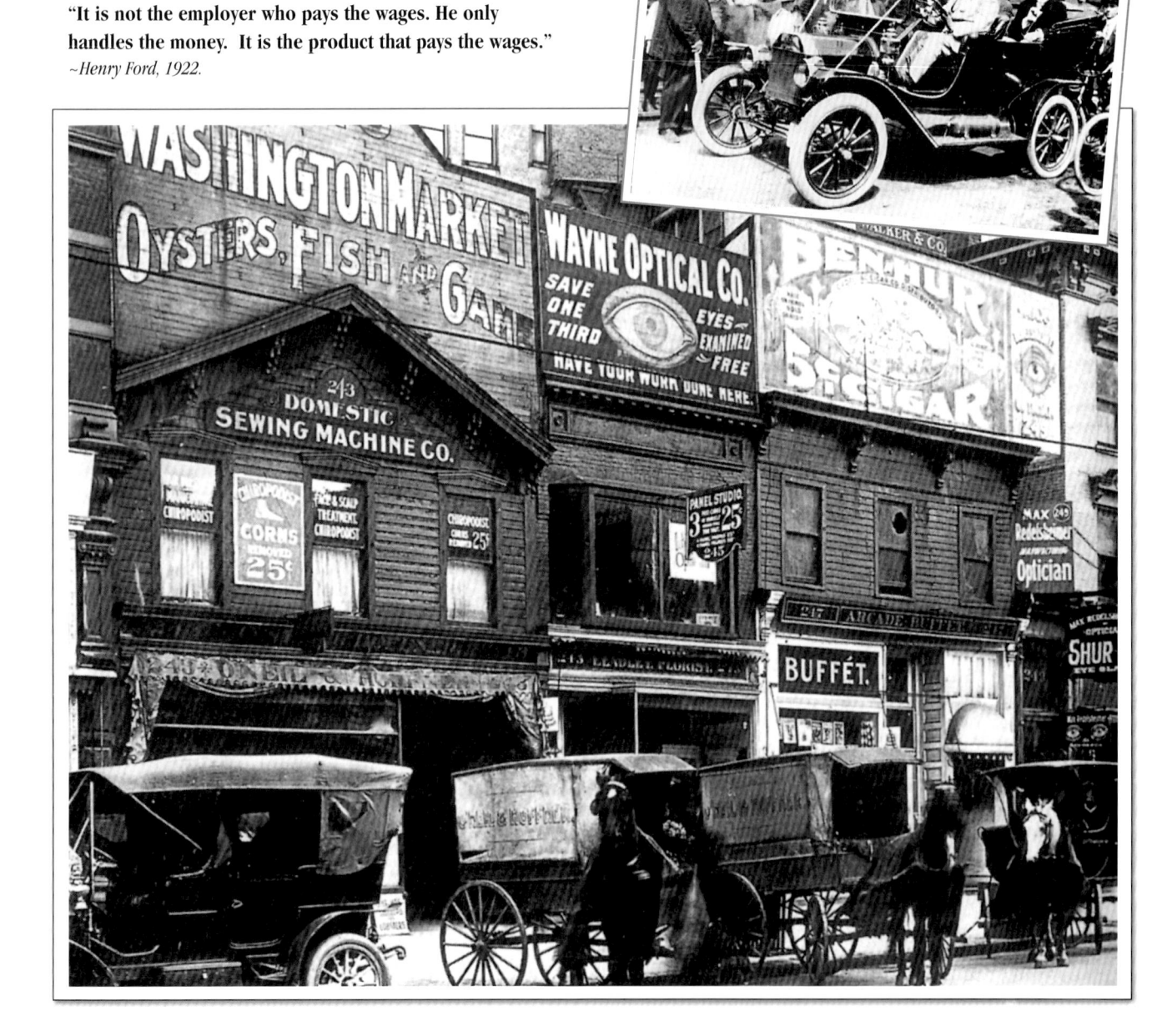

"It is not the employer who pays the wages. He only handles the money. It is the product that pays the wages."
~Henry Ford, 1922.

142 • birth of the auto

Above:
This photo may be the earliest in existence of the inside of the Ford Motor Company Plant in Windsor (formerly the Walkerville Wagon Works), 1904-05. The plant was torn down in 1914 to make way for a massive expansion. Photo: Ford Canada Archives

Right:
At the dawn of the auto industry, visual inspections were carried out by workers; this unidentified man checks the crankshaft of a Model A. Photo: Windsor's Community Museum

Below:
A 1919 Ford Model T, also known as the "Tin Lizzie." Here, workmen hoist the back end, attach a drive belt to the rear wheel and – presto! – enough power to drive a circular wood saw. Photo: Ford Canada Archives

best of the times • 143

Earliest known image of Ford workers in existence is this photograph of paint department employees taken on the front porch of the Walkerville Wagon Works building in 1906. Note their low-tech paint cans and brushes. Back row from left: Andrew "Andy" Moir; unidentified; Hilaire "Frenchy" Perrault; Fred Renaud; Leslie Burns; unidentified and George Williams. Front row: Percy Jacques; unidentified; Alfred Jacques; unidentified and L.V. Spur.
Photo: Ford Canada Archives

The streetcar parked next to the Model T in front of the Old Ford City post office was affectionately called "Galloping Gus" by Ford workers, who commuted from Windsor to Ford City. When stuffed with Ford factory workers, the trolley didn't have enough power to climb up the Peabody Bridge; a few workers would jump off and give old Gus a little help. Note the stylized Ford logo above the door of the post office.
Photo: Ford Canada Archives

144 • birth of the auto

Above:
Teamwork: Windsor Ford employees in 1940, the same year the machine shop (Plant 2) expansion was completed.
Photo: Ford Canada Archives

Above:
The Walkerville Wagon Works became Ford Motor Company in 1904. The East Windsor Ford site soon dominated the riverfront, witnessed in this 1934 photo.
Photo: Ford Canada Archives

Left:
Riverside Drive and Drouillard Road, 1919. In this same year, the first Ford truck, the Model TT, came off the assembly line.
Photo: Ford Canada Archives

best of the times • 145

Top: Non-powered moving assembly line producing Model "T" Fords in 1913. Photo: Ford Canada Archives; Soap car derby participants at the Windsor Ford Test Track in the 1950s; "T" Roadster, 1921. At left, the old style (U.S.) and at right the new style (Canadian). Photo: Ford Canada Archives

146 • birth of the auto

Paupers to Multi-Millionaires
The Dodge Brothers

from "Pioneering the Auto Age," by Herb Colling & Carl Morgan, and the archives of Daimler-Chrysler

During the childhood of the Dodge brothers, there was nothing to suggest that they would one day rank among the most important American motor manufacturers as well as among the richest U.S. citizens – both of them grew up in poor conditions.

John Francis Dodge was born in Niles, Michigan, some 90 miles away from Chicago, on October 25, 1864. His brother Horace Elgin Dodge was born almost four years later, on May 17, 1868, also in Niles, Michigan. Their father Daniel Dodge and his brother ran a small smithy and mechanical workshop, earning just enough money to make ends meet.

"We were the most destitute kids in town," John Dodge would tell a journalist at a later stage.

In Niles they were known as "the brothers," and the two redheads always did everything together – until their deaths. They were hard-working, hard-drinking, tough businessmen and master machinists. They ignored all correspondence not addressed to both, and even capitalized the "B" in "brothers" as if it were a proper name.

Their career began in their father's workshop. And soon their strengths came to the fore: both had a great talent for mechanics but Horace was the more brilliant technician, while John developed great business and management acumen. In 1886, they began working for Murphy Engine Company in Detroit, where they gained experience for four years and John was promoted to foreman after just six months.

Founded in Windsor

In 1890-91, John and Horace took up jobs as machine operators at the Canadian Typothetae Company in Windsor. John was soon promoted to workshop manager and married Ivy Hawkins in 1892. Horace married Anna Thompson in 1896 and one year later was granted a patent on an adjustable ball bearing for bicycle hubs.

With the financial support of the Detroit-based entrepreneur Fred S. Evans, the brothers rented the printing company – and began production on Evans & Dodge bicycles which soon made a name for themselves as E & D bikes. Their shop was at the top of "Ferry Hill" on Ouellette, which led down to the steamers. They continued building bikes for four years, then sold their start-up company to National Cycle & Automobile Company and retained key positions in the company.

Alongside bike manufacturing, the Dodge brothers had started producing parts for the automotive industry, still in its infancy at the time, as they foresaw a great future for automotive production – quite rightly so, as it turned out.

By 1901, they had acquired an excellent reputation for top-quality products and with their savings of $7,500, they founded their own

Above: John and Horace Dodge in the first Dodge production car, 1914, driving past their Boston Boulevard estate in Detroit. Photo: National Automotive History Collection

best of the times • 147

John Dodge & Horace Dodge. Photo: Daimler Chrysler Archives

company, Dodge Brothers in Detroit's on Beaubien Street. With half a dozen mechanics and as many trainees, they produced parts for bicycle manufacturers as well as mechanical components for motor vehicles. In "Automotive Quarterly" edition 17/1, 1979, Stan Grayson wrote that "John and Horace worked alongside their employees in the workshop during the day. At night, John did the accounting and dealt with the customer correspondence. Horace worked on new technical developments and projects."

At the time, the Dodge brothers even supplied complete engines to Olds Motor Works (Oldsmobile) – though still in rather modest numbers. In March 1901, the factory of Ransom Eli Olds burned down but Olds reconstructed it quickly; from then on the Dodge brothers featured as gearbox producers in the company's supplier files.

Production at the Olds Motor Works increased rapidly as if the fire had not left any traces. With his 1.5 liter single-cylinder Oldsmobile Runabout, which was to go down in history as the "Curved Dash" at a later stage, Ransom Eli Olds had designed the right car to appeal to the public. Starting with just 425 units of the robust and plain vehicle in 1901, production figures rose to 2,100 in 1902, to 4,000 in 1903 and to 6,500 in 1905 – between 1903 and 1905, Olds was the world's largest motor manufacturer.

The Dodges in the Motor City:
The world's largest automotive supplier

In Olds' wake, the Dodge brothers came up with another superlative: when Ransom E. Olds ordered 3,000 gearboxes from them in 1902, the Dodge brothers' company became the first large supplier in automotive history through the first – documented – major order.

In response to their endeavors to supply nothing but the best quality, the success of the Dodge brothers grew, and as early as 1901, they opened a new factory on Hastings Street at Monroe Avenue in Detroit.

On February 28, 1903, the Dodge brothers signed a supplier contract with Henry Ford to produce and supply eight-horsepower two-cylinder engines and transmissions for the Ford Model A, the hot new car of the times. Like the majority of motor vehicles built at the time, Ford's creations were put together from components from a large number of supplier companies – and the Dodge brothers assumed responsibility for the "heart" of the first Ford in large-scale production.

By producing initially 650 engines, transmissions and axles for Ford, they earned $162,500. In 1903, the Dodges abandoned their bicycle manufacturing business and concentrated exclusively on automotive components, with a workforce of 150 – and with Ford as its largest (and virtually only) client.

A Dependence on Ford

The drawback, however, was that they became heavily dependent on Ford. They even discontinued supplies to Olds, although Olds was a flourishing corporation at the time and Ford Motor Company had not even been founded yet. When Ford had to pay the first $5,000 installment to the Dodge brothers in March 1903 and the next $5,000 dollar installment for April became due, Ford had to establish Ford Motor Company as a stockholding company to be able to raise this money, and when Ford officially launched his company on June 16, 1903, the Dodge brothers were among the first twelve major stockholders. John Dodge became one of five Ford presidents with far-reaching competencies.

Ford, however, continuously tried to disengage himself from his parts' suppliers and eventually founded the Ford Manufacturing Company in 1905 to produce the company's own engines for the Ford Model N. But the Dodges had a say in this matter – John Dodge did after all, hold the position of vice president of Ford's engine factory. And when one of the top-ranking executives of Ford Motor Company died in 1906, John also took over as vice president of Ford Motor Company. When Ford sold its stock in 1908 to raise capital for his rapidly growing corporation, John and Horace came into the possession of 1,000 Ford shares each.

Business was booming – for both Ford and Dodge. In 1910, Dodge opened a new, almost 300,000 square foot factory in Hamtramck, a suburb of Detroit with a large Polish population, thereby consolidating its position as the world's largest automotive supplier. But partnering with Ford was not always easy.

Says author Stan Grayson in *Automobile Quarterly*: "The men were fairly close friends in their private lives but business negotiations – specifically the annual negotiations of new prices and contractual terms – were always characterized by fierce controversies."

Henry Ford continued in his endeavours to become independent of suppliers, and this did not exactly improve the atmosphere. The brothers soon left Ford and founded their own company, Dodge Brothers Incorporated, and began to manufacture their own car.

But fate intervened, and in 1920, the brothers died of pulmonary pneumonia during a flu epidemic. The Dodge name refused to die, however. Shortly after their passing, Dodge Brothers of Canada Ltd. was founded in Walkerville, and Dodge vehicles were assembled using imported parts from Detroit. In 1924, the company settled into a larger facility on Walker Road. Eventually, the company moved to Toronto to produce both Dodge and Graham Brothers trucks.

In 1929, the Dodge name returned to Windsor under a new Chrysler insignia, at the new facility at Walker and Tecumseh Roads. Soon after, the "Brothers" portion of the name was eliminated and became simply the "Dodge" division.

The First "Modern" Automobile

from the archives of Daimler-Chrysler

When Walter P. Chrysler presented the first car bearing his name as a trademark to the public at the New York Motor Show on January 5, 1924, he had pulled off a major coup: his Chrysler Six, marketed with the model designation B-70, because of its top speed of 70 mph (approx. 110 km/h), set new standards in the category of mid-sized U.S. cars. What's more, the first Chrysler became a bestseller – and the foundation for Chrysler Corporation.

Over and above this, Walter P. Chrysler reached one of his great personal goals with this car, an achievement he had been pursuing since 1908. In that year, he bought his first car, a Locomobile, while still working as one of the youngest top managers in the American railway industry. He disassembled his new acquisition in order to analyze its engineering.

According to Chrysler's biographer, it had been his dream to become active in automotive production from the moment he began disassembling the Locomobile. He decided to turn his back on railway management and to become a motor manufacturer.

He pursued his aims with single minded determination, thereby creating the conditions for the assembly of the first Chrysler cars in the Chalmers plant on Jefferson Avenue in Detroit on brand-new production facilities on December 20th, 1923. Even before the public launch at the New York Motor Show, Chrysler was thus able to present the new creation of his team of engineers, Fred Zeder, Owen Skelton and Carl Breer, to a select circle of bankers, suppliers, car dealers and important automotive experts at a trial driving event.

The new Chrysler Six met with spontaneous enthusiasm. The few skeptics were impressed, at the very latest, after the first trial driving. One dealer, for instance, expressed his doubts about the car's alleged top speed of 70 miles per hour. But when Chrysler's marketing manager Tobe Couture accelerated the test car to 70 mph on a wet road, with the skeptic in the passenger's seat, then took his hands off the steering wheel and slammed on the brakes to demonstrate the car's track-holding stability, this dealer was convinced, too. His signature under the purchase contract is said to have been a bit of a scrawl, however as the man was still shaking.

A top speed of 110 km/h may be ridiculous by today's standards – but it was breathtaking for drivers back in the 1920s. The Chrysler was only insignificantly slower than straightforward luxury cars like the Packard Eight that sold at twice the Chrysler's price. The Chrysler Six also proved to be highly superior to the competitors in its class in terms of its other design features and qualities, so it assumed the position of "best in class" immediately. In his article entitled "The Chrysler Six – America's First Modern Automobile," which appeared in the January 1972 edition of the Antique Automobile magazine, automotive historian Mark Howell wrote that its influence on motor history only compared with that of the Ford Model T, and that this car clearly defined the parting line between 'old' and 'new' cars in automotive history.

Above: Walter P. Chrysler took over Dodge Brothers in 1928. The photo shows him with the first Chrysler model, the 1924 Chrysler Six. photo: Daimler Chrysler archives

best of the times • 149

The Chrysler-Windsor Connection

by Elaine Weeks, Issue #2, May/June 1999

Chrysler Canada's local roots extend back to 1916, when the Maxwell Motor Company of Canada built a new passenger car plant in Windsor on Tecumseh Road East. Maxwell was challenged by many competitors, including the Chalmers Motor Company of Canada, which also began car production that year.

The two companies merged in the early 1920s under the name of Maxwell-Chalmers Corporation of Canada and moved car production to Tecumseh Road. By the time they merged in 1925, Windsor was Canada's largest and most important auto manufacturing centre. The company was soon renamed Maxwell-Chrysler, a forerunner to Chrysler Corporation, which was founded in 1925.

Over the next two years, it became apparent that demand for Chrysler products exceeded plant capacity. In 1927, Chrysler leased land occupied by the former Fisher Body Company of Canada Ltd. on Edna Street. The new plant in Walkerville was used for the assembly, painting and trimming of passenger car bodies.

The end of the 1920s also saw more expansion for Chrysler. In 1928, the company bought 70 acres of farm land in Walkerville for a passenger car assembly plant that went up that year. They also acquired the Dodge and Graham Brothers' operation in Toronto and moved it to a facility at Tecumseh and McDougall Road in Windsor. The first Dodge trucks rolled off the assembly line in 1931, and four years later, the Fargo began production.

Despite the Great Depression, Chrysler produced a record 30,000 cars and trucks in Canada, and opened a brand new engine facility in 1936.

Also at this time, union involvement in the automotive industry took centre stage in the United States. Taking their cue from their counterparts south of the border, auto workers in Canada began to organize. From 1938 to 1942, a large number of Chrysler workers waged a bitter battle for union recognition amidst an atmosphere of police arrests and blackballing.

Above: In 1928, the company purchased 70 acres of farm land in Walkerville for a passenger car assembly plant, shown here under construction.

Left: Chrysler picketers in the 1970s.

In 1936, Windsor Kelsey Wheels workers were the first to organize under the United Auto Workers as Local 195. Other small plants and then the Big Three, including Chrysler, began to organize and join up with 195. In 1942, 3,600 Chrysler workers secured a wage of 90 cents an hour in their first contract. Today there are 74 plants in Local 195.

Also established in that contract agreement was the grievance procedure, giving employees an avenue to settle any issues with management. Before the agreement, workers had no recourse when they were subjected to hardships on the job, health hazards, discrimination or abusive treatment.

The Local, re-organized into UAW Local 444 under Charlie Brooks, was the driving force in pioneering pre-paid drug plans through Green Shield and coverage through S. & A. Windsor Medical and Ontario Hospital Plan.

At the end of World War II, Chrysler Canada moved into a new administration building on Drouillard Road. During the next two decades, production expanded, and the Windsor facilities grew by leaps and bounds.

By the 1970s, the company experienced what can be charitably described as tough times. Chrysler then entered the most critical phase of its history. It seemed likely that Chrysler would be bankrupt, plants closed and thousands put out of work. The consequences for Windsor seemed dire indeed.

Lee Iacocca, who had developed the Ford Mustang, was unceremoniously fired by Ford; he would become the saviour of Chrysler. When Iacocca was hired to salvage the company in the late seventies, Chrysler was in debt to the tune of $160,000,000. The Chrysler "deathwatch" was on – The Windsor Star was preparing a series detailing Chrysler's collapse and its impact on the city.

Iacocca discovered that Chrysler executives were out of touch with reality; he immediately fired 33 out of 35 U.S. vice presidents, introduced just-in-time delivery, sold the overseas operation, unloaded the tank factory in Detroit, laid off thousands of workers and cut costs to the bone. Iacocca dropped his salary to $1, asked for and received concessions from unions, suppliers and loan guarantees from the government.

By 1983, Chrysler's recovery seemed to be taking hold. Iacocca's next move was even bolder – he stripped Windsor's entire Plant 3 to the walls, retooled and prepared to build his dream vehicle: the minivan. The conversion was a huge success, Chrysler paid off its bills, hired more workers, tore down old plants and built new ones in Windsor.

Today, Chrysler Canada has been folded into a merger with the German-based Daimler Corporation. Daimler-Chrysler is the last auto manufacturer still producing automobiles in Windsor.

Above: Chrsyler chairman Lee Iacocca displays the first Chrysler minivan in 1984.

Below: The Chrysler Corporation of Canada Limited was incorporated in Windsor, Ontario, on June 17, 1925, only 11 days after Walter P. Chrysler founded the Chrysler Corporation in Detroit. Chrysler Corporation of Canada was the successor to the former Maxwell-Chalmers Motor Company of Canada. In this photo Chrysler's first unit in its initial year of operation employed 181 people and built 7,857 cars.

postcard:: Dave L. Newman Collection

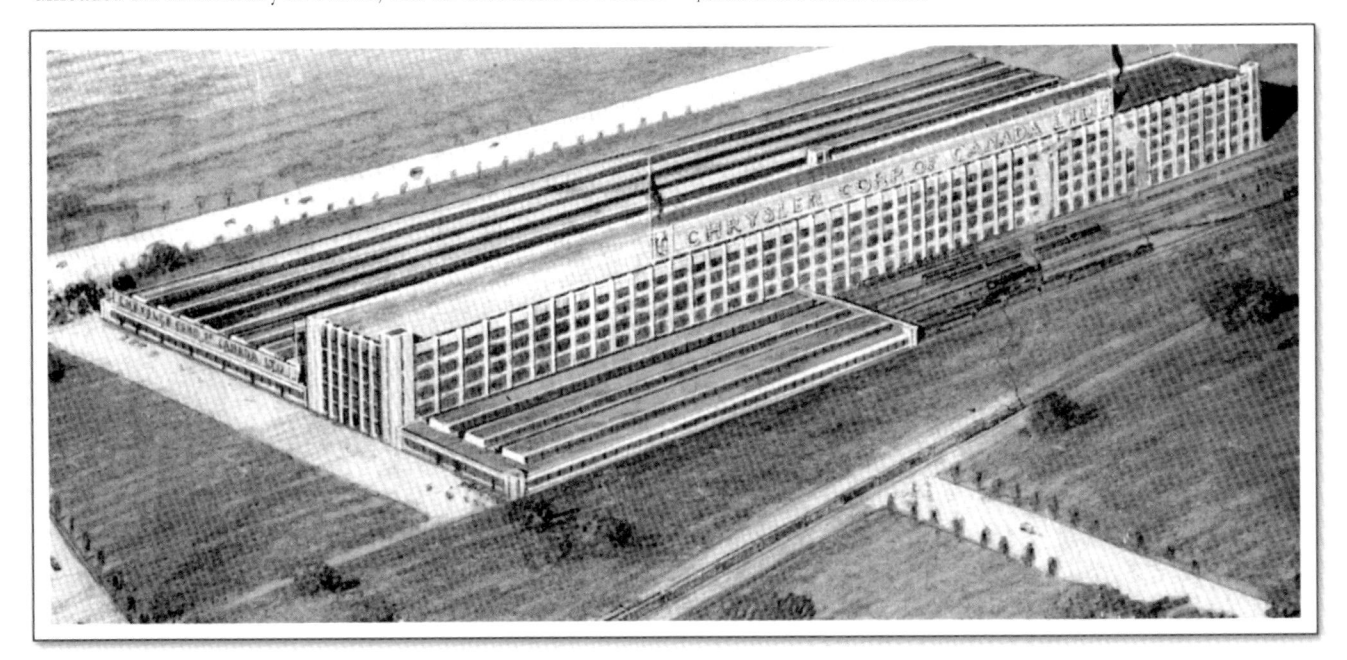

Essex Stock Yard 1885 – Future Site of G.M. Transmission Plant

General Motors in Walkerville
From Cows to Cars

by Elaine Weeks, Issue #4, September/October 1999

General Motors has been part of the Walkerville landscape since 1919. But before this industrial giant's days, things were decidedly more bucolic. Shorthorns, Aberdeen Angus Polls, Jerseys, Percheron and Roadster horses, Shropshire sheep and Berkshire pigs roamed a 1,000 acre stock farm owned by Hiram Walker's & Sons became the site of Windsor's 2nd major auto company.

Unlike Walker's stockyard on what is now Tecumseh and Walker Road, where cows were fattened and shipped to England in time for Christmas feasting, the animals at his Essex Stock Farm were bred to stock his extensive agricultural operations in Essex County.

An article in Canadian Live-Stock Journal from 1885 humorously describes the buildings located on his stock farm: "These are plain and unpretentious, the aim being rather to produce good animals than to furnish fine buildings with only inferior specimens within, as is so often done in the erection of dwellings for human habitation." Walker was also interested in raising children's saddle ponies and in 1883, an Exmoor pony was imported from England.

According to the Live-Stock Journal: "He is now being crossed with Canadian ponies, which it is confidently expected will produce a valuable pony paheton driver, and also a fine specimen of children's saddle ponies."

Since Hiram Walker encouraged business and industry to set up in Walkerville, it was only a matter of time before his rural properties were overtaken by the "wheels" of progress.

The World's largest automobile manufacturing company was founded on September 16, 1908. Its creator, William Durant, was a man who just five years before had known nothing about automobiles yet was convinced of their future importance. Once he became an automaker, Durant — energetic, ingenious, farsighted and a natural salesman — began to assemble a group of companies intended to build a range of cars in every style and price group. It was primarily because of his ability that General Motors grew to be the complex and highly successful organization it is today.

Canadian Products Limited, a subsidiary of General Motors Corporation was established on Walker and St. Luke Roads in 1921; it produced auto engines and axles but ceased operations in 1923.

In January 1928, the Walker Road Plant was re-opened as a branch plant of General Motors of Canada, Ltd. for the assembly of truck chassis and in 1929, operations were extended to manufacture truck and bus bodies. For a short period during 1929 and 1930, Chevrolet and Pontiac automobiles were also assembled in the Walker Road Plant.

In 1930, GM hired 575 men to assemble Chevrolet engines and then Pontiac, Oldsmobile, Buick engines, and also G.M. truck engines on Walker Road. When the Depression hit, the plant was re-tooled to produce engines.

GMC trucks and bodies were built under the direction of the Fisher plant for a short period in the 1930s. Border Cities Industries Ltd., a subsidiary of General Motors of Canada, was built in 1940 on adjacent property to the GM engine plant bordered by Kildare Road.

Former art deco-style headquarters on Walker Road. photos courtesy Dan Garneau – G.M. Transmission Archives.

During World War II, 25,000 Browning Machine Guns, 10,000 Palstin automatic rifles and several thousand naval gun mounts were produced. In 1945, this property was sold to the Sandwich, Windsor & Amherstburg Railway Co. (SW&A), only to be repurchased in 1978 as the GM Transmission Plant – a whopping $1 billion investment! Unfortunately, the Art Deco GM adminstration building on Walker Road was demolished and replaced by a shipping area; the familiar GM water tower was also dismantled.

During the 1950's, GM continued to produce engines, but a crippling 148-day strike in 1955 left a scar on labour relations.

In June of 1964, the engine plant was converted to the manufacturing of Synchromesh and 2-Speed Automatic Transmissions. The Walker Road plant's record of quality control and efficiency resulted in GM Corporation's decision to expand and convert the plant for production of THM 3-speed automatic, transaxle transmissions in 1978.

In 1965, Canada and the United States signed the Canada-U.S. Automotive Products Trade Agreement (Autopact). The agreement allowed GM of Canada to increase its production capacity dramatically. More recently, the North American Free Trade Agreement (NAFTA) between the U.S., Canada and Mexico has led to wide-open automobile trade in North America.

GM also built a trim plant on Lauzon Road in 1965, a $20,000,000 investment that boosted the fortunes of Windsor. Eventually, the plant was spun off to the Lear Company. The company continues to be a major employer in the city.

GM in 2004

Today GM of Canada has the capacity to manufacture more than one million units in a single year – generating significant export earnings by shipping about 90 percent of those vehicles to the United States. It also satisfies a third of Canada's 1.2 million unit market, the ninth largest automobile market in the world.

General Motors of Canada presently employs 22,000 employees working in manufacturing, marketing, engineering, customer support and other staff areas. General Motors of Canada has seven assembly and component plants within Ontario as well as several General Motors Acceptance Corporation (GMAC) and Motors Insurance Corporation (MIC) branches located across Canada.

Over the past two years, over 300 engineers have been hired in the new Canadian Regional Engineering Centre (CREC) located in Oshawa.

Over 800 General Motor's dealers employ 32,000 people in the sales and service of General Motors vehicles. Across Canada, over half a million Canadians are employed in sectors including 184,000 in the manufacturing, 145,000 in retail and 225,000 in aftermarket. GM of Canada sells over 90 models of cars, trucks and SUV's across an 800 dealer distribution channel. No other automotive manufacturer offers more new models through the largest network of dealers.

Above: GM worker displaying broken safety glasses, 1950.
Photos courtesy Dan Garneau – G.M. Transmission Archives.

W.E. Seagrave Fire Apparatus Co.
Birthplace of the Modern Firetruck

by Carl Morgan, Issue #7, February/March, 2000

Like the vast majority of people who travel Walker Road on a regular basis, you have probably seen it without really seeing it – or, more importantly, without knowing that it was home of the first company to produce a motorized fire engine in Canada.

Until recently, it was believed that the building at 933-963 Walker Road near Niagara had been erected sometime between 1895 and 1904. However, a search of the Town of Walkerville assessment rolls reveals that as late as 1904, a row of six private homes (lots 37 to 47) were located on that stretch of Walker, or 5th Street, as it was known at that time.

A year later, the registry shows the lots were owned by W.E. Seagrave, the head of W.E. Seagrave Fire Apparatus Company of Ohio (established 1881).

We can surmise that it was Seagrave who built the building, as the Canadian subsidiary of his successful Ohio fire truck company.

Walt McCall, retired Manager, Public Relations at Chrysler Canada, is one of this country's leading authorities on fire apparatus equipment and companies. According to McCall, the Canadian Seagrave operation was essentially an assembly company, using materials shipped to Walkerville from the manufacturing plant in Ohio.

In 1907, Seagrave assembled its first motorized fire apparatus, shipping three engines to Vancouver. In 1910, the city of Windsor bought a Seagrave aerial truck and in 1914, bought a Seagrave motor powered pumper which was in use until 1947.

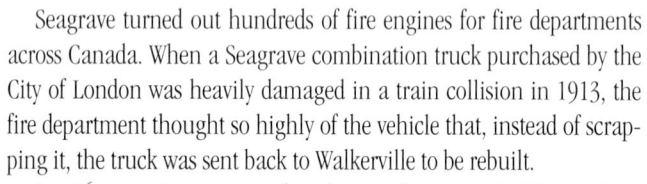

Seagrave turned out hundreds of fire engines for fire departments across Canada. When a Seagrave combination truck purchased by the City of London was heavily damaged in a train collision in 1913, the fire department thought so highly of the vehicle that, instead of scrapping it, the truck was sent back to Walkerville to be rebuilt.

For 16 years, Seagrave produced air and water-cooled fire engines but found himself in financial trouble when rival American-LaFrance set up in Toronto in 1915. To save his company, Seagrave tried merging with Loughead Machine Company in Sarnia and produced a line of heavy-duty trucks. The move failed and the company closed its doors in 1923.

Today, the building appears to be down-at-the-heels, but its historical importance overrides its physical condition. It is one of the last known industrial buildings still standing in Walkerville that can trace its roots back to the early years of the 20th Century (despite the fact that in its heyday, Walkerville was the site of dozens of different industrial companies).

What fate awaits this 100-year-old building is uncertain. In larger urban centres, it would probably be snapped up for converting into fashionable condos, studios, boutiques or a combination thereof.

Above: Site of the former W.E. Seagrave Fire Apparatus Company of Canada, founded in 1904; 933-963 Walker Road near Niagara Street, still stands today.

Below: 1914 pumper built by W.E. Seagrave Fire Apparatus Company, Walkerville. Purchased by City of Windsor and nicknamed "Old Mike," it was one of the first motorized fire engines in Windsor.

The Ghost of Seagrave

by Walt McCall, Issue #8, April/May 2000

You never know what history lies in your own back yard! For several years, I had noticed a domed private mausoleum in Windsor Grove Cemetery, about two miles from my Victoria Avenue home.

One day, I embarked on a purposeful drive through the cemetery to take a closer look at this odd structure, clearly visible from busy Howard Avenue. I was amazed to find the name "Seagrave" carved in stone above the iron door. I knew the Seagrave Company of Columbus, Ohio had established a Canadian branch plant in Walkerville at the turn of the century.

There were certainly no other families with that famous name in the area. I made an appointment to stop in at the cemetery office to look at the burial register. The handwritten ledger was fragile, but readable. I carefully scanned the long list of "S" internments and was absolutely thunderstruck to find not only the name of Frederic Scott Seagrave himself but that of his wife Adelaide, too. Mr Seagrave had been entombed in February 1923, and his wife nine years later.

The next chapter in this fascinating saga took place on Labour Day, 1984. I wanted to take a picture of my very own Seagrave fire engine in front of the last resting-place of this great company's founder. I had carefully positioned my 1925 Seagrave pumper in front of the mausoleum when a woman tending some nearby graves strolled over and politely asked why I was taking a picture of a fire engine in a cemetery.

I showed her the oval Seagrave nameplate on the radiator of my truck then pointed to the name over the door of the mausoleum. "Is that... him?" she asked. I nodded and proceeded to tell her how Mr. Seagrave had started out making ladders for Michigan's apple orchards over a century earlier, and had gone on to establish one of the largest and best-known fire engine companies in the world – a company still in business today, 119 years later.

Ironically, the Seagrave nameplate returned to Olde Walkerville in 1991, when the Windsor Fire Department's Station No. 2 at Walker Road and Richmond Street was assigned one of two new diesel-powered Seagrave pumpers. Seagrave Fire Apparatus, a direct descendant of the original Seagrave Co., relocated from Columbus to Clintonville, Wisconsin in 1964, had built engine 2.

Engine 2's big lime green Seagrave pumper was stationed on the same block of Walker Road, on the same side of the street where the former W.E. Seagrave Fire Apparatus Co. plant still stands – 96 years after it was built.

On the night of June 30, 1985, the old fire engine factory almost went up in flames when the former Gotfredson Corporation plant across the street was destroyed in one of the most spectacular fires in Windsor's history. It's unlikely that the firefighters who kept the raging flames to the east side of the street knew the heritage of the structure across the street they were protecting!

Frederick S. Seagrave, and W. E. Seagrave, established the W. E. Seagrave Fire Apparatus Company in Walkerville in 1900 to build and sell Seagrave fire apparatus in Canada. The firm featured a complete range of horse-drawn fire apparatus, including chemical hose combinations, hose wagons, hook and ladder trucks and spring raised three-horse hitch aerial ladder trucks. Unfortunately, intense competition from LaFrance Fire Engine Co. Ltd., a subsidiary of American-LaFrance, which built a plant in Toronto in 1914, put W. E. Seagrave out of business by 1919.

Top to Bottom: Seagrave firetruck; founder Frederic Seagrave, far right, and son W.E. Seagrave (wearing light jacket & white boater) deliver Ottawa's first motorized fire truck in 1911; a pyramid of men aboard a 1914 pumper in downtown Winnipeg; Seagrave firetruck; Walkerville's fleet of motorized fire trucks lined up on Walker Road, 1913. *All photos courtesy Walt McCall*

Dump Truck owned by artist Scott Gregory

The Lincoln Toy Factory

by Andrew Lochead, Issue #9, June/July 2000

Collecting has been documented as far back in history as ancient Egypt. Whether fine art, beanie babies or sports cards, collecting has moved from being a small time personal obsession to a billion dollar industry – thanks to the internet.

One passion with the potential to tell a great deal about ourselves is collecting toys. It is within the annals of toy collecting history that we find the story of Walkerville's own, "Lincoln Specialties," or as it was more commonly known, "Lincoln Toys." This local company's products, almost fifty years after its demise, are sought after by toy enthusiasts all over the world. In fact, one collector notes the average "Lincoln" toy can fetch $100 to $600, depending on its condition.

Founded by father and son team, Haven and Fredrick Kimmerly (who at the time resided at 2448 Gladstone and 1009 Windermere respectively), the business made its first appearance in the Windsor city directory in 1946.

In 1941, the Kimmerlys and close family friends, the Lynns, amicably split their small metal stamping business, LK Metals, into two companies. The Kimmerlys opened "Kay Manufacturing" at Lincoln and Erie, while the Lynns carried on as LK Metals. The two companies remained connected, with Kay Manufacturing making components for some of LK Metal's products, such as gas heaters, in addition to their own product line which consisted (in part) of fireplace covers and stove pipes.

There is a saying that when paraphrased, states that: "There is nothing better for the economy than a good war." With the Second World War raging in Europe, the Canadian economy was slowly rising out of the last grips of the Great Depression.

Business was good for Kay Manufacturing; they received an official government contract to build ammunition boxes and fenders for the Canadian Army. The Kimmerlys made a decision to change the business name to "Windsor Steel;" they also diversified the range of their manufactured products. These new products included bicycle carriers and kickstands as well as the now ultra-collectible steel "Coca-Cola" licensed coolers and automobile visors.

By 1945, the wartime economy had slowed down and Windsor Steel required new products to replace the loss of the government contract. Although their flourishing automobile products division, which included gas tanks and mufflers was keeping the business steady, the Kimmerlys required something that would put the business "over the top."

That same year it was suggested that the company focus its direction on the large post-war toy market. So, it came to be that Haven and Fredrick Kimmerly set up "Lincoln Specialties" in 1946 in order to market their new "Windsor Steel"– made commodity. The first offices and showroom were located in the original Kay Manufacturing building back at Lincoln and Erie and John Milner was hired as company president.

Ironically, the very first "Lincoln" toy was actually a small wooden Jeep. This mini Jeep was comprised of two halves connected by a single joint. The joint allowed the toy to make smoother turns and handle more wear and tear on the uneven surfaces on which so many children like to play. This was also the only wooden toy ever marketed by Lincoln Specialties.

Some of the first metal toys made by Windsor Steel for Lincoln were the "817 dump truck" and the "No.54 Repeater Canon" which actually fired small wooden cannon balls with the aid of a spring loaded crank mechanism. The "Repeater" was also the first "Lincoln" to appear in a major store catalogue, making its debut in the 1946-47 Eaton's Fall & Winter catalogue.

After such a short time in operation, Lincoln Specialties, which also handled the marketing of Windsor Steel's other products, began to focus energy on their ever-widening selection of toys.

By 1953 the selection had grown to over 24 different styles of trucks in three different sizes and two different cab designs. This was largely possible due to their close relationship with Harry Ellwood, a Windsor toy maker who had relocated to Tilbury. Mr. Ellwood's company, "Ellwood Toys" manufactured all "cab over" style trucks marketed by Lincoln Specialties and would eventually purchase the bulk of Lincoln's dies upon their closure.

Also included in Lincoln's toy roster were cranes, power shovels, several variations of the Massey-Harris 44 tractor and other various farm implements such as combine harvesters. One of Lincoln's most interesting products however, was a toy airplane. Considered a rarity in its time and even more so today, the plane featured the colours and logos of the now defunct Trans-Canada Airways.

With so many toys being manufactured, the facilities at 1701 Shepherd could not adequately meet the storage needs of Windsor Steel. It was about this time that the company designed its own warehouse and showroom at 2892 Walker Road. Built by Mark Glos, father of Windsor architect Randy Glos, the building served as the home of Windsor Steel until the company's eventual closure.

Lincoln Specialties outgrew their Erie Street location within three years and relocated to 1200 London (now University) Street, in the old SW&A streetcar barns. Both companies also maintained other warehouses across the city of Windsor.

Locations changed frequently for the Kimmerly families as well, with Haven, his wife Minerva and their younger children living at 1175 Kildare and 1192 Devonshire, and Fredrick, his wife Muriel and their children residing at two locations on Willistead Crescent and at one point in Cottam.

Unfortunately, despite their success, both companies fell victim to the unstoppable juggernaut of time. Increased foreign competition and unsuccessful bids by Windsor Steel to win back automotive contracts abandoned during the toy boom forced Lincoln Specialties out of business. It made its final appearance in the Windsor City Directory in 1958.

Windsor Steel continued to operate in a limited capacity but closed only a year later, dissolving officially in 1959.

After Windsor Steel's closure, Haven's son, Edward T. Kimmerly maintained the family's presence at Lincoln and Erie by continuing the "Lincoln Casket Company," a business founded by Fredrick prior to the demise of Windsor Steel. Eventually the business relocated to Sydney Street before being sold to a larger casket company.

Meanwhile, Haven's other child William (Bill) Kimmerly, with help from his father, began Dayton Manufacturing on Crawford Avenue. Dayton also relocated to Sydney Street, less than a block away from where brother Edward's operations were conducted. They have remained there ever since and continue to manufacture custom bathroom vanities for major retailers like Sears & Roebuck Canada.

Fredrick A. Kimmerly moved his family to the United States and eventually returned to Canada where he launched Standard Printing, located on University Avenue West where Ho & Wong's Chinese restaurant now stands. The family-run business eventually returned to Walkerville, moving into the former Studebaker offices at 530 Walker Road, and relocating to 3500 Ontario in 1993 where they continue to serve the public's printing needs, under the stewardship of Fredrick's eldest son Paul, his wife Lori and their two children.

Through their successes and failures, the popularity of the Kimmerley's metal toys remains highly appreciated by collectors and offers us a whimsical glimpse back in time.

You may leave for the attic now... happy hunting!

Connecting the Dots

I have a connection regarding two photos that appeared in the April 2002 edition of The TIMES. On page 21 (April 2002 Photo Issue), there is a picture captioned "Ford Motor Company's provisional store enables employees to buy food and clothing at low prices." Most people called the store The Ford Commissary. In the first year or two or operation, it was meant for Ford employees, but eventually opened to the public.

After losing money for about four years, the Ford store ceased operations. At this time, Mrs. W.R. Campbell, wife of Ford of Canada president Walter Campbell, suggested to Walker Jenkins that he open a meat market in Walkerville. Shortly thereafter, Walker Jenkins and Chester Bear, formed a partnership and launched Jenkins and Bear Meat Market in the Imperial Building on Wyandotte Street in Olde Walkerville, about 1930 or '31.

My uncle Bill Blackmore was another butcher who also worked for Ford. He was hired by J & B so it was through this connection that I became the delivery boy while attending WW Tech. I worked from 4 pm to 6 pm, Monday to Friday and 8 am to 6 pm Saturdays.

As an aside, I worked as a delivery boy for Bill James' Meat Market in Olde Walkerville prior to working for J & B.
Frank Pengelly, Oshawa, Issue #38, October 2003

Above: Ford Motor Company's provisional store enabled employees buy food and clothing at low prices. Photo courtesy Ford Motor Company archives

Left: The Imperial Building, 1900 block, Wyandotte Street E., c. 1950. l-r, Stephen's Bicycle Shop, GoodYear Tires, A.H. Black Jewellers, Walkerville Paint and Wallpaper, J & B Market, Walker Insurance Co. Not shown on far left, Coles Models.
Photo courtesy James D. O'Neill

158 • birth of the auto

For Many Upstarts, the Road was Short, Rough... and Unforgiving

by Herb Colling and Carl Morgan, condensed from "Pioneering The Auto Age"

Packard – A Car For the World's Elite

James Ward Packard bought an early model automobile at the turn of the 20th century, and was so angry with its performance that he wrote a letter to the manufacturer: "I got one of your damn cars. It's no good! I could make a better one myself..." Putting his money where his mouth was, he produced one of the finest automobiles of its day.

Packard launched his business in the U.S. at the turn of the century, producing a powerful, heavy, well-built machine with distinctive hub caps and radiator. Body changes were infrequent and advertising boasted that the Packard remained new for 10 years. By 1914, the U.S. company was selling to the world's elite: the Czar of Russia, a Maharaja in India and a Viscount in New Zealand.

Production of Packards in Windsor began in 1931 at Chatham and Church Streets. While sales dropped in the U.S., Canadian production climbed to 500 cars a year; the company could not keep up with demand, even during the Depression. The first Windsor-made Packard rolled off the line draped with a Union Jack. Guests included Windsor mayor David Croll, Packard President Alvan Macauley, and Hugh Greybiel, publisher of The Windsor Star. A reception was held at the Prince Edward Hotel where Macauley installed the hubcaps to complete the car.

The vagaries of the auto industry caught up with Packard by 1935. Packard was a conservative car builder, and once he established a model, it remained unchanged for years. As competition increased, sales faltered.

He tried winning back market share with a new V-8 engine and banked heavily on his reputation as a quality car builder. Twelve thousand orders poured in for the new car before it was built, but the final product fell short of public expectations and sales immediately dwindled.

In Canada, production peaked in 1937 with 2,500 cars. In 1941, Packard turned his Windsor plant over to the war effort, but by 1944, construction began on a new building on Huron Church Road between College and Millen (currently the University of Windsor's LeBel Building).

Packard planned to sell lower priced cars to boost sales. His new building was designed as an assembly plant but was used as a parts warehouse for the 200 Canadian Packard dealers. Conditions deteriorated and by 1958, Packard shut down.

Studebaker and the EMF

Studebaker, with its distinctive, futuristic, post-war styling was one of the more romantic names in the auto industry. Ahead of its time, it was popular with car buffs for its "get-up-and-go."

Its Windsor roots trace back to 1908-09 when an American firm called the E-M-F Company bought the Globe Furniture Factory on Montreuil Road to produce the E-M-F 30 and Flanders 20; it was one of the busiest car plants in Windsor.

Using Canadian capital, E-M-F built its first cars in 1910. The humble Flanders was well-received, featuring right hand drive, an open front and big brass headlights, fueled by acetylene tanks. A solid, peppy performer, it could reach speeds of 45 miles an hour.

The E-M-F, on the other hand, was dodged by trouble and generally disliked. Two years after the launch, a dispute erupted between E-M-F and Studebaker, the company's American distributor. The dispute was settled and led to takeover of E-M-F by Studebaker – which found itself thrust into the Canadian manufacturing scene.

The Studebaker Corporation of Canada's offices were at 530 Walker Road. Flanders became vice-president and continued producing E-M-F's until 1912, when they were renamed Studebaker 20 and 30. At one point, Studebaker was second only to Ford in employment and output in Windsor. In 1913, Studebaker introduced a successful line of five cars ranging from $900 to $1,800; more than 3,000 were built the first year.

Studebaker suffered its first major setback in 1927 when it gambled on a lower-priced Erskine, named after company president Albert A. Erskine. More trouble followed when Studebaker united with Pierce-Arrow. The company set up a distribution/sales office in Walkerville in 1928 and a small number were actually assembled. Trouble was, Pierce-Arrow had been in financial straits for 10 years, even though it was a car of distinction – the choice of kings and sultans. The most expensive model in the U.S. was sold to Persian Shah Riza Khan, who ordered a gold radiator and diamond studded convertible top – the price: a cool $25,000.

Above: 1929 Studebaker at Willistead Gates and The Canadian, probably the first commercial vehicle manufactured in Windsor.

When the Depression hit, Pierce-Arrow went begging for buyers. Instead of producing a smaller, cheaper car, the company stuck with an expensive 8 and 12-cylinder gas-guzzler; by 1933 the company was in receivership.

In 1937, after dropping price as low as $700 without buyer response, the company folded. In 1939, with the introduction of the low-priced Studebaker "Champion," there were talks of reopening the Canadian plant in Windsor but the war intervened. The company made a comeback in 1949, working out of a former munitions plant in Hamilton. It ceased operating in South Bend, Indiana, in 1963 and in Hamilton in March 1966.

Gotfredson Built A Name In Trucks

The name Gotfredson doesn't roll off the tongue with the easy familiarity of Ford or Chrysler, but the Walkerville company became one of the major truck manufacturers in North America.

Gotfredson built medium and heavy trucks with a reputation for a distinctive, highly-polished cast-aluminum radiator shell. They sold coast-to-coast, advertised as "the best truck in the world."

In 1923, Gotfredson-Joyce produced a truck called the "G and J." Two years later, the firm reorganized as Gotfredson Truck Corp., merging with the American Auto Trimming Company Ltd., a Walkerville parts supply company established in 1911 by Benjamin Gotfredson of Detroit.

During World War One, Gotfredson produced gun carriers and army trucks; later it manufactured buses, taxis, fire engine chassis and passenger car bodies for Studebaker. The company became a major supplier of parts and truck bodies for Ford, and a distributor of diesel engines. It employed more than 400 men and women at its peak.

In 1925, the Windsor police bought a Gotfredson truck for use as a patrol wagon. Gotfredson was popular in Canada, where production reached 2,000 units a year, well ahead of the U.S. Although the Canadian operation outlived its American counterpart, it ran into money problems and bankruptcy proceedings were started in 1929. Studebaker rented the buildings, hired the 110-man staff and took over production of Erskine and Studebaker bodies. The company continued building auto bodies and parts until the 1960s, long after the truck manufacturing ended. The final vestiges of Gotfredson in Windsor disappeared on Canada Day in 1985 when two large buildings on Walker Road at Niagara Street burned in a spectacular fire, one once occupied by Gotfredson.

The Hup Mobile

In 1911, the Hupp Motor Car Company was founded by Robert Hupp, a Detroit engineer. The firm manufactured the famous Hupmobile or "Little Red Car," a low-slung angular machine with high-perched headlamps. It sold for under $1,000 though the top doors and acetylene lamps were extra. It was such a popular little car that the company outgrew its space at the Medway Power Building and moved to new quarters at Giles and McDougall.

Hupmobile was one of the first North American cars to use a pressed-steel body. By 1914, some models even came with full electrical equipment at no extra charge. It was advertised a "Guaranteed for Life."

Hupmobile production ended in 1914 when the firm retreated to the U.S. It returned to Canada between 1933 and 1936, and then imported cars again until 1941.

Canadian Commercial Motor Car

In 1911, the Canadian Commercial Motor Car Company Limited, 509 Goyeau Street, was probably the first Canadian firm to manufacture a commercial vehicle. Included was the light delivery wagon called, "The Canadian." It had a screened-in body and ebony steering wheel – all for $1,600. The company motto had an uncharacteristically patriotic ring: "Deliver the Goods the Canadian way." Records are unclear about the company's lifespan, but it may have been in the business as late as 1933.

Publisher's Note: We've only scratched the surface in this article. Read the fascinating account of the more than 100-year history and struggles of the automotive industry in the Border Cities: "Pioneering the Auto Age," by Herb Colling with Carl Morgan, Travelife Publications, 1993.

All in the Family

Below are three generations of the Mollard Family, owners of "Producers Cold Storage" in Windsor. Each year, they purchased a new Studebaker from my father Ed Dela Haye's car lot (right) at the corner of University and Campbell. My father owned Dela Haye Motors for over 35 years, until they stopped making Studebaker cars. This photo was taken in 1947 by the renowned photographer Sid Lloyd. **Nancy (Dela Haye) Carter, Windsor**

An early Windsor tool and die plant. photo courtesy Windsor's Community Museum

A Salute to Windsor's Tool and Die Industry
In Good Company

From "Made in Windsor – The Anchor Lamina Way"
by Clare Winterbottom with Chris Edwards

The arrival of a 19th century technology altered the landscape of a sleepy backwater community located on the south bank of the Detroit River. In 1854 the Great Western Railroad had come to Windsor. This much-heralded event served to stimulate the growth of industry in the community. Soon, entrepreneurs provided services revolving around the main requirements of the district – the support of flourishing inland agriculture communities, the railroad, and shipping.

By the 1890s, small gasoline and steam engines were being built locally for marine use. There was also a thriving carriage and wagon industry catering to the requirements of the farmers of Essex County. It was but a short step to marry an engine to a wagon and in 1900, or shortly thereafter, William Bulmer did just that. He had no intention of entering the automobile business, but it was reported that he used his primitive motor vehicle for about a year.

Two men who did enter the automobile business were brothers John and Horace Dodge. They first made a name for themselves in bicycle production in their shop located at the top of "Ferry Hill" on the corner of Ouellette and Sandwich (Riverside). They sold their business to National Cycle and Automobile Co. (listed in the Windsor City Directory for 1900), but retained key positions in the company – at the same time producing parts for the automotive industry. The brothers envisioned a world of motor-powered vehicles and sold their Canadian operations and moved across the river to Beaubien Street in Detroit in 1901. With their savings of $7,500, the two founded their own company, Dodge Brothers.

In 1904, G.M. McGregor and his partner obtained a franchise for Canadian manufacturing rights from the owner of a new and struggling Detroit automobile manufacturer – Henry Ford – who cannily obtained a 51% interest in the new venture.

"There are men in Detroit like Henry Ford who say every farmer will soon be using an automobile. I don't see why we can't build autos right here (in Windsor)," McGregor said.

The first Canadian-made Ford was produced in August 1904. A better

Windsor's Kelsey Wheel Company. photo: David L. Newman Collection

best of the times • 161

word might actually be "assembled," as the heaviest piece of machinery in use at the Walkerville Wagon Works was a drill press. Ford assembled cars in Windsor until 1954, and still maintains a major industrial presence through its engine and casting plants. Ford of Canada was always export-oriented and Canada proved to be a convenient conduit for American companies to sell their cars to the British Empire; high tariffs discouraged direct sales from the United States. A Windsor-built Ford was shipped to Calcutta, India in October 1905; the first shipment to New Zealand took place one month later.

Numerous American and Canadian automobile makers followed Ford into Windsor and the surrounding area. Many of those names have since passed into the annals of time: the Chatham Motor Car Company (later Gray-Dort Motor Co.) founded in 1906, the Menard Auto Buggy Co. founded in 1908, the Everett-Metzger-Flanders Co. (EMF) founded in 1909, which became Studebaker Corporation of Canada in 1912. In 1911, the Hupp Motor Car Co. (maker of the Hupmobile) established a presence in Windsor.

In 1916, the Maxwell Motor Co. of Canada built a factory on Tecumseh Road. Maxwell merged with the Chalmers Motor Co. and became the nucleus for Chrysler Canada in 1925, currently the largest manufacturing operation in Windsor.

In the 1920s, jobs in the Canadian auto industry doubled to 16,000. Windsor – the heart of the Canadian auto industry – saw its population increase fivefold between 1904 and 1929. Canadian auto output was 170,000 units in 1927 and 240,000 units in 1928.

The Parts Makers

With the assembly of automobiles taking place in Canada, and more especially in Windsor, it is no surprise that parts manufacturers either established operations or set up Canadian subsidiaries. Canadian Auto Top Co. (established 1910 by Edmond G. Odette) was an early parts supplier. In the same year, Dominion Forge Co. began the production of axles, fenders, gas tanks and running boards, initially for Ford, but then for other manufacturers.

A year later, American Auto Trimming Co. Ltd. was established to manufacture trim and tops. In 1912, the Fisher Body Corporation of Canada launched a plant in Windsor to manufacture bodies for Ford and, from 1920, for General Motors. The Kelsey Wheel Co. commenced manufacturing in 1913; Champion Spark Plug, another early local automotive parts pioneer, dates from 1919.

It was only a matter of time before the skills necessary to support a tooling industry began to develop, assisted in large measure by the need for high-tolerance manufacturing of war material in 1914-1918.

In 1920, P.J. McConnell, George J. Schengle and William E. Tregenza, established Canadian Engineering & Tool Company and incorporated two years later. Schengle was head of the Ford tool department for six years while Tregenza, formerly tool department head at Packard, spent the war in charge of Canadian Aero Planes' tool department in Toronto. Canadian Engineering remains one of the larger firms manufacturing tooling in Windsor; Don Tregenza, grandson of William Tregenza, manages the third-generation company.

A "List of Industries Operating at the Border Cities" compiled in November 1922, includes five other tooling companies: Connor Machine Co. Ltd., Parent Machine Co., Windsor Machine and Tool Works, J. Bertram & Sons Co. Ltd., and Wilson Bros.

In 1923, realizing the business opportunities arising from the growing automotive industry in the area, Ernie Lanie and Lorne Wilkie founded Windsor Machine, incorporated in 1927 under the name Windsor Tool & Die Ltd, and once located at Langlois and Wyandotte Streets. Among other pioneering tool and die manufacturers were Windsor Match Plate & Tool Ltd., Border Tool & Die, and Nickleson Machine and Tool.

Above: Factory floor, Windsor Tool & Die c.1920s
photo courtesy Windsor Tool & Die

Below: The 1953 Plymouth and Dodge Metal Shop.
Photos: Hugh Durnford and Glenn Baechler, Cars of Canada, McClelland and Stewart Ltd., 1973

Influence of World War II

The Windsor-Detroit manufacturing sector became the "Arsenal of Democracy" during World War II, and the tool and die industry expanded rapidly.

At the end of the war in 1945, a new industry emerged employing the design and manufacture of plastic moulds. Windsor Tool & Die, under the leadership of Walter Doster, was an early entrant in plastic mould making, specializing, in those days, in toy moulds. In September 1944, Doster lost an enterprising young employee, the flamboyant and ambitious Peter Hedgewick, who launched his own startup, which eventually became International Tools Ltd. – later ITL Industries Ltd. – at one time the largest mould shop in the world.

The 1951 Directory of Manufacturing Industries for the Windsor region lists 19 businesses involved in TDM, most of which were in the categories of 1-25 or 25-100 employees.

Over the years, both tool and die and mouldmaking had become increasingly complex. New markets emerged, especially in the automotive sector. In 2003, there were approximately 500 plants in the Windsor region, with production related directly or indirectly to the automotive industry, employing more than 48,000 workers.

Almost half of all Canadian mouldmaking is located in Windsor. The industry, like others that rely on highly skilled employees, is chronically short of personnel. St. Clair College specializes in the training of tool and mould makers and has partnered with industry to develop one of the most advanced training – facilities in the world.

Opportunities Ahead

The tooling business has generally been known as a "silent" industry that receives little flourish and less ceremony. But for all that, it is a vital component of the Canadian economy. Largely established by skilled immigrant workers, the industry heavily relies on local secondary educational institutions and St. Clair Community College to provide a pool of trained workers who are high wage earners in largely non-union shops. Many Windsor tool and die and manufacturing firms remain privately owned entities run by self-made entrepreneurs with little formal education yet who possess highly technical backgrounds.

It is generally and justifiably believed that in the next few decades, the Canadian industry will depend on brains and skill and that mainly unskilled operations will inevitably move to less developed countries. The skills of the tooling industry's employees and the capital investments of its companies will provide the industry with the means to an important and successful future.

The tooling sector has a great importance within the automotive industry and consequently the metalworking and plastic moulding industries and the industries that depend upon them. Yet the tooling sector is rarely covered in writing on the automotive parts industry, in spite of the fact that it provides the skilled input that assists and accommodates changes in technology and permits ever-increasing improvement in productivity for its customers. The tooling sector is important in the U.S. and Canada, and particularly in the Windsor region, which is known for its tooling cluster.

The area's tool and die makers, ship in excess of $100 million a year and employ over 1,500 workers. Die set manufacturers and other

Top:
Champion Spark Plug Company staff, circa 1920
Photo courtesy Champion Spark Plug Company of Canada

Centre:
One of Windsor Tool's oldest customers is Zalev Brothers who own a scrap yard on Grand Marais. Windsor Tool has repaired its cranes for many years; photo of Zalev Brothers delivery truck, circa 1917.
Photo courtesy Zalev Brothers L:imited

suppliers to the industry contribute sales of another $150 million a year in the Windsor area. The 2005 Manufacturers Directory for Windsor and Essex County listed 118 tool and die makers and 103 mould makers.

Despite the technical and manufacturing complexity of what they make, die and mould shops are typically quite small. Although there are a few plants with more than 100 employees, the Windsor tooling sector consists mainly of small firms with fewer than 30 employees.

The Windsor tooling cluster owes its development to a combination of a favourable location, the role of ITL in the early formation of the cluster, and the way in which firm spin-offs and the transfer of local tacit knowledge between plants has fostered incremental learning and innovation. The presence of good basic technical education through the secondary schools and the local community college has been important. Tacit knowledge development on the shop floor, however, appears to have been crucial to the largely incremental system of innovation in the cluster.

The automotive machinery industry in Windsor was hit hard by competition from Germany and Italy in the 1990s. Today, Windsor mould makers are concerned with increasing competition from Chinese firms. New supply chain management practices are having an adverse impact on the tooling sector though price squeezing and the appropriation of intellectual property. With increasing frequency, Windsor mould makers are being called on to provide mould design and engineering development work, but seeing the actual production of the mould outsourced to low-cost producers in countries such as China. A critical question is how sustainable the current situation is for continued innovation within the cluster.

In 2004, the federal government and Ontario committed a combined billion dollars to lure new auto industry investment in Canada. That was enough to persuade Ford Canada to commit $1 billion (including $200 million in government money) to expand its plant in Oakville, Ontario.

On March 2, 2005, GM Canada announced the largest-ever investment in the auto industry in Canada – $2.5 billion (including $435 million in government money).

In 2005, the Canadian auto industry has momentum that has not been seen in the past decade. Ontario surpassed Michigan in auto production for the first time in 2004.

Notes: In 1991, David Fry was commissioned to research and write a history of the tool and die industry for inclusion in the 1991 Anchor Lamina Inc. annual report. Portions of this text were excerpted in this piece, with new materials researched and written by Chris Edwards and Renka Gessing.

In a foreword to the 1991 Anchor Lamina Inc. Annual Report, David Fry wrote: "Anchor Lamina asked me to write a brief but snappy article designed to be a tribute to the Tooling Industry of Anchor's hometown, Windsor. The Windsor Centennial (1991) is an event that deserves recognition. Windsor is, after all, the mother of the Canadian automotive industry, and by inference, those industries that contribute to its success.

I would like to thank those who helped in this project: old-timers, Bus Lossing, Clyde Wheatley and Bill Ryan. Also many thanks to Alan Douglas, former curator of the Hiram Walker Museum for providing much interesting background on the history of Windsor, and to the ladies of the Windsor Public Library who put up with a lot of rummaging through their newspaper files, blue cards and books. And thank you to Anchor for asking me to undertake the project."
David Fry, Toronto, November 1991

15 Minutes of Fame
The Ford Family of Riverside

by Anne Rochon Ford, Issue #14, March 2001

Depending on your age and where you were in 1965, you might remember an ad that appeared in major newspapers across Canada for nearly a year with the catchy headline: "Why Ford swears by Volkswagen."

The ad went on to win a gold medal prize from the Art Director's Club of Toronto and a couple of years ago, it appeared as part of an exhibition of award-winning ads from the past 50 years at the Royal Ontario Museum. It's now part of the ROM's permanent collection.

This famous ad was about my family.

At the time we lived in Windsor (then Riverside) on Riverside Drive. A clever copywriter with the Ronalds-Reynolds advertising agency had learned from my father, John Ford, who worked in photography, that he had nine kids and a Volkswagen bus. From this, he came up with the catchy slogan, and thus the ad was born.

To say I remember the day we were photographed like it was yesterday would be, well, stretching the truth. But, I do remember the bus well. I can remember the feeling of the wind in my hair as several of us hung out of the sunroof, waving to friends, catching flies in our teeth, my mother at the wheel, pretending she didn't know the shenanigans we were up to. The VW bus had come to symbolize our family in that Windsor neighbourhood where we lived. When people saw the bus coming down the road, they knew: "Yup, there's the Fords."

That's me, eleven years old, second from the left with the big cheesy grin.

When my dad arrived home with news that we had been chosen to be in the advertisement, I was thrilled at the prospect that I might get some new clothes for the occasion which, of course I did, after a thrilling trip to the new Devonshire Mall with my sister, Mary.

That's Mary to my left, four years older, and upstaging me by not only wearing an outfit she had personally made but by making the tunics worn by our two younger sisters, Kitty and Liz. And, in the centre of the photo is my older brother, John, who probably spent forever up in his room before the shoot, making sure the crease on the pants was just so.

My three middle brothers – Bill, Pat and Mike – would have been completely oblivious to the fashion dictates of the day. I remember that Matt, the babe in my mother's arms, cried a lot that day, as only a few weeks before he had been diagnosed with a medical condition that left him in a great deal of pain.

Above: The Ford family of Riverside (now part of Windsor, Ontario) appeared in a national ad for Volkswagen in 1965. Anne Rochon Ford is second from left.

In front is our neighbour's dog, Pesky, who, seeing us all lined up so dutifully, voluntarily joined us in the picture. In the background is the wonderful house that my parents purchased from my grandparents as a cottage and later renovated into a home large enough to accommodate our crowd. The location where the photograph was taken is now called Stop 26 Beach.

Shortly after this picture was taken, our family moved to Toronto in the middle of the school year. Our move coincided with the release of the ad in newspapers across Canada. While we were all thrilled at home to be seeing ourselves in print, the ad had mixed consequences at our various schools.

I'm sure my face turned a bright and very hot red when the ad was passed around my classroom with all kinds of nasty graffiti having been added to it while my fellow classmates snuck a peek at the new girl who'd just arrived from Windsor.

On the other hand, my brother John acquired a certain notoriety as the new boy in school whose whole family was on a full page in the Toronto Star!

After visiting the exhibition when it was on at the ROM, I was anxious to talk to my parents about it. At that time my father told me of another consequence of our celebrity that I had never known. When Ford of Canada, another client of my father's employer, learned of the ad, they withdrew their business from the agency, even though my dad had been reassured that Ford had okayed the idea of the play on names.

Motivated by the urge to see his family in print, the loss of this account was, for my father, a harsh slap in the face.

That evening, after hearing my father's story, I looked with fresh eyes at that photo as I passed it in the hallway outside my son's bedroom. It saddened me to think that while I know he was infinitely proud of all of us, my dad had paid a price professionally, and had kept that to himself.

I took in this new information through the lens of a parent, as someone also trying to make it professionally, though ten years older than my father was at the time that picture was taken.

My father never did see the exhibition at the ROM. I can't say I blame him. But I'm heartened and relieved by his parting words after we spoke that evening:

"It's still a damned good ad."

Pillon Family Nearly Auto Pioneers

My dad's family originally settled in the Amherstburg area around 1790 or 1800, and used a lot of the old French names, as that area was primarily French in those days. My dad was given the name "Theophile Albemee Pillon" although he was known in Walkerville only as Phil or T.A., for obvious reasons.

His father and grandfather were blacksmiths and had a shop on the Pike Road not too far from what is now Walker Road. At one time, dad's father and uncle operated a wagon works in conjunction with the blacksmith shop, making carriages for the local gentry.

Who knows? We might have been early automotive pioneers if the shop hadn't closed before 1900. There are pictures in the Amherstburg historical museum of the Pillon Carriage Works.

In my dad's Walkerville Fire Department days, when we lived on Monmouth Road, the alarm system was set up so that it would ring in our house; Dad would pull on his boots and gear and run to either Wyandotte or Walker Road to jump onto the rig as it passed by. He explained to me that the horse harnesses were suspended above the stalls and were dropped on to the horses to save time. He was very proud of his experience with the department and during the war years in Walkerville, when we had air raid drills and blackouts and he acted as block warden in charge of "incendiary fire action."

Those were strange days!

Incidentally, my mother, who was a Drouillard, was a descendent of an early French Canadian settler family who established the first grain milling shop in the River Canard/LaSalle area. But that is another story.

Ray Pillon, Mississauga

Look Twice! *Ernie St-Louis poses with his 1935 Ford in front of a mural of himself on Drouillard Road near Riverside Drive in Ford City. According to a plaque at the site, "Ernie has dedicated himself to reviving the neighbourhood. He helped promote the East Windsor Citizens' Committee...to aid area residents and to enhance the life in the neighbourhood." Ernie's Ford was built in Windsor; he holds a trophy awarded to this local classic.*

Lincoln Toy Story

Thank you so much for the article on the Lincoln Toy factory (Summer 2000). My grandfather Tom was Haven Kimmerly's brother and I will never forget either of them. I started out my play time with one of the toys from Uncle Have's factory in the 1960s. I never did get the whole story on the venture and am proud to include this in with my Kimmerly family information.

Randall Kimmerle Wonsch, Windsor

Lee Sunshine poses for a Muntz sportscar ad, around 1950. The Muntz came equipped with a telephone and a built in bar! photo courtesy Larry Burchell

The Muntz Sports Car

Lee Sunshine, a well-known local entrepreneur who passed away in 2003, once owned Brownie's Marina in St. Clair Shores and the Dock Restaurant in Leamington. He was also a sales representative for the Muntz Sports Car Company in the early 1950s. Lee poses with a Muntz, above, and this image appeared in advertisements for the fledgling car company.

Earl "Madman" Muntz made a fortune selling Kaiser-Frazer automobiles in LA, and earned his moniker with flamboyant advertising and wild deals. His motto was "I buy 'em retail and sell 'em wholesale. It's more fun that way!"

Muntz acquired a second fortune by being one of the first producers of affordable television sets after the war. In 1948, Muntz had a falling out with Kaiser-Fraser and developed his own car, a 4-seat sportster he dubbed "The Muntz," offered with a choice of Lincoln or Cadillac engine. The Muntz also came equipped with a telephone and a liquor bar built into the huge rear armrests; one of the armrests was actually an ice box! Muntz is also credited with being one of the first auto maker to offer seat belts.

About 400 cars were built before production ended in 1953. Muntz later said that every car was sold at a $1,000 loss, which translates into a loss of about $400,000 during the car's four year stint. But Muntz wasn't washed up yet!

He thought music should be more portable, so anyone could listen to songs of their choice while cruising. The 4-track tape, developed in 1956, was deemed "unmarketable" and remained on the back burner until the early 1960s, when Muntz exploited its potential and began producing the Muntz Stereo-Pak, a 4-track tape system for cars.

Bill Lear, inventor of the Lear Jet, rode in a car outfitted with a Muntz stereo in 1963, and was so impressed with the sound that he signed a deal to distribute Muntz systems. He installed some in his Lear Jets, but, being a tinkerer, began taking the players apart and found ways of improving them. Thus was born the 8-track tape system.

All-in-all, Muntz made and lost three fortunes. He once said that he didn't mind losing a fortune, "cause it was so damn much fun making the next one!"

4
Crime
in the City

An ankle flask for the female tippler (1922) illustrates how the term "bootlegging" was coined. photo Library of Congress

Detroit –
Prohibition Trial Run

by Chris Edwards, Issue #32, March 2003

During the 1920s Prohibition not only failed to prevent the consumption of alcohol, the movement led to an extensive production of dangerous, unregulated and untaxed alcohol, the growth of organized crime, increased violence, and massive political corruption. Amazingly, some people still insist that Prohibition was a success! Prohibition clearly benefited some; notorious bootlegger Al Capone made $60,000,000 per year (untaxed!) while the average industrial worker earned less than $1,000 per annum. In the Border Cities – Windsor, Sandwich, Walkerville, Ford City and Riverside, one out of every four people were directly involved in bootlegging.

The temperance movement in the U.S. is documented as far back as 1733 when the colony of Georgia became the first to establish a prohibition decree; it was revoked in 1742.

In 1789 farmers of Litchfield, Connecticut began the first loose association of a temperance movement in the US by prohibiting its workers from drinking alcohol.

The first official association of the movement was founded in Boston in 1826 as the American Temperance Society. Emerging unions also dictated abstinence from alcohol to its members. The "Anti-Saloon League" was founded in 1892 in Oberlin, Ohio by Rev Howard Russell and is credited with leading the charge toward a dry nation. The theatrical, hatchet-wheeling antics of Carry Nation brought additional attention to the effort.

The temperance movement was much stronger in Michigan than in Ontario. In the 1800's, this influenced both Hiram Walker and J.P. Wiser's decisions to move their distilleries to Canada.

By 1911 forty of Michigan's eighty-three counties were dry. Then,

The saloon and the bartender were often the targets of Prohibitionists. This cartoon was one of a series published during the campaign for the Eighteenth Amendment.
photo courtesy The Library of Congress

on May 1, 1917 state legislation took effect and all Michigan went "dry" – saloon dry not liquor dry. But, due to a peculiar federal law, it was illegal to buy or make alcoholic beverages in any state where their sale was illegal.

Michigan, and Detroit specifically, became the national test site for prohibition. Thus began a steady stream of vehicles to the Ohio border; soon multitudes who discover a closer source for running rum (and other alcoholic beverages) – across the waters in the Border Cities.

The war effort had an effect on prohibition in the U.S. as well. On December 1st, 1918 under authority of the Food Control Bill, President Wilson prohibited the use of barley for brewing.

In 1919 the Damon Law, legislation that enabled Michigan to enforce its prohibition law, was ruled unconstitutional by a technicality. Soon after, however, the federal Volstead Act – prohibiting the manufacture, sale, and transport of all beer, wine and spirits – was put into effect on January 16th, 1920. This law gave authorities new support in their fight against the booze drinking public.

This legislation ushered in an era of corruption and chaos. By the late 1920s the federal government was expending 27% of its enforcement budget in Michigan. Interestingly, Michigan was the first state to ratify the 21st amendment, thus rescinding prohibition.

The temperance movement won the battle to legislate prohibition, but it would lose the war to enforce it.

Carry Nation

Hatchet wielding Carry Nation, who literally busted open rumshops in the U.S. at the turn of the last century, symbolized early prohibition movements. She was famous for leading groups of raiders, who wrecked saloons with rocks and hatchets.

Photo courtesy "The Rumrunners, a prohibition scrapbook" by C.H. (Marty) Gervais

FACT:

- Those who chose total abstinence, or "TA," were known as teetotalers.
- In the 1800s, "coffee breaks" for labourers were often "whisky breaks."

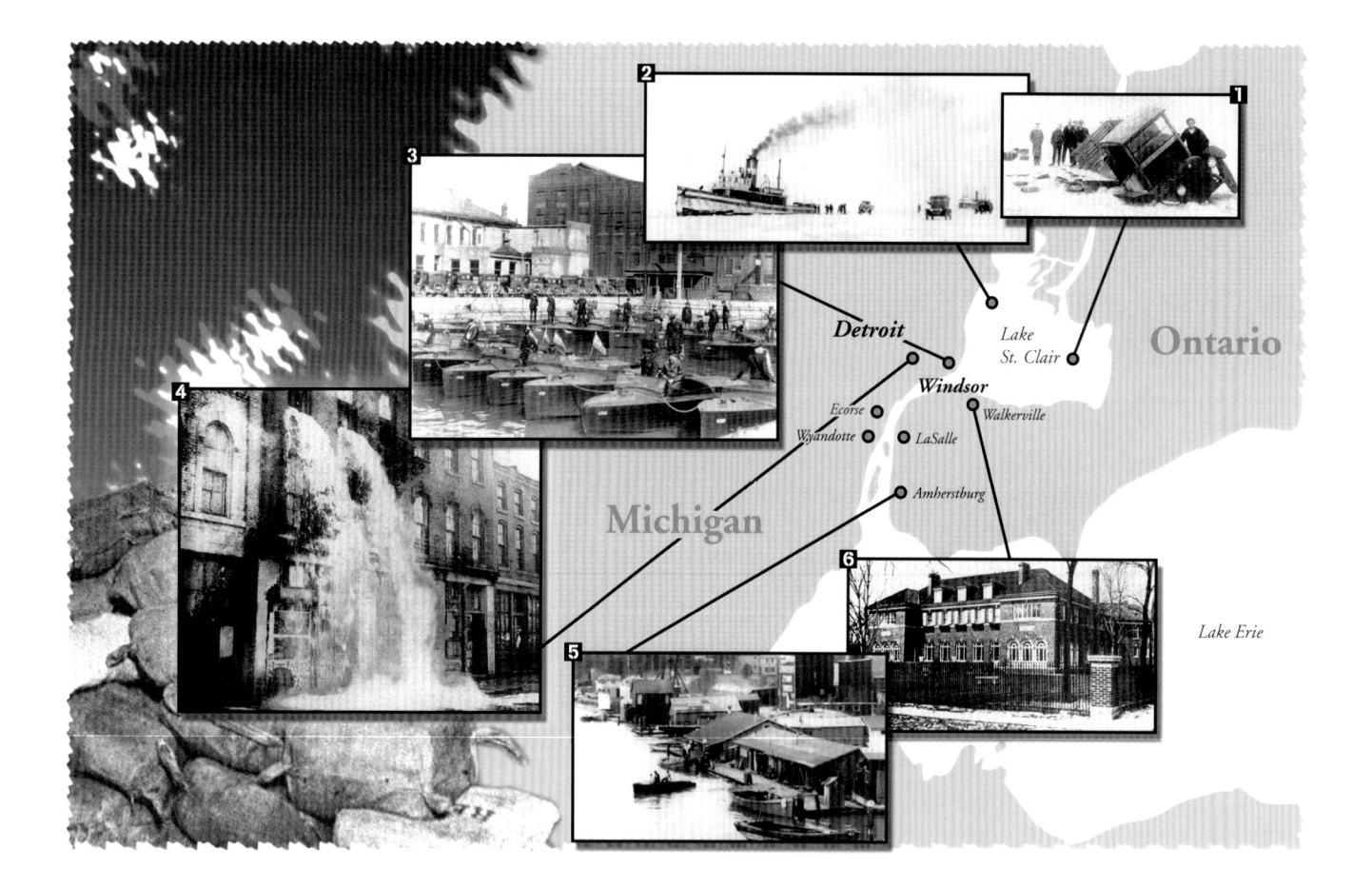

Windsor Went Wild in the Roaring Twenties

by Elaine Weeks, Issue #33, April 2003

From top right, counter-clockwise:
1. This smuggler's beer-laden truck was too heavy for the Lake St. Clair ice in 1933 (The Detroit News);
2. Jalopies were used to load contraband Canadian liquor from vessels in Lake St. Clair (Dossin Great Lakes Museum);
3. Detroit police at river patrol headquarters, foot of Riopelle St. 1932 (The Detroit News);
4. A waterfall of booze cascades out windows of a still on Gratiot Avenue (The Detroit News);
5. Rum runner leaving "export dock" at Amherstburg (Detroit News);
6. Rumrunner Jim Cooper's Walkerville mansion. Also pictured at bottom left are cases of liquor packed in jute bags; thrown overboard, smugglers could return to fish the bags out by hooking the jute's "ears." collage by Chuck Ress

Canada and the United States were witnessing the dawning of the modern age. In the U.S., the 1920 census reported for the first time a majority of Americans living in urban areas. An explosion of new inventions and technological breakthroughs would soon transform North America. Jazz, Wall Street speculation, women's suffrage, radio, Hollywood, air travel, telephones, a shorter work week and increased wages would converge to a revolution in communications, transportation and recreation.

On January 16th, 1920, the U.S. Eighteenth Amendment banning the sale, manufacture or transportation of "intoxicating liquor" took effect. An atmosphere of general lawlessness was bred by prohibition, bootleggers and gamblers. Gangsters fought to secure a share of the lucrative business and corrupt politicians turned a blind eye as mobsters like Al Capone terrorized entire cities.

Most Canadian provinces went dry at the same time the Eighteenth Amendment came into being. The Liquor Control Act in Ontario (LCA) forbid public or hotel drinking but did not prohibit the manufacture and export of liquor.

For border cities like Windsor, this loophole in the Act set the course for a wild decade not seen before or since. Opposite Windsor was big parched Detroit and beyond, the entire U.S. with its tongue hanging out. It didn't take long for enterprising businessmen in the Border Cities to set up "export docks" to supply thirsty Americans.

The docks were often simple frame sheds, which dotted the shoreline from Lake St. Clair to Lake Erie along the Detroit River. Every inlet, every bank that would support a dock was used. It was the perfect setup to make a quick buck – or an easy million.

Liquor moved to the docks by trucks, protected by a "B-13 customs form," a document for liquor in transit. Consigned to parties in Mexico, Cuba, Bermuda or St. Pierre and Miquelon, liquor was loaded in speedboats or rowboats, which theoretically, then headed for Cuba or Mexico.

In reality, these boats made a short trip across the Detroit River where the booze was then easily smuggled into the U.S. Boats cleared for Cuba in the morning, and returned in the afternoon, only to clear for St. Pierre in the afternoon; nobody asked any questions.

At the turn of the 20th century, Petit Cote, six miles downriver from Windsor was a quiet village where people spoke French and attended church on Sunday. On weekdays they cultivated their radish patches.

The radish-growers soon learned that if they rowed to Detroit with a bottle of whisky they could double their investment. Soon they were selling cases instead of bottles and travelled by launch instead of rowboat. They built big docks and imposing houses and even changed the name of one section of Petit Cote to LaSalle, which sounded swankier.

At one point, more liquor moved across a couple of miles of waterfront at LaSalle than across any other couple of miles on earth!

Local police were aware of these operations and it was their job to ensure that the liquor did not get "short-circuited" back to Windsor's blind-pigs once it left the docks.

In 1953, Windsor Police Chief Carl Farrow recounted his experiences as a Provincial Constable in the late 20s to the Windsor Daily Star. "One day you'd see a fellow rowing across the river from Detroit, in a small rowboat. He'd buy a couple of cases of liquor, and then row back. In a little while, he'd row back over to the Canadian side and buy three or four cases. Next day, when he came over, his boat would be powered with a shiny new outboard motor. He'd buy more liquor and make more trips. Then one day he'd show up in a big speedboat. He'd keep making his trips, then suddenly disappear. Months later, he'd come back with his rowboat and start all over again. This sort of thing was happening all the time."

Farrow also described how things were done in the winter. "In Amherstburg, they'd take an old sedan, put chains on it, cut the top off it and load it up with whisky. They crossed the ice of Lake Erie and carried planks to help them across cracks in the ice – it would be black with cars... heading for the States. The highways all along the riverfront were just black with trucks carting liquor to the export docks."

Constable Farrow recalls meeting two of the biggest Chicago gangsters: the notorious Al Capone and Bugs Moran. While they ran outside the law in their own country, they came to Windsor as two gentlemen in speedboats, conducting a simple business transaction.

Around Windsor, inns sprouted up overnight and were packed. This outraged Rev. Leslie Spracklin of Howard Avenue Mission whose impassioned speeches induced authorities to appoint him

Top: A lookout on a Canadian dock with binoculars to spot the signal from the American side. A rumrunner is loaded and ready to cross the Detroit River. Photo courtesy Larry Burchell

Left: In Elk Lake barrels of the best Canadian whisky were destroyed when a blind pig was discovered. Photo Archives of Ontario

best of the times • 171

DETROIT MUG SHOTS

The Purple Gang, as they came to be called, quickly rose to power and wealth. Law enforcement officials were powerless against the high-profile tactics of the gang.

Harry "Happy" Millman

Known as a hard drinking, fast living, hot tempered gunman, "Happy" Millman earned his nickname from his perpetual sneer. He survived several attempts on his life, and his car was blown to bits by dynamite. In eight years of crime, he was arrested 28 times for assault, armed robbery, kidnapping, extortion and murder, but never spent a single night in jail. He was assassinated in November of 1937 in a bold daytime attack in Boesky's Deli on Hazlewood and 12th Streets. His killers were reportedly the ruthless Murder Inc., of Brooklyn, NY, hit duo of Pep Strauss and Happy Maione.
Cause of death: Lead poisoning (bullets!)

Zigmund "Ziggy" Selbin

Ziggy Selbin was considered a loose canon in The Purple Gang. His specialty was extorting money from local merchants and hijacking blind pigs. Ziggy was known as a mean drunk. During one binge, he asked a patron for his ring. The man refused and Selbin beat him senseless. When Selbin couldn't remove the ring, he cut off the finger – ring and all. He was only 22 years old when he was shot in cold blood.
Cause of death: Executed by mobsters.

Abe "the Agent" Zussman

A killer for hire, Zussman acted as an agent for several prominent bootleggers during prohibition. He would follow victims into movie houses, take a seat directly behind them until a noisy scene and run his knife through the back of the chair. When the movie ended, house attendants would find a "sleeper" who never woke up. He was rumoured to have enjoyed his work so much that he would occasionally kill someone as a favour, free of charge.
Cause of death: Unknown

Photos & descriptions from "The Purple Gang – Organized Crime in Detroit 1910-1945" by Paul R. Kavieff

---

a "special temperance enforcement officer" with the right to carry a gun.

Spracklin swaggered around with armed bodyguards raiding inns. They once raided a private yacht without a warrant. The owner sued them for the illegal search and was awarded nominal damages by Mr. Justice Latchford of the Ontario Supreme Court, who commented that Spracklin and his pals, boarding the yacht, "displayed their pistols like veritable pirates."

In 1921, Spracklin and his men climbed through the windows of the Chappell House on the city's west end, and were surprised by Babe Trumble, the proprietor. After an argument, Spracklin shot Trumble dead. Charged with murder, he testified that Trumble had moved a hand as though reaching for a gun. He was acquitted on a plea of self-defense although it was clearly shown that Trumble was unarmed.

American crooks sought control of the export business and gang warfare broke out across the border, led locally by the Purple Gang. Things also turned nasty along the Windsor waterfront. Horace Wilde, a photographer for the Windsor Daily Star, was taking pictures at the Amherstburg export docks, when he was roughed up and his camera smashed. He was abducted, and shackled in chains and would have ended up at the bottom of the river, but was saved at the last moment. Constable Farrow arrested one of the men involved in the abduction (see story page 172).

The government soon cracked down on the exporters. There was debate over what "in transit" meant. Farrow participated in raiding parties and began seizing export docks and the liquor stored in them. On one occasion, he watched highjackers working from the river and boats, attempt to steal the stock at an export dock. The thieves tossed their guns into the river when police approached.

Top: A blind pig at 917 Farmer Street, Detroit, is padlocked by a Detroit Police official, June 1924. Photo The Detroit News
Bottom: Results of a state police raid on a Detroit speakeasy. Photo Michigan State Archives

The Roadhouses

compiled from "The Rumrunners – a prohibition scrapbook" by C. H. (Marty) Gervais, 1980, printed in Issue #33, April 2003

The roaring twenties in the Border Cities. An era when men wore floppy tweed caps, slicked their hair back like Valentino, sported spats, smoked Omar cigarettes or Player's Navy Cut and carried revolvers. An age of kiss curl ladies, chiffons, printed art crepes and hats with vagabond crowns.

An age when parents washed their children with Lifebuoy soap and their clothes with Rinso "the cold water washer," then sped to the roadhouses for a night out to take in a little Bye Bye Blackbird, the Charleston, jazz band; and, of course, to roll the dice and drink.

The shoreline of the Detroit River was like a diamond-studded bracelet, each glittering jewel a roadhouse. Americans nightly traversed the mile-wide river to moor their yachts until the first glimpses of dawn.

They came to the Canadian shoreline to feast upon hearty seafood and chicken dinners, soak up the lush, elaborate speakeasies and toss away easy-come, easy-go money in long, bustling, upstairs rooms crammed with gambling tables and flappers.

On those enchanted evenings, music filtered out from wide verandas and gingerbread barrooms of fabulous roadhouses. Everyone within was caught in amid a whirl of music and dancing, safe in the knowledge that although it was illegal to guzzle and gamble, trusty beady-eyes "spotters" stationed in second-storey windows or makeshift towers were ready to sound the alarm, warning of a police raid.

And if the law successfully got wind of the illicit gambling and liquor, it was only a matter of minutes before the booze was stashed behind false walls or into hideaway cupboards, along with gambling paraphernalia. All that remained on view were huge steaming platters of perch, frog legs and chicken, hastily carried out to bored customers accustomed to such interruptions.

Few of these roadhouses exist today. In the west of Windsor, the Chappell House dominated. Built within a few feet of Sandwich Street, it had a sign over the entrance, which read: "At All Hours." There were accompanying signs on the railings advertising frog legs, chicken and fish dinners. This roadhouse, with its prominent veranda, was actually a second incarnation of the Chappell House. It was built by two brothers – Henry and Harley Chappell. They opened their first in 1865 on the Canadian Steel Corporation property in nearby Ojibway. They eventually sold it and bought the Mineral Springs Hotel in Sandwich; in 1897 they opened up the second Chappell House. Later, it became The Lido Tavern, RumRunners Bar, [and finally The President's Club, which caught fire on May 27, 2006 and may have to be torn down.]

To the east were Abars Island View, Edgewater Thomas Inn, the Rendezvous, among others. Michael Vuicic, one-time general manager of the Rendezvous, said the food may have been good in the twenties…but the meals were really "a front" for gambling and drinking.

"You could eat all the perch you wanted downstairs for fifty cents; and upstairs there was gambling and booze."

When the old bar was removed and replaced years later, a simple but reliable, old buzzer system was torn out. "This place was wired together with four other roadhouses – the Edgewater Thomas Inn, Abars Island View, the Golden House and Tecumseh Tavern. One would buzz that the police were on the way and all the stuff would be stashed."

Vuicic said bottles were often flung from the second-storey windows into a moat fronting the building. It was also from this second floor that spotters were positioned to watch for police raids. Old photographs of the Rendezvous (opposite page) reveal just how deliberate the builders of the roadhouse were in the placement of the windows; they face east and west to watch the road. If a raiding party was spotted, the buzzer would sound to also warn the other hotels to stash the contraband.

The only surviving hotel wired to the Rendezvous is Abars Island View. The name is derived from the Hebert family, the original owners. Henri Hebert, a local fisherman, registered the name "Abars," in 1893 because he thought the French pronunciation of his name was more easier to pronounce. The hotel remained in the family for three generations, and the name was synonymous with fine cuisine.

Built to serve the stagecoach lines, the hitching rail at the front entrance remained long after automobiles made their appearance. At the turn of the century, the roadhouse became a leading nightspot on the waterfront and lured high society visitors from Detroit. Formal dress was the order of the day and local patrons were sometimes discouraged from dining there.

Above: Edgewater Thomas Inn: a high-class blind-pig in Riverside – secret passageways and hidden wine cellars. photo David L Newman Collection
Left: The Rendezvous' bar was wired into four other roadhouses to alert owners about police raids. Photo "The Rumrunners, a prohibition scrapbook" by C.H. (Marty) Gervais

Rendezvous Tavern – strategically designed look-out windows.

At the entrance sat the flamboyant Mrs. Hebert, dressed in jewels and furs, greeting her guests – the Fishers, the Dodges, the Fords, Jack Dempsey, Al Capone. Or members of the Detroit Tigers and New York Yankees who yachted to Abars as regulations forbade them to be seen in Detroit speakeasies. They directed their launches into Abars' docks at the mouth of the Detroit River, and its magnificent view of Detroit.

But of all the inns and roadhouses of the day, the Edgewater Thomas Inn was the most fashionable eating and drinking spot in the area. Owned

Bertha Thomas: eccentric roadhouse pioneer. David L. Newman Collection

by the eccentric Bertha Thomas, she was considered "a pioneer" in the restaurant and roadhouse business in the Detroit-Windsor area.

Formerly Bertha Haf of Detroit, she came to Windsor as a widow and purchased a small three-room Riverside eatery, cooked meals and waited on customers with a dream of owning a bigger place.

By the twenties, her Edgewater Thomas Inn, with gingerbread entrances, mahogany-paneled walls, plush interiors, fabulous "shore dinners," and hideaway gambling, became the favourite haunt for Detroiters.

As business increased and her popularity as a hostess grew, Bertha added more space. At the time of her death in 1955, Bertha operated one of the most widely known and patronized dining and partying establishments in the area.

But it was in the roaring twenties when Bertha earned her reputation. Thomas' inn was equipped with secret passageways and hidden wine cellars. During prohibition, it only took the "tip of a stick" and the bottles of liquor slid down a chute. Moments later soft drinks would magically appeared in their place. If Thomas' inn was the target of a police raid, musicians had duties too. Their task was to rush to customers' tables and dump glasses of liquor on to the well-padded carpets.

On one occasion when a band member missed the rug and booze splashed all over the dance floor, it was mopped up by the raiding party – with charges laid against Bertha. But the clever roadhouse owner wasn't to be outdone. She proved that the dance floor had been recently varnished and the varnish contained, curiously enough, alcohol.

Bertha's parking attendants also performed double duties. Louis Baillargeon was officially employed to park patron's cars, but in fact was used as a "spotter."

He was hired as a young boy by Bertha, who felt Louis lacked the proper homelife and advantages of other children. She paid for his schooling and kept him at work. Before directing him to park cars, she sequestered Louis in a strategic window location of the hotel where he was duty bound to do his homework and keep his eye on the movements of the police.

Bertha would often try to bribe police during a raid. One legendary tale recounts how she placed ten-dollar bills on the floor in a trail leading from the entrance of the hotel to the back door exit. The police simply followed the path strewn with money – and left the inn without charging her.

Bertha's became quite wealthy, and throughout the years following prohibition she dispensed it generously to the community. She often helped struggling friends by paying their mortgages. In later years, she threw fabulous Halloween parties for children in Riverside.

"If she didn't like you, you were in trouble," remembers a former Riverside police officer, who added, "but if she fancied you, it was OK."

The officer added although many believed Thomas' inn was a fashionable nightspot, it really was "a high class blind pig," and, when it caught fire in 1970, the legendary hidden rooms were revealed.

"She had all kinds of places to hide the booze, and there were buzzers all over the place, outside under the window sills or in the little shack they had for the parking boys. There were buzzers inside near the bar and in various other rooms…and there were false walls that would open up…she had it all figured out."

Bertha, he recalls too, was "a real show girl," One time, a Detroiter fell into the river near one of the docks behind the roadhouse. "Bertha jumped in after her, and of course, the police then had the task of saving them both."

No matter how many time the Edgewater Thomas Inn was raided by the police during the twenties, it was always back in business in less than ten minutes. "A fine was nothing to her," another policeman said. "It was just part of the operating expenses for Bertha."

Bad Boys: The Purple Gang pose for a police line-up. Photo Burton Collection

Mobsters, Mayhem & Murder

by Chris Edwards, Issue #34, May 2003

ONE OF THE GREAT IRONIES *of Prohibition is, instead of creating a perfect society by banning the consumption of liquor, the era produced one of the most violent, crime-ridden periods in American history. Prohibition was the perfect mix for crime bosses and syndicates that have become the stuff of legends, including Chicago's Al Capone and Detroit's Purple Gang.*

The Detroit-Windsor "Funnel"

Detroit was the first major U.S. city to ban the sale of alcohol in public establishments. By 1918, the city was completely dry, giving it a one year lead as prohibition became the law of the land in 1919. A year for gangsters and bootleggers to build a network for the transfer of booze from Windsor to Detroit. A veritable river of booze, which led to an huge increase in the consumption of alcohol. It was an era of ingenuity, crime and gangster rules.

Although individual provinces, including Ontario, outlawed the retail sale of liquor, the federal government approved and licensed distilleries and breweries to manufacture and distribute alcohol "for export only."

The Detroit River was a smugglers' paradise; twenty-eight miles long and less than a mile across in some areas, with thousands of coves and hiding places along its shores and islands. Along with Lake Erie, Lake St. Clair and the St. Clair River, these waterways carried an incredible 75% of all liquor supplied to the United States during prohibition.

It was a match made in heaven: Detroit, gateway to a huge market of thirsty Americans desperate for prohibited alcohol, and its sister city Windsor, legally capable of producing and exporting beer and whisky in large quantities.

The Colour Purple

In the midst of its first great automotive boom around 1910, Detroit witnessed an influx of immigrants seeking employment in the emerging auto capital of the world. It was a tough town, and the lower east side near the Eastern Market incubated poverty, crime, and violence in the early 20th century.

Ben Bronstein paid a heavy toll for hijacking liquor from The Purple Gang.
Photo: "The Purple Gang– Organized Crime in Detroit 1910-1945" by Paul R. Kavief

best of the times • 175

Photo: David L. Newman Collection

One group that flourished in the years just preceding World War I became notorious: The Purple Gang. Legend has it that the gang received its colourful moniker as a result of a conversation between two Hastings Street shopkeepers. Both men's shops had been terrorized, shoplifted and vandalized by Jewish kids in Eastern Market. One of the shopkeepers exclaimed, "These boys are not like other children of their age; they're tainted, off colour."

"Yes," replied the other shopkeeper. "They're rotten, purple – like the colour of bad meat – they're a purple gang."

Most of the young Purples were children of Russian Jewish immigrants, who worked hard to scrape out an honest living for themselves and their families in the Jewish quarter near Eastern market on Detroit's lower east side.

The young delinquents quickly graduated from petty street crime to armed robbery, hijacking, and extortion. The gang became notorious for its high profile management style and its savagery for dealing with enemies.

In the early years of prohibition, sugar houses supplied corn sugar for home brewers, who were allowed to brew a set amount of liquor for personal use. The sugar houses were a valuable resource for illegal stills and breweries, and one of the biggest, the Oakland Sugar House, was controlled by mobsters.

The men known as The Purple Gang were young, but became valuable assets to the older Sugar House Gang. And when the opportunity came to "import" liquor from Windsor, the Purple Gang was organized – and ready. They would soon dominate the rumrunning business and connect with Al Capone's Chicago syndicate.

By the early twenties, the Purples had developed an unsavoury reputation as hijackers, stealing liquor loads from older and more established gangs of rumrunners.

Hundreds of docks, boat slips, and boat canals lined the Detroit River from Toledo to Port Huron; they were a haven for rumrunners seeking shelter from patrol boats. Above, the steamer Columbia (later famous as the Bob-Lo boat). An innocent passenger was wounded on the deck of the Columbia by stray bullets from a border patrol boat shootout with rumrunners.

1918
1,534 licensed establishments and 800 estimated blind-pigs (unlicensed).

1923
Between 15,000 and 25,000 unlicensed blind-pigs in Detroit

Newspaper cartoonist reflected public opinion about the failure to enforce Prohibition.
Cartoon from Detroit Saturday Night, August 7th, 1926

176 • crime in the city

Sarcastically called "The Jewish Navy," The Purple Gang preferred hijacking to rumrunning – and their methods were often brutal. Anyone landing liquor along the Detroit waterfront had to be armed and prepared to fight to the death, as it was common practice for the Purples to steal a load of liquor and shoot whoever was with it.

The Bernstein brothers – Abe, Ray and Izzy; Harry Fleisher, Abe Axler and Phil Keywell – were a few of the names that became well-known to Detroiters during Prohibition, when most of America was forced by the 1919 Volstead Act to buy wine, beer and liquor from the underworld.

The Purple Gang sought control over the alley breweries and stills, and fought with other gangs for dominance of booze flowing into blind-pigs. Prostitution and gambling went hand in hand with the speakeasies, and was valued by the mobsters.

A Detroit Mob War soon broke out between Italian, Irish and Jewish bootleggers fighting over territory. The Purples fought a vicious turf war with the Licavoli Squad led by two psychotic brothers, Tommy and Pete Licavoli. When anyone was shot, newsboys would hawk a special edition The Detroit Journal, with extra pages devoted to all the gory details.

The Purple Gang rapidly rose to prominence after a machine gun massacre at the Milaflores Apartments in March of 1927. Three out-of-town gunmen suspected of killing a Purple Gang liquor distributor were butchered in the ambush. Fred "Killer" Burke, famous for his role in the St. Valentine's Day Massacre in Chicago in 1929, was hired by the Purples as the machine gunner.

To ensure the safe passage of liquor to other cities, The Purple Gang developed the fictitious Art Novelty Company. Smuggled liquor coming into Detroit was repackaged and shipped under false label to St. Louis, Chicago, and other cities; Chicago mobster Al Capone was one of their main customers. This arrangement was made after Capone was told by the Detroit underworld to keep his operation out of the city. Capone thought it more prudent to make the Purples his liquor agents rather than go to war with the gang.

Hollywood actor Robert Blake (centre) portrayed a gangster in the 1960 movie "The Purple Gang"
Photo from "The Rumrunners, a prohibition scrapbook" by C.H. (Marty) Gervais.

One of Capone's shipments was hijacked by Bugs Moran's Chicago gang, and led to the famous St. Valentine's Day Massacre in 1929.

By the late 1920s, The Purple Gang reigned supreme over the Detroit underworld, controlling the city's vice, gambling, liquor, and drug trade. They also ran the local wire service, providing horse racing information to local horse betting parlors and handbooks, including many in Windsor.

For several years the Purples enjoyed almost complete immunity from police interference. Witnesses to crimes were terrified to testify against any criminal identified as a Purple Gangster.

Reporters covered the war between the authorities and the bootleggers and between rival gangs, with a vengeance. Two new dailies joined the

FACTS:

▶ The Purple Gang became the first criminals in Detroit to use Thompson submachine "Tommy" guns. After mowing down three rivals, a newspaper reporter counted 110 bullet holes.

▶ During prohibition, illegal liquor was the 2nd highest industry after automobiles, grossing over $200,000,000 each year.

Right: In August of 1937, Purple Gang member Harry Millman's LaSalle Coupe was blown to smithereens (left). The blast killed a valet (who had been sent for the coupe) outside the 1040 Club in Detroit, a favourite Purple Gang watering hole.
Photo The Detroit News

best of the times • 177

The Horace Wild Story

Kidnapped by Rumrunners

condensed from The Rumrunners – A Prohibition Scrapbook, by C.H. (Marty) Gervais, printed in Issue #34, May 2003

Rumrunners were accustomed to being chased by United States patrol boats, being fired upon with "tommies," battling off hijackers – but were unaccustomed to having their work documented by news photographers who wanted to blaze their faces across the provincial dailies.

Angus Munro was right when he said newspaper photographers from that era were noted "for their sheer crust in getting the pictures" they wanted. This was particularly true in the case of Horace Wild, a Border Cities Star employee, who took his son, Noel, with him on assignment to photograph rumrunners in action.

We tried running but they grabbed dad and me and smashed his cameras. They didn't find the film dad had hidden but they smashed everything else.

Noel Wild recalls those events of June 29th, 1929 vividly:

"In 1929, the Border Cities Star decided to do a feature on this rumrunning business. A friend of the paper had a big speedboat on Riverside Drive. My dad, two reporters and I went to Amherstburg where we knew there was some running going on from the dock."

"It was a nice, calm day. We cruised back and forth along the river. There were cases of the stuff piled up on the docks and men loading the boats to take it across the border."

When they saw was us taking photographs they got really upset, so we turned around and tried to get away. They loaded about four carloads of fellows and others got into a couple of boats to give us chase, but their boats weren't as fast as ours.

But the rumrunners cars followed the road from Amherstburg. We decided to let them catch the boat, pulled over just about where Calverts (Seagram's) is today, put in at the point and jumped off. My dad and I grabbed our cameras and ducked into the woods.

But these boys weren't so dumb. They came along the road and caught sight of us. They wheeled around and came back to get us. We tried running but they grabbed dad and me and smashed his cameras. They didn't find the film dad had hidden but the smashed everything else.

They took my father back to Amherstburg. They left me because I was only sixteen years old. I informed the Provincials (police) when they came along the highway a little later.

Horace Wild's kidnapping by American rumrunners was front page news in 1929. Reprint from Larry Burchell

They took my father, bound him in chains and were going to throw him in the river. These kidnappers weren't from Amherstburg; they were from the States... there must have been 40 of these guys.

The Provincials managed to stop them from doing away with dad. They got there just in time apparently. Dad was a little upset. I know he was, because he told me afterwards. And of course the Star really blew up the story about him being kidnapped by rum runners.

In those days these were regular export docks. They were allowed to export out there... well they were supposed to be exporting the liquor to South America or to Europe or somewhere but not to Detroit. But we were photographing all these guys... you could see every one of them in our pictures. If those had appeared in the paper, every cop in the States would have been after them – that's why they came after us.

I managed to get a few pictures out, but they didn't use any of them. In those days we were using the Speed Graphics. They were awfully heavy to carry, but we were used to them, and besides, that's all we had in those days."

News, Free Press and Times in covering the mayhem. Competition was fierce and extras were printed almost continuously. Impartiality was the order of the day; many reporters drank in the same blind-pigs as the bootleggers; they knew the gangs as well – or better than the police.

The gangs meanwhile grew increasingly violent and brazen. Hijacking and kidnapping were rampant, as was murder of rivals. Innocent pleasure boaters or fisherman could hardly go on the river or lake for fear of stray bullets from Customs agents or gangs. The innocent and guilty were subjected to searches of their property, homes and persons.

By 1929, illegal liquor was the second biggest business in Detroit at $215 million a year, second only to auto manufacturing. Public opinion was squarely against the liquor ban – no mayor was elected in Detroit who expressed favourable views of prohibition.

People drank everywhere, from speakeasies to private clubs, to established restaurants, to storefronts – and of course they drank at home. Cocktail parties were all the rage, and workmen wanted beer with lunch or dinner.

One could buy a shot from a car in the parking lots of the Hamtramck auto plants or in one of the four hundred 'soft drink parlors' licensed there in 1923.

When the state police raided the Deutsches Haus at Mack and Maxwell, they arrested Detroit Mayor John Smith, Michigan Congressman Robert Clancy and Sheriff Edward Stein.

From St. Clair Shores' Blossom Heath on Jefferson to Little Harry's downtown, to the Green Lantern Club in Ecorse, Detroit's most upstanding citizens fed the coffers of the gangs that were reaping huge fortunes from their appetite for alcohol.

The Purple Gang became arrogant, even sloppy to the point where they were terrorizing Detroiters with street executions of their enemies, killing a police officer and in 1930, murdering well-known radio personality Jerry Buckley in the lobby of a downtown hotel.

In 1931 an inter-gang dispute resulted in the murder of members of their own gang. The three victims had violated an underworld code by operating outside the territory allotted to them by the Purple Gang leadership.

Known as the "Little Jewish Navy," this splinter group of Purples owned several boats and participated in rumrunning as well as hijacking. They decided they would break away from the gang and become an underworld power. The three men, Hymie Paul, Isadore Sutker (aka Joe Sutker) and Joe Lebowitz were lured to an apartment on Collingwood Avenue on September 16th, 1931.

They believed they were attending a peace conference with Purple Gang leaders. In reality, they were being set-up for a

Sneaky Smugglers

Smuggling has always been a way of life in the Border Cities. During prohibition, sneaking liquor across the border was almost a badge of honour. It was estimated that one-quarter of locals were involved in some form of smuggling alcohol into Detroit.

The Legend of the Egg Smuggler

A story has come down through the years that illustrates the tricks liquor smugglers would use. U.S. Customs officers noted an increase in the export of eggs from Windsor to Detroit. One day in May, 1920, a man carrying a large market basket disembarked from the Windsor ferry and was struck by a taxicab near the foot of Woodward in Detroit.

A crowd gathered; there was an unmistakable aroma of whisky in the air. Several dozen eggs were spread out on the pavement. The man, not seriously hurt, was obviously ill at ease. As soon as a police officer approached, he ran away. The basket, with some eggs intact, remained in the middle of the pavement. Upon examination, the basket contents revealed eggs filled with liquor and carefully resealed. From that day on, all baskets of eggs were suspect.

Photo Hiram Walker & Sons archives

Pulling the Plug

"Muskrat La Framboise had a boat with a plug in it like a bathtub. When the police spotted him, he'd just pull the plug and the boat would sink. Later, he'd return to where it sunk and when no one was around, he'd dive for the stuff. He was really good at this, and with the whisky being in these jute bags and tied together at the top, the bags had "ears" on them. When they were dumped overboard, you could dive down and pick them up by the ears and haul them to the surface." *Photo Burton Collection*

The Belt System

"We'd take bottles across the border. My lady had a rig she would put bottles in. She had belts she'd strap to her body, beneath her dress. One time, we got to the border and they asked us to get out. She got out on her side, I got out on mine and we were looking at each other over the roof of the car w e the Customs man searched the car. All of sudden she got a terrified look on her face... smash smash smash... one of the belts let go." *Photo Hiram Walker & Sons archives*

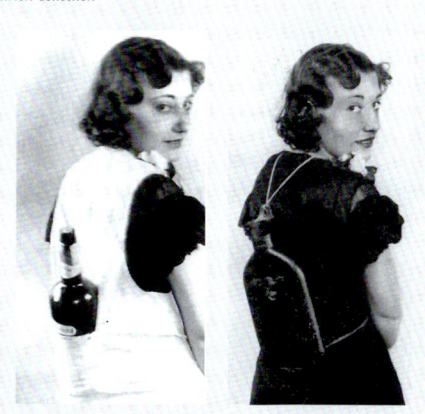

Text from "The Rumrunners – a prohibition scrapbook" by C.H. (Marty) Gervais

best of the times • 179

Smugglers load their cargo onto a ship at Windsor headed for "Cuba," while an official looks on.
Photo Larry Burchell Collection

Granny by Day, Bootlegger by Night

As a direct descendent of Mary Pugsley, Crawford Avenue's bootlegger, I feel qualified and privileged to share the colourful background of my grandmother. She lived eight houses from me on Crawford Avenue, on the west side of Windsor.

In an upstairs duplex, she was "granny" during the day – sporting a white starched apron, busy baking chocolate chip cookies in her small kitchen. By late afternoon, another woman emerged. Out came the spirits she doled out sparingly to off-duty railway men who had ended their shifts and wound their way through the fields on Crawford Avenue (where CBC now stands). They climbed the rickety stairs to "Bootlegger Mary's" for an evening of chatting and drinking.

The honour system was in place; the men dropped their coins in a cup on the round dining room table while Granny busied herself at the kitchen sink. Cigar smoke whirled over their heads, filling the small parlour as the men struggled to solve the world's problems. Granny's blue budgie lived in a small cage and had to be frequently covered up as he could pick up a colourful vocabulary. Granny did her best to shield us from this too.

Next day we were invited over for chocolate chip cookies and the opportunity to rifle through the old mohair couch cushions. Whatever coins we found we were able to keep. What fun!

Granny's business lasted well past her 70th birthday. She was an entrepreneur of prohibition days. "Bootlegger Mary" once ruled supreme. Today, the Devonshire Seniors' Residence stands on the site of my Granny's blind-pig. ***Judy (Robinson) Vien, Windsor***

"Bootlegger Mary" and Fred Pugsley in front of their home on Crawford Avenue (a blind-pig) in Windsor

---

mob assassination. After a brief discussion, the three unarmed Purples were shot to death by the very gangsters they had gone to meet.

A bookie named Sol Levine, who had transported the three men to their fatal rendezvous, was arrested soon afterwards and quickly became the State's main witness to the murders.

Levine had been allowed to live because he was a friend of gangster Ray Bernstein. The State finally had a live witness who could testify against The Purple Gang, and Levine's testimony was devastating. Three of the four Purples involved in the Collingwood Manor Massacre were quickly arrested. Irving Milberg, Harry Keywell, and Raymond Bernstein, three high ranking Purples, were convicted of first degree murder in the Collingwood Manor Massacre and sent to prison for life.

The demise of The Purple Gang occurred when government agents enlisted the support of the Italian mafia, who soon traded places with the purples and took control of Detroit's criminal underworld.

Although the Purples remained a force in Detroit until 1935, long prison sentences and inter-gang sniping eventually withered the gang's manpower. The predecessors of Detroit's modern day Mafia family simply stepped in and filled the void as The Purple Gang self-destructed.

The stock market crash in 1929, together with the start of the 10-year Great Depression, signaled an end to the Roaring Twenties and an era in bootlegging that will never be seen again.

To learn more about one of America's least known, yet most powerful and notorious gangs of thugs and mobsters read the gripping account by Michigan historian and author Paul R. Kavieff, "The Purple Gang- Organized Crime in Detroit, 1910-1945"

Below: Five prominent Detroit women took an active role in the successful "American Repeal Prohibition" campaign. In 1931, the Women's Organization for National Prohibition Reform presented "The Money Box Revue," drawing attention to the need to end prohibition in the United States. L-R: Mrs. C. A. Dean, Jr., Mrs. David McMorran, Mrs. Fred Alger, Mrs. Thomas F. McAllister, and Mrs. Catherine D. Doren. Photo Burton Historical Collection

Detroit police at river patrol headquaters at the foot of Riopelle Street ready for patrol, April 20th, 1932.
Photo Detroit News

More Sneaky Smugglers

Text reprinted from "The Rumrunners, a prohibition scrapbook" by C.H. (Marty) Gervais

Hazards of the Trade

"(The smugglers) were just like ants. And a lot of them went through the ice. In June 1928, we fished out about 28 bodies from the Detroit River and Lake Erie. They had either fallen through the ice into the water, or out of their boats, or they had been hijacked. It got to be quite a job pulling them out and it wasn't very pleasant."

Photo The Detroit News

Sea Cruise

"90% of all liquor illegally imported into Michigan was by boat. They differed widely in size, type, shape and appearance. Steamers, tugs, fast motorboats, sailboats, rowboats and even canoes were employed. All had one purpose: using high-speed, evasive tactics, camouflage and surprise to dodge U.S. Revenue cutters and police boats waiting on the shore." *Photo courtesy "The Rumrunners, a prohibition scrapbook" by C.H. (Marty) Gervais*

Tempting Fate

One rumrunner hauled liquor in a Studebaker – he took the back seat out. One day he pulled up to Customs and said: "I'd like to speak to you fellows." The bootlegger asked if a deal could be struck. "I come over loaded, and I will give you so much per case."

The Customs officer was very honest, and he also thought he was quite clever, so he agreed that next time the bootlegger came across, he would give him the go-ahead sign and let him through Customs.

At the appointed time, the bootlegger drove over, and Customs agents were ready for him. They searched the car from one end to the other and tore out the front seats. Someone got underneath and they looked under the hood.

Nothing – not a drop of liquor.

The Customs agent asked the bootlegger: "I thought you said you were going to bring over a load?" The smiling bootlegger replied: "No, the day I was talking to you was the day I had the load." *Photo Dossin Great Lakes Museum*

best of the times • 183

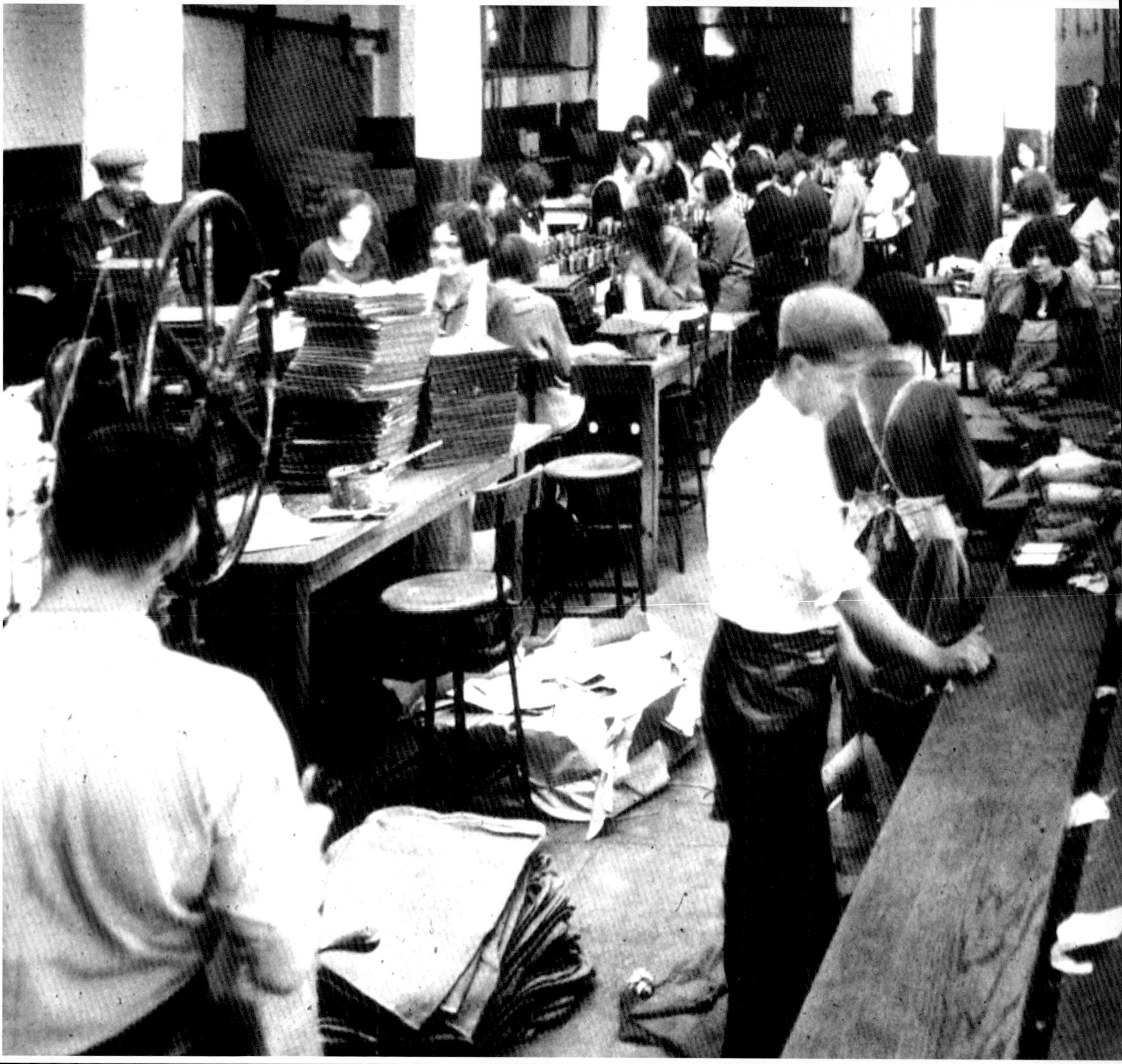

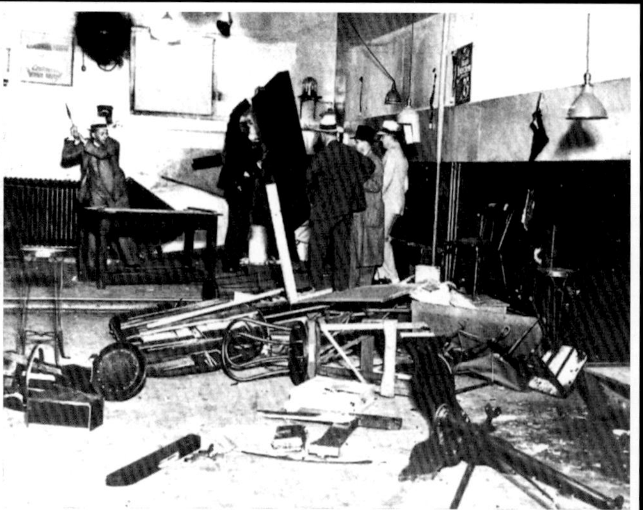

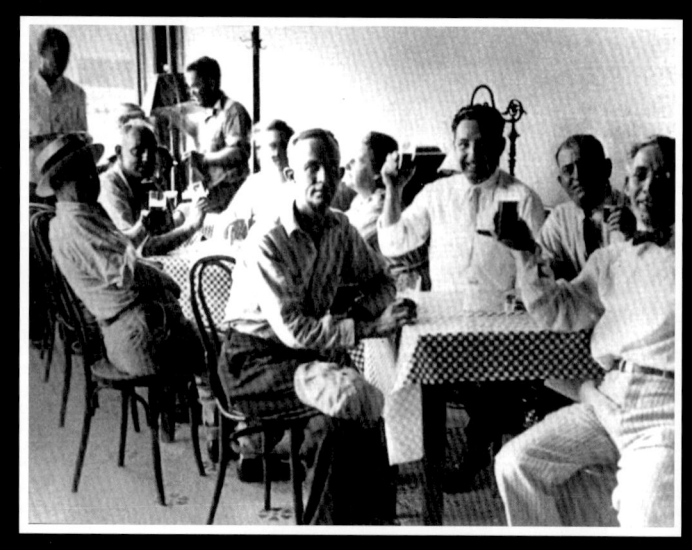

Tunnel Vision

During the Civil War in the 1860s, a Canadian dollar was worth a whopping $2.50 U.S. (those were the days!). Being a visionary, Hiram Walker purchased as many U.S. dollars as he could.

At the same time, demand for alcohol was so great that his distillery was busy loading whisky into boats headed for thirsty Americans. By the time the war ended and the U.S. dollar returned to par, Walker was a rich man.

Walker's success made competitors envious; from a place called "Swill Point" in Detroit, a concocted story emerged that Walker had constructed a whisky pipeline under the Detroit River from his distillery in Walkerville to his Detroit property at 35 Atwater Street to avoid customs inspectors and tairiffs; variations of this legend persist to this day.

Walker did use pipelines to move mash from his distillery on Sandwich Street (Riverside Drive) to his livestock barns at Tecumseh and Walker. The photo above, taken by Monmouth Road resident Peter Angermann, shows a 5' long section of wooden mash pipe unearthed on Monmouth Road during water main construction in 1994. Walker used Cypress trees from Florida as piping material since the wood was waterproof and durable.

Fact:
The Purple Gang was immortalized in the classic 1957 Elvis Presley tune, "*Jailhouse Rock*": "...the drummer boy from Illinois went crash, boom, bang, the whole rhythm section was The Purple Gang."

Clockwise from top left: During Prohibition, Walkerville's Hiram Walker & Sons continued to bottle large quantities of whisky for "export" (Hiram Walker & Sons archives); Ontario Export Dock no. 4 on Windsor waterfront (Wayne State archives); Men toasting the end of Prohibition (Larry Burchell); Police raid and destroy a speakeasy at 2942 Woodward Avenue, Detroit (The Detroit Free Press).

King Canada

from "The Rumrunners – A Prohibition Scrapbook"
by C. H. (Marty) Gervais, printed in Issue #34, May 2003

I was called "King Canada" because that's how I wanted to be known in the United States. I gave myself that name because here in town if the law comes looking for King Canada, well, nobody's going to know who that is. The people in town know me as Blaise Diesbourg but they don't know King Canada. If the law comes to me and asks, I say I don't know. I did this so the law couldn't keep track of me and what I was doing.

The King and Capone

Al Capone came to see me at the Mexico Export Dock, and asked if there was anybody that could handle that stuff for him. And I was the only one that could. I mean Capone was getting the stuff by boats…but he wanted the stuff everyday, by plane. I was the only one that could give 'em that.

So we go in the house of my brother Charlie, in the cellar, and we talked. There was another fellow with him. I said, "Listen, I am King Canada, and you know you can't fool around with me. I know every move in Chicago every move you make."

He says, "How?"

I says, "What do you think I am? Don't you think I know something through the government of what's going on in Chicago?"

"Yeah," he said. "Yeah," I said.

Capone was kind of a tough man but, oh, he was a good guy, you know. He was about, oh, I guess five-foot ten or eleven but smooth. He was never tough with me. I met him only two times once here in Belle River when he came to see me and once more in Chicago when I went down there with his pilots.

Capone had his own planes…old bombers…each had a pit long enough to hold twenty-five cases of whisky. At six o'clock in the morning I'd meet the pilot there in one of the five fields.

Capone would order from the export dock and it would be delivered to my field. I would load up the plane when it landed…that was my job. The pilot used to pay me money in a bundle from the bank. And it was stamped on the back how much it was. I never counted no money. He would give me the bundle and I'd throw it on the floor of the car. Never had time to count it. Because I only had five minutes to load the plane…300 bottles of whisky.

One time a pilot said, "Capone wants you to come to Chicago." So I got in the plane and went to the Sportsman's Park Racetrack in Chicago. And Capone was there with his big car. I got in with him. We had three motorcycles with machine guns, three in the front and three in the back. And we had nine miles to go to the place they called the Fort.

So Capone says, "I want to show you a good time tonight." We started drinking and he had about fifty girls…young girls about sixteen, seventeen. He put on a real show! All dancing and everything! I got drunk and forgot where I was. Well, the next morning I had to take the plane because one of the men I had hired was waiting in the field with the load…back in Belle River.

Everyday I sent a load to Chicago. I never had them land in the same field. And Capone was a nice fellow. Oh yeah. But they say that you couldn't double-cross him, because you'd be a dead goose.

Anyway, I'm the only one – the King of the Airplanes.

The King and The Purple Gang

I had a gang in Detroit I used to deal with called The Purple Gang; they were tough. But they didn't bother me. They had a big bar over there, and you knocked at the door, and a guy would say, "Who do you want to see?" Well, I knew the guys there, and he'd holler to another fellow to go get my friend. When my friend came, he'd say, "Oh, hello, it's King Canada! Let him in! Let him in!" and I'd go in and they'd bring champagne…anything I wanted."

"I made a lot of money in those days working for The Purple Gang. I was rich at one time. I had money, but just like that – it was gone. And you know when you get too big in business – you become too big as a man – you lose out. I bought an airplane, paid $12,000 for it."

"Well, this guy form The Purple Gang, he made two trips – I couldn't fly myself – and busted it up on the other side. He landed in the field where it was rough. They busted up the undercarriage, and set fire to it."

"The registration was under my name, so if anything happened, I'd told them to set fire to it. Get rid of it. I don't want no trouble."

"Well, that gang in Detroit says you better buy another one. I load them up in my field, but the engine wasn't working right. He just made it over the fence, and he crashed. Right away, he set fire to it."

"The Purple Gang had the pilot…a good pilot, too, most of the time…but I just wasn't lucky. Anyway, I lost $24,000, crashed up two planes, a month apart. Yeah. They were $12,000 a piece. "

Top Right: King Canada (l) and Al "Scarface" Capone, king of Chicago gangsters during Prohibition. (photo: "The Rumrunners, a prohibition scrapbook" by C.H. (Marty) Gervais and www.discovery.com).

295 Bottles of Liquor Seized at Hotel *(Top right)*
No, this isn't a scene from a liquor store. It's Constable Bryce Monaghan, of Riverside police, checking a seizure of 295 bottles of assorted brands of liquor discovered at the Island View Hotel (formerly Abar's Inn) on Riverside Drive. The liquor was listed and checked at the Riverside police station, where it was taken following the arrest of Nick Vujatovich, the proprietor, for illegal purchase. That trunk full of whisky (bottom right of photo) is exactly as they found it, police state. Vujatovich was unable to produce purchase slips for the cache, a veritable oasis in a liquor-parched community.
Reprinted from 1943 clipping from The Windsor Daily Star, provided by Richard Monaghan of Windsor. During WWII, liquor was in short supply in the Windsor area but was available on the black market.

Bookies and Bootleggers Abound
Born on the seven hundred block of Gladstone, I had to wait a few months before the family moved to the eight hundred block of Lincoln in order to attend King Edward School and Walkerville Collegiate. Being an adventurous lad I discovered a number of things in Walkerville. In the middle of the late '30s, very few homes had a black telephone like ours did. Imagine my surprise when a friend took me to his father's neighbourhood "store" and in one room, 12-15 telephones were all being used at once by shirt-sleeved men. Well, bookies will be bookies.

A girl in the neighbourhood's father spent a lot of time at the movies but didn't know much about the pictures being shown there. It seems the Tivoli Theatre had special rooms where card games were played on a regular basis.

Venturing out of Walkerville to Pierre Avenue, one of my newspaper customers had a very large four-door automobile in his driveway (a Reo, I believe). Unable to understand why a car had truck wheels I finally asked about it and the owner allowed me inside. The interior was plush with crystal flower holders on the wall. I was then shown how the many compartments in the walls and seats that featured hidden containers used to smuggle booze across the border during prohibition. The enormous gas tank had a one-quart capacity while the rest of it was a specially sealed whisky container. Ordinary car wheels and tires would not have been able to withstand the weight of these liquids.
Don D. McCartney, Oakville

Prohibition Artifact Still Making Music *(right)*
Just read the piece on (rumrunner) James Scott Cooper in the April 2003 issue. Did you know that the "colossal organ" from his Cooper Court mansion in Walkerville currently resides in the chapel of Morris-Sutton Funeral Home? "Colossal" seems an exaggeration – it is rather a small organ as pipe organs go– but it is an interesting and unique instrument. I'm not sure the organ receives the kind of professional service an instrument of that significance deserves. It ought to become designated and protected as a Walkerville heritage instrument as it is a part of our local history. People should stop by the funeral home and have a listen!
Rev. Murray B. McLeod, Westminster United Church, Windsor

Breakfast with Marty

by Laryssa Landale

He's an accomplished author, poet, play-wright, and columnist; founder of The Black Moss Press (Windsor's first publishing company); managing editor of The Windsor Review; University of Windsor's Resident Writing Professional. His list of literary achievements includes several collections of poetry, a children's book, a history of Policing in Windsor, a play, and most recently, a history of the Italian Men's Choir in Windsor. Perhaps Marty Gervais' most renowned literary accomplishments however, is the 1980 publication "The Rumrunners: a prohibition scrapbook."

I met with Marty one foggy March morning for breakfast at The Lumberjack in Windsor to discuss his fascination with this subject. I left with a full stomach and a brain packed with interesting details about this bygone era.

Ironically, as the title suggests, this book is literally a compilation of leftovers.

Marty originally began researching local prohibition stories in search of a plot for a play he had been commissioned to write for a University of Windsor drama department's showcase production. He thought a play on the prohibition era would be interesting, but wasn't sure what angle to take. During his investigation Marty came across the story of J.O.L. Spracklin and "Babe" Trumble.

> "...the King was asking for more (books). Marty soon discovered that he was selling them in Belle River. He was still making money from the rumrunning days!"

Their feud represents "the epitome of prohibition" says Marty. Spracklin was a local Methodist minister chosen by the Ontario government to enforce prohibition in the Windsor area. Trumble was saloonkeeper of The Chappell House (appropriately renamed "Rum Runners" bar for a while.)

The two had known each other since childhood, and there was no love lost between them on opposite sides of the prohibition issue. Marty saw Spracklin as representing "the forces of good... in) excess." He paints the picture of Spracklin as a pistol-packing Methodist minister, "marching up and down the Detroit River... like Wyatt Erpp." Babe Trumble, on the other hand, "represented the excess of prohibition." One fateful night in November 1920, Spracklin confronted Trumble and shot him, claiming Trumble had flashed a gun. The details of this circumstance were intricate and intriguing.

Marty's investigative efforts culminated in the production of the play "The Fighting Parson." But the scraps left over – all the *other* stories and information on prohibition that he had collected – became the makings of "The Rumrunners: a prohibition scrapbook."

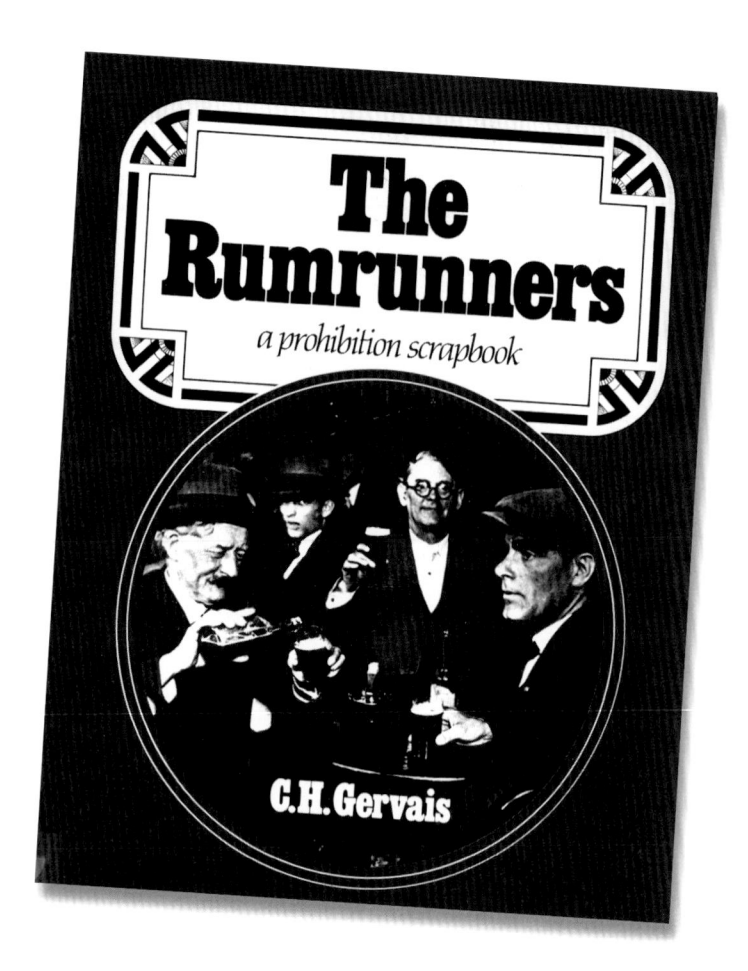

Marty's research experience itself would make a good book. It seems, even in the late 70s, many of those involved in rum running were still hesitant to speak of it – nearly fifty years after prohibition had ended.

"These people lived through it," he said, "some of these people didn't want these stories told again... when you live through something you don't think of it as history."

Marty came across several stories that no one was willing to talk about. There are stories that should be in the book, but aren't because he was not given permission to print them. Many of the old-timers still feared arrest or "having the income tax department hit them up for money," he says. "However," Marty continues, "when the book came out it suddenly made it okay. So now people are saying, "well, you don't have my story" or "why didn't you print my story?" "Well, because you didn't let me.""

Their attitudes were that they had been keeping these secrets for most of their lives, and weren't about to let them out now. Apparently Marty has hours and hours of taped interviews that never made it into the book. Do I smell a sequel?

Marty then explains hoe he was able to obtain as many stories as he did. "These guys aren't stupid... (they) made money during prohibition era... So when I asked them for their stories, they said, "what do I get out of it?" So I had to make deals with these people."

King Canada seemed the least demanding with his request for five copies of the finished book. Two weeks after the King received them he contacted Marty to request ten more books for relatives in Florida.

Not long after that, the King was asking for more. Marty soon discovered that he was selling them in Belle River. "He was still making money from the rum running days!"

Walter Goodchild was another interesting character. He had a goldmine of rum running photos – many taken in broad daylight – which had been sought by other writers. Goodchild had been put off by the pretentious attitude of other journalists that had an interest in his information. They had come to the house for a television interview and begun rearranging everything without permission. Goodchild kicked them out. When Marty contacted him in regards to these pictures Walter told him "yeah, I've got pictures... but I'm not going to give 'em to you."

Marty went out anyway. Their first two visits consisted of much conversation – about everything but prohibition. The third time Marty went out to see Goodchild he brought a forty-ounce bottle of Canadian Club whisky. Things loosed up, and Marty was successful in getting not only Walter's story but the copyright to his pictures, as well.

One of the other guys who agreed to talk to Marty had him drive out to his home in Belle River. When Marty arrived the old man was waiting with his coat on at the front door. He jumped in the car and said, "Lets go." Marty was intrigued. He figured they were off to see some of the old rum running haunts.

They ended up at the relatively new Gordon's grocery store. At that point Marty thought "this must be the site of..." so he (the rum runner) said, "Come on." So I go inside the grocery store. He grabs a shopping cart. Starts going up and down the aisles filling the shopping cart.

So I said, "what are we doing here." He said, "well I needed a ride to the grocery store. I usually take a taxi, because you know... I'm a pensioner... and you want a story for the rumrunners." "Yeah, well where do I fit in?" "Well, you've got the car. You've driven me over here, so I'm going shopping and I'll talk to you while I shop."

"The Rumrunners" book was, without question, the definitive work on local prohibition. It whetted an appetite in area residents that has yet to be satiated. The book became a best seller (it is currently out of print, but Marty has recently announced that the second edition will be reprinted in 2005).

We still crave details about the cultural anomaly known as the Roaring Twenties, an exciting era that has become legendary throughout North America.

Marty added one final observation of the prohibition circumstance during our breakfast: "The ironic thing is that this area voted overwhelmingly against the repeal of prohibition. Turns out that this area of the country (Windsor) made more money from prohibition than any other area!"

Prohibition certainly was a colourful era, filled with characters and stories the likes of which we may never see again. If not for Marty Gervais' research into the phenomenon that was prohibition, many of these stories would have disappeared with the passing of its leading players.

A ROARING TWENTIES GLOSSARY

Rumrunning and the Roaring Twenties, Philip Mason, Wayne State University Press, 1995.

BARREL HOUSE
A place where liquor is sold illegally.

BARREL HOUSE BUM
A drunkard.

BEERAGE
Prominent people whose wealth has come from the manufacture and sale of beer.

BEEROCRACY
People who have made fortunes by the sale and manufacture of beer. A member of this group is a beerocrat.

BLIND-PIG OR BLIND TIGER
A place where liquor is sold illegally. Term originated from the practice of a shrewd Yankee who evaded law against the sale of liquor by placing a blind pig on a box inside of a tented enclosure and announced, "See the blind pig. Ten cents a look." With each payment he gave a way a drink of rye or bourbon.

BOOTLEGGERS
One who sold liquor illegally. Term originally applied to one who hid liquor in his bootleg.

FLAPPER:
Young female of the 1920's. Term signified young woman with a cynical attitude; an interest in daring fashions and indifferent morals.

GIN MILL
A low dive; a saloon.

SHORT-CIRCUIT
Booze that was to be exported from Canada to "Cuba, Bermuda or Mexico" but came back into the country, ending up in roadhouses and Blind-pigs.

SPEAK EASY OR SPEAK
A place where liquor was sold illegally or after legal hours. Term first used in the nineteenth century to mean, "speak softly when ordering illicit liquor."

Above: From the looks on their faces theses Windsorites were enjoying their evening at a Windsor speakeasy. Photo courtesy Larry Burchell

The Ride of a Lifetime

The homes and names of Rumrunners Low and Cooper were well known to me as my father drove a delivery truck for the Canadian National Express (forerunner of Purolator and U.P.S.). We delivered many parcels to these homes, especially at Christmas, when everyone wanted to make sure they were remembered.

I worked at Hiram Walker and Sons my entire career. At one time I was the clerk in the blending department. Most of my duties included keeping track of all the alcohol to within three percent of a proof gallon each month. Across from me was a federal exercise officer doing the same thing. He was a very fine gentleman by the name of Harry Moss.

One day he looked at me and said "The name Busby seems to ring a bell with me. When I was younger I was in charge of issuing Export Permits at a small dock in LaSalle, one of the boat owners made two or three trips a week to Bermuda or Havana under the alias of Stan Lee. I later learned his real name was Stanley Busby – any relation?"

I asked my parents that night at dinner. My father told me Stan was one of his cousins from Detroit, and between my mother and my dad this tale evolved:

"Stanley asked my parents if they would like to go for a boat ride on the river. It seemed a good idea, so why not? He picked them up at our house on Lincoln Rd. and took them out to LaSalle to his boat. This surprised them as Stan lived in the far west end of Detroit.

Stan's boat turned out to be a very large speedboat with a WWI Liberty aircraft engine in it. Stan's boat was loaded with boxes covered with burlap. After a quick call to the weather station to see if the coast was clear, they left port.

They were only a short way out when a U.S. Coast Guard boat started to follow them. The Liberty revved up and Stan took the fully loaded speedboat on a quick trip to the American side, where they weaved in and around ships waiting for their appointed berths. At last they felt confident enough to head for pre-arranged landing place. Here they were "entertained" by a rough looking group while the boat was unloaded. They waited around until they received a phone call saying it was safe to leave.

They were hardly under way when another U.S. coastguard hailed them to stop. Stan immediately told his crew of three to "dump the meat choppers;" two machine guns went overboard. Stan told my parents that with no booze and no guns, they were just a family out enjoying a boat ride. If guns were found aboard they all could've served eleven years in Federal Prison.

My parents got home in one piece, but they never accepted the offer of another boat ride from Stan."

Many years later I met Stan and I told him about Harry Moss. He laughed and said "those were the days." Then he told me that he once received a letter from a bank in Ojibway saying the branch was closing and that he needed to move the $50,000 he had in the account. It wasn't his; he had never made any deposits. Obviously someone had used his name to hide some money. He would not and could not pursue this matter as he could not prove that it was his cash. Like many businessmen during prohibition, he ended up living a frugal life.
Edward Busby, Windsor

The Smuggler's Choice

During Prohibition, Studebaker's seven-passenger E.K. "Big Six" was a favourite of rumrunners. With the back seat out, it could carry 50-gallon jugs. Known as the "Whisky Six," the car could rev up to 80 miles an hour. The $3,000 pricetag was chalked up as the cost of doing business. In 1921, the Windsor Police Department bought its own Studebaker chase car – though they called it the Police Flyer instead of a Whisky Six.

Generally, Packard's, Cadillacs and Lincolns were used to run booze. One of the most unusual belonged to the notorious Al Capone who frequented the Border Cities. His "made-to-order" car was a 1928 bullet proof Cadillac protected by half-inch boilerplate and inch-thick glass. The gas tank was shielded by sheet steel and the car was equipped with a siren and secret gun lockers. It also had a roll down rear window.
From Pioneering the Auto Age, Herb Colling and Carl Morgan

Above: Brick door stops, each concealing a quart of whisky, was a common smuggling method. Photo: Cleveland Public Library

The end of this story?

by Laryssa Landale, Issue #34, May 2003

"So convinced were they that alcohol was the cause of virtually all crime that, on the eve of Prohibition, some towns actually sold their jails." (The Anti-Saloon League of America Yearbook, 1920)

As we have seen, prohibition ushered in wild, unbridled social conditions that define the Roaring Twenties. Instead of stopping alcohol consumption, and eliminating crime, it encouraged both. Statistics indicate that annual pre-war alcoholic consumption was at a rate of nine gallons per capita. After prohibition legislation took effect, the numbers show consumption at a staggering 102 gallons per capita in the U.S. In addition, the lack of quality regulations on homebrews enabled many dangerous concoctions to reach an unsuspecting public and caused much physical damage.

Bootleggers were initially average folk, smuggling a bottle or flask of genuine whisky for personal consumption or selling a few cases to the local speakeasy. Smalltime gangsters soon got in on the act and crime rates skyrocketed. Organized crime had been handed a lucrative business that produce revenue in excess of $200 million dollars annually by 1929 – second only to Detroit's automotive industry!

Not only were undesirables drawn into the liquor business by prohibition but upstanding members of society were forced out. Hiram Walker & Sons, Ltd. was sold outside the family in the late 1920s. Though the manufacture of spirits was quite legal by then in Canada, the business' reputation suffered by being loosely associated with rumrunners. In an attempt to avoid the social stigma associated with earning a living in a business connected to bootleggers and their illegal activities, Hiram Walker's descendents sold the business and even went so far as to keep future generations of the family in the dark about the origins of their wealth.

But some good came out of prohibition, including a platform for women to become involved in politics. The formation of the Women's Christian Temperance Union ultimately led to the women's suffrage movement and the achievement of the right to vote. Women gained another freedom from the prohibition era. Oddly enough, it was during prohibition that it became socially acceptable for women to drink alcohol. The temperance/prohibition issue became a catalyst for – and creator of – social equality for women.

Prohibition also created financial prosperity for many. There was virtually no unemployment as fast money could be made by almost every citizen in the Windsor-Detroit area through participation in bootlegging.

Alcohol smuggling funneled millions of dollars of revenue into Canada and its government in the ten-plus years that it was in full swing. As a result of all the alcohol that flowed across the border during prohibition, many Americans developed a taste for Canadian whiskies and ales. This preference has continued, and seventy odd years after the booze ban was lifted, liquor remains one of Canada's largest exports.

Prohibition may have failed to accomplish its objectives, but some good did come out of it. As for the rest of the story – what an incredible time to be alive in The Border Cities!

Above: Headline proclaims the renewed flow of beer at local hotels in 1928.
Photo: Larry Burchell Collection

Left: After the repeal of prohibition in Ontario in 1927, Windsor boys lined up with their wagons outside provincial liquor stores to assist customers in transporting whisky and beer to their homes.
Photo: The Detroit News

The Legacy of the 1943 Detroit Riots

by Chris Edwards, Issue #26, July/August 2002

While the Detroit Riots of 1967 remain etched in our collective memories, seeds of discontent were sewn much earlier. Even as World War II was transforming Detroit into the Arsenal of Democracy, cultural and social upheavals brought about by the need for workers to man the bustling factories threatened to turn the city into a domestic battleground.

Recruiters toured the South convincing impoverished whites and blacks to head north with promises of high wages in the war factories. They arrived in such numbers that it was impossible to house them all.

Blacks who believed they were heading to a "promised land" found northern bigots every bit as mean and violent as had been left behind in the deep south. And southern whites brought their own traditional prejudices with them as both races migrated northward.

In the Motor City, black workers mixed with European immigrants on the assembly lines and in the city, and violence often broke out, despite everyone earning wages beyond their wildest dreams.

Between 1933-43, the number of blacks in Detroit doubled and racial tensions in the city grew accordingly. Blacks were excluded from all public housing except the Brewster project, and housing shortages were acute.

The Detroit Housing Commission chose a pilot housing project site for blacks in a predominantly white neighbourhood, called Sojourner Truth; growing resentment by whites led to riots in 1942.

Local and national media anticipated more trouble; Life Magazine called the increased tensions "dynamite."

On June 20th, 1943, blacks and whites clashed in minor skirmishes on Belle Isle. Two young blacks, angered by being ejected from Eastwood Park five days earlier, went to Belle Isle to even the score. Police searched cars filled with blacks crossing to Belle Isle but not cars driven by whites. Fighting on the island began around 10 pm, but police declared things under control by midnight. More than 200 blacks and whites had participated in a free-for-all battle.

Leo Tipton and Charles (Little Willie) Lyons told a black crowd at the Forest Social Club that whites had thrown a black woman and her baby off the Belle Isle Bridge. More than 500 angry and indignant patrons took to the streets. The crowd moved toward Woodward, near "Paradise Valley," and began breaking windows and looting stores.

Nearby, just west of Woodward in an area inhabited by southern whites, a separate rumour swept the neighborhood – blacks had raped and murdered a white woman on the Belle Isle Bridge. An angry mob of whites spilled onto Woodward near the Roxy Theater around 4 am, beating blacks as they were getting off streetcars.

The toll was appalling; six Detroit policemen were shot in the melee, and another 75 were injured. The 36 hours of rioting claimed 34 lives – 25 of them black. More than 1,800 were arrested for looting and other incidents, the vast majority black; thirteen murders remained unsolved.

As a result of the 1943 riots, improvements to the plight of Detroit's inner city blacks were promised, yet little changed. In an era of growing disenchantment, racial tensions would boil over almost 24 years to the day after the riots of '43.

The First "Black Day in July"

On a hot, humid Motor City summer night, events in 1967 seemed routine: police raided an illegal bar in the inner city, known as a "Blind Pig"– a place to get a drink after the bars closed. A small crowd gathered to protest the raid and arrests. Within a short time, mobs of young men were engaged in burning, looting, and acts of random violence – the embers of the 1943 riots were rekindled and it would be some days before the fire was extinguished.

Earlier riots had been blamed on police "overreaction" to minor incidents; authorities did not dispatch large numbers of officers to quell rioters. They tried to keep things in check – based again on presumed lessons from disturbances elsewhere – by persuading the media to impose a news blackout. Neither tactic worked, however, and things were soon completely out of control.

Rioting quickly spread to encompass over fourteen square miles in Detroit. The '67 riots were indiscriminate: mobs torched and plundered black businesses as freely as white ones and burned down many black homes. Both blacks and whites participated in looting, burning and rioting.

Forty-three people lay dead by the time the 1967 Detroit riot ended five days later on July 28. Beyond the statistics are the human stories.

The following accounts are by those who witnessed what Gordon Lightfoot called "Black Day in July."

Previous Page: Rioters overturn a car on Woodward at Vernor; Detroit police arrest a group of blacks when one was found carrying a knife during the February 1942 disturbances. From top right: Flaming car on Woodward; a white mob overturns a car belonging to a black man on Woodward; burning cars.
Photos Burton Collection

Recollections of Life during the 1967 Riots
Panic in Detroit

by Leah Behrens, Issue #26, July/August 2002

On Sunday, July 23rd, 1967, Detroit police raided a 'blind pig' – an illegal after-hours bar – on 12th Street near Clairmount on the city's near west side. A large crowd of African-Americans gathered as arrests were made and they began taunting the police. Someone threw a beer bottle through the back window of a cruiser; the crowd became increasingly agitated. More patrol cars arrived but the police did nothing to quell the disturbance, so rioters seized the opportunity to start looting. It wasn't long before a wave of more than 200 people surged through city streets – Detroit's riots of '67 had begun.

There were less than 200 officers spread over the entire city that morning. The mob became unstoppable as it carved its path of destruction. Rioters smashed, burned and looted everything in their path; they set fire to businesses and homes. Police and firefighters were met by sniper bullets as they tried to contain the riot.

Detroit became a war zone.

The last major Detroit race riot had occurred in 1943. On the night of June 20th, fights broke out between whites and Afro-Americans near Belle Isle. Before long, the mob had grown to over 5,000 and the Detroit riot squad was called in. By the time the riots of '43 were over, 34 people lay dead, hundreds injured, 1,800 arrested and property damage was estimated in the millions.

While the rest of her family headed north, 20-year-old Linda Parrott was home with her husband in east Dearborn. The glow from the television lit up the living room. To Linda, as she watched what was unfolding in Detroit, the events seemed like they were happening in another world.

EVE OF DESTRUCTION: *A National Guardsman watches the city burn. This famous photo, taken by renowned Detroit Free Press photographer Tony Spina, was published around the world and won a Pulitzer Prize.* Photo Walter P. Reuther Library, Wayne State University.

Victims of the '67 riots included:

- **Krikor "George" Messerlain:** 68 years old, beaten to death defending his shoe repair shop.
- **Clifton Pryor:** 23 years old, killed carrying a mop and bucket on the roof of his apartment. He was mistaken for a sniper and was shot by a National Guardsman.
- **Jerome Olshore:** The only policeman killed in the riot after a commotion began in a local A&P Supermarket and random gun shots were fired.
- **Emanuel Cosby:** 26 years old, shot and killed by police after failing to surrender while looting in a local N&T Market.

Dearborn was a 'closed' town; Mayor Orville Hubbard made sure no blacks lived there. The rioting in Detroit didn't affect Linda's job at Ford Motor Company. It was business as usual, even for her worried father who would be coming home from work as soon as he was back from dropping off her mother, brother, and two sisters at the cottage.

Meanwhile, Kathy Parrott sat in the back seat of the packed family car heading north, and stared out the window. "He never explains anything," thought the 15-year-old as she looked at her father. "What exactly is going on?"

That same question echoed across the nation as the Motor City riot spread to other Michigan cities. Pockets of violence broke out in Pontiac, Grand Rapids, Kalamazoo, Flint, and Saginaw.

Elna Browder of Detroit had just put her 15-month-old daughter to bed. Glued to the TV, Elna thought of her husband Richard, a four year veteran police officer with Detroit's 15th precinct. When the riots started, he was ordered to patrol the worst neighbourhoods, working 12-hour shifts, from noon to midnight. Their second child was due any day.

The phone rang again. It was another anxious relative. "I heard a policeman got killed! You think that was your husband?" Elna had no idea. She could only pray that he was safe.

"People are just stealing to be stealing," officer Richard Browder mused, as he watched looters running out of an emptied gas station with nothing more than a credit card stamping machine. Wherever he travelled in riot-torn areas of Detroit, there were the looters. Generally, he would arrive on the scene and they would flee – cat and mouse; the Detroit Police force was out manned and overworked.

The riots seemed to be about racial rebellion. Most of the police and guardsmen were white, while nearly all the rioters were black. However, a bizarre fellowship formed between looters that defied racial boundaries. United in a spirit of anarchy, looters of all races helped each other 'clean out' merchandise from stores.

Peace officers like Richard Bowler, who was African American, realized that, black or white, they were in this together. It had become a field day for thrill seekers, uniting people so hopelessly trapped in poverty that they had nothing to lose.

To help police restore order, the state governor brought up the National Guard.

"They're just young guys from upper Michigan," observed Richard. He and four national guardsmen saw looters robbing a convenience store. As he went in to investigate, he looked over his shoulder.

"All they do is just stand their with their rifles in front of them," he thought; "they don't move or anything!"

Richard arrested a few perpetrators, then called for backup – busy. Suddenly, he was attacked from behind. As he shook the hoodlum off his back, Richard looked up to see a mob gathered across the street, advancing towards him, throwing bottles and rocks; he had to get out of there.

He released the looters, and he and the guardsmen scrambled into the cruiser. He groped for the keys; someone must have taken them!

In desperation, Richard searched the cruiser as the crowd moved in. "The glove compartment! There are extra keys in the glove compartment!" He grabbed them, started the car, and raced away.

Four days into working the most dangerous shifts of his policing career, Richard's wife gave birth to their son.

"I want out of here," Elna told him. "I don't want to raise my kids like this."

Within six months, Richard quit the Detroit force and moved his family across the river to Windsor.

On the night the Detroit riot broke out, 21 year-old Phil Chauvin was working as a waiter in the Garrison Lounge at downtown Windsor's Seaway Hotel. The borders were clamped shut early Sunday morning. The rooms at the hotel began to fill up as American clientele who found themselves trapped in Windsor, unable to get home.

"Where can we get some beer and whisky?" someone asked the young waiter.

The toll of the '67 riots included:

▸ **467 injured:** 181 civilians, 167 Detroit police, 83 Detroit firefighters, 17 National Guard, 16 State Police, 3 U.S. Army.

▸ **7,231 arrested:** 6,528 adults, 703 juveniles; 6,407 blacks, 824 whites. The youngest, 10; the oldest, 82. Half of those arrested had no criminal record. Three percent of those arrested went to trial; half of them were acquitted.

▸ **2,509 stores looted or burned:** One month after the riot, a city tally showed 388 families homeless or displaced and 412 buildings burned or damaged enough to be demolished. Dollar losses from arson and looting ranged from $40 million to $80 million.

(source: Detroit 300)

Phil thought fast. The liquor stores closed at 6 p.m. and they don't open on Sundays, but he knew how he could help them out.

I guess this would be called 'bootlegging', he says with a chuckle. He had managed to set up a few of the Americans with some whisky. 'Fix 'em up, for a price!' Phil slipped the money into his pocket.

Meanwhile, across the border, traffic was backed up along Riverside Drive as carloads of residents flocked to the riverfront to watch the 'fireworks' over Detroit. Early Monday, July 24th, the Windsor Fire Department received a call from Detroit for assistance; the W.F.D. responded immediately. When they arrived in the riot district, it was like a scene out of war movie.

They were instructed to tackle the worst blazes. For three days, Windsor firefighters worked alongside their beleaguered American counterparts.

Meanwhile, the death toll climbed. By the end of the week, the panic in Detroit claimed 44 lives and 7,331 arrests had been made.

Walter Perry paced in his office. The 1967 Windsor Emancipation Day festivities were scheduled for next week. He was in charge, and pressure was being applied to cancel the event – the first time in its 35-year

National guardsmen on the lookout. Photo Walter P. Reuther Library, Wayne State University.

Like an Army of Ants

On Sunday, July 20th, 1967, my family was visiting friends in Grand Rapids, Michigan. As we drove along on that hot, sunny day, I heard my parents briefly talk about breaking news heard on the radio concerning trouble in Detroit. I recall my parents discussing the significance of the news but there seemed nothing to worry about.

Late that afternoon we headed home to the inner city of Detroit, specifically, LaSalle Garden South off of Lindwood only four blocks from the soon to be notorious Twelfth Street. The grade school I attended for eight years was located on that now historic street and perhaps only a mile or less from the blind pig where the riot broke out early that Sunday morning.

Although as we made our way into the city via the John C. Lodge Expressway around nightfall, we saw that our city, indeed our neighborhood, had erupted into something terribly frightening. Numerous buildings were engulfed in flames; fire engines, police cars, military vehicles and people were racing from point A to B. Seeing the chaos around us, my father ordered us all down on the floor of our station wagon.

When we arrived at our parking spot in front of our house at 2479 LaSalle Gardens South, we raced to safety as soon as the car doors were flung open. My oldest brother greeted us at the front door with a baseball bat spiked with six-inch nails. He had been home the entire day and was ready to defend our sanctuary.

As the evening wore on, my mother and six of us kids eventually went up stairs to try to sleep on the floor of one of the bedrooms. The night was frightfully hot. Surreal echoes of sirens punctuated by periods of complete silence replaced the usual neighborhood sounds from our playmates, their siblings and the summer street traffic.

Early the following morning my dad drove everyone, except my oldest brother, across the border to Oxley, Ontario, outside of Windsor. My parents arranged for us to stay with friends until the turmoil ceased.

On the drive down Fourteenth Street to the Ambassador Bridge, we witnessed a mob of looters racing like an army of ants, running in and out of stores. Men, women and children were carrying anything of value out and into their homes or waiting cars or even wheel barrels.

I stayed in Canada for most of the rest of that summer. Being only 12 years old, I quickly forgot about the chaos in my native land – thanks to the peace and quiet of my sanctuary – south of the border.

Richard Klein, Farmington Hills, MI

history. The situation across the river was too serious, he told himself; too much of a gamble to hold the 1967 celebration.

On Thursday, July 27th, The Windsor Star broke the news. "We called it off to be on the safe side and to protect all citizens in Windsor," Walter was quoted.

While tensions remained high, the rioting was finally quelled by the end of the week. Relief projects for Detroit riot refugees were quickly established. Windsorites contributed, as well; tonnes of food and clothing were collected and sent over to help their neighbours.

When the border crossing reopened, the brave and the curious wanted to see where the rioting had happened. Carole and Manfred Behrens decided to take a Sunday drive across the bridge to check out the damage.

"It's like a war zone!" said Carole. Whole city blocks were completely destroyed. Her husband shook his head." Stores, businesses, everything burned out," he said in disbelief. "Why would they do this?"

Too Painful to Look Down

My memories of Detroit of "old" are tangled in a fine weave of sentiment and nostalgia. The Hudson building was magic during the Christmas season and we all waited with baited breath for our trip up the elevator to Santa's floor.

The lunches in the Hudson cafeteria, heavenly, hot bittersweet sundaes at Saunders, Vernors at the soda fountain in their warehouse building, and the bustle on Woodward Avenue, congested wall to wall with people. That was the Detroit I remember.

Through a set of circumstances none of us could comprehend, that city is no more.

The 1967 riots broke out in downtown Detroit on the day I was to fly to Las Vegas to visit a fellow Windsorite, Erica Gardner. Her uncle and his family resided there, and she was working as a counsellor in a summer day camp, attending to the sons and daughters of the rich and famous.

I was 16 and scheduled to fly alone from Metro Airport in Detroit to stay for a week. When the officials closed the border, I was left holding a non-refundable ticket on the Canadian side of the border. What to do?

Being resourceful, I, along with others in my predicament, managed to rent a four-seater aircraft that was flying from Windsor Airport to Detroit Metropolitan Airport.

The Detroit I saw from above at close range was at war. Fires burned and people were running up and down the streets. The National Guard tanks were everywhere; soldiers were on every corner. The sky was smoky and the air was foul.

I moved away from Windsor a few years later. After 22 years in Toronto, my family and I returned to once again reside in Windsor.

Detroit and I have had a long hiatus from one another. We have both come a long way since that day in the sixties when it was too painful to look down.

Sheryl Davies, Windsor

People Crying for Help

The Riot of 1967. When those words are spoken or written, the sounds and feelings surge back as if it happened just yesterday. Little is forgotten.

I lived on Riverside Drive West. Radio reports of events were confirmed by a short walk along the Detroit River to look across and directly up 12th Street; we could also hear the gun shots.

I worked for MichCon then. On Monday morning, the day after the riots began, I approached the tunnel with trepidation. I knew that only emergency personnel would be allowed to cross, but I tried to explain that because MichCon is a utility I thought I might be needed; I was turned back.

On Tuesday, I was allowed to cross the border. The Tunnel Bus only went through the tunnel before turning back. When I knew had to walk the rest of the way to work, my stomach sank. I walked up the stairs and crossed in front of Ford Auditorium. There were no pedestrians on the streets, only myself and the National Guard – young men with rifles. The hair on the back of my neck bristled; I was afraid. My impulse was to duck.

I arrived at the MichCon building and it was ringed by the National Guard. I had to explain, timidly, what I was doing there. A man smiled and motioned me on.

photo: Spike Bell, PPA Certified, M. Photog., M.P.A.

As I sat at my desk, the calls pleading for help came in – someone's house was on fire at the gas meter or the house next door was on fire because of a broken meter. People explained their situations between tears and begged for help; the pleas were heartbreaking.

One woman asked for help to save a soldier in Vietnam's car in her care. "As soon as we can get a National Guard escort we will be there," I said. It sometimes took hours before they were available.

While all of this was going on, I was trying to call my grandmother, an elderly woman all alone and now isolated on the east side of Detroit. When I finally got her on the phone, the National Guard had been there and had told her to get her most important items and wait on the front porch; she was scheduled fo evacuation.

Although the riot was not in her neighbourhood, it wasn't far away. I was in a panic. Where was she going? Would her house and possessions be destroyed? Would she be safe? There was no way I could get to her.

Eventually more staff members were able to come into work. My grandmother wasn't evacuated from her home, but it was a while before I really settled down again.

Helen Brumpton, Windsor

The Riot Sale

During the '67 Detroit riot, we had a pawnshop in our furniture store on 12th Street. It was well protected with locks and an alarm system, or so we thought. Rioters knocked down the front of the building by backing a truck into it, then proceeded to clean out the place.

The police cautioned us not to go into the area as it was considered too dangerous.

We were told that people were running down streets and alleys offering stolen items at a fraction of their value – shoes were 50 cents a pair, TVs for $100. Some people took advantage of this "sale" but many did not buy anything being too afraid to be seen by neighbours, etc.

Truly these were hectic and precarious times.

Ed Chanko, Windsor and Martin Adler, Hamtramck

Portrait of a Scandal

by Robert Earl Stewart, Issue #22, March 2002

All photos courtesy of Windsor Star archives.

For a $2 ride in and out of the compact blocks of Windsor's business section, any cab driver would point out which of the dingy rooming houses, pool rooms and tobacco stores along Pitt, Sandwich, Assumption and Pelissier Streets, behind whose false fronts you could get a girl, buy a drink or place a bet.

Maclean's Magazine, May 1, 1950

What is it about the graft that turns ordinary men into devils?

Is it the graft – abusing political influence by accepting money or gifts – or is it the fallibility of ordinary men that's to blame? It seems that all too easily certain people can be coaxed away from their ethics by overtures of covert personal gain. How quickly morality falls by the wayside.

So why is it that so many of those unable to resist graft seem to end up in public office?

Juicy scandals involve money and greed on some level.

But the juiciest scandals have money, greed, pay-offs, alcohol, gambling, violence, murder and sex in their dark, velvety hearts.

The Windsor Police Scandal of 1950 had all that and more.

Border City Blues

The 1950s are often depicted as idyllic and quaint, full of good clean living and prosperity. The reality is that there were lots of places, Windsor being one of them, where prosperity was often connected to what the police like to call vice.

In 1950 downtown Windsor – a hotbed for illegal gambling, prostitution, after-hours drinking, gunplay – had a reputation as "sin city."

Larry Kulisek, a University of Windsor history professor, specializing in urban and local histories, including Windsor and Essex County, stated: "A certain latitude towards gambling and bootlegging and other vices can be expected in a border area. The police weren't on a moral crusade, there was just an expectation that 'this is life'."

This is not to say certain kinds of late-night entertainment don't exist today, because, for better or for worse, they do. Ironically, many of the vices from the past – including gambling, escort services and late-night drinking – are now legal.

But in 1950, reports in the media elevated vices to the level of entertainment and Windsorites eagerly followed the exploits of downtown bookies, pimps and bootleggers in the daily papers and around the lunch counters.

Windsor gained a nationwide reputation as a wide-open town.

915 Shepherd Street raid by city police turned up bookies but no evidence of betting.

The Secret Room

March 11, 1950: the pages of The Windsor Daily Star are filled with stories of gambling and violence, including a page-one story about a two-year-old Detroit murder case connected to a Windsor bookie joint, the Polo Club.

Also on page one, a less violent but no less sensational story about a bonanza of illegal liquor located in a room nobody can find.

This "Secret Room," as the Windsor police referred to it, was apparently located somewhere in the Sandwich Street residence of one Joe Assef.

A raid on Assef's property on January 1, 1950 had turned up hundreds of bottles of illegal booze. On March 7, Assef plead guilty to a charge of keeping illegal liquor for sale and running a speak easy at the Sandwich Street address.

During the lengthy court proceedings, it was established that large quantities of booze might still be stashed somewhere in the house. Subsequent searches of the property turned up nothing and Assef was mum on the whereabouts of the rest of his illegal booze cache (insiders said it was under the breezeway's cement floor).

Little did anyone know that this mysterious but relatively unassuming event would kick-start a scandal that would result in accusations of widespread "moral laxity" on the part of the Windsor Police Department, and resignations amongst the City of Windsor's top cops, lawmakers, administrators and politicians. Even the mayor was painted with the scandalous brush.

The Whistleblower

Whether he intended to or not, Magistrate J. Arthur Hanrahan, who sentenced Assef to six months in prison, blew the lid off the graft and payoff racket that had fuelled a booming Border City vice trade.

During Assef's eight-week trial, Liquor Control Board of Ontario investigators raised questions as to how Assef had received 5,400 deliveries of beer and liquor over a 90-day period late in the previous year.

At a rate of 60 deliveries a day, it seemed impossible that no one, including members of the police department's five-man morality squad, had witnessed suspicious activity at Assef's residence.

Hanrahan found answers in a few other items uncovered in the Assef raid – several liquor delivery receipts bearing the home addresses of some of Windsor's most prominent citizens and 16 Windsor policemen. The implications were obvious: the Windsor police were on the take.

On the day of Assef's sentencing, a shocked and embittered Hanrahan unleashed a diatribe against the Windsor Police Department. He openly referred to what he called "moral laxity" on the police's behalf and suggested Assef's uninterrupted bootlegging was possible only through police complicity. Hanrahan said it was also likely the Windsor police force was "rendered impotent" by the booming vice trade around them.

Magistrate J. Arthur Hanrahan: "I have had a growing conviction that things were seriously wrong in this city."

The Fallout

There are those who suggest if the Assef trial had taken up less of Magistrate Hanrahan's time, he would have been in a better mood on the day of the sentencing and let the 16 delivery receipts slide.

Criticized by Mayor Art Reaume for putting negative images of Windsor in people's heads, Hanrahan went on the offensive. "I have had a growing conviction that things were seriously wrong in this city," he told reporters. "The judgement I delivered on Assef was intended to bring this to the attention of the people."

His bold words in the courtroom were heard as far away as Queen's Park. Within days, The Windsor Daily Star reported that Attorney General Dana Porter was grilled on the floor of the provincial legislature for his apparent lack of action on "the allegations of police laxity in Windsor."

Porter returned from his upbraiding in Toronto with "sweeping powers" to call in witnesses and follow up statements made in the police commission probe; the city of Windsor braced itself for a public inquiry. Clearly, the city's moral laxity had become a thorn in the Province's side.

The Probe

The first probe into the Windsor Police Department's moral laxity began on March 16, 1950. The probe was conducted by a committee comprised of three men: Judge Albert J. Gordon (the past chair of the Windsor Police Commission) would chair the probe, Chatham Crown Attorney A. Douglas Bell (appointed commission counsel by Porter), and Mayor Art Reaume.

The Police Association retained James S. Allan, K.C., as their solicitor. Magistrate Angus W. MacMillan, serving as the police commission chair at the time of the probe, had replaced Judge Gordon the previous month.

There was substantial newspaper coverage during the days leading up to the probe. Citizens who had any information about corrupt police dealings were asked to come forward.

---

577 Pelissier – Illegal gambling house operated in plain sight.

Heightened media and provincial scrutiny during the probe did little to slow down the drinking, prostitution and gambling in Windsor's dens of iniquity. The following quotes appeared in the March 14, 1950 edition of *The Windsor Daily Star*: "The devil himself lacks the persistency, defiance, the outright gall of bordello and bootleg operators…The open defiancy displayed in Windsor's tenderloin districts still goes unchallenged by cities of comparable size…There was a meaty influx of American Army personnel in the city and the solicitous women in bars enjoyed a veritable field day."

Rumours circulated throughout the city of a secret witness list, which supposedly included the names of several Windsor and provincial policemen. The Windsor Daily Star reported Chief of Police Claude Renaud, Deputy Chief W.H. Neale, Magistrate Hanrahan and the infamous Joe Assef were among those scheduled to take the stand.

Yet for all the hype leading up to it, the hastily assembled Windsor Police Commission probe revealed very little. The 16 policemen denied having any connection to Joe Assef and his bootleg liquor and Police Chief Claude Renaud was convinced of the loyalty and moral righteousness of every man on his force.

After rough treatment while on the stand from the three-man commission, Hanrahan told reporters "the attitude that has been shown to me here as a magistrate does not augur well for the treatment that would be given to the public who may appear here to give evidence."

Despite the provincial and public heat, the Windsor Police Department appeared to be getting a break. The probe wrapped up on April 15, when Gordon made a motion to adjourn. Bell went on the record saying Hanrahan's statements regarding moral laxity were "exaggerated" and "unjust."

The Mayor
Although Art Reaume's political career in Windsor lasted until 1967, his reputation was never the same after the police commission probe. Some of the only salient information revealed during the probe was in relation to Reaume's character, which, until the allegations of moral laxity against the police force, had been considered unassailable.

On the day before the probe it was revealed that Reaume had met privately with four members of the police association two nights earlier urging them to convince the police force to endorse a resolution denouncing Hanrahan's allegations of moral laxity – the very allegations he was appointed to investigate.

The police force, surprisingly, turned down Reaume's proposed resolution by a 74 to 12 margin. Instead, they issued a statement of complete confidence in Chief Renaud and Deputy Chief Neale.

Reaume vehemently denied the story told by the officers, saying only that he had met with four officers to advise them that no statement should be made during the course of the probe, but it was within the police association's rights to seek counsel to protect their name.

"The mayor was an ex-officio member of the police commission board," explains Kulisek. "If it wasn't a statutory provision for the mayor to be on the board, he would have been kicked off. It didn't work out well for (Reaume). The probe tarred him with the brush as well."

On the second day of the probe, Mrs. James Shearon, a Windsor Avenue resident, stood up in the large gallery and made an unscheduled allegation. She claimed Mayor Reaume had accepted graft, in the form of "hush money" from her brother, a slot machine operator, in 1933 when Reaume was Mayor of Sandwich. Reaume's only response was that Mrs. Shearon and her brother would have to appear on the stand and make the allegations public before any action could be taken.

Mayor-In-Waiting
It was several years after the Windsor police scandal that the important role Albert Howard "Bert" Weeks played was revealed.

A watch repairman and jewellery shop owner, Weeks formed the Citizens Action Committee which pressured the municipal and provincial governments to investigate "police indifference to widespread lawbreaking in Windsor."

Weeks met secretly with OPP officers in Detroit on several occasions to pass on information regarding Windsor police corruption.

Taken back to Toronto, the information lead directly to Attorney General Dana Porter's scathing report on policing in Windsor.

Weeks ran with his success, gaining public office as an alderman in 1954.

After an unsuccessful attempt at provincial office, Weeks was again elected to Windsor city council in 1965. In 1975 he was elected Mayor of Windsor, serving through 1982. His fiscal responsibility was often met with derision, but his three terms as mayor marked a period of prosperity and balanced, conscientious spending at City Hall.

A Tale of Two Mayors: Art Reaume's (left) career was tarred with the scandal brush. Bert Weeks' (right) three terms as mayor marked a period of prosperity and balanced, conscientious spending at City Hall.

The Report
Six months had passed since the probe. Renaud and Neale remained as the city's top cops. Magistrate MacMillan and Judge Gordon continued on as top police commissioners. With the exception of a few crack downs and raids at certain bookie joints, Windsor's gambling, bootlegging and sex trades continued unabated.

Then, on September 14, 1950, a report from provincial inspectors, Frank Kelly and W.H. Lougheed, based on Bert Weeks' information, was released by Attorney General Porter. It was a scathing denunciation of police work in Windsor. It called for "round-the-clock" morality policing, an increase of 50 police constables, and an immediate end to the vice trade in Windsor.

"Most of the troubles of the Windsor police department can be laid on the doorstep of the morality detail," the report read. "It is difficult to understand why the executive officers should permit this important phase of law enforcement to become neglected and undermanned, especially since the whole administration has been under fire repeatedly in the press..."

The provincial inspectors made six recommendations:

1. A permanent morality squad should be created and put under the direction of an inspector. It should be adequately staffed to provide 24-hour morality policing and raiding parties.
2. That members of the morality squad be carefully selected from the force and paid a wage equal to the detective force.
3. That the police headquarters be enlarged to accommodate more staff. Sub stations were to be built to patrol the city's south east side.
4. That 50 additional constables be added to the force immediately.
5. That the chief and deputy chief be required to give written reports of their activities to the police commission board.
6. That the police beats in the city's business section be revamped so foot constables are directly responsible for locked-up property.

The Windsor Daily Star published the complete text of the condemning OPP report in a two-page spread.

The Resignations
Immediately upon the release of the provincial report, Magistrate MacMillan and Judge Gordon resigned from the police commission, eager to protect their courtroom reputations. The Windsor Crown Attorney, E.C. Awrey, was removed.

Windsor Police Association President Gilbert Ouellette resigned too, but said it was not connected to the probe and the "shake-up."

Windsor Police Chief Claude Renaud: forced to retire due to "massive incompetence"

AXED
Magistrate Angus W. MacMillan and Judge Albert J. Gordon resigned from the police commission.

Windsor Police Association President Gilbert Ouellette resigned, but said it was not connected to the probe and the "shake-up."

The Windsor Crown Attorney, E.C. Awrey, was removed as well.

Chief Claude Renaud and Deputy Chief W.H. Neale, both with over 30 years of service with the force, forced to "retire." Both men were given full pension rights.

Less than three weeks later, the newly formed police commission, now under the direction of local businessman Lt.-Col. Roland Harris and Judge Archibald Cochrane, met for the first time and called Chief Renaud to the stand.

Renaud was immediately singled out for massive incompetence when it was revealed through questioning that he knew very little about the operations of his own department, particularly the beefed up morality squad.

Renaud, who was warned several times about smoking cigarettes while being questioned, told the commission the morality squad was Deputy Chief Neale's territory, which was in direct contradiction to policies laid out in the provincial recommendations. Renaud also had officers remove identification numbers from their uniforms.

Mayor Reaume, still an ex-officio member of the commission, attempted to defend his Chief, but his efforts were for naught.

Further investigation of the activities of the top cops revealed Neale was the owner of the Police Equipment Company which sold $2,500 worth of police equipment to the City of Windsor on an annual basis.

Under oath, Renaud denied any knowledge of Neale's interests in Police Equipment Co. but there was ample evidence to the contrary.

On October 25, Chief Renaud and Deputy Chief Neale, both with over 30 years of service with the force, were forced to "retire." Both men were given full pension rights.

Mayor Reaume also denied any knowledge of Neale's connection to the company and let his highest ranking policemen take the fall. OPP Inspector Edwin McNeill was appointed as interim chief.

Within days, the Windsor Police Scandal of 1950 was nowhere to be found in the newspapers, all but forgotten and left for historians to quibble about the details.

"The police scandal was part of a general drive for reform and moral purification in Windsor," says Kulisek. "The 'full disclosure' policies of the 1950s were meant to help in municipal healing."

It was in the wake of the scandal that Windsor's municipal government was reformed to include a city manager or chief administrator. In a backlash against Mayor Reaume, the ward system was adopted, ending a tradition of at-large politics.

A tradition that didn't die is that of the public expecting a certain level of ethical behavior from elected municipal officials and city administrators. It took a gutsy, would-be mayor and the province's intervention to get the mess straightened out 60 years ago.

The Great Bank Robbery of '59

by Currie Bednarick, Issue #21 February 2002

Little do the patrons of a local hair salon know they are being pampered in a building that was the site of a real cops-and-robbers drama.

June 9th, 1959 was an unforgettable day to anyone who lived in or near the Bank of Montreal at Chilver and Wyandotte in Olde Walkerville. Two men, Nicholas Hamilton (alias McCormick) of Vancouver and Kenneth Irwin of Toronto, wearing white jackets, hoods, and sunglasses, entered the bank that afternoon, armed and ready to get their black-gloved hands on some easy cash.

Adele Paré, a local housewife, was making a withdrawal when one of the men thrust a gun into her back and grabbed her, exclaiming, "This is a stickup. Do as we say or you'll get it, and we mean it."

The men forced her and another customer into a corner of the vault along with the bank's 15 employees. The chief clerk, Norman Wingrover, tripped the alarm along the way. The three female tellers were robbed of a total of $10,733 before the pair attempted to make their getaway.

The first officer to arrive at the scene was Const. Brian Pickup. He had spent eight years as a policeman in his native England before moving to Windsor and joining the force in 1957. Forty years later, Pickup can still recall the incident quite clearly. "A call came over the radio saying there was a robbery at the bank. When I got there a large group of people had gathered around the building."

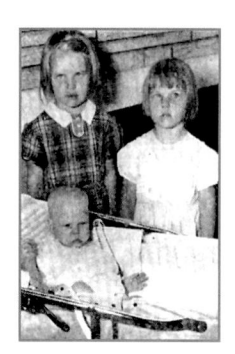

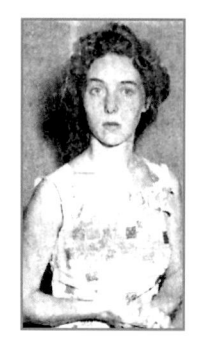

He had only seconds to take in the scene. "As I got to that block, I saw a woman with her hands in the air, and then a man with a bag in one hand and a gun in the other. I didn't draw my gun because a stray bullet could have gone into the crowd."

Instead, Pickup lunged for the robber, Nicholas Hamilton, throwing him over his shoulder onto the sidewalk and kneeling on him to hold him down until the other officers arrived.

Unfortunately, he was unable to see inside the bank, and assumed that the man he was holding captive had been working alone; that mistake could have cost him his life.

"The second man came out and I heard a shot." He was hit! The bullet slammed into his back, exited his stomach and went into his knee, but still he held onto his catch.

Pickup emphasizes the names of the officers who came to his assistance and arrested the shooter, Kenneth Irwin.

"Constables Washbrook and Rowley saw that the man was going to shoot me again, and shot at him;" a gun fight ensued. Washbrook and Rowley fired from behind the back of a station wagon as their

---

Top: Neighbours mill around the scene of the crime at Chilver and Wyandotte
Left: Constable Brian Pickup shortly before the robbery; Pickup's wife Vera and kids; Vera was told her husband would probably not live.

202 • crime in the city

One of the bullets took out a tail light on a nearby parked car.

In January 2002, retired Constable Brian Pickup revisited the scene where he was gunned down.

assailant returned their shots from the other. Approximately six shots were fired (one of them smashing a car's tail light) before Irwin finally gave up, lowering his weapon. Pickup held onto Hamilton and they arrested him as well.

After the incident, an inspection of the getaway car resulted in the discovery of a suitcase in the back seat containing another gun. The car had been stolen in Kingston a week earlier, just after the thieves had been released from Kingston Penitentiary.

Brian Pickup was taken to Metropolitan Hospital where he endured a four-hour operation. His wife, Vera, kept a vigil at the hospital as he fought for his life. "He wasn't supposed to live through the night," she told reporters a few days after the incident.

He did make it through the night, however, and made a full recovery after seven weeks in the hospital, and another six at home. He recalls his recovery time clearly as well. "It was incredibly difficult, since my weight went down from 180 pounds to 118. It was quite a while before I could walk and drive again." The only repercussion from his injuries is a bit of stiffness in his one knee. All in all, he says, "I think I came out pretty good."

Nicholas Hamilton (charged as McCormick) was sentenced to 15 years in the Kingston Penitentiary. Kenneth Irwin, the shooter, was sentenced to 25; he died of natural causes in prison five years later.

A year later and fully recovered, Pickup received a letter from Ottawa, marked "Confidential." He didn't notice the three letters that followed his name until he opened the envelope.

"I have the pleasure of informing you that Her Majesty the Queen has been graciously pleased to approve my recommendation of the award to you of the British Empire Medal for Gallantry in recognition of your bravery. In accordance with Section XXXVI of the Royal Warrant instituting the British Empire Medal, you are now entitled to have placed after your name the letters B.E.M."

The letter was signed by Canada's Secretary of State, Leon Balcer – the first British Empire Medal awarded to a Canadian police officer.

"I was surprised," Pickup states simply. "All I knew was that I had been recommended for a police medal."

Did the award affect the way he was treated by his co-workers? "Not really, but I did get a lot of support from the other officers."

The incident, he says also, didn't change the outlook of his profession. Pickup remained on the force until 1988, when he retired and became a travel agent, a job he's still enjoying today. Two of his daughters work in central records for the Windsor Police.

Pickup held onto the bullet that had travelled through his body until just two months before this article was written.

Special thanks to Joan Urie, one of the tellers involved in the robbery, who provided us with news clippings about that fateful day. She recalls a big gun in her face and the words "Move or I'll shoot!" She, along with 14 other bank employees and two customers were herded into the vault until help arrived.

1st Fallen Officer in Windsor's History

On May 5, 2006, Constable John Atkinson was shot and killed while questioning two suspicious teenagers he observed at a convenience store in the city's east end. This was the first murder of an officer in the line of duty in the 120-year history of the Windsor Police Department.

Thousands of mourners attended Windsor's largest funeral along with dozens of RCMP in their red formal uniforms and hundreds of blue-clad police officers from across Canada and the United States. All wore black armbands with Atkinson's badge number – 6744.

Constable Atkinson had served with the agency for 15 years. He is survived by his wife and two young children, shown here by his coffin.

Photo: Spike Bell, PPA Certified, M. Photog., M.P.A.

The Slasher

by Melanie E. Namespetra, Issue # 48, October, 2004

The sentence of this court upon you, Ronald George Sears, is that you are to be taken from here from whence you came and there to be kept in close confinement until Tuesday, the third day of December, 1946; upon that day you will be taken to the place of execution and there be hanged by the neck until you are dead, and may God have mercy upon your soul.

In fewer than ten minutes on 3 December 1946, a Windsor, Ontario man was sentenced to hang for the murder of Sergeant Hugh Blackwood Price, committed in August 1945. This was for one of two charges for murder, and of three for attempted murder that were yet to be tried.

Two long summers of panic ended in the city. Men had been attacked and stabbed late at night around Dieppe Park, known then as Government Park. These stabbings first occurred in the immediate aftermath of WWII when stories of the European front continued to dominate media attention; the first attempted stabbing received little attention in the *Windsor Daily Star*, the community's prime news source at the time.

On 23 July 1945, the first stabbing occurred when victim George Mannie received two deep stab wounds in his back while walking at Government Park. A few weeks later, on 8 August 1945, a second stabbing attack resulted in the death of fifty-six year old Frank Scigeslski. He was stabbed seven times in the back and his backside was repeatedly slashed by a knife. Immediately following his attack on 16 August 1945, a night watchman named William Davies was beaten to death while on guard at work on his midnight shift at the downtown G. Easton Tate Garage. This murder was at first attributed to the 'Slasher' but was soon disregarded by police as connected because different motives and methods became clear. Lastly, on 17 August 1945, Sergeant Hugh Blackwood Price was attacked on the grassy grounds near where the current CBC Broadcasting station stands; he was stabbed 14 times in the back. The *Star* immediately dubbed the attacker "the Windsor Slasher" for his compulsive slashing of victim's clothes and bodies.

Windsor police detectives increased the amount of men on duty by 50 percent as a result of these serial attacks and murders. With the aid of the Ontario Provincial Police, dragnets were conducted on all roads leaving the city and the search for suspects was extended as far as Chatham; every car was searched. Police rounded up several suspects but none were charged due to lack of tangible evidence. Due to all the publicity allotted to the stabbings in the *Star*, a panic ensued in the city, which escalated throughout the remainder of the summer of 1945. A note found scribbled on a men's washroom stall in the Detroit-Windsor International Tunnel, claimed to be written by the 'Slasher,' stated that the next

---

Above: A Windsor detective checks the crime scene on August 8th, 1945, where Frank Scigeslski, one of the Slasher's victims, was found near Crawford and Riverside Drive, (now CBC TV and radio).
Photo courtesy Windsor Police.

victim would be female. Rumours then spread throughout the city that two young girls were found murdered in Amherstburg and that a radio announcer was killed in Jackson Park. At least ten people were rumoured to have been killed by the 'slasher' in one weekend.

Despite the Police Department's exhaustive efforts at capturing a killer, they did not have any concrete evidence to charge any one suspect. After the third murder, the attacks ended and the case went cold. Other pressing issues such as the Ford Strike of 1945 overwhelmed police and they concentrated their efforts and manpower to ensure that the city remained clear of labour strife and any possible related incidents of violence.

Summer of '46 brought further unexpected stabbings; it seemed that the killer from the previous summer had returned. On 24 June 1946 Alexander Voligny was stabbed by a man while walking at the waterfront. Two weeks later on 5 July 1946, city resident Joseph Geleneser was also stabbed while at a waterfront park. The police resurrected the 1945 'Slasher' case file and City Council doubled the $1000 reward offered by the *Star* the previous summer in an effort to capture this serial attacker. Once again police hours were increased but they still did not have any concrete leads to help them solve this case until they published a photograph of the weapon found lodged in the back of a surviving victim.

The 'Slasher' was finally arrested on 6 July 1946 on a report of suspicion by the killer's sister-in-law. Mrs. Dorothy Sears reported to police that the knife used in the stabbings and held by a police officer in the photo was similar to one she was missing. She believed her brother-in-law to have had it in his possession last.

Eighteen-year-old Ronald George Sears was taken into custody and shortly afterward made four separate, yet different, confessions to Windsor Police detectives about the stabbings and murders.

Following detention by police, Sears confessed to murdering two men and attempting to murder three others. He claimed in each case that the men he stabbed were sexual perverts and suspected homosexuals and that they had made unwanted sexual advances while he was walk-

Windsor Police Inspector Dave Rossell with clippings about the Slasher, including a court sketch (the only likeness available) on view at the Windsor Police Museum. (by appointment only) photo: E. Weeks

ing in the parks. With only his confession and one eyewitness account, his trial date was set for 11 September 1946, and at the opening of the trial Sears denied all charges against him. Hesitantly the judge deemed his confession admissible, and proceeded with a jury. Despite only one week of trial, circumstantial evidence, and expert witnesses and testimonies, the jury rendered a guilty verdict in less than two hours. Immediately following their decision, the judge sentenced Sears to be executed within months. This would have been the last execution in the city but Sears appealed his case immediately following the decision.

While Sears awaited his death sentence, the Ontario Court of Appeals decided that his confession should not have been considered admissible and granted him another trial; this time he was charged solely on one count of attempted murder for which they had sufficient tangible evidence to charge him. By February, 1947, Sears' original verdict was overturned. He was retried and sentenced to a mere twelve years in prison. After serving his sentence, he died in an institution.

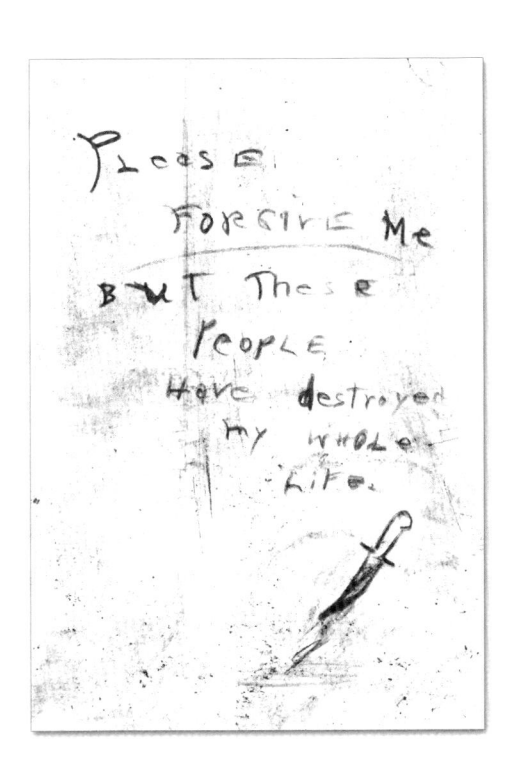

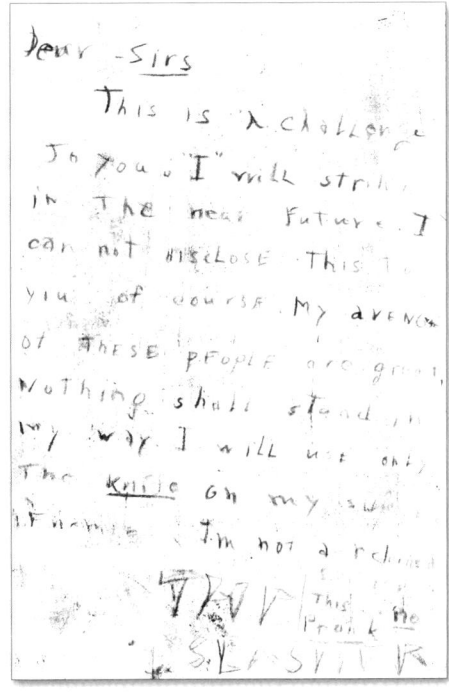

Front and back of a letter mailed to Windsor Police headquarters by Ronald George Sears, the "Slasher," written four months prior to his arrest:

"Dear Sirs, This is a challenge to you. 'I' will strike in the near future. I can not disclose this to you of course. My avenge of these people are great. Nothing shall stand in my way. I will use only the knife on my supposed enemies. I'm not a returned solider. This is no prank. The Slasher

Please forgive me but these people destroyed my whole life."

(The grey cast on the pages is from finger printing dust used by the police in a fruitless attempt to lift one of the Slasher's prints.)

5
The Mysterious & the Disastrous

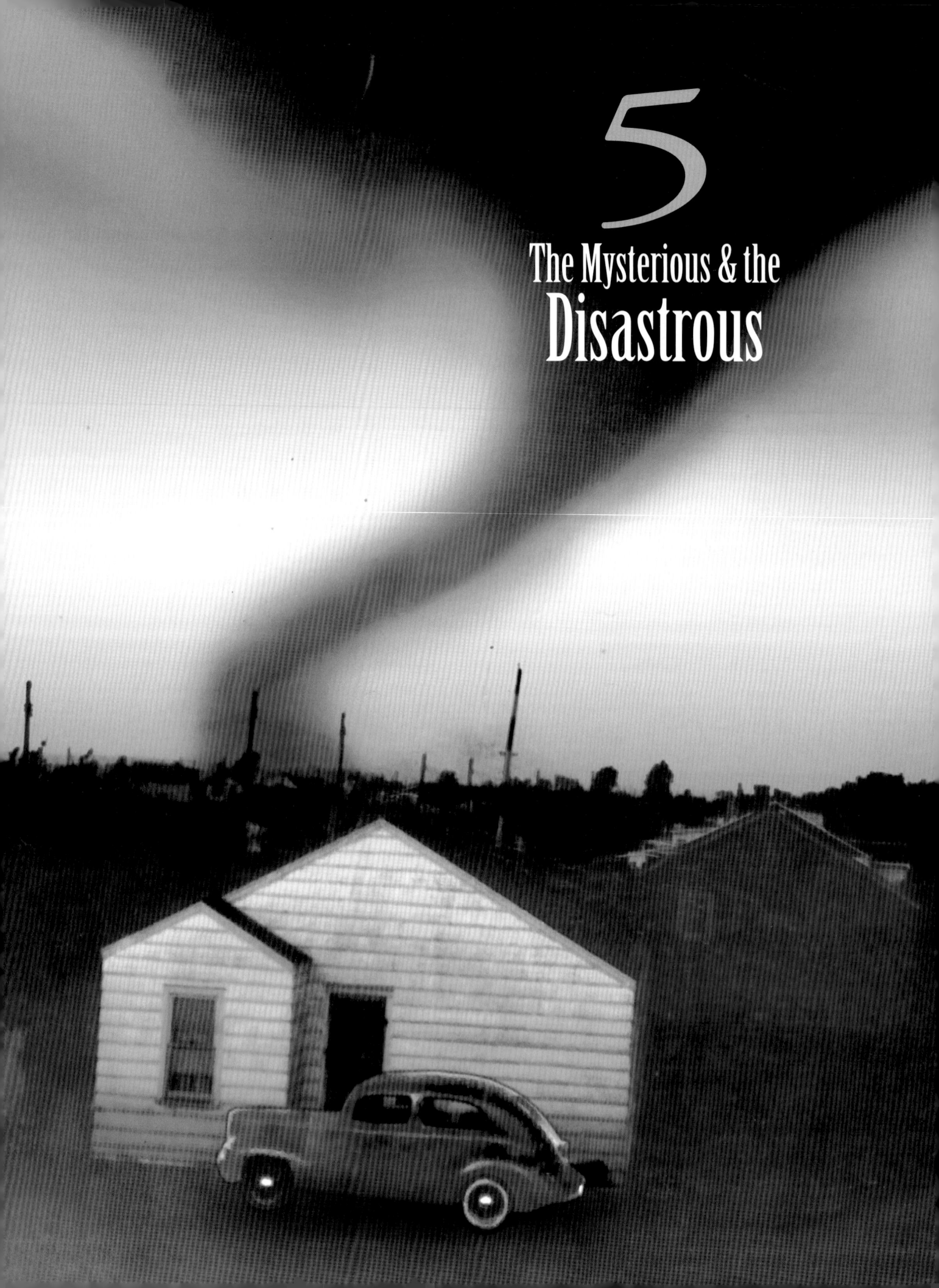

the Curse of Peche Island

by Elaine Weeks, Issue #18, October 2001

The little island lies just offshore in the Detroit River, about two kilometres east of Belle Isle. Possibly you've noticed its calming greenness as you hurry to work along Riverside Drive. Maybe you've been curious enough to have motored across the water in your boat to explore it. Perhaps you might even remember when the island was supposed to have been developed into everything from a swanky housing development to an amusement park and have wondered why those plans fell through.

According to descendants of the French family which once settled the island for almost 100 years, there is a good reason why Peche Island, also known as Peach Island, only a five minute boat ride from Windsor, is today a virtual wilderness: it has a curse on it.

The Native Legend

Before delving into the story of the curse, it is worthwhile to reflect on the fascinating Native Canadian legend describing how Peche Island was formed from *Legends of Detroit, Marie Watson Hamlin, 1884:*

The spirit of the Sand Mountains on the eastern coast of Lake Michigan had a beautiful daughter whom he feared would be stolen away. To guard against this, he kept her floating in the lake inside a wooden box tethered to the shore.

The South, North and West Winds battled over this maiden, throwing up a huge storm. The girl drifted away and washed up at the shore of the Prophet, the Keeper of the Gates of the Lakes, at the outlet of Lake Huron. He was happy to find the beautiful castaway.

The Winds soon found her again and teamed up to destroy the Prophet's lodge. The maiden, the box, parts of the lodge and the Prophet were swept into the water and drifted through Lake St. Clair to the Detroit River. The remnants of the box formed Belle Isle and the old Prophet was lodged further upstream to form Peche Island.

The French Connection

On the earliest French maps of this region, the island was named either Isle au Large, or Isle du Large. Possible meanings include "at a distance," since Peche Island is the farthest island upstream from Detroit before entering Lake St. Clair or, "keep your distance," because of dangerous shallows on the north side.

The island was next called some variation of Peche Isle, including Isle aux Pecheurs and Isle a la Peche, the French word for fish – the island was once used as a fishing station.

In 1789, what is now Ontario was divided into five administrative districts for the regulation of the land. The Board of the Land Office for the Windsor region needed title to the island, which was mostly in the hands of the Indians in order to issue land grants. A treaty with the Indians was accomplished in 1790 for lands in the western Ontario peninsula, but it excluded Peche Island possibly because the Ottawas, Chipewas, Pottawa-tomies and Hurons who signed the treaty wished to retain the island as a fishing ground.

Local businessmen possibly did not notice that Peche Island was not among the lands transferred to the Crown and began petitioning for grants for the land. Alexis Maisonville was among them and it seems that he eventually obtained some sort of title to the island and it even became known as Maisonville's Island for a time.

Perhaps the first permanent residents of the island were a French Canadian family named Laforet dit Teno. Evidence suggests that the family moved to the island somewhere between 1800 and 1812 and possibly earlier – an entry in surveyor John A. Wilkinson's notebook for December 27, 1834 says the family had been living on the island for 34 years.

Irvin Hansen Dit Laforet, a descendant, believes the family settled the island even earlier. In his article, "Peche Island: Occupancy and Change of Ownership 1780-1882" he describes how Jean Baptiste Laforest was granted the island in 1780 for his service in the British military as a guide and interpreter and for his family's steadfast support of the Crown. (No deed was ever found, however, nor was there any evidence of a grant recorded in the land office).

Jean moved to the island with his wife and his five-year-old son Charles. Jean built a homestead to verify his claim and passed the title onto Charles. In January 1781, Jean Mary Laforest was the first Laforest to be born on Peche Island. They had seven other children.

Apparently, they shared the island with a group of local natives who occupied the western portion, keeping the eastern side for themselves. According to Laforest family legend, Jean bartered with the natives to gain ownership of the island, closing the deal with the exchange of some livestock. The Laforest family lived on the island confident of their ownership for almost 100 years.

By 1834, Charles and Oliver Laforet (the 's' had been dropped by this time) maintained their large families on the island. At that time about 25 acres had been fenced and were under cultivation. The settlers had constructed a house and a barn, but there is no further information about their petition for a grant to the island.

In 1857, Peche Island was finally transferred to the Crown by the Chippewa Indians, but there was no great rush to acquire grants perhaps because local people believed that the island legally belonged to the Laforet family.

Benjamin Laforest was involved in a lawsuit with Hiram Walker over ownership of land on Peche Island.

In 1868, someone did attempt to purchase it, but because of the belief that it belonged to the Laforet family, no further action was taken.

"They and their ancestors, having been in possession for a long series of years, and having always regarded the place as their home, and considered that they would be awarded at least squatters' privileges in respect of the said Island. ...the island may if sold, be sold to the said Laforet or Teno family, provided they are willing and able to pay a fair price therefore."
Essex County Council, Minutes, June 1868 – June 1873

The last Laforest on the island were Leon (Leo) Laforest and his wife Rosalie Drouillard.

Leo was the grandson of Jean Baptiste and had been born on the island in 1819. He and Rosalie, who had been born on Walpole Island and was the daughter of a Native interpreter, had 12 children, the last being born in 1880.

They raised livestock, grew crops and engaged in commercial fishing. Rosalie supplemented their income by weaving straw hats and selling them in Detroit.

When a deed for the land could not be found, Leo staked out four acres in 1867 when it became part of Canada. He paid taxes on this property until he died in 1882.

In 1870, Benjamin and Damase Laforest, cousins of Leo had entered into an agreement with a local Windsor businessman named William G. Hall concerning commercial fishing. Benjamin filed a quit claim deed at the local township office giving him squatter's rights.

Many years later, an affidavit confirmed that Leo LaForest had agreed orally to the commercial fishing contract, but he had never signed his name to anything. Hall applied for a land patent of 106 acres in 1870, which included the whole island except for Leo's four acres. Hall eventually received title to the island, minus the four acres for a payment of $2,900 to the Crown.

After Hall's death in 1882, his executor advertised that Hall's estate would sell the island, with fishing privileges and this sale raised the question of title.

Hiram Walker's sons purchased the property from the Hall estate on July 30, 1883, as a summer home for their father. Benjamin Laforet filed a claim on the 1st of August stating that he and his brother Damase had a one-third interest in a certain parcel of land that was described in the patent from the Crown to Hall.

The case was settled and the Hall Estate was authorized by the Supreme Court of Canada to give the Laforets a one-third share of the $7000 that Walker's sons paid the estate.

Leo Laforet died on September 26th of that year. According to the Laforet descendants, a group of Walker's men forced their way into Rosalie's home and made her and the oldest boys sign the deed over to the Walkers. In Laforest's article, he writes, "They (Walker's men) threw $300 on the table and told Rosalie to be out by spring of 1883."

That winter, while Rosalie and her family were away in Detroit on business, someone came onto their property and ruined the winter stores. Because Rosalie was knowledgeable in the ways of the Natives, they were able to survive until spring.

Hiram Walker had canals dug on Peche Island, allowing boats to bring in supplies and ensure the flow of fresh water. photo Chris Edwards

When it was time to leave, Rosalie got down on her knees and cursed the Walkers and the island. "No one will ever do anything with the island!" were her apparent words.

Walker's Folly?

Despite his sons' hopes that he would use the island as a retirement spot, Hiram Walker occupied himself for many years attempting to develop it. For five years, he had canals dug to allow boats to bring in supplies and to ensure the flow of fresh water through the island from Lake St. Clair. Two yachts were purchased – the "Pastime" and the "Lurline" for travelling to the island from Walker's office and for cruises and parties on the river and lakes.

Walker built what has been described as either a 54-room or 40-room mansion. He planted hundreds of trees, put in an orchard, and built a green house to cultivate flowers. He also put in a golf course, stables a carriage house and installed a generator for electric lights.

It was widely thought that this was no summer "home" for Walker but an attempt on his part to create a resort. The only problem was, his intended market, the society people of Detroit, all went to nearby Belle Isle.

The Curse Takes Hold

Willis Walker, Hiram's son and a lawyer who had handled the purchase of the island, died soon afterwards at the tender age of 28.

Hiram did not enjoy the island for long. In June of 1895, he transferred the land to his daughter Elizabeth Walker Buhl because of ill health. (Apparently, she was not a benevolent Walker; legend has it that she did not let the locals pick the island's abundant peach crop, as had been the case for many years. She had them dumped into the river; the locals came in boats to scoop them up).

Hiram was quite ill while he worked on his Peche Island project, suffering a minor stroke before dying in 1899.

Edward Chandler Walker died relatively young in 1915. Prohibition caused embarrasment for Walker sons and grandsons who were American but operating a Canadian based distillery. They didn't want to be seen as bootleggers so they sold their father's empire in 1926, only 60 years after he established it.

Hiram Walker & Sons distillery was purchased by Toronto's Cliff Hatch in 1926 ending the Walker dynasty. The Walker family leaves Walkerville and abandons the town their father founded in 1858. Some remain in the Grosse Point area. At the time of amalgamation with Windsor in 1935, no Walkers lived in Walkerville.

Curse Affects Island Development

Elizabeth Buhl sold the island to the Detroit and Windsor Ferry Company in 1907. At that time, the president of the company, Walter E. Campbell stated that the island would be made into "one of the finest island summer resorts in America," and that "the big house... at the upper end of the island... has 40 rooms and will be easily converted into a temporary pavilion at least" according to the Detroit News, November 11th, 1907.

Mr. Campbell apparently died in the home on the island that same year. The property fell into a state of disrepair. In 1929, the house burned to the ground. Some say a huge lightning bolt hit it.

Needless to say, nothing ever came of Campbell's plans to create a park on the island. Although the island still legally belonged to the Detroit, Belle Isle and Windsor Ferry Company and, after 1939, to its successor the Bob-Lo Excursion Company, the island remained deserted except for picnickers, young lovers and probably rumrunners during prohibition in the 1920s and 30s.

It is believed that the Bob-Lo Company bought the island to deter development of another Bob-Lo Island (an island further down the river near Amherstburg that had was developed as an amusement park until the latter part of the last century).

Peche Island was so neglected that as late as 1955, the employee who guarded the island for the Bob-Lo Company spent his spare time there fishing for sturgeon, trapping muskrats, and hunting ducks.

Despite vigorous efforts by local groups to have the island purchased by some government agency for use as a park, the Bob-Lo Co. retained the island until 1956 when it was sold to Peche Island Ltd. Their plans included filling the island's water lot in to create a residential area. With this aim in view, the remains of the Walker house were removed in 1957.

The scheme was abandoned that same year, reportedly because of a lack of suitable landfill. Local rumour has it that the plan was in some way connected to the fact that Detroit was short of space for a garbage dump.

Other proposals for the island followed quickly but nothing concrete happened until 1962, when Detroit lawyer and investor E. J. Harris purchased it. His plan included dredging the canals and creating a ski hill and protective islands. A few years later, Sirrah Ltd. purchased the island and its water lot. This despite strong resistance by many Windsor delegations and groups who wished to see the island turned into a public park. Under the direction of E. J. Harris, Sirrah planned and actually began work on an extremely elaborate park area for the island. He constructed several buildings and sewage, hydro, water and telephone were connected to the mainland. The project operated for one season with ferry boats from Dieppe Park and barges from Riverside. Due to financial difficulties and mismanagement, Sirrah declared bankruptcy in 1969. He also lost the 50-acre Greyhaven estate in Detroit.

R. C. Pruefer of Riverside Construction purchased the island around that time with the view of developing it into a residential area or commercial recreation park that would have included a marina but due to financial restrictions and other commitments, was forced to sell the island.

In 1971, due to tremendous lobbying by various local conservationist groups, the island was purchased by Government Services with the department of Lands and Forest as the managing agency. The island

The ruins of Hiram Walker's Peche Island mansion. photo Chris Edwards

was also to be used by nature study students. The government planned to spend a couple of million dollars on nature trails, picnic shelters, etc. but there were no funds. In 1974, the property was designated a provincial park for administrative and budget purposes.

Currently the island is a Windsor municipal park, and the city has no immediate plans to develop it, apart from bathroom facilities. Other than part of the foundation of Hiram Walker's home, a bridge, some dried up canals and a piles of old bricks here and there, it is pretty much the way it was before the Laforets were forced off the island.

Perhaps Rosalie's curse came true.

Curse Caused by Conniving Conspirators

In one of your website archives, I came across the story on "The Curse of Peche Island." I have known about this story for ages through my own family history. The Laforets, who were forced off the island by Hiram Walker, were my ancestors and Leo's great granddaughter, Rose Laforet, was my great grandma. To be honest, I'm glad Rosalie cursed the Walkers because, from what I was told, Walker threatened them by telling them to either leave or be murdered. I'm glad the island remains undisturbed to this day because I'm sure the Walker family, along with Hiram Senior, got what they deserved after they all passed on.
Ryan Gauthier, e-mail

From the Editor:
The Curse of Peche Island is a very intriguing story but I have a feeling, based on the research we have on Hiram Walker, that he wasn't responsible for the mistreatment of Rosalie and her family. I don't think that Hiram realized exactly what was going on – if he had, he wouldn't have stood for it.

It's possible that his sons may have been overzealous in their efforts to encourage Hiram to retire from the business so they could run it and were seriously intent on taking control of the island so he could enjoy it as a retirement spot. Work was all Hiram knew however, which is most likely why, rather than take it easy, he decided to create a resort on the island.

Peche Island Query

I enjoyed reading "The Curse of Peche Island" article. For years I have been going over there with friends and family. No one that I know has ever seen a picture of what the main house looked like on the Island! Just wondering if you have seen a picture and if so it would be great for all to see.
Garry, via email

Editors Note: Sorry, we don't have a picture of the house; it was on the island for only a short time before it burned down in 1929, but perhaps there is a picture out there somewhere. We do have a photo of the caretaker's house (above).

Explosion Shattered Essex in 1907

from "The Three R's of Essex – Riches, Rags, Recovery,"
by Evelyn Couch Burns, Revised 2nd Edition, 1982
Issue #38, October 2003

Saturday, August 10th, 1907. At the Canadian Imperial Bank in downtown Essex, eighteen-year-old Edwin Beaman was working his first shift as a teller – a day that would go down in infamy for the townfolk of Essex. The new bank at the main intersection was under the management of J.M. Kairns and was a progressive addition to the bustling little town.

Walking to the post office around 9 a.m., Beaman considered the promise of a very warm day. He thought he heard rifle shots at the nearby Michigan Central Station. Later known as the New York Central, the railway ran through southwestern Ontario, connecting Detroit and Buffalo; the sound of gunfire unnerved him.

"Before the new bank was built, I performed the night watchman duty in the small office that served as a bank until the new one was finished. I slept on a cot with a safe on one side of me and a .38 revolver on the other side, at a salary of 50 cents a night. The town policeman told me that he always met the night train because some shady looking characters sometimes debarked. I was never able to go to sleep until after the train left town and anything that sounded like rifle shots at the station would make me prick up my ears."

At 10 minutes before 10 a.m., Beaman was in the teller's cage, chin on hands, meditating on his new surroundings when the earth seemed to shudder and the plaster ceiling came down in huge chunks. Beaman was protected by his teller's cage; no one in the bank was hurt although one man was nearly buried in a pile of rubble. The force of the blast created a vacuum so great that the window glass was hurled into the bank and then blown back out.

Rear view of the Michigan Central Station in Essex after the great explosion.

Twenty miles away plaster fell from the ceiling and the walls of the Windsor city hall and windows rattled in Detroit. When the dust settled it was learned that a boxcar loaded with 5,000 pounds of nitro-glycerin had exploded at the MC Station, about a quarter of a mile away from the bank. Two men were killed, a quarter of a million dollars worth of property was destroyed, dozens of residents were injured and the town was thrown into a panic. The rifle shots Beaman thought he heard were drops of glycerine on the tracks, exploding as the shunting train ran over them. This is the story of how it happened.

Explosives were being shipped by train to Amherstburg for dredging operations on the Detroit River. The explosives had been brought in on a boxcar on Friday night, to be switched to the Amherstburg train.

The yard crew was "shunting" the cars — coupling them to the other train. David Cottrell, the engineer, and J. Madigan, the fireman, were in the engine. Thomas Berry, the conductor, was standing in front of the station. Leo Conlon was riding on the car containing the explosives, hanging on to the ladder on the north side; Joseph McNary was alongside to give signals to the engineer.

As the trains came together, the contents of one car exploded, probably ignited by a spark on the track. The two young trainmen from Amherstburg were blown asunder. The burned torso of Joseph McNary was found in a crater under the train car. Only pieces of Leo Conlon were found, as far away as 400 feet. Bits of flesh and blood smeared the branches of the elm trees. McNary's right hand was found near Trimble's home and part of his body was found lying by G. J. Thomas' fence, 200 yards north of the railway.

The crater under the car was 20 feet across and 10 to 12 feet deep.

The conductor told reporters, "I saw both my trainmen blown to atoms, just a few feet in front of me. We had noticed the glycerin leaking so we went into the car. Some of the boxes had fallen down so we stood them up again. Conlon and McNary stayed near the car but I went across the street as I did not feel any too safe, even there."

The engineer and the fireman were hurled from the engine. The blast's force knocked down many men and seriously injured others. A horse standing nearby was killed when a piece of rail pierced its body.

As is often the case in disasters, there were many people who by strange coincidence escaped death. A few yards away in the planning mill, George Wyman was turning veranda posts on a lathe. He usually laid the finished posts flat on the floor but he stood them up that morning. When the mill collapsed the posts held up the roof — saving his life.

A barber in his shop two blocks away was shaving a customer when a piece of flying metal broke the razor in his hands. An excursion train from Brantford to Detroit with a crowd of holidayers was due at the station seconds before the explosion. Fortunately it was running late that morning.

The town's doctor, James Brien, who had been ill, died about two hours after the tragedy of natural causes (possibly from shock). So much plaster fell off the walls and ceiling of his home and so many windows were broken, that his funeral was held on his lawn.

The telephone switchboard was operated by Mrs. Flossie and May Cockburn, in the stockroom of the drugstore. Even though May was seriously injured, Flossie stayed on duty for over 13 hours to send help and to answer the continuous calls from worried relatives. Through her efforts a special train from Windsor brought doctors and nurses to aid the injured.

Front view of the Michigan Central Station after 5,000 pounds of nitro-glycerin exploded in 1907, killing two men and causing enormous property damage thoughout Essex.

Back at the bank, Beaman at first thought that the bank was being held up. He ran down to the basement to lock an outside door in order to apprehend the culprit. It was then that he saw a huge black cloud and realized something terrible had happened. The five employees of the bank were required to remain at their place of work and did not learn any details until later in the day.

To restore order, the first task was to board over broken windows to deter looters and keep out rain. A rail had been blown through the boiler of the hydro plant, cutting off electricity; but even without power, business continued somewhat as usual with oil lamps. A glass strike in Europe, the only source of glass at that time, made it necessary for stores to operate windowless and boarded up for weeks after the blast.

Pieces of rail up to two feet long were thrown as far as 1,500 feet. The Methodist Church, the planning mill, grist mill, electricity plant, carriage works, warehouse and elevator, the Michigan Central depot and freight shed, as well as several homes, were completely destroyed.

John McDougall lost his home aand his livery stable and carriage works. A large piece of rail was hurled through the back window of Robert Wolfe's home on Arthur Avenue. It broke through an inside door and landed near the front window. Another two-foot piece of rail landed on the verandah of D.C. Hopgood's home on Irwin Avenue.

Chief Police Robert Wolfe put fourteen constables on duty the day of the blast and throughout the following week.

By early afternoon, Highway 3, then a dirt road from Windsor, was one continuous cloud of dust as good Samaritans rushed to Essex in every conceivable contraption. Later, curiosity seekers crowded into the overburdened town. Since few people were able to return home, accommodations were exhausted and food supplies ran low.

A disgusted reporter from The Windsor Record wrote, "With almost ghoulish glee they searched over lawns for bits of the dead bodies and exhibited anything they might find to the morbid crowd."

Reports by the local newspaper office, dated August 23rd, 1907, described the cause of the explosion. The tubes of dynamite were packed 25 to a box; each boxful of cartridges was required to be wrapped in paraffin paper before being boxed to reduce the danger of concussion, and to prevent seepage if the nitro-glycerine leaked from its absorbent. With one or more of the boxes broken, the tubes of dynamite burst and the liquid was released.

The news story continued: "The inquest into the deaths of Leo Conlon and Joseph McNary will be held at the town hall today (13 days after the explosion). Besides representatives of the MCR and Canadian Railway Commission, the Power Company is expected to be represented by counsel. The Power Company will endeavor to see that the blame is not laid at their doors, while the Railway Company will seek to have themselves blameless."

The account provided much description of the condition and injuries of each victim. The following is an example of the style of reporting at that time: "Mr. Stimers was taken to the hospital Saturday afternoon (note the delay). He suffered internal injuries as he vomited considerably on Sunday and Monday. He has also been suffering from shock but on Monday evening his temperature was normal and condition favourable."

A box car destroyed by the explosion, August 10, 1907

"While his arm was very badly lacerated, the physician states that he will not lose same. Large slivers were taken out of his back. Mr. Stimer's hearing was seriously affected but the attending physicians now hope that he will not lose same; his arm is giving him much pain."

The MCR had been taking dynamite to Amherstburg for a number of years. According to reporters at the Essex Free Press, the crew had seen it leaking at other times and had avoided shunting the cars anymore than absolutely necessary. Officials, according to the report, believed nitro-glycerin simply melted in the heat of that August day. C.E. Naylor, J.H. Carlton and Wallace Ritchie, who said they had seen the explosives dripping from the boxcar, also gave testimony at the hearing.

At the investigation it was established that the dynamite was improperly cured, and the railway was held responsible for careless handling of an explosive. The company was fined $125,000 for money to repair the damage to the town.

Only one month later the town acted as host to a Liberal Party picnic, but some of the buildings were not replaced until the following summer.

Blown Far & Wide

Below: The Royal Hotel Parlour after the explosion

End of break-beam in Laing Ritchie mill	**50 yards**
Corner plate of car found at Coulter's office	**150 yards**
Break-beam at Perry's foundry	**175 yards**
Razor broke in hand of Barber Roberts while at work	**180 yards**
Piece of galvanized car roof blown into Laing & Moore's store	**200 yards**
Piece of switch-block thrown through S. Smith's stock room	**375 yards**
Piece of steel track thrown through E.L. Park's upstairs window, breaking the bedstead	**400 yards**
Piece found on bowling green	**400 yards**
Piece steel rail, 40 lbs., thrown on D.C. Hopgood's verandah	**500 yards**
Piece steel found in J. A. Coulter's meadow	**550 yards**
Piece of steel track found on John Laing's lawn	**600 yards**
Piece of steel rail, 25 lbs., thrown over W. H. Ritchardson's residence, eight blocks away	**700 yards**

1809-1909
Executions in Sandwich

from "The Township of Sandwich Past and Present," by Frederick Neal (1909), Issue #38, October 2003

During the early part of Sandwich's existence as a District or County seat, punishment was dealt out with a liberal hand. In those days the law read "Murderers, horse and sheep thieves shall be hung in some public thoroughfare and remain in full view of passersby until the flesh rot from their bones." It is said that a woman and a man were gibbeted on the brow of the hill near Mill Street and known as Lot 4, East Russell Street (near the Duff-Baby House). The crime for which they are said to have suffered for was murder.

During the time when the office of Sheriff was held by William Hands two young men, both of Chatham, (one coloured and one white), were gibbeted on the brow of the hill on Russell Street, nearly opposite of what is known by the citizens as Cook's Canal. At that time Bedford Street terminated at South Street and the public thoroughfare continued down South Street to Russell, down Russell for a short distance and then gradually ran towards the river until the River Road was reached along by the Pittsburgh Coal Company's dock and fish hatchery at the intersection at McKee Road.

> ...a white horse was seen in the immediate neighbourhood of the gibbets, and next morning, not a sight was to be seen of the bodies...

The iron frames, or "gibbets," consisted of an iron bar, which when placed on the person to be punished reached from the back of the neck to his heels. To this perpendicular bar was clasped an iron ring which clasped the neck, another encircled the waist, while two others firmly held the ankles.

The "gibbets" stood on an elevation overlooking the road. This big-boting made a great commotion in the neighborhood, and the exposed remains became so offensive as to excite the strongest opposition to the law." The dreadful smelling things must be cut down and buried" was the cry. But who was to do it? Such an action would be in defiance of law and might bring unknown severity upon the heads of the people who interfered. There seem to have been few brave enough to attempt the noisome work.

Sheriff Hands was a man of courage and decision, a conspicuous character that rode about mounted on a strikingly white horse.

One dark night during the heat of the argument regarding the occupants of the gibbets, a white horse was seen in the immediate neighbourhood of the gibbets, and next morning not a sight was to be seen of bodies. No arrests were made and the worthy sheriff refused

Condemned men hang in their "gibbets" overlooking the town of Sandwich as a symbol and a warning of how crimes are punished.

to talk on the subject and took no action to discover the person or persons who defied the law.

In 1889, the property on which the bodies of these two men were buried was purchased by Calvin Cook and made into a gravel pit. One day while the labourers were engaged in digging they came upon a quantity of bones and iron frames. The writer, hearing of this discovery, visited the gravel pit and succeeded in saving and securing the complete skeleton of one of the men and the gibbeting irons in which it was enclosed. The discovery and a complete history of the incidents was published in columns of the Windsor Record at that time.

A day or two afterwards, Calvin Cook, the owner of the property, demanded possession of them and the writer very reluctantly gave them up. These "irons" have since passed on to other hands.

The Condemned

As far as can be ascertained all the executions that followed up to the present time (1909) took place at the Sandwich jail, the condemned men being hung by a rope from a scaffold.

A man named "Bird" was hanged in 1834 for killing a peddler in the Long Woods, in Kent County. Bird met his victim in Chatham and followed him to the place where the crime was committed. When arrested he had the peddler's pack with him.

In 1840 a man named Huffman was hanged for murdering his daughter's illegitimate child in Kent County. Huffman was a Methodist preacher and had a beautiful daughter by whom he fathered a child. His child was found drowned in the Thames River.

In 1838 a man named Fitzpatrick was executed for committing an unmentionable crime on a daughter of a prominent family in Amherstburg. He protested his innocence to his last days. Some years after a man named Sellers confessed on his deathbed guilt of the crime for which Fitzpatrick had suffered.

Alfred Young was tried September 27th 1858, and sentenced to be hung on February 20th 1859. Young came with his wife to Windsor from Paw Paw, Michigan, during the fall of 1858. The day of his arrival he wandered with his wife to a lonely back street in Windsor and there shot her to death.

Before the day of his execution, he succeeded in making his escape, it is said, by burning a hole in the floor and then digging his way out from under the building. When he made his escape from prison he left a very sarcastic letter addressed to Sheriff McEwan.

Those familiar with the details of this horrible crime looked upon "the burnt hole in the floor" story with grave suspicion. The hole in the floor would scarcely admit of a child passing through it, and the actions of the jailor in charge at that time were considered not above suspicion and it was openly hinted that he had a hand in the supposed escape.

At any rate a change was made and a new jailor appointed. Young was the first man sentenced to be hanged after the MacKenzie brothers built the new jail and courthouse.

Above: Before and after of an unknown condemned man, being hanged in the town of Sandwich. Photo taken by Frank G. Kiborn, 1313 Sandwich Street E., Windsor. (Windsor Directory 1923-24)

St. John's Cemetery Vandalized

Two hundred-year-old tombstones were damaged during a senseless rampage through St. John's Anglican Church cemetery in Olde Sandwich. About 100 tombstones were toppled during the night hours of Friday, May 23rd, 2003.

One of the damaged tombstones marks the grave of William Hands, a sheriff in the early 1800s (William Hands Secondary School was named for him). Others buried in the cemetery include Alexander Grant, once the President of Upper Canada, and the family of Col. John Prince, often considered the first man of wealth to settle in the area.

Among the tumbled monuments were granite tombstones weighing more than two tons. Others showed evidence of chips and cracks from crowbars and other tools.

There were no witnesses to the devastation, and although the cemetery is located across from a police station and the Windsor jail, the vandals were not deterred from their frenzy. Thanks to efforts from the community, the tombstones have all been repaired.

The distinguished Col. John Prince was laid to rest in St. John's cemetery.

Tornado! 1946

Issue #38, October 2003

It was just after 6 p.m. on June 17th, 1946, when storm-darkened clouds collecting over Southwestern Ontario suddenly broke with all the fury of nature-gone-mad and unleashed death and destruction on the unsuspecting city of Windsor. When the final tally was taken 17 persons were dead, almost 200 injured, and property damage was estimated at half a million dollars. Before the night was done The Windsor Star made plans to meet with the community leaders and thus was born "The Windsor Star Tornado Relief Fund." Calls for aid spider-webbed the continent and when an official report was issued a year later, it showed $231,768.40 had been raised. The money was used to treat the injured, bury the dead and rebuild homes demolished by the maelstrom.

William A. Taylor climbed onto the roof of his home (right) at 2957 Walker Road to snap a shot of the tornado as it approached. In the photo at right, the tornado appears to be in the vicinity at Walker Road and E.C. Row, or possibly even the Walker Farms area. According to Taylor family legend, William retreated from the roof just before the tornado took the back wall and a section of the roof off of his house.

This photo was colourized and featured as our cover image in the October 2003, Issue #38 edition (see page 390).

Tornado Survivor Played Hooky

I am an avid reader, and occasional contributor to your magazine (I supplied the cover picture of Windsor's 1946 tornado, taken by my grandfather, for your "Doom, Disaster, & Destruction," Issue #38, October 2003). As I was anxiously leafing through your 3rd Annual Photo Issue #43, April/May 2004, a certain picture caught my eye. The photo showed a young man standing in front of a destroyed home. That young man is my father, Tom Taylor, who now resides in McGregor, Ontario. I visited him a few days after I had discovered the photo, presented him with a copy of the magazine and showed him the picture.

He recognized it immediately. My mother still has a copy of this photo, albeit now a little ragged and yellowed, which was re-published in the Windsor Star's Centennial Edition in 1967. They were quite pleased to have a new pristine copy of the picture once again.

I asked my father to tell me about the photo and he smiled as he began to tell me his story. It seems that the photo was taken on June 18th, 1946, the day after the tornado had struck. The home was that of the Potvin family, who lived four doors to the north of my father's home in the 2900 block of Walker Road. As you can see, the home was a total loss.

On a humourous note, the day that the picture was taken, my father was suspiciously absent from school (at that time the Ivor Chandler Public School). When questioned about his whereabouts the following day, it seems young Tommy had been quite ill and unable to attend school.

One can only imagine their surprise when both young Tom and his teacher opened the daily newspaper later that evening, only to see the young truant posing for the camera, and not "deathly ill" as he had claimed earlier that day.

To this day, I have not received any information concerning his resulting punishment!

Richard E. Taylor, Windsor

Windsor Twice Engulfed in Flames

excerpts from the Border City Star and Garden Gateway by Neil F. Morrison, Issue #48, October 2004

On the night of December 1, 1867, six months after Confederation, Detroit fireman saved Windsor from being burned flat. It was the most disastrous fire of the century up to that time.

The fire originated in the barn of Thomas Chater, which was consumed within the space of minutes with the loss of two valuable horses and some sporting dogs. Buildings nearby were also ignited. Mr. Chater's hotel, The Great Western Hotel, was burned with little time for saving furniture and bedding, or his hobby of a collection of valuable stuffed birds and rare living ones. His losses were estimated to be $10,000 with only $3,000 of insurance. He had not taken the precaution to insure his large stock of fine liquors in his wine cellar. In addition to his loss he was left with his business temporarily suspended.

Mr. Rolff, a hardware merchant, suffered losses of $8,000 with only $400 insurance. Solomon White, owner of the building occupied by O'Connor and White as a law office, and by the cellars of the Canadian Wine Growers Association, estimated his losses at $9,000, of which $4,000 was covered. Mr. Rice, the cabinet-maker, lost $1,000; Mr. Haggerty the jeweler, about $600.

Windsor Fire Department of 1885.

Much property was stolen during the fire, especially jewellery from the hastily removed stock of Mr. Haggarty. Thieves of both Windsor and Detroit were responsible.

The firemen of both communities were heroes, notably the large number of firefighters who came across the river to help. John Joseph Maurer, hotel and restuarant proprietor, earned the thanks of his fellow citizens by working through the entire night to provide the firefighters with hot coffee and substantial food.

At its next meeting, the town council voted two hundred dollars in gold to reward the visiting firemen. Steps were taken to raise six thousand dollars for the purchase of a new fire engine and hose. Limits also were set within which no future buildings of wood could be erected. This area was defined as Sandwich [Riverside] on the north; Pitt on the south; Church on the west and McDougall on the east.

The little community of Windsor was sadly handicapped for water supply, especially in case of fires. Indeed, according to the Record, a pump on the river front constituted the "water works" of the time. As late as March 1871, water carts still circulated through the streets, selling water for drinking purposes at one New York shilling per barrel.

Windsor's most reliable fire-fighting equipment in the early 1860s was still the bucket brigade. A "goose-neck pump" was purchased, but it failed to work effectively. When placed along the high bank of the Detroit River, the hose was too short to take the water. When moved down to the beach, the suction drew sand with the water. At best, it failed to produce a strong stream. A small, single-storey, frame fire hall, which served as headquarters for the volunteers, stood in a central location on Sandwich Street between McDougall Street and Windsor Avenue, near the Town Hall.

Four years later, the city firemen from across the river responded again; early in the morning of October 12, 1871, Windsor had its biggest fire of all, when 100 buildings were destroyed.

The blaze began at the rear of McGregor's livery stable, northeast corner of Ouellette and Pitt Street. At this hour of heavy sleeping flames can prowl like thieves and cut-throats unnoticed. Before the alarm was given and the firemen responded, a raging inferno was kindled, burning the stable, the bank and the post office. Frame buildings in their path were devoured like heaps of kindling wood. Within half an hour Windsor's fire department was in action, but without a piping system the hoses of the steam fire engine were quite inadequate. The citizens' bucket brigade, feeble enough with one burning building, was absolutely powerless against whole blocks of fire. As promptly as possible, Detroit's fire engines and men rushed across the river by ferry to aid in checking the spread of destruction.

Dawn lighted a dreadful scene of ruined buildings, blackened fire fighters still struggling with the danger, homeless families and broken hopes. Over one hundred buildings were destroyed, wholly or partly. The old Town Hall and a few other brick buildings stood amid the long lines of wreckage. Loss was estimated at $158,000; insurance $68,000.

A major loss was suffered for all future writers of Windsor's story. By a strange freak the town records had been removed from the town hall (which survived the fire) to a printing office to be copied. The printing establishment went up in flames with all of its contents.

As a result, valuable minutes, records of taxes and official documents of all kinds were lost.

A devastating fire destroyed the Jackson Park grandstand in July 1957. The grandstand was the last vestige of the Windsor Jockey Club Racetrack. Named after former Windsor Mayor Cecil Jackson, Jackson Park was once called the Driving Park (fairgrounds) and later the Windsor Jockey Club (1883-1928). The ban against horse racing in Michigan was rescinded in 1933 and brought an end to a profitable sport in Windsor; the site was sold to the city of Windsor for $685,442 in 1928 for park and school purposes. *Photo Jack Renner*

Last One Over!

by Corky Dier Rawson, Issue #18, October 2001

Funny what you remember about the Hallowe'ens of your growing years. It's amazing too, how the people around the block remain in your memory in every detail.

I recall a woman named Hattie McKinley who was always polishing her windows. She cleaned office buildings downtown for a living but on her days off, she liked to look at the world through spotless glass.

She had a daughter Aileen of eighteen years as I recall, and a son Donald who would soon be ten, and Hattie was proud that she'd managed to keep them together through the worst of the Depression with its soup lines and apple stands. Her husband had taken his own life after the crash of '29 and overnight she'd become the head of the family without knowing much about the job.

Monday evening's twilight was beginning to deepen quite swiftly, and Hattie realized with a twinge that not only another winter would soon be upon them, nothing had been done about Donald's birthday on November the first.

He was such a good, thoughtful, tidy boy and with many of the neighbourhood kids in trouble of one kind or another with the police or school authorities, both mother and sister were proud of young Donnie and the way he was growing up – straight and forthright. He was a little overweight, but then he did have a good appetite.

His best friend Sylvester had nicknamed him "Pecker" because of his beakie little nose and a habit of nodding "yes." He swore Donald looked like a woodpecker when he bobbed his head like that, and the kids on the block took it up with relish. "Pecker" he was to be for the rest of his days.

Hallowe'en was on Saturday that year so Donald's birthday would land on Sunday. Hattie rejoiced as it meant she could make him a special dinner, one he'd remember for a good long time.

When Saturday came, Mrs. McGrath stopped in with Sylvester to visit and leave a gift for Donald. The boys went into the sunroom, which doubled as a bedroom for the only male member of the McKinney family. They dug around in ragbags and closets for old funny getups they could wear that evening. Every year they'd gone "trick-or-treating" with the Wahley twins and this year they wanted to dress in such a way that nobody would ever guess their identity.

They roared into the kitchen with an urgent request. "Well what do you want twenty cents for, Donald?" Hattie put down her teacup and folded her hands in her lap, waiting for a reply.

Her son was excited and making motion with his hands, to convey the guaranteed success of the costumes the boys had rigged up for themselves. But to make them really WORK, they needed the gruesome, contorted false-faces they'd seen in the window of Mrs. Barnes' corner store.

Sylvester was working on Mrs. McGrath's sympathies at the same time, and both women gave little sighs of compliance and ended up fishing for change in their purses. They counted out the nickels and pennies for the ugly lacquered papier-maché masks that seemed to be a matter of life and death to the ten-year-olds. Donald worked the coins down into his pocket with his chubby fingers since his pants were a tight fit over stomach and hips. They ran off giddily to purchase their masks, planning to put on their costumes as soon as they returned.

A Tight Squeeze

"Somebody HELP me – Aileen – Mom – oh quick he-e-elp!" Aileen and Hattie ran to Donald's room to find an exasperated bundle of anguish. He was half in and half out of a satin sheath, caught up in several loops of braid that were supposed to hang loose.

Aileen roared with laughter. "Well now what on earth d'ya think you're doing, Donald? Now just calm down and hold still. You've gone and got your arm all hooked up in these hoop things. Will ya stand still son, and let me take the thing off. We have to start from scratch!"

"Jeeze! How do ya stand it?" Donald wheezed once he was freed, "Goin' through that every day! It's harder' n I thought bein' a girl!" He was all pink and puffing, and little beads of sweat glistened under his eyes.

With four expert feminine hands the lad was slip covered successfully in the narrow rust satin dress. It was tight at the ankles, being cut along the old hobble skirt lines and Hattie was sure he'd fall and break both arms, so a slit was opened in the seam on either side. The hideous false-face of bilious green was applied after hasty kisses from Hattie and Aileen, and the treats bag hooked over his short thick forearm.

Puffing with exertion and confinement inside the satin tube, Pecker banged sharply on McGrath's door. It opened. A dark form, Sylvester, emerged in floor-length velvet that had seen better days. Down the block they joined forces with Eric and Simon, dressed as twin hobos.

They all exchanged punches and squeals of delight, tried comic voices on each other to throw people off and, leaping with joy and excitement, began their door-to-door ritual of treat-or-threat. Doors were opened, they were gushed over, play-acted with, teased, asked to sing or dance, treated and laughed at, and told to come again. Even better than all the gleeful hospitality and candies, was the fact that nobody could tell who they were. Oh – sweet success at last! The boys congratulated themselves right and left.

On the second leg of their journey, the jolly quartet ran into a motley gang disguised as a gypsy band. They were from Marentette Road over by Langston Park. The Hogarth kids were invited to go along and join the raid on the cemetery just for fun. The last one over was a rotten egg and had to forfeit his bag of goodies to the others, as a penalty.

Everyone had to get to the little marble mausoleum, touch the wall, make it back over the fence, and meet in the alleyway off Penbury Street. The trick was to keep perfect silence for fear of rousing the caretaker, who made his rounds with two big German Shepherds on chains. He'd be listening for every sound tonight, ready to leap! To add to the challenge, the graveyard was surrounded by a black iron fence six feet high, with sharp spikes at the top so that scaling it was some feat in itself. Sylvester and the twins were among the first over, being light of frame and cat-like. They were good, swift runners, but poor old "Pecker" had a time clearing the fence in the tight confines of his satin getup.

As his feet hit the ground, he noticed that some of the kids were already returning to the fence, having touched the mausoleum in the centre of the graveyard. They were passing him all the way to the mausoleum, swearing in whispers as they stumbled along the way. Finally he reached the mausoleum, and stumbled his way back.

Pecker wished he was a better runner and not so fat. "It really gets in a guy's way at a time like this," he admitted, kicking for a foothold. He worked his weight up the fence, up towards endless stars that winked like tiny acetylene flares, hard and remote, in a sky as black as a witch's hat.

"Let's see, everybody here now?" asked the kid from Sklar Street, as he looked around the alley, taking charge like a true leader. After some confusion, they discovered that all were accounted for but the little satin chub.

They opted to wait, and to pass the time, they rummaged around in their bags and started eating BB-Bats, Tootsie Rolls, popcorn balls and taffy apples. They waited, swapping stories, knock-knock jokes, and relived the current Captain Marvel serial playing at the Tivoli on Saturdays.

Suddenly Sylvester jumped to his feet, saying it was getting late and wondering what could be wrong. He walked to the end of the alleyway where it ran into Penbury and peered through the dark where the fence should be. The gang followed him, declaring they'd waited long enough. The ragtag band of mummers formed a curious column across to the corner of Hogwarth, where the streetcar tracks shone silver in the lamplight.

They crossed there, under the streetlight, and cut sideways to the dark space where they'd gone over the fence. There was a hush and a gasp! They stopped cold in their tracks. Oh GOD, THE FENCE! There was something crimson and rusty, shining there, dangling over the top, spilling down. As they drew nearer they saw the satin chub, caught in a tangle of looping fringe, hanging like a side of beef on a hook.

A spike was buried in the soft pink of Pecker McKinley's throat. His eerie green mask stared down while the ostrich feathers on his hat moved prettily in the wind.

The Hunchback of Oakview Avenue

As 9-year-old Maggie lay motionless in her bed, she heard it: the slow, steady sound of footsteps making their way up the stairs. A shudder ran down her spine as her eyes darted over to her bedroom door. She willed the footsteps not to stop outside it. But they did – as always.

Maggie normally left her bedroom door open just a trifle so that the hall light could penetrate the darkness. It helped her sleep. Now, the door was slowly creaking open. Maggie held her breath. The door closed again leaving just a sliver of brightness to cut across her room. Then the dim light from the window illuminated the shadow of a figure – small in stature, hunched over and moving slowly along the wall toward the closet. The door to the closet (which housed the entrance to the attic) swung silently open and the shadow was gone.

Maggie was frozen with fear. She lay in her bed for what felt like an eternity, until she mustered enough courage to leap from the concealment of her bedsheets and bolt down the hall to the sanctuary of her brother's room.

Shortly after her family had moved to the house on Oakview Avenue in Toronto, Maggie's night visits had begun. They continued for years – not every night, not consistently, and sometimes more frequently than others.

Amazingly, Maggie grew used to the sights and sounds of her guest. Her parents, busy in their adult world, chalked it up to youthful imagination with nonchalant comments like, "That's interesting, dear." Her second oldest brother, Henry, (two years her senior) found the story useful ammunition for frightening and teasing her. However, one night, a few years after her first eerie encounter, Henry sprinted into her room with a terrified look on his face. His eyes wide, he whispered, "I saw the hunchback man!"

When Maggie was about 17, her girlfriend, Elizabeth, came to live with her family on Oakview Avenue. Elizabeth stayed in Maggie's oldest brother's room as he was away at college. There had been a long lull in the ghost's appearances. Maggie hadn't remembered seeing it for nearly two years. Several months after moving in, Elizabeth commented "you know you have ghosts in this house?"

Maggie's jaw dropped. Then she asked her to explain. Elizabeth described the same hunchback shape that had been so familiar to Maggie. The ghost was back.

Until she moved out of the home on Oakview to attend college in September of '61, the hunchback man continued to appear to Maggie every now and then. Over 40 years later, she has not seen or heard of him since, but will never forget her encounters with the supernatural.

"Maggie" now lives in Windsor.

Laryssa Landale, Windsor

illustration by Chuck Rees

Local Bed & Breakfast
Serves Up the Occasional Ghost

by Renka Gesing, Issue #18, October 2001

Ghosts were the furthest thing from his mind when Wayne Strong purchased the house at 1104 Monmouth Road at Richmond Street in Olde Walkerville. Wayne, a labour relations and business improvement consultant, had planned to open Ye Olde Walkerville Bed & Breakfast in 1996 simply as a financial investment.

Now, in the words of one of his guests, the B&B business, the house itself and its history is a "passionate hobby." Part of that hobby now includes researching the family who originally built the home, and especially the life of one person from the home's past – someone who seems happy to occasionally wander through the home and make herself known to special people who, according to Wayne, "have a gift."

After check-in, each guest of the elegant manor, which was built around 1903, receives historical information about the Walkerville area and also gets a tour of the building highlighting the detail of restoration efforts. Invariably Wayne is asked if there are any ghosts on the premises. "My answer is always I don't know," explains Wayne. "I haven't seen anything move, no shadows, no encounters of any sort. I possibly don't have the gift to communicate with the here after, but I know there's something beyond just this." As far as believing in ghosts, Wayne says he's open to it.

"I mean there are documented experiences of 'ghosts' which inhabit homes. The book, 'Life after Life' details out-of-body experiences, and police departments bring in psychics to help them solve crimes. Surely there's something to all that."

And, if he had any doubts, they dissipated after two certain guests visited. Britt-Marie Karlberg arrived with her husband one day last year to the Walkerville B&B, her first visit to North America from Sweden. Partway through the usual tour, Wayne thought Britt-Marie asked the usual question. Her husband, who was more fluent in English, explained to Wayne that she was telling him there is a ghost in the house, not asking him if there were any.

The next morning, Britt-Marie revealed a dream to Wayne about a woman who was living in the house, who appeared to her as a kind woman with long, dark hair; wearing a long, white, flowing dress; between 35 to 55 years old. She felt the woman was either a family member, maid or worker at the home and died in the month of March or April.

The "ghost" told Britt-Marie she is very happy in the house and is pleased with what Wayne has done to the home. And she somehow shared her name to Britt-Marie; it sounded like Maggie, Magee, Macghee or Mackee. "She kept rolling these names out; all a variation of Maggie and Magee and Mackee," recalls Wayne.

In Wayne's earlier research of the house, he discovering that a Robert Leishman had purchased the land from E. Chandler Walker (Hiram Walker's son) in 1903. He also discovered that Robert was a machinist at London Bridge and that his wife Mary worked at Hiram Walker's. He had paid little attention to the detailed history until Britt-Marie revealed her experience. With renewed interest Wayne re-read the file. In the Windsor Directory of 1903, which listed all family members living at each address, he found Maggie Leishman, one of the eight Leishman's living in their previous home at 224 Monmouth – Robert & Mary Leishman and their six daughters. While Wayne remained slightly skeptical, he provided this informa-

photo illustration Vanda O'Keefe

The Disappearing Picture

I live in the old Chilver family farmhouse. I believe the house is haunted. On time, my mom gave me a picture of my deceased grandma, which I hung on the wall beside my dresser. The day after I hung it up, it was gone! My girlfriend Nancy and I looked for it but couldn't find it. I told her to say a prayer, and she said, "How about the one your Grandma liked, the prayer to Saint Jude?"

I looked for the copy of the prayer that I had put in my Bible, but that was gone too!
Mike Last, Walkerville

Right: The Chilver farm house (circa 1915) on Chilver Road, south of Wyandotte

220 • the mysterious & disastrous

The Walkerville Bed & Breakfast in 2003.

tion to Britt-Marie, who agreed to try to reconnect with her visitor.

The next morning Britt-Marie told Wayne that there is something to do with a large pile of dirt on the south side of the building, and reconfirmed that the woman had some connection to the home.

Spurred on by this information, Wayne continued his research. He found a newspaper article noting that Robert Leishman died at his residence May 25th, 1923, survived by his widow and six daughters, one of whom was Mrs. William McGhee. The name McGhee jumped off the newspaper page and by process of elimination, Wayne concluded that this was Maggie.

"This was what she was trying to tell me," Wayne recounted. "Britt-Marie nailed it. How could she have possibly known the history of this area? She was pronouncing the full name all the time – the ghost's name is Maggie McGhee."

But this was not the only time Maggie made an appearance. Carol Malewicz, a local teacher, stayed at the B&B last December while in between house moves. As she related to the Times: "I was sitting in the main living room, and just had a sense of needing to look up. She sort of floated across from the front door, reddish hair, white, silky, very flowing type of gown. I saw her a second time in the dining room." As was the case with Britt-Marie, Carol had no previous knowledge of Maggie or of the Leishman family.

Wayne is obviously now intrigued and convinced that Maggie indeed resides at the B&B and he continues to try to uncover what happened to her, when she died, and where could she be buried.

The Times managed to track down a relative of the original Leishman family, Phyllis Gervais, who was also born in Walkerville. "Maggie was my aunt," recalled Phyllis, surprised that Maggie should have made these appearances. "She was older when she died. She did suffer with her heart. Old Doctor (Clare) Sanborn attended to her for years and years. I used to go visit her quite a bit. She was a nice, quiet lady."

Phyllis believes Maggie is buried in the Windsor Grove Cemetery, but has no other information.

Wayne Strong would like to know more about the life of his "ghost" Maggie and why she has chosen to "haunt" his B&B. If you know anything, contact Wayne at Ye Olde Walkerville Bed & Breakfast, 1104 Monmouth Road, Windsor, N8Y 3L8, phone (519) 254-1507.

Wayne Strong in Corinna's room, where Maggie made her first apperance.

When Corpses Rode the Bus

"Corpses may be accompanied by an adult holding proper transportation on presentation of legal form of transit permit properly filled out and signed, showing that the body has been prepared for shipment in accordance with the law. Fare between any two points $2."
From 1928 Hydroelectric Railways Local Passenger Tariff

Windsor's bus depot opened Saturday, May 31, 1940. Homes line the east side of Goyeau (now occupied by a park and tourist welcome centre). In the distance, All Saints' Anglican Church pointed steeple.
photo courtesy Bernie Drouillard

best of the times • 221

Ghosts of Our Highways

adapted from a story by K.V. Moore, B.A., written in 1959
Issue #19, November 2001

Please remember when you visit our county that we have byways as well as highways. Remember, too, that we have soil where the feet of many generations have trodden. Soil where Indian warriors have crept stealthily, in order not to break a twig lest they startle and warn hearers whom they were attempting to surprise. In at least one case, however, it was the stealthy creeper who was surprised.

"Sketches of the Wyandots," published in 1870, tells of an Indian scout who was exploring around a local white man's fort and settlement one very dark night. As he crept cautiously up a southern slope, his hands encountered a cold, round object with a smooth, glossy surface. Groping to avoid this mysterious and possibly hostile form, his knees bumped into something cold, round, and still larger. Hastily and silently he changed the angle of his advance. But a third round, cold body rolled down upon him. Terrified by the unknown way in which the spirits of night were conspiring to entrap him, he fled. Thus the white settlement was saved from this autumn raid – saved by its melon patch.

The Indians were very superstitious. But that is a trait which characterizes many races. Ancient history relates how the Romans watched the flights of crows and sparrows for good or bad omens. Or a senator or tribune might go out to his poultry yard in the morning to observe the avidity with which the hens ate their grain. According to his chickens' vigour or languor in feeding he would judge his own prospects of success or failure in political or military struggles.

The White Panther

Thus, the Wyandots of this area many decades ago had a superstitious fear of a peculiar sulphur spring at the western end of Lake Erie. The water rose and fell regularly as if the movement was caused by the breathing of some submarine monster. Warriors brave enough to venture into this vicinity at night saw weird flashes of light. Sometimes they heard rumbling subterranean thunder and felt the earth trembling beneath their feet.

In spite of their fear, intellectual curiosity prompted some of the braves to penetrate the hidden mystery. They camped beside the haunted spring. They armed themselves with special wooden arrows cut from the red willow and sharpened and hardened with hot embers. Then their medicine man called upon the spirits of the spring to arise. A loon came up uttering its haunting cry. But the shaman shouted, "Not you," and the loon vanished. Then the otter appeared, but it too was dismissed.

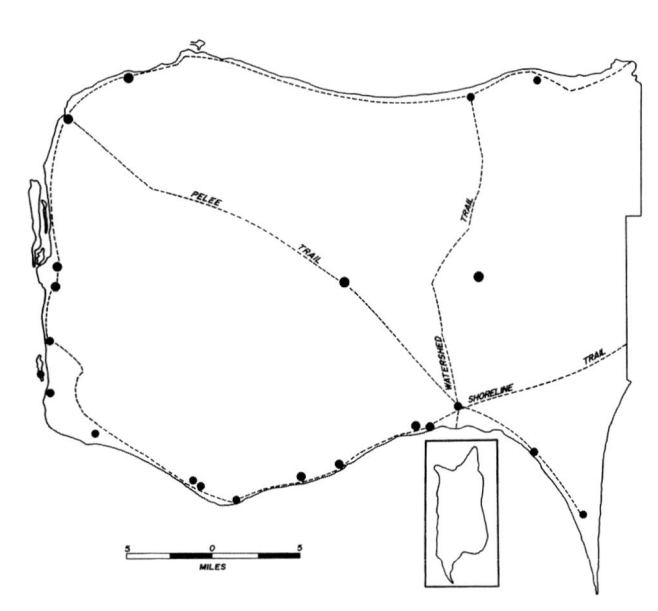

From research compiled by former Walkerville C.I. history teacher, the late Georgina Falls

"Suddenly, a tall red coated figure appears..."

Again he called for the mysterious spirit. Slowly a huge white panther emerged from the waters. The Chief shot it with his red willow arrow. From its blood they made charmed articles which brought good luck to the hunter in the frigid winter chase, and to the squaws making maple sugar in the spring woods. So efficient were these charms, or at least so firmly believed in, that the good priests along the Detroit River found special difficulty in converting the followers of the deified white panther.

Some of you may not believe in ghosts because you have never seen one. Yet, I presume, you have never seen an atom bomb or a hydrogen bomb.

Imaginatively, I ask you to believe for a few moments in ghosts. Just as we believe in them theatrically – for example, the ghost of Hamlet's father; the ghost of Banquo at Macbeth's coronation feats; the ghost of Julius Ceasar appearing in Brutus' tent.

Now, imagine a lone motorist at midnight on the highway approaching Windsor. Suddenly a tall, red-coated figure appears. He raises his arm with a commanding military gesture. The motorist retains sufficient self control to come to a cautious gradual stop. The red-coated, sword-girded figure still maintains its exact position just outside the driver's window.

"What is your hurry, sir?" the night visitant asks, "I was once in a great hurry to get to Fort Malden along the Detroit River, but I would never have dreamed of going your speed. Yet I was going to capture Detroit and the territory of Michigan – a great objective...

After a pause, the stranger identifies himself as Sir Isaac Brock. "Yes, we captured Detroit. A very interesting event in military history. I doubt whether you were taught the correct details in your school classes, sir. Let me tell you. General Hull was the American General and the Governor of Michigan at that time. There were practically no roads in Michigan then – 1812. No roads on the Canadian side of Lake Erie either! No roads meant no supply line for food, ammunition, and reinforcements. General Hull knew of the position was untenable. Therefore, we surrounded one August Sunday afternoon – without striking a blow. And after we got it, we couldn't hold it either. That's what I said. General Hull knew the position was untenable.

The delayed motorist, whose reputation evidently depends upon doing so many miles per hour in his particular make of car, grows impatient. What do the lives saved 150 years ago mean to him? It certainly wasn't his life. He doesn't think far enough back to realize that his great-great-grandfather's life may have been saved – an event which would have influenced his existence. The impatient driver suggests: "Would you like a lift going west, General? Then you could go on with your story while we're travelling."

"No thank you, sire," Sir Isaac replies, "I have never heard of a ghost in an automobile. I hesitate to establish a precedent which might be rather unnerving for drivers. Moreover, my little fleet is just a few miles south of here along the Lake Erie coast. I'll go back and join it."

The motorist says incredulously, "Your 1812 fleet floating along the lake! I've never heard tell of anyone who has ever sighted it."

A voice replies, "Oh, you people go by so fast in your motor cars and motor boats that you miss many things worth seeing."

The words fade and the motorist is alone, a sadder and a wiser man.

"Maybe I was going too fast," he murmurs to himself. "Well, a thing like that is a warning."

"Madam, don't you recognize my George III medal?"

Now, imagine a woman driving east in Central Essex County on a foggy autumn night. A mud-splashed figure waves a burning torch at a dangerous curve. The woman brings her car to a standstill.

"Thanks, sir," she says gratefully. "I don't know whether I would have remembered this curve or seen it in time."

The torchbearer demands, "Madam Paleface, what are you doing driving a gasoline horse on a night like this? Our good squaws always remained by the tepee fire when the night blotted earth, sky, and water together."

With outspoken curiosity the lady asks, "Well, what are you doing here yourself sir? And who are you?"

The guttural voice answers her: "Madam, don't you recognize my eagle head dress, beaded buckskin, and George III medal? Also, I never miss an anniversary of the Battle of Moraviantown – October 5, 1813. I'm on my way there, now."

The motorist remembers: "Oh, yes, Tecumseh! Well, thanks for warning me at this danger point."

The Chief, who knew his obscure trails with unerring instinct, replies: "These roads were once our Indian paths, quiet, narrow – we loved them! Now, madam, if you wish me to do so, I'll go ahead of you eastwards. Follow the fiery spirals of my torch!"

The lady driver used to say to her friends for weeks afterwards, "Girls, of course, you won't believe it! But nothing could blur those swirling gleams that danced before my eyes! I just wish one of you had been with me following Tecumseh and his pine torch!"

Many of these trails have become unrecognizable, but let not all the poetry and legend of the past dry up and shrivel in all our minds. When you come to our county bring, above all, your sympathy and imagination. There are no weight limits, customs duties, or national barriers and boundary lines for these we hope. Bring all the creative fancy and understanding that you can, and take back from us your trunks, your cars, and especially your hearts full of our imagination and sympathy.

Ghost Sent Packing

Re. "The Ghost of Colonel Bishop School" in your October 2002 issue. I was a student at the school before it closed in 1983. I recall the ghost very well (although I never saw or heard anything). Everyone thought it lived in the boiler room, which was next to the gym so no one ever went near there. The ghost was absolutely part of growing up and part of the thread of that school. Everyone knew about that ghost and when it was time to move to the new school, Sandwich West Public School, we Grade 7's "boxed" the ghost up and took it with us!
Jeff Renaud, Windsor

Burnt Matches

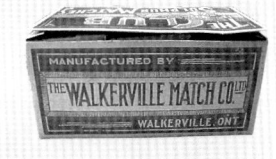

Brock Macpherson of Kingston, Ontario, recently submitted photos of Walkerville Match Co. products, hoping that someone could help provide the date of the company.

According to the Evening Record of January 26th, 1901, the Walkerville Match factory burned down on January 25th, 1901. It was a disastrous fire that included two explosions. A wall collapsed killing two firemen and people were injured from bricks that flew everywhere when the wall fell down. In all ten people were injured and two people were killed.
Don Tupling, Windsor

best of the times • 223

The Ghost of Colonel Bishop School

by Phil Hernandez, Issue #28, October 2002

As a new teacher at Colonel Bishop School, I was quite eager to do a lot of extra planning during the Christmas vacation. I borrowed one of the three keys available to teachers and headed over to the school which was located on Hazel Street in La Salle.

I arrived at about one o'clock in the afternoon. The day was rather gloomy; it had snowed earlier and the sky was still overcast. I entered through the front door of the old school, which had an old pneumatic spring to pull the door closed and made a loud hissing noise while doing so.

My classroom was around the corner of the gym. You had to pass through the gym in order to get from one side of the school to the other or to get to the rooms down the hall from my room.

I was working quietly for an hour when I heard the front door open, someone stamp their feet on the carpet and proceed to walk across the gym floor to the other side of the school. I heard several doors, all much in need of oil, creak open. I never gave much heed as to who it might be, as I knew other teachers had also borrowed keys for the building.

After a half hour, I decided to check who else was in the school. I went through the gym to the staff room, which was about half way down the hall on the other side, and put on the kettle to make coffee for myself and the other teacher.

I went through the creaky doors and looked into the hallway only to find them in darkness. Both of the classrooms on the lower level were empty and dark. I turned on the light to go up to the second floor; I peered down the hall from the top of the stairs – none of the rooms had any lights on.

I decided I had been very involved in my work and whoever had come in had already left. I went back downstairs, made myself a coffee and returned to my room.

About fifteen minutes later I again heard the front door open, someone enter the building, stamp their feet to get the snow off of their shoes, and proceed across the gym floor. This time I got up right away to see who had come into the building. When I entered the gym, the footsteps suddenly ceased. There was no one there.

I was stumped for a moment; it must be the neighbourhood kids, who

Phil Hernandez circa 1970, was a teacher at Colonel Bishop School in La Salle. He retired from teaching in June 2002. In his opinion, the spirit of a long-ago teacher, who died at the school, and not Colonel Bishop, is the "ghost."

were fond of playing tricks on the teachers. They had ways of getting into the school and playing with the gym equipment on bad weather days; you could often see their muddy footprints on the gym floor when we returned after a weekend.

Well, I thought, if you want to play tricks, I can play too. I sat on the front stage, which was just inside of the entrance of the gym, but in a place where you couldn't be seen, and waited.

I only had to wait for about five minutes before I heard the front door open (without the sound of a key going into the lock), someone enter the building and stamp their feet on the carpet. At that point, I jumped down and went around the corner to confront the culprit – only to find no one there!!! To say I was surprised would be an understatement!

I glanced down on the carpet to check for unmelted snow from someone's shoes, to see just the watermarks left from my own shoes. I was flabbergasted.

I turned and began walking back to my classroom. Suddenly, I could distinctly hear the sound of footsteps following me. I was too frightened to turn around to see what was making them. They followed me all the way to my classroom door.

I went into my classroom and closed the door behind me. I still didn't look back. My room had a fire escape, which led directly outside. I exited through that door, went around to the front of the school and checked that the front door was locked. I got into my car and drove home, shaking all the way.

On my return after the Christmas vacation, I told my story to the elderly Irish caretaker who had worked at the school for about twenty years. "Well, you've met him," he announced. "Our beastie. Our Ghosty!" He then proceeded to tell me all of the strange happenings that had taken place at the school during his tenure there.

Many other strange occurrences happened during my twelve-year stay at the school. One time a psychic (whom I don't believe in, incidentally) visited and she told me that she could definitely feel a presence in the building.

The students playfully named our spirit the "Ghost of Colonel Bishop." Indeed, they could tell many stories of their own. It was an experience I'll never forget.

Colonel Bishop School closed in 1999 and is now the Colonel Bishop Community Centre.

Who Was Billy Bishop?

Colonel Bishop School in La Salle, Ontario was named for WWI Canadian Air Force hero Billy Bishop. From growing up on Third Avenue West in Owen Sound, Ontario to the battlefields of France in World War 1 and England in World War II and beyond into civilian life, Bishop dedicated his life to aviation.

He received the Military Cross for action over Vimy Ridge in WWI and was awarded the Distinguished Service Order for attacking three planes, sending two down while under attack by four other planes.

In World War II, Billy Bishop helped bring world recognition to Canada's air force and the British Commonwealth Air Training Plan which became a model for other countries of the free world.

Does Elizabeth Haunt the Duff-Baby House?

by Marie Nikkanen, Issue #25, June 2002

The Duff-Baby House on Mill Street in Olde Sandwich (built 1798)

The year is 1812 and the war on the Windsor-Detroit frontier rages as desperately as the cruel winter, bringing scarcity of food, illness and death in its wake.

Elizabeth, wife of James Baby, Lord-Lieutenant of Kent County, gathers her six children and they flee to the safety of family in Quebec.

But alas, Elizabeth does not survive the journey. Never again will she return to her spacious Georgian home, flanked by graceful gardens and fruit orchards overlooking the Detroit River.

At least, not physically.

Elizabeth's home, now 204 years old and known as the Duff-Baby Mansion, has long been rumored to be haunted. Government office staff have been startled by self-slamming doors, have heard running water sounds from the basement but find no substantiating events, and have noted movement tracked by the alarm system triggered by... no one.

Jo-Anne Rafuse, a psychic residing in the Windsor area who provides both client and location/building readings to Windsor residents and international clients alike, believes the house harbours a number of spirit entities within its clapboard frame.

In late 2001, Jo-Anne, (who had no previous knowledge of the history of the Mansion or its previous inhabitants), and several Windsor locals spent several hours on different nights in the mansion which is located at Mill Street and Russell in Old Sandwich. During Jo-Anne's visits, she sensed both 'psychic imprints' – events or activities that have occurred in the past – and the current presence of entities whose energies still remain in the building.

One entity that Jo-Anne senses died on a trip away from the mansion due to a combination of dreary cold, dampness and a virus or flu, glides from the second floor down the main staircase to the first. This is a very calm, detached female who seems to be waiting for someone. Her spirit has returned to the mansion, patiently waiting for the others to return to the home she loved.

During his years at the mansion, documented owner James Baby travelled away for long periods of time. Perhaps it was a ritual that his wife Elizabeth performed many times, longing for the sight of her husband returning from his business travels, drifting hopefully down to see whether he had finally come home. There would, at least, be no mistaking the stairs today for they are entirely original, creaky with their comfortable wide, solid, steps intact, including the centuries of wear.

Jo-Anne also senses a heaviness to a room on the third floor. The old iron wood-stove, with the words 'Good Cheer' cast into it, still stands against the outer wall, the foot railings inviting you to prop your boots against it to get warmed. But this wood stove provides no comfort for the other occupant of this room. Jo-Anne feels an elderly gentleman lies very sick here. Endlessly calling for help, he is unable to get up from his bed, and no one in the house hears his anguished calls for help. It seems he has not realized that he has passed on. Jo-Anne said prayers to send him to the light and to allow him move on. There is no documentation identifying this man.

On the narrow wooden steps leading to the attic, Jo-Anne senses the psychic imprint of trauma, of a black man harboured in the attic, who was abruptly and aggressively removed. Could this trauma be connected to Andrew, a fleeing slave documented to have worked as a servant in the mansion? His former Kentucky master came in heated pursuit of him, but Andrew fled to York. Now lost, but once photographed, there was a wooden, carved figure of a seated slave found in the mansion. Was this of Andrew, or made by him?

Overall, Jo-Anne finds the energies of the mansion as a whole to be good and calm. Come and experience the Duff-Baby Mansion and learn more about the historical past of this remarkable 'frontier' Georgian home. There's a lot more going on behind its placid walls than you might imagine, and perhaps you too will suddenly come upon the gentle, peaceful wraith of Elizabeth still faithfully waiting for her Jacques to come home.

(This article was written in collaboration with Jo-Anne Rafuse.)

Historical Source: 'A Mansion on the Detroit Frontier, The Duff-Baby Story, a bicentennial celebration, Les Amis Duff-Baby, 1998,' available for purchase at the Windsor Community Museum, and "Souvenirs of the Past," by William Lewis Baby.

Centre: Jacques Baby, one of the Canada's most influential men..

6
My Old House

Unknown woman at 549 Chilver Road c. 1890.
photo courtesy Charlie Fox

2014 Willistead Crescent
The Crassweller Home

by Renka Gesing, Issue #17, September 2001

We had to move. We didn't want to, but a new career in the Detroit area for my husband meant a new city for all of us. Our initial disappointment at having to leave Kingston in 1997 evaporated when we first saw Olde Walkerville, and especially when we discovered a beautiful old house for sale on Willistead Crescent.

Our "new" home's history started calling out to us as we began peeling away layers of paint and wallpaper. Curious to learn more, I visited the City of Windsor's Building and Planning Department to pour through all those hand-scripted entries in the assessment roll books. And there it was – the first entry for what was to become 2014 Willistead Crescent: "24 August 1924, actual value of property $2,310." Then came the house: "17 August 1925, value of building $11,000."

I was hooked! I had to find out more.

Heritage planner Nancy Morand directed me to the Central Public Library's archives, to investigate a historical designation under the Ontario Heritage Act.

The first challenge was to find the original address, since Willistead Crescent wasn't always Willistead Crescent. As was revealed in the impressive leather-bound council minutes of the time, initially it was comprised of two parallel streets running from Devonshire Road east through to Monmouth Road. As recorded in the minutes, By-Law No. 1294 in 1930 asked: "That the names of the highways in the Town of Walkerville known as Navaho Street and Cayuga Street be changed to Willistead Crescent." When our house was originally built in 1925, it was located at 86 Navaho Street.

The more people we met who implied that the house does indeed have many stories to tell, the more we wondered about its former occupants. We of course had met Helen Channen, the previous owner, who ironically moved to Kingston. She and her family lived in the home from 1973 to 1999.

We also knew the earlier owners, Arthur and Sheina Handscomb, since they still lived on the Crescent a few houses down until a couple of years ago.

Nancy's impressive report filed with the request for heritage designation filled us in on the first owners, Dr. Henry Crassweller and his wife Mara. Wrote Nancy: "Prior to moving into their new home, the Crassweller's lived at 534 Ouellette Avenue (near Tuscarora), which was owned by Mara's father, James Anderson, the general manager of the Sandwich, Windsor & Amherstburg Railway, the predecessor of Transit Windsor.

Young Dr. Crassweller originally had his offices at 16 Wyandotte Street East, but relocated in the 1950s to 1011 Ouellette Avenue Of interest are articles in the local newspaper from November and December 1918, which describe Dr. Crassweller's experience as a prisoner of war in Germany during World War I."

Dr. Crassweller's son and daughter, Dr. Peter Owen Crassweller and Barbara Hill, both live in the Toronto area. Peter kindly answered my request for information about his Windsor home with a letter and the above photograph.

"The Crescent at the Monmouth end had no buildings on it on either side of the road, and it served as a playground and kite flying field," he reminisced. "My memory tells me that the house has been made to look as it did when my father died and it was sold."

And that's exactly what this "Colonial Revival style" home makes you do – respect its original elegance. We greatly value the gumwood trim, the impressive central staircase (and the separate "maid's" staircase), the original wood frame double-hung windows, the butler's pantry, the fireplace featuring special Pewabic tile, even the original ice box.

The more I delve into my home's past, the more privileged I feel to own such a wonderful piece of Walkerville's history.

Top: Peter and Barbara Crassweller in front of 2014 Willistead Crescent, c. 1925

719 Victoria Avenue
Treble-Large House

by Renka Gesing, Issue #33, April 2003

For Daniel Imeson, the present owner of the magnificent Treble-Large house, his home is far more than a place to hang his hat. Instead, it represents one of Windsor's last remaining downtown heritage homes. "They're all gone," he says. "This is the foothold; we've saved it."

The Treble-Large house, as it is known for its heritage designation, was built in 1895 by a Mr. C. A. Sullivan on the lot he purchased in 1893 for $2,400. The history of the house is intertwined with the Treble-Large family history – family members owned the property for over 100 years.

Elizabeth Treble (née Sinclair), purchased the house shortly after it was completed for $5,000 and moved in with two of her daughters, Mable and Violet. Elizabeth, who was a widow at the time, had eight children. "Four boys followed by four girls," explains Margaret Large-Carduso, one of Elizabeth's granddaughters. The sons and two older daughters were already on their own when their mother moved into the Victoria Avenue house. Margaret's mother, Mable, "became a Large at the age of 37.

Sketch of 719 Victoria by Jonathan Gillespie

We had no need for men in our family," jokes Margaret, who herself first married at the age of 59.

Margaret's recollections of the house goes back to 1919 when, at the age of three, she moved to Windsor from the west with her mother and sister, who was also named Violet. "Aunt Vi" invited Mable to come back to Windsor to help look after their mother, in return for assistance with her two daughters. "Grandma died very shortly after that," recalls Margaret.

Although she has few memories of her grandmother, Margaret remembers in great detail her life with her mother, sister and Aunt Vi, in the "lovely old home:" the call buttons for the maid (although they never did have a live-in maid), the Christmas tree in the alcove, ("a scraggly tree" purchased on Christmas Eve, to save money), the robbers ("my aunt went down with a shoe to clobber him with the heel!"), Aunt Vi shoveling coal into the furnace. "Then there was gas. We remember thinking that little blue flame isn't going to heat the house!" Although Margaret moved out soon after starting her post-secondary studies, her sister Violet Large lived in the house until she sold it in 1991 to Tony Fardilla, who sadly, died soon afterwards.

While growing up in Windsor, Daniel Imeson passed by the house regularly; whether on his way to Saint Anthony Grade School, Forester High School, choir school, choir practice at St. Alphonse's School, and much later to the antiques store he ran in Walkerville. The Treble-Large house now serves as his home with his partner Jonathan Gillespie, and provides an ideal ambiance for the French antiques he sells through his business, the Imeson Collection.

Elizabeth Treble, first occupant, in a 1910; photo showing detail of front porch.
photo: City of Windsor, Heritage Planning Department

"There were Victorian antiques in our house," says Margaret, while expressing her joy that the home has such a dedicated owner. "We were tickled to death when they bought it. We were so afraid we'd have to sell it to doctors or lawyers who would change the façade."

People are drawn to that façade, which is typical of the Queen Anne style of home (Queen Anne, who reigned from 1702-1714, actually had nothing to do with this style of architecture). The Queen Anne style is asymmetrical in design, with wings, porches and round towers and turrets. It also features many decorative details including wood shingles and trim in various patterns. By the end of the 19th century, decorative architectural products were pre-built and readily available to builders through catalogue orders (*Living Places, A Teacher's Guide to Domestic Architecture*).

Daniel and Jonathan value those unique details. When roofing companies balked at rebuilding the conical roofs, Jonathan did the reconstruction himself. A 1910 photograph Margaret sent them of her grandmother Elizabeth on the front porch encouraged them to hire Essex County craftsmen to carve new wooden posts using original designs. Other striking features include decorative chimneys, curved glass in the north tower windows, and carved interior wood trim, including the elaborate stair banister with an electric lamp on the landing post. The owner's current challenge is to find protective storm glass for the 84" tall curved windows.

"Basically, we're caretakers," says Daniel.

"You don't live forever. You just take care of it, and hopefully pass it on for someone else to love."

The garden and rear view of home at 719 Victoria Avenue. photo E. Weeks

A Brief History of Victoria Avenue

From "A Walking Tour of Victoria Avenue" compiled by Windsor Architectural Conservation Advisory Committee (WACAC)

James Dougall, developer of Victoria Avenue, was born in Paisley, Scotland in 1810, arrived in Windsor in 1830 and established the first general store, called "Dougall Emporium." The enterprise was located on Sandwich Street (now Riverside Drive), near the present Cleary International Centre.

Victoria Avenue (named for his daughter) was intended to be a gracious, residential street. In fact, the Windsor Land and Building Company placed conditions on buyers of building lots stipulating a minimum set back of 20 feet, a house value of at least $3,000 (considerable for that time), and assurances that any business carried on would not be deemed a nuisance to a private residential street.

As a result, the earliest houses, built between 1890 and the Stock Market "Crash" of 1929, show diversity of design and, in spite of recent renovations, quality of material and fine workmanship. They were the valued residences of some of the most influential and respected families during this middle period in Windsor's evolution – doctors, merchants, lawyers, educators, politicians and industrialists whose ideas moulded this municipality.

An old-timer, recalling the 1930s in Windsor, said, in that decade, "real estate was worth nothing... a house on Victoria Avenue would sell for $40,000 just before the "Crash," and afterwards... if you had a mortgage, they either pressed you for it or took it away from you."

Dougall was elected to the first village Council in 1854, the first town Council in 1858, and mayor 1859-1861 and again, 1867-1869. He donated land for the first school near his residence on Riverside Drive.

Top: Victoria Avenue, early 1900's. photo: David L. Newman Collection

393 Caron Avenue
Charles McLerie House

Issue #35, June 2003

Photos and research submitted by Marilyn McLerie Hayes, South Carolina Architectural information; McKay history provided by Nancy Morand, Heritage Planner, City of Windsor

Recently, Pat Lewis Lehrter (whose family owned Lewis' Flower Shop on Ouellette Avenue) told me about your publication and lo, and behold, another friend gave me a subscription.

I was particularly interested in the article entitled "The Treble-Large House" on Victoria Avenue ("My Old House," April 2003). The sketch looked very familiar; at first I thought it was my grandfather Charles McLerie's house at 393 Caron Avenue, built prior to 1900. This home was built near the Detroit River and was a fine home in its day.

McLerie Family History

My great grandparents, John and Mary Allen McLerie came to Canada in the summer of 1855 from Kilbarchan, Scotland, a suburb of Glasgow. Mary was the first cousin of Sir Hugh Allan who founded the Allan Steamship Lines. His first vessel, "The Canadian," had its maiden voyage in 1855. He was also 'famous' for his part in "The Pacific Scandal," (charges were made in Parliament that the Conservative administration of Sir John A. Macdonald had accepted campaign funds from Sir Hugh Allan in return for a promise to award Allan's syndicate with the contract to build the Canadian Pacific Railway).

The youngest of their nine children was my grandfather, Charles William McLerie, born May 5th, 1862. He married Annie Dickson and they had three sons. He once served on Windsor city council. On June 13th, 1904, Charles fell down the stairs inside the house at 393 Caron Avenue, broke his neck and died. At the time, his son Allan Gordon was 15, Roy Dickson was 12 and my father, John Stuart, was 5. Allan had just entered McGill University but instead of continuing his education, he went to work to support his mother and brothers.

Despite their father's untimely death, Charles' three sons went on to achieve success in life. In 1916, Roy entered the Canadian army and became a captain. My father Stuart also joined the Canadian army in 1916, barely 17 years of age, and became a corporal. In 1917 Allan joined the Royal Flying Corps/Royal Air Force in Canada. Between 1921 and 1922, he was the first pilot to fly a winter mail route in Canada.

My uncle Allan died three months before his only daughter, Allyn Ann was born in Grand Mere, Quebec. Shortly after her birth, she and her mother moved to Brooklyn, New York. How proud he would have been of his daughter.

Allyn Ann began a professional life at age 16 as a singer-dancer on Broadway. She later went on to play in various Broadway plays such as the hit "One Touch Venus." She made her movie debut in the 1948 MGM feature "Words and Music."

Top: The Charles McLerie House as it looked not long after it was built (sometime between 1888 and 1896). Once occupied by Charles McLerie and his family c. 1900, it became the J. A. McKay residence in the 1910s.

Left: J. A. McKay residence, 2003.

Built by Frank MacDonald

I wanted to bring your attention to the houses my maternal grandfather, James Francis (Frank) MacDonald built. My mother, Thelma MacDonald McLerie was an only child. In 1912, when she was ten years old, her parents Frank and Jean Fuller MacDonald, who were living in Tillsonburg, flipped a coin to see if they would move to Toronto or Windsor; Windsor won.

Frank was multi-talented; he was a farm implement dealer, real estate and insurance broker, and building contractor. He built a home at 1017 Victoria Avenue near Erie Street. The family lived there until he completed the duplex across the street at 1022-24 Victoria Avenue; they lived in the lower half.

He also built several houses on Ontario Street in Walkerville. One was purchased by Mr. B. R. McKenzie (owner of a sand and gravel company), another by a dentist and a third by a mortician named Mr. Beuglet. My grandfather lost everything in the Great Depression.
Marilyn McLerie Hayes, South Carolina

Top Right: The Frank MacDonald house, 1017 Victoria Avenue, 2003.

Far Right: The Frank MacDonald duplex, 1022-1024 Victoria Avenue, built prior to 1917, in 2003.

Right: A fine example of one of the homes built on Ontario Street between Devonshire Road and Kildare Road by Frank MacDonald.

Concerning the House

The 2 1/2 storey, single family dwelling at 393 Caron was built around 1888-1896. Its original Queen Anne Revival style boasted clapboard, plate glass windows quarrelled transoms, ornamental crowns on the brick chimneys, wooden spool trim on the wooden verandah and balconette, and metal roof cresting and finial.

In narrow architectural terms, Queen Anne Revival refers to a London-based revival of the ordinary red-brick building of the 17th and early 18th centuries. In North America, however, the term was more loosely applied to describe an eclectic style incorporating architectural elements borrowed from a variety of historical periods.

The Queen Anne architectural style was most popular in the U.S. from 1880-1900, and in Canada from 1890-1910. It is the most eclectic style of the Victorian era. Queen Anne style represents the culmination of picturesque, romantic styles of the 19th century. The style itself is based on "decorative excess" and variety, and the rule of thumb is "anything goes." This architectural style does not focus on specific historical detailing, but, rather, combines various forms and structures.

Some identifying features of Queen Anne Revival are: steeply pitched, irregularly shaped and multiple roof; dominant, front-facing gables; patterned shingles; bay windows; polychromatic and decorative ornamentation; partial or full-width one-storey verandahs; multiple gables and dormers; towers and turrets; the use of various surfaces on the same building, especially brick, wood shingles, stucco and half-timbering.

Who Was J. A. McKay?

393 Caron Avenue was purchased by John Alexander McKay of Woodstock, Ontario around 1910. John worked at the Woodstock Sentinel Review and, in 1890, married Miss Margaret Brotchie of Woodstock. In November of that year, they moved to Windsor so Mr. McKay could join Archibald McNee as a business partner in the Record Printing Company, Limited, publishers of The Evening Record.

McKay would become sole owner of this publication from 1906 until 1918, when he sold the paper to W. F. Herman, who renamed it The Border Cities Star (now The Windsor Star). John McKay was also quartermaster of the 21st Regiment, Essex Fusiliers, with the rank of captain.

Research indicates that around 1905, John and Margaret had four children: Kenneth D., Margaret Brotchie, Douglas A., and Catherine Scobie. The exact year in which the McKay family became owners of 393 Caron Avenue is unclear. However, there are records of it as "The J. A. McKay House" as early as 1913.

3164 Sandwich Street
Solomon Wigle House

by Renka Gesing, Issue #34, May 2003

Situated in historic Sandwich (west Windsor), a diminutive red brick home may be as old as the former town itself. According to WACAC, (the Windsor Architectural Conservation Advisory Committee), the Solomon Wigle house, "a vernacular Georgian cottage... could be considerably older than the estimated construction date of 1890." Since no record of habitation occurs until about 1890, it is presumed that the house was built in that year.

The Crown transferred the land on which the house stands to Francois Baby in 1801. The Babys were a wealthy French Canadian family who lived in the area for years in the 1800s. The Duff-Baby House, built in 1797, is a block away from the Wigle home.

"The municipal history of the Town of Sandwich begins with the year 1858," wrote Frederick Neal in his book, "The Township of Sandwich (1909)." The first European settlement west of Montreal, reaches back even earlier."

The civil history of the Village of Sandwich really commenced in 1788... "the British Government paid to the Chiefs of the Wyandottes or Huron Indians, the Chippewas and the Ottawas, the purchase price demanded by the joint tribes, for the peaceable possession of a piece of ground one mile square. Part of the newly acquired block of land was immediately surveyed and plotted into one-acre lots for settlement and the future county town was given the name of Sandwich."

Although the book doesn't reveal origins of the name, Alan Douglas, former curator of Windsor's Community Museum, figures the name Sandwich came to the area with others from the County of Kent in Southeast England. Years ago, he drew up a map of the county that highlights names familiar to area residents such as Chatham, Dover, Maidstone, Colchester, West Tilbury, and Raleigh as well as Sandwich. The name itself is Saxon in origin, and means

The Solomon Wigle house, 3164 Sandwich Street, is thought to have been built earlier than its estimated construction date of 1890. Sketch from Sandwich walking tour booklet, compiled by WACAC in 1986.

sandy place, or the place on the sand, and that, according to one web site (www.sandwich-kent.co.uk), goes back to the first recorded mention of the town in 640 AD.

Ruth Sharon, a local cook book author, was born in the Solomon Wigle house in 1923. Although her family moved out of the house when she was four years old, she has many memories of her first home, with its deep set front lawn. "We always called it the little red brick house. There's one window facing the road upstairs – that's the room where I was born. Behind the house I remember the horse stalls. We didn't have a horse even though in those days, bread, milk everything was delivered by horse and wagon. I remember waiting for my father to get off the streetcar with my mother and the new baby." Ruth lived in the house with her parents, two older sisters, a brother and "the new baby" – a younger sister.

The streetcars stopped running in 1939, but the little red brick house, now owned by dentist Greg Hanaka, remains an important part of the streetscape.

"We moved in 1968," says Greg. "My father wanted a cheap house – paid $6,000 for it." That wasn't much more in contemporary dollars than the $1,217 Solomon Wigle spent to purchase the property. Wigle was a land speculator who likely built the cottage as a rental income property.

A Conservative, he was Essex County's first member of the Ontario Legislature. He defeated Windsor lawyer Alexander Cameron in 1867. Wigle was the descendant of pioneers who had settled in Gosfield South back when they had to follow Indian trails through the woods. He owned a store in Leamington and had a contract for two four-house stage and mail coach routes connecting Windsor and Kingsville and Blenheim and Amherstburg.

His son Lewis (1845-1934) was even more successful. According to Neil F. Morrison in "Garden Gateway to Canada," Lewis was one of "two men (who) stood out prominently in the agriculture of the time. (The other) was Hiram Walker...

Gaining Heritage Status

There are many reasons to consider gaining heritage status for your old house or building. Properties with heritage designation are selling for about 10% higher in the Windsor area and are eligible for grants or loans from Windsor's Community Heritage Fund for single family homes. The designation is based mostly on exterior details so there is no restriction on interior changes. Plus, property owners get a bronze plaque presented during a special ceremony at City Council.

Your first step: get the "owners' request to designate" form from Windsor's Heritage Planner, 255-6770 x 4449

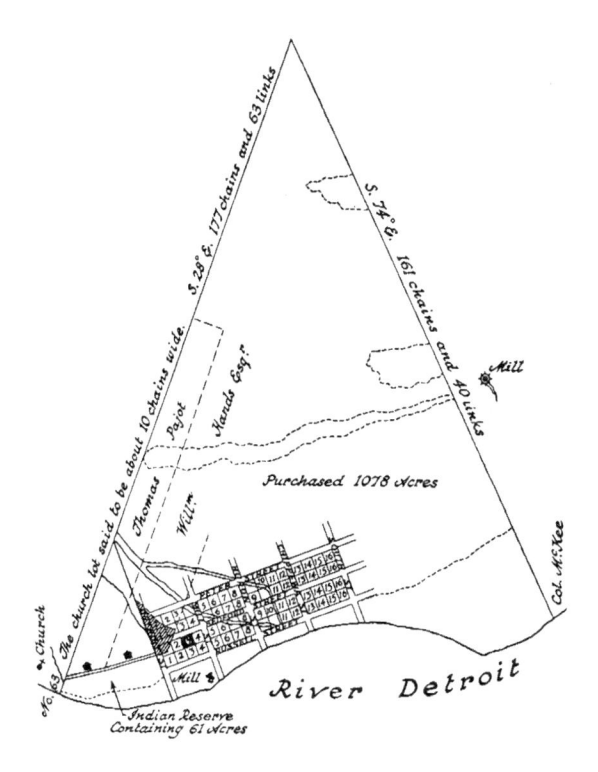

Lewis was a businessman, politician, purchasing agent, shipper, railway promoter, with farming and horse racing interests... On November 12, 1897... he went through Colchester South and Malden and purchased 600,000 lbs. of tobacco for shipping." Lewis was only 29 when elected to the Ontario Legislature, the beginning of a long political career.

The house may have been in better shape back in the 1890s than when the Hanakas moved in over seventy years later. "It wasn't much more than a glorified outhouse," jokes Greg, who was raised by his father, Frank in the house with his sister and twin brother. The previous owners had "destroyed the inside." The Hanakas restored the house and it was designated in 1993 under the Ontario Heritage Act.

The reasons for designation include the historic structure: "Local brick with radiating brick voussoirs in segmental arches around windows and doors." Voussoirs are wedge-shaped stones used to make up an arch.

The house is also known for its triple brick walls and its "shotgun" layout, in which front and rear doors are aligned. The story is that this allows shotgun pellets to be fired through the front door to pass all the way through the house without hitting any barriers. Shotgun houses, more prevalent around New Orleans than Windsor, are usually one room wide and one or two rooms deep under a continuous gable roof. Some scholars have suggested that they evolved from ancient African "longhouses," but no one really knows for certain.

"I don't think he was looking at its historical value," says Greg concerning his father's decision to buy the house but the family came to appreciate its historical value. Greg decided to keep the house as a rental property after inheriting it from his father in 1984. He restored the home between 1995 and 1996, and he set up his dental practice next door. "It was like coming home," he says of his choice of location.

Above: 1797 plan of the purchase of the Huron Reserve, containing 1078 acres, including the Town of Sandwich. The town lot contained one acre at right angles, being three chains and thirteen links every side, the street one chain wide.
photo: Public Archives of Canada

Fumigated Parcels & Cobblestone Streets

I was raised at 606 Argyle at the corner of Wyandotte St. E. in Walkerville. My siblings were Paul, Ferol, Doreen, Kenneth, Eugene, Bernadette and Ruth Ann (adopted). Mom had so many kids with birthdays in June the Windsor Star ran our picture with our huge cake!

Our house was originally a cottage but my dad added to it quite a bit. For a while he ran his business (National Fumigating & Pest Control) out of a small front room that was first a porch, then a sun porch. He later moved the business to Riverside at Louis.

Argyle was a type of cobblestone street that flooded when it rained too heavily; we would splash about and have a ball. When you're small, that much water seems like a lake! I even placed some of my artwork under the new cement sidewalk years ago (1961?) in a plastic bag and hoped it would be discovered in the "future." I thought I might become famous, I suppose. I bet it is still there.

Michael Parent, B.C.

Remembering The Henkel Home

The Henkel home pictured in the June 2003, 2nd Annual Photo Issue was located on the southeast corner of George and Riverside Drive. Robert Henkel owned Henkel Flour Mills of Detroit; this was the family's summer home.

When the family moved away in the mid-40s, the home became the Frontier Badminton Club and was open for wedding receptions; it was torn down many years later. A road called Henkel Place still exists, which ran behind the house, and was named for it.

Terry Marentette, Windsor

Henkel Housed Escaped Poles

Henkel Place (Issue #36, July/August 2003), did not exist at least until some time after the 1940's. All the property from Riverside Drive to Wyandotte was part of the Henkel estate and was surrounded by a fence. As a young fella, my chums and I walked along the west side of the property on George Avenue on our way to the Ford City Bathing Beach (East Windsor Beach).

During World War II, a contingent of troops was billeted there. They were Polish military personnel who had escaped from Poland to England at the beginning of the war. I am not sure whether they were billeted in the house or in the large two-storey carriage house located about midway toward the back of the property. We would watch them quite often in the mornings when they would form up in front of the carriage house and board army trucks which would take them away for the day, presumably for training at some other location.

Allan R. Clegg, via email

The Robert Henkel summer home, 1913. photo courtesy George White

The Yellow Brick Question

by Elaine Weeks, Issue #37, September 2003

A reader's architectural query opens the door to a fascinating time in Windsor's history.

I moved to Windsor in 1969. The Windsor, Walkerville and Sandwich areas are such great places in which to live. My question is, why are there so few soft yellow brick buildings this side of Chatham? If one travels to Chatham, Sarnia or London, the number of soft yellow brick buildings from the late 1800s and early 1900s is significant.

Why does Windsor and amalgamated communities have so few of these brick buildings? The only one from that era I can think of is McEwan Manor at 131 McEwan.

Robert Schmidt, Windsor

Steeped in history... 131 McEwan Avenue, built in 1872.

Your interesting question was passed on to Fred Cane, Heritage Conservation Advisor. According to Mr. Cane, the colour of brick depends on the amount of iron naturally found in the clay. Most communities obtained their brick from a local brickyard using local clay. The buff or yellow brick found so commonly in southwestern Ontario has less iron in it than the clay that produced the orange or red brick seen in other areas. Red brick was used more in the Windsor area and in Amherstburg than buff. The answer may lie in the proximity of Windsor and Amherstburg to the St. Clair River. The clay deposits along the river may have a higher iron content than those farther away. Mr. Cane says he's "no geologist so I can't explain how that would have come to be, but I suspect that this is the reason." There are exceptions like Mackenzie Hall and Assumption Church. As buff brick was preferred for important buildings, the brick for these buildings may have been intentionally sourced from a different location.

In 1955, the entrance was switched from Riverside to the McEwan side.

Now that I am more aware of brick colour, I have noticed several homes and small apartment buildings dotting the neighbourhoods of Windsor and area that are yellow brick. Thanks to Robert, we thought that in this month's My Old House, we would profile McEwan Manor, also known as the Sheriff John McEwan Home, as well as have a look at the fascinating life of its first inhabitants, John McEwan and his family.

Sheriff John McEwan Home

This unique Italianate house with Flemish gable is comprised of brick, stone, terra cotta and wood. It has a square plan with two stories, low hipped roof, a north side projecting central bay with semi-parapeted gable, eight chimneys and a frame addition on the south façade. The Italianate style was in popular use for town houses about the time of Confederation (1867).

In 1929, the house served as a temporary home for the Sisters of the Good Shepherd for a year. The current owner is John Hyatt who has lived in the Sheriff McEwan home since 1998 when he purchased it from his parents, Frederick and Ruth Ann Hyatt, owners since 1977.

John Hyatt has in his possession a copy of a local newspaper page from 1872 describing the progress of the house's construction and indicating that it was nearing completion. The home was built to face the Detroit River. John Hyatt guesses that occurred sometime in the 1950s, the entrance was switched to face the McEwan Avenue side.

A 1955 snapshot of the home given to his parents by the previous owners shows the house facing McEwan and a vacant lot to the north, (now occupied by a residence). Although the photo is black and white, the red paint that once covered the brick is evident. John thinks that the reason the house was painted was possibly because the light-coloured brick had been discoloured by coal as it was dropped down the chute into the basement.

The Manor was converted into a multi-unit home several years ago with the main (north) entry bricked in (a bathroom has been built in what was once the entrance). A large wooden front porch has been added. Despite the changes to the home, John has worked hard to preserve as much of the remaining character as possible. The high ceilings, the many tall windows, the ornate fireplaces and much of the original wood remain.

Who was John McEwan?

John McEwan was born in Saratoga, New York in 1812. As a small boy he moved to Gananoque, Ontario and grew up along the St. Lawrence River. He married Margaret Arnold, daughter of Richard and Ann Arnold, and granddaughter of Benedict Arnold, of Revolutionary fame.

In 1846, John and Margaret McEwan settled in Sarnia where he engaged in the timber business. In 1848, they relocated to Windsor and a year later, he was made Clerk of the Court, a position he held until 1853 when he engaged in the warehouse and lumber business. When the Great Western Railroad was completed, the right of way led through his lumberyard, which required him to sell the land and close his business. In that same year he accepted the position of Station Agent for the railroad.

In 1856, John McEwan was appointed Sheriff of the County of Essex, a post he held until 1883. John was also editor and owner of Windsor's first newspaper "The Windsor Herald," which he started in 1855. Later he became promoter of the Canada Southern Railway, school board trustee and municipal councillor.

The children born to John and Margaret McEwan were Charles, Patrick Anderson of Illinois, William J., Margaret, James, Porter, and Christine.

Construction of his fine new home on what became McEwan Avenue began in 1871. According to the custom of the day his daughter, Margaret, drove around in a horse-drawn buggy to invite guests to attend the reception in the new home.

The property at that time and for years afterwards, ranked as an estate and stretched south from the river to London Street (University Avenue). A hired man's house stood on the grounds about 200 feet back of the McEwan home, which originally faced the river. Just south of the house was a splendid well and it was said that even people from the east side of Windsor would come to drink its water.

In 1872, John's son James was appointed Crier of the Court of Essex County. In 1881 he married Amanda M. Rogers. They had four children: Grace Margaret, Arnold, John, and Anderson. When the Humane Society was formed in 1895, James McEwan was chosen as head of the organization.

John McEwan died in 1892 and is buried in St. John's Church yard.

James lived in the old homestead until his death in 1917. Four years earlier his daughter, Grace (Mrs. J.W. Hanson), opened up McEwan Avenue between Sandwich (Riverside) and London (University) Streets, in response to the needs of the new industrial age, which was then causing rapid growth in Windsor.

McEwan Tried to Save Stricken Norwegian Immigrants

In an article by Alan Abrams, which appeared in the Windsor Star on March 20, 1982, entitled Black Hole of Baptiste Creek, 57 Norwegian immigrants – men, women and children – died of cholera when they arrived in Windsor by train from Hamilton on July 2, 1854. These immigrants were part of a large group that had sailed to Quebec from their homeland and were heading to Detroit from Windsor, where they were to take a train to Chicago and eventually end up in settlements – in Wisconsin and Minnesota.

In her book, *A Scandinavian Heritage: 200 Years of Scandinavian Presence in the Windsor-Detroit Border Region*, Joan Magee notes that the Norwegians had been exposed to cholera a number of times while enroute to Windsor. She reveals that because the train service from Hamilton to Windsor had just started that year, overcrowding was common as the railroad was anxious to accommodate the massive traffic to increase the rail line's profitability. The Norwegians were therefore crammed into freight cars, which had no windows.

As Abrams put it; "100 years later, similar box cars were used in Germany to transport Jews to the death camps."

As the train neared Windsor, it was stopped because a gravelling engine had derailed due to the rails expanding from the intense summer heat. The first class passengers were transferred to another train but the immigrants were left at Baptiste Creek, in the

Top: Current photo of the living room on the main floor. photo E. Weeks
Below: John McEwan, a man of many faces.

township of Tilbury, for two additional days without the provision of food, water or shelter from the heat. They resorted to drinking the water in the creek (also referred to as a swamp).

When the immigrants finally reached the newly established village of Windsor, the journey had taken its toll – one Norwegian was dead and 33 others collapsed on the platform at the station house. In 1854, Windsor only had a population of 750. There was no hospital and only one doctor, Alfred Dewson, who set up a cholera hospital in the Great Western storehouse at Moy Avenue and Riverside Drive.

When word of the plight of the Norwegians spread, the McEwans and a Mr. Blackadder went to the storehouse to help the sick foreigners, but in spite of their efforts and the risk to their own lives, (John McEwan himself contracted cholera) many died.

One Norwegian couple left two children behind in their deaths, and Mrs. McEwan did not hesitate to take care of them for several years, until they could look after themselves.

Originally the railway agreed to defray the expense of providing coffins and burial of the immigrants but the company reneged on the offer. Ironically, as a token of appreciation, the railway presented Mrs. McEwan with a gold watch on January 1, 1855. It was inscribed with the words, "Presented to Mrs. John McEwan, of Windsor, Canada West, for kind and Christian benevolence to the poor sick Norwegian emigrants in July, 1854."

As there was no cemetery in Windsor, nor a Lutheran church to perform the burial rites, one can only speculate as to the place where the bodies of the cholera victims were buried. Abrams noted that historian Alan Douglas recalled incidents of Windsor homeowners in the Moy and Hall Avenue areas (near Riverside Drive) having uncovered human skeletons and bones within the last 20 years and wondered whether they might have been the remains of the Norwegian immigrants.

This incident is still one of Windsor's great mysteries. Not only are the graves of these victims unknown but their names are equally elusive. There were no records kept by either the shipping companies or the Canadian government for these immigrants. According to Magee, the event didn't even make the pages of the newspapers in Canada, Norway or Detroit.

As there was no cemetery in Windsor, nor a Lutheran church to perform the burial rites, one can only speculate as to where the bodies of the cholera victims were buried.

Today in 2003 local archaeologist Rosemarie Denunzio confirms that no remains of the cholera victims have been discovered. The bones that have turned up over the years have been determined to be that of Native Canadians who lived in the area hundreds of years ago.

It has long been thought that the bodies of the cholxera victims were buried near where they died. Several archeological digs have been conducted along the waterfront over the years in an effort to discover the remains of these immigrants, including under the Peabody Bridge at Chilver and Riverside Drive but nothing has turned up.

Denunzio explains that even back in the 1850s, the locals would have known not to bury diseased bodies near the source of their drinking water, in this case, the Detroit River. As to the location of the bodies, she says they are still a mystery. "To people of those days," 'near' was a whole different concept from what it is today. They thought nothing of walking miles to get somewhere."

The bodies were definitely buried or disposed of somewhere in the Windsor area. Denunzio cautions anyone who discovers bones to call the police. "And don't touch them," she says. "If they belong to one of these immigrants they can still carry the infection."

Sources:
The Township of Sandwich, Past and Present, 1909 by Frederick Neal (reprinted 1979 by the Essex Historical Society)

"Black Hole of Baptiste Creek" by Allan Abrams, Windsor Star, March 20, 1982
Garden Gateway, 1854-1954 by Neil F. Morrison, PH.D., 1954 (1st printing)
Architectural Information: Nancy Morand, City of Windsor Heritage Planner
John Hyatt, current owner of home

Above: View of Detroit from the Great Western Railway in Windsor, circa 1860. In 1854, the small depot at left served as a temporary hospital for Norwegian immigrants stricken with cholera (from" A Dutch Heritage - 200 years of Dutch Presence in the Windsor-Detroit Border Region," Joan Magee, 1983)

509 Crawford
The John Wesley McConnell House

by John McConnell, Issue #53, May/June 2005

My old house is located in the centre of Windsor, but when it was built over 100 years ago, it was at the western edge of town. It was built by my grandfather, John Wesley McConnell in 1904, after he purchased the land on August 12, 1903 for $240. The original deed was prepared by Oscar E. Fleming, a barrister-in-law. Fleming was the Mayor of Windsor from 1891 to 1893.

My grandfather married Mabel Louise Lofthouse in Komoka, Ontario on June 21, 1904. They immediately returned to Windsor to begin building the house on Crawford. A mortgage was taken out for $1,200. Surprisingly, the mortgage rate at that time was 5 1/2%, payable twice a year, which is about the same as current rates.

The house was very large with two apartments upstairs. The main floor, where my grandparents lived, featured eight large rooms including a sunroom and a library with a fireplace. The two upstairs apartments had five and six rooms and a two-story garage at the back of the property. My grandparents raised a brood of eight boys in the house.

In 1924, my grandfather was elected alderman and served on Windsor City Council from 1924 to 1927. He also served as chairman of the Light and Street Opening Committee. In 1928 he became Chief Engineer at the newly built $500,000 Metropolitan General Hospital, where he was responsible for all building and plant maintenance.

In 1933, my parents, Ronald and Ruby McConnell, moved upstairs into the larger apartment. I lived there for the first twenty years of my life. My grandfather passed away in September, 1954 and the big old house we all knew so well was sold shortly after.

I have many pleasant memories of life on Crawford: Sunday family dinners and special occasions and holidays with relatives from Ontario and Michigan who would visit and spend the afternoon sitting on the front porch having long conversations into the early evening. I still have the large Union Jack that hung on the front porch every Victoria Day.

I watched the city expand around us and the house on the corner of Crawford and London Street (University Avenue) expand into a major hospital. I remember Saturday afternoon walks to the Capitol, Empire and Palace where western double features played on the big screen. I remember spending hours on the banks of the Detroit River watching passenger boats, Bob-Lo boats and railway ferries make their way down the river.

These were the carefree days of my youth, and every time I pass the big old house on Crawford Avenue I am stirred up with wonderful memories.

Crawford Avenue

Crawford Avenue has an interesting origin. Until 1880, this road formed the western limit of the town of Windsor. It was founded and named after Alexander Crawford, a prominent local citizen. Crawford was active in public affairs. In 1875, when Windsor was still a small town, he built the Crawford House on the corner of Sandwich (Riverside Drive) and Ferry Street. For a time, it was the largest Canadian Hotel west of Toronto.

Four blocks west of Crawford Avenue and University Avenue, in the Church of the Ascension, a large three-panel stain glass window looms over the altar. This Ascension window was a gift from the Crawford family in 1927, replacing an earlier Ascension Window destroyed by fire in 1926. The inscription below the window reads, "To the glory of God and in loving memory of Alexander Crawford and his family."

Top left: John Wesley McConnell House, 1932. Right: The house in April 2005.
Photo: Sherrill Tucker
Above: John McConnell, centre, in front of his family home, c. 1939.

342 Rosedale Boulevard, Sandwich
The Amedee Marentette House

by Terry Marentette, Issue #40, December/ January 2003-2004

When my mother worked for Western Union in Detroit over eighty years ago, my father Amedee Marentette, aka "Mid," was the sole proprietor of the Acme Hardware store in Sandwich. Since he didn't have anyone but himself to account for, once in a while he would take some time off to meet my mother for lunch in Detroit. At this point in time, they weren't married yet, although they had been engaged for almost ten years.

With his impending marriage on his mind, (scheduled for 1923), my father saw a sign advertising the sale of all materials from the demolished Pontchartrain Hotel. Upon investigating, he was pleased to discover that the prices were very low. He wanted to build a dream house, or in his words, a "grand house" as a marriage gift, perhaps because my mother had been waiting so long.

After inquiring about getting the materials to his store in Sandwich, he felt that he just about had everything in place to put his plan into action.

Thus, our house at 19 Rosedale Boulevard (now 342) was born.

Dad purchased doors, window frames, tiles, electrical switches, fixtures, brick and part of a central vacuum system (in 1920?), which did not work then, and does not work now, according to the current owner. The master bedroom had a master panel with about 24 switches, which were two way – they could be operated from two locations. Therefore, any noise in the night meant that one could turn on lights and fixtures anywhere in the house!

The bedroom doors, and all the closet doors had one-inch plate mirrors on the backs. All remain to this day, except for one. When I first met the current owner, she asked me why the built-in buffet and china cabinet had drawers marked with "Pontchartrain Hotel – Detroit, Michigan."

For many years, there was a small, three-foot solid brass drinking fountain in the foyer, which was the same as the children's fountains in the old J.L. Hudson Department Store in downtown Detroit. I suppose it was there so that my mother could play bridge and not be interrupted if my brothers needed a drink. The light fixture from the porch (which was installed in a later home) appears to have been from an indoor fixture in the hotel.

Mrs. J. J. Grozelle, whose husband was the manager of the Home Bank (later the Imperial Bank) at Sandwich Street and Mill, in Sandwich, often mentioned to me in later years, that she would have liked to have seen the house fully furnished. Apparently, all the money went into the building of the home. I guess that with a 28-

---

Top: Bits of the Pontcharrain Hotel were incorporated into this Sandwich home, photo circa 1922.

foot living room, if you sat in front of the fireplace, you would have had to scream at someone sitting in one of the few chairs across the room, in order for them to hear you!

All the tile in the kitchen and bathrooms were unglazed and a day lady once told my mother, "the man who put these tiles in here was trying to kill his wife." Dirt would accumulate rapidly on the tiles and in the grout and they were very difficult to clean.

I have no record of what the house cost. We did have a bill that itemized walnut doors: 90 cents each, duty: 20 cents. The beveled glass front door was one of two that came from the entrance to the dining room of the Pontchartrain, and remains in the house.

At the time that this house was built from my father's plans, I believe that John L. Forster's house to the south of ours was already built. Mr. Forster was principal of Sandwich Collegiate, now Forster Collegiate. The house to the north was, for many years, the residence of Mayor Arthur J. Reaume.

The house originally had a large brick garage. My mother often regretted not renting it during prohibition to a man who said he needed storage for "food products." We knew what these products were strictly of the liquor variety, as he was obviously a bootlegger.

Sadly, we lost the house in the Great Depression and had to move into my grandmother's house on Elm Avenue in Windsor. Though I never lived in the house on Rosedale, (I was born after we moved), it remains close to my heart.

The "PONTCH"– Then & Now
Detroit's Two Pontchartrain Hotels

When Detroit's first Pontchartrain Hotel was demolished in 1920, the interior elements were sold off and some found their way into Amedee Marentette's matrimonial home on Rosedale Boulevard in Sandwich.

The original Pontchartrain Hotel was located at Woodward and Cadillac Square in downtown Detroit. It was built in 1907 on the site formerly occupied by the Russell House, which was Detroit's premiere hotel from the late 1800s. The Pontchartrain's spacious, glittering saloon was a famous enclave for auto pioneers and featured a painting of Comte de Pontchartrain, the French minister responsible for sending Cadillac on his voyage to Detroit. The Pontchartrain quickly became the city's leading hotel and its barroom was frequented by financial magnates of the time. However, in 1915 the new Statler Hotel opened and immediately became a chief rival of "The Pontch." The Statler raised the standards for Detroit hotels so much that, in an effort to remain competitive in the hotel business, five floors were added to the original ten-storey structure in 1916.

The Pontch only stood until 1920 having been trumped by the newer hotels. When it was demolished, the National Bank Building (today's First National Building) designed by Albert Kahn, was built in its place.

In the 1930s, in a time when Detroit was without a Pontchartrain Hotel, the Pontchartrain Wine Cellar restaurant opened on Larned near Washington Boulevard in a building from the 1880s. The Ponchartrain Wine Cellar was regarded as one of Detroit's best restaurants, and was in business for around 50 years, closing in the 1980s.

The second Pontchartrain Hotel was built in 1965 by architects King and Lewis. It was erected on Larned directly across from the Pontchartrain Wine Cellars restaurant – on roughly the same site as the French explorer and fur trapper Antoine de la Mothe Cadillac's Fort Pontchartrain du Detroit, which was built in 1701. The new Pontch was designed so that each room had an angular bay, thus allowing a view of both the river and the city. The "Top of the Pontch" restaurant closed several years ago, but can be rented out for parties.

Issue #40, December/January 2003-2004

Above: The new Pontchartrain Hotel, built in 1965. Each room has an angular bay window affording a view of both the river and the city.

Left: Detroit's first Pontchartrain Hotel, built in 1907 at the southeast corner of Cadillac Square and Woodward Ave. Notice the five stories that were added to the top in 1916; it was torn down 4 years later.

The Griggs House

by Asha Tomlinson & Elaine Weeks,
Issue #8, April/May 2000

Adolphe and Lydia Morrill cherished the sweet melodies floating from their baby grand piano in their new home's music room. The year was 1919, WWI was over and the future looked bright. Listening to their daughters play the piano buoyed the Morrill's optimism.

After a falling-out with his business partner Lorne Wilkie, Adolphe had sold his half of Windsor Machine and Tool. The family had been living in a house on the business property, located just west of downtown Windsor near Riverside Drive. The sale of his business shares provided Adolphe with enough money to buy the stately Stephen A. Griggs home in the prestigious town of Walkerville and start over.

Dennis Rowley, grandson of the Morrill's, heard many stories about the house from his mother, Grace Morrill, who was raised in the home.

"Grandpa was full of ideas" says Rowley. "One time, he decided to breed canaries as a hobby in the attic. He begged and borrowed canaries until he had 300 of them; but one day, the birds flew against the screen window and they all got away. Grandpa had to pay back all the people who had lost their birds. Grandma wasn't too happy – needless to say."

He also remembers his mother telling him that his grandfather was able to rekindle his machine tooling business in the garage on the property. "He was doing work for the Heinz Co. back there and even Henry Ford!" marvels Rowley.

Life in the Grigg's house was not always melodic for the Morrills. Tragedy struck when daughter Lydia died at age 15 of rheumatic fever; years later, the Morrill's ended up divorcing and the house went back on the market.

In 1952, it was purchased by Dr. Walter Percival; the family lived in the house for 45 years. Aware of the historical significance of the home, Dr. Percival succeeded in having the house designated; his efforts are marked by a small plaque attached to the front gate.

Current owners Sharon and Berkley Curtis transferred back to Windsor from Germany in 1997. "The company gave me a week-long house hunting trip," recalls Berkley. "I was visiting friends on Chilver, who said a house on Kildare was for sale. When I went through the place, I knew that this was the house for me."

Situated at the gates of Willistead Manor on the corner of Niagara and Kildare, the house was designed in 1905 by the talented American architect, Albert Kahn.

The house is named after its first owner, Stephen Griggs, vice-president of the Walkerville Brewery Company. Nine years later he would purchase the brewery from the Walker family.

Designed in the Arts & Crafts style, the home has a very English country look. The main floor layout includes a sunroom, living room, formal dining room, half bath, butler's pantry, kitchen and cloak room.

Four bedrooms, the main bathroom plus an ensuite bathroom occupy the second floor and two more bedrooms are located on the third.

One of the home's most unique features is the Dutch front door. The three to four inch think door splits so you can open just the bottom of the door or the top, supposedly to keep out squirrels on those hot days before there were screen doors.

"When we bought the house, we didn't know how much work it would require. It was intimidating!" Sharon admits. "Every single room

---

Griggs Granddaughter

A friend who recently moved to Windsor, picked up your paper in the lobby of her apartment building, and sent it to me. I am delighted with your paper and am looking forward to future issues. I was born on what was then Victoria Street (now Chilver) in Walkerville.

My father built our home on Willistead Crescent (the first house there). His father was a close friend of Ed Walker (E. Chandler Walker, Hiram's son and owner of Willistead Manor) and moved to Walkerville to operate the Walkerville Brewery for him, which my grandfather subsequently bought. As for me, I went to school in Walkerville, but took off for Toronto when university days rolled around.

I married a fellow law student, and we eventually ended up in Montreal, where we lived from 1940 on. My husband died seven years ago, and I now live in a residence for elderly women in downtown Montréal, just a short walk from a park, which provides me with views of the St. Lawrence River, evoking fond memories of walks with my father along the Detroit River.

Detroit was his family home until he came with his father, mother and sisters to Walkerville. My grandfather built a house opposite the Willistead Gates, facing St. Mary's Church; I do not remember the street names [Kildare Road at Niagara]. I'd like to have a map to identify them. Keep up your good work.

Margaret (Griggs) Abbott, Montreal, Issue #8, April/May 2000

in the house needed work. It was something we weren't prepared for but it has been kind of fun too."

The Curtises feel fortunate the house came with so much property. "It's really rare to find this much space in the middle of this old neighbourhood. The inground pool is very private thanks to the stone fence around it – and the large garden is certainly a bonus," says Sharon.

The historical designation meant the Curtises were prohibited from changing the original architecture on the outside the house. Berkeley said restoring this aspect of the home was quite an effort.

"It took two to three months of solid work to restore the garden brick wall. We took it down brick by brick, cleaned each one by hand and then re-layered them. That's been our lengthiest restoration project so far."

While restoring the interior of the home, the Curtises discovered a few surprises, such as solid maple and oak countertops, oak floors and oak ceilings hiding under Formica, linoleum or paint; the paint on the fireplace was stripped to reveal the original mahogany.

The Cobbles

Houses are usually made of bricks or wood to stand tall, represent a place one can call home, and to last for years to come. But one house, located at 849 Kildare Street near St. Mary's Church, gives new meaning to "home." This ten-bedroom, brown cobblestone house known as "The Cobbles," served as home for Polish Army officers and the Canadian Women's Army Corps during the Second World War. In addition, it was a temporary Metropolitan Hospital School of Nursing in the late 1940s.

The Cobbles was built in 1906 for Victor Williamson, who lived there until 1924, when it was sold to Earl C. Drake. Williamson was an independent contractor and builder in Walkerville at the time. The Walker family controlled development of Phase Two planning in Walkerville, encompassing an area south of Wyandotte. The Walker's did allow independent builders in the area, which may explain the unique design and fieldstone construction. One outstanding feature of The Cobbles is the roofline of turrets, stone chimneys and the variety of dormers. Its slate roof, so in keeping with a stone house, was recently replaced with asphalt shingles.

Williamson became a joint partner in a real estate/insurance firm in 1911 and was president of the construction company that built King Edward School (demolished in 1993 and rebuilt in 1995) and many other area landmarks. The Cobbles, now a family residence, is a lasting testament to Williamson's unique interpretation of home.

Janice Domingo, Issue #2, May/June 1999

photo: C. Edwards

An intriguing find was a safe hidden in the basement. A room much like a large-sized bank vault was found within the panel walls. It has no handles or doorknobs so the room is never completely shut because the Curtises fear their children might get trapped inside. Berkeley believes the room was used during the prohibition to store bootleg liquor.

The couple is keenly aware of the house's historical significance, considering the many people in the neighbourhood who have lived long enough to know stories attached to the Griggs house.

"After we moved in, folks would tell us stories about the house – we began to appreciate that it is a very significant part of Windsor's history," said Sharon. "We want to do everything we can to preserve the history of the house while making it comfortable enough to be a family home."

1136 Devonshire Road

Mrs. C.H. Ramin lived at 1136 Devonshire for 38 years; the Ramins purchased the home in 1939. While re-decorating, they discovered the date "1929" written on a wall and assumed this was when the house was built. (Based on deed information for 1129 Devonshire, 1136 was likely built before 1920).

In an issue of *The Walkerville Times*, a reader wrote that Harry Low, the infamous local rumrunner, lived in the house at 1144 Devonshire, next door to 1136.

According to Mrs. Ramin, Harry Low lived at her house, not at 1144 (Lowe later built one of Walkerville's most elegant mansions at the corner of Ontario and Devonshire, subsequently lived in by former Prime Minister Paul Martin).

After selling the house, Mrs. Ramin was surprised to get a call from the new owners telling her they had found about $90 in the staircase.

"I had forgotten all about it! I used to keep 'mad money' in the secret hideaway in the third step of the inside staircase. When I came by to claim it, the owners gave me a tour. I was happy to see that they had restored the stove in the kitchen with its big warming oven. They had also painted and redecorated, and I hardly recognized my house.

I couldn't go upstairs as there were too many memories…"

This house at 793 Argle Road, Walkerville, was built around 1900 and was purchased by Charles Fox Sr. in 1917. His wife Mary is sitting at left with friends on the front porch. Son, Charles Fox Jr., still lives in the home.

Photo courtesy Charlie Fox

40 Elm Street, Kingsville

The Davis H. McCay House

by Renka Gesing, Issue #52, March/April 2005

It was a big gamble, and it all started with a telephone call in November of 2003. Kingsville auctioneer Jean-Marc Lacasse was set to auction off a beautiful old house at 40 Elm Street in Kingsville. He knew Ken Turner had a great interest in local history and called to ask if he could find out when it was built. "I'll not only tell you when it was built, but I'll be there to bid on it," answered Ken.

"Of all the houses I've seen when I drive around Essex County, this is the one I really liked, but I never thought I'd have a chance to own it," declared Ken. "There haven't been many chances to buy the place. It's only been for sale four times in the past 120 years."

The current owners wanted it sold as quickly as possible, and auctioneering rates are 1/2 that of real estate fees.

Even though Ken and his fiancée, Yvonne Harrison, loved their previous home – another heritage Kingsville house built in 1925, formerly owned by Harold Cull, one of the town's early mayors – the McCay house already had a hold on them.

Ken and Yvonne went to the auction – the required $10,000-deposit in hand – wondering if they were taking too big a risk. "We thought we were going to stop at a certain price," said Ken, recalling the bidding. Even though they did go over their predetermined limit, the two were very happy with their final bid – "a very reasonable price" of $225,000 for a unique home complete with an acre of land.

It's amusing to compare this dollar amount with past selling prices. Ken discovered that: "The 1884 tax assessment for the house and property valued both at a total of $325. In 1952 it sold for $7,500. In 1962 it sold for $7,400. At this time it was in a state of some disrepair and had water in the basement, knee deep."

Fortunately for Ken and Yvonne, by the time they moved into the house in January 2005, it was in much better shape, thanks to the care of the previous owners, the Runstedlers. "All the plumbing and electrical had been upgraded. Most of the work required was cosmetic – re-plastering, repairing clapboard siding, having some stained glass releaded."

Ken and Yvonne threw themselves into that cosmetic work, doing as much as they could on their own during holidays and weekends. They spent last summer stripping and repainting the entire house and windows and Yvonne stripped and painted all the detailed dentil moulding.

"In the peaks are different designs," said Ken, "sunburst, flower designs – there's a lot of wood moulding. We used colour to accent it and bring it out." They stayed with traditional historic colours: red river and Vandeusen blue for the mouldings, alum and Broad Street Beige for the siding.

Darrell Shad and Shadow Construction repaired the damaged clapboard and wood mouldings on the front of the house as well as part of a corner of the fieldstone foundation. They also repaired and reconstructed the intricate wood mouldings and spindle work on the front porch and reconstructed and mended the porch pillars. "They did such a good job, you can't tell it's been repaired," said Ken.

And Essex Stained Glass expertly repaired the leaded glass windows.

Ken spent hours researching their new home. "I like all things historic. Yvonne and I are big fans of architecture, especially of the Victorian era – and Queen Anne is our favourite style." Ken has a degree in history and, as president of the Essex County Historical Cemeteries Preservation Society, works to locate and restore pioneer cemeteries.

Their Victorian home, he discovered, was built by Davis H. McCay in 1884. McCay started his working life as a carriage and wagon maker, then became a builder of many of Kingsville's landmark buildings. He also opened McCay's Hardware Store, worked as a special constable, and served as a town councillor. He even tried his luck in the Yukon gold rush of 1898.

The home was built on property belonging to one of the area's original pioneers – the Ulch family. R. Ulch was McCay's father-in-law.

People often ask if the house is haunted. Answers Ken: "We haven't experienced any ghostly experiences. We do know there were two births, four deaths, two funerals and a wedding in the house. Ours will be the second wedding." Ken and Yvonne have put off their wedding until the

Builder of home, Davis McCay (with mustache) and family in front yard, early 20th century. photo courtesy K. Turner

house is completely ready to hold their reception.

Their guests will be sure to admire the home as a classic example of Queen Anne Revival style. One special feature, besides the beautiful dentil moulding and intricate woodwork, is the two-storey open turret porch. Also noteworthy are the uncut fieldstone foundation and, on the inside, the wood flooring and paneling, and the wonderful windows.

The floors are of alternating oak and cherry. The main floor has sycamore paneling throughout, while the trim upstairs is oak. The ceilings are 10 feet high in the living areas; even the basement has high 7-foot ceilings. The attic is unfinished, but Ken and Yvonne have plans to convert it into a library or loft space.

"The house was built without a fireplace, which we thought was unusual," said Ken. He then determined that McCay was the proud owner of one of the very first forced coal burning furnaces – "a status symbol; you didn't need a fireplace when you had the latest technology."

Ken and Yvonne look carefully each time they expose some older spaces. "We found a 1917 Kingsville Reporter newspaper, printed just after the Halifax explosion." They're really hoping to find a stash of gold nuggets from McCay's prospecting days, which would be a gold lining to a lucky bid at an auction – but no luck just yet.

What, exactly, is Victorian?

Many people use the term to describe an architectural style. However, Victorian is not really a style but a period in history. The Victorian era dates from about 1840 to 1900. During this time, industrialization brought many innovations in architecture. There are a variety of Victorian styles, each with its own distinctive features.

The most popular Victorian styles spread quickly through widely published pattern books. Builders often borrowed characteristics from several different styles, creating unique, and sometimes quirky, mixes. Buildings constructed during the Victorian times usually have characteristics of one or more these styles:

Gothic Revival Architecture: Victorian Gothic and High Gothic buildings feature arches, pointed windows and other details borrowed from medieval cathedrals.

Victorian Italianate Architecture: Rebelling against formal, classical architecture, with low roofs, wide eaves, and ornamental brackets, Italianate is sometimes called the bracketed style. Second Empire or Mansard Style: Characterized by their boxy mansard roofs, these buildings were inspired by the architecture in Paris during the reign of Napoleon III.

Folk Victorian: Just plain folk could afford these no-fuss homes, using trimwork made possible by mass production.

Shingle Style Architecture: Often built in costal areas, these shingle-sided homes are rambling and austere. But, the simplicity of the style is deceptive. The Shingle Style was adopted by the wealthy for grand estates.

Victorian Romanesque Architecture: Designer Henry Hobson Richardson is often credited with popularizing these romantic buildings. Constructed of stone, they resemble small castles. Romanesque was used more often for large public buildings, but some private homes were also built in the imposing Romanesque style.

Above: McCay house in the early 20th century. There are a few subtle differences – steps were wood – now stone, finial post on tower is now missing, kitchen added to rear. Notice horse hitching post in front. photo courtesy K. Turner

811 Devonshire Road

Foxley

by Chris Edwards, Issue #53, Summer 2005

In the early 1900s, Walkerville expanded from a small village into a boomtown. Development pushed south toward Wyandotte from the site of Hiram Walker's distillery along Riverside Drive.

The Walkerville Land and Building Company controlled all the land from the Detroit River south to Ottawa Street between Kildare and Walker Road. After the death of Hiram Walker in 1899, the Walker Brothers, Edward Chandler, Franklin and Harrington embarked on an ambitious scheme to construct executive residences south of Wyandotte, in Phase 2 of their Garden Plan, a concept which separated industry from residential areas by streetscape design; Walker Road housed numerous factories.

The Walker brothers, through their Walkerville Land and Building Company, instituted a rule that houses within the expanded garden community around the newly constructed St. Mary's Church should be no less than 5,500 square feet on two floors, presumably to keep the riff-raff out.

As an apprentice for the Detroit firm of Mason and Rice, an aspiring architect named Albert Kahn had earned his stripes by working on the interior of the Hiram Walker World Headquarters. When he was commissioned to build a manor home for Edward Chandler Walker and his wife Mary (Willistead Manor 1906), he soon found favour with other Walker executives seeking homes in the Willistead Crescent district.

The Walker brothers commissioned Kahn to build for Clayton Ambery, secretary and director of Hiram Walker & Sons, a house worthy of a Walker executive on a lot at the corner of Devonshire and Cataraqui. Kahn drew references for the house's design (dubbed Foxley) from the English countryside's "cottage style." Foxley features a "mock tudor" design, highlighted by picturesque half-timber second and third stories trimmed in cypress wood. Two Carved faces peek out from under the front rooflines – one happy, one miserable.

Although Kahn never received formal education he produced buildings that have incredible scale and detail. He had unusual design instincts and an intuitive sense of domestic design that resulted in homes considered as masterpieces by students of architecture. He was a hands-on architect who supervised all work on his projects during his early domestic period (pre-1920).

Foxley is set equidistant on a triple lot – the front and backyards are exactly 80 feet in size. Kahn recognized that placing a home in the middle of the lot afforded its residents panoramic views of the gardens from all main floor rooms. In some rooms the views extend to three sides. To improve these panoramas, Kahn installed an astonishing 118 windows throughout the house, (all were painstakingly removed, painted and reinstalled by its current owners). The attention to detail, scale and balance at Foxley is amazing. One outstanding feature is the low-slung fireplace in the front den, bedecked in Marovian tile that heats the room perfectly.

Above: Painstakingly restored (above November 1994) by its current owners who possess a special affinity for the work of its designer, architect Albert Kahn, Foxley, built in 1907, is one of Walkerville's premiere residences.
Next Page: Foxley vault

Foxley soon rose to national prominence after an article appeared in The American Architect in 1910, highlighting Kahn's distinctive design. It is much larger than it appears from the street and features four stories, including a full finished basement, encompassing almost 10,000 square feet of living space. There was once a top floor poolroom for the men to enjoy cigars and after dinner drinks, and a storage vault in the basement, purportedly used for valuables such as paintings, jewellery and silverware when the owners were away.

Under construction while Kahn finished work on Willistead Manor (1906), Foxley forms an important part of Albert Kahn's early domestic architecture period. As Kahn received more commissions to design factories for the captains of the auto industry, his domestic design commissions increased dramatically (see sidebar: Kahn Goes Domestic).

Commissioned in 1906 and completed in late 1907, the Ambery's moved in for Christmas in 1907. The Walkerville Land and Building Company retained title. Kahn even designed furniture for the house, which forms part of the current interior and is the perfect match for the carved woodwork within its walls.

One unusual feature of the house was a very large battery charger (discovered in the garage by Foxley's current owners) for an electric car built in 1907; Mrs. Ambery donated the unique vehicle to the Walkerville school system.

An interesting anecdote concerns tunnels that run next to Foxley from the river to Willistead – reputed to be used during prohibition to stash contraband liquor headed to the USA. As it turns out, the tunnel was filled with coal and moved by a giant screw that would feed the coal to the boiler rooms.

Clayton Ambery died suddenly in 1915 at the age of fifty; he was the second Walker executive to pass away within a five-week span, the other being Hiram Walker's son Edward Chandler, who lived at Willistead Manor. Both men are buried in the cemetery at St. Mary's Gate. According to an obituary in The Evening Record, Ambery was a man "of simple habits and retiring disposition (who endeared) himself to the entire community."

As the Walkerville Land and Building Company still held title to the house, the Walker brothers placed his successor, William Isaacs, in the house. Isaacs was instrumental in negotiating the deal that led to Harry Hatch purchasing Hiram Walker & Sons' distillery in 1926-27. The house's title was then transferred from the Walker holdings to Mary Isaacs, William's spouse, after the deal was consummated.

Issacs passed away in 1941 but his wife Mary remained in the house until her death in 1964. Little work was done on the house under Mary's watch, and after her death at 89, the house was bequeathed to the Children's Aid Society, which sold the house for $28,000 to the McVickers family, who came to Walkerville from Cape Breton. Foxley was almost sold to the same developer who razed the fabulous Pentilly Mansion at Tuscarora and Kildare to build the unsightly apartment blocks next to Walter Kelly Funeral Home. But the developer went bust and Foxley was spared the wrecker's ball.

When purchased in 1993 by its current owners who possess a special affinity for the work of Albert Kahn, the grounds around the house were in a state of disrepair. The house could not be seen from the road, as plant life had completely overtaken the lot. Thirteen trees were removed and the hedge that surrounds the house (which is original) was trimmed to expose the house from the street.

The house has been painstakingly restored; everything within is authentic and very little has been modified from Kahn's original design. Although the kitchen has been totally rebuilt, it retains the same shape and design; in fact, the original stove has been stored in the attic. All fixtures that were removed and replaced (by exact copies) have been wrapped and stored in the attic. The landscaping emulates what Albert Kahn would have envisioned.

The current owners have updated the wiring, plumbing and have installed a state-of-the-art heating and cooling system, a new cedar roof and copper flashing.

Empire Brick was hired for the brick restoration. This took three weeks and invovled the house and the garage. According to Glen Beecroft, Brick Manager for Empire Brick, "The before and after were amazing. The condition of the brick was good considering the age of the house but it was definitely time for a complete maintenance. Now the house is good for another 75-80 years."

The exterior features cypress wood trim, which lends to the Tudor feel, unfortunately painted in the 1960s. Normally, cypress weathers like driftwood but the paint pigment stained the wood and cannot be stripped without damaging the beams, so must remain painted.

The striking woodwork inside, including paneling and beams, is of museum quality. While the house is very large it does not feel overly spacious, another Kahn specialty.

Walkerville real estate remains the best value in the country if one considers the quality of the homes, the neighbourhood, the lifestyle and the well-preserved Garden Plan neighbourhood envisioned by the Walker brothers more than one hundred years ago. And Foxley is certainly one of the finest private residences within this remarkable district.

7
Places
We Remember

Pitt Street and Trolley Station, 1911. photo David L. Newman Collection

Long Live Bob-Lo!

by David L. Newman, Issue #21, February 2002

A hot summer day, a few dollars in your pocket and the urge for fun was once a recipe for a trip to Bob-Lo Island, a Canadian island with a strong American accent. Who could forget the Wild Mouse roller coaster, the Dodge-em cars – or Captain Bob-Lo putting his hat on some lucky kid?

Situated eighteen miles southwest of Windsor, Bob-Lo was named Bois Blanc by the French, due to the birch and beech trees that once covered the approximately half-mile wide by three-mile long island.

The area's non-French residents called the island Bob-Lo, since they couldn't pronounce Bois Blanc properly. The name stuck for years and was officially accepted by the owners and area residents in 1949.

The island's written history dates to the 1700s when French Catholic priests set up a mission for the Huron Indians residing in the area. During the War of 1812, the great Shawnee Indian Chief, Tecumseh, set up his headquarters there. Three block houses were constructed on the island in the 1830s and Bois Blanc was a stepping stone for runaway slaves during the American Civil War.

A lighthouse was built in 1839 on the southern side of the island to guide ships into the narrow straights behind Bois Blanc. In the 1850s, Colonel Arthur Rankin purchased the island from the government for $40 including 225 acres, but could not buy the remaining 14, as they were leased for life to the lighthouse keeper, Captain James Hackett.

In 1869 the island was sold to Rankin's son, Arthur Mckee Rankin, a well-known stage actor in New York. He built an elaborate home and held grand parties there.

Rankin also stocked the island with deer, elk and wild turkey.

The island was later sold to Colonel John Atkinson and James A. Randall, who built a home on the site of one of the block houses. The island's next owner was the Detroit, Belle Isle and Windsor Ferry Company. In 1898 the Bob-Lo Excursion Company was born.

The Bob-Lo Steamers

The first steamer to carry passengers to Bob-Lo was the ferry Promise. Frank E. Kirby designed the next two steamers: the Columbia, built in 1902, and the Ste. Claire, built in 1910. The Columbia's first trip was July 8th, 1902; the Ste. Claire's launching was May 7th, 1910 and her first trip was later that year. The Ste. Claire was named after Lake St. Clair and St. Clair River, which in turn reflects the fact that the explorer Robert de La Salle paddled through the two waterways during the feast of Ste. Claire. The Columbia, named after Christopher Columbus, celebrated her 100th birthday in 2002. She is the oldest steamer in the USA, with the exception of vessels classed as ferries.

Top: The Ste. Claire, built in 1910, carried passengers for over 70 years.
Right: The Bob-Lo dock in Detroit, early 1900s – price of steamer ride to "Bois Blanc" was 25¢.
Photos: Dave L Newman Collection

In 1958, Bob-Lo added trains rides that circled the park. Above is the S.S. Ste. Claire (a Browning Line) at Bob-Lo dock and one of two scenic railway trains making a two mile trip around the island. Photo David L. Newman Collection

Both steamers are propeller driven, as were all North American steamers. The Ste. Claire is 197 feet long, 65 feet wide and 14 feet deep. Her tonnage is 870 grt and 507 nrt. The engine is a triple expansion steam with 1083 horsepower; she can carry 2,500 people.

The Ste. Clair and the Columbia, which served 81 years on a single run – a record unequalled in U.S. Maritime history – are the last of the classic excursion steamers in the U.S.

U.S. Military Invade Bob-Lo

The first attractions to the island were quite simple. There was the trip to the island, picnicking and a carousel. Henry Ford had famous Detroit architect Albert Kahn design and build the stone pavilion.

During World War I, U.S. military personnel were not to leave the country when on leave in Michigan. The military officials, however, made an exception for Bob-Lo, deeming it a hardship not to let military men relax there with their ladies.

The Papoose IV once sailed between Amherstburg and Bob-Lo Island every 30 minutes.
Photo: David L Newman Collection

An Amusement Park is Born

In 1949, bankruptcy threatened the island park. Windsor Mayor Art Reaume wanted the island to be designated a National Park but the Browning family stepped in and bought the property and the steamships.

The Brownings transformed the island into an amusement park. They built roller coasters, rides, a ferris wheel, a fun house, a dance hall and an antique car exhibit. The zoo held 300 exotic animals – in 1972, seven baboons escaped their pens and roamed free; the last one was finally captured after being coaxed out of the fun house. The miniature railroad that went around the island was built in the 1960s.

In 1961 the dock area was upgraded. The freighter Queenston was stripped and sunk in place as a dock.

In 1972, three people were arrested for causing a disturbance on one of the ships. They ran around yelling, "the ship is sinking!" Twenty-three people were injured in the melee.

In 1973 the Thunder Bolt roller coaster was constructed. Built of steel, it thrilled the crowds that lined up to ride it. The next addition was a log flume. In 1978, the 100-year-old carousel was restored and returned to active service.

Captain Bob-Lo

Getting to the island from the Canadian side was easy. A small ferry called the Papoose carried passengers to Bois Blanc from Amherstburg. From the American side you boarded at the foot of Woodward Avenue, later the Cobo Hall area, then lastly the Gibraltar area.

Once on the Columbia or Ste. Claire, you could take in the beautiful view of the shorelines on both sides for the trip, which lasted over an hour.

For the children there was Captain Bob-Lo! He was a small man appropriately named Joe Short, who amused the children as a clown for the Ringling Brothers Circus. In this 1960 photo (at right), he has a good grip on the arm of a little girl who happens to be my girlfriend, Joan. Her brother, Robert is to his right. Captain Bob-Lo would hand out colouring books and small items to

The Bob-Lo steamer Columbia, seen next to one of the two miniature trains, was built in 1902, and named after Christopher Columbus, celebrated her 100th birthday in 2002. photos David L Newman Collection

amuse the kids on the trips. He always wore an oversized hat, binoculars and carried a sceptre. Joe worked on the ships until he retired, at 90 years of age. He passed away the following year.

Island for Sale
The Brownings sold the island in 1979. Several owners followed, including IBC (owners of the Harlem Globetrotters) and AAA Michigan.

In 1987, U.S. Immigration people and Ontario officials spent all day on the island, rounding up members of the Outlaws, a motorcycle club.

End of an Era
In 1990 the old carousel, whose figures were made by famous carousel maker Marcus Illions, was auctioned off. The top price paid was for a deer – $34,000 U.S. Next was a horse that went for $21,500 U.S.

Labour Day 1991 – the last ferry ride, the final bag of cotton candy – Bob-Lo Island closes. In 1992 the two steamships were named as national monuments. So ended a long and illustrious era for Windsor and Detroit residents. All that remains are snapshots, souvenirs and memories.

LONG LIVE BOB-LO!

Adults and kiddies' fire engine, Bob-Lo Island Park. Lea and Michael Appel of Windsor are the last two riders in this photo.

R.J. Cyr & Bob-Lo Connection
I read David Newman's article with great interest, as I have many fond memories of the island.

By way of correction, however, the Log Flume was installed in 1972, followed by the Thunder Bolt roller coaster in 1974. The roller coaster was an innovative design for the time and one of the first all-steel rides in North America. It was designed and fabricated in Japan, and when the amusement park closed, it was unbolted and shipped to Mexico.

Both rides were installed by R. J. Cyr Co. of Windsor. The rides were initially tested using sand bags, but when it came time to be the first human riders, Lorenzo (Red) Browning, owner of the island and my dad, Ray (R.J.) Cyr took the front seats. After they had deemed it "safe," they consented to give my sister and I the second seats.

Randy Cyr, Windsor, Issue #22, March 2002

Bob-Lo Perks
My younger brother and I were still in school during WWII and one of our summer jobs was on Bob-Lo Island. It was probably 1943 or '44, and it was as much fun as it was work. I don't recall the pay, but it included room and board. We stayed on the island for the summer in a 'men-only' dormitory. The female summer help had to leave on the Papoose before it quit running each night. My brother and I worked at the coffee/hamburger stand, which was at a corner of the cafeteria building. Getting to know the operators got us some free amusement rides – just one of the perks. I think Matti Holli led the dance band at the big pavilion that summer. It had a very impressive wooden floor as I remember.

The souvenir shot-glass [right] was picked up at a yard sale in 2001 in Charing Cross, just south of Chatham. I was going to send one to my brother but never got around to it.

Ron Lemon, Blenheim, Issue #27, September 2002

To the Mettawas!

Photo: National Archives of Canada

by Chris Edwards & Elaine Weeks, Issue #26, July/August 2002

To serve his business interests, Hiram Walker built the Lake Erie, Essex, & Detroit River Railway. For his recreation, he designed a grand resort on the main line of the railway, in Kingsville, on the shores of Lake Erie – The Mettawas Hotel, opened in 1889. The elegant hotel was torn down in 1902, but memories live on, particularly for Kingsville residents, and through "The Walkerville Mercury," published by Hiram Walker himself.

From The Walkerville Mercury, June 28th, 1890

There is a wise old proverb: "all work and no play makes Jack a dull boy." Perhaps at this time of the year, when the days are longest, and the sun is at its zenith of power, this adage is brought more forcibly to the mind of the wearied statesman or the toiling banker, merchant, and over-brain-worked professional man than at any other season of the year.

Although the custom is pretty general in most parts, another writer has just said, "In no other part of the world is the custom of seeking an annual change of air and scene so general or the provision for the habit so universal as on this continent.

Upon the coasts, in the mountains bordering our lakes, great and small, in fact wherever invigorating breezes prevail or climatic conditions are favorable to the constitutions or ailments of our people, are to be found hotels, which in numbers, dimensions and luxuriousness, excel those of any other country.

Notwithstanding the fact that there are so many places to choose from, the greatest difficulty arises in finding the right place to suit the habits and temperament of each member of the family or social circle, as the case may be. This place is too gay, that too grave; this too quiet, that too boisterous; and in trying to please all in the party or family in arranging the summer holiday, the cry is given out, "Where shall we go?"

…the place that suits the tastes and habits of each individual member of the party best will be Kingsville, on the Essex shore of Lake Erie, and that the Summer Resort Hotel, where the guest will find all the comforts and luxuries of a refined home, coupled with those out-door amusements which refined tastes and good manners demand, is The Mettawas, situated as it is, on the north shore of Lake Erie, the very waters of which lap the beach and feet of the hotel's lawns. To arrive at this delightful spot let all intending visitors by rail meet at Walkerville station, the chief station and starting point on the Lake Erie and Detroit River Railway Company's system, situated in the rising Town of Walkerville, and of easy access by ferry boat or street car from Windsor and Detroit, a good converging point from all parts of this continent.

When at Walkerville, board the 5:28 p.m. saloon car of the Mettawas Special, and for some 30 miles the visitor will pass through, alternately such sylvan and pastoral scenery that has justly earned this Essex peninsula the name of "The Garden of Canada."

Although one of the earliest settled parts of the Dominion, until opened up by the L.E. and D.R. Railway, it has hitherto remained but little known to the outside world, except to citizens of Detroit and some American sportsmen who have

Mettawas Lighter
Danny Pepper of Walkerville found this cast iron match lighter in the ruins after a fire at The Mettawas, many years ago.

Robin Hood on the Dance Floor

The excellent article on the old Mettawas Hotel in your July/August 2002 issue brought back many memories – especially the picture of the now long-gone outdoor dance floor and band stand that stood next to the cliff at the Lakeshore Hotel which had replaced the Mettawas.

I had occasion to be in Kingsville about four years ago (1998) and visited the site. Much to my surprise, the old dance floor is still there, although weeded over. In 1945 the dance floor was very much in use with "dime a dance" activity three or four times a week. A number of my friends from Assumption College and I had formed a dance band the previous winter called "Robin Hood and his Merry Men." We had introduced this band to the public at the old K of C hall, upstairs next to the old Vanity Theater, to try and lure away some of the teens who were going to hear Hal Campbell at the Masonic Temple at Erie Street and Ouellette Avenue, or Al Edwards at Coral Gables. We weren't great but the dancers seemed to like us and we were apparently good enough to be asked to play the summer of '45 in Kingsville at the Lakeshore.

Playing three nights a week, and sometimes to midnight Sunday when there was a holiday on Monday, was pretty rough, especially with most of the players holding down day jobs in Windsor.

However, there were some offsetting benefits, not the least of which was the billeting of a large number of farmerettes next to the hotel who were working on farms during the war for their summer vacation from school. With the girls outnumbering the guys about four to one, it made for interesting social activities. But, that could be an article in itself.

In 1945 gas rationing was still in effect, but the teenage musicians used a lot of imagination in working out transportation. We always managed to get ration coupons and borrowed pick up trucks with mattresses in the back to get there. We were young and didn't seem to mind travel discomfort.

Many of the players went on to become well-known in business, music and teaching. Readers might remember some of them (some are still playing) – Phil Murphy, Jim Collins, Roydon Smith, Bill Meloche, Gord Jupp, Pat Mullin, Jerry Nantais, Vance Hardy, Bill Peterson, Jerry Nantais, Gord MacMillan, Lenny Booker, J. Jack Amos, Jerry Brannigan and myself, of course! When the war ended in August, gas rationing ceased and a lot of young people from Detroit started coming to Kingsville to dance, which added much more activity to the Lakeshore and eased the transportation problems as well.

Sure, the war was still on with Japan until August, but the young people who attended the dances at the Lakeshore pavilion wanted to enjoy themselves in their time away from their work and "Robin Hood and his Merry Men" did its best to help them. The man who ran the dances at the Lakeshore, and I believe the hotel itself, was Joe McManus whose brother, Pat McManus, was a well-known and well-respected teacher at the Windsor-Walkerville Vocational School (W.D. Lowe).

Ray Pillon, Mississauga, Issue #28, October 2002

Dime a Dance Romance
Above: The Bandshell. Dancing under the stars was a popular event in the 1930s and 1940s, and certainly the outdoor dance floor by the lake in Kingsville was one of the most popular spots. Many area residents will remember the fun nights that were enjoyed at the outdoor dances in Kingsville at this bandshell.
Photo: Marie Sims, "Kingsville 1970-2002 – A Stroll Through Time" by Kingsville Gosfield Heritage Society.

---

been allured to its solitudes in search of game, and to the adjacent Island of Pelee after the finny tribe, for which the waters surrounding it are famous.

Passing quickly through the pretty hamlets and villages of Pelton, Oldcastle, Paquette, McGregor, New Canaan, Marshfield, Harrow, and Arner, and only 50 minutes after leaving the Walkerville station the visitor will alight at Kingsville station, and within five minutes' drive from the Mettawas, whose well-appointed omnibus and luggage car are always in waiting for guests and their baggage.

"Kingsville is one of the most delightful haunts of health and pleasure seekers, and enjoys the distinction of being the most southerly incorporated town in British America – a fact which has led to its receiving the sobriquet of 'The Sentinel Town.'

It derives its name from Colonel King, who early in the present century erected the first house within its limits. For some years the natural beauty of the locality and its reputation for healthfulness have attracted to it a steadily increasing number of summer visitors, and it was to meet this demand for accommodation that The Mettawas was built. The streets of the town are well shaded by maple trees, thus forming cool promenades."

Leaving the saloon cars at Kingsville station the visitor enters the omnibus and is driven along the well-made entrance road of the hotel and grounds, which is lined on both sides with young trees, and in a few minutes finds himself under the carriage-way portico at the main entrance hall of The Mettawas, a magnificent pile of buildings, constructed after what is known as "the American style of architecture."

Millennium Milestones: 1900/2000

The 3-story Mettawas was built of piled fieldstone with shingled gables, and contained 120 bedrooms. The exterior was impressive; seven balconies on the third floor, four on the second, and a white columned veranda stretched across the south side of the building, running the full width to the north side.

Designed by Mason & Rice Architects of Detroit, the Mettawas was reported to have cost $250,000. Well-to-do Detroiters would arrive at the fieldstone Kingsville railroad station. They then rode the three short blocks to The Mettawas in the hotel's carriage.

To supply the resort with the water, Hiram Walker had a complete water pumping system built at the bottom of the hill below the hotel. The pumphouse equipment also supplied the entire town with water and was eventually purchased by the town and from this nucleus was developed the modern plant that supplies pure water to the town today.

One of his sons, Franklin Walker, maintained a summer home in Kingsville for many years after Hiram Walker died in 1899 (it was called Birchlea Villa and was located on Park Street, near where Southgate Residence now stands).

In 1901, W.P. Beyer purchased The Mettawas. By 1902 bitterness developed between Beyer and the town authorities over property assessments. Unable to have the assessment reduced, Beyer made a final decision and the elegant Mettawas was torn down just 13 years after it was built. Gone was the splendor such as Kingsville would never see again. It was the end of an era. Only the casino and the servants' annex were left standing.

When the Windsor, Essex and Lakeshore Electrical Railway was opened in the early 1900's, the financial interests controlling the railway bought the Mettawas property. New owners built a little neat hotel called The Mettawas Inn on part of the foundation of the grand structure. The new summer hotel opened in 1914. This hotel was operated by the owners and several subsequent owners for many years with varying and rather different results and was eventually renamed "The Lakeshore Terrace Hotel."

After World War II, the notable casino was torn down. Leaving a faint memory of the original Hiram Walker family's presence in the town were the annex of the present building, which now stands uninhabited; the remains of a water pumping station, which has since been demolished, and a unique fieldstone railway depot, which once welcomed the well-to-do to Kingsville.

Top: The casino, part of the original Mettawas hotel, opened in 1890. A separate building west of the main hotel, it featured a bowling alley, dancing hall, billiard room, card room, lounging room, etc., but apparently no gambling area. Although the main hotel was torn down in 1903-1904, the Casino building remained intact until well after World War II. Photo courtesy Barbara Healey.

The Kingsville Train Station

Hiram Walker commissioned the eminent Detroit architects Mason & Rice to design and build the Kingsville train station, in anticipation of the railway line reaching Kingsville from Walkerville, in the spring of 1889. The interior layout included gentlemen and ladies' waiting room, ticket office, freight and baggage area, covered porch, porte-cochere, and a second floor bed chamber. Built of stone, complete with a slate roof, the station was equipped with gas heating and lighting brought in from natural gas fields nearby. Fares round trip to Windsor were 80¢ for adults 40¢ for children; the station has recently been restored.

Gone and Mostly Forgotten
The Old CPR Station

by Sherrill Tucker, Issue #11, November 2000

My friend Elaine Weeks (Managing Editor of the Walkerville Times) and I were jogging west along the riverfront path that links Walkerville to my old neighbourhood.

Left once again in Elaine's wake I took a breather by the railroad bridge, at the foot of Caron Avenue. While admiring the brickwork, I noticed the eastern portion of the bridge contained a convex arc which appeared to be the foundation of a building. I could also see a bricked up door and window. When Elaine returned, we decided it must be what's left of the old CPR station. But what happened to it, we wondered?

I decided to find out the whole story.

I thought this would be a pretty "cut and dried" tale. Not so. I was disappointed by the lack of information in our local public archives and the history section of the Windsor Public Library.

I called local rail and bus historian Bernie Drouillard hoping he would know something about this building but to no avail. A call to the archives at Canadian Pacific Railway in Montreal revealed only that it was built in 1890.

As Windsor was an integral link to the United States and all points east, it would make sense that ours would be one of the first stations built. CPR built 70 stations between 1886 and 1896.

Following this early phase, an eighteen-year construction blitz lead to more than 700 stations being built or replaced on their lines. The bulk of these stations were similar in style to the ones that existed in the town of Walkerville and downtown Windsor.

Most kept architectural embellishments to a minimum. Our CPR station was unique in that it featured a turret (only one other similar station was built in Smithville, Ontario).

Windsor Salt commenced business in 1892 and housed their first offices in the tower of the CPR station, though their main business site was on the south side of Sandwich (now Riverside Drive).

A major salt deposit was discovered right below where CBC Place now sits, on Riverside Drive West at Crawford. The only evidence today of this is that on occasion, sink holes have been known to appear in CBC's front lawn hence the wrought iron fence erected last year, for insurance purposes.

The CPR station was abandoned in the 1920s when a new one was built at the foot of Pelletier Street to accommodate train passengers coming through the (now electrically lit) train tunnel from the U.S.

Evidently, Windsor's turreted station was demolished some time during the 1930s. All that remains is a small portion of its foundation and a few photographs.

That its brief existence has not been well documented exemplifies how a piece of our history can be gone in the blink of an eye.

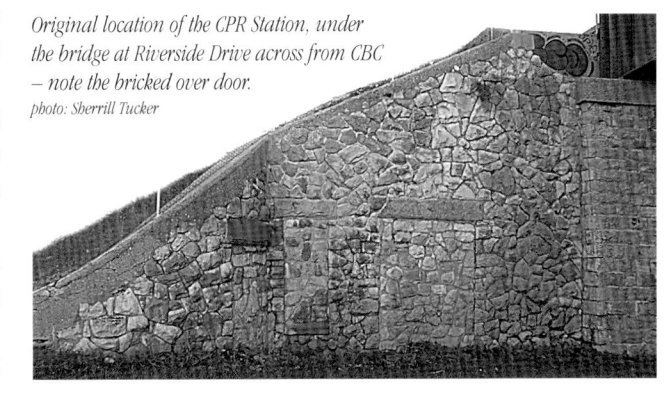

Original location of the CPR Station, under the bridge at Riverside Drive across from CBC – note the bricked over door.
photo: Sherrill Tucker

The Chilver Family of Walkerville

by Elaine Weeks, Issue #19, November 2001

"Subdivision of the Chilver estate, coming with the first glimmerings of development, marked the end of the farm as one complete strip of land, and ushered in an era of advance that is seen today in the lavishly-built area that borders on Victoria [Chilver] Road." The Border Cities Star, 1920s

You may think Chilver Road starts at the Detroit River and runs south a few kilometres to Memorial Drive in South Walkerville. But Chilver Road is much longer than that. Its roots stretch all the way back to Plymouth Rock in 1620 when a descendant of the wife of its namesake, Charles Lewis Chilver, crossed the Atlantic to the New World from England.

Arriving in Plymouth, Massachusetts on the Mayflower, this adventurous family eventually settled in Philadelphia. They proliferated and around 1760, a child named John Casper Fulmer was born. Sometime during the Revolutionary War of 1776, John settled in Mersea Township, in the County of Essex. He moved further north to Concession 3 and eventually owned nearly 700 acres of land. He found a local girl to his liking named Ann Fox and they married and had seven children.

A son named John married Betsy Wilkinson, who bore him four children. Their son, Francis Casper Fulmer, was born in 1835. At the age of 16, he took over his father's farm, then moved to Windsor in 1871 to start a livery business and a hack and sale stable. He did very well buying and shipping horses to the United States for use in the cavalry. Phoebe Jane McQueen became his bride in 1856.

Previous to this, Victoire Maisonville, whose husband had served in the War of 1812, received a Crown grant of land in what was to become Walkerville. One of their daughters, Eliza Grier, married Captain Thomas Chilver, a prominent figure in early "border city" days. He was owner of the ferry "Gem" which ran between Detroit and the Canadian side.

Almina Elizabeth Fulmer, first-born daughter of Francis and Phoebe, married Charles Lewis Chilver, son of the captain and Eliza in 1879. They had seven children: Henry Lewis, Frances Warren, Charles Alonzo Grier, Florence May, Mildred Priscilla, Lettie Elizabeth and Almina Jane.

Charles Lewis Chilver was the owner of the Chilver Land

Top: Charles L. Chilver in the early 1900s, riding to his farmhouse on Chilver Road (near Wyandotte) before it was paved; the house still stands.
Left: Almina Jane Chilver (mother of George E. White).

The Chilver farm house circa 1915, Chilver Road, south of Wyandotte.

The farm house as it appeared in 2003.

and Building Company and subdivided his grandmother Victoire's grant, which had become the family farm (farm plot #23), and extended from the Detroit River south to Tecumseh Road along the line now defined as Chilver Road.

Among Chilver's buildings were the commercial buildings on Wyandotte between Chilver and Jubilee Park (Peerless Ice Cream is in the corner unit), the commercial building at the corner of Chilver and Ottawa going east, the terrace homes on Chilver just north of Cataraqui (named after two daughters: May and Mildred) and the large frame house on Chilver and Cataraqui on the northwest corner.

The family farmhouse used to sit on the corner of Chilver and Wyandotte but was moved back to allow for the building of the Merchant Bank (later Bank of Montreal). The farmhouse still stands next to a parking lot. A small log home opposite the Victoria Tavern on Chilver near Assumption was once the stable.

A member of Walkerville town council, C. L. Chilver was also a member of the board of education, Chief Magistrate and Mayor of Walkerville in 1909 and 1910. He was born Dec. 10th, 1850 and died in the 1920s in his home in the Grier apartments (still standing on Riverside at Chilver), which was owned and built by himself and named for his mother Eliza, on the site where he was born in the pioneer border days.

Chilver Road, originally named Susan Road, was renamed Victoria Road, after Charles' grandmother Victoire. When Walkerville was amalgamated with Windsor, the road's name changed to Chilver as there was already a Victoria Avenue in Windsor.

Charles' daughter Almina Jane Chilver married Windsor pediatrician Dr. George E. White. Their children included George E. White, who was the owner of Geo. E. White & Son, Ltd. (building supply – see story in Legacy Profiles section). George and his sister, Ann Jasperson of Stouffville, provided The Times with information and photos about their family.

Above: Chilver stable, opposite Victoria Tavern, Chilver Road near Brant.

Left: May, Annie, Lettie and Mildred Chilver in front of Grier Apartments (Riverside Drive at Chilver Road) April, 1925.

All photos courtesy George White
(except 2003 photo of farm house – E. Weeks)

best of the times • 255

Angus Mackintosh
Ruler of Moy Hall

by Trevor Price, Issue #8, April/May 2002

Why is the beaver widely regarded as the national symbol of Canada? Because its fur was once in great demand. When the French first came to the shores of the St. Lawrence River and met the native peoples, they were greeted with enthusiasm since the Indians were anxious to trade furs (including beaver) for goods of European manufacture. This trade came to dominate the relations between Europeans and the native peoples of eastern North America during the 17th and 18th centuries. It influenced the patterns of exploration, the conflicts between natives and Europeans as well as the global conflict between Britain and France.

The French and their allies – the Huron Indians, gained access via the St. Lawrence to the major fur bearing territories of North America on the Canadian Shield. The British were able to out-flank the French by establishing trading posts in Hudson Bay, closer to the sources of the fur-bearing animals in Western Canada. The French responded by penetrating further into the Midwest into what we now know as the Great Lakes and from there down the Mississippi to the Gulf of Mexico.

The great French explorer – Samuel de Champlain who pioneered the Ottawa Valley Route into Lake Huron, led much of this exploration. Having obtained an overview of the dimensions of the Great Lakes, the French established key fortifications at such strategic locations as Niagara, Michilimacinac and Detroit.

Detroit was an especially favoured settlement because it had a climate, fertile land, and was a key link between the upper and lower Lakes, as well as a Garrison, which could threaten Anglo American penetration into the Midwest.

The British conquest of New France in 1760 gave control of the Midwest to Britain. Detroit became a British outpost and, as in the time of French rule, Detroit naturally focused on Montreal as the center of fur-trading enterprise. In Montreal, the French were replaced mainly by Scots and English traders who created the Northwest Company to compete with the Hudson's Bay Company.

Angus Mackintosh was one of the Scots traders who arrived in Detroit around 1787. He was originally from Inverness, Scotland, where his family had suffered from supporting the Jacobite cause in the 1745 rebellion against the Hanoverian monarchy of Britain. Mackintosh became a partner with other traders in the fur trade and prospered.

In 1796 the British agreed to evacuate the post at Detroit since Michigan and the rest of the Northwest Territories was allocated to the Americans by the treaty of Paris of 1783, at the conclusion of the war of Independence.

Above: Amherstburg artist Peter Rindlisbacher's painting of the HMS Schooner Nancy setting sail from Moy Hall on the Detroit River. Moy Hall was located on Riverside Drive, between Hall and Moy Avenues.

Macintosh was faced with the choice of staying on the U.S. side of the Detroit River or crossing to Upper Canada, which remained under British rule. In 1797 he purchased a tract of land just west of the site of present day Hiram Walker's. There he constructed a large wood frame building, which he completed by 1799. This became the focus of fur trading along the Detroit River and Macintosh himself became the chief representative of the Northwest company in this area and as such a figure of some prominence.

Although Macintosh and his enterprise at Moy Hall (named for the ancestral home of the clan Mackintosh in Scotland) is not sufficiently esteemed today for its local economic significance, it may be considered in many ways to be the forerunner of economic activity and wider trading relationships on the Canadian side of the Detroit River.

Moy Hall was a centre for the distribution of all kinds of trading goods such as blankets, kettles, tomahawks, knives, liquor and firearms. Macintosh traded with local farmers for grain and meat products, which were used in the fur trade to supply such an important link as Fort William at the head of the Great Lakes. Whisky distilling and the making of highwines (brandy) served to create products of higher value in relation to their volume as compared to trading the much bulkier and less valuable grains. This was important when distances were great and all goods had to be transported by canoe over water.

Rendering of Moy Hall
(courtesy of Windsor Community Museum)

Macintosh was also responsible for beginning a shipbuilding industry in the Walkerville locality when he brought the Jenkins family in to construct some of the earliest sailing vessels on the Great Lakes.

Mackintosh stayed in this area until 1828, when he was called back to Moy Hall in Scotland, after the death of his elder brother. Moy Hall was demolished in 1912 to provide room for new residential development.

"Amherstburg Shoreline, 1804"
by Peter Rindlisbacher

Local artist Peter Rindlisbacher has painted many scenes of local historical significance.

This scene is meant to depict a typical summer day along the waterfront of Amherstburg in 1804. At the time, the community was only about seven years old, so there was still much building yet to be done. The town was laid out in the area south of present-day Richmond Street; the area north of this was designated as "Naval Yard and Fort property."

In the painting, this division is marked by the palisade that runs past the red and yellow blockhouse, down to the water's edge. The placement of the buildings in this scene is taken from a photo of a scale model of this portion of the town, constructed using an 1804 site plan. Colouration of the buildings was taken from the Margaret Reynolds' watercolour of Amherstburg, done in 1813.

At this time, there were several schooners in the area, some in the late stages of their operating life. The anchored and partially de-rigged schooners in the centre and right of the painting might be the Francis and Maria. Because the river close to Amherstburg had the only reliable deep-water channel, one would typically see American ships passing by on their way to and from Detroit. A small American coasting schooner, perhaps the General Wilkinson, can be seen navigating around the downbound raft in this narrow stretch of the Detroit River.

Peter's quest for accuracy and attention to detail in his work is apparent when studying the step-by-step display he created to accompany "Amherstburg Shoreline, 1804." All of Peter's paintings make the viewer wonder if he somehow has travelled back through time. Peter (at left) also enjoys participating in military re-enactments. Here he is dressed as a provincial marine lieutenant from the Battle of Lake Erie, 1813. photo E. Weeks

best of the times • 257

Memories of St. Joe's

by Cathy Nantais, Issue #12, December 2002

The Windsor-Essex Children's Aid Society began as St. Joseph's Manor, a mansion housing kids in need. A former resident remembers life in this special place, known as "St. Joe's."

Children were brought to St. Joseph's on Riverside Drive in Walkerville because of abuse, abandonment, or for adoption placement. There were also some just hard to handle kids like me – usually teens or pre-teens who had gotten out of hand at home and were placed at St. Joe's where social workers helped the Sisters of St. Joe's keep us in line.

Usually a child would live at St. Joe's for a week to a month and then would either return home, be adopted or go to a foster home. When I went to St. Joe's in the 60s, I was a pretty cocky young girl. On my first day, I saw some girls cleaning and I asked one why she was washing the floor. She replied, "We all have chores here." I said, "Oh ya, well not me." About a year later, I was cleaning and a new girl came in and asked me what I was doing cleaning. When I explained she replied, "I sure won't!" I just turned my head and grinned. Was she in for a rude awakening!

The older kids also helped out with the younger ones, including the babies. One winter night around two or three in the morning, the teen girls were awakened by one of the Sisters to help some new arrivals. The police had brought in three abandoned kids wrapped in blankets. The youngest was barefoot, as the police couldn't find any shoes in their house for her. They all looked like they had rolled in dirt; their hair was matted, one had gum in her hair, and one had to have his head shaved. They were all very thin and frightened but they didn't cry – I don't think they had the strength.

It wasn't until they were bathed and put in pajamas that they began to smile. We fed them a snack and put them to bed and in the morning they ate everything they could. I was glad for them knowing the Sisters would take them under their wing and try to make their world a happy one. Then one day I came home from school and they were gone. No warning, just gone.

Then there was Janice, a little girl who had spent most of her home life in a closet. She was about four or five and she had been so traumatized she couldn't speak. Eventually, with love and patience on the Sisters' part, you couldn't keep her quiet. She followed me everywhere so we became "buddies." I was happy when she was placed in a very caring home.

St. Joe's was a huge place – I can't imagine that at one time a single

Above: Stately St. Joseph's Manor, located on Riverside Drive at the foot of Windermere Road. Photo: Windsor-Essex Children's Aid Society.

family had lived there. One of the rooms had been converted into a chapel with pews and an altar complete with stained glass windows. The Sisters always seemed to be in there although one would stay behind with us because if they all went in, they would have to take turns coming out in the middle of prayer to break up a fight, soothe a skinned knee, or answer the phone.

Despite their frequent visits to the chapel, you couldn't get away with much – the Sisters always caught you. My theory was God was on their side!

Fortunately, there was a huge playroom where we were allowed to cut loose. When we were given a snooker table we were in heaven. All good things come to an end however. The ball kept bouncing onto the tile floor making a racket and I think the sisters feared one of the younger kids would get hit with it. The table went into the basement so the boys had it to themselves because the girls didn't want anything to do with that skanky place. The only reason we would go down there was to get fruit and vegetables out of the cold cellar. When a new girl came we would spook her and tell her that a girl had once seen the ghost of a nun flying around the basement.

There were about six or seven bedrooms upstairs – two for the Sisters, four for the kids and one for the babies. Part of upstairs was off limits and I'm sure it held a quiet room for the Sisters. Lord knows they needed it with up to fifteen kids running around.

I shared a bedroom with the other teen girls. We spent a lot of time there and if we got bored, we would listen to music and dance in front of the big mirror. Sister Carmichael would come in and say something like, "Shame on you, don't be so vain!" but we could see the little smirk on her face. She was a wonderful nun but I remember she was always ill and one day she just wasn't there anymore.

We had our own bathroom off of our bedroom and once another girl and I decided to dye our hair black. When we woke in the morning, our faces were black too and our pillowcases had not fared any better. Soap and water couldn't remove the evidence. Passing the nuns to get to breakfast, we heard laughter and a warning not to repeat that mistake again from Mother Superior.

At Christmas the playroom looked like a picture from a fairy tale. A donated tree that seemed at least ten feet tall was decorated with hun-

The wading pool at St. Joe's. Photo: Windsor-Essex Children's Aid Society.

dreds of lights, ornaments and tinsel from top to bottom. All of us would just sit and stare at the tree wondering what Santa would bring. We had special guests at Christmas and now that I look back, no doubt some families wouldn't have had Christmas without St. Joe's.

St. Joe's yard went from Riverside Drive right back to Assumption Street, with an eight-foot high fence out back. There was a flower garden and a few wide steps that led into a huge backyard.

At night the backyard was very dark and on occasion a boy or two were known to jump the fence. Sisters wore habits in those days and had long beads that rattled when they walked. By the time one of the Sisters got out to the backyard the boy would be gone. But I am sure the Sisters weren't deaf and could hear the fence rattle as he made his escape.

The driveway went all the way back to what was probably at one time a carriage house. A groundskeeper/driver would take the Sisters to appointments, shopping, doctor's appointments, etc. In bad weather he would bring us back and forth to school (St. Anne's on Monmouth).

There were two covered verandas on the west side of the house, upper and lower. Sometimes we would sit in the upper one and look out at the river thinking that if we could we would take a boat and run away. A girl and I did just that except we escaped by foot. We were gone about 24 hours and were grounded upon our return.

I was lucky enough to have a terrific social worker named Marion Bednarski. She was gentle and compassionate. Alas I lost her too; she left and I was heartsick, but life went on.

A family in Riverside was going to take me in as a foster child but the husband was in a bad accident and they had to back out. I never got to meet them. I was put in a different foster home but I was so unhappy there I asked my social worker to take me out. She wouldn't so I ran away. When I ran away a second time I was finally moved back to St. Joe's. I went to live with my sister when I was 15.

Now that I'm grown and married with my own children, I look back at St. Joe's fondly. Memories of my two years there will live forever in my heart.

St. Joe's Tidbit *(at right: Cathy with her brother)*

When Cathy composed her memories of her life at St. Joe's, she included some questions that had never been answered for her: Who were the original owners of the home? How did it become St. Joe's?

Two manors once stood on the present Children's Aid Society's property; one owned by Hiram A. Walker and one by Chandler Merrill Walker (both nephews of Hiram Walker). Hiram A. was mayor of Walkerville from 1890-92, Chandler from 1894-95. Hiram A. Walker did not live in the manor that became St. Joe's as is commonly thought. His cousin (or possibly his brother) Chandler did.

The Manor was named for St. Joseph, the patron saint of children and families, and was opened in 1936 as a receiving home for the Roman Catholic Children's Aid Society. The Manor was torn down in 1969 when an Ontario Supreme Court grand jury determined it did not meet the Ontario Fire Marshall's building requirements. A second building was constructed in 1970, and named in honour of Roy J. Bondy, who served as the local Director of the RCCAS for 25 years. It too, was torn down, and the present building was built in 2003.

Cleary's First Auditorium

by Sherrill Tucker, Issue #7, February/March 2000

One building I've always loved is the stately, two-and-a-half-storey, red brick house at 274 Crawford.

The public archives at the Central Public Library on Ouellette satisfied some of my questions about this house. The old fire insurance maps are a great resource as they reveal how the city's streets were laid out back to 1924.

I got a kick out of the information in the large, dusty voters' registration ledgers. Here one can find obvious information and some curious: the occupation of the owner – gentleman, spinster, baker, etc., the numbers of persons living at the address, the heads of cattle and how many dogs they owned.

I felt like I was on some kind of wonderful treasure hunt, especially when I discovered that the Crawford house was once the home of Francis Cleary, a name that is ingrained into the local psyche.

Cleary served on our city council from 1882 to 1885, including three years as mayor. He was a barrister and Clerk for the County Court, founder and president of the Essex County Historical Society at the turn of the century, and patron of the (now defunct) Cleary Auditorium. Cleary was instrumental in opening Ouellette Avenue to the water's edge for a permanent ferry landing.

Cleary was not the original owner of the home. John Armour, gentleman/agent/accountant, had that distinction. It appears he purchased the property in 1866 for $102 from Mr. A. Crawford for whom the street was named.

Until the home was built in 1869, the voter's registration ledger states that the property was occupied by one dog. The Armour family lived there until the late 1880's when Francis Cleary and his family moved in.

The style of architecture appears to be a blend of Queen Anne/Victorian Gothic styles. Supposedly based on the simple elegant English architecture typical of Queen Anne's reign in the early 1700's, the style began to accommodate features of other periods including medieval, Tudor, Elizabethan and Jacobean. When the fashion reached North America, French, Flemish, and sometimes swiss elements were added to the already complex mixture. Irregularity of outline and floor plan became hallmarks of the Queen Anne style, with projecting sections, bay windows, towers and turrets adding complexity to the roof line.

I spoke with the current owner, who has lived there since 1956 and had received a citation from the Windsor Architectural Conservation Committee in 1983.

The only major changes she has made are in the upgrading of the kitchen and bath and removal of the slate roof. The original moldings and trim are apparently still intact, as is the very imposing 8' tall front door. The third floor no longer houses servants who would have used the back stairs on their way to the kitchen each morning.

This beautiful home, with its wrap-around verandah (replaced by a front stoop) was host to many a grand party in the Cleary days, according to an old neighbour who's since passed away.

Carriages would pull up and discharge their fancy passengers at the front entrance and their buggies were parked around back, by the carriage house (where we can assume the drivers had their own little gathering).

Clay tennis courts on the property south of the house kept many prominent ladies and gentlemen entertained during the warm weather. The Cleary Family held title on the home until 1935.

The house was vacant when the Salvation Army Grace Hospital purchased it to use as a nurse's residence in 1940. Some of these nurses maintain fond memories of life in the old house.

At a class reunion in 1983, many knocked on the door, anxious to tell stories... most memorable being that the bathtub was so large two woman would sit, one at each end, to soak after a long day on the wards. Apparently, the house was also a home for unwed mothers, no doubt during the ownership of Grace Hospital.

In 1954 the Sun Oil Company bought the property and put up a gas station on the tennis courts' site. They sold the home to a Mr. Tesloff who had plans to use it as a nursing home.

Surprisingly, this property is not designated under the Ontario Heritage Act, according to information received from our City Planning Dept. Hopefully, the historical and architectural significance of this building will be recognized and will ensure that the building will remain for future generations to enjoy and appreciate.

Above: Built in 1869, in the Queen Annex/Victorian Gothic style at 248 Crawford is a west end classic.

c. 1878
Dominion House

by Bill Marentette, Issue #13, February 2001

The Dominion House is the oldest remaining continuously run tavern in the Border Region. From its inception, when the stagecoach ran between Windsor and Amherstburg, it has served local residents and numerous travellers. When Frederick Neil published "The Township of Sandwich Past and Present in 1909," the Dominion House, owned by John McCarthy, had been operating at its present location for 26 years; 118 years later, it operates in the same building and location, having survived fifteen or sixteen different innkeepers.

The Dominion House was named by Frank Dent in 1878 when it was on the west side of Bedford Street (Sandwich Street), although it had been a hotel dating back to 1859, operated by James Cotter and owned by Charles Askin.

Albert Lininger ran the old hotel until it burned to the ground on the night of February 23rd, 1883. In March of the same year, Mr. Lininger reopened the hotel across the street in an existing building, built by Francois Janisse, a local contractor, with a clapboard exterior, and a front porch and side topped by a railed veranda. The grand porch and veranda were removed in 1945 or 1946.

By the late 1880s, my grandfather, Daniel Marentette, operated the house until his untimely death of heart failure at the bar on Saturday evening July 28th, 1902. My father often spoke of living at the hotel with his two sisters, and his mother cooking meals on a large wood stove. They raised hogs for personal use and to feed patrons; a garden behind the hotel supplied fresh vegetables, etc.

Father told of farmers from LaSalle and River Canard hauling their produce by horse and wagon to Detroit's Eastern Market, crossing the river by ferry on Friday night and returning Saturday. The horses would automatically turn into the lot on the west side of the building where a watering trough and well were located and refresh themselves while the owners would do likewise at the bar.

The Dominion House played a role in the history of Sandwich, and as my father often recalled, juries from the old County Court house would dine at the hotel and Essex County Council members who would also spend off-session time at the hotel.

No Place Like Home:
Standing next to the man on the bicycle is Dominion House operator,
Daniel Marentette and his son Amedee. Standing on the upper veranda, left to right are
Florence and Corrine Marentette, both born in the hotel, and their mother Edwidge (née Janisse).

Following the death of my grandfather, my grandmother sold the hotel to Eugene Breault, a long-time friend of the family, later elected Reeve of Sandwich and Police Magistrate in 1909 Following Breault's ownership, the hotel was purchased by Capt. John J. McCarthy, then Lorne White (1920-1922), was innkeeper during the first years of prohibition 1920-1922.

The next owners, William and Jean Boyer (1923-1948) faced many problems, as did most hotel owners during the twenties and thirties including prohibition, the Depression and rationing of beer and restricted hours during WWII. It was not the best of times to run a tavern. One bright spot during this time was the construction of the Ambassador Bridge; Bill and his wife housed bridge workers at the hotel.

Sid Walman arrived from Toronto after working for the Paramount Hotel in the Spadina-Dundas district, looking to buy into the local restaurant business, put off by the high prices in the Toronto area. After 25 years, the Boyers sold their business to Walman in 1948.

Soft spoken and congenial, Walman put the "DH" on the map with hospitality, good food and a great staff, catering to the University crowd, and the locals. He opened a basement lounge for poetry readings, etc. and many university professors held regular classes at the DH.

In 1989 after 48 years, Sid sold his tavern to Amanda Heiser & Co., a long-time employee; by 1993, Ann Peterson, a former DH bartender, became a partner.

The Corporation of the City of Windsor designated the properties, including the lands aand buildings known as "The Dominion House (Tavern)" as properties of architectural and/or historical value of interest under Part IV of the Ontario Heritage Act in March, 1993.

In 1994, Ron Limarzi and Sam Simoff, both experienced food handlers, took over operation of the DH. Within two years, they sold the business to Mike Balun and Natalie Bouliann, who operated this historic roadhouse until it closed in May, 2004.

In January, 2006, four Windsorrites took over this historic social landmark that has enjoyed so many generations of patrons: Wes Balazs, the Di Pierdomenico borthers Brad and Brian, along with Scott Sharon. All have fond memories of the DH, having attended the University of Windsor.

postcard: David L. Newman Collection

C. H. Smith's Department Store

A retailing giant in Windsor for more than 60 years, C.H. Smith, founded in 1914, was the city's largest and most popular department store through to the 1960s. Smith originally opened a store on Pitt Street, and then moved to its famed Ouellette Avenue location (near Pitt Street) in 1919. Its imposing architectural design altered the entire appearance of lower Ouellette Avenue. The building was torn down in the 1970s. Smith opened a 90,000 square foot store in the Devonshire Mall on October 23rd, 1974. The British firm, Marks & Spencer, bought Smith's on October 10th, 1975; it closed on August 14th, 1976.

Aboard The Aquarama

by Bonnie (Hazen) Nelson, Issue #10 September/October 2000

One summer's day in 1957, grandma's tenant, Miss Thelma Montrose, a secretary for Hiram Walker's & Sons, arrived at grand's door all in a dither. She just had to go to the third floor to look down the river from Milly Morrow's apartment.

By the state of her I was sure a relative of hers was lying in the Detroit River! Off we went to the third floor. Milly let us in and we all peered out her dining room window. To our astonishment there lay a huge black hull on its side in the river half out of the water – the Montrose – no relative but the name was the same. For a few weeks we kept an eye on that ship, driving down to the shore to watch the process of raising her. Then one day she righted herself and was towed away.

That story brought back memories of another ship that passed briefly through my family's life – the Aquarama. She spent one glorious summer on the Detroit River moored on the American side. Not too long into that summer, my parents booked a day trip for our family, down the river and out to Lake Erie. There are always specific highlights in a person's life and that was mine. Mom, dad, grandma and me – thirteen years old – on that great ship.

It was a world unto itself; my parents had taken cruises the odd time, but this was my first. We boarded on the Detroit side of the river. I recall a huge dance floor and a live band, numerous dining rooms and to my surprise, escalators. Lunch was a smorgasbord of mind-boggling delights. Most of all, I remember my first time dancing with my dad, a very special moment in a young girl's life. I didn't give my dad a moment's peace once I discovered dancing. Mom and Grand visited with other passengers and sipped on sarsaparillas, while I discovered another world.

Living just two blocks from the Detroit River always afforded great adventures. Across the tracks and down to the water or a walk along the tracks keeping an ear and eye out for trains. Big shiny new black steam engines like the 5588. They were a real part of kids' lives who lived in Walkerville below Wyandotte. Spewing black smoke makes me wonder how any white laundry ever survived hanging out on a line.

Counting boxcars and seeing where they originated from was something to do on a summer evening. Boxcars brought hobos in those days, and the old Peabody bridge was a refuge for them. Off limits for myself and friends, but we knew we could see through those iron bars (beside the ramp that let you walk across the bridge) into the nooks and crannies where hobos used to spend the cool summer nights, waiting for the right train to move slowly through Walkerville and out into southern Ontario and points unknown.

Until I was four, my parents and I lived in Grand's third floor apartment; the river was in full view over the treetops. Last year, I videotaped this grand old river for my children to see. I taped

Looking down on the "Club Deck" of the Aquarama.
Photo: David L. Newman Collection

the Detroit skyline at night and the ghostly ships slinking through her black waters without a hint of noise, only to be detected by moving lights. That river was so much a part of my life.

I have always lived on the water, no matter where my travels have taken me. Be it the Detroit River, Lake Erie, Lake Ontario, Georgian Bay, the St. Lawrence and now, Passamaquady Bay off of the Bay of Fundy, water has been a constant in my life. And now my children reflect on their times to remember and tell me they will always be beside the sea.

If the Detroit River could speak, the endless stories it could tell — of love and romance, intrigue and tragedy.

Publisher's Note: According to a website maintained by James Neumiller of Harrow, Ontario, the Aquarama (originally called the Marine Star) spent six years in dry dock in Windsor in one of the old slips on Russell Street.

Orchestra on main stage, main dance deck on upper deck.
Photo: David L. Newman Collection

Shop, Stay, Save, Play

Remember the big electric sign installed on the top of the tunnel ventilation building... the one that flashed on and off and read *"Windsor – Shop Stay Save Play/C'mon Over?"* It faced Detroit of course. The fortieth anniversary of turning it on was in January. There was much fanfare but by 1968 it was structurally unsound and they pulled the plug.

Another milestone of sorts is the fortieth year of the completion of the "Jackson Park Overpass;" that one has had a longer run.

The S.S. Noronic was before my time but one of the last regularly scheduled passenger vessels not mentioned at all in your feature (Oct. 2002) was the *"Aquarama."* Does anyone remember this one? I saw it sail past Windsor several times in 1959 and 1960 when I was a lad and I seem to recall it kicked up quite a wake. I also remember the Aquarama's modern design and the fact that it even rated a mention in a Pepsi radio commercial sung by Joanie Sommers.

What a fantastic read *The TIMES* is. Non-baby boomers look out. There will be more from our generation in the future no doubt. Ya gotta remember.

Peter Faulkner, Calgary, Issue #31, February 2003

Editor's Reply: The Aquarama was a former Liberty ship, built in 1945 in Chester, PA for the Second World war, but it made just one trip across the Atlantic before the war ended.

This sign lured Americans to Windsor; it was located on top of the tunnel ventilation building, and torn down in 1968.
Photo: David L. Newman Collection

It was designed for 35 to 40 years of service, but during the last six decades it has actually been in service for around five years. A Detroit industrialist eventually bought it and spent $8 million converting the USS Marine Star into a cruise-ferry ship that took passengers between Detroit and Cleveland in the late 1950s and early 1960s.

The new Aquarama had nine decks containing four restaurants, four bars, movie theatres, recreation areas and room for 160 cars and 2,600 passengers. But it was remembered as much for its mishaps as for its Great Lakes grandeur. The Aquarama is currently docked at the Cargil Pool Elevator Pier in Buffalo, N.Y. awaiting possible restoration.

Fifties Chic: the viewing lounge. Photos courtesy David L. Newman Collection

S.S. Aquarama, Great Lakes passenger ship.

Last Paddle Wheeler on the Great Lakes
The Lansdowne

by Charmaine LaForest, Issue #16, Summer 2001

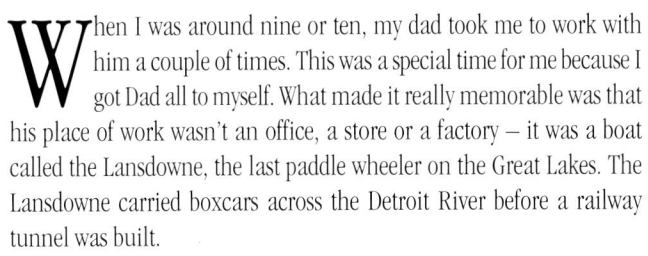

When I was around nine or ten, my dad took me to work with him a couple of times. This was a special time for me because I got Dad all to myself. What made it really memorable was that his place of work wasn't an office, a store or a factory – it was a boat called the Lansdowne, the last paddle wheeler on the Great Lakes. The Lansdowne carried boxcars across the Detroit River before a railway tunnel was built.

The Lansdowne was almost like a barge, except it was propelled by a paddle wheel on the sides. It had two sets of railroad tracks running end to end. The steering was done in the wheelhouse, which was about 30 feet above the deck. When docking in Windsor or Detroit, the boat's tracks had to be lined up with the tracks on the shore so the boxcars could be pushed by an engine onto the ferry.

Dad took me with him when he worked the evening shift when the boat was docked – his job became that of a night watchman. There wasn't much for my father to do on the watch shift so we'd sit and watch the sunset, which always seemed softer when we were on the boat. Dad told me that you could predict the next day's weather by the sunset or sunrise. There was an old saying he told me: "red sky in morning, sailor take warning, red sky at night, sailor's delight."

At around eight o'clock, we'd eat the lunch my mother had packed for us. My peanut butter and jelly sandwich always tasted better – creamier and sweeter – than it did at home. Dad had a can of sardines, a couple of hard-boiled eggs and some buttered bread.

We'd sit and watch the Detroit skyline as lights started to blink on like the stars in the sky. Dad would smoke his pipe and drink his coffee. The two odours would mingle together with the sound of the waves gently lapping against the boat. The smells made everything seem right in the world.

Once it got dark, Dad would hang a lantern over the side of the boat to attract fish so we could catch some for Friday's dinner. All kinds would swim by to check us out – short, squat perch, the longer more streamlined, yellowish pickerel, and the fat, whiskered catfish. We'd stop after catching four or five perch. Dad would wrap them in newspaper to bring home.

I'd get sleepy before the shift was over so Dad would take me up to the wheelhouse. There was a brown, stuffed leather bench just big enough for me to curl up on. It had a slightly oily smell that reminded me of my baseball glove after I'd treated it with linseed oil.

Dad would cover me with an old woolen blanket that pricked my skin and made me itch. The soft starlight and the gentle whoosh, whoosh of the waves mixing with horns would soon lull me to sleep.

When his shift was over, Dad would gently wake me and carefully lead me down the stairs from the wheelhouse holding a lantern, so I wouldn't trip. Then we'd walk over to the bus stop about three blocks away for the ride home.

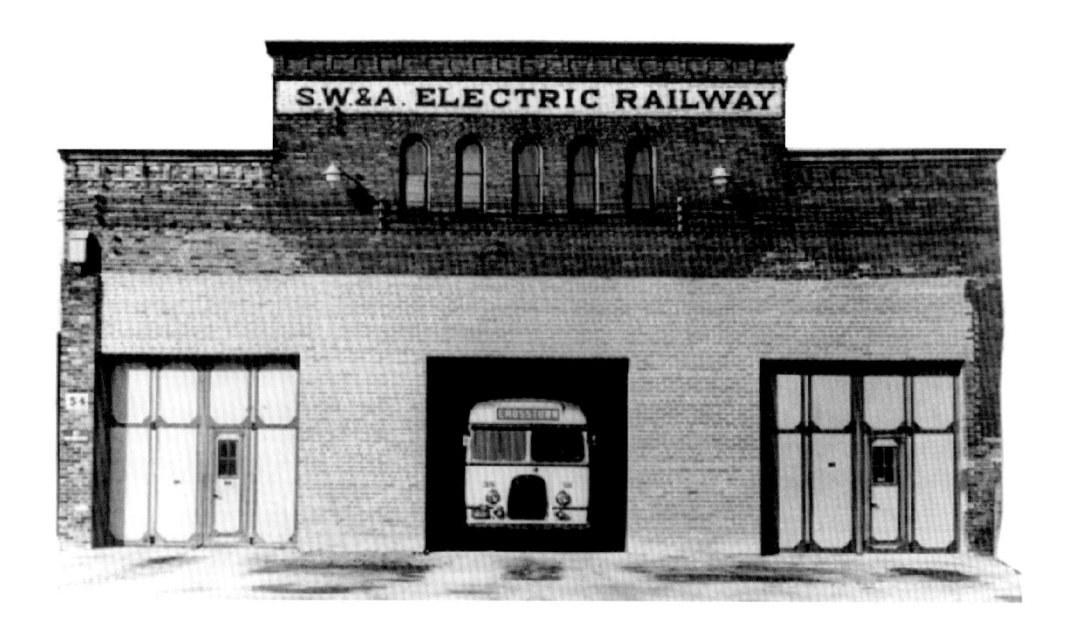

Birthplace of Windsor & Area's Transit System

The Junction

by Sherrill Tucker, Issue #8, April/May 2000

One hundred and fifty years before the Casino attracted thousands of tourists to Windsor every day, another local tourist attraction was a *real* hot spot!

In the mid 1800s, thousands came to Windsor every summer to visit the sulphur springs in Brighton Beach, just outside of Sandwich. In order to accommodate the thousands of mostly American tourists flocking to the area, the Ontario Legislature passed an act in 1872 approving a horse drawn street car line.

The City of Windsor cleared a 100-foot wide swath of land from Bruce west to Huron Line to create London Street (now University Avenue). The six car trolley line opened on July 20th, 1874. Rates "from any point in Sandwich" to Assumption Church were six cents; to Campbell, seven cents; and eight cents to Windsor.

During the very snowy winter of 1875, the railway substituted sleighs for the horse-drawn streetcar. Thus began a nearly 100-year tradition of street car companies being responsible for plowing and cleaning our main roads.

The original streetcar line did not prosper and changed hands many times (even Americans were involved at one point) until the Sandwich, Windsor & Amherstburg Railway commenced operation in June, 1887.

In 1891, a powerhouse (to equip the road for electric operation) and the London Street trolley barns were built just west of the Michigan Central Railroad Bridge. The powerhouse apparently also 'sold' electricity to its neighbours during its brief history.

The first electric streetcar ran between Windsor and the town of Walkerville. The one-and-a-half mile long line was officially opened on June 9, 1886, with a travel time of 12 minutes to Walkerville. It is thought to be the first electric streetcar in North America but our Municipal Archives has no information that would back up this claim.

While the trolleys disappeared in 1937, the London Street Trolley barns still exist (though another smaller version out back is long gone, as are the street rails) on University Avenue West at the foot of Wellington Street.

The S.W.& A. ran their operations there from 1887 until 1947, with a freight office and barbershop to the east. The Windsor Rollerdrome (1949-52) was located in the building, which most recently held "The Junction," a family entertainment facility.

Windsorite Brenda (Gallimore) Gall loved rollerskating and remembers going to the Rollerdrome as a young teenager with her

Above: A bus ready to leave the Junction on University. photo courtesy Bernie Drouillard

Trolley cars and depot. photos courtesy Bernie Drouillard.

babysitting money. "The floor was so smooth and there was never any drinking or fighting – you were kicked out if you started anything."

There were unofficial 'races' on Saturday afternoons bringing people from all over the county for the good-spirited competition.

Other neighbourhood girls from those days whom I spoke with indicated that they "weren't allowed to go," and others "didn't have money for that kind of thing."

Both of these buildings and the adjacent property were onces owned by the M.G. (George) Butler family and were managed by Doug Butler, Sr. (one of George's sons) and Doug Jr.

In 1951, Michael George Butler bought the buildings from the S.W. & A. and started the family business. Calling themselves 'Industrial Distributors,' they warehoused "a little bit of everything:" maintenance and janitorial supplies, hoists, chain, all kinds of rope, hoses, valves, tools, etc… I even saw 'wellies' and rain slickers. All the things a hardware store junky like me loves.

Blueprints provided by local bus historian Bernie Drouillard, show that when the powerhouse was in use, tracks brought the coal car right into the building, to a small room behind the boiler room. Upstairs in the back the original trusses are exposed.

Patrons during the trolley barn's sever-year incarnation as the family entertainment facility, "The Junction," were likely unaware that remnants of a maintenance pit, which hearkens back to the building's garage days, were still in the building. The original heavy sliding doors had been moved and were used as wall dividers throughout the building.

The scene of many children's parties (even adults were known to have whized down the curvy slides), came to an end in 2005 due to competition from other entertainment attractions and establishments throughout Windsor and Essex County.

Over the past year the M.G. Butler and Sons building housed a tow trucking company among others things, while The Junction remained vacant. These two fine historical buildings face an uncertain future.

Left: The SW&A Terminal Yard (Junction) in the late 1930s. Both buildings still stand on University Avenue West. The building on the left was the Street Car Barn.

Photo courtesy Bernie Drouillard (found on Andrew Foot's website: internationalmetropolis.com)

Right: A full lot of parked buses, foot of Wellington Road. photo courtesy Bernie Drouillard.

best of the times • 267

Hudson's North Pole

story and photos courtesy John J. Vallance, Windsor
Issue #30, December/January 2002-03

Christmas season just isn't the same without the once-traditional visit to Hudson's in downtown Detroit for a trip to the North Pole, and a seat on Santa's knee.

The adventure always began with a bus ride through the tunnel from Windsor to Detroit. Stepping from the warm bus into the frosty air of Cadillac Square, the busy sidewalks would be crowded with throngs of holiday shoppers.

Snowflakes landed in your hair and the wind was cold, but you didn't care. You were heading to some place very special.

As you drew near, the building stood tall against the cold, gray sky, its display windows filled with the colours of the season. In contrast with the dark red brickwork, several thousand white twinkling lights formed a huge Christmas tree that stretched from the ground floor window awnings clear to the tip of the tenth floor! You had arrived.

As you pushed through the heavy revolving doors, the smell of bus fumes quickly dissolved into the lovely scents coming from dozens of cosmetic counters. Those who entered from Gratiot Avenue were greeted by the aroma of candy and freshly baked chocolate chip cookies.

You made sure to hang on extra tight to Dad's hand – he might never find you should you happen to get lost in this vast crowd. Still a long way up to your destination: the North Pole.

As you wait for the elevator a group of Christmas carolers entertains the crowd while noisy children take turns getting a sip of water from one of the sleek brass drinking fountains.

A lady operates this elevator – sharply dressed in a gray uniform with white gloves. Floor after floor glide by until finally, you arrive at the North Pole – in reality, the large store auditorium on the twelfth floor.

Stepping from the elevator, you stare in absolute wonder at an entire indoor forest of trees decorated with more lights than you could ever count. As you walk through the forest you see elves, reindeer and even chipmunks hard at work helping Santa get ready for his big night. Finally, to a long line of eager and restless children and you know soon you'll meet the famous jolly man himself.

After your turn on Santa's knee, you simply have to visit the spectacular Toy Department conveniently located on the same floor. What a department it is – an entire jungle of stuffed animals, dolls from around the world, games of every description, and speeding slot-car races! When you look up there are model airplanes hanging at crazy angles – some of them look as if they are about to crash into the bridges, castles and other fabulous creations built with Lego Bricks and Lincoln Logs.

You press your nose against the glass to watch several tiny trains make their journey over what seems like miles and miles of miniature electric track. You don't want to ever leave!

This was the special childhood magic of a visit to Hudson's on one cold December Saturday in 1964.

Hudson's was more than a store. It was a unique part of Detroit and Windsor's way of life for nearly a century. It was not just a place to buy things, but a place to be amazed!

Top: The Hudson's store consisted of six different buildings, built between 1891 and 1946. Together, they covered an entire city block at Woodward and Gratiot Avenues in downtown Detroit.
Left: Hudson's employees march in the annual Thanksgiving Day Parade dressed as toy soldiers, clowns, elves, and gingerbread men.

Hudson's seemed to have an unmatched sense of style and a one-of-a-kind flare for display. A trip to Hudson's was never just a shopping trip – it was an adventure!

By the time Hudson's reached its final Christmas season in 1982, the huge store was only a shadow of its former glorious self. Thirteen floors of merchandise had dwindled down to only seven. Only one restaurant was still serving meals. Although the fabulous Christmas decorations remained inside the store, the incredible animated window displays and giant tree of lights were gone from Woodward Avenue.

Following a gigantic January liquidation sale that nearly emptied the huge building of merchandise and fixtures, the lovely old department store turned out the lights and locked the doors for the last time on Monday, January 17th, 1983.

The demise of the store (1983), the building (1998), and the Hudson's name (2001) have left quite a vacancy in the downtown Detroit scene. At present, a brand new office and retail shopping development is under construction on the large site where the former red brick giant once stood.

But one thing is for sure – it will never be the same.

The sun sets for a final time on Hudson's Department Store, October 24, 1998. This surreal photo was taken by Detroit artist and internet pioneer Lowell Boileau from the 1st National Building, immediately to the south of Hudson's. Photo: Lowell Boileau (www.atdetroit.com)

Hudson's in Detroit: A Timeline

January 13, 2001, www.freep.com

1846	Joseph Lowthian Hudson is born in England.
1877	J.L. Hudson comes to Detroit.
1881	J.L. Hudson, age 35, opens a men's and boys' clothing store in the old Detroit Opera House building.
1891	J.L. Hudson builds an 8-story building at Gratiot and Farmer. This store, plus a 1907 addition, was demolished in the 1920's.
1881	Hudson opened his first store in the Detroit Opera House.
1911	J.L. Hudson's on Woodward opens. There were additions to this building as late as 1946. The store added an L-shaped, 16-story addition, a portion of which extended into a 25-storey tower. The addition was built between 1925 and 1928. A 12-storey addition at Woodward and Gratiot, site of the former Sallan Building, was built in 1946. By then, Hudson's contained 2.2 million square feet and 49 acres of floor space.
1912	J.L. Hudson takes a trip to England, and dies of pneumonia. His sister's sons take over the store.
1923	World's largest flag is first displayed on Hudson's store.
1927	J.L. Hudson's becomes the nation's third-largest department store, behind R.H. Macy in New York and Marshall Field's in Chicago.
1954	Hudson's opens at Northland Center in Southfield. Northland is the nation's first large suburban shopping mall.
1957	Hudson's opens at Eastland Center in Harper Woods.
1965	Hudson's opens at Westland in Westland.
1969	J.L. Hudson and Minneapolis-based Dayton Co. merge.
1970	Hudson's opens at Southland in Taylor.
1976	Hudson's opens at Fairlane Town Center in Dearborn and Lakeside Center in Sterling Heights.
1983	Hudson's closes its downtown store.
1976	Hudson's opens in the Fairlane Town Center, Dearborn, MI.
1984	Hudson's announces it will move headquarters to Minneapolis.
1998	Hudson's downtown building on Woodward is imploded.

2000 Minneapolis-based Dayton Hudson Corp. changes its corporate name to Target Corp.

2001 Target Corp. decides to change the names of its 60 full-line department stores, including Hudson's, to Marshall Field's, "increase the company's brand and strengthen its competitive position."

Left: The line-up to sit on Santa's knee.

Last Roar at "The Corner"

by Chris Edwards, Issue #5, November 1999

It's just a building.

From the outside, it looks more like a giant airport hangar than one of the most treasured landmarks in this area. But once through the gates, down the long corridors – a field of dreams. Do you remember the first time?

"I'll never forget the first time I saw it," says Al Kaline. "I had to convince the guards that I was a player – I was only 19 years old. When I walked in, I saw the most beautiful place I have ever seen, before or since. It was all green – the grass and seats. I'll never forget it."

Green in the shades we never knew existed. The sound of the crowd and vendors. And the smell of the place – didn't the air seem fresher, cleaner?

Just a building...

The corner of Michigan and Trumbull Avenues in Detroit has hosted baseball since the first game at the old Bennett park on 1896, making it the oldest continuing home to professional baseball in the world. Until now.

In the winter of 1912, the wooden Bennett Park was torn down, home plate was moved from right field, and a renamed concrete and steel Navin Field was built. Navin Field was expanded three times, the last coming in 1938 when it was renamed Briggs Stadium and the ballpark assumed the current structure that we know today.

A place that has served as a connection to life during turn-of-the-century America. Where we could visit the past. For over five generations,

From the dirt and cobblestones
An origin so humble
Emerged the famous Corner
Michigan and Trumbull.
– Ernie Harwell, the Hall of Fame voice of the Tigers –

a place to forget one's troubles. A healing place during depressions and riots, where spirits could be raised, hungry for something that could provide hope for tomorrow. A place to come together as a community. Common ground.

The Tigers played 6,873 regular season games at Tigers Stadium, where they had a won-lost record of 3,764-3,090 and 19 ties. In that time, there were only four World Series Champions; this was not a place of baseball dynasties. Maybe that's why the ones we remember seem so special – 1984's "Bless You Boys," the 1968 miracle team, or for the oldtimers, the 1945 post-war victory or the 1935 team, when the city partied through the night, a collective amnesia from the grips of the Great Depression. This event propelled baseball into the status of a civic religion, with the ballpark as its cathedral.

Above: Ty Cobb, called a genius in spikes, was arguably the greatest hitter in the history of baseball. photo: Detroit News Archives

Briggs Stadium under construction in 1937. Photo: Detroit News Archives.

They played football in the park too! Photo: Detroit News Archives.

Just a building…

For those of us on this side of the river, perhaps a trip across the ferry to the Jos. Campeau or Walkerville docks, in times that have been softened by memory. On a streetcar through downtown Detroit to the old ballpark. Years later, we'd travel by car or bus to a park that was always closer in proximity for us than for most Detroiters.

The Lions played football here, boxing matches were contested, opera and rock concerts performed, Mandella dropped in on his Freedom tour. For a people who had been through personal struggle, Mandella's visit to the corner joined Detroiters in celebration. Another moment that proved this was much more than a baseball park – it was a place that defined the city.

Still, this has always been a place for baseball, a mythical game that so succinctly defines the American spirit – a game of heroes – Cobb and Kaline, Kell and Crawford, Greenberg and Gibson. Tiger Stadium was one of the last bastions of an era that has almost completely disappeared – a time when it was a game, not a business, before the mass and crass commercialization of a sports machine that feels compelled to tell us when it is time to cheer.

Only two of these parks will carry the old tradition into the 21st century – Wrigley Field in Chicago, probably the purest baseball park left on the planet and Boston's Fenway Park– on the endangered species list. The Cubs are famously stubborn in their traditions – the team bans advertising signs on the field and features ivy against its outfield wall. Wrigley has less than 40 sky boxes in an age when many clubs claim 100 luxury boxes are essential to help financially support a team; it is a huge tourist draw. But Boston's Fenway Park will probably be toast in the next five years.

Hey, they're just buildings…

Why are these places so important? And why do we feel a pang when they are taken away? Notably, the crowds on the final day at Tigers Stadium booed whenever the new "Comerica" Park was mentioned (shamefully, the new park's name won't even be include Tigers!).

In the end, it is important to note that baseball is now a huge business. Players' salaries have changed the entire game, resulting in the need for owners to generate staggering sums of money every year. New parks serve that purpose, with their corporate boxes and sponsorships. And in 100 years, maybe they'll be saying: *"Isn't it a shame they're tearing down that old place – Comerica Park."*

Ghosts, Thrills and Voices Heard at the Final Game

"For that one particular year (1984) it was like a dream come true… they don't make them like this place anymore."
Alan Trammell, member, 1984 world champion team

"To play in the next century, you need a different outlook on the sport of baseball. You need a financially viable franchise to compete."
Bill Freehan, member, 1968 world champion team

"Today was as close to a perfect day as you can get.
Lance Parrish, member, 1984 world champion team

"When fans think about Tiger Stadium, they think about the people they were here with."
Jack Morris, member, 1984 world champion team

"The greatest thrill was to be on that team that won in 1945 – this place will always be special for me."
Billy Pierce, member, 1945 world champion team

"One of the nice things about getting old is, you forget a lot of things."
Dick Tracewski, member, 1968 world champion team

"Walking into Comerica Park, I hope some of those old memories don't die."
Dan Petry, member, 1984 world champion team

"In those days, the crowd didn't need to be prompted – they knew enough about the sport."
Gates Brown, member, 1968 world champion team

Bennett Field was built on the site of a haymarket in 1896.
Photo: Detroit News Archives.

photos: Windsor's Community Museum P5807K; PC-5725

Kresge's Department Store

When Sebastian Spering Kresge opened a modest five-and-dime store in downtown Detroit in 1899, he sold everything for 5 and 10 cents. The low prices appealed to shoppers and soon Kresge expanded to 85 stores by 1912, with annual sales of more than $10 million. Kresge changed the entire landscape of retailing. In Windsor, the S.S. Kresge store opened in the early 1920s on the main floor of the Victoria Building (at left), built in 1883, located at the southwest corner of Chatham and Ouellette. The building was destroyed in a spectacular fire on Christmas Eve, 1945, and reconstructed on the same site on June 24th, 1948. Its lunch counter was a popular congregating place for a cross-section of the people who were employed downtown. The site is now a Royal Bank Building.

photo David L Newman Collection

Elmwood Hotel

Famed 103-room hotel located on a 11-acre lot on Dougall Avenue, the Elmwood was a fine example of an art deco-style hotel. It enjoyed a run for almost 30 years until its owner, Al Siegel, filed for bankruptcy in December of 1974. Many top name entertainers highlighted the nightly floor shows: Tom Jones, Tony Bennett, Liberance, Ella Fitzgerald, Sammy Davis Jr., Jimmy Durante, Sid Ceaser, Milton Berle, Wayne Newton and Englebert Humperdink.

The Elmwood fell on hard times, as it could no longer afford the stars it had supported throughout the years. It was closed in December 1974, and re-opened as the Brentwood Recovery Home in October of 1983.

Street Life

Two views of the corner of Riverside (Sandwich) and Ouellette, at the turn of the 20th century. The Dominion Bank of Canada (top postcard postmarked May 6, 1911, photographed by renowned photographer Louis Pesha) formed part of the Norwich Block (Richmond Landing, on the southwest corner). The elegant Beaux Art style bank featured a marble façade. The adjoining buildings included the Dominion Security and Credit Company, W. Boug Clothier and a dentist. This entire block was razed in 2000 to make way for the DamlerChrysler headquarters. The Bank of Commerce (bottom) stood on the southeast corner. Travellers coming uphill from the ferry dock made many enquiries here. *postcards: David L. Newman Collection*

Above: Ouellette Avenue was little more than a dirt track in this image, postmarked June 14, 1908, facing north toward the Detroit River from Chatham Street; the Royal Bank (Manning Hotel) with awnings is at right on Pitt Street, and the old post office building is at left. postcard: Tim Baxter Collection

Below: Parade on Sandwich Street (Riverside Drive) in the 1890s; the Windsor Opera House can be seen in the lower photo (the large structure at left).
photo courtesy Georgina Falls

Market Life

North America's first farmer's markets imitated ones from our European ancestors; farmers rode into town on horse-drawn carriages to sell their cash crops to the city folk. The city market was located on this site in one form or another from at least 1877, until it made way for Casino Windsor in 1996. The market reopened as Market Square on Ottawa Street at Walker Road. *postcard courtesy David L. Newman*

The old City Market, Pitt Street at McDougall Avenue. In the photo above, circa 1910, plenty of horse-drawn carriages remain in use, side by side with the still newfangled automobile. *photo courtesy George White.*

Right: An even older scene of the market in 1905.

Business Life

Ley's Block was once the north block of Sandwich Street (now Riverside Drive) extending west from Ouellette Avenue, (pre-1871). The two-story wooden Record Building at right, (36 Sandwich Street West), was replaced by a brick structure after it burned down in the great fire of 1871. The Windsor Record was purchased by W.F. Herman, who renamed it the Border Cities Star. After amalgamation in 1935, the name changed to The Windsor Daily Star and finally, The Windsor Star.
photo courtesy Georgina Falls

best of the times • 275

FERRY LANDING, WINDSOR ONT.

Foot of Ouellette Avenue

Known for decades as "Ferry Hill," the foot of Ouellette Avenue was a bustling port, serving as the principal ferry gateway to Detroit and to cruiseships on the Great Lakes. In the photo at top, taken around 1908, the automobile has yet to become the dominant mode of transport. Several years later, an expanded landing features a mix of cars and horse-drawn carriages. postcards David L. Newman Collection

Farewell to the Ferries

Top: After the international train tunnel, the Ambassador Bridge and the Detroit-Windsor Tunnel were constructed, passenger and train ferry traffic between Windsor and Detroit diminished significantly. The days of the ferry steamers were numbered and eventually, passenger service was discontinued in 1942. The photo at top shows the Windsor ferry docks shortly before they were closed and then torn down.

Middle: Panorama of Windsor, circa 1910. *postcard David L. Newman*

Bottom: The Detroit and Windsor Ferry Comapny, founded in 1877, operated a fleet of steamers between Windsor and Detroit, including Belle Isle, Bob-Lo Island and many other Great Lakes destinations. The company ceased operations in 1938 when competition from the Ambassador Bridge and the Detroit-Windsor Tunnel sunk its business. Large advertisements on the riverfront buildings facing the river targeted visitors and locals alike. Postcard postmarked 1914. *postcard David L. Newman Collection*

best of the times • 277

Above:
Ferry boats LaSalle and Britannia, at the Windsor docks. Built in 1906, the Britannia was the final steamer added to the Detroit, Belle Isle & Windsor Ferry Company fleet. In 1925, when the Belle Isle bridge was built, the Britannia was refitted as a ferry boat, one deck was removed and a central structure built on the lower deck so cars could easily move on and off the boat.

The LaSalle was pressed into service in 1922 and ran between Windsor and Detroit until its final crossing in 1938. This steamer could handle up to 3,000 passengers and 75 cars. After the demise of the Detroit-Windsor Ferry Company both ferries were conscripted into the U.S. Coast Guard fleet.
photo David L. Newman Collection

Right:
Looking more like a scene out from the Mississippi Delta, the crew from the Detroit-Windsor Ferry boat "Excelsior" (built in 1876 by John Horn) pose at the Windsor ferry docks, c. 1890.
David L. Newman Collection

Above: Sheila, Brenda and Daisy Weeks watch the Bob-Lo boat Ste-Claire sail past.
photo courtesy Barb Moluchi

Right: The Aero-Ride at Bob-Lo Amusement Park
photo courtesy Bill Marentette

Below: On the way to Bob-Lo passengers enjoy the view from the Bob-Lo boat deck.
postcard: David L. Newman Collection.

best of the times • 279

The Fate of the Tashmoo

For decades, she was the best-loved vessel on the Detroit River. The Tashmoo, with a capacity of 4,000 passengers, sailed the Detroit, Tashmoo Park and Port Huron route for only 50 cents. Tashmoo Park was once an immensely popular resort near Harsen's Island at the north end of Lake St. Clair.

The ship once broke loose from her moorings near Woodward Avenue during high winds with no one aboard, and slammed into the old Belle Isle Bridge on December 8th, 1927.

On June 18th, 1936, she was chartered for a moonlight ride by the Pals Club, a Hamtramck, Michigan social group. A crowd of 1,400 gathered at the foot of Griswold. On her way home, a shock was felt throughout the ship at ll:20 p.m.

Passengers were told that there was engine trouble. Jean Calloway's orchestra played on and the dancing never was more lively. But in the engine room, it was a different story. The Tashmoo had struck a submerged rock. The wound was mortal. As water poured in through a hole in the hull faster than the pumps could handle it, the engine room crew stoked the boiler fire in a swirling, waist-deep flood. Capt. Donald MacAlpine called for full speed ahead. Ten minutes after the shock, the Tashmoo docked at the Brunner-Mond Co. coal wharf above Amherstburg on the Canadian side. Only after passengers and crew were safely ashore did the grand old steamer sink to the bottom in 18 feet of water (small photo centre). Deemed unrepairable, she was eventually scrapped and the Tashmoo's days of glory were over.

The Detroit News archives, painting by Peter Rindlisbacher, postcard: David L. Newman Collection, photos courtesy Bill Goddard

Classy Victorians

Construction of Hotel Dieu Hospital (right) on the "outskirts" of Windsor (Erie Street and Ouellette Avenue) began on October 10th, 1888 and it opened in February, 1890. The building was in the Norman style of architecture and featured three turrets. It cost of approximately $40,000. The three-storey brick building had a capacity of 100 beds. It was demolished in 1963 when the current Hotel Dieu opened.

Best of the Times publisher Chris Edwards attended Patterson Collegiate (below) in its final year of existence (1973). Located at the corner of Goyeau Avenue and Elliot Street, it originally opened as Windsor Collegiate in 1888 to service Windsor's growing population. It remained the only public high school in Windsor until the 1920s. Demolished in 1979, the site is now a parking lot and grocery store.

postcards: David L. Newman Collection

Ouellette Avenue

Ouellette Avenue was named after Vital Ouellette who in the mid 1800s owned this land.

Top: Windsor's Ouellette Avenue, running south from the Detroit River, around 1923; Busy Ouellette Avenue near Park Street, looking north sometime in the mid 1920s; The intersection of Wyandotte Street West and Ouellette Avenue, c. 1940.
postcards David L. Newman Collection

282 • places we remember

The Prince Edward Hotel

Opened on June 6th, 1922 and billed as Windsor's first major hotel, the Prince Edward stood at the northeast corner of Ouellette Aveune and Park Street. The gala opening of the nine storey, 215-bedroom hotel was the social event of the season, attended by more than 1,000 guests.

Named after the Prince of Wales, the building served as a hotel and community centre for teas, bridge parties, dinner dances and other social events.

The hotel enjoyed a long run, but became riddled by debt, and saddled with owners who refused to invest any more money, after buying it in 1954 for $1.7 million.

In 1967, a Vancouver-based consultant claimed the hotel was run down and could only be classified as "third rate." It was eventually demolished in 1976. The site is now home to a branch of the Bank of Nova Scotia.

Norton Palmer Hotel

Located at the northwest corner of Park and Pelissier Streets, the Norton-Palmer Hotel opened in December, 1927. At 12 stories high and containing 250 rooms, it was Windsor's tallest building in its day.

It took a mere nine months to build, and was named after Charles W. Norton, a veteran Detroit hotelier who was born in a tavern in Brighton, Michigan and Perry C. Palmer, its treasurer and resident manager.

Once a popular haunt, it experienced declining revenues and closed in 1974.

postcards: David L. Newman Collection

best of the times • 283

When Hotel Dieu Hospital was unable to meet the health-care needs of a burgeoning population, the Salvation Army purchased the former Henry Ellis home (a lawyer for whom Ellis Avenue is named) at Crawford and London Street (University Avenue), and established Grace Hospital (1918). Originally opened as a maternity hospital, the need for general hospital care was acute. Plans were modified and Windsor soon had its second hospital, open to all.

In 1922, a wing was added to Grace Hospital, increasing its capacity from 28 beds to 122 beds. In 1942, another wing was built, but on June 60, 1960, a fire destroyed a large part of the hospital. Grace Hospital closed its doors February 1, 2004, and was sold to private developers; its future remains uncertain.
Photos: David L. Newman Collection

Life of a Salesman

At left is my father Fred Jones in the early 1920s, in his general store at 1037 Assumption Street. This building, located directly behind Begley School, still stands and is currently a small apartment or home. He owned and operated the store for about ten years before selling it to become a travelling salesman (commercial traveller). He then made his way to London, where he opened another general store. He was forced to sell it during the Depression and returned to Windsor.
Gloria Snyder, Windsor

The Amherstburg Stagecoach; here a traveller is preparing for the often bumpy and arduous journey. This scene was shot in 1907 near the end of the stagecoach area. photo courtesy Georgina Falls

The Amherst House, Amherstburg, Ontario, was served by the Sandwich, Windsor and Amherstburg trolley. postcard: David L. Newman Collection

best of the times • 285

Top:
The Walkerville Beltline Car, c. 1913. Photo Courtesy Bernie Drouillard. (Andrew Foot Website: internationalmetropolis.com)

First Windsor-Tecumseh street car, 1907. Conductor William McGuigan is at extreme left and motorman Arthur Geauvreau is on the running board.

Elegantly attired Windsorites boarding street cars on Sandwich Street (Riverside Drive) near Ouellette Avenue in the early 1900s.

286 • places we remember

The Lost Resort

Above is a postcard of the Shore Acres Hotel, built on the site of the Rankin home that once stood on University Avenue facing the Detroit River. In October, Andrew Foot sent in a postcard of a home also called Shore Acres with Windsor, Ontario printed on the front. Dave Newman thought it was the Shore Acres pictured here. I know that this is not so, because I was a patron of the hotel for many years.

The Rankin home was demolished in 1925, following a fire set by vandals. The hotel opened in August 1925, with a dining room for 400, overflow space on the verandah and a large ballroom where a five-piece orchestra played. It had modern sleeping accommodations, shady porches and beautiful lawns, with a splendid riverfront view as well as ample parking. They specialized in roadhouse dinners, fish, frog, chicken, and steak. Province-wide serving of 4.4% beer and ale was approved in May 1925, by the Ontario Government.

The beer on opening day was supplied by Kuntz Brewery of Waterloo, Ontario, serving "Ye Olde Inn Ale" and "Olde Dutch Lager." I spent many an enjoyable evening on the verandah of the Shore Acres Hotel with my friends, drinking beer in 10 oz. glasses at ten cents each. It was operated by Mr. and Mrs. Herman Sutton, her two sons and their wives, from 1937 until the early 1950s. The hotel was torn down in 1954 to make way for the Rotary Club Swimming Pool.

The Rankin House was built in 1842 for W.R. Wood. It was sold to Col. Rankin and occupied by him and his family until his death in 1893. It was then purchased by his daughter, Phyllis McKee Rankin, wife of Frank Davenport, a famous American actor. She had the home renovated, with the intention of occupying it, but unfortunately never did. It was sold to Robert Segal, a Detroit department store owner, who held it until it was sold to make way for the hotel.

I too, have the identical postcard owned by Andrew Foot. My card was post-marked Athens, Ontario, June 1912. So the mystery of the card is still unsolved. Perhaps there is a Shore Acres in the village of Athens?

Bill Marentette, Windsor, Issue #21, February 2002

8
Black History

Dreamland
p.139

Amherstburg & Windsor Terminuses
The Underground Railroad

by Elaine Weeks, Issue #18, October 2001

News of the abolishment of slavery in Upper Canada reached slaves in the southern U.S. in 1813, when the American Army invaded Essex County. The slaves who accompanied their masters to Canada brought the astonishing news with them when they returned home, and it spread quickly.

Many slaves headed to Canada to escape slavery, and by the 1850s, between 35,000 and 40,000 slaves found freedom with the help of the Underground Railroad. This was not an actual railroad at all, but in fact a network of people who helped the fugitives make their way to Canada. In Detroit, they were usually hidden in the livery barn of Seymour Finney's, on the northeast corner of State and Griswold streets. After hiding in the stable until the way was clear, the runaways were escorted across the Detroit River to Canadian sanctuary.

A large number of slaves journeyed across the Detroit River at its narrowest point into Amherstburg, to be temporarily hidden in cellars from the American bounty-hunters in search of them. Many of those fugitives found protection in Amherstburg's Nazrey Church, using it as a resting place until permanent housing could be found. Most of them lived in Windsor's military barracks, which stood where Windsor's City Hall stands today.

By 1855, it was estimated that of Windsor's 1,400 residents, 259 were black, with 22 black refugee families in Sandwich. Four years later, it was thought that Windsor had 700 to 800 black residents out of a total population of 2,500. In addition, there were large numbers living as farmers in Sandwich East, (now the area in Windsor east of Glengarry Road).

In the village of Colchester (home of Elijah McCoy, famous inventor and subject of the catch phrase "the real McCoy"), many freed slaves built small cabins. They had little or no money, so grew crops, kept animals, and worked for farmers as hired hands to support themselves. Despite their freedom from slavery, some blacks were still treated unfairly and distrusted whites, though some were treated kindly by them.

Fugitive slaves recognized the need for education, and strongly supported the formation of schools in the 1840s and 1850s. However, many whites did not want their children associating and learning with black children. This offended some blacks, while others felt their children would receive a poorer education if they studied alongside white children. In spite of the arguments, black children were eventually allowed into white schools.

Still, there were many disputes between blacks and whites, and between the blacks as well. Justices of the Peace often had to deal with their disputes over land and money, and occasionally physical altercations and acts of violence.

Detroit, Windsor, Sandwich and Amherstburg played pivotal roles in providing sanctuary for more than 40,000 enslaved people seeking freedom from slavery. Pictured above is the Windsor monument located just north of Pitt Street near City Hall Square, one of two monuments honouring the Underground Railroad. Created in honour of Detroit's 300th birthday in 2001 by sculptor and first black astronaut Ed Dwight, the monuments face each other across the Detroit River. photo C. Edwards

The Legacy of John Freeman Walls
If These Walls Could Talk

by Laryssa Landale, Issue #31, February 2003

The story of John Freeman Walls is as unique as it is familiar. It is but one of several million stories of enslavement in the southern United States during the 1800s. John Walls left the south with his master's widow and her four children in 1842. In 1845 they landed in Amherstburg and he claimed his right to freedom. A year later the family settled in Puce just east of Windsor where John, a skilled carpenter, built a two-story log cabin home.

John's life of hardship in the aptly named Troublesome Creek, North Carolina was unfortunately commonplace in those times among those of African descent. His story begins with his close friendship with his master's son, Daniel, born in the same year, 1813. It was this relationship that provided John with his first experience of interracial equality and respect – a rare gem in those troubled times. The uncommon friendship between slave and slave master's son set the stage for this saga. Though it would not always serve to ease the burden of enslavement, in the end, this bond provided John with his freeman papers and entrusted him with Daniel's wife and children. The circumstances that arose from Daniel inheriting the Walls' plantation, and his untimely death, would ultimately usher John onto his incredible journey.

The story's uniqueness is furthered by John's flight to freedom – scholars estimate a mere 40,000 to 100,000 slaves travelled the road to liberty in the north. (By 1860 some four million enslaved blacks lived in the southern United States.) Unlike the main character from the groundbreaking 1852 novel "Uncle Tom's Cabin," John Walls was not reconciled to die within the confines of racial discrimination. The mere fact that he would challenge the status quo and strive to make his dream of a better life become reality makes his story extraordinary.

Enormous courage and strength were required on the road north. The slave patrollers and their hounds were often near. The fate that awaited a captured fugitive was unspeakable. To make John's situation even more unusual was the fact that his future wife Jane was white and his former master's widow. They travelled with her four white children and Corliss, a house slave from the Walls' plantation. Such an unmistakable group of sojourners would not easily go unnoticed.

The first half of the journey they navigated themselves with only the words learned during John's childhood: "the side of the tree that moss grows on and the North Star are the way to Canada and freedom" to guide them. For weeks they travelled under the cloak of night before stumbling upon sympathetic abolitionist Quakers, Ephraim

Canada was the first country in the British Empire to legislate against slavery. Upper Canada's first Lieutenant Governor, John Graves Simcoe, was a pioneer in anti-discrimination policy. In 1793, he saw legislation passed that outlawed importing new slaves into Canada while granting freedom to those slaves born after 1793 once they reached 25 years of age.
On August 1, 1834 slavery was abolished throughout the British colonies by King William IV, pursuant to the Slavery Abolition Act of 1833.
But in the U.S., slavery remained. With thoughts of sweet freedom in the north, thousands of slaves began the perilous journey to Canada.
Here is one of their stories.

John Freeman Walls refused to be photographed, for fear of being discovered and sent back to a life of slavery in the South. The drawing of John, above, was sketched by a Detroit-Windsor Police composite artist in 1985, after conversations with Walls' grandchildren, Stella and Frank Walls (his image, along with his wife Jane's, are from the jacket of "The Road to Discovery," a video about Walls' life and the John Freeman Walls Historic Site.) Above the portrait is a photo of the log cabin built by Walls in 1846. It stands today as a focal point of the John Freeman Walls Historic Site and Underground Railroad Museum in Puce Ontario.. The original sketch of John is displayed inside.

Dr. Bryan Walls chronicled his great grandfather's life in his book "The Road That Leads To Somewhere"

and Mary Stout, in Indiana. It was through them that John and Jane learned of the Underground Railroad. This secretive, unorganized movement of abolitionists — some white, some free blacks and some formerly enslaved blacks — offered food, shelter and guidance to those seeking freedom.

Railroad terminology was adopted by the movement as a measure to confuse slave hunters. (The image of a secret underground railroad was so effective that in the 1800's, many people actually believed that a train ran from the south to freedom in the north).

This network of individuals employed several ingenious methods to secretly convey directions and information to other members and to the freedom seekers fortunate enough to encounter the Underground Railroad. By the 1830's several routes to the northern free states and Canada had been developed. Travellers were being sent into the south to teach songs encoded with information to enslaved blacks. One such song was "The Drinking Gourd Song" which instructed slaves to leave in winter or early spring and follow the North Star along the bank of the Tombigbee River, and look for dead trees that were marked with mud and charcoal drawings. The following verses led the freedom seekers to the Ohio River, usually a year later, when it was frozen over and, thus, more easily crossed. On the other side they were reportedly met by "conductors" from the Underground Railroad in the free states and transported to Canada.

The Walls family was not fortunate enough to have had previous knowledge of this great freedom movement when they set out on their journey from Troublesome Creek in the spring of 1842. However, they did benefit greatly from it on the remainder of their journey. It was also from their safe harbour with the Stouts, and with new knowledge of underground "stations" along the way, that Jane and Corliss were able to return to the Walls' plantation and lead seven more toward freedom.

Their long road reached freedom in the summer of 1845 on the shores of Amherstburg on the Detroit River. From there the Walls family would travel across the county to settle in Puce and build a homestead that stands today.

John and Jane raised ten children in their homestead and engrained in them the necessity of love and harmony toward all. Their home would also become a terminal on the Underground Railroad for other blacks seeking salvation from slavery.

The Legacy

John and Jane's journey inspired many – both during their own lifetime and in the more than 160 years since they first headed north in search of a dream. Strong beliefs of equality and freedom were taught to their children, and have been passed down through eight generations. These descendents expressed those same convictions in several creative and powerful ways.

In 1976, Dr. Bryan Walls began four years of research that culminated in the book "The Road That Led To Somewhere." His Aunt Stella, granddaughter to John and Jane, told the majority of the stories included in this epic to the author.

She was about twenty-three years old when her grandparents passed away in 1909 and 1910. And those years before they died were richly steeped in oral history. Bryan's grandfather Frank, some thirteen years Stella's junior, confirmed many of the stories that form the basis for his book.

In 1980, the family self-published Bryan's fictionalized biography of his great-great-grandparents' fascinating lives. Written from the point of view of his Uncle Earl, 1952 Canadian heavyweight boxing champion, the book allows the author to span over a century and comment not only on the treacherous journey that his ancestors endured to reach a land of freedom, but also about the legacy that has been passed down through generations of their descendents.

This documentation of the Walls' family's beginnings in Canada not only provides their relatives with a concrete family history, it also offers local, national and international communities a glimpse into a significant part of their own past.

The novel made its way into the hands of a government official who felt it an important part of Canadian and American history. Thus, the land on which the original two-story log cabin was built became a historical site. This property, and the desire to preserve it, were catalysts for the creation of the book. Through the diligent efforts of Bryan, two of his brothers, Allen and Winston, and with the aid and constant support of the rest of their families, the historical site has since been expanded to include an Underground Railroad Museum.

This small plot of land has been transformed into a fascinating tourist attraction that offers visitors a trip back in time to where the story all began – Africa.

The Real McCoy – Born in Colchester, Ont.

Elijah McCoy was born in 1843 in Colchester, Ontario. His parents had escaped slavery in Kentucky via the Underground Railroad. At age 15, he was sent to Scotland to study engineering; upon his return to Canada, the only job available was as a railway fireman (stoking the engine's furnace with wood). It was during this time that his mind started to look for better ways to do things.

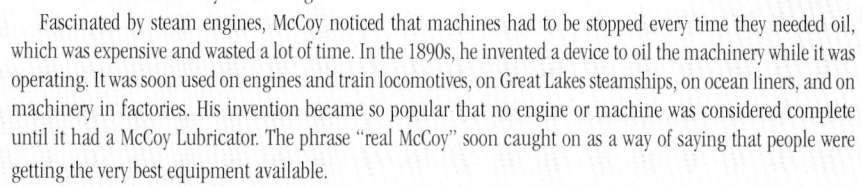

Fascinated by steam engines, McCoy noticed that machines had to be stopped every time they needed oil, which was expensive and wasted a lot of time. In the 1890s, he invented a device to oil the machinery while it was operating. It was soon used on engines and train locomotives, on Great Lakes steamships, on ocean liners, and on machinery in factories. His invention became so popular that no engine or machine was considered complete until it had a McCoy Lubricator. The phrase "real McCoy" soon caught on as a way of saying that people were getting the very best equipment available.

By 1923 McCoy was known throughout the world. His inventions were patented in Great Britain, France, Germany, Austria, and Russia as well as in Canada and the United States.

Issue #10, September/October 2000

Visitors are then led both verbally and physically, on a journey that takes them symbolically across the Atlantic, then through the slave states toward freedom. They are guided through the woods with a narrative that instills the urgency of a fleeing slave. They learn of the creative and frightening feats that these fugitives would perform on their trek northward. They emerge triumphant at the border of the heaven sung about by enslaved blacks – Canada.

Patrons culminate their tour at the original log cabin built in 1846. They are also invited to experience the Freedom Train Museum (housed in an old railway car on-site), the Sir John Graves Simcoe Educational Resource Log Cabin, and the Peace Chapel built in honour of Mrs. Rosa Parks, a frequent visitor to the museum.

The Walls story is featured on two videos. "The Road to Discovery," the first video, is a creative rendition of the John and Jane story, filmed at the historic site. It highlights some fascinating aspects of the journey taken by visitors at the Puce museum. The second video is a NASA (National Aeronautics Space Administration) production entitled "The Underground Railroad: Connections to Freedom and Science." It focuses on the scientific skills that enslaved men and women used to navigate the Underground Railroad. Explanations of mathematics, geometry, astrology, and horticulture are given as they related to this specific challenge. It also encourages youth to consider science as a way to fulfil their own dreams.

In January of this year, Bryan participated in launching a mutual respect campaign with the Toronto Police Service. His efforts were focused on the creation of an audio/visual CD-ROM entitled "Only the Rainbow." This project is a tribute to the heroism that prevailed in the aftermath of 9/11. It is also a recruiting tool for the Toronto Police Services. Included on it are two original compositions and a short digital video. The full album "The Road That Led To Somewhere" by Stephen Bard is forthcoming.

More recently, the novel, videos and CD, along with information on their sister museum, Motown Museum, Hitsville USA in Detroit, have been combined to create a teachable unit. This package has been introduced into the elementary school system and is being taught in roughly thirty schools in Essex County, as well as some in the Toronto area. Winston Walls and his wife, Chris, have written a teacher's guide to support the implementation of this educational program. A field trip to the museum often transforms this unit of study into a tangible experience for the students.

It is the family's hope that people will leave their historic site with a "greater appreciation of the importance of freedom and the importance of making the best of their talents in whatever arena they are working in or are challenged by." And it seems to be effective. In fact, some youths later reported having had revelations of sorts at the museum – even overcoming feelings of personal despair. Vincent DeForest explains this potent connection felt by many in the NASA video. He states that "this is not an African-American story but a story of liberation" – one that is creating a universal impact, despite its geographically and ethnically specific details.

The Walls family is quick to point out that Canada had inherited a legacy of nondiscrimination, which predated, and thus facilitated, the Underground Railroad movement. Dr. Bryan Walls emphasizes the fact that as far back as 1793, John Graves Simcoe, Upper Canada's first Lieutenant Governor, was instrumental in passing Canada's first anti-slavery law. It outlawed the buying of new slaves, and immediate freedom was granted to those slaves who outlived their masters. This legislation laid the foundation for the abolition of slavery in Canada. Bryan's belief is that "democracy may not be... (perfect), but show me a better (system). Canada may still have problems in terms of race relations, but there is no better country in the world for a visible minority to live than in Canada." On January 17, 2003, Dr. Bryan Walls learned he had been appointed to the Order of Canada for his efforts in preserving Canada's black heritage. He had previously been honoured with the Order of Ontario.

The destruction of the institute of slavery was certainly not the work of one single group. It was the culmination of many dedicated, courageous individuals working through various facets of society for the common good. John Freeman and Jane King Walls surely played an active role in the roots of this movement. Their descendents have inherited their strengths. The family's desire to preserve their own heritage has mushroomed into an ongoing effort to promote the legacy of mutual respect and "equal sisterhood and brotherhood of humankind." John and Jane could not have imagined where this road to somewhere would one-day lead.

Walls' great-great-grandsons Allen (at left) and Winston Walls, with Anna Davis' photo, "Equal Sisterhood and Brotherhood of Humankind."

Delos Rogest Davis
First Black Lawyer in Canada

information provided by The North American Black Historical Museum, Amherstburg, Ontario

story Elaine Weeks, Issue #13, February 2001

James Davis, a former slave from Virginia, relocated to Colchester Township in 1850. Determined that his children not be enslaved by ignorance, Davis hired a private teacher to instruct his children until a school could be built.

In order to further his education, his son Delos worked as a deckhand on the steamer *Forest City* and as a fireman on the tug *Castle*. Obtaining a teaching certificate, he taught school in his hometown of Gilgal, South Colchester Township, Essex County (between 5th and 6th Concessions on Walker Road near Harrow) for four years before he pursued his ambition to enter the legal profession. Gilgal was once a hamlet of over two hundred black people who settled in the area as part of the Matthews Settlement for former slaves. At his own expense, Hiram Walker, founder of Canadian Club, built the community a brick school, one of the finest in the county. Today, Gilgal is a ghost town – all that remains is the cemetery.

In 1871, Davis was appointed commissioner for taking affidavits. Two years later he was appointed a notary public but racism prevented Davis from becoming a lawyer. It was a requirement of the Law Society of Upper Canada that individuals studying law must article for a period of time with a lawyer prior to taking the entrance exams for admission to the bar of Ontario.

However, no lawyer would hire Delos Davis to article under them. For eleven years, Delos Davis studied and practiced law at the level of legal clerk – he was prohibited from handling most legal matters – not having been admitted to membership in the Ontario bar.

Versed in the law and certain to pass the final examination of the Law Society, Davis applied to the Ontario Legislature to pass a private member's bill to authorize him to practice as a lawyer.

The bill was introduced by W.D. Balfour, M.P.P. for Amherstburg. On May 25, 1884, "an act to authorize the Supreme Court of Judicature for Ontario to admit Delos Rogest Davis to practice as a solicitor" received Royal Assent.

This act provided that Davis be permitted to take his final law examination in order to obtain admission to the Law Society of Upper Canada, notwithstanding the fact that he had not complied with the articling requirements of the Law Society. On taking the examination, Davis stood first in the class of thirteen candidates and was admitted to the Ontario bar on November 15, 1886.

Delos R. Davis, 1846-1915, was counsel in six leading murder cases in Essex County; he won every case.

Great grandson Lloyd Dean is a Windsor-based Ontario Court Justice

In the spring of 1892, Davis and his wife, the former Nancy Jane Mitchell, moved to Amherstburg where Davis established a law office on Ramsay Street. He also opened an office on Goyeau Street in Windsor and soon became a noted criminal lawyer. During his career, he was counsel in six of the leading murder cases in the county, defending five and prosecuting one. He won every case. Davis was also solicitor for the Town of Amherstburg and the Townships of Anderdon and Colchester North.

On November 10, 1910, his merits were recognized by the Ontario Government, which appointed him a King's Council, *"the first black so appointed in the United Kingdom of Great Britain and Ireland and the British Dominions."*

Davis' eldest son followed in his father's footsteps. Frederick Homer Alphonso Davis (1871-1926) became the second black lawyer to be called to the Ontario bar when he graduated from Osgoode Hall in 1900, joining his father in the Amherstburg law firm of Davis and Davis. Another son, Delos Rogest Davis, Jr. (1875-1921), became a conveyancer and notary public.

While still a law student, Lloyd Dean, great grandson of Delos and now an Assistant Crown Attorney, was instrumental in establishing the Delos Rogest Davis, K.C. Memorial Scholarship in 1990, a permanent fund available for any deserving third year law student attending the University of Windsor.

Street Named for Slave Descendant

by Elaine Weeks, Issue #21, February 2002

Like many other escaped black slaves, Allen Watkin's final destination was the Windsor area. He fled from a life of misery in the U.S. in the 1830s and settled in Sandwich, a town that now forms the west end of Windsor. Along with other members of the local black community, he soon helped construct a place of worship on what became the "Watkin's homestead," the northwest corner of Lot and Peter Streets.

The Sandwich Baptist Church was originally a log cabin and the men who helped erect it were buried nearby. The gravestones marking their place of burial, however, have been missing for many years.

The existing brick church was completed in 1851, and on August 1 of that year, which marked the 18th anniversary of the freeing of the slaves by the British, the structure was dedicated.

After emancipation, a number of Allen's 11 children returned to the U.S. but his son William chose to remain. William Watkins also built his own home at 3616 Peter Street and like his father before him who had built a home at 3540 Peter Street, his son Homer Watkins, born 1893, did the same at 375 Lot Street when he was just 20 years old.

As a boy, Homer Watkins lived near the church his grandfather helped build, which by then was the oldest Baptist Church in the city of Windsor. Homer owned a confectionary and grocery store at Lot and Peter Streets.

"I remember when there was nothing but woods on that side of Peter Street. Up at the corner, a family was digging to put in the foundation for a new house and turned up $1,500 that someone had buried there."

Howard Watkins, Homer's son and a former Windsor detective, remembered how they would fish and hunt near his home; he could look out his window and see wild animals.

"From my own porch at 3603 Peter Street, I could toss a stone and hit the house where I was born, or the house where my father was born, and if I had a good enough arm I could even hit the house where his father was born."

An employee of Ford of Canada for 30 years and before that of the Windsor Salt Company, Homer Watkins kept his family's spirits high during the tough Depression years with his songs and dances, occasionally bringing home a basket of groceries when he was declared the winner of a vaudeville competition.

In 1963, with over 100 years of Watkin's history tied to Lot Street and as a tribute to Homer Watkin's numerous contributions to the community of Sandwich, the city of Windsor formally announced that Lot Street would become Watkins Street.

Since that day, there has always been at least one Watkins living on the street that bears the family name. Currently, Homer's daughter Charlotte, a former opera singer, resides in the home at 375 and her daughter lives in the house next door. Since Charlotte is the mother of four children, is the grandmother of nine as well as the great grandmother of three, chances are, there will always be a Watkins on Watkins Street.

In addition to the street naming, Homer Watkins (centre), was honoured by Homer Watkins Days held annually in Sandwich.

Still a Watkins on Watkins Street

After researching the history of Watkins Street for the previous story, I wondered if forty years after its naming there still was a Watkins on Watkins Street. I looked up the name in the Windsor phone book and, lo and behold, there was a C. Watkins at 375 Watkins, the very house that Homer Watkins had built.

"Yes," said the woman who answered, "I'm Charlotte Watkins, Homer Watkins' daughter." She sounded almost as if she was expecting my call. I explained that I was planning a story to commemorate Black History month. Would she be interested in an interview?

A few days and one major winter storm later, I was slowly cruising up Watkins Street looking for Charlotte's home and there it was – looking somewhat as I imagined – a neat and trim blue frame house that appeared to be about 80 or 90 years old. I was excited – it wasn't every day that I met someone with a street named after them!

My interview with Charlotte proved to be informative and inspiring. I learned that Charlotte Watkins was the great-great-granddaughter of Carolyn Quarreles, the first run-away slave to arrive in this area. Carolyn was the daughter of a slave and a slave master. She could pass for white and she became the mistress' first slave. She was taught how to do lace which was something of an honour. She had very long hair and was caught by the mistress looking at herself in the mirror. Her hair was cut off in punishment.

Carolyn ran away, arriving first in Wisconsin and, after a long, hard journey, all the way to freedom in Canada in 1840. She married a man named Arthur Watkins whose family had escaped through Chicago. Freed slaves were deeded 300 acres of land by Queen Victoria and Carolyn and Arthur received their share in the southern end of Sandwich. They farmed it and built a house, probably in the 1860s, which still stands.

Charlotte has a granddaughter who looks much like Carolyn. She is the model for a bronze statue that is being made of Carolyn for permanent display in Wisconsin. A book about Carolyn's life is being written and it will parallel her life with Charlotte's, who had various hardships due in part to being of a generation that grew up with overt racism and prejudice.

"I remember when I was a little girl, my mother tried to explain to me why I wasn't invited to a white classmate's birthday party and everyone else was," recalled Charlotte who was the only black child in the class. "How do you explain prejudice to a child?"

When she got older, Charlotte's father told her that in order to get ahead in this world, she would have to do what he did. "He was very 'Uncle Tom,' explained Charlotte. "He knew that in order to get what he wanted, he would have to act subservient. He was manipulative and used his intelligence. As a result, he was the first black person at the Power House at Ford's" (Ford of Canada in Windsor).

But Charlotte was a rebel. She remembers one particular incident when she was travelling in the States. "I was in the Cincinnati railway station and a man with a baby told me to 'Get out of the way, nigger.' In so many words I told him I would not. He stomped his foot and said 'What did you say?!' I took off and ran across the station not knowing what he would do to me."

As a black person in medical transcription in the 1950s – then a white person's field – Charlotte faced many obstacles. She was told that black people would not be able to learn the medical terms – "It was very difficult but I knew I had to do it. I was divorced and had four children to raise. I was determined not to go on welfare." Thoughts of what her great great grandmother went through helped inspire Charlotte to persevere. And thoughts

[My great great grandmother] had very long hair, and was caught by the mistress looking at herself in the mirror. Her hair was cut off in punishment.

of her mother, who had worked as a servant kept her going too. "I wasn't going to answer to anyone's bell," said Charlotte grimly.

When her children were small, Charlotte took them with her to work. They helped her with stapling or photocopying. "They all have excellent work ethics now," she smiled.

What Charlotte really wanted however, was to pursue her love of music. A talented pianist and singer, she had hoped to travel to La Scala, Italy when she was a young mother but family obligations held her back.

At present, Charlotte continues her work as a medical transcriptionist part-time and devotes a great deal of time and energy to her piano and voice students as well as to her various grandchildren.

She preferred not to be photographed but allowed me to snap a picture of her beautiful grand piano. "I bought it years ago from the daughter of a chemist in Indian Village [in Detroit]. She was an only child and had nothing to call her own except this piano. She sold it to me for $450 so she could elope!"

Charlotte is the only descendant in the area now bearing this historic family name, although, she said, "My children have talked about changing their name from Maxie to Watkins."

by Elaine Weeks, Issue #21, February 2002

Charlotte Watkins, a former opera singer, still teaches music to Windsor children. She purchased her grand piano from a woman who needed money to elope. Charlotte covered all her windows, in lace in memory of her ancestor, Carolyn Quarreles; before Carolyn escaped, she was the first slave of a white mistress, who taught her to make lace.

Sandwich First Baptist Church

by Sherrill Tucker, Issue #10, September/October 2000

*I am on my way to Canada
That cold and distant land
The dire effect of slavery
I can no longer stand
Farewell, old master
Don't come after me
I am on my way to Canada
Where coloured men are free*
(Anonymous)

When I was a kid growing up in the richly diverse university area, I went to most of the churches with my sister Shelley in tow within walking distance of our home. I loved singing in the choir and tried them all: Sandwich (now Bedford), United, Knox Presbyterian, Campbell Baptist, Church of the Ascension and Central United. The joy of singing was the only thing I took away from those experiences.

When I discovered the Sandwich First Baptist Church on Peter Street near Prince Road in 2000, I found what I'd been missing. Entering the sanctuary, the hair all over my body stood on end. I sensed that a spirit in this church is alive, and I'm certain it lies within the bricks of the structure itself.

The original church (c.1820) was housed in a log cabin. When the congregation decided to replace it with the brick structure, every able-bodied male member of the congregation was required to make a certain number of bricks, using clay from the Detroit River. Many of these bricks were made by slaves escaping through the underground railroad as payment for the meal and safe haven that had been provided by a member of the congregation. The church was completed in 1851, after eight years of hard work.

At that time, American bounty hunters were still allowed to track slaves who had escaped to Canada, and they would invade Sunday services in their quest. Little did they know that those escapees were always seated in an area of the church where they could easily escape through a passageway in the floor of the sanctuary. From there, they would make their way to the back corner of the church, where a tunnel ran all the way to the river's edge.

Queen Victoria herself deeded the land for the church and graveyard (they're still trying to find the graveyard) and the documentation is on display in the church. The property ran from Peter Street all the way to the river where the baptisms were held.

Unfortunately, there is virtually no documentation of the church's history to be found. When the church was abandoned in the 1970s for nearly ten years, the registry's pages were torn from their bindings. There are still some members who are descendants of the original congregation, but with little to no proof, it is a bit frustrating for research purposes. They've recently formed a History Committee that will endeavour to preserve what's known of the Church's past for future generations.

Currently, the church hosts many Underground Railroad bus tours, especially from the United States. These tours are usually lead by their volunteer Pastor (yes, that's volunteer, as in no salary), Owen Burey or Charlotte Watkins (Watkins Street is named after her family), a descendent of one of the original congregation members.

There is a restoration/renovation program in progress, where one can purchase bricks to aid their fundraising efforts. Plans include reaching farther out into the community by forming an Education and Cultural Centre at the church.

I cannot tell the story of this wonderful church without honouring its Pastor. Owen Burey, originally from Jamaica, began his professional career as a teacher. When his children were grown, he decided he needed a change, and he literally found his "calling."

Owen has been volunteer Pastor of the Sandwich Pastor Church since 1985. He has helped galvanize the community to understand the historical significance of this church, and has been tirelessly in efforts to preserve it, ensuring the soul of the church lives on. Thanks to Owen, the church was designated a "National Historic Site" by Parks Canada (in July of 2000). Owen watches over a flock of just over 20 families at the church. He resides with his wife Detha in Chatham.

Owen would love to find the escape tunnel and the graveyard, and hopes someday to come across someone with the proper sensing equipment to locate them.

(Owen Burey passed away in 2004. The tunnel and graveyard have still not been found. Times Graphic Designer, Chuck Rees, created the ghostly composite of the church on the previous page.)

It's Black & White

On page three in the February issue of *The TIMES* (Issue #31, 2003), my father is the boy holding the slate in the 1893 school picture at right. His name was Walter F. Brooke and he was five at the time; his brother Harry is standing behind him. My father told me that by looking at that picture you could tell there was discrimination in the school – all the whites were on the left side of the picture and all the blacks were on the right side. You can even see the slight gap at the point where the two groups are next to each other.

Walter's father T.W. Brooke started T.W. Brooke & Sons, a painting and decorating company. He was a member of the first Town of Windsor council and then also the first City of Windsor council.

Walter and his brother started a picture framing business at home and then moved it into their dad's shop on Pitt Street (part of the Norwich Block in downtown Windsor, recently torn down to make way for the Chrysler Building). The business was sold in the 1970s.

Mary Calder, South Windsor, Issue #33, April 2003

Above: Children from Goyeau Street School in Windsor pose on the front steps for this class photo in 1893. Once known as the Windsor High School, it stood on the east side of Goyeau Street, opposite St. Alphonsus Hall. It was built as a separate school, and then served as the high school from 1877 to 1889. It was turned into a 2-room grade school after Windsor Collegiate (Patterson Collegiate Institute) was built in 1888-89.

It DID happen here...
Local Racism in the 1950s

Issue #31, February 2002

The following excerpt is evidence compiled over half a century ago by the Windsor Council on Group Relations on black discrimination in local hotels and taverns. In 1951, this information was sent to all local MPPs, the Premier of Ontario and the Liquor Control Board of Ontario, requesting action. (Please note that the term "Negro" was commonly used at that time when referring to people of African descent.)

July 14th, 1951

"Practically all public houses, hotels, and taverns will serve Negro men in their men's beverage rooms. A couple of places serve Negro men and women in rooms separate from the ones in which white men and women are served, although white men and women may be served where the Negroes are served, if they wish.

About half a dozen places give equal service to all, both men and women. But here is the general policy: a vast majority of licensed establishments will not serve Negroes in any room where men and women are generally served. A few will not even serve Negro men in the men's room. Below is a list of the licensed places against which the Council on Group Relations has received complaints of racial discrimination in one form or another during the past year [1951]:

The Commodore Tavern [now Jason's], Rowsons' Tavern [near the Top Hat], Killarney Castle, Shanghai Tavern, The Elbow Room, Rendezvous Tavern, Shawnee Gun Club, Elmwood Tavern, Thomas' Edgewater Inn, Mario's Tavern, Hollywood House [on Howard], Grand House [corner of Erie and Howard], Border House, Anderdon Hotel.

All the licensed outlets in East Windsor, as far as we know, have been fair to all; also the St. Clair and British American [Hotel] downtown. There may be others but we're not sure.

It is our intention to protest the renewal of licenses to the following hotels, taverns and public houses of which the proprietors have continued to deny any service to members of the Negro race or who have segregated, or in any other manner outlined herein, exercised racial discrimination.

DISCRIMINATION EVIDENCE IN LICENSED ESTABLISHMENTS

Commodore Tavern

In March 1950, Mr. G., Manager, after having refused service to a group of Negro people, admitted before a committee of the Windsor Council on Group Relations, namely, Miss Dorothy Carthas, Bond Collier and Lyle Talbot, and again before Mr. Talbot and Mr. Les Dickirson and Mr. Bushel, District Supervisor for the Liquor Licensing Board, that "in the best interests of his business" he found it necessary to refuse service to persons of Negro origin in the tavern and lounge of the Commodore Hotel. Mr. G. further stated that he had no intention of changing his policy until he was forced by the authorities to do so.

On June 12th, 1951, Mr. Eugene Kersey, Negro, 1120 Marion Avenue, Windsor, was refused service at the bar of the Commodore.

Killarney Castle

Mr. D. of the Killarney Castle Tavern admitted before Mr. Talbot, Mr. Dickirson and Mr. Bushel that it is his policy to refuse service to all persons of Negro origin. He repeated this statement to Miss Carthas and Messrs Talbot and Dickirson on June 25th, 1951, further stating that unless compelled by law, he would continue his policy of racial discrimination. He made reference to the type of clientele that patronizes the Killarney and stated that he does not cater to "gamblers, bookmakers, alcoholics, street-walkers, prostitutes or Negroes." When asked how he could tell a bookmaker from any other person unless he knew him personally, he replied that he "guessed he couldn't tell," but he "could tell a Negro when he saw one." On that basis he admitted his policy of racial discrimination.

Rowsons' Tavern

Mr. Carl Overton, a Negro and a member of the Essex Regiment, was refused service at Rowsons' while in the company of other members of his regiment in uniform. This tavern has a policy of demanding reservations of all Negroes, although reservations are not generally required of those who enter the establishment. On June 25th, 1951, a committee of three from the Windsor Council on Group Relations entered Rowsons' Lounge with the intention of seeing the manager. The committee, made up of Misses Alvira Brush, Phyllis White and Mr. Lloyd Jenkins, two of whom are Negroes, were met at the door by the hostess, who asked if they had reservations. While they were waiting to see the manager, who didn't put in an appearance, several parties entered and were seated and served without being asked for reservations.

Mario's Tavern

While in Windsor on business for the C.N. Railway, Mr. Husbands, a Negro resident of Levis, Quebec, was refused service in Mario's dining room on Ouellette Avenue.

"Reservations" are sometimes demanded of Negroes at times when they are not required of white people, if the tavern is busy or the Management for any other reason decides not to give service to a Negro party.

White's Tavern [on Pitt Street]

Mr. L., proprietor of the establishment, stated before Miss Brush and Miss White and Mr. Jenkins, that he serves Negroes if they are "outstanding, dignified, well-dressed and respectable" in the dining room. Negroes are not served, however, in the "Elbow Room." Mr. L. places the responsibility of refusing service on his waiters.

In spite of Mr. L.'s claim that he serves Negroes in the dining room, Rev. C.L. Morton, a respected Negro citizen, was refused a meal at White's dining room in June 1951.

NOTE: In order to avoid embarrassment, American Negroes often enter an establishment and inquire whether the management serves Negroes, while Canadian Negroes enter an establishment and expect to be served. Consequently some proprietors of eating and drink establishments are able to differentiate between American and Canadian Negroes, and discriminate accordingly.

We contend that in order to hold a license to operate a public house, hotel or tavern under the Liquor Control Board of Ontario all licensees should be required to refrain from refusing service to or segregating persons because of their racial or ethnic origin."

Genuine and effective action against discrimination did not occur until the enactment of the Ontario Human Rights Code of 1962, which was a consolidation of all earlier human rights statutes enacted by the Province of Ontario since 1944.

This information was provided by Les Dickerson, a member of the Windsor Council on Group Relations and still active in local human rights issues.

Previous Page: Mario's Tavern, once located on Ouellette near Elliott.

Above: In 1939, The Commodore was the hot spot in downtown Windsor for dining and libations. The building still exists, yet its façade is barely recognizable in its present incarnation as Jason's, a popular strip club. Photos courtesy W. Marentette

Black Curfew in Walkerville

In 1913, my father, Robert Daniher, constructed a building on the southwest corner of Lincoln and Erie, as well as several other houses in Windsor. The Lincoln and Erie building had flats above and businesses below. We lived upstairs (where I was born) and I remember Lil Butcher's soda fountain and ice cream parlor with the fancy white wrought iron chairs and six or seven tables, a grocery store, a garage on the alley and a tailor shop run by Mr. Basden.

Mr. Basden lived in Windsor and had to ensure he left Walkerville by sundown, because he was black and that was the rule; this was in 1924.
Ruby Lennon, Walkerville

Right: Proprietors of Butcher's Ice Cream Parlour, Erie and Lincoln in the 1920s.

Black Cemeteries a Mystery

by Elaine Weeks, Issue #51, February 2005

Are slaves buried in Amherstburg? The Elliott Northern Plantation was situated near the old Bob-Lo dock and parking lot south of Amherstburg's town centre.
postcard David L. Newman Collection

Once a major depot for the Underground Railway, Essex County may be home to more than ten black cemeteries, including Canada's only black slave burial ground. Ken Turner has spent a decade looking for long-abandoned cemeteries in Essex County and believes there is a large burial site for a black settlement just south of Amherstburg that pre-dates the arrival of runaway slaves in the 1800s.

Matthew Elliott, an Indian agent for the British government, is known to have brought 50-70 black slaves to help clear forests from Bois Blanc Island (Bob-Lo) in the 1790s. Turner, president of the Essex County Historical Cemeteries Preservation Society, thinks a cemetery used for a black settlement is somewhere on a large chunk of land near a former dock and parking lot, south of the Amherstburg town centre, once occupied by the Elliott Northern Plantation.

A preliminary archaeological survey of this site, now a farmer's field, was performed in the summer of 2003. Local archaeologist Rosmarie Denunzio was involved and says that without doing an excavation, it's impossible to determine if the cemetery is actually on that site.

"Artifacts on the surface or other evidence of archaeological significance such as stains in the soil are indications of habitation but in the case of a lost cemetery, the only way to ascertain its presence is to dig six feet down."

Turner found references to the black settlement on the Elliott property in papers belonging to the late David Botsford, former curator of the Ford Malden National Historical Museum, which has an extensive collection of information about Elliott, including one of his uniforms.

A native of Ireland, Elliott came to the Detroit area with other well-known Loyalists such as Alexander McKee. Elliott played a key role in rallying Indian support for the British against Americans in numerous battles along the border. Elliott was later elected three times to the Ontario Legislature for Essex South.

The archival evidence found in Botsford's papers regarding Elliott's and a neighbour, John Caldwell's use of black slaves, is fairly detailed.

Two other abandoned cemeteries in Malden and Colchester South were used by blacks who fled slavery in the U.S. in the early 1800s and Turner fears they too are in danger of becoming lost. What was once the Mount Pleasant Church in Malden had an adjacent cemetery, but is now being farmed, as is the site in Colchester South. Dorothy Shadd Shreve's history of black churches in Canada, "The AfriCanadian Church: A Stabilizer," indicates the Mount Pleasant Baptist Church was active from 1843 to at least 1910, with a congregation of 52 at its peak.

According to curator-director Elise Harding-Davis of The North American Black Historical Museum, a national historic site in Amherstburg, they have a few headstones from Mount Pleasant donated almost three decades ago. Harding-Davis commends Turner's efforts to find and preserve black cemeteries in this area. She agrees with Turner that the Elliot estate property should be carefully explored, as well as other historic black cemeteries like those of Mount Pleasant, Colchester South, Harrow, and New Canaan in Gesto, where Canada's first black lawyer, Delos Davis, rests. Fences should be built, graves tended, and historical plaques erected to preserve the names of important figures like Delos Davis, says Harding-Davis, (no relation). "When the graves and the names of people and things belonging to black history are eradicated, we cease to exist," she says.

Turner has been using old land survey records and newspaper obituary notices to piece together the locations of cemeteries. Unfortunately, the Cemeteries Act is "very weak" and lengthy delays often ensue before digs are ordered to confirm or refute evidence of abandoned cemeteries, he says.

According to retired Harrow history teacher Gerald Pouget, before the American Civil War ended, about a third of Colchester South's families were black. After the Civil War some returned to the U.S., including large numbers who went only as far as Detroit.

In the case of the Elliott property, the estate, which was built in the late 1800s, fell into disrepair in the early part of the 20th century. In 1956, the last remaining structure caved in after a heavy rain. The property has been a registered archaeological site since at least the 1970's and a historic plaque referring to Colonel Elliot was placed on the property near the former Bob-Lo Island ferry parking lot.

Now the property of Kanata Lving Inc., the owners are aware of the historical significance of the site and have financed two archealogical surveys which have revealed evidence of native habitation dating back 10,000 years. There is no sign of the black cemetery yet but it is thought it could be situated in another part of the property further south. Several "hot spots" were found however, which will be further investigated in case there are graves. If so, they would likely contain the remains of the Elliott family; documentation shows several members were buried on the property.

Says Turner, "Not only is this site significant in terms of the black history connection but it also has tremendous significance because of the Native occupation of this land."

And if future archealogical surveys do reveal the location of a black cemetery, the revelation that slaves once lived in a major terminus of the Underground Railroad would be very ironic indeed.

Mary Ann Shadd: Founder of Provincial Freeman

story provided by Windsor's Community Museum

Mary Ann Shadd was born on October 9, 1823, to a family of free black abolitionists living in the slave state of Delaware. In 1833, the Shadd family moved to West Chester, Pennsylvania, where Mary attended a Quaker school for black children. After completing her studies in 1839, Mary became a teacher at the age of 16. For the next decade, she established or taught in schools for black children in several free and slave states.

When the United States Congress passed the Fugitive Slave Act in 1850, Mary migrated northward to Canada to escape the threat of unlawful enslavement. In 1851, she settled in Windsor and opened a school for black refugees. Mary described Windsor as a hostile and segregated place.

"This is by universal consent," she wrote, "the most destitute community of coloured people, known in this province."

During the 1850s, Mary was one of the most outspoken anti-slavery activists in the region. She felt strongly that "caste" or segregated institutions were inappropriate in a free country, and only contributed to racial discrimination. Mary believed that integration was the surest route to "race improvement" of Canadian blacks. To promote these views Mary helped found the Provincial Freeman, a weekly newspaper for the black community of Upper Canada that began publication in 1853. Although listed on the masthead as "M.A. Shadd, Publishing Agent," in reality, Mary was the editor of the paper.

In 1854, Mary faced discrimination of a different sort when she decided to correct the "misapprehension" that M.A. Shadd was a man. "It was," she wrote, "a mistake occasioned, no doubt, by the habit we have of using initials. We would simply correct, for the future, our error, by giving here the name in full (Mary A. Shadd) as we do not like the Mr. and Esq., by which we are so often addressed."

This revelation unleashed a wave of "sex discrimination" that threatened to close the Provincial Freeman. Mary urged readers not to abandon their support of the paper simply because "it had editors of the unfortunate sex." After advising readers that a new "gentleman editor" had been secured for the paper, Mary bid "Adieu" to Freeman readers.

In the late 1850's, Mary wed Thomas F. Cary of Toronto and resumed her teaching career in Chatham. During the American Civil War, she returned to the United States where she recruited black soldiers for the Union army. After the war, Mary (by then a widow), moved to Washington, D.C., where she taught school for many years, worked for the welfare of emancipated blacks, and studied law at Harvard University (she graduated in 1883 at the age of 60). Mary Shadd died of cancer in 1893; she was 70 years old.

photo courtesy National Archives of Canada.

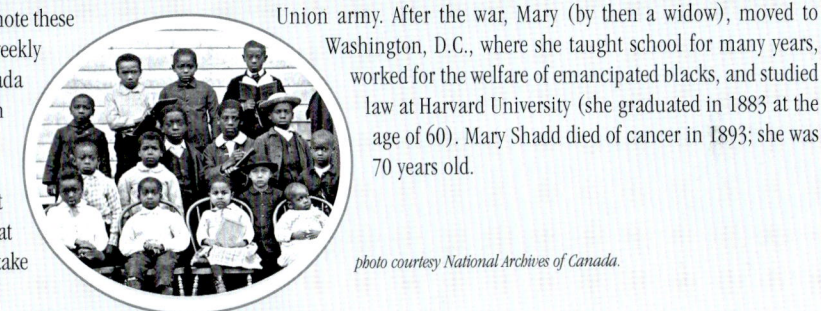

19th century postcard, promoting cockfights in Windsor.
David L. Newman Collection

Left, officers and men of the Afro-Canadian unit at Windsor; these men were part of the No. 2 Construction Battalion. The battalion was based in Nova Scotia, but a recruiting centre was located in Windsor. During WWI, blacks were not allowed in combat, so they formed a special unit for other duties. This photo was taken in November 1916; there are no names for any of the faces.

1930 Boys' Swim Team, Central Collegiate
l-r: C. Peck, R. Ortner, H. MacLellan, B. Howe, S. Hull, J. Farmer
photo courtesy Don Parsons

9
Sports Heritage

Reno Bertoia
Tiger by Day, Student by Night

by Shelley Divinich Haggert, Issue #15, May 2001

What Little League player in Windsor hasn't dreamt of playing Tiger ball? The vision of stepping up to the plate at the corner of Michigan and Trumbell has been replaced by the dream of Comerica Park, but it's still the same dream – Windsor boy makes the big time.

Reno Bertoia did just that.

Born in Italy in 1935, Reno's family took up residence in Canada when he was 22 months old. Like all immigrants, the Bertoias came in search of a better life. Reno's father worked at Ford Motor Company, and the family settled on Hickory Road.

Reno first started playing ball in the neighbourhood – the schoolyards, vacant lots and parks of East Windsor. His role model was next-door neighbour Hank Biasotti, who had played major league ball for the Philadelphia Athletics.

Reno followed a similar path – Gordon McGregor School, Assumption College, and then the major leagues. He started following the Tigers when he was a young newsboy, and the Tigers won the 1945 World Series when he was 10.

From the diamonds at Stodgell Park to Class –'D' ball at Northwestern Field in Detroit, under the supervision of Father Ronald Cullen (who still coaches past the age of 80), Reno moved toward the ultimate – his 1953 signing with the Detroit Tigers

An eighteen year-old 'bonus baby,' Reno was luckier than most. His initial contract included not only his signing bonus and salary, but also a trip to Italy for his mother and a commitment from the Tigers to pay for his university education. His 1954 Topps card lists him as the only Italian-born player in the major leagues.

In August of 1953, Reno was voted Most Outstanding Prospect in the City of Detroit, and sent to play in the Hearst All-Star game in New York City. He'd also been given a baseball scholarship to the University of Michigan. After New York, John McHale, general manager for the Tigers pursued him, and offered Reno his first major-league contract.

For the kid from a small Canadian town, the major leagues were a culture shock. Most of the Canadian players at the time were pitchers – there were few fielders. In fact, in 1958, Reno was the only Canadian in an opening day lineup. The pressure was the worst of it – but Reno was hardest on himself. "I worried too much," Reno said candidly in his interview for this story.

Required to forfeit his scholarship to U of M, Reno continued his education at Assumption University in between ball games. Friends would forward class notes for him during spring training, and he'd play second base by day, and write exams at night.

Reno's parents were proud of his accomplishments – his dad would often be found in the stands at Tiger Stadium. Reno's mother watched while he faced the illustrious Satchel Paige in his first game at Tiger Stadium. He got spiked at second base and she never attended another game.

Reno's major league career didn't end with the Tigers. Over the next ten years, he would play for the Washington Senators (later the Minnesota Twins) and Kansas City (now the Oakland A's) and back to Detroit. It was easier, he says, to play for the distant teams. "There was less pressure. At home, everyone wanted to know what you were doing, how you were playing," he recalled. "I was always afraid of disappointing somebody."

Reno's fondest memories of the game involve the people and players he met. He shared the game with some of baseball's greats – Ted Williams, Satchel Paige. For five years he roomed with Al Kaline, and recently reconnected with Kaline at spring training in Florida.

After leaving the major leagues, Reno settled in Windsor to raise his family. "Windsor was home – it never really occurred to me to go anywhere else." The teaching career that had started as a winter job in 1958 continued for 30 years at Corpus Christi,

Reno at bat, circa 1950s

Assumption and Holy Names. Reno also spent time scouting for the Tigers and Blue Jays after his retirement from professional play.

Reno agrees that baseball has changed – not just the economics, but the caliber of play. "If you look at the stats now, these are big players – most of them over six feet. But there are some darn good players."

Reno likes Comerica Park, and enjoys going to games. The Tigers have been good to him, he says, but he has no airs about his major league career. "I had my fifteen minutes of fame."

Reno Bertoia was inducted into the Canadian Baseball hall of Fame in 1988.

Baseball in the 20s
The Walkerville Chicks

by Mary Feldott, Issue #14, March 2001

Back in the 1920s, there was a semi-professional baseball team in Walkerville sponsored by a very successful local business man named Thomas Chick. Called "The Walkerville Chicks," they were quite a sensation. My father, Charlie Gatecliff, played infield. He was a good player and my grandmother collected hundreds of newspaper articles about him and the team. For over 50 years they were stored away.

Reading many of these articles and studying the pictures of these earnest looking young men, I came to realize that these articles are more than just about a baseball team. They are stories about Walkerville and its people. These young guys were having the time of their lives; baseball was their great love and they were good at it.

They knew the value of hard work, fair play, teamwork, giving it your all, while playing in tough conditions. One article described the Chicks playing in the snow when the season ran unusually long due to playoff games; another mentioned how spectators turned on their car lights to illuminate the field when a game continued after sunset.

The Chicks were subject to the baseball politics of the day when games were delayed or the opponents didn't show. They played with primitive equipment and without a team doctor – when they were injured they kept right on playing.

They often attracted huge crowds for the big game – one report noted that 5,000 people attended a play-off game and that the townspeople from small towns enroute to the tournament, stood by the side of the road and cheered them even after they had beaten their home team!

The Chicks were local heroes and pioneers of the game, the team few could beat. The Chicks stayed on top by recruiting the best players from the area. Prospects developed their skills by playing on a junior team called the "Chicklets."

My father's baseball career ended when he broke his leg trying out for a spot on a professional baseball team. He never shared this part of his life with me – being a kid I never thought to ask him about himself.

The articles end in the fall of 1929 leaving me with many questions: Whatever became of the Chicks? How long did they continue to play as a team? Did any of the guys ever make it to the major leagues? Were the Chicks one of the many casualties of the Depression?

Even if the players were unable to make it to a big league ball team, they were "big leaguers" to the people of Walkerville.

Photos and captions from The Border Cities Star, highlight the activities of the Walkerville Chicks in the 1920s. courtesy Mary Feldott

ON the trail of triumph tomorrow, this veteran hurler, Jack Smith of the Chicks, will be at work tomorrow against Steve Paris Shines, attempting to set the Windsorites back in the second game of the Southern Ontario baseball play-off. Facing him, for the Shines, will be the youngest ball-player in the game, Dave Kay, clever Windsor right-hander.

THE former Windsor battery that put Walkerville out of the 1927 race carried the Chicks to victory at Strathroy on Saturday. Bill Burnie, inset, blew his fast ball past the batters for nine innings and should have had a shutout if not a no-hit game. "Tel" Johnson, his catcher, led the clouters for the afternoon with two triples, a double and a single. Both may be in action against Niagara Falls here on Wednesday.

The "Major"
Olympian Ian Allison

by Shelley Divinich Haggert
Issue #10, September/October 2001

Walkerville Collegiate students called him "The Major." His friends called him Al. And history will remember him as a member of the only Canadian basketball team to ever win a medal at the Olympics.

Ian Allison was born in Greenock, Scotland. As a boy, his family emigrated to Canada and lived on Monmouth Road across from Walkerville Collegiate, where he would eventually win numerous medals for basketball, soccer and track and field.

Ian was an all-conference halfback in football at Assumption College, and played for the championship squad at the University of Toronto. After college, he returned to his roots, teaching and coaching at Walkerville for 40 years – from 1933 until his retirement in 1973.

In 1934, Ian and Jean, a Walkerville secretary, eloped in Bayfield. They had two daughters, Heather and Jane. Jean accompanied Ian to Berlin in 1936, where the boys from Windsor represented Canada at the Olympics. According to Jane Peckham, (née Allison) her parents often spoke about the military presence in Berlin. Soldiers were everywhere and swastikas draped the streets. Hitler watched the Games carefully, but refused to attend the medal ceremonies when African American Jesse Owens was recognized for his gold winning performance in track and field.

Nineteen-thirty six was the first year basketball was played as a medal sport at the Olympics. Team Canada, formerly known as the Ford V-8's, performed admirably. On outdoor courts, they defeated Brazil, Latvia, Switzerland and Poland, with Ian scoring 20 points total in those games.

Their gold-medal opponents were none other than the boys next door – Team U.S.A. Ian's teammate Jimmy Stewart exclaimed, "Oh, Al, they're so tall!" To which Ian replied, "That's okay, we'll just run between their legs!"

Playing in a steady downpour, the Canadian team ultimately lost to the Americans 19 - 8, with Ian Allison scoring four points. They proudly brought home the silver medal for Canada.

One of Ian's memorable moments from those Olympics was meeting Dr. James Naismith, a fellow Canadian and the founder of basketball. Ian's daughters still have their father's Berlin picture, autographed by Dr. Naismith, and Jesse Owens.

Returning to Windsor, Ian resumed his teaching career. Four years later, he was back on European soil, with a very different kind of team. Attached to the Calgary Tank Corps, Major Allison saw action at Dieppe and Monte Cassino, again bringing home medals, but this time for bravery.

When World War Two ended, Major Allison was back at Walkerville Collegiate. Teacher, coach, and athletic director, he was often seen in the halls carrying his trusty pointer or yardstick. The "Major" was well

Part of the V-8 Team: Ian Allison, centre middle row between Bud Wiseman & Ed Dawson, Front Row: Don Gray, Joe Marcel, Ernie Williams; Back Row: Percy McCallum, Tom Pendlebury, Ellis Millard

respected by his colleagues at Walkerville and was known for his poise and credibility. Early on, he coached his basketball team to victory over the previously unbeaten Assumption Purple Raiders, 19 – 16, to win the WSSA title. Ian also took great pride in the track and field athletes he worked with, like Richard Rau, and Jack Cowan. (He even taught Times editor Elaine Weeks how to hurdle.)

There is a story, confirmed by a colleague as well as Ian's daughter, about the day in 1965 when Walkerville flew the new Canadian flag for the first time. As the students gathered on the front lawn, Major Allison, a staunch Union Jack supporter had the honour of raising the flag. As the flag unfurled at the top of the flagpole, everyone looked up to admire the red Maple Leaf – flying upside down.

Just before his retirement in 1973, Ian and Jean moved to Kingsville. Following Jean's death in 1979, Ian relocated to London, Ontario to be closer to his daughter Jane. His love for sport continued. According to Jane, "Dad got a big charge out of watching his grandchildren's sporting events."

Ian Allison died on August 3rd, 1990. His three granddaughters and three grandsons have continued the family tradition of excellence in sport. One granddaughter is currently attending Colorado State on a volleyball scholarship, and a grandson will be attending Ohio State on a volleyball scholarship in the fall.

Although Mr. Allison's Olympic feats were often taken for granted by his daughters when they were younger, his grandchildren are very impressed by his record, prompting his grandson Scott to even consider changing his last name to Allison.

In 1981, the V-8 team was inducted into the Canadian Basketball Hall of Fame, and in 1988, Ian Allison was inducted into the Windsor-Essex County Hall of Fame.

Special thanks to Mrs. Jane Peckham (née Allison) of London, ON for sharing her memories.

Windsor Boxer
Harry Marshall

by Shelley Divinich Haggert, Issue #17, September 2001

It would be impossible to calculate the number of Windsor boys whose lives were changed because Harry Marshall taught them how to throw a punch without getting into trouble.

Born in 1923 in Liverpool, England, Marshall moved to Windsor with his parents when he was five and grew up on Bernard Road. While a student at W.D. Lowe, he was an all-city track star but found his true calling in the boxing ring.

Marshall's father, a boxing enthusiast and coach, introduced him to the sport early. The oldest of five boys, Marshall was the only one to pursue boxing. While serving for the Canadian Army in England during World War II, he became the Army Lightweight Champion in 1945.

Back from overseas, he turned pro. Fighting in the Windsor and Detroit area for the first few years, Marshall's career progressed but could only go so far. Hoping to achieve national champion status, Marshall and his manager moved to New York City.

In one hundred fights, he suffered only two knockouts and seven losses. Ring Magazine ranked him the #3 lightweight in Canada in 1942.

One of Marshall's favorite memories of his amateur days was the opportunity, while overseas, to spar with Canadian champion Danny Webb. Great friends, but competitive in the ring, the two would often work out together. While they never fought one another officially, Marshall did score a knockdown against Webb during their informal sparring.

Marshall resettled in Windsor and married Patricia Crilley who had grown up in the same neighbourhood as him. He had developed a reputation there for showing off his athletic abilities – his favourite trick was walking on his hands.

Tom Marshall, youngest of their three children, remembers a story of his dad showing off during his courting days. One day when his mother went to the Marshall home, she was met by her fiance walking on his hands – down a flight of stairs.

A labourer at Chrysler's for 30 years, Marshall inspired physical fitness in the workplace before it became standard to provide employees with such outlets. Convincing his employer to allocate space on the second floor, he brought in medicine balls, speed bags and other equipment to give workers the opportunity to work out on their breaks.

The YMCA allocated space to Marshall for a time, as did the Jewish Community Center. After founding the Windsor Amateur Boxing Club in 1968, Marshall petitioned City Council to donate a former storage building, and the WABC moved into its permanent home on Grove Avenue in 1970.

Ringside Magazine ranked Harry Marshall #3 lightweight in Canada in 1942

Marshall then approached various businesses in Windsor for donations, such as Pazner Scrap on Drouillard Road, which contributed iron to build the ring, and fellow Chrysler employees donated their time welding it together. Even the canvas and ropes were donated.

Marshall's wife got into the spirit by obtaining her license as an official judge, and attending matches regularly. Tom Marshall entered twenty amateur fights, winning 19, with – the other resulting in a draw.

"Dad taught me the science of keeping my hands up, scoring points and not getting hit."

Marshall's love of the sport, and his desire to instill confidence and skill in young men motivated him to open his club's doors to the youth of Windsor. Regardless of background or past history, prospective boxers were welcomed at the club, as long as they followed the rules. WABC also provided opportunities for men in local drug rehabilitation programs and St. Leonard's Halfway House to work out as part of their therapy.

WABC has produced its share of stars. Pete Pestowka became Canadian Amateur Middleweight Champion and Jim French and Charlie Stewart won gold medals at the 1972 Canada Winter Games in Saskatoon. In 1973, the WABC team won the Michigan Golden Gloves championship, and became the only Canadian boxing club to defeat the famous Detroit Kronk and Brewster Clubs.

Sportsmanship and hard work have always been more important than winning to Marshall, and that principle is held in high regard in the Marshall family.

In 1972, Harry was voted Kinsmen Club of Windsor Sportsman of the Year, and was recently nominated for induction into the Windsor-Essex County Sports Hall of Fame. He passed away in the fall of 2004.

Don Parsons
One Man Basketball Team

supplied by Bob Weepers, Issue #44, June 2004

Basketball is played by two to five players on the floor at any one time. Well, to quote a line from an old Hertz commercial, "not exactly." Don Parsons, a former Walkerville resident who now resides in Kingsville, can dispute that fact. Playing for Central United Church on April 21st, 1956, in St. Catharine's, there was a time in the game when he no doubt felt like a shipwreck survivor marooned on an uninhabited island, all alone and not a soul to talk to.

In a bizarre situation, he was the only Central player on the floor for the final 45 seconds of the game against St. Catharine's CYO in the first of a two-game total points series for the Ontario Amateur Basketball Association Intermediate "B" championship. All of Parson's teammates had fouled out.

Parsons performed beyond the call of duty, holding St. Kitts to only two points with his one-man defence over the final 45 seconds. He also didn't foul out, which would have caused Central to forfeit the game, and maybe even the series.

Central ended up on the losing side of a 96-77 result but, by not allowing St. Catharine's a bundle of points, Parson kept Central from absorbing a larger deficit on the final score, which would have made it very difficult for them to overcome in the second and final game of the series.

Only six Central players made the 200-mile trip to St. Catharine's, but they came out of the first half with a 36-34 lead, and minus no players, due to foul disqualification, but John Forsyth sprained an ankle and had to retire to the bench. He was forced back into action when two teammates fouled out in the third quarter.

Central started the fourth quarter with only three players, but still protecting a 10-point lead. Forsyth fouled out with four minutes remaining in the game, leaving Parsons and Don Echlin to fend off the opposition, reduced to just three players itself. Echlin fouled out with 45 seconds left on the clock, setting the stage for Parson's heroics, which certainly made him a candidate for a Medal of Honour.

What strategy does one employ in a one-versus-three situation? Parson's choice was to drop back into the free throw lane to better protect the basket, and grasp any rebounds. On the offensive side of things, the $64,000 question is, how did he in-bound the ball after a score or turnover by St. Catharine's? Having taken a referees course earlier so he could join the Windsor & District Referees Association, Parson knew his options: once he bounced the ball off a referee, and twice off opposing players.

When he put the ball in play his dribbling enabled him to avoid the 10-second rule to get the ball over half-court, and effectively play keep-away from his three pursuers and run time off the clock. He launched one shot at the opposition's basket. Not to be overlooked is the fact that Parson was Central's top scorer in the game with 19 points. The remainder of Central's points were distributed among Jack Boyce (16), Hugh Murray (18), Forsyth (16), Echlin (4) and Warner Day (4).

Parson's efforts also had a huge effect on the eventual outcome of the series, and they boded well for St. Central's chances in the final game at home, adding fuel to their confidence playing the deciding game on their home court.

They had little difficulty. Central made up the 19-point deficit quickly in the first half and by halftime they were seven points up on the round. They won the final game 82-58, and the championship, taking the total points series 159-154. Parsons scored 15 points in the final game.

Top Left: Don Parsons, March, 1952. Right: in 2004, photo E. Weeks

Ernestine Russell
Canada's First Female Olympic Gymnast

by Shelley Divinich Haggert, Issue #11, November 2000

Ernestine (Ernie) Russell, grew up at the ballet bar. Her mother, an examiner for Britain's Royal Academy, was in charge of her dance training. Problem was, Ernie didn't have a ballerina's body

A neighbour, former Member of Provinicial Parliament and teacher Bernie Newman, had formed the Vocational Boy's gymnastics team. Newman suggested that the frustrated ballerina try the trampoline. According to Ernie, "I got on, and I never got off."

Competing for the first time when she was 13, Ernie eventually won nine Canadian championships. Newman's dream was to see Ernie and team member Ed Gagnier compete in the Olympics.

Canada had never had a female gymnast at the Olympics. At 17, Ernie became the first, participating in the Melbourne Australia Olympics Games in 1956.

Ernie just recently realized how significant that was. "In those days," she recalls, "I just went and did my gymnastics. It was just one more place to compete."

Windsor track star Johnny Loaring, a competitor in the 1936 Games, had advised Ernie not to be overwhelmed by the "bigness" of it all but arriving in Melbourne was still a shock for her. The women's compound was fenced; Ernie remembers watching the Russian team do their warm-ups, using the fence as a ballet bar. Their swan-like poise and grace impressed her.

By contrast, Ernie was ill prepared. She remembers, "We didn't even have a pianist for the floor routine." The Czechoslovakian pianist volunteered and accompanied Ernie with music provided just minutes before so there was no time to rehearse together.

In addition to the floor competition, Ernie's events included the balance beam —her favourite, followed closely by the vault. She represented Canada well, finishing less than a point behind the gold-medal winner, but did not medal.

Ernie often wondered how different things might have been with just a little more training. The reality is a lone athlete without a team doesn't have much chance of winning a medal.

Gymnastics continued to be a major focus of most of Ernie's life. She graduated from Kennedy High School in 1956, and four years later, was one of two Canadian women to compete in the Olympic Games in Rome. She went on to win five gold medals for the U.S. in the 1959 Pan-Am Games.

After earning a degree in physical education and dance from Michigan State University, Ernie taught high school for five years, then returned to coaching at Michigan State. Coaching positions at other U.S. colleges, including the University of Florida followed.

At Florida, she worked with a young Elfie Shlagel, the former Canadian gymnast who became a sports broadcaster for NBC.

In 1977, Ernie became head coach for the U.S. gymnastics team. She has been inducted into the Canadian Hall of Fame, and may be one of Kennedy's most outstanding female athletes.

Ernie also serves on the Board of Directors for the International Hall of Fame. Now living in Las Vegas where she works in a physical therapy clinic, Ernie continues to be involved in gymnastics clubs.

The Canadian Gymnastics Federation invited her to the Sydney Games in 2000. Unable to attend, she watched the Games with interest from her home and was pleased to see one of her club members compete.

One of Ernie's clearest memories of her childhood in Windsor is practising her twists and flips in the vacant lot at the corner of Chilver Road and Tecumseh Road East, where Windsor Chapel Funeral Home is now located.

Although the U.S. has been her home for many years, Ernie's peers still call her "the Canadian." The sight of the Maple Leaf being raised in Sydney brought tears to her eyes. "It's something that's always a part of you," explains Ernie. "It's still my flag."

Ernie Russell shows her form.
photo: Bernie Newman

Helped Ernestine Fly

I read the story of Ernestine Russell on your web site. In 1951, I was 'dating' Ernestine's older sister, who was an instructor at the Barrett-Russell School of Dance. She and I used to help Ernie practice her early leaps and bounds. We attached a leather belt around her waist with metal hooks on the sides. Ropes were attached to both sides and Ernie would race up to the mat and fly though the air while we held on to the ropes to guide her in those early gymnastic moves. She was a feisty little girl and would never give up until she got it right. We spent hours working with her and it was a lot of fun. I joined the RCAF in 1953 and didn't realize Ernie had done anything with her talent until I saw a newsreel in France where I was stationed with the Air Force. I was amazed but not surprised.

Ray Stone, Ottawa, Issue #54, Summer 2005

Roseland Park Country Club

by Jeff Mingay, Issue #36, July/August 2003

Throughout a career in golf course design that spanned nearly four decades and spawned 399 courses, it is estimated Donald Ross designed fewer than 15 courses in Canada. Curiously, two are in Windsor: Essex Golf and Country Club and Roseland, once known as Roseland Park Country Club.

It was Harry Neal, a successful local entrepreneur and avid sportsman, who first brought Ross to Windsor in 1926 to lay out an 18-hole course as the centrepiece for Roseland Park, a stately residential neighbourhood he was developing on the city's south side. Neal's plan was for those who purchased homes in Roseland Park to automatically become members of Roseland Park Country Club, completed in 1928.

In October 1929, development in Roseland Park stalled with the onset of the Great Depression. The sale of homes and lots surrounding the course, from which Neal and his brothers expected to recoup their investment in the golf course, ceased.

The Neal brothers managed to endure until 1933, when, faced with an unbearable financial burden, they were forced to turn over Roseland Park Country Club to bondholders.

"There was no bitterness," Harry Neal wrote in his memoirs many years later. "The Neal brothers were victims of the times. They had lost, but they took with them full realization that they had built a championship golf course."

Since 1972, Roseland has been owned by the City of Windsor and operates as a public golf course.

Above: An aerial photograph of Roseland taken by Frank Wansbrough in August 1956. The ninth green is seen at bottom-centre. Above it, adjacent to the pro shop building, is the 18th green. And, at top-left, the 10th, 11th, 12th and 14th holes are clearly seen, with Donald Ross' original bunkering schemes still intact. The driving bunkers at the 10th and 11th, seen in this photo, have since been removed, and the course has been heavily planted. The treed area at bottom-left, above the original clubhouse building, is now the site of Roseland's nine-hole par 3 course.

Harry J. Neal

Henry James "Harry" Neal was born in Morpeth, Ontario on October 9th, 1883. In 1915, he was appointed president of his family's Neal Baking Company based in Windsor. After having assisted in expanding the company's operations to include additional Ontario bakeries in London, St. Thomas and Sarnia, Neal sold the business to a national conglomerate in 1925.

Neal also dabbled in politics, when necessary. But, most of all, he enjoyed sports. Particularly baseball and golf. Neal was in fact one of Windsor's first golf enthusiasts. He and others, including Clarence H. Smith, established the popular Essex-Kent Boys Golf Tournament at Roseland Park Country Club in 1928.

Neal and his wife, Jane, had five children. Their youngest son, Fredrick, who was popularly know by the nickname "Shin," became a fine young golfer, In 1933, Shin Neal won his first of two consecutive Essex-Kent titles at Roseland.

Today, both the Roseland golf course and the Essex-Kent Boys Golf Tournament serve as lasting tributes to Harry Neal, who died in 1961 at the age of 78.

by Jeff Mingay, Windsor

photo: One Hundred Years, A History of Essex Golf & Country Club: 1902-2002

An Architectural Marvel

Ross was the most sought after golf architect in the world when Neal invited him to design Roseland Park. Between 1919 and 1925, five of seven United States Open championships were contested on courses designed by Ross.

In late July 1926, Ross personally visited the proposed site for Roseland Park, during which he devised a routing for 18-holes and drew rough freehand sketches of the proposed greens and their surroundings. Neal was anxious to begin construction, so Ross hurriedly mailed his preliminary drawings to Pinehurst, North Carolina, where they were formalized by his chief draftsman, Walter Johnson.

"This is a rush job," Ross explained to Johnson in a letter dated August 3rd, 1926. "I would like you to lay everything aside and do the general plan first. They will want to start clearing the fairway widths. It is very urgent, so give it your best attention."

The Roseland Park site was poorly drained and absolutely flat, much like the Matchette Road property Essex directors would present to Ross two years later.

"The main ditch which I have shown in front of the Club House and across #8 and #9 holes, is at present located through the lot lines back of the Club House," Ross continued in his letter to Johnson, "but it is to be changed to suit the golf course. The swales which I have shown in red are subject to slight adjustments as the construction work progresses but as the land is dead flat and badly drained those swales could be very useful both for filling material and drainage purposes."

Ross' routing of 18-holes at Roseland Park took full advantage of a featureless 124-acre tract bordered on all sides by home lots. Aside from back-to-back par 4s at the 10th and 11th, no two consecutive holes play in the same direction and the variety in the types of holes is equally impressive.

The par 3's are particularly varied. The fourth and 16th holes, 182 and 172 yards long respectively, are both medium in length, but they play very differently: the green at the fourth is open in front and angled to prefer a shot on a right-to-left trajectory. The 16th green is perched high on an artificial plateau, defended in front by a deep sand bunker and is more likely to accept a soft cut shot from a right-handed golfer.

The 183-yard 8th was originally planned to play as long as 210 yards. It was a diabolical par 3 with a creek cutting through the line from tee-to-green only a few yards short of its relatively small putting surface. The creek has since been converted into a grassy swale.

Offsetting the 8th was the 140-yard 13th, which somewhat resembled the short par 3 seventh hole at Essex, with its tiny pear-shaped green virtually surrounded by sand. It has since been lengthened to 177 yards through the extension of the tee.

The most interesting holes at Roseland Park were the short par 5's at the 2nd, 5th, 12th and 14th – none of which were longer than 470 yards. Originally, these holes were wide open and littered with sand bunkers that set up a number of alternate routes to their greens. Today, many of those original bunkers are missing and have been replaced with trees that have significantly narrowed corridors of play.

Roseland's 3rd and 15th holes are still neat little drive-and-pitch affairs that call for delicate second shots to tiny, heavily bunkered greens.

And the closing stretch, beginning with the demanding par 3 16th, is indeed of championship caliber. The 434 yard 17th, with its sublimely contoured green, and the mammoth 449 yard finishing hole can easily destroy an otherwise good round.

The greens at Roseland, none of which have been altered from their original design, are most conspicuous. Predominately pitched from back-to-front, they are typical of Ross, with multiple tiers, diagonal swales and centre ridges dividing each into a number of distinct "cupping areas;" not a single one resembles another.

Indeed, there are many similarities between Roseland and Essex – and one marked difference too. Whereas Essex was a "design and build" contract, Donald Ross and Associates were hired to lay out the Roseland course only. Ross' detailed plans were handed to a construction company without previous experience in golf course construction. As a result, Roseland's tees, bunkers and greens have an abruptness about them – they "pop up" out of the ground and do not tie into neighbouring features.

In contrast, there is a relatively seamless flow to the Essex property. Tees flow into fairways, fairways into greens, and greens into tees.

On paper, Roseland and Essex are comparable golf courses. It is the detail work that separates Essex from its sister course; a craftsmanship that is attributable to the on-site presence of one of Ross's top associates (either Walter Hatch or James McGovern) and the knowledge and experience of green keeper John Gray.

Roseland 1947

Originally featuring some 90 sand bunkers, Roseland was almost completely devoid of trees in 1947. The course is very heavily treed today, and left with fewer than 60 bunkers total– as illustrated by the corresponding aerial taken in 2000.

Note the absence of homes around the perimeter of the course in this 1947 aerial photograph. Today, Roseland is surrounded by residential development– referred to as the Roseland district of the City of Windsor.

The original frame clubhouse at the foot of the circular drive in the top right corner of this photograph was torn down and replaced with a new clubhouse and curling rink in 1978.

The original golf shop between the first tee and the 18th green was also replaced in 1999.

The sparsely treed tract of land to the immediate right of the clubhouse area in this photograph is today occupied by a nine-hole par 3 course, constructed in the mid-1960s.

Roseland 2000

A comparison between this 2000 aerial photograph of Roseland and the 1947 aerial illustrates many changes to the layout of the course and the surrounding area over half a century. The planting of hundreds of trees has significantly narrowed corridors of play throughout the course; a local myth persists that Donald Ross designed the course around the tress. And nearly 30 original sand bunkers are missing today. The par 3 course, with its two ponds (used to store irrigation water for both courses), can be seen at top right in this photo, adjacent to the clubhouse and curling rink. The large, open area between the 13th and 18th holes is the golf course maintenance facility.

From: "One Hundred Years, A History of Essex Golf & Country Club: 1902-2002" by Jeff Mingay with Dick H. Carr. produced by Walkerville Publishing.

GOLF FINALISTS TO PLAY 36 HOLES ON
Feature Matches Are Due in Tennis Tournament as Events

Sixteen Boys Who Get Company Golf Kits in Roseland's Tournament

Al Langford (4th from left,) was one of the sixteen boys who won golf clubs in 1928 at the 1st Annual Essex-Kent Boys Golf Tournament at Roseland.

Goofy Over Golf

I was introduced to the grand old game when I was about 13. My uncle, Phil Larsh Sr. was my teacher. We played on the course inside the Devonshire Race Track; Bob Whittle was the Pro. We had to climb over or under the railings of the track from time to time and the tees were sometimes on grass. There were no wooden gadgets to peg the ball in those days; instead there was a box of wet sand to place the ball to tee off. The "greens" were not much more than pasture land.

Then Roseland Golf Course opened (I think it was in 1926 or '27). It must have been about that time because I played in the 1st Annual Essex-Kent Boys Golf Tournament in August of 1928. There were 162 of us who teed-off for the qualifying round.

The lowest 16 boys qualified for the Championship Flight, the rest would be made up of flights of 16. There were six flights altogether; 66 of the boys failed to make any of the flights (Joe Merovitch took approximately 292 strokes for 18 holes!). Most of the boys were caddies at courses in the Chatham-Kent Area. Caddying was a good way to make a few extra dollars in those days.

It was a rather tight group. Every boy had a club member who preferred him, so, if you didn't know some member, you sat in the caddy shack and waited for a "carry." I tried a few times at Beach Grove with no luck.

(I also had a job after school and on Saturdays as an office boy. I licked stamps etc. at McLarty & Fraser Law Office and at M.D. MacPhail's Real Estate.)

Here were the scores: Joe Bialkowski, a 15 year-old caddie from St Clair Golf Club was the medallist with a score of 85, Alcide LaBute, 15, of Essex, 86, Bill Moynihan,15, Tecumseh 86, Paul Cantin,15, Essex, 87, Charles Christian, 13, Beach Grove 87, C. Charbonneau, 15, Essex 89, Albert Langford, 16, Windsor, 90, Howard Schneider, 15, 91, Arno Seegar,16, St. Clair, 91, George Smith,15, Monmouth Road, 91, Sam Holt, 14, Westminster Boulevard, 93, Malcolm Wiseman, 15, Felix Avenue, 94, Emerald Awad, 14, Moy Avenue, 94, John Corlett, 15, Bernard Road, 94, Jack Popp, 15, Chippawa Street, 94, and Tom Fullerton, 14, Brock Street, 95.

Match play began the next day. The low man, Joe Bialowski (we called him "bottle-o-whisky,") played Tom Fullerton and beat him 6 and 5 (Joe was 6 strokes up and only 5 holes to play). The rest of the winners in the 1st round were: Alcide, Bill, Paul, Malcolm, Charby, Al, and Howard.

Joe and Alcide were the finalists and the match was touch and go all the way. Alcide beat Joe on the final hole. Joe redeemed himself in 1929 by beating Alcide. Sad to say, your hero, Al, lost in the next round to Howard Schneider.

There were lots of prizes. Each one of us in the championship flight won a set of golf clubs. Each player who made a birdie on any hole (one under par) received goodies in trade from the concessionaire; Norm Meisner and Jack Popp had two of them. Your hero drove the fourth green and missed a hole-in-one by 12 inches. As a side note, on one of my visits to the sports department of Hudson's, that wonderful store in Detroit, I saw a "spoon" (now known as a 3-wood). It had a beautiful white hickory shaft and it felt great to swing it in the store. I saved for quite a while until I purchased it. After a year or so the shaft developed a curve (warped) but I still used it for quite a while.

The Roseland officials handled the tournament very well and saw to the needs of all participants. The members loaned their clubs to any who needed them – golf balls, too. Two sandwiches and a bottle of milk were available at the ninth hole. We even had quite a few spectators. Unfortunately, no slo-mo replays (I'm glad they didn't analyze my swing!).

Al Langford, Windsor, Issue #38, October 2003

On the porch at Walkerville Country Club, circa 1900

100 Years of Golf at Essex

by Jeff Mingay and Richard H. Carr, Issue #25, June 2002

Today golf is one of the most popular sports in the world. But one hundred years ago, golf in Canada was in its infancy. Recognized golf clubs had been established in Victoria, British Columbia; in Brantford, Toronto, Kingston and Niagara-on-the-Lake in Ontario; and Montreal and Quebec City. But there were few others. And those that did exist had a very difficult time recruiting members to sustain themselves.

Walkerville Country Club

As is the case with many seminal local historical events, this story begins in Walkerville. Legendary American businessman Hiram Walker developed a fine reputation for the quality of his whisky. From the remarkable success of Walker's industry was born a prosperous little town bearing his name.

With success comes expendable time and monies that could be dedicated to recreation and leisure. In the late 1880s, Walker and his family established the Walkerville Country Club.

Although the game of golf was by no means a popular activity at the time, Walker laid out a rudimentary nine-hole course for members of his country club at some point prior to 1900 on the current site of Walkerville Collegiate High School and Willistead Crescent. This makes Walkerville Country Club one of the first golf courses in the Windsor-Detroit area.

For the record, the Country Club of Detroit, which is generally acknowledged as the oldest golf-related club in the area, was established with an 18-hole golf course in 1897. Two years later, Detroit Golf Club was incorporated.

Due to the absence of proper engineering, the Walkerville course drained very poorly and was unplayable for extended periods of time following rain. There was also an absence of ground contour, sand bunkers and other obstacles, which made golf in Walkerville rather bland.

George Mair and a number of other disgruntled Walkerville golfers soon decided that a more suitable course was not only desirable, but necessary.

By 1902, assisted principally by his wife and a "Mr. Greenhill," Mair had successfully solicited support from an enthusiastic group of Walkerville and Windsor area golfers – enough support to warrant the establishment of a new club, which they called Oak Ridge Golf Club. Appropriately, Mair was elected the new club's first president.

Men like Mair who were involved with the organization of North America's first golf clubs, could not have imagined that 100 years later historians would want to know how and when the game took root in their city. As a result, historical documents, photographs and other information regarding the establishment of many golf clubs are scarce.

Oak Ridge Golf Club

Fortunately, the establishment of Oak Ridge was chronicled, albeit briefly, in the January 1916 edition of The Canadian Golfer magazine.

"It was about fifteen years ago that Windsor and Walkerville had a joint club at Walkerville, but the course was not a very suitable one, becoming almost unplayable in wet weather. Through the kindness of Mr. Thos. Austin of Detroit, son-in-law of the late Mr. Yawkey, a multimillionaire, who owned a large tract of land in and adjoining Sandwich, Mr. Mair, the first President of the new club, and the members were most generously offered the use, free of charge, of a thirty-four-hundred-yard golf course on his farm."

The club was successful from its inception, and subsequently 44 acres were rented adjoining Mr. Yawkey's farm from a Mr. Freeman of Detroit. Largely through the efforts of the late Mrs. Mair, who secured subscriptions from members and friends, a small clubhouse was erected on this property and the game of golf prospered apace.

For nearly a decade, Oak Ridge Golf Club enjoyed great success on the Yawkey and Freeman Farms in Sandwich. Enthusiasm for the game of golf and the general activities of the club had grown tremendously in just eight years.

Besides the fact Oak Ridge directors could no longer justify the exorbitant cost of leasing the Yawkey and Freeman lands, the golf course and clubhouse were quickly being rendered incapable of accommodating the increasing demands of a growing membership.

Plans to move the club were underway in 1909 when Oak Ridge directors exercised an option to purchase a 53-acre property, located at the intersection of Centre Road (today Prince Road) and the Essex Terminal Railway line in Sandwich from the heirs of the late Colonel John Prince.

Having essentially been evicted from the Yawkey and Freeman owned lands, Oak Ridge members were granted permission to play golf on the old, hapless Walkerville course while their new layout on the Prince Farm was under construction.

During their first season spent golfing at Walkerville Country Club in 1910, Oak Ridge members exhibited a ripe, infectious enthusiasm for their ambitious plans. Soon, a significant number of Walkerville golfers opted to join Oak Ridge. The end result was a genuine amalgamation between the two clubs that warranted the creation of an entirely new club.

Above: Rare photograph of golfers on the Prince Farm course were taken for an advertisement for Ford Motors Co. in 1919.
Right: Members of Oak Ridge Golf Club lounging on the front porch of the clubhouse on the Yawkey Farm in Sandwich, Ontario, circa 1909.

Birth of Essex

In October that year, with a formidable capital of $40,000, Essex County Golf & Country Club was incorporated under an Ontario Provincial Charter. Despite this, Essex members were forced to play on the Walkerville course for yet another season. The new Essex course opened for play on the Prince Farm in the spring of 1912, and the old Walkerville layout was happily abandoned.

It is unknown who originally laid out the Prince Farm golf course, which consisted of just nine holes during its first two years of existence.

In 1913, Essex directors secured a $20,000 loan from a "Mr. Arthur Doumouchelle" of the Township of Sandwich West in order to purchase a 54-acre property adjoining the existing course for the sole purpose of expanding it to 18-holes. No records have been discovered indicating who laid-out the nine-hole addition. Nonetheless, an 18-hole course was in play by the spring of 1915.

And yet, many Essex members were still dissatisfied with the overall quality of the Prince Farm course. There was a definite consensus that it had too many short holes and not enough in the way of sand bunkers and contour in the putting greens.

During the club's annual meeting held on January 24, 1916, Essex director Gordon M. McGregor, suggested that more land was required if indeed Essex was to have "the best 18-hole golf course west of Toronto. But, at the time, the club could not afford to purchase more land, nor pay an expert to renovate the course.

This, however, did not discourage McGregor, a self-made millionaire who co-founded the Ford Motor Company of Canada along with Detroit industrialist Henry Ford in 1904. Shortly thereafter, McGregor personally purchased an additional seven acres of adjacent land owned by the Woollot family for $5,000. He then agreed to sell the property to the club at cost when appropriate funds were readily available.

Unfortunately, no photographs of the Prince Farm course have been located. And its exact layout is a distant, incoherent memory.

Gordon McGregor: "the best 18-hole golf course west of Toronto"

Donald Ross: Golf's first "superstar"

Move to Matchette

By 1919, there was a general feeling amongst Essex members that the club was losing its "country club" appeal to the rapidly growing City of Windsor. There was concern that the Prince Farm would soon be engulfed by urban development, and further expansion of club facilities would be severely limited. Property taxes were steadily rising as well with the growth of the area.

Moving the club to a more rural location – where a new and improved golf course and an attractive new clubhouse could be constructed – became a popular option.

Almost immediately a tract of land in the village of St. Clair Beach along Lake St. Clair was considered, but not purchased. Presumably, the establishment of the St. Clair Golf Club (today Lakewood Golf Club) in 1919, and Beach Grove Golf & Country Club in 1921, deterred Essex directors from venturing east of the City of Windsor.

Essex directors purchased 14 individual farms on Matchette Road, bounded by what were planned to be International Avenue to the north and Marcella Street to the south, Matchette Road to the east and the Essex Terminal Railway line to the west. The total land purchase amounted to exactly 125.39 acres, and a total cost of $106,049.50.

Caddy Shack at Essex Golf and County Club

The next step was to select an architect to design the course that would indeed be the "best course west of Toronto." As a side note, Gordon MacGregor passed away in 1922 and did not get to play on his vaulted dream golf course.

By the time Essex directors decided to engage Donald Ross to layout the club's new "18-hole championship golf course" on Matchette Road in LaSalle, Ross had completed several notable courses in the Detroit area; fifteen in all, including the famous North and South courses at Oakland Hills Country Club, 36 holes at Detroit Golf Club, Grosse Ile, Franklin Hills, and Windsor's Roseland Park.

His talent and abilities as a golf architect were well advertised to Essex directors. They were easily convinced Ross was indeed the man for the job. In fact, there is no evidence another golf architect was considered.

Ross' remarkable reputation as a competitive golfer, a respected teacher and an accomplished greenkeeper preceded him as well. He is widely acknowledged as America's first golf superstar.

Today, he is credited with laying out some 399 golf courses across North America. According to his biographer, Bradley S. Klein, author of "Discovering Donald Ross, the Architect and his Golf Courses" (Sleeping Bear Press, 2001), Ross visited approximately 75% per cent of those courses in person. This in an era when the principle mode of transportation was by train!

Donald Ross designed the Matchette Road course, but it was Essex' longtime greenkeeper, John Gray, who built it.

When it came time for Ross to appoint a supervisor for the construction of the new Essex course in 1928, Gray's previous experience in golf course construction was invaluable.

There are certain Ross courses, such as Essex, acknowledged to be superior to others. Some benefited from the natural topography of the given land, or a healthy construction budget. Others profited from Ross' personal time on site.

With Ross' frequent absences, however, the man charged with supervising the course construction had a significant impact on the overall quality of the finished product. Modifications to an architect's drawn plans are not out of the ordinary. Thus, an educated, experienced foreman is required to successfully execute those necessary changes in the field.

Construction of the Matchette Road course began in May 1928. It was to be the last of 16 Donald Ross-designed golf courses constructed in the Windsor-Detroit area between 1910 and 1929. When he arrived at Essex, Ross was arguably the busiest golf architect in the world. Based on accounts, he visited the Matchette Road site personally at least once. However, there is no evidence suggesting a second visit.

Throughout 15 months of construction and grow-in on Matchette Road, Gray supervised up to 135 men and 80 teams of horses. The Matchette Road course was completed in 1929.

It is interesting to note that Ross' original plans for the course do not denote par. According to "Pinehurst, North Carolina's Outlook" newspaper, Ross was" "of the puritan school, a lover of the old Scotch foursome." He abhorred the lavish use of a scorecard.

When the new Essex opened for play in July 1929, it measured 6,683 total yards and played to a scorecard par of 72. Then, the 461-yard fourth hole was labelled a par 5. It was amended to par 4 in 1965 on advice from Royal Canadian Golf Association officials who rated the course that year.

As a result, total par for the course is now a challenging 71. Its total length has changed very little in the intervening years, measuring 6,703 yards from the back tees today.

John Gray was greenkeeper at Essex until his sudden death in 1958, at the age of 73; he was simply "Mr. Essex" to all who knew him.

Essex Golf and Country has earned a deserved reputation as one of the finest courses in North America – if not the world.

The course has hosted major tournaments, including the Men's Canadian Open Championship in 1976, the LPGA du Maurier Championship in 1998, the 2002 AT&T Canada Senior Open.

According to golf architect Bruce A. Hepner of Renaissance Golf Design, Inc., "the original design at Essex is the perfect blend of complex putting surfaces matched with the varying lengths of tee and approach shots. It is a golf course that, throughout the years, has challenged every type of golfer from the greats of the game to your average "Sunday afternoon" member.

Remarkably, many years after it opened for play, the Matchette Road course continues to exemplify Ross' brilliance as a golf architect and John Gray's labour of love.

Above: John Gray: "Mr. Essex"

Left: Golf legend Jack Nicklaus, on the tee at the 1976 Canadian Open.

Photos from One Hundred Years, A History of Essex Golf & Country Club: 1902-2002. By Jeff Mingay with Dick H. Carr.

Searching for "Mr. Walkerville"
Issue #24, May 2002

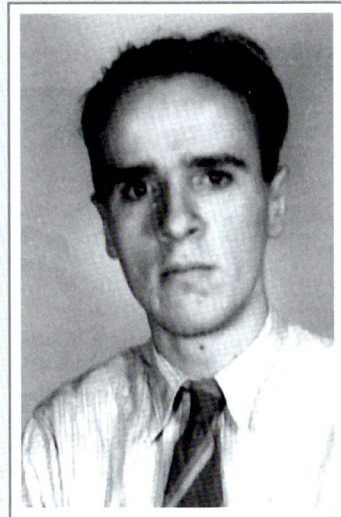

Cecil Gawley as a student at Walkerville Collegiate in the 1940s

Mr. Walkerville: Cecil in 1997 at Walkerville C.I.'s 75th Reunion

photo courtesy: Glenna Houston

Anyone Seen Cecil?
My brother, sisters and I (Patti, Mike and Sue – students at W.C.I. in the 70s and 80s), were chatting the other day and we remembered an older fellow who was always at the various W.C.I. sporting events. I believe he walked with a limp and his name may have been Cecil. We remembered that we used to see him at the football, hockey and basketball games, but I don't think we ever knew the story behind him. If anybody has any information, it would help the four of us.
Steve Hodges, via email

Mr. Walkerville
As always, the latest issue of *The Times* evoked many memories for this born-and-raised-in-Walkerville senior. Regarding the letter about Cecil the sports fan – I remember Cecil Gawley well as he and I shared many Latin classes with Mr. Fred Burr at Walkerville C.I.

Cecil had a congenital problem that resulted in a severe limp and thus the inability to play sports. Cecil rarely missed a sporting event however. He was a real fan. He was also a clever person hampered by poor communication skills. In retrospect, many people chose to ignore him rather than be a friend probably because of his disability and the fact that he was "different."

For those who attended W.C.I.'s reunion in the 70s, you may remember that Cecil was recognized for his contribution to the history of the school as its most devoted sports fan.
Winifred Auld Sinclair, Windsor

#1 Tartan Fan
I have just finished reading the latest *Times*. What a wonderful magazine you are putting out. As I live and work in the Walkerville area, I look forward to each edition.

A recent letter to the editor from Steve Hodges inquired about a man named "Cecil" who attended all the Walkerville C.I. sports events. The gentleman's name was Cecil Gawley. He attended Walkerville in the early 1940s and for many, many years was the #1 Tartan fan.
Glenna Houston, Office Staff, Walkerville C.I.

From Cecil's Niece
Steve Hodges inquired about a man named Cecil, who attended all Walkerville C. I. sporting events. I am enclosing a few facts your readers might find interesting. Cecil Gawley was my uncle. His older brother, Edwin, was a teacher and later became audiovisual coordinator for the Windsor Board of Education. His sister, Elsie, was a homemaker.

Cecil loved sports. He was born with a club foot and could not participate, so he became a super fan. For years he went to all Walkerville's games, home and away, even after graduating. In appreciation for his loyalty, in the mid-nineties, he was named "Mr. Walkerville" and received a free pass to all Walkerville sporting events. He was also invited to ride on the Walkerville float in the Santa Claus Parade.

Cecil died in 1997 at the age of 71.
Irma Gerard, Windsor

A Sports Gallery

Hiram Walker's 1937 Detroit Triple A Fastball Team
Left to right – Back Row: Elmer Bauer, Clarence Bruggeman, Fred Bolter, Jack Smith, Bill Hudson, Robby Robson; Front Row: Pip Weaver, Buck Nantau (trainer), Fred Nantau (manager), George Mosley (coach), Bernard Parent, Ross Newitt; Front: K. Nantau. Not in Photo: Joe Levine, Fred Sargent, Joe Rubinsky, Harry Heydo. Photo courtesy Hiram Walker's & Son

Walkerville C.I. Basketball Champs - 1925
Edith (Edie) Helps Snyder is seated in front at left. At 94, she gave her daughter Barbara the names of the other champions without hesitation. They are, standing: Edith Gauthier, Esther "Bill" Churchill, Marian Bull, Audrey Brown. Middle: Viola Agla, Coach Jean Leishman, Jessie Churchill, Assistant Coach Jean Beasley, Lillian Bull. Front: Edie, Gladys Bergin. Photo courtesy Barbara Snyder.

Above:
Windsor Rovers Football Club, 1913-14. *Source unknown.*

Above right: **Elaine Weeks**, University of Windsor Sports Hall of Fame inductee, winning 60 metre race at 1984 Ontario University Championships. *Photo Windsor Star*

No, They're Not Hockey Players!
This is Windsor's Brophey Wolves football team, circa the early 1900s. They were the only team in town so they travelled to Detroit to play teams there. My grandfather is the centre fellow, Alvin Lorange – I think. It's a pretty good guess, but I don' know any others.
Name unknown, via email

Hockey Night in Windsor

Above: the Canadian Navy Hockey Team, formed in Windsor during the Second World War.

Little is known of the team or the identification of the team members. They apparently were quite a powerhouse in hockey circles at the time. My guess is this photo dates to 1942. I know the first lad in the front row left was Ernie Page, the father of a local dentist, Dr. Denis Page.

We believe that the Detroit Hockey Club supplied all the team's equipment and thought so highly of the team's athletic abilities that they were interested in signing some of the players to play for Detroit after the war.
Jack Collins, Windsor

Below: Ford City Baseball Team cira 1920s.
Photo courtesy Annie Lazurek, Windsor

Essex Scottish Hockey Team Champs, Windsor League 1931-32. R. Anderson, Coach (Dorothy Krause's father), Slim Gray, Asst. Trainer, Ptes. J. Stewart, F. Whitesell, G. Spring, R. Cooper, A. Nosotte, Cpl. F. Briggs Sergt. W. Sharpe, Trainer Cpl.C. Bondy, Ptes. H. Ralston, S. Sharpe, Jackie Fryer, Mascot, Ptes. G. Godwin, B. Gallaghor, Cpl. J., Manager.
Photo courtesy Dorothy Krause

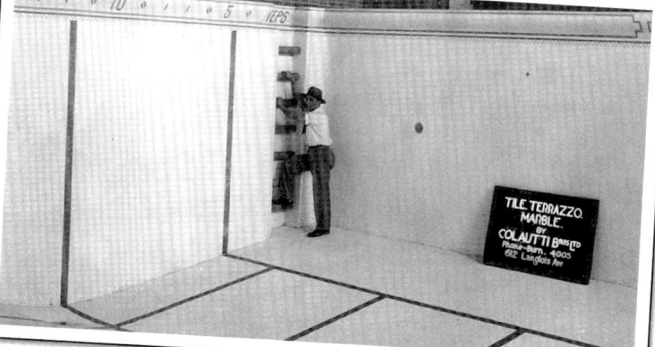

Kennedy Collegiate High School Pool, October 6th, 1929
Colautti Tile of Windsor founder Baldo Camilotto stands in the finished tiled indoor pool at Kennedy Collegiate.
Photo courtesy Clorinda Camilotto

best of the times • 319

10
School Daze

Unidentified pupils being measured by the King Edward School nurse, 1926.
(source unknown)

School Days - 1907

by Camilla Stodgell Wigle, Issue #10, September/October 2000

I started school at five or six years of age, 92 or 93 years ago. I just can't believe it's been that long. I went to S.S. 1, Township of Sandwich East Public School – later Riverview Hospital on Riverside Drive, where all classes from grades one to grade eight were taught by one teacher. We didn't seem to mind and each grade had their own sitting place and as we were assigned to our work or studies, we seemed to concentrate on what we had to do. We didn't listen to the teacher talking to other students of different grades.

Classes would be asked to go to the front of the room, in a line to be asked questions and to write on the blackboard, or do arithmetic that was fun. I must say some of the girls and boys in lower classes would listen in to what the teacher would be teaching the upper classes and this way gain knowledge. Sometimes, when a know-it-all spoke up, they would be called "Smart Alec."

A potbelly stove at the front of the classroom gave us heat in the winter. Sometimes the back of the room would be so cold! When the stove needed more wood to burn the teacher would say, "Billy would you please go out and bring in more wood for the stove." In cold weather, that was a shivering job – poor Billy's hands would be so cold, he would stay for a while beside the stove until his hands warmed up.

School started at 9 a.m. and at 10:30 we all had to go out for recess. Only those who had a cold or something would stay inside. To have a drink of water, there was a pump outside with a handle on it and I remember a tin cup on a chain, and a hook to hang it on. Oh how cold that water was! Water fights often occurred and then we had to stay in at recess for punishment.

I often wonder how the new generation would cope. We didn't have the conveniences then as now, and we had two outhouses to go to when nature called – one for the boys and one for the girls and we had to use newspapers or pages from magazines for hygiene sake. Can you believe this? I bet its hard for you even to think of those days – but I lived through them and I don't think it hurt one or any of us. It made us strong, obedient and truthful.

We adored our teacher and respected her wishes. When we didn't obey, our parents would enter into the scene and would reprimand us for disobedience. We had to respect religion too and always began our school day with the Lord's Prayer. Sometimes, one of the older pupils would read scripture. No matter what colour or religion the pupils were, they all knew their God was the one they worshipped, so all was harmonious among us.

We had great holidays too. On Dominion Day, as we called it, we all gathered around the flagpole when our national flag was raised, stood at attention and saluted our flag with dignity and pride, our voices wafting toward the sky, as we looked at the flying flag with love for our Country. When we sang O Canada, I can remember having chills running through me. I guess I was just happy for all the good things I had.

Our one room school became too small in a few years and a new room was added on – what a thrill it was to know we were to have two rooms. Boy oh boy! Not to have a crowded room was great. Things changed a lot. New ideas were put to practice but we always had the inner feeling of closeness and friendship, which never died even when we graduated.

That fellowship never left us when we left our dear school for good to enter into higher horizons of learning. Although we had a hollow feeling inside, we hoped greater things were in the future for us.

I hope all those who were my friends and companions remembered our one room school house, with great joy and through the years gained more knowledge, thanks to our beloved school teachers.

Three I remember to give them honour: Miss Hand, Miss Richards and Miss Briody.

Also see "A Remarkable Life," the story of Camilla Wigle, in the Walkerville Chapter, page 61.

Above: Camilla Stodgell Wigle's family in 1907 L-R: Grandmother Emily Stodgell, Grandfather Simeon Stodgell, Father John Stodgell, Brother Simeon, Brother Charles, Camilla, Mother Emma

Home of the Tartans
Walkerville Collegiate Institute

by Sonia Sulaiman, Issue #17, September 2001

Esto perpetua...

79 years ago, a beautiful new school opened its doors in Walkerville. Designed by architects Pennington and Boyle in Collegiate Gothic (the traditional style of the 1920s), Walkerville Collegiate Institute cost $600,000 at a time when the town of Walkerville had a population of 7500.

Official opening of W.C.I. was November 2nd, 1922. Celebrations included a luncheon, a dance, a swimming exhibition and a program of "moving pictures."

In that first year enrollment was 195 students. The staff included Principal Robert Meade and nine teachers. The original building contained 22 classrooms and other areas including: manual training for the boys, household science for the girls, a wood paneled library, a 48 by 80 foot gymnasium, an 800-seat auditorium with a 42-foot stage and a pool known as "the Plunge."

Walkerville's pool affectionately called "The Plunge"

Also during the first year, W. D. Lowe Vocational School used the second floor of W.C.I. until moving into a building on Giles the following year. Walkerville Collegiate also housed the offices of dentist Dr. Dean, Dr. Phelps, M.D. and school nurse Miss V. L. Leavette.

In 1923, lunch was served in became the Family Studies room and usually consisted of soup and crackers or hot dogs and beans for five cents. The kitchen and cafeteria were completely renovated in 1990.

When the town of Walkerville amalgamated with the city of Windsor in 1935, enrollment grew; soon all the rooms at W.C.I. were in use.

The students and staff of Walkerville developed a fierce pride in their school, which was renowned as one of the top schools in the province. The famous Cameron-kilted Cadet Corps, with its own bagpipe band, were the best in the province. Walkerville also had a reputation for consistently producing champion athletic teams.

As the school's population grew (peaking in 1970 at 1287), new rooms were added: in 1955 a music room, rifle range and, quartermaster stores (later converted into an industrial arts facility and now a media arts facility including a dark room and computer lab, a new gym and cafeteria); in 1966 the main office was revamped, a new library was built, as well as more classrooms.

Today, the Walkerville student council is still known as the Agora, taken from the name of the public square in Athens built in 500 B. C. Agora evoked the spirit of democracy for it was in the Agora of ancient Athens that the assembly met in session and its officers were elected by the citizens.

Agora membership was voluntary in 1934 and required a fee of 15 cents to cover expenses. Today members are elected by the students and the fee has increased tenfold to $15.

The Agora established the Honour Society in 1960, to recognize individual effort in academics, athletics, service and clubs. Honours

322 • school daze

included everything from medals to having one's picture hung in the library – a supreme honour.

Currently, Walkerville is known for its excellent art program – the Windsor Centre for the Creative Arts. Previously, the visual arts program was centered at W. D. Lowe until the principal at Lowe decided to convert the art room to a weight training room.

The W.C.C.A. began with 171 students studying dance, drama, piano, vocal and instrumental music as well as visual art. Today, 225 W.C.C.A. students attend classes at Walkerville while a further 120 commute from other areas of Windsor as well as Essex county.

Even before the W.C.C.A. moved to Walkerville in 1989, music and drama were an important part of the school. The school orchestra formed in 1927 and prospered until 1947, when it was the only concert orchestra in the city.

The first music classes began in 1949. In 1967, Mr. Bruce Curry formed "The Tartan Players." Curry's cast and crew of approximately 200 students put on performances for the community until 1982.

With the arrival of W.C.C.A. came two dance studios, two additional music rooms and the enlargement of the stage (to twice its original size), with new lights and sound equipment.

Having taken classes at W. C.C.A. since grade 9, I can vouch for what a singular experience it has been. Admission to the W.C.C.A. is by audition and students must maintain a 70% average to stay in their program. They are taught by specialist teachers augmented by professional musicians and artists from the community.

Walkerville has more than its fair share of talent. The W.C.C.A has toured Europe four times, and recently returned from a tour of Alberta and British Columbia. They annually showcase dozens of plays, musicals, art shows, dance performances and concerts with support from local businesses.

Probably the most unique aspect of WCI is the Community Living program which transferred to Walkerville in 1986. This program helps integrate developmentally challenged young people into our school's society. All Walkerville students come away learning something about accepting others.

From top to bottom: Boy's Swim Team, 1947; Orchestra for W.C.I.'s presentation of "Fanny" in 1973. Conductor Mr. B. Curry; Cadet Corp Inspection, 1945; Cheerleaders, 1973. Left: Students get into the spirit on "Slider Day," 1972
photos: The Blue & White Yearbooks

best of the times • 323

The Bare Naked Truth

by Sonny Batstone, Issue #52, March/April, 2005 and Issue #53, May/June 2005

I decided to go to Lowe Vocational Technical Institute along with all my neighbourhood buddies. That's what kids did in the '50s; boys went into auto mechanics and girls took the commercial courses like typing, shorthand, and filing.

I sure was happy to be out of King George Public School. I wasn't a really bad student but I had a lot of run-ins with certain teachers that landed me in the principal's office. I was never destructive or disrespectful – just a smart-ass.

By mid-August I was still waiting for information; all my buddies' classes had been confirmed – even the ones who just squeaked by with a pass grade from "Fagan's" office. Fagan was our King George principal, Mr. Mallory.

My sisters and brother also went to KG so our family was well known in Fagan's office. My greatest school and family pride was the fact that when my older sisters, Lois and Bev were sent to Fagan's office for some infraction and received four straps on each hand, they never even cried. And they were girls!

When boys were strapped, you could hear it throughout the first floor and their howling would reverberate through the whole school. I think that was the secondary purpose of the strappings – to teach others to behave or this could happen to you too!

One morning in August, Mom said I had better start looking for used schoolbooks for my classes. When I said I didn't know what books were required she handed me a list Dad had given her. It read, "Books Required For Walkerville Collegiate Institute – Grade 9C."

I was already registered at Walkerville and didn't even know it! Can't argue with Dad. Looks like I'm collegiate bound. Well the good side of it was, the school is only two blocks away from my front porch so I would have an extra hour sleep time in the morning.

Come September, I straggled off to WCI with a few of my graduate acquaintances from KG and St. Anne's Catholic School. Things started out okay. Most classes were about what I expected except for one: the PE/Health class. To this day, I have never figured out why the boys had to go swimming in the nude.

Swimming was a two-class period once a week. On the first day of gym, our instructor, Major Allison, explained that notes from mothers for exemption from this class were not accepted – only a certified document from a doctor and only for a serious ailment like tuberculosis, polio, or the plague.

This must have been WCI's policy for changing their public school recruits into men of the world!

What quiet fear and utter panic this instilled in most of the younger students! Hell! Most of these kids hadn't even seen their own body naked and now were supposed to parade around the swimming pool like a page out of "Nude Sunbathing!" What about that "be modest" and "cover-up" attitude we were taught to respect? Was it now going to be a "Look at me" and "Let it all hang out" environment?

I bet ten-to-one that the girls didn't go swimming in the raw.

Thirteen years old is an awkward and insecure transition period for most boys. Pubic hair, erections, and female genitalia were all key subjects on our minds and not meant for public discussion. You could mask your shortfall of knowledge in the booth at the local corner store but you were still in the dark as to what sex was all about and what your role was in it, and how would you handle a "hot girl" if she came on to you.

No way could you or would you ask someone in your family a sex-oriented question – this subject was strictly taboo. I just couldn't see myself asking about sex at the supper table. Would I say, "Dad, pass the carrots please," and then, "Mom, what is this talk about women's periods?"

I don't think there would have been a piece of me left together any larger than a thin dime.

And now into this confusing mix of pubescent emotions came the edict that we were to disrobe in front of our entire school class, shower together, swim together and even play water games in the nude.

Only three days to our first swimming class. I wondered if I could get the Black Plague by Friday.

I was one of the smaller guys in my class. Many boys were a couple of years older as they were immigrants from Europe and they had been held back in the Canadian school system so they could learn the language.

I couldn't help but visualize the whole male class lined up beside the pool's edge, hip-to-hip, bent over the water and ready to dive. Looking down the line one would be able to judge the manly features on a comparative basis for the whole class.

I had a feeling where I would stand in this unjust contest.

Furthermore, embarrassment, a cold shower, and cold pool water would all add to "shrinkage." I feared that maybe I wouldn't even have a penis – just a dimple in my crotch. Oh gawd! I'm done!

Wait until this got back to the classroom after gym. There was no way it could be kept a secret from the girls. How would I survive their snickering, whispering, and laughing?

Sarah, the girl who I was secretly in love with, would know my life's shortcomings.

Maybe I'll become a monk.

No one talked about swim class during school breaks or on the way home from school. I felt like I was the only one concerned. I did mention it once but all the guys would say is that it would be great to swim in the wintertime. Granted, this wasn't said with too much conviction; the smaller guys said nothing and looked away.

I knew we were all feeling the same way.

Nothing we could do though. This was school policy and a WCI tradition, like the school's Essex Scottish Cadet Corp and the Pipe Band.

Third period was the witching hour. Two boys were noticeably absent from class; one was a class sissy so his absence was expected but the other was just a regular guy. I hoped aliens had abducted them because they were going to go through hell in the next PE/Health Class. Major Allison didn't seem the type to give too many chances.

There were no lockers in the pool dressing room. You just stripped off your clothes and left them on the benches or hung them on hooks above the benches. Floors were terazza and icy cold. There were three large shower stalls with wide entrances and no doors. Each stall was equipped with about six shower nozzles for community use. Everyone was to shower before swimming. From the showers a short hallway led to the pool and your fate.

Major Allison was there to greet us. He carried a light bamboo type stick under his arm, much like the swagger stick he carried while in uniform. He had been a decorated front line soldier during WWII and had seen plenty of action.

I knew that the stick he was carrying had also seen action as his poolside enforcer. It was well known and rumoured to be partly responsible for many of Walkerville's swimming trophies.

When everyone crammed into the dressing room Major Allison shouted we had five minutes to undress, shower, and line up beside the pool. The room was packed as there were about 35 students from two classes – 9C and 9D. The older and bigger kids undressed quickly and swaggered into the showers and beyond, oblivious of their nudity.

The younger, shyer ones stalled, hoping for a little privacy that was not to come; their faces were to the wall, only their shirts were off, and they were bent over engrossed in untying their shoelaces.

Then another yell, "Hurry up you babies! Get into that shower now or I'll drag you in!"

That was enough for most – me included – to take the final step: remove our underwear and sidle into the shower. All those bare bums together in that small space! You could see that everyone was trying not to touch the person next to him – heaven forbid!

Crotches were not visible as we were all hunched over like monkeys screwing a football. Barely wet I tried holding my knees together and in a semi-hunched, knock-kneed position, waddled my way through the doorway and into the pool to line up as instructed.

This was the first time I had been in an indoor pool. The pungent smell of chlorine was overpowering and the tiled room made every sound reverberate. It was not a pleasant experience and I had the sense this was not going to be the last unpleasant episode of this day.

We were all poolside now, but no! Two boys were still missing: Michael and Paul.

Then, a horrible scream from the dressing room/shower area; it was Michael. We could visualize tears streaming down his face.

"No! No! Please don't make me take my clothes off! Please! Please! I don't want to go swimming!" he pleaded.

And then came the coarse and commanding order to "Get those god damned clothes off or I'll whip them off! Both of you get a move on and into that shower!"

More shuffling noises, more crying sounds, and then through the door from the shower came a naked and completely subdued and defeated Paul, red-eyed but alive. A minute later in strode Mr. Allison – but no Michael. I'm sure we all thought the same thing: Michael was dead!

With both hands behind his back, a silver whistle around his neck, and clasping his bamboo switch, up jumped Major Allison onto the diving board. He walked to the end, stood at attention, faced the new recruits and barked out the order "Attention!"

We all knew that this didn't mean to pay attention. This was a military order to stand at attention. Out of fear and with many knees a knocking, the class came to attention with a "Sir!" as rehearsed from our parade ground training.

Here we were, some thirty-odd newly initiated teenagers experiencing life as we never thought possible. Just a few short weeks ago, we had lounged our summer days away at Wilson's Drug Store counter with thoughts of pretty high school girls and maybe even a steady. Pretty girls and dates were far from everyone's mind now as we stood beside the pool, cold, shivering, naked and scared to hell.

What was he going to do to us now?

From the diving board the Major recited all the class rules and penalties – and there were dozens of them, from peeing in the pool to keeping your hair cut short.

"In-one-ear-and-out-the-other" was the best way to explain our

Nice "Swimsuits:" 1953 Walkerville Boys W.S.S.A. Swimming Champs

comprehension of these rules. We were not interested in learning the rules at this time, just worried about surviving the next thirty minutes.

Then came the class routine. First of all, we were to jump in and hold on to the side. Then, as commanded, flutter kick for two minutes on our front and then turn for two minutes on our back. All by whistle command.

This was our warmup. Then we were to swim widths of the pool on command from the Major — free-style, backstroke, or whatever he stated. Later we would all take diving lessons, front and back flips, gainers and twists and things.

Hell! Most of us couldn't even swim. But the Major didn't ask if anyone could. We all just came out of the showers and lined up by the pool. The first ones through the shower lined up by the shallow end and the last by the deepest end.

The biggest guys were now near the shallow end. I wasn't the only one to realize this; when there was finally a break in the Major's instructions and he was about to give the command for us to jump in and start kicking, LeRoy, one of the kids in 9D, managed to blurt out "Sir, I can't swim. Can I please move down to the shallow end? I'm scared of the deep water."

"You stay just where you are, young man. It's the same distance across the pool at either end," responded the Major.

I think this was his attempt at humour, but it fell on deaf ears with the exception of Homer and his friend Billy, who were both repeating grade nine. They managed a stifled laugh that the Major seemed to appreciate. LeRoy looked panicky and before he could say anything else, the Major blew his silver whistle and barked, "Into the pool!"

Major Allison had locked the door after his entrance; the key was around his neck with his silver whistle so there was no escaping. It must have been like WWII again for him. His troops were poised for imminent attack and he would personally shoot the first coward to show signs of retreat.

I was huddled midway along the poolside and didn't know the depth of water below me. A blast of the whistle and I leaped into the water without further thought — as close to the edge as possible. I maybe could have made the width of the pool, but would never have tried by myself without a strong incentive.

Under I went and up I came, grabbing for the pool's edge.

It wasn't too bad. I could touch bottom, just barely, on my tippy-toes so I knew I could keep alive when the time came for us to cross the pool.

That is, if the Major didn't have some strange rule that we would have to change positions every now and then.

The fact that I was naked and in the pool with 35 other naked guys suddenly didn't seem to be as important or embarrassing as I had thought. Shaking the chlorine saturated water from my face and eyes, I looked up on the pool's edge to see LeRoy and two other boys still standing.

The Major was on his way off the diving board, swagger stick in hand.

The whole class, minus the three on shore, were bobbing by the pool's edge and watching this drama play out before our very eyes. It was going to be a tragedy, for these three in the path of the Major, and maybe a few more like Paul who had managed to jump into the deep end and had resigned himself to his last hour of life.

The trios' behaviour was definitely insubordination and they weren't going to get off lightly with a sentence from a court marshall. It looked like a battlefield firing squad, based on the Major's walk. At a military "quick pace" he was beside the guilty in an instant, but not before LeRoy, in a brilliant and wise move jumped into the pool's deep end holding his nose and I'm sure with a "Hail Mary." The other two faced Major's wrath.

Both boys were cowering, knees together, shoulders hunched and hands crossed in front of their crotches; the Major didn't hesitate for a moment. As soon as he reached within whipping range he let off a sizzling bamboo swat across the ass of the nearest malingerer.

The tiled swimming pool prison suddenly erupted into sounds of an unreal reverberation of pain and fear that must have been heard down at the Principal's Office. This lasted only seconds and then into the pool fell, jumped, or was pushed, the first casualty of the confrontation, his cries muffled only as the water engulfed his body. He was quickly pulled to the pool's edge by fellow students and still sobbing, hung on.

Now only the howling of the last survivor could be heard, crying out for understanding and sympathy. I felt ashamed that I couldn't or wouldn't say something on his behalf. I knew it would be useless but, for the luck of the draw, that could have been me up there. I did feel sorry for him but not enough to jeopardize my mid-pool edge position.

He was now curled up in a ball on the tile floor, crying, and saying over and over, "I can't swim, I can't swim, I'm scared!" The Major was standing over him with his switch resting on his shoulder, looking down on this sorry specimen of a first time swimming student.

"Get up, get dressed and wait for me in my office. Move! Now! Quickly!"

Even then the boy didn't move quickly but sat with his head bowed and waited while the Major opened the door to his freedom.

Now he had us all where he wanted us, all lined up poolside – petrified and not knowing what to expect next. No doubt existed amongst us concerning his methods toward achieving his goals. We had seen him in action. It was now time for us to be ordered out of the trenches and charge headlong into enemy lines. Except we had no guns and we didn't know who or where the enemy was.

After relocking the exit door, Major Allison hopped back on the diving board and blew his whistle for our attention.

Yeah, as if we weren't watching his every move.

Not a word was spoken concerning the rapid departure of the "scared stiff" student from the pool, or prior incidents in the dressing room. The Major continued with his instructions as if we were atending a church outing to the beach. We were informed that after the warm-up kicking at the poolside, we were to swim freestyle across the pool and then wait for his signal to return to the other side on a backstroke.

A backstroke! Hell! I could hardly do a front stroke. I thought – again incorrectly – that our instructor was going to teach us something, such as how to swim, not just 'tell' us to swim to the other side.

Then, for the first time in the period the Major said, "Any questions?"

Before anyone could open their mouth, he continued, "Fine, now let's get a move on, the period's almost over."

Oh, how sweet those words sounded. It was the first glimmer of hope that there was an end to this torture. Down from the diving board came the Major and he strode to the opposite side of the pool. Bending down, he placed his swagger switch on the floor and picked up a ten-foot bamboo pole.

Oh, my Gawd, no! Now he had a pole he could use to whomp us even as we swam!

One long blow on the whistle got us flutter kicking and after we finished both sides of that exercise, another blow and threatening command signaled the dash to the other side of the pool. Throughout, the Major paced back and forth on the far side of the pool while shouldering his pole.

Panic and bedlam followed. Thirty-some kids lined the sixty-foot poolside like sardines bobbing on the inside of a sardine can, fin-to-fin. That left only an unmarked swimming lane of about a two-foot width per swimmer. Most could not swim while some could only dog paddle or tread water.

Sixty arms, sixty legs, instantaneously thrashed the bleach-spiced water, creating a frothy scum and spray which hid most of the participants in this race for survival.

With a hard push, I launched off the side, thrashed my arms and kicked as much as possible. By my side, the others did the same. One stroke, two strokes, and then the swimmer on my left crossed in front of me; I swerved into the swimmer on the right who was treading water as the swimmer on his right grabbed his foot while he was sinking.

Down the line, with few exceptions, the mass swim had bogged down into a sputtering, thrashing, coughing, yelling befuddlement. I dog paddled to stay afloat; around me, swimmers were slapping about, expressions of panic in their eyes as they tried to ascertain the location of the pool's far end.

In the middle of this madness, the Major, looking nonplussed, wailed on his whistle and barked: "Back to the start line, now!"

Half the class was already on their way back so only the residual swimmers were left sputtering off to one side.

Were we now going to face the wrath of the Major for this failure, as we retreated to our trenches, unsuccessful in our attack? Would this be the first defeat of his glorious Essex Scottish Regiment?

Surprising everyone, he showed his first sign of humanity.

Three boys were still thrashing about while slowly sinking. "Come on now, you can make it back," barked the Major, holding the bamboo pole almost within their grasp, and one at a time, the Major herded them toward the pool's edge.

"I can't reach it, I can't reach it!" shouted one, Paul, as the Major edged him closer to the pool's side while the security of the bamboo pole loomed ahead.

"Keep on kicking those legs, you're doing well, you're almost there!"

Suddenly, all three realized they were within grasp of the pool's edge, and they forgot the pole and lunged the last couple of feet to the safety of the ledge. Huffing, puffing, and gasping, they wedged in among the other sardines, looking almost proud of their ability to stay alive.

"I made it halfway across the pool and back; I never swam before. I can't believe I did it!" Paul shouted, seeming to forget about the ignominy prior to entering the pool.

We all were back in line; were we going to regroup for another charge? Did the Major have some hidden agenda for us?

Back at the diving board with his swagger stick under his arm, he surprised us all with his next statement.

"Well, we have used up all our scheduled time for instructions today. The last fifteen minutes are free swimming time. I always give this when a class does well. You have done well. Enjoy yourself and exit the pool on my next whistle. See you next week and don't forget – showers before entering the pool."

Wow! He said we had done well even though very few made it across the pool, one never made it past the dressing room, one chickened out poolside, and two had to be forced into the water. If we had done well, what happened in the other classes?

During the last fifteen minutes, the class split up with the swimmers in the deep end and the paddlers and non-swimmers toward the shallow end. Paul stayed in the deep end holding the side and kicking.

The whistle sounded and everyone headed to the shower and dressing room, bare bums and crotches openly exposed and not quite the big deal they were forty minutes ago.

Though still self-conscious as I dressed, as were many of the others, I could see how, in time, this would seem a normal way to swim. And if Paul was an example, everyone in this class would become great swimmers.

'Major' Allison gets a new stick: retirement in 1973. Principal Dave Mallendar & Jean Allison are highly amused.

Edith Cavell Public School in 1934. photo: *Jim Cornett*

From Learning to Living
Edith Cavell School

by Natalie Atkin, Issue #18, October 2001

On October 7th, 1915, Edith Cavell, a British nurse, was sentenced to death by German authorities. Her crime had been to provide refuge to British, French, and Belgian soldiers in her Berkendael Institute in German-occupied Belgium. The soldiers successfully escaped from the Germans.

Three years later, a school was constructed in present-day Riverside on land originally owned by Gilbert Parent and named in Edith Cavell's honour. Located on the corner of Ontario Street and Esdras, Edith Cavell Public School opened in 1919 in the Township of Sandwich East with Mrs. Gilbert Parent as its first principal.

When the town of Riverside was incorporated in 1921, the land from Tecumseh Road to the river was all farmland. Flipping through the school's 65th anniversary program from May 1984 brings one back to when streetcars paused at Stop 10 (present-day Jefferson) along Ottawa Street (now Wyandotte). There were creeks along Homedale, Ford, Glidden and Jefferson, that, once spring rains came, some neighbourhood boys actually navigated.

Most of the housing was north of Wyandotte while construction to the south was just in its infancy. Many new residents were Ford workers who built their houses at night, lit only by hurricane lamps.

Between Prado and Villaire, there was a "Town Tap" – a community water tap that people used to do their laundry. The trees of the orchard near the corner of Glidden and Wyandotte often served as a boxing ring for spontaneous matches between neighbourhood boys.

As Riverside grew and modernized, so did the school. When it opened, Edith Cavell was just two rooms, accommodating grades one through eight. In 1924, additional classrooms were added and in 1936, a gym was built. The school continued to grow in 1958 when a whole wing was added.

In 1942, the school began accepting pupils through grade ten and in 1944 and its name was changed from Edith Cavell to Riverside Continuation School. The next decade witnessed major changes as the school dropped its elementary grades, becoming a high school with grades nine through 13 and changing its name to Riverside High School in 1956.

Once present-day Riverside High opened in 1964, Edith Cavell returned in name and the school converted to a senior public school for grade seven and eight students.

Like most neighbourhood institutions, Edith Cavell was much more than a school. In the 1920s and 1930s, the school hosted concerts, films, card parties and dances and served as the center of the community. The congregation of Riverside United Church began services at the school before

Honouring Edith Cavell
I read your article on Edith Cavell School in the October 2001 issue and thought you may like to see a scan of an old postcard I have of Edith's grave and of her (top left corner).
Chris Gall, Walkerville

Ed: Thanks Chris. Edith Cavell was a British nurse who was sentenced to death by German authorities in 1915 for providing refuge to British, French and Belgian solders. In 1918, a school was constructed in Riverside and named in her honour.

construction of its current building in 1929. Edith Cavell also housed Board of Education offices at one time.

Several generations of Riverside residents attended Edith Cavell throughout its sixty-eight year history. Harold Dresser, a life-long resident of Glidden Road, was a student from 1936 through 1947, and his children attended in the 1960s and 1970s. The Monaghan family raised three generations on Ford Boulevard and all three generations were sent to Edith Cavell.

Bernard Monaghan and his brother Bryce, the former Riverside Police Chief, attended in the 1920s. Bernard's son Richard Sr. was a student in the 1940s and his sons were schooled there in the 1970s.

By the 1980s, Edith Cavell was too small to serve as a high school and too large to be a grade school. This part of Riverside now had more updated elementary schools such as Princess Elizabeth. In 1987, Edith Cavell officially ceased to be a public school.

Closing ceremonies were held in June 1987, but the school remained open to house F. J. Brennan's overflow and later King Edward students during that school's reconstruction.

As Windsor is faced with additional school closures, questions arise over what to do with the old schools. Edith Cavell, along with St. Genevieve School in central Windsor, are now being converted into condominiums. While some other schools have become community centres, Cavell and St. Genevieve are the only Windsor schools to date to be turned into condominiums.

Converting schools is not without controversy. Many neighbours near Edith Cavell oppose condominium construction. Members of Riverside United Church, which stands directly across the street from the school, encouraged neighbours to voice their opposition to the development.

According to Church Secretary Nina Dresser, the Church was eyeing the lot for additional parking and for possible single-detached

House at 957 Ford Blvd. served as the original school. photo courtesy Jim Cornett

housing. Members were disappointed to learn that the lot was purchased by a developer who was planning to keep the building intact and redevelop for condos, all of which needed rezoning and city approval. Eventually, the Church was able to purchase part of the property and gain 57 parking spots.

Surrounding neighbours who opposed the conversion, believed that condos did not fit the fabric of the neighbourhood and they feared traffic and sewer problems associated with denser development.

When the Planning Committee and City Council sided with the neighbours the developer appealed to the Ontario Municipal Board which overturned the local decisions in June 2000 and opened up the way to condos at Edith Cavell.

Edith Cavell Place Condominiums are scheduled for an early 2002 occupancy with twenty units planned.

The condos represent a viable way to preserve by-gone architecture. The converted structure introduces a new type of housing into an established neighborhood, a trend that may become increasingly attractive to city developers and planners.

*Blue and White,
Blue and White
These are the colours
for which we'll fight!
Rah, Rah, Rah
Ziss Boom Bah
Edith Cavell School!
Rah Rah Rah
(1920s school cheer)*

Edith Cavell grade 8 class, 1943

October 1960
The Sock Hop

by Richard Hughes Liddell, Issue #28, October 2002

The four of us begin sidling around the perimeter of the gym eyeballing the females, in particular the Grade 9 girls, since it was the first dance of the school year. Dave Goodbrand, Charlie Meanwell, Brian McCabe and I perform this ritual at every sock hop, too terrified to ask any girl to dance. We are Grade 10 nerds.

Suddenly something deep inside my primordium stirs and I break rank and wander into the unknown. I have spotted "that girl" who I have been eyeing since the first day of school. She is without a doubt the most beautiful vision I have ever seen.

I feel my heart racing as I approach her. Sweat starts beading on my forehead. She is talking to another Grade Niner from my public school, Hugh Beaton, who recognizes me and says, "Hi, Richard." I start to respond but suddenly realize I lack the sufficient saliva to utter a word so I just nod my head in a very cool way and walk on.

It would take two more danceless Sock Hops for me to get up the nerve to approach her again. As I draw near her at the Christmas Dance, my heart is still racing and the sweat is still pouring but this time, I have gulped a huge drink of water and I hear myself say, 'Would you like to dance?'

She looks into my eyes and offers a smile from heaven. Her dark eyes are hypnotic, her teeth are perfect and I barely hear her confident response, "Yeth pleathe."

We head to the centre of the floor just as the disc jockey announces, "Here's one from a couple of years ago, the Teddy Bear's singing 'To Know Him is to Love Him'."

I take her hand in mine, place my other arm around her waist and begin my famous box dance step taught to me by my Mom and sister, Joanne. Suddenly she draws me nearer, pulls me so close that my pocket protector is jammed into my left breast (thank goodness, I took my geometry compass out before the dance.)

She places her head close on my shoulder and starts to lead me around the dance floor. Her mother and sister were much better dance instructors than mine because the two of us literally glide to the music (Arthur Murray, eat your heart out!)

I see Dave, Charlie and Brian watching with their mouths open. At this moment I should be in heaven: she's drop dead gorgeous, she dances close – very close, she has her head on my shoulder and she moves like Ann Margaret.

But I just want the dance to end. It does and I return her to her friends and mumble a thank you. My three buddies catch up with me but all I can say is: "She has a lisp."

Dave looks at me and says, "Are you nuts?"

In the life of a snowman, there is a point when the sun commences its inevitable melting process.

A pool of water expands as the snowman slowly sinks to the ground. The sun continues to do its work and gradually the water in the pool starts evaporating until the last molecule of H^2O is set to become water vapour. At this point it could be argued the snowman is at his smallest.

That night on the dance floor I wanted "that girl" to be perfect but I could not rise above the fact that she had a lisp. That night I was at my smallest.

In retrospect, that sweet voice was cute. In retrospect, I wish I had a second chance but I never took it. Instead, the four of us continued our ritual prowl around the gym.

Above: Walkerville Collegiate Sock Hop, 1954
Left: Richard as a nerd - circa 1960

Illustration by Pat Kelly

The Mad Chemist

by Stanley Scislowski, Issue #27, September 2003

Whenever I happen to run into old classmates of mine from Windsor Vocational School (later known as Lowe Tech), class of 1940 or '41, we invariably reminisce about some of the zany incidents that took place in that "one of a kind" school.

Back then, I was known to the guys as the "Mad Chemist" since I specialized in chemistry, the only student in the whole school of close to 2000 who dared take up the subject, and as "Homer" because I wrote a couple of poems. The account I'm about to relate is not about my dubious talent of composing deathless poetry, it's about my dangerous preoccupation with properties hazardous to life and limb of both myself and those close by.

The one occasion that stands above all others is when Lorne McGee, the chemistry instructor, was absent for six weeks due to a serious operation, and I was left with no assignments to carry out. Since I was the only student occupying space in the lab, I decided to make chemistry far more interesting.

What enthralled me was to concoct any mixture that either made smoke, fire, stunk to high heaven, produced fancy colours or made a heck of a lot of noise. As I leafed through a thick book on organic compounds I came across something that captured my attention: methyl mercaptan, said to be amongst the most smelliest compounds known to man and used as an additive to natural gas (which is odourless) so that it could be detected in case of leaks.

Fine and dandy! An overpowering desire enveloped me and I set about to make the stuff-in the fume cabinet, of course. There were several stages of production involving the simple mixing of three compounds, each of which did not have the pleasant odour of roses. Then there was a distillation, followed by another form of distillation known as refluxing. As is natural for budding chemists, my nose gradually became desensitized to the developing stink.

As I waited for the final stage of manufacturing this horrendously stinky concoction, I strolled over to the windows on the Parent Avenue side of the classroom to see what might be passing by, only to be shocked to discover what seemed like the entire student body out on the badminton courts and on the sidewalk, all looking up at where I stood at the window. In my naivete, – I muttered to myself, "Gee, I never heard any fire drill bells go off. I wonder why everybody's outside."

Just then into the laboratory rushed Mr. Lowe the principal with a flushed and pained look on his face, holding his nose, exclaiming through convulsive gasps, "Stanley, Stanley, what have you done? I've had to evacuate the whole school!"

For this misadventure, I thought I'd be expelled or at least receive 10 sharp lashes of leather belting on each hand, but I did not. All Mr. Lowe did was mildly admonish me and suggest that I should choose something far less discomforting to compound during Mr. McGee's absence.

I was not to be denied the lure for the spectacular however. A couple of weeks later I decided to make the most sensitive explosive ever known: nitrogen iodide, which was not a high explosive, but was in the class of those known as initiators that set off high explosives. My eyes sparkled at the thought of what I could do.

A very simple mixture it was, which I will not divulge here for obvious reasons. It was so sensitive that it was too dangerous to work with. The book said that it would explode at room temperature, and could go off even when a fly walked across it. Again, those sparkling eyes of mine, or maybe this time, it was a mad chemist smile that flickered across my face.

And so I set to work. No sooner had the last drop of ammoniacal liquid exited the funnel in which sat the filter paper holding the mass of explosive iodide, when a crystal popped, sending the filter paper flying onto the floor and scattering hundreds of crystals. "No problem!" I thought. "I'll just get a wet rag and wipe them up and bottle it with all the crystals and take them home to have my fun."

Suddenly, in swarmed a class of rowdy students. Five of them, instead of turning sharply left and walking past the blackboards to the lecture room, walked straight ahead to where I was about to mop up. Crystals began popping under their feet with machine-gun rapidity. Pretty soon half the class got into the act, stomping away with great glee. Man! You'd think there was a battle going on by the sound of things.

Thank god Mr. Lowe was never aware of this latest misadventure of mine or he'd have sent me packing for sure.

Lowe Tech

Knuckle Sandwiches and Scoffed Textbooks

by Al Roach, Issue #10, September/October 2000

There is now less flogging in our great Schools than formerly, but then less is learned there; so that what the boys get at one end they lose at the other. – Samuel Johnson

Mr. Harrison: "Tim, if you found 45 cents in one pocket and 35 cents in the other, what would you have?"

Tim C.: "Somebody else's pants."

Joke in "The Towers," W.D. Lowe's yearbook, circa 1960.

W.D. Lowe Technical School (successor to the Windsor-Walkerville Technical School). 1650 students. All boys. A no-nonsense school. Run by Lee F. McGee, who used to boast that he operated a "tight ship."

A school where the appearance of the boys hulking through the halls between classes belied the strict discipline of the institution. Skin-tight pants, narrow ties, pointed shoes, white socks, duck-tail haircuts, pink combs protruding from rear pockets.

But no hair on the face. Any boy adventurous enough to sprout a cookie-duster was promptly sent home to shave by the first teacher who spotted the fuzz.

A few years later Vice-Principal "Scrubby" Aitchison would keep an old, painfully dull electric razor in his desk drawer for the rent-free use of any boy looking five o'clock shadowish.

It was a tough school where threats of "knuckle sandwiches" (sometimes brought to realization in nearby alleys) were the order of the day.

But a school with a province-wide reputation for excellence in the trades. A Lowe grad had an edge on the graduate of any other school when applying for a job in the trades anywhere in Ontario.

And the boys knew it. They had a sense of pride in their school, which sometimes descended to snobbery. I recall lecturing the boys in assembly one day for their lordly and patronizing attitude toward the students of "mere high schools."

Not that the academic side of education was ignored. When Lowe's first Grade 13 class wrote the Ontario Departmentals in 1966, the boys scored the highest average of all secondary schools in Windsor.

Strict discipline was part of the explanation.

"Yup," replies a careless boy, in reply to a query from his teacher.

"I beg your pardon!" "I mean 'yes.'" "Yes, what?"

"Yes, Sir!" "That's better."

The strap was never far away. It could be and was applied for such infractions as the use of profanity. And several sharp raps on the cranium, administered by the teacher's knuckles, was the accepted method of attracting the attention of a daydreaming lad.

Discipline? Well I guess! In the early 1960s the boys at Lowe still carried in the halls a "paddle" (a small piece of wood bearing the number of the classroom from which the boy had been excused). And woe betide any student caught in the halls without it.

Needless to say, theft was at a minimum, but a boy, when asked for his

W.D. Lowe Technical School: 1940s class photo. photo courtesy Charlie Fox

missing textbook, would often reply: "Somebody scoffed it, Sir."

But discipline was already waning. An edict from on high called for teachers to surrender their classroom straps. Nearly 100 per cent did. Nearly. A Board of Education mogul appeared at the class room door of Pat McManus, who had taught at Lowe for 100 years, to demand that he surrender his strap.

"Take it away from me," replied six-foot, three-inch Pat. The strap stayed.

A school with 25 shops, including three for autos where the boys would repair my old 1957 Pontiac and I could rest easy in the knowledge that the work would be excellent. We had no "recalls" in those days.

A tough school, but in some ways "oh, so gentle." With a literary page in the yearbook. And no one laughed at the contributors of the poems. Not unless he wanted to pay to have his teeth rearranged as a postscript to the conversation.

A school with:

John Murray, the great coach of the 1940s and 1950s who produced more championship basketball and football teams than anyone could remember. Easing off a bit in the classrooms of the early 1960s.

Bert Weir, artist unique, sporting his little goatee, the first beard of any staff member in the Windsor school system.

Col. Bill Malkin, academic director, whacking the flat of his hand on the office counter and thundering at some cowering lad: "I don't give a cuss why you were late! You'll serve a detention!"

Syd Levine, proving over and over that all of those Italian boys were musically inclined.

Great shop teachers such as Charlie Murray, Clarence Cole, Fred Barnes and William Anderson, all bringing a natural dignity into their shops and classrooms.

A continuous noon hour staff room crib game involving Messrs. Ryan, Sherman, Aitchison and Sivell.

Mrs. Merle Worthy's smile bringing a beam of sunshine into the front office.

Another joke in the yearbook:

Coach (pointing to a cigarette butt in the shower room): "Is that yours, Matthews?"

Don: "No, Sir. You saw it first."

King Edward School Gallery

Above: Nursing Station, 1926; unidentified pupils with school nurse, source unknown.

Below: Gr. 2/3 class, 1964, teacher Mrs. Goldhawk. Top row ?, Bodhan Toreshanko, George Jovanovic, Mike Dulmage, Mike Sankof, Randy Dixon, John Henderson, Scott MacPhee; Third row: Elaine Weeks, Anita Gordon, Susan Hadden, Kristen Tanner, Candice Johnston, Debbie Legace, Robin Ritchie, Elaine Gosnell, Suzanne ?; Second row: Ginny Asselstine, Brenda Newman, Mary Anne Prattes, Sabina Balazs, Melissa Mrkonjic,?, Janice Wild, Janet Easton, Vera Danculovic, Cheryl Clark. First row: Dave DeYoung?, Alan Winterbottom, Leonard Kander, Danny Bougner, Barry Salmon, Wayne McConnel

King Edward Public School (top left) built in 1906 by Vic Williamson and designed by Detroit architect Albert Kahn.

Gr. 3 or Gr. 4 class (above), November 1926, source unknown. Note the girls' stylish coats.

Below: Home Economics, 1920's. Dorothy Woodall, 2nd row 4th from left. Photo courtesy Audrey (Woodall) Harris.

*Many King Edward students went on to Walkerville C.I. while **W. N. Ball** was principal (1943-1956) at right. "Mr. Ball had a big, gruff exterior but a big heart. If it weren't for him, I wouldn't have gone to university. If he knew you had something in you, he prodded and poked to get it out."*
Charlie Lee, Windsor
Photo: The 1947 Blue & White yearbook

best of the times • 333

Above: Dougall Avenue School, approximately 1927. Nancy (Dela Haye) Carter is sitting 1st row third from right (on the curb)
Photo: Nancy (Dela Haye) Carter

Left: The Cast of "Youth's Highway" and "The Birth of the Infanta" from Hugh Beaton School, 1934. Photo: Jack Creed (2nd from l. bottom row)

Bottom right: Gr. 1 class, King George School, October 1926.

Bottom left: Gladys Chapman was the Senior Representative for Central Collegiate (now Riverside High School) in the Windsor Public Speaking Contest in 1930. In her speech, "The Stranger Within Our Gates," she explained how foreign immigrants are necessary to the development of Canada.

Above:
Grade 8 Class, St. Alphonsus Separate School – June 12, 1940
A partial list of students (but not in order): Anita La Branche, Rena Canil, John Buffon, Joseph Zakvor, Jack MacIntyre, Ermida Muggin, Mary Stephens, Helen Bruna, Shirley Smith, Bridget Fergusen, Rosemary La Price, Frank Macconi, Jim Asmar, Bernice Corrigan, Tom Hennessey, Betty Sylvain, Mary Jane Zakoor, Rose Canil, E. Canor Shaloub, Norma Alsin, Norman Dority, Patricia Alise, Henry Haberg, Cecile Anderson, Roland Anderson, Elia Zorzit, Lena Bastianon, Terry Clonnell, Bruno Reh, Vincent Fagg, Jack Artiss, Gordon McNamara, William Taylor.
photo courtesy Herb Millis, Windsor

Holy Name School, Grade 8, 1945
Front row (l-r): ?,?, Mary Levko, ?, Kate Wall, Mar-Jo Boyde, Edith Wilhelm, Mary Lyons, ? 2nd row: ?, Angelina Trnka, ?, Joan Fader, Catherine Recker, Mary Forrest, Shirley Reddam, Joan Johnson, ?, ?, ?, ?, ?, Pauline Gillis (glasses on far right) Boys: Emmet Garter (top left), Jack Tourangeau (3rd from left), Daniel McLellon (6th from left) & Clifford Sutts (8th from left).
photo courtesy Jack Boyde, Windsor

Walkerville Collegiate Cadets – 1939
*Top l-r: Dick Carr – lived at 274 Devonshire, now 1100 block;
Jim Scorgie – retired Hiram Walker & Sons Limited executive;
Jack Morris – R.C.A.F. veteran;
Bill Chilver – from the Charles Chilver (Road) family;
Jack Stodgell – father was Sim Stodgell, brother of Camilla Stodgell Wigle.
Bottom l-r: Jim Bartlet – lawyer with Bartlet & Richardes, lives on Willistead Crescent in home built by Bill Chilver's father;
Bob Daniels; Berrien Easton.*
photo courtesy Dick Carr, Grosse Pointe, Michigan

best of the times • 335

Christmas 1946, Gordon McGregor School presented "The Toy Maker" – based on "Babes in Toyland."
photo courtesy Ed Agnew

Remembering Christmas at Victoria Public School

"Here is a picture of my Grade 1 class at Victoria Avenue Public School, at the corner of Ellis and Victoria in Windsor, from 60 years ago. The back of the classroom was decorated to celebrate Christmas and a make-believe Santa was coming down the chimney. Mrs. Hurst, (inset) Superintendent of Reading for the Windsor Board of Education, was reading "The Night Before Christmas."

As far as I can remember, the children in the photo are from left to right: Joanne Marshall (the girl in the striped top), me, girl in white dress unknown, not sure of name of girl sitting on the floor but possibly Ilene, Jamie Murdock, Elizabeth MacLuckie. Our teacher, (not shown) was Betty Strain.

This scene preceded our Christmas vacation, which was always welcomed as we loved to play in the snow. We seemed to have much more snow then and we certainly didn't have school buses or fancy backpacks to carry our supplies. Our snow suits were stiff and heavy and we could hardly move but we would build snowmen, lie in the snow and create "snow angels," throw snowballs, etc. We pushed our dress shoes into goulashes and they laced up over our shoes.

Shirley (Rising) Kussner, Oxford, Michigan

Right: Mrs. Clarissa Hurst is the teacher pictured reading above. "She loved her work," says her granddaughter Joanne Marshall, one of the students in the photo. "She co-authored several student readers, including, 'My First Primer' and 'Peter, Pepper and Fluff.'"
photo courtesy Joanne Marshall

336 • school daze

Assumption High School band. photo: Sid Lloyd

Hugh Beaton Elementary School 1934, possibly first Safety Patrol in Ontario. Photo courtesy Jack Creed, standing at extreme left

best of the times • 337

11
Why We Must Remember

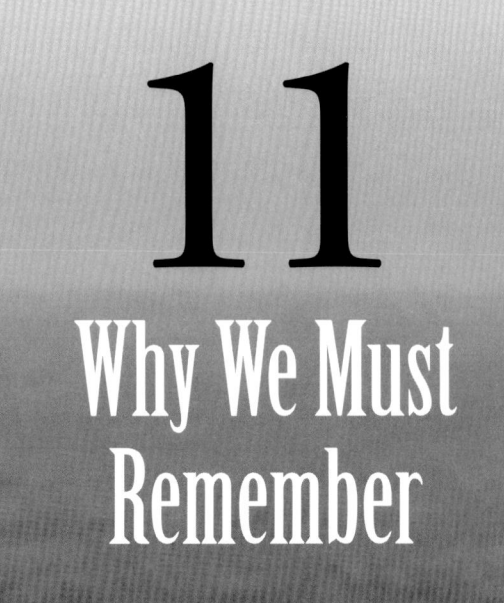

Ann Rudinkoff, Pearl Trudelle, Winnie Jackson and May Scales, of the Windsor branch of the Canadian Red Cross Corps. relax on the grounds of the Oxley Retreat House during WWII.

Sergeant Cameron D. Myers. 1923-1943

Forever Young

Margaret Myers Stokes Remembers, Issue #5, November/December 1999

"While I was going in, Ohmand was giving the Jerry a burst, and soon I saw a puff of black smoke from one of the engines. Almost at the same instant my machine was smothered with oil. I pulled up to one side and saw two of the enemy crew smash the hood and try to get out. Before they could manage, the JU-88 dived into the sea, leaving only bits of wreckage and a lot of swirling water." Sergeant C.D. Myers

My two brothers and I were born in Walkerville. Both Malcolm and Cameron were born on Windermere; Malcolm in a house near Ontario, (a short distance from the "edges" of town!) and Cameron in a flat on the corner of Cataraqui. Cameron was a kilted cadet in Walkerville Collegiate's Marching Band (around 1937). He lived to fly and was always making balsa wood model aeroplanes. As a kid, he would rush outside to see a plane and leave the back door wide open which would make Malcolm, who was 8 1/2 years older angry, especially in the winter.

Both brothers served in WWII. Cameron enlisted in the R.C.A.F. in Windsor in February, 1940 and received his wings in November, 1941. He became a Spitfire Pilot and went overseas a few weeks later. On his first mission, (July 1942), he and a fellow pilot shot down a "Junkers Bomber" into the North Sea. On May 15, 1943, at age 20 he was shot down over the English Channel.

He was missing for 6 months and then presumed dead. My mother went to a fortune teller who said, "his feet were in the sand, but he's not there any more."

We received information about where he was buried from the Swiss Red Cross. His body washed up at the mouth of the Cayeux River in France. The Germans buried him in the World War I Cemetery at Abbeville, France.

My parents grieved themselves to death. My father died of a heart attack in 1944 and my mother died in 1949. My doctor told me, that my mother had made a shrine of Cameron's pictures and letters and it helped destroy her.

Before my mother died, Paul Martin Senior assisted my mother in helping have Malcolm released from Service on compassionate grounds. Malcolm came home from Italy in 1944 after having gone through the horrors of Mount Cassino. Before the war, Malcolm had worked in Hiram Walker's offices and they immediately gave him his old job back.

Above right: Sergeant Myers recounts his first aerial victory. Left: Cameron as a cadet in Walkerville Collegiate's Marching Band.

best of the times • 339

Graveyard of the Atlantic
I Crash Landed on Sable Island

by Flight Lt. Al Early, D.F.C., Issue #5, November/December 1999
(as told to Dick Halvorsen, Men's Life Magazine, 1954)

It was wild and dark that day over the North Atlantic and the low gray clouds threw thundering gusts of snow and sea spray against our plane as we began the long haul back to base.

Then things began to happen. The No. 2 engine of the big four-engined Liberator quit dead. Ice began to creep into the carburetor opening on the No. 1 engine and the manifold pressure began to wobble and drop. My guts grabbed as I realized we were still hundreds of miles from base and were in for a dunking which would be wet – and if we couldn't free our bombs – loud as hell.

Over the intercom, I called Harry Head, my navigator whose office was in the nose of the aircraft, and he came scrambling back through the knothole passage below the catwalk. I gave him a quick rundown of the situation and told him we'd better jettison the bombs. Harry opened the bomb doors and shouted an order and one after another the bombs fell away.

Suddenly Harry cursed and dropped to the floor and began to lower himself through the opening. "One of the bombs is stuck in the rack!" he yelled, and disappeared.

I yelled for Roy Hoag, my co-pilot, to get into his seat. We'd picked up some height after dropping our bombs but suddenly No. 1 engine went dead with an angry splutter.

Harry gave me our position a few minutes later, reckoning us to be 160 miles east of our base at Dartmouth, N.S. "But we're only fifteen minutes Sable Island vectoring 270 degrees."

"Sable Island," snorted Roy. "The graveyard of the Atlantic."

"Appropriate," I said, thinking of the bomb which was still lodged in the rack.

There wasn't a chance of getting back to Nova Scotia so Roy and I wrestled the aircraft around and made for Sable, a curved finger of sand about twenty miles long and half a mile wide, paralleled by treacherous sandbars. I'd buzzed the island a couple of times and knew there was danger at the north end in the shape of 100-foot dunes. I ordered the wireless to send one last message, "Crash landing on Sable Island," and to screw down the key for the bearing.

The snow was a white wall in front of us and as darkness settled I ordered a flare dropped and slowly Roy and I hauled at the controls to bring the ship around in the a long sweep before coming in to land. Harry kept his eye on the altimeter as we eased off, barely maintaining airspeed.

"Now!" he shouted, and Roy and I yanked back, trying to bring the 30-ton bomber in on the skid. We hit hard but right and just before she pancaked we hit water and were thrown forward as she stood on her nose in the water.

I held on, rigid in my harness, my mouth full of cotton, waiting to hear from the bomb. I looked over at Roy and he was white but grinning. The crew came forward and clambered out the escape hatch and up onto the wing, while Harry and I stayed behind and destroyed all the codes, instructions and secret equipment. I grabbed a pistol and went topside.

Above: Flight Lieut. Alan Early (inset) took this picture as his crew returned to his plane, the Liberator, for equipment the morning after it crash landed on Sable Island.

The plane was sheathed with ice and the wind ripped at us with gale force as we clung to the direction finder and the handholds by the hatch. Off in the distance the rotating beam of the lighthouse spun, barely visible in the snow. I fired a flare from the pistol.

The islanders had heard our motors and seen our first flare. Half an hour later a lifeboat appeared near the end of the wing.

"You were quick," I told the skipper when my teeth held still.

"On this island we've got to be," he said. "The wrecks happen awful fast."

Discovered some 300 years ago, there are over 200 known wrecks lying above or beneath the sands of Sable. Lodestone in the sand was blamed in the old days for fouling compasses causing ships to wreck but modern ships with modern equipment keep piling up there too. And now the Liberator was to be added to the hulks of dead ships that lined its shores.

While we waited for the weather to brighten, my aircrew and I wandered around the island accompanied by a succession of off-duty rescue workers as guides. Every few feet brought a new tale of disaster as we went over the island.

"Must be hell for the ships to start sucking toward the island when it's really rough," I said to one man.

He nodded. "They don't stand a chance. The whole bleddy Atlantic just picks itself up and throws itself onto Sable Island. Waves are twenty-five feet high but they look higher on a account of they're techin' the sky."

There was not a tree on the island and not a bush higher than a man's waist. Somehow horses, not much bigger than Great Danes, ran wild on the island. Apparently surviving on seawater, wild peas, berries, kelp and grass that's so sharp it would cut your mouth, the horses have populated the island at least 150 years. The islanders think they're descendants of a cargo of cavalry horses that swam ashore when a French supply ship was wrecked there during the French and Indian Wars.

Five days passed before the sea was calm enough for a PBY4 Canso to land a mile off the lee of Sable island.

"Glad to get off that bloody place," I said to Harry as we circled away.

Upon his return to base, Early was greeted by some top brass. Instead of hearing congratulations for saving his crew, Early was asked, "Just what do you think you were doing hitting that trawler with your garbage?"

A bag of garbage Early's crew had dropped at 10,000 feet prior to their adventure on Sable had landed on an ally Russian trawler. Thinking it was deliberate, the captain complained to Moscow and the garbage was eventually traced to Early's plane.

Early replied, "If you think that I could have aimed that bag of garbage at that trawler from 10,000 feet up, in cloud cover, then I think I deserve a raise in pay or a new rank!"

For his action in saving his crew by so skillfully landing his plane on Sable Island, Flt. Lieut. A.A. Early was awarded the Distinguished Flying Cross. After the war, Early returned to South Walkerville and resumed his job with the Ford Motor Company.

Above: Al Early points to his WWII crash site, among hundreds of wrecks on Sable Island.

Front row right, Marjorie's father, Piper R.F. Millar

Vet Returns to Vimy in 1936

The 26th of July, 2002 was the 66th anniversary of the dedication of the Vimy Ridge Memorial. My Father, Piper Robt. F. M. Millar of the Essex Scottish Pipe Band, (based here in Windsor), a veteran of WWI, and a survivor of Vimy Ridge, was chosen to be a part of the contingent sent from Canada to attend this prestigious ceremony in 1936. The following is an excerpt from his journal:

"July 26th, 1936. Reveille 7:00 am. Breakfasted. Left for Arras Station and played on platform while pilgrims were arriving. After a short ceremony at the Cenotaph outside the station in Square we were inspected by Field Marshall of Belgian Army. Busses back to school and dinner. Left for ceremony at Ridge at 1:30 pm. Busses drove to within 100 yards of monument. Took up our places on the opposite side of driveway from French Colonial Mounted troops. His Majesty arrived at 2:15 pm. Inspected Naval and Returned Men's Guard, and then band. He mentioned to Hodrum and I, 'I am a bit of a piper myself. I play a little.' And we knew it too – by the hours the band had to practice 'Mallorca,' which was composed by His Majesty.

After the departure of His Majesty, the bands were mobbed. We could not throw our drones on our shoulder to play. Autographs! Autographs! Autographs! At 4:30 pm we left the monument for a short service in a cemetery for unknown soldiers, near the monument. Then we returned to the main road to get busses but the traffic congestion was dreadful. We waited for busses until 7:10 pm, but none came. Col. Dupuis decided to march back to Arras, which is nine miles. The high spot of the trip was the march back. Both bands played all the way. We stopped at Nouvelle St. Vaast for refreshment but I could not recognize the burg. I tried to figure out where Jerry took down the four observation balloons but could not. We arrived at Arras at 9:30 pm and were very, very tired."

Marjorie Luno Stepp

Turning Point of WWII
The Taking of Xanten

by Colonel Alfred Hodges, Issue #5, November/December 1999

The cream of the Nazi forces – the oft-tested Paratroops, defended Hitler's last stronghold west of the Rhine. They met their match in the form of the 4th Canadian Brigade comprising the Royal Regiment of Canada (Toronto), the Royal Hamilton Light Infantry and the Essex Scottish. The Essex Scottish Regiment was to seize objectives in the northwest suburbs of Xanten, while the RHLI advanced on the right. When they were both in position, the Royals were to pass through and advance further into Xanten.

Our commanding Officer, Lt. Col. John Pangman, issued his orders at 4 pm. on March 7th, 1945. He had flown over the area in an artillery spotter plane and concluded that the area was weakly defended. This was borne out by evidence from other sources – prisoners, patrols and Army Intelligence. How wrong they were!

Lt. Col. Pangman's plan was for a two company assault, with two companies in reserve. Leased companies were A on the left and B on the right. I was in command of B, a rifle company with about 100 men. A creeping barrage laid down by medium and field artillery supported the attack. Zero Hour was set for 5:30 am., 8 March 1945.

The ground we had to advance over was rough farmland, interposed with many drainage ditches, bordered with barbwire; no place for tanks.

Reveille was at 3 am. There was the usual confusion, forming up in the dark. Then, promptly at 5:30 am the first great shells of the artillery passed overhead; the lead platoons started off, 300 yards behind the bursting shells. Barking N.C.O.'s drove their men to keep them as close as possible to the covering shells.

B Company was attacking with 10 Platoon on the right, 12 Platoon left, 11 Platoon in reserve. All platoons had groups of buildings to attack and occupy – those of the reserve platoon to the north of the others were supposed to be cleared by the RHLI. Little did I know that two whole companies of the RHLI would get lost in the darkness and this would not get done.

Before Company Headquarters & 11 Platoon could take off, we were hit by artillery fire with numerous casualties. I was blown flat and came to hours later surrounded by what I thought were at the time, fatal casualties.

Eleven Platoon and C Company were nowhere in sight. I was close to being panic-stricken. I HAD TO FIND MY COMPANY! Quite honestly, I was more afraid of not being able to do my job (I was in awe of the Colonel) than I was frightened of the Germans!

I took off across country and shortly encountered a file of our troops, moving west to east, headed by a young lieutenant. Poor chap, he was

---

Above: Part of Essex Scottish Regiment. L-R Capt. David McWilliams, Capt. Tom Simpson, Col. Walter McGregor, Major Bryan Wilson, Major Bill Grant, Lt. Joe Campeau, Lt. Don Wicham, Major Ken Kersey, Major A. Hodges, Lt. Art Bond.

lost and almost off his head. He asked who I was and then, pointing his pistol at me, said, "You're now part of my platoon – fall in at the rear – or I will shoot you." This I did and continued walking.

We eventually came to a road running north and south and here I found our Mortar Platoon digging in. The Platoon Commander gave me my position on the map. I discovered 11 Platoon was in a house only a half-mile or so down the road.

When I arrived, the back door was open. I walked in and was greeted by a German paratrooper pointing a bazooka at me. I covered him with my trusty pistol and he, thinking I had troops with me, gave in. I got him outside and indicated he should start walking north. Now, of course he could see I was alone, so he performed an admirable unarmed combat job on me and took my pistol. I hit him on the right jaw with my left hand, and to my surprise, knocked him down. I regained my pistol and shot him where I imagined his heart should be and then, put another shot through his head. After all, he had just taken ten years off my life.

I then found 10 Platoon, which had been unable to undertake its objective due to the fact that their lieutenant had been wounded. I instructed the Platoon Sergeant to take half a dozen men and a few hand grenades to clear their target building. About 25 prisoners were taken and were dispatched, along with the wounded, to Battalion H.Q.

Empire Day: Windsor men who fought under British Flag in five wars, including the Riel Rebellion; Major Hodges stands at left.

I then turned my attention to 12 Platoon. They had command of the ground but could do nothing about a large, fortified, heavily sandbagged house with an impressive moat. I told them to continue to contain it.

Returning to 10 Platoon, I discovered that the Germans on 11's objective had come to life and vehicles could no longer pass down the road. Two lost RHLI signalers appeared and commandeering them, I had them put me in touch with Brigade H.Q. in the hopes that a "Crocodile" – a flame equipped British Churchill Tank, could be provided.

About an hour later, the tank lumbered into sight. I had no choice now but to go out in the open and with hand signals, guide it into position and give it instructions. It positioned itself in front of 11's house then let loose a couple of rounds of cannon fire, followed by a burst of flame. The door of the house shot open and a horde of terrified enemy rushed out, waving sheets, pillowcases, anything white. Another 50 Germans were soon headed north to prison camp.

The tank then slowly turned to face 12 Platoon's fortified house. Out rushed a crowd of Germans, waving their white "flags." The battle was over for B Company. The other three companies, A, C & D, also took their objectives and within a couple of days, Xanten was ours.

The victory at Xanten directly paved the way of the crossing of the Rhine and the termination of the war in Europe in exactly two months.

(While we didn't know then the pivotal role we had played, we were gratified to see that the farm property we had occupied had a nice herd of cattle. My company mechanic, a butcher in civilian life, was able to see that we ate well when we returned for a couple of weeks' rest.)

Left: Major Hodges, 1999. photo E. Weeks

best of the times • 343

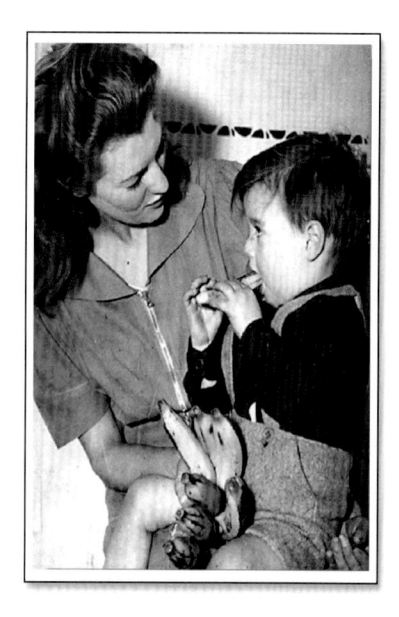

A Family Affair

by Norma Heath (Niven) Chantler, as told to Elaine Weeks
Issue #5, November/December 1999

*In fourteen hundred and ninety-two,
Columbus sailed the ocean blue.
In nineteen hundred and forty-two,
Hitler tried to do it too!*

At the outbreak of WWII, I lived with my parents on Walker Road directly across from the old Walkerville Train Station. It was from this station that my uncle, George Dixon, left for England with the Essex Scottish. I was about two when we all gathered there to see him off. He, along with his friend George Hardcastle, were both trained in England and sent to Dieppe. Only one George returned.

There are many photographs to remember Uncle George by. There's a picture of him on the ship that carried him over to France, one of him being inspected by King George VI and another in front of the NCO mess hall.

While in England, Uncle George met and married an English woman name Irene Lyons. They had a son whom he never saw. After the war, Irene and her son were paid by Canada to come to live in Windsor. They lived first with my grandfather Dixon, then with us until they were accommodated in wartime housing on Felix Street in the west end of Windsor.

My mother's other brother Dick served in the war as did my Uncle Kenny Clark and Uncle Jack Gibson. I had two cousins in the war on the Dixon side of my family as well.

When the men were away, the women worked. Aunt Evelyn and Aunt Grace were able to work at Kelsey Wheel making wheels for the Lancaster bombers. (You've heard of Rosie the Riveter?) These women grew very independent while their husbands were away.

During the war, even children's games were influenced. A skipping song went something like this, "Tramp, tramp, tramp, the boys are marching, who's that knocking at the door? If it's Hitler let him, and we'll kick him in the shins and we won't see Hitler anymore, slam the door." The radio played songs like "The White Cliffs of Dover," "Goodnight Irene" and, "I shall fight my country's battles on the land or on the sea." Movies showed short features geared to the war and patriotism and even the Seven Dwarfs in Snow White taught us songs like, "Whistle while you work, Hitler was a jerk. Mussolini was a 'Sheeny,' whistle while you work." We also repeated a rhyme that went like this, "In fourteen hundred and ninety-two, Columbus sailed the ocean blue, In nineteen hundred and forty-two, Hitler tried to do it too."

War bonds were sold vigorously, even at King Edward Public School, which I attended. Through these bonds my sister Isabel bought her first bike and skates. My music teacher at King Edward, Mildred Strauss, had a photograph of her husband who had died during the war on her desk.

Our clothes were geared to the armed services. Girls wore replicas of the Waves and Wacs in army greenish/brown or air force grey/blue, or navy pinafores, and boys wore variations of these. The boys played mock war games with wooden rifles, which shot strips of tire inner tubes and they fashioned pistols out of clothes pegs.

Top left: Wedding photo: Irene and George Dixon.
Middle: Irene (Lyons) Dixon, with son Thomas, son of late Pte. George Dixon, enjoying bananas, a rare treat.
Top right: Norma Chantler is determined to preserve her family's past for generations to come. photo: E. Weeks

Food rationing was in effect. My parents had food stamps for certain products like sugar, salt, meat, butter, gasoline, etc. Each member received a certain number of stamps per household. Some fruits like bananas and lemons were very hard to get, so they may have been rationed too. We saved tin cans for the war effort and bottle caps even, which were turned in at the movies for a show.

While my uncles were fighting on the war front, other men like my father, Alexander Heath Niven, served on the home front in the Civilian Defence in the Air Raid Squadrons. The neighbourhood had air raid drills, where the windows were blacked out at the sound of sirens. My dad had a special flashlight, hard hat and boots for this work.

He was finally able to obtain full-time employment during the war at Ford Motor Company because so many young men had gone to war. I remember my father talking about the many instances immediately after the war when there were skirmishes at Ford between Canadian soldiers with newly arrived immigrants who had served for Germany.

I remember vividly the day the war ended. The weather was warm. Now living on Sandwich Street (Riverside Drive), we organized a giant neighbourhood parade. The adults marched with pots and pans and every available noisemaker they could find, singing all the while and cheering. The children rode on their bikes with streamers, and we Niven children pulled our wagon on which sat our huge stuffed lion.

We were all very happy and the adults cried tears of joy.

What Did You Do in The War Daddy?

My father, Lance Corporal Leon Lucien DeSalliers, was a member of the 1st Canadian parachute Battalion. He was killed in action on March 24th, 1945 in Wessel, Germany. His unit was involved in the last major operation of the war in Europe: the crossing of the Rhine River. Excerpts from a letter written by his commanding officer, Lieutenant C. B. Browne, can best describe his part in this operation. My mom received this letter several weeks after Dad was killed and our lives were forever changed.

Dear Mrs. DeSalliers,
It is with deepest regret that I inform you of the death of your husband. This letter is written, not in the official capacity, but with a deep sense of personal loss on the part of myself and all other members of Lou's unit. You, knowing him so well, will appreciate how keenly we feel the loss and how deeply we sympathize with you and your son and daughter. Lou was everyone's favourite and all the men, not only those under his command, looked up to and respected him as a man and a soldier. His courage and coolness became a byword in his platoon and company. As his platoon officer I would like to tell you the story of how he died, as he had lived, helping others.

When his platoon reached their objective after dropping just north of the Diersfordter Wald (northeast of Wessel on the Rhine River) they were being hampered by snipers. Four men volunteered to help out by going forward and clearing out the Huns, and Lou was one of them.

When this party reached a point about three hundred yards forward of the platoon area, they were suddenly cut off by heavy machine gun fire from a hidden German position between them and our own lines. Lou immediately got his Bren gun into position and opened fire on the enemy.

The sergeant told the group to move back under cover of the riverbank to our position. But Lou, seeing that this could hardly be done if the Huns were allowed to fire at will, refused to leave his position and continued firing on the enemy. By this brave and unselfish act he enabled two of the party, one badly wounded, to reach the safety of our own lines. In saving two lives he sacrificed his own.

"Greater love hath no man than this: that he should lay down his life for his friends." It will be of some consolation to you to know that Lou did not feel any pain. When we carried him back to our lines, after wiping out the Germans, he had a smile on his face.

My mother became a widow that day, at age 29 with two young children to support – my brother, Leon, was 13 months old and I was 6 1/2 years. As I look back over the last 57 years, I believe our mom has also lived her life with courage and coolness. Through the challenging task of earning a living and raising a family on her own, she taught us determination, independence and to have a sense of humour.

The letters that my father wrote to us during the war have been shared with his three grandsons and five great-grandsons. They show his zest for life and his compassion for his fellow man. Although he died young, his legacy lives on and I believe that he would be proud of whom we have become.

Annabelle Desalliers Grainger, Frankenmuth, MI
Issue #29, November 2002
Ed: Annabelle grew up in Windsor and attended John Campbell School from 1945-50. Her mother also attended John Campbell and was a student when the school opened. Annabelle returned to Windsor recently to attend the 75th reunion of the school with her mother, now 87 years old, who still resides in the city. Annabelle lives in Frankenmuth, Michigan and writes a small monthly column titled "Trivial Delight" for her brother-in-law's paper, "The Frankenmuth News."

September 1944 - Lieutenant Corporal Leon Lucien DeSalliers (six months before his death), with his children Leon, 7 months and Annabelle, 6 years old.

The War Bride

by Elaine Weeks, Issue #5, November/December 1999

In 1939, Danny Pepper, was faced with the prospect of losing her husband of one year. War had just broken out and Howard had joined the Navy.

"We had all been brought up on the horrors of WWI," recalls Danny, "We were pacifists but when this war broke out, yet young men flocked to join. We felt it was a just war even though an Oxford poll taken before the war had shown that people felt that there was no need for it."

The turning point was the sinking of the Athenia, a civilian ship, by the Germans on Sept. 4th, 1939. One hundred and eighteen people perished.

"Many of us knew people on that boat," explains Danny. "Then, when the first fighting ship was sunk, it really hit home. If they were able, the men were not going to stay behind."

Danny decided she wasn't going to stay behind either and through a code arranged with her sister in Halifax, was able to visit with her husband while he was based there.

"My sister would wire me saying, 'Why don't you go see your aunt in New York which meant that I could spend a little time with Howard so I would travel to Halifax and see him for maybe one day and a night."

Howard Pepper was a top scholar and athlete at Walkerville Collegiate and was one of the few students to receive the coveted diamond lapel pin upon graduation. Being that it was the middle of the Depression however, he was unable to go on to university, but managed to get a job in insurance. He returned to the insurance business after the war and he and Danny enjoyed 50 years of married life.

Danny Pepper has lived in Walkerville most of her 85 years. She is a poet and has published three books of poetry, including "Caught in Amber, In War With Time" and "Love Poems with Several Men." A collection of poems, "The War Brides, Remembering the War Years," based on her war diaries, was published by Black Moss Press.. Above: Walkerville Poet Danny Pepper and her true love, husband Howard Pepper. photo: E. Weeks

---

Jim Cody: First Local WWII Loss

I was happy and saddened to see Ernie Creed's picture in the September 2003 issue (Flashbacks: First WWII Casualty). He was my husband Howard's best friend, and one of mine. Ernie was in the Air Force and Howard in the Navy during the last world war. I have carried a picture of them in uniform in my wallet for over sixty years.

I would like to clarify who the first local war casualty was. Here are two quotes from my "War Diaries."

November 2, 1939: Tonight I can hardly write because of the tears still swimming in my eyes. Yesterday came the news of Windsor's first war casualty: Flight Officer Jim Cody, twenty-three, died in a plane crash in England on the eve of his promotion to rank of Pilot Officer. It has devastated me. As his poor mother said, "This is one. There will be many others." It is terrible to think of the young boys we know dying…God knows why? I remember Jim, brother of my dear friend Marg Ashley, and my sister Joan's first serious beau. I remember Jim's dog Heinie (from Heinz 57 Varieties!) marching in the cadet parade at Walkerville Collegiate season after season. Everyone in town knew them.
Halifax, August 14, 1941: Howard got in from three days at sea and I had to tell him the ghastly news about his best friend Ernie Creed, who had introduced

Howard Pepper, Aug. '42; Ernie Creed Aug. '41

us on a blind date. Ernie was a handsome golden-haired man who played the piano magnificently. My most vivid memory of him in uniform was when he came to say goodbye to my mother. Instead of using the door to get into his open roadster, he swung his long legs over the side, jauntily tipped his cap and was gone. We wrote to him in Summerside, P.E.I. to tell him the good news I was pregnant. In his letter congratulating us, he promised to fly to Halifax to see us on his next leave but went down instructing a young air trainee. Such a waste.

Leila Pepper, Walkerville

Tom Paré, (hand to face), and his squad

From Windsor to Korea

by Tom Paré, Issue #29, November 2002

For the most part, the boy's youth was spent on Josephine Avenue in Windsor. Those were his happy times, sharing wars, and baseball, and girl-dreams with his gang. The other gang members all lived on Josephine except for Phil Power who lived with his mom and dad on Bridge Avenue. He was allowed in because his brother, Frank, had been killed in a RCAF Lancaster, shot down over Germany. That made Phil a hero also, and that's what the Josephine Avenue gang was all about.

After all, they had lived through World War II, and they had all prayed to be part of an Allied victory, which arrived before any of the gang was old enough to enlist.

All went well until one fateful day when the boy's parents announced that they were moving to the United States. Despite his protests the house was sold, their belongings packed and the family moved away. In July of 1950, a very bitter and disenchanted boy of 16 and his four brothers arrived in the United States. To make matters worse, it was his senior year at school, and he would be forced to find a whole new group of friends.

Soon the boy graduated from high school and joined the Army to help fight a new battle. The Korean War had started in June, 1950, and the United Nations Allies were fighting the North Korean Communists. He looked forward to the adventure and the opportunity to leave a neighbourhood in which he never felt comfortable.

After training with the famed 101st Airborne Division at Camp Breckenridge, Kentucky he was sent to Fort Bragg, North Carolina, and at Christmas 1952 orders were issued to report to Seattle, Washington for shipment to Inchon, Korea.

Boyhood Was Over
Inchon at Dawn – December of 1952

The USS General McRae lay offshore in the Yellow Sea, arguably the ugliest body of water in the universe. At least it seemed that way to a boatload of soldiers lined up at the rail, preparing to disembark and board a flotilla of landing craft, which would deposit them on the beach at Inchon, Korea.

Carrying full field packs and holding tight to newly-issued M-1 rifles, the roughly four thousand or so replacement troops stared quietly at the beach. From a little further out, a navy ship fired its quad-fifty guns toward the shore, and in the pre-dawn darkness, the red glow of the overhead tracer bullets was plainly visible to the nervous men waiting to clamber into the barges for their three-quarter of a mile trip.

With no incident at the beach, the men proceeded inward to a holding area where non-coms with a foot of stripes and hash marks on each sleeve, read off names and directed the respondents to waiting trucks, whose motors and drivers rumbled impatiently, and corporals flipped their cigarette butts out of the windows into the frozen morning.

So this was Korea! With a temperature equivalent to Northern Michigan, some war correspondents called the U.S. troops the "frozen chosen."

The soldiers stood at ease in formation awaiting their vehicle assignments, wondering silently where they were going; they knew little about the country or the war. Like cattle they awaited the prodding of the men who controlled them, cajoled them, lined them up and told

Tom (right) on his way to the Hook

them to move forward, then yelled at them to "go back two paces and smoke 'em if you got 'em."

Nothing seemed to make sense; they just followed orders blindly, knowing that they would end up wherever they were supposed to be.

An eighteen-year-old private from Michigan adjusted his pack and nervously fingered the blue barrel of his M-1 rifle. Some of the young soldiers tried to use humor to temper their worry and confusion. Some milled around staying close to someone they just met, in the hope that the new friend knew what to do next. None of them really had any idea. "When your name is called, sound off with your first name and serial number," yelled a sergeant. "And when I check you off, get on the truck, and keep quiet. There will be no further smoking until we say so. Is everything clear?"

"Sergeant, when do we find out what unit we are going to?" asked the kid from Michigan.

"When you damn well get there," was the response.

And then the boarding began. One after another, the big trucks were loaded; about twenty-four to a vehicle, sitting across from each other, silently looking down at their shoes, or off into a now-purple dawn. A few talked to no one in particular, showing off their bravado, false or otherwise, as the trucks began to move.

"Wonder where the hell we're headed. Probably around Porkchop Hill - lot of action there," said a curly headed kid who looked no older than seventeen. "Yes, sir! Action! That's why I joined this man's army. Or could be down around Pusan or Koje-dotoo."

"My buddy from home was with the 2nd Infantry Division," the Michigan kid offered. "He got the Silver Star and Purple Heart at Heartbreak Ridge."

The truck eased to a stop and the sergeant came around to the rear.

"O.K. Listen up. As I call your name, sound off, grab your gear, and get your asses down here lined up to my right," he ordered.

"Johnson Michael."

"Yo, Sergeant," answered the young kid.

"Brown, Willard." "Yes, Sergeant."

"Herkowski, Felix." "Here, Sergeant."

A lieutenant and a master sergeant greeted the new replacements and they were ushered off toward a group of men in a lunch chow line. Then, like a city bus that had just dropped off some passengers, the truck lumbered ahead. This scene was repeated five or six more times.

And now there were only two men left: the kid from Michigan and another guy from Chula Vista, California. His name was Alfredo Gonzalez and he was the first Hispanic guy the Michigan kid had ever met. By this time it was late afternoon, and the two were hoping to be assigned together. The truck jerked to a stop and the driver put it in reverse for a couple of hundred yards. It stopped again, and the sergeant appeared at the tailgate.

"Hey, Gonzalez," he shouted.

"Yes, sergeant."

"O.K. boy, off you go. That nice corporal there is waiting to take you home."

And now there was just the kid from Michigan. He didn't realize it, but the truck had been heading northeast in the general direction of the front lines. Suddenly, he felt alone and scared. It was late in the day and he didn't know where he was going. He could hear muffled booming sounds from somewhere.

The truck slowed as it started up a hill and then, as the corporal shifted gears, it surged forward until the next incline and then more gears and another climb. He watched through the opened canvas in the back and saw the road disappear behind each curve. And now the truck stopped. The doors opened, and the corporal and the sergeant climbed out and both appeared at the rear opening. Another master sergeant joined them and he peeked into the truck.

"Just one?" he asked.

"That's all she wrote," countered the corporal. "Hey, boy! You're the only one in there aren't you," he laughed. "Hop down, kid. You're home. This mean-assed sergeant is going to show you around."

The kid climbed down and reached back for his pack and his rifle.

"Hello, kid," said the new sergeant. "Welcome to the 2nd Infantry Division. You are now a member of Dog Company, 38th Infantry Regiment. I am Sgt. Rhinehardt and I'm the 1st Sgt. of this chicken-shit outfit. You are currently in what is called the 'Hook Sector.' Much of our area is under enemy observation, so you better stick real close to somebody until you learn the ropes. I'm going to have you stay near Corporal Bish for a while and you listen to everything he tells you. O.K.?"

"Yes, sergeant," the kid answered.

The 1st Sgt hollered over to a dirty-faced corporal standing in the chow line. "Hey, Bish. See that this kid gets some chow, and then the two of you come over to the command post. We've got a commo line blown out near the machine gun platoon trenches."

"O.K. Sarge," Bish hollered back and then motioned to the new guy to join him in line for what was to be his first of many unusual meals.

"Where you from, kid?" asked Bish.

"Detroit area, corporal," answered the kid. "Hey, just call me Donnie," said Bish. "And I'm from Toledo. Hell, we're almost family, you and me." By now, the other guys in line started to come over and ask the kid about things back home, and how are the girls looking, and suddenly, just like that, he didn't feel so lonesome and scared. Just cold. It was about fifteen degrees and starting to get windy. Everybody stomped their feet and kept their hands in the big pockets of their parkas. "OK, kid, let's go to your new house," said Bish, after they finished eating their cold corned beef hash out of cans.

The Hook

It was almost dark now as Bish motioned the kid through a black-tarped curtain into a sandbagged bunker where two other soldiers were sitting on a dirt floor. One was writing a letter and the other was cleaning his rifle. Neither one looked up.

"Hey you guys! Here's our new man from Detroit, Michigan, just up the road from my hometown. This colored guy is Farrell and he comes from Washington, D.C. The Spanish guy is Chico Ayala and he's from New York City, by way of Puerto Rico." Farrell grunted and Chico greeted him with girl questions.

Bish showed him how to dress for the cold and how to put his rifle in his sleeping bag so it wouldn't freeze up. And he explained to the kid that you also kept your extra socks and underwear in the bag. And it might be a pretty good idea to keep your bayonet in your bag too and that they usually kept their boots on while they slept. This last part sounded a bit ominous. The kid remembered an old movie called "They Died With Their Boots On."

Bish helped him unpack and showed him what to throw away, pointing out all the unnecessary items.

"You only need a spoon, to hell with the fork and knife," he said. "They clang together and old Joe Chink will put a mortar right up your keester in half a minute, once he picks up on that noise. Whenever you go to the latrine, make sure you take your weapon, and for Chrissakes, don't call it your gun," warned Bish. "Another thing, whenever you go out, and that includes the latrine, always wear your flak jacket. We could get hit at anytime. The old man tells us to always wear our steel pots, but they don't push that too much as long as you're wearing the helmet liner. Questions?"

"Naw, I guess not. I'll just watch you and Farrell and Chico. Oh yeah! One question. Where do we sleep?"

They all laughed. Especially Chico.

"Hey Hombre," he laughed. "You don't sleep with me, unless you're real name is Chiquita."

Bish answered, "This is our house, kid. We take turns sleeping. Two men on guard and two sleeping. On two hours and off two hours. One man outside and one in here on the PRC-10 radio. For the first couple of days, you will work with me until you learn the codes for battalion and regiment. We have to check in with the rear echelons every two hours. Also we have to report any incoming rounds or enemy activity in our sector. Don't even try to make sense of all this yet."

"OK rookie, you and me are on a mission. We have a blown out commo line somewhere around the machine gun platoon. Right now, all we have is radio communication with the platoon, and we need the telephone lines. I'm switching you over to a scatter-matic carbine instead of that heavy bastard of an M-1. We can have ninety rounds of ammo in that carbine instead of that little old clip in your rifle. The M-1 is more accurate – up to five hundred yards or more, but who the hell needs that when we are over-run in a trench by little gooks just ten feet away. Leave everything else here but your carbine, put on your flak jacket and this time, we wear our pots. Let's move out. I'll drive because we won't be using lights, and you will ride shotgun. OK?"

The kid just nodded. He had no idea what to say to this corporal who seemed to have no fear. He silently vowed to be like this man if he ever got to be a leader.

Bish revved up the communications jeep, and they started out on a road that the kid couldn't even see. Up and around curves, down steep grades, bumping over craters and ruts, and finally gearing down to a stop without braking, to avoid the tell-tale brake lights.

"Here we go, kid. Stay right with me and stay as low as you can. When we get to the trench, we roll into it, and then keep your head and your ass down. You are just here to watch this time. We are right now on the MLR, which is the main line of resistance. The gooks have this position under constant watch, and they have our position coordinates tied right into their mortars. One mistake and our asses are mud."

Strangely enough, the kid's fear was replaced by excitement. "Jeez," he thought. "I am in a war. I am really in a war!"

Bish was on his hands and knees following some wire and feeling out in front for a line break. Every twenty-five yards or so he would strip a piece of the wire and attach it to a telephone-type device called a TS-10 soundpower. He would whistle into the mouthpiece, and if that segment of the line was working, Chico or Farrell would whistle back. Then he would go on and try another segment until there was no response from the command post. He then moved back retracing his crawl until he finally found the break or bad part of the line. Then he cut the line and re-wired it to the good part, and tested again with the TS-10. If all was well, he then advised the guys to try telephone contact with the machine gun platoon leader. After a few minutes, we heard a whistle on the soundpower and Bish whistled back. Everything was working fine.

"Let's go kid. We're through here for now," Bish said.

As they started to turn back to where the jeep was parked, the rookie forgot all his instructions, half stood up and peeked at the now purple

Corporal Bish

mountains out in front of the MLR. They reminded him of his train ride to Seattle on the way to Korea, when he had woken up, just before dawn, and right out in front of his window were the Dakota Badlands with their purplish stone monuments jutting up from the ground. But this was not the Dakotas. This was a different kind of Badlands, and his corporal let him know it immediately.

"I told you to keep down, Goddammit! Now grab the dirt. Jesus Christ," he swore to himself. "Maybe they didn't see you. Maybe it's still too dark." But it wasn't. It seemed like just seconds, and then they heard the dull "whuump" of the mortars. And shortly afterwards, about a dozen rounds of white phosphorous rounds exploded all around them. The kid dug into the ground with his fingers and laid his cheek flat against the damp cold dirt. He heard his own voice. "Mom, mom! Jesus Christ! Oh mom! Jesus, Jesus!"

And it was over.

He and Corporal Bish drove back in silence. There was nothing the kid could say and nothing the corporal wanted to say at that time. Once they got back, Bish radioed in to Battalion Headquarters that they had been hit by twelve rounds of "willie peter" with no injuries. He then gave them the coordinates of the incoming rounds and the approximate range of the Gook position. He leaned back against the sandbags in the bunker and lit up a Luckie.

"Any problems out there, amigo?" Chico asked.

"Nah! Smooth as silk," replied Bish. "We got us a good one here with this guy."

And then he winked at the rook.

The kid vowed again to be just like his corporal.

Wounded at Lamone River

On this Remembrance Day, I will think about landing on the southern shores of Sicily near Pachino. It was July 10th, 1943 almost a year earlier than D-Day at Normandy June 6th, 1944.

We were part of the British 8th Army, 2nd Field Regiment, Royal Canadian Artillery, I was with the 10th Battery from St. Catherines. The others in our regiment were 7th Battery from Montreal and 8th Battery from Moncton. The 10th Battery mostly supported the 1st Canadian Infantry Brigade, the 48th Highlanders from Toronto, the Royal Canadian Regiment, RCR's from London, the Hastings and Prince Edward Regiment, Hasty P's (from Bellville area I think) and the Canadian Army 1st Division. A little later we were joined by the 5th Division and fought our way courageously from Sicily to northern Italy against an efficient and seasoned enemy over a very difficult and often torturous terrain. Our guns (25 pounders) were sometimes bogged down in the mud – that darn Italian rain.

Some of the places I remember in Sicily are Assoro and Leonforte. We crossed the Messina Strait and landed at Reggio D Calabria in Italty. As we made our way northward the names that come to mind are the Gustav Line, Hitler Line, Monte Cassino, Gothic Line and especially Ortona.

Then on December 10th, 1944, I was wounded at the Lamone River by shrapnel from those German 88's. I was in the hospital for a month. Well it worked out for me because the wounds weren't that bad but I was there for Christmas 1944.

Soon I was back in uniform. For the next little while we were mostly on the Adriatic Coast. Then early in 1945 we left Italy and fought with the other Canadians in Europe. I managed to survive in the trenches until the war ended later that year.

Frank Palmer, Issue #29, November 2002

Major Frederick A. Tilston, V.C.

Frederick Albert Tilston was working as a sales manager for a drug manufacturing company when he voluntarily joined the Canadian Armed Forces in 1940. He was 34 years old. Having quickly ascended to the rank of Major, Tilston lead a company of the 2nd Canadian Division, Essex-Scottish Regiment, in an assault on the heavily fortified Hochwald Forest defence line in Germany on March 1st, 1945.

In the early hours of the battle, Major Tilston was wounded in the head, but continued to lead his men forward. When his platoon came under heavy machine-gun fire, it was Tilston who dashed forward and silenced the enemy gun with a hand-grenade. Tilston was the first Allied soldier to reach the enemy position, and the first to take a German prisoner. Determined to maintain the momentum of the attack, Tilston ordered his men to press on.

Shortly thereafter, he was wounded again. Still, Tilston struggled to his feet and rejoined the assault.

The Germans retreated, immediately regrouped and counterattacked. Tilston repeatedly crossed the bullet-swept battlefield carrying ammunition and grenades to his troops on the frontline. He also repaired a damaged wireless set to re-establish communication with battalion headquarters.

Then, he was wounded for a third and final time, sustaining injuries that subsequently resulted in the amputation of both legs from the knee down. The Allies were eventually victorious at Hochwald Forest. For his gallantry, Tilston was awarded the British Commonwealth's highest honour for valor, The Victoria Cross. He is one of only seventeen Canadians to receive that prestigious decoration in WWII. Shortly after his return from Europe in 1946, Major Tilston, V.C. was welcomed home by thousands of Windsorites during a special ceremony held at Jackson Park.

Tilston was named honorary-colonel of his old regiment, since re-named The Essex and Kent Scottish. The regiment's armory in downtown Windsor was named in Tilston's honour as well. A resident of Toronto, where he was born in 1906, Tilston died in 1992 at the age of 86. His family presented his Victoria Cross to the Canadian Military Institute in Toronto.

from "100 Years: A History of the Essex Golf and Country Club, 1902-2002," by Jeff Mingay

photo: National Archives of Canada

Searching for Subs on the Detroit River

by Tom Paré, Issue #19, November 2001

Sitting on the seawall in the dark, a boy watched the Detroit lights dance across the tops of the murky waves that came alive as they approached the spiles of the railroad docks. The river announced its arrival with rhythmic lapping sounds as the water ended its mile-and-a-half long journey to Canada.

It was the boy's favourite place in the entire world.

1943 was a fine year for a ten-year-old boy. And it was a good time to ponder things like life and battle and triumph. It was surely a time for patriotic imagination.

The war, now in its fourth year, stirred manly thoughts and feelings as he looked out over the mystery of the darkened water. He wondered if enemy submarines lurked out there, perhaps to deposit foreign raiders or saboteurs on the Canadian shore. He thought it very unlikely, especially since this was the exact place that the Queen of England stood on her yacht and waved to crowds just a few years before. For assurance, he looked over his shoulder at the marquee of the Coronation Hotel, named in her honour.

Tom Paré with Grandpa Gignac

The boy decided to watch for enemy activity; at night the subs were known to surface. So far, none had been reported.

During the day, the boy warily scoured the white-cropped wave tops searching for oil slicks and periscopes. After all, this river would someday carry home all our heroes from the battlefields. There would be welcoming fireboats spraying the bows of the returning hospital ships and city bands would play, probably right where he stood. He read of such things in the war reports.

At the theatre newsreels, he saw huge boats sailing under the Golden Gate Bridge. And the boy remembered seeing a troopship entering the harbour in New York, passing right under the arm of the Statue of Liberty.

As he looked to the west, he imagined that the Ambassador Bridge would serve just as well as the Golden Gate and what better Statue of Liberty than the huge Penobscot Building, probably the tallest skyscraper in the world except, he guessed, the Empire State Building. For many years, he had watched the red blinking ball at the top of the Penobscot from his bedroom until he fell asleep. It was a symbol of safety to him during his very young life, just as the Statue of Liberty is the beacon for others in the world.

On this day, he watched the steamers Ste. Claire and Columbia leave their moorings, with a full load of passengers headed for Bob-Lo Island. He imagined them as massive troopships on the way to the battlefields, with troops hanging over the rails waving goodbye to families.

Within a couple of hours, the boats would return and pass under the Ambassador Bridge with a new load of passengers, this time undoubtedly carrying the wounded heroes. As the Ste. Claire reappeared under his Golden Gate, he silently cheered and stood erect as if at attention, with his hand on his breast. And when the Columbia followed shortly afterward, he was sure he saw decorated veterans, probably from France or Morocco.

Suddenly from behind him came the sound of a train as it chugged through the underpass at Wellington Street and made the turn westward along the riverfront. Although the locomotive bore the Canadian National Railway letters on its boiler, it was a certainty that the train was actually carrying fresh troops to relieve those soldiers returning on the steamers.

In war, the government couldn't be too careful, he reckoned.

As the train slowly passed, the boy heard the sound of an engine and turned back to the river just in time to see a small boat racing to intercept an up-bound freighter. When the smaller ship pulled up to the starboard side of the vessel, he could plainly see the markings.

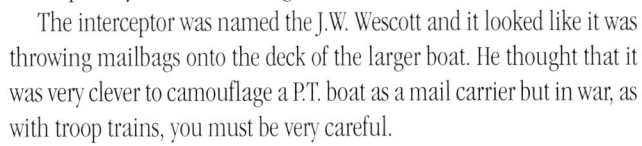

The interceptor was named the J.W. Wescott and it looked like it was throwing mailbags onto the deck of the larger boat. He thought that it was very clever to camouflage a P.T. boat as a mail carrier but in war, as with troop trains, you must be very careful.

When the small boat finished its investigation, it backed off the side of the freighter, which resembled a Canada Steamship Lines ore carrier, and raced back to shore where it laid in waiting for the next ship.

From under the Ambassador Bridge came the low rumblings of two more boats, and the boy recognized them immediately. They had come to haul the troop train boxcars across the river, where they would join the Americans for another allied attack, probably in Berlin or Munich or Tunisia. The flat black boats named the Manitowoc and the Pere Marquette loaded up and returned to their ports, awaiting further orders.

As the boy watched the waters of the river, the twinkling lights of the Detroit skyline started to come alive, and he glanced up at the Penobscot building turret to make sure that the red ball had resumed its watchful blinking. Behind him, he heard the hissing of the steam-engine locomotive waiting for a new load of troops.

He then looked westward, and satisfied that the Ambassador Bridge lights were working, he turned from his boats and his trains and his river and slowly walked up the street to his home, glancing back once or twice, just to make sure.

On this day in 1943, all was well in the Border Cities. The boy felt good about himself.

Too Young To Die

by Stanley Scislowski, Issue #19, November 2001

The night was black as pitch – no moon, no stars, no flash of artillery fire to light the way for the Canadian infantry moving forward to the start line of their next attack. It was unusually quiet, as though both armies facing each other in the flatlands of the North Italian plains had gone to bed early. The only sound came from the scuffle of the infantrymen's boots on gravel as they worked their way forward

To a man, as always, they fervently hoped that the advance would be a 'walkover,' but it was not to be. The enemy had not gone away, and they had not gone to bed early. Except for those momentarily relieved of weapons post duty, the enemy was very much awake and alert.

They were in positions all through the area with their weapons trained at the single point where they were sure the Canadian attack would come in on them, and that was the roadway crossing the Fosso Munio stream.

In the lead section of the lead platoon of the Perth Regiment from Stratford, Ontario spearheading the attack was a 17-year-old Windsor lad. Too young to have been inducted into the army, Lance Corporal Freddie Lytwyn must have lied about his age to get in.

But he was a veteran now, a veteran of several hard-fought battles. As he marched on towards yet another battle, this one only five days before Christmas, he hoped as all men do when going into battle, that it would be an easy affair and that he would come out of it okay.

Undetected thus far as they approached the start line at the roadway crossing of the insignificant narrow watercourse, they entered a roadside drainage ditch, and with stealth, made good time on the way to their first objective. They strained their eyes to peer into the black fields around them to catch signs of enemy presence. They would evade them if they could, or throw fire at them if necessary.

The immediate danger, however, was not in the open fields to their left, nor was it in the impenetrable darkness on their right. It was straight ahead along the line of the ditch. An enemy machine-gun crew hidden behind a stone culvert waited for them, their lethal weapon pointing down the centre of the ditch. This weapon, an MG 42 rated at 1200 rounds per minute, almost twice as fast as the Bren, could in the narrow confines of the ditch, do considerable slaughter. There was no way the man behind the gun could miss the unsuspecting approaching platoon.

At 25 yards range the enemy Fusilier squeezed the trigger, the gun ripping off a long burst. 400 steel-jacketed slugs slammed into the bodies of the lead two sections. Twelve men died instantly, their bodies literally torn apart in the slash of bullets. Farther along the column, others a little slower to react to the 'ripping canvas' sound of the gun, threw themselves onto the slick sides of the ditch, but delayed only by seconds, their own deaths.

Somewhere in that pile of torn bodies was that of a 17-year-old Windsor lad. He was too young to have to die in battle... he was too young to die anywhere. He, like so many countless others of our generation, had been denied by the cruel fates of war to reach manhood, to love, to marry, to raise a family, to enjoy all those things that we as survivors have taken for granted.

And so, in eternal thankfulness to God that somehow we were spared a similar fate and allowed to live out our lives as He had intended, it is only fit and proper that on Remembrance Day we should pause and pay tribute to their supreme sacrifice.

Private Stanley Scislowski, Perth Regiment

I have taken the liberty of describing the last moments in the life of one inordinately young Canadian who represents the hundred thousand and more other Canadians who laid down their lives in war. I have done this for a reason, that reason being that it is much easier to focus the memory onto one individual than it is onto a faceless multitude. In remembering one... you remember all.

Faces Emerge From the Past

Gale Hopkins (back row 5th from left) was reading Issue #51 and was amazed to see himself in this War Bond photo. He was able to identify a few other faces: Eddie Ingram (b. row 7th from l.), Joe Delani (f. row 3rd from l.) and Red Kennedy, Personnel Manager, far right.

They're posed in front of the Employment Building next to Chrysler's Plant 3. Eventually, workers from this building moved across the street into the Personnel Building. The Plant 3 manager was Kels Cameron; employment manager was Dave Courtney.

Issue #51, February 2005. photo courtesy Ted Ryan

A 25-Pounder Fieldpiece in action, Torelta, Italy, October, 1943, National Archives of Canada

When The Sky Was Falling

**by Stanley Scislowski, Issue #11, November 2000
from his book, "Not all Of Us Were Brave," Dundurn Press, 1997**

I began wondering if any of the guys in my platoon got hit in that first flurry of MG fire. I got to thinking maybe I was the only guy still alive – how would I know? Were they all sitting at the bottom of trenches like I was? Or had they managed to get back out of line of fire, leaving me here all alone? If that was so, then I knew I'd just have to wait it out and make a break for it as soon as it got dark.

During a lull in the MG fire and a slackening in the rate of mortar fire I heard someone hollering, but couldn't make out who it was and what it was all about. At first I thought it was someone calling out for a stretcher-bearer, but I detected a tone of calm authority in the voice. "Who in the hell's stupid enough to be out there in the open? The sonofabitch'll get himself knocked off if he doesn't smarten up."

With care I stood up to see who it was. First I put my helmet on the muzzle of my rifle and lifted it above the lip of the trench. When no shot drilled, I took a chance and stuck my head out to have a quick look around. That's when I saw Gord Forbes, Jimmy Ees and George Simeays hot-footing it for the protection of the gully. And not ten yards behind them sprinted Ken Topping, Walt Thomas, Bob Wheatley, Cec Vanderbeck and Bill Robotham practically falling all over each other in the flight to safety, with bullets chewing the ground at their feet and snapping past their ears.

How the Jerry gunners failed to plink any of them will forever remain a mystery to me. Was it a miracle? Was it divine intervention? Or was it simply that the MG 42 wasn't the magic weapon everyone touted it to be? Had the Jerries used Brens, it's not likely the boys would have made it. I watched them as they ran, admiring their guts for getting out of cover to run the gauntlet. I was thinking "they've got a hell of a lot more guts than I've got!"

I hesitated for at least five minutes trying to screw up courage, and then without really being conscious of what I was doing, I was up and out and picking the old feet up and laying them down, tearing off across the open ground like a scatback in a football game, dodging tackles, but hundreds of steel-jacked 7.92 mm rounds snapping and cracking all around. I knew that if I threw myself on the ground I'd get stitched up from asshole to breakfast in nothing flat.

And then, to speed me on my way even faster, a mortar bomb dropped out of the gray sky and exploded with an earsplitting crash not twenty yards to my left. With the stink of the HE (high explosive) burning in my nose I pelted right on as fast as my furiously pumping legs could carry me. That seventy-five yards seemed more like three hundred. With my lungs on fire I hurtled into the cover of the embankment. In doing so, I damn near bowled over three of my buddies, who were watching my desperate flight as I had watched theirs.

As soon as I hit the protection of the embankment I flopped on the ground on my back gasping for air, my heart pumping away at breakneck speed like a runaway engine. I don't think it was because of the energy expended that I was near done in. Blind fear had to be a good part responsible. And then after my respiratory and heart rate returned to near normal, I realized what I'd just gone through and felt proud of myself.

H.M.C.S. Calgary, c. 1940

We Took Our Harbours With Us

by Gordon Dalgleish, Issue #19, November 2001

On June 11th, the S.S. Partridge was sunk with no survivors. The following day, we endured the worst storm in 40 years. Although our ship survived, some of the tugs lost their tows, which forced us to send distress signals. On June 13th we were strafed from German planes but suffered no casualties. Our ship even had a torpedo fired at it. Thankfully, it did not hit its mark.

I was a telegraphist aboard the H.M.C.S. Calgary, which was a corvette in the Royal Canadian Navy. It was our job to escort the ocean-going tugs that towed artificial harbours to France across the English Channel. The Germans did not make it easy for us. They thought that their harbours were well fortified and that they would simply shoot us when we tried to land in France. Little did they know that we wouldn't allow that to happen. Instead, we planned to build and install our own harbour at Arromanches, France.

The project began in 1943 as the brainstorm of the British War Office. They knew the small fishing villages they could capture would not be able to handle large ships bringing supplies to back up the landing.

The British engineers built huge concrete caissons that were assembled near the channel coast. They were made to float. There were six different sizes to suit various depths of water. The smallest would weigh 1,672 tons, the largest, 6,044 tons.

Seven miles of pier equipment were prefabricated in sections 480 feet long (small enough to be towed across the Channel). Some of these caissons were built like ships, as tall as large houses. Early on, Nazi aircraft spotted them but couldn't have known their purpose. We were spared any attacks for the time being.

On the morning of D-Day, along with the first assault waves, Marines ran small boats toward the beaches. Instead of landing with the rest, some ships stopped off shore. German observers must have thought them insane, for they proceeded to throw lines overboard as if they intended to spend a quiet morning fishing. In reality, they were re-surveying the offshore bottom, double-checking a survey made months before by commando crews.

Late in the afternoon the first warships arrived. These sacrifice vessels ran directly up to the beach. Before the charge, they made a turn and tied up to a flag buoy already placed by the survey crews. They dropped their anchors, lowered their lifeboats and allowed most of their crew to leave. A few men stayed aboard to perform the delicate job of detonating the dynamite charges that would blow holes in each ship's bottom.

By nightfall, there was a tight line of a dozen warships on the bottom about 1200 feet offshore sticking high out of the water. The tides rose their allotted 22 feet, but the whole thing had been planned so neatly that the highest tide never topped the vessels.

Meanwhile, a fleet of ocean-going tugs, 165 in all, had started to tow the giant caissons across the English Channel. This was the most dangerous part of the entire operation because they stood high out of the water and were perfect targets for Nazi E-boats, planes and subs. Their speed was three knots per hour. It was our job to protect them.

Gordon Dalgeish in 1945

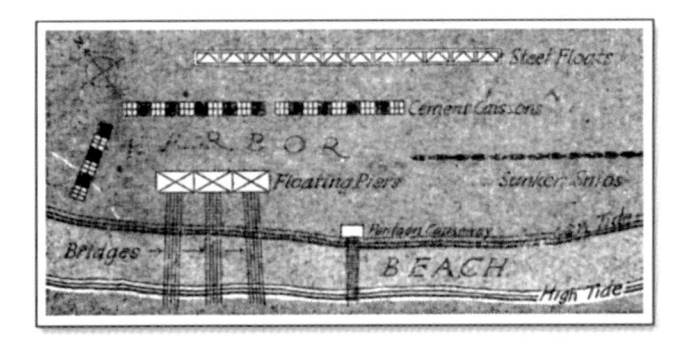

The next three days were the aforementioned attacks coming between June 11th and June 13th. Thwarting the attacks, the caissons made it to their destination.

The caissons were designed to be sunk in five and a half fathoms of water, permitting ships of 30-foot draft to lie behind them at low-tide. It was necessary that they sink accurately into place, while a riptide was running, and within the shortest possible time. It took exactly one hour and one minute for the concrete wall to touch bottom. By the third day of having the wall in place, more caissons were arriving at the rate of four to six a day. The concrete sea wall grew. Eventually it enclosed an area the size of the Port of Dover and could be used as a place where great ships unloaded in safety.

With the wall in place, the purpose of the 15,000-ton steel floats that accompanied us became apparent. The British engineers knew that Channel waves, swelling up to 12 feet high, beat against the Normandy coast. There was grave danger that the very force of such waves might topple and destroy the concrete caissons. Ships waiting outside the artificial harbours could be torn loose from their anchors and sent careening into caisson walls. To provide a safe outer harbour for ships awaiting unloading or making up convoy to England, huge steel floats were anchored in a line a mile or so outside the concrete harbour edge. Large, dangerous waves were reduced to ripples.

At the end of the battleship line, another steel float was used as a central anti-aircraft battery, office and control point. From its main mast, signals were flown by port-control officers.

Westward of the "Old Boy" battleship was the main channel entrance, more than 600 feet wide, through which large ships could pass toward their berths. Beyond this, providing unloading facilities for as many as seven Liberty ships at once, were the concrete caissons.

Within the harbour, another invention came into play. The British designed bridge piers to serve LSTs (Landing Ship Transport) and coasters. Here, again the tides had seemed to present an insurmountable obstacle. A pier could stand above the water at high tide and would be far above the decks of the ships at low tide. A low-level pier would be under water when the tide came in. Their difficulty was overcome by devising a new type of pier that rested on hollow steel legs. When the tide was low, the legs touched bottom and rested firmly, bringing the pier floor even with the average ship's deck. At high tide, the pier floated on its hollow air-filled legs, rising just enough to keep its floor adequately above water. The floating piers solved the problem.

Once the Nazis realized what was going on and how greatly these ports threatened their defence plan, they made frantic assaults. It was too late. We now had anti-aircraft fire from the "Old Boy" battleship and army anti-aircraft protection from the shore. Each ship and caisson flew its own barrage balloon and there was a constant cover of fighters maintained by the air forces.

It was not planned to use this port indefinitely, only until the forces could capture Cherbourg. It was hoped that the harbour could at least last through the great winter storms that lashed the Channel. The important thing, while the harbour was standing, was to get heavy equipment ashore quickly. This was something that had never been done before in any beachhead landing operation.

On November 5th, 1944 we had leave to go ashore at Arromanches to see the marvellous job that we all had done. Sadly, on December 29 of the same year, there were two ships lost. The H.M.C.S. Calgary took 37 survivors. Many of these men were badly burned and covered in oil. While we didn't have a doctor aboard, we did have a sick bay attendant. We all pitched in to help.

I was proud of the participation from the many Canadian ships in the operation. They did the job so admirably.

The H.M.C.S. Calgary has had a noteworthy presence since our crew manned her. She has since rescued 30 survivors from a Greek cargo ship that was sinking in the Atlantic and played a part in the sanctions against Iraq.

I have attended two reunions of the crew of our ship. One of the reunions took place in Calgary, Alberta in 1989. The other was in 1995 in Victoria, BC where a new ship bearing the H.M.C.S. Calgary name was commissioned, not as a corvette, but as a frigate.

I lost many friends in WW II and I think of them at times like this. I still keep in touch with some of the crew that served on the original H.M.C.S. Calgary, and I will never forget them.

Gordon was injured while loading a depth charge. A dud, it dropped off the end of the thrower and landed on his knees. He spent two weeks in hospital in Chatham, England and when the swelling went down, was released. The injury did not heal, however, and plagued Gordon for many years until he finally had a knee operation in June, 2001, 56 years after the accident.

Above: These British floating harbours helped the Allies win WWII
Below: Gordon (centre) at 1989 H.M.C.S. Calgary reunion

best of the times • 355

M.I.A. – Presumed Dead
Ross Mingay

by Bob Hogarth, Issue #29, November 2002

Ross Mingay served in the Royal Canadian Air Force. He was always reluctant to talk about his experiences during World War II, but when he did, he would enthrall his listeners.

Shot down over Belgium during his very first bombing raid, Ross and the surviving crew members of his Halifax bomber bailed out deep over enemy territory.

Seriously injured, and in excruciating pain, Ross lay immobile in a farm field for over two days. In desperation, Ross stumbled and crawled his way to a nearby farmhouse. Quickly deciding that capture would be no worse than his present situation, he knocked on the farmhouse door.

The lady of the house was alone at the time, and showed little sympathy for his predicament. This was understandable, as it was not uncommon for the Nazis to masquerade as allied airmen in order to infiltrate the underground network. The woman helped Ross to the barn, and told him she was going for the authorities.

She subsequently returned with her husband and several associates. Ross was interrogated at some length, and eventually convinced them that he was in fact, an allied airman. He received shelter and badly needed medical attention, and eventually made contact with the underground chain that would aid in his escape back to Britain.

Ross had seemingly vanished from the face of the earth. As a result, his name was listed in the dreaded "Missing in Action" notices in the local newspaper. Later his status was changed to "Missing in Action – Presumed dead."

The grieving Mingay family accepted condolences from the Governor General, the Prime Minister and countless relatives and friends. They arranged for a stained glass window to be installed at their church as a memorial to the young airman.

Meanwhile, Ross was making his way through the underground, posing as a French national. Little did he know that the leader of their small group was a double agent, who would turn them over to the Gestapo when they reached Bordeaux. It was 1943, and Ross spent the remainder of the war in a prisoner of war camp.

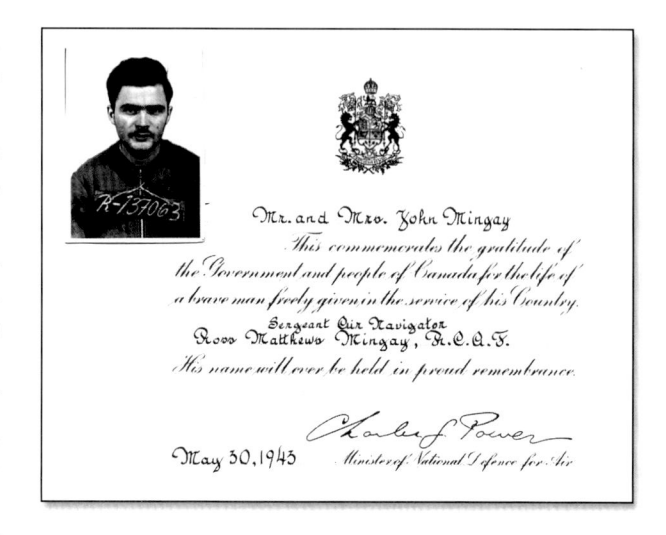

In 1966, Ross and his wife Betty returned to the Continent to retrace his steps through the underground. They visited all the homes where he had been harboured, and he renewed his acquaintance with those families who had sheltered him. On his visit to the Belgium farmhouse, the family returned his flying boots and the remnants of his parachute, most of which had been used for clothing by the family during those difficult times. Ross, understandably, had great admiration and respect for this family, who had rendered assistance, at great personal risk.

In 1991, a Belgium writer researching a book on the German air war, wrote to Ross seeking information on the fate of his crew. This gentleman also sent Ross a photograph of the twenty-two year old German fighter Ace, who had shot down his Halifax bomber on that fateful night.

Ross' wartime experiences had a profound effect on him, and certainly influenced his zest for life. He exhibited an interest and concern for everyone he came into contact with, and enriched the lives of us all. Ross had a great sense of fair play, and would always remind you that every story had two sides.

If Ross Mingay ever did have an enemy, he surely would have made that enemy his friend.

WWII Comrades

Raymond Laframboise (far left) and members of his crew during WWII, 1944. Raymond also appeared on the cover of the 56th edition of The TIMES Magazine to the right of his buddy. See page 385.

Photo courtesy Raymond's granddaughter Vanda O'Keefe

Issue #56, November/December 2005

Churchill to Mackenzie King:
"What About Your Women?"

by Elaine Weeks, Issue #29, November 2002

1941: After two years of what was proving to be a devastating war, British Prime Minister Winston Churchill asked the Canadian government for more men to go into active duty. When he was informed that there weren't sufficient numbers available, his response, "What about your women – why are they not replacing men as cooks, waitresses, stenos, telephone operators and so on...?" was to change the course of history for the women of Canada.

The Canadian government had already been experiencing incessant pressure from women's volunteer corps who wished to serve their country. With Churchill's request and the reality of dwindling "manpower" making it impossible to send over enough men, a reluctant Army allowed women to serve in supportive roles. For the first time in the nation's history, women were invited to enlist in the rank and file of the Canadian Army.

The Canadian Women's Army Corps was part of the Canadian Army's support system – working at home, and short distances behind the frontlines as need arose – which freed fighting men for action overseas and in battle. The 21,624 C.W.A.C.s who served for their country from 1941-1945 facilitated the release of more than a full division of male troops for combat service.

Theirs was an unsung role, created to get a job done – despite opposition to women in the military from both within the Canadian Army and from the Canadian public, including their own families.

"We were the first liberated women," declares Margaret Jobin, current president of C.W.A.C. Windsor Association which formed in 1947. "Many women in Windsor were already working in the war plants before they joined. Our jobs had already changed from traditional 'women's work'."

Local C.W.A.C. Memories

Verna Kavanaugh drove ambulances for 3 1/2 years including a stint in England, meeting trains and ships to transfer wounded soldiers. She has kept through the years, an ID card of "Peanut Pewee," a small dog which "adopted" CWACs stationed in Brockville, Ontario.

Betty (Clifford) Stewart's job was to pack parachutes for paratroopers. From 1944-45, Betty worked in a Manitoba hanger carefully folding and packing 80-yard, nylon parachutes. "We worked at long tables – the parachute would be tied to one end," recalls Betty. "It would take about 45 minutes just to pack one chute."

Rita (Berthiaume) Wessel vulcanized rubber tires for trucks (upgraded old tires for reuse). She remembers that the tires were larger than her. "I could stand inside of them," she laughs.

Thelma (Wighton) Waldron worked in London, Ontario processing monthly leaves and then discharges for the Canadian army. One day, as she was bent over writing a form, she heard an order, "I want to go to Windsor on CP and make it snappy sister!" It was her brother William whom she hadn't seen in four years.

After the war, women veterans were not allowed to join the Legions. *Beth (Friedl) Anderson,* a C.W.A.C. from Saskatchewan, who also was a regular on a radio show during the war, moved to Windsor with her husband, (also a war vet) in 1941. She was refused membership to the Legion. In her defence, her husband did not join the Legion, either.

Margaret (Tobin) Jobin, president since 1983 of the C.W.A.C. Windsor Association, was stationed in Ottawa in the Department of Military Training as a secretary in the Russian section of Foreign Publications during the war. In 1995, she travelled with some other C.W.A.C.s to Holland for the 50th Anniversary of the Liberation. "It hit us hard to see the graves of the boys, the brothers and husbands that we knew from Windsor. And then to see some of their real ages – 15 or 16! These boys had lied about their age to get into the army and their parents hadn't known they'd enlisted until it was too late."

Three thousand C.W.A.C.'s served overseas in Great Britain, Italy and Northwestern Europe during WWII.

Shortly after its creation in 1941, Canadian Women's Army Corps selected "Athene" as its symbol (above) and with it, the motto, "Dulcit Amor Patrice" (In Love of Country, We Serve). In "Homer," Athene is the Goddess of Wisdom. In "The Iliad," Athene appears as the goddess of Counsel, a true friend of bold warriors.

Canadian Women's Army Corps Pay Scale 1941-45
(1/3 of what the men earned for the same work)

Private: 90 cents a day
Extra pay for trades: A Trade: extra 75 cents
B Trade: extra 50 cents
C Trade: extra 25 cents

Women Treated Poorly on the Home Front

After reading the "Why We Can't Forget" feature in the November 2000 issue of The Times, I would like to try to explain what it was like as a young woman of 18 living and working in Walkerville during WWII.

Many women were treated poorly by men turned down by the army and left to show women how to run the machines. The women took courses at Lowe Tech to prepare for the factories. Then we were sent to Port Credit where we worked at Small Arms in Long Branch – 12 hour shifts for 35¢ an hour making bayonets. We experienced awful things: women caught in the big machines and new born babies found in waste baskets in the washrooms.

After three months, we were sent back to Windsor to work making airplane parts. When the foreman saw me standing on top of my shoes because my feet were sore and swollen, he fired me.

But jobs were plentiful then and I got a job at Gelatine Products (now Shearers) making capsules. I could sense the man showing the women how to run the machines was not happy about this so I tried to set the machine up myself for the next run. I got my hand caught between the dies but this man could care less. Thank God a nice young man of around 18 years old came right over and stopped the machine before any major damage was done. Then he went over and grabbed the other man by the collar and let him know that you don't treat women like that.

Some of the capsules we made there included tiny red bottle shaped ones that we filled with lighter fluid – these were sent overseas for the soldiers to refill their lighters. We were young and didn't realize the extent of the danger we were in doing this job – we could have easily been blown up.

When the war ended, the women had to give up their jobs to the returning men. What the war did to these men later forced women to lie and do things they wouldn't ordinarily do to get a job to make ends meet. The only place for the men to go was the Legion to drink for hours to drown their sorrows and their pain, only to face it again the next day. The women stayed home and took care of their children and took the brunt of everything.

Society played a big part in teaching young men how to treat women and that women were taught to accept this behaviour. The government knew exactly what to do to prepare us for the war and its aftermath but did nothing. So many men and families were destroyed as a result.

I never could muster up the courage to say how I really felt until I met a young woman named Sherrill Tucker who encouraged me to write. I am ever so grateful for being introduced to your paper and finally having the opportunity to do this. I know there will be many who will disagree with me but I have learned I have every right as anyone to my opinion.

I would like my memories passed on so the new generation can understand what it was like in the hopes this never happens again. Thank you for the opportunity to speak out.

Kitty Hyttenrauch, Windsor, Issue #13, February 2001

Keeping Track of the C.W.A.C.'s

I was very pleased to see an article on the C.W.A.C.'s, Issue #29. It has been a long time coming. I am writing regarding what you wrote about myself. The information regarding the joining of the legions at that time is so true. I had already been a member of the RCL Branch in Bienfait, Sask., and upon arriving in Windsor I wished to join Branch 12 with my husband. I was told they did not accept women veterans and that I could join the Ladies Auxiliary. After serving for 3 1/2 years in the army I felt I deserved the same recognition by the Windsor Legions as I had received from the Saskatchewan Legion. Needless to say, neither my husband nor myself became members then. I did join Branch 225 in the 1990s.

Beth Anderson, Windsor, Issue # 30, December/January 02-03

C.W.A.C. Windsor Assoc. members c. 1968. Pictured above, also in 2002 group photo (below): far left, middle row Mildred Blyth, 3rd from left middle row Pearl Hatton (founder of the group), 6th from left middle row Thelma Waldron.

Canadian Women's Army Corps Windsor Association members in 2002. Back row, l-r: Margaret Jobin, Stella Cookson, Betty Stewart, Beth Anderson, Vera Haines, Lorraine Labute, Cecile Treleaven, Louise Vincent, Jean Forbes, Mildred Blyth Front Row, l-r: Christine Lewis, Thelma Waldron, Rita Wessel, Verna Kavanaugh, Eva MacEachern and Sheila Seal. photo E. Weeks

Four representatives of the Canadian Women's Army Corps filed past the coffin of Corporal Ronald Culpan, the first soldier buried in Windsor to die of injuries from overseas enemy action in WWII. Culpan was wounded while with the Essex Scottish Regiment, in the raid on Dieppe, on August 19th, 1942. Pictured is Margaret Tobin (saluting) with Tina (Virgina) Yusaw on her right.

Safe Haven

by Elaine Weeks, Issue #39, November 2003

The Ford Motor Company of Canada played an important role in the Second World War. Many Ford men were sent to Britain to design Canadian Military Pattern vehicles under great secrecy. In addition, a number of Ford men and women gave their lives in service for their country.

On the home front, thousands of trucks, scout cars, and Windsor carriers were manufactured in the Windsor Ford factory and shipped overseas to aid the Allies. The assembly lines were devoted entirely to military production from May 1942 to June 1946.

But perhaps the most intriguing component of Ford's involvement in the war was their Evacuee program, popularly known as "Bundles from Britain." Over 100 British children – the sons and daughters of British Ford employees from the London area – became the guests of Windsor Ford executives, dealers and the employees of feeder plants that supplied the auto industry, from 1940 to 1945. Wallace Campbell, the President of Ford of Canada, and his wife Gladys, dreamed up the idea of offering the children safe haven.

Campbell and Lord Perry, the Chairman of Ford of Britain, worked together to transport the children to the Windsor area. Because of the German bombing blitzes in London, British parents were willing to entrust their children to caring families in Windsor until the end of the war. Since the London-area Ford plant was producing armaments for the war, it was an obvious target.

The children, who were also referred to as the "Blitzkrieg Kids" started sailing across the Atlantic and arriving in Windsor after bombs began falling in London in July of 1940. Some of these children were only 4 years old.

The Campbells personally hosted 23 children, ranging in age from 4 to 14. The family converted the top floor of Edgewood, their large home on Richmond Street opposite Willistead Park, into a dormitory. Many other children also stayed with them for a brief while, before being situated in area homes.

Often, the only contact that the children had with their parents back in England was through letters that would often arrive with sections blacked out by military censors.

Unfortunately, not all of the children were given warmth and affection; some were treated more like servants than refugees and a few even ran away.

In April, 2003, several child guests, now in their sixties and seventies, who were among those that had chosen to emigrate to their adoptive country, gathered at the University of Windsor to attend a ceremony, where a collection of interviews, newspaper clippings and other memorabilia of that time, was presented to the University and the Ford Motor Company. These documents represented 13 years of work by UNI-COM, a volunteer group of retirees coordinated by Bill McRae, who realized that this significant era of our local history shouldn't be forgotten.

Peter Horlock, one of the Blitzkrieg Kids and now a resident of Mississauga, Ontario, was one of the attendees and is also keen to help preserve the memory. He donated the trunk that was given to him as a child to transport his belongings to his temporary home in Canada, to Windsor's Community Museum, where it is currently on display. His story about returning to England after his stay in Windsor follows.

Top: Ford of Canada President Wallace Campbell with his British war guest David Leon at Edgewood, Campbell's home in Olde Walkerville.

British boys in front of the Angstrom home, Amherstburg, 1940

Reflections of a Blitzkrieg Kid

by Peter Horlock, Issue #39, November 2003

The war had been progressing for about a year when the time came for Britain to batten down the hatches. After Dunkirk the bombing raids were beginning in earnest. Through the generosity of the Ford Motor Company of Canada and its employees, an evacuation scheme was put into operation for the safekeeping of the children of Ford Motor Company of England employees.

At 13, I was one of those children lucky enough to be a part of this scheme.

In the spring of 1940, we lived in Hornchurch, Essex near the Dagenham plant where Dad worked. This area is almost a suburb of London and was also home to an RAF base and therefore deemed a target area.

Mom and Dad wanted me to go to Canada to be safe from the bombing and that soon I would be back with them when the war ended. It was a big rush getting outfitted, buying a trunk to put it all in, seeing all of my aunts and uncles, getting documents from school and saying goodbye to all my friends. To say I was thrilled was putting it mildly.

I was completely oblivious to the effect this would have on my parents.

In no time it was mid-July and we were at the train station saying goodbye – shaking hands in manly fashion with Dad and being embarrassed by a long hug from my Mom. (She told me years later that she ran down the station platform, to try to take me off the train.)

We were chaperoned all the way by Ford Motor personnel and finally arrived in Liverpool to board the CP ship "Duchess of Bedford." It was a fast liner and so was able to travel alone. It was an exciting time, meeting the other evacuees, learning lifeboat drills, and generally getting in the way.

I attended most meals while we were in the North Atlantic, getting only mildly seasick. Then we were traveling down the St. Lawrence River where we really marveled at all the sights down to Quebec City.

One of Mr. Campbell's sons (Noel I believe) met us and organized our train trip from Quebec City to Windsor. I remember that it felt like a luxury train after the British commuter trains we'd been using to get in and out of London.

After a long journey we arrived at the Windsor train station at the foot of Ouellette Avenue on the Detroit River. There were a lot of people there to meet us and help everyone get sorted into the various vehicles that would take us to the staging locations. I was one of twelve boys who were put on a bus with a chaperone and taken to the home of Mr. and Mrs. L.C. Angstrom and their daughter Barbara on Riverfront Road in Amherstburg.

Upon arriving we were all awestruck at this beautiful home and its park-like setting. Overlooking the Detroit River at its widest point, the property had a curved driveway leading to a huge house with a separate garage and two monstrous barns, plus equipment sheds for the farm machinery.

The Angstroms had things well organized for us and soon we were sitting down to our first Canadian meal. We were housed in a large room at the top of the house that had been turned into a dormitory. There were two American boys there also, who were waiting to join the RCAF. They looked after us younger ones and organized activities, etc, while we were getting Canadianized and waiting for the "foster parents" to come out and pick up those boys who had been assigned to them.

Towards the end of this period, Mrs. Angstrom asked me if I would like to stay with them as part of their family until the war ended. I couldn't believe my luck! Of course I said YES! Thus began a wonderful friendship with a great family, which still exists to this day.

Mr. and Mrs. Angstrom were now Aunt Hazel and Uncle Carlton and Barbara became my older "sister" Barb. My room was a huge bedroom on the north end of the house with a great view over the

Detroit River. They owned a 200-acre farm that stretched down the 10th Sideroad to Malden Road and as well, they were leasing another 800 acres across the road, to assist in the war effort. There were Belgian horses, milk cows, Berkshire hogs and Leghorn chickens, plus various crops. Uncle Carlton and the farm manager, Bert Madill, showed me how to look after the animals and generally be a "regular farmhand."

About three weeks after arriving, I had my 14th birthday and coincidentally, the first letters arrived from my mother. That's when it really hit me how much I missed her but the Angstroms understood and provided lots of comfort. When September rolled around I started school at General Amherst High in Amherstburg. It was strange at first being in a co-ed class, but I was really made welcome by the teachers and classmates.

After school I would help on the farm, "mucking out" animal stalls, collecting eggs, etc. Dinners were formal affairs, so I had to clean up after chores before sitting down to eat. Then it was homework time before I went off to bed. I was also involved in after school activities such as lacrosse, DCRA shooting team, school play and, as it was wartime, all male students, who were not conscientious objectors, were involved in the RCAC cadets. It was a truly great experience that guided me in later life.

Aunt Hazel made sure I wrote home to my Mom and Dad every week and it was always an event when my parents' letters arrived.

The school year had several highlights, of which the November 11th parade was the first. In 1940 all cadets were issued WWI uniforms from the school stores and it was a riot trying to get the things to fit. Uncle Carlton had quite a laugh helping me wind the puttees and tie them off.

We were a small school with only 200 students, so in order to have a marching band, we enlisted the girls into a drum and bugle band. Another highlight was Christmas, which was very nice as there was snow in the area back then. We always had a play and a Christmas Social.

The big event of the school year was the annual cadet inspection in May and the Cadet Ball. This event became quite impressive after 1941 when we were issued our new, modern uniforms, which complemented the girls' formal gowns at the Ball.

The scholastic side of my education was good, as I had to master French and Latin, plus various Maths, a new style of History and Geography, various English components, Phys. Ed. and Shop.

In 1941, I had my tonsils out at Hotel Dieu Hospital and I was "obligated" to eat ice cream to "ease" my throat. Another highlight was attending the wedding of Wallace Campbell's daughter Glad to Nelson Works.

Although gasoline was rationed we did save enough for Uncle Carlton

"Child Guest" Peter Horlock in 2003 with his boyhood trunk (on display at Windsor's Community Museum)

to drive us to Toronto and the CNE. The visit to the exhibition is sketchy, but I do remember driving along the QEW, only two years after it was opened. In December came the "Day of Infamy" and I remember listening to the news flashes on the radio with the Angstroms while we were all in the study. The next day, we heard President Roosevelt's speech and realized the war was being brought home to all of us.

Nineteen forty-two was not a good year in general, and the entire Windsor area was particularly hard hit with the news of the Dieppe raid. I remember Aunt Hazel going in to Windsor to comfort several friends who had lost loved ones in the raid.

One day, as a reward for our hard work we were allowed to go to Detroit to see and hear Glen Miller and his orchestra at the Michigan Theatre. He was playing between movies and just afterwards, he and his group joined the army.

After my 16th birthday in the fall of '42, Aunt Hazel took me to get my temporary driving license. I was then allowed to "put the car away," that is, drive it from the back door of the house to the garage, but eventually I was taken on the road for lessons. Gasoline rationing had been tightened up by this time and therefore I didn't get to drive too much.

I remember that my mother's letters were beginning to look like paper cut outs from the censor's scissors.

Soon it was 1943 and the war had taken an about turn. The Allies were no longer consolidating, but were starting to advance in both Europe and the Pacific. At home, we were starting to talk about when the war would be over. I had passed my Departmentals for grade 11 and spent the summer planting and harvesting on the farm.

In the fall I started grade 12. Patriotism was running high at this stage of the war, so along with a group of friends I made a pact to join the RCAF when I graduated. I wrote and asked my parents, who wrote back and agreed.

Before I could graduate however, the long arm of the British Government reached over the Atlantic and beckoned me. It was time to come home and do my duty. I had a conversation with Aunt Hazel about the RCAF, but she felt it would be better if I went home, as I would get to see my parents for the first time in 3 years.

When all the official papers had been filled in, there came several rounds of long and very, very difficult goodbyes. I left the Windsor area from the station at the foot of Ouellette Avenue on Christmas Day 1943. I left behind very enduring memories of some wonderful people who I came to love as my own parents.

To Uncle Carlton, Aunt Hazel and Barb, you were a part of my life that is unforgettable.

A British Child Guest Remembers

by June Jolly, London U.K, Issue #29, November 2003

During WWII, several Rotary Club members in Windsor opened their homes to children of Rotarians in England. I arrived in Windsor as a 12-year old girl with my 9-year old sister and 6-year old brother.

We had traveled across the Atlantic – criss-crossing to avoid the U-boats – and were somewhat shell-shocked. We had been living on the southern coast of England where an invasion was expected at any time. The feeble defenses in that area consisted of barbed wire fences and mines on the beaches. The war was long over before these armaments were removed.

My siblings and I were welcomed into three separate families; my sister went to a home in Riverside, my brother moved in with a Grosse Pointe, MI family and I spent four years with Walkerville pediatrician Dr. George White, and his wife and family. I attended King Edward School and Walkerville Collegiate along with the White's children, Dordie (George) and Ann. These were happy years for me, highlighted by annual holidays with the YWCA camps at Orendoga and Tapapwingo.

School in Windsor was very different from in England; the lack of uniforms and the inclusion of the opposite sex were foreign to me. I am certain my teachers were appalled by my accent and writing skills, as all I could do was upright, "joined-up" printing. Mrs. McLaren, our Grade 8 teacher, was the first to instill confidence in me and I ended up winning the annual school medal – which I treasure to this day. I learned to spell, which I am doubtful I would have accomplished elsewhere. I was instructed in public speaking, health studies, and music and art appreciation, and benefited from a much more liberal education than was available to me in my home country.

Outside of school, we made candy to sell and filled "ditty bags" for sailors to help with the war effort. In winter, Ann and I often skated up the road to join in the fun when Willistead Park was flooded to make an ice rink. As soon as spring came, we played hopscotch and baseball on the vacant lot opposite our Devonshire Road home.

Hallowe'en was another mystery to me. I shall always remember my foster father having us all duck for apples before we were given our treats. Christmas and the real trees were another wonder. I especially remember the year our tree was sprayed white by the local garage and decorated with blue fairy lights.

On Christmas morning we shouted our greetings to my family in England, just after the King's speech, knowing that my parents were doing the same. Later, it was possible for us to have a short phone call, but these were never very satisfactory.

My parents somehow managed to send over my bicycle in the middle of the war. It was very different from the Canadian cycles. I even had a little pump attached to it to blow up my tyres, which was a great bore. I was delighted when they were adapted so that I could use the local air pump on Wyandotte Street.

Memories of milk shakes and sodas at the Peerless Ice Cream Parlour and the downtown movie theatre are also fondly recalled. It was after experiencing these treats that I was introduced to hotdogs, hamburgers and, wonder of wonders! a coke – all things I longed for after my return to England, where rationing continued for several years after the war.

Another great treat was our annual trip to Bob-Lo Island. As it was leased to the United States, Canadians were allowed only three days per year to enjoy the fun. As British Child Guests (BCG) we were given free tickets and could go on the rides as often as we liked.

Left: Anne White with British guest June Jolly during WWII.
Right: June and Anne reunite in recent years.

British kids in Windsor enjoying a game of baseball in 1943, (l-r): John Shackleton, Mary Phillips, Neville Haslop, Jeanette Rothwell, Dennis Drew, Jacqueline Eastman, Kenneth Pendergast (batting) and Mamie Bain, catching. photo courtesy Anne White

We never had to queue as we went in through the exit gate and must have been a real pain to everyone else who had to patiently wait their turn. This excursion was one of the few occasions that I saw my sister. Strangely, I saw my brother more often as I was invited to stay with his foster family, the Hendersons, in Grosse Point.

I would like to take this opportunity to thank everyone who was so kind and patient with us. When I left England I had been cross to think that I had to leave friends and family in England during the bombings so I was not a particularly grateful guest at the time.

I shall be eternally thankful to all the people who sacrificed for my family and me. Later I learned that these generous individuals received no compensation whatsoever for their kindness.

Canada will always remain part of my life and a treasured memory as I grow old. Thank you all at The TIMES for reviving my many memories.

Father & Sons: Served and Survived

In 1918 my Dad, David A. Weir was in Europe with the 20th battalion serving as a stretcher bearer on the battlefields.

In 1941 my brother, one year older than I, joined the Royal Canadian Air Force. By 1945 he had completed his tour flying Halifax heavy bombers, had won the Distinguished Flying Cross, and was back in Canada.

I joined the R. C. A. F. in October 1942. I trained as a pilot, washed out and moved into the air gunner stream. I graduated from #9 Bombing and Gunnery School in Mont Joli PQ and was soon on my way to England on a troop ship.

As part of further training, our crew of seven airmen were sent to #82 Operational Training Unit. It was our introduction to bombers. We flew training missions on Wellington two-engine aircraft.

One evening my crew was scheduled on a cross-country flight with a pilot instructor. I was assigned to another crew to do some exercises on air-to-air firing and air-to-sea firing. As the Wellington I was in was flying back toward base we heard an aircraft call the tower to ask for a priority landing. Their port engine had stopped and they were flying on just the starboard engine. The hydraulics for the undercarriage and turret come from the port engine. The green light in the cockpit signaling the undercarriage down and locked had come on and then gone off again.

As the plane I was in circled the airfield, we watched the landing aircraft as it lined up with the runway and descended to the ground. As it touched down, the undercarriage collapsed and the Wellington skidded down the runway on its belly with sparks following the tail turret. Soon it was a sheet of flame. The aircraft stopped and the tracer bullets of the machine guns began streaking off in all directions.

We landed on another runway. As I entered the debriefing room, I found my crew sitting around without their usual banter and kidding. They had been the crew of the burned Wellington. Besides my crew and the instructor pilot, they had carried an air cadet, probably on his first flight. The air cadet had crawled out the usual entrance and exit which now sat partly on the ground. We never saw the air cadet again; probably he'd gone off to join the navy. The airmen had escaped out through the escape hatches. Our bomb aimer's foot had landed partially on a strut injuring his leg. We could not wait for him to heal so we were assigned a new bomb aimer and continued on towards 433 squadron. We completed our tour with 22 missions over enemy territory flying Halifaxes and Lancasters but that's another story.

For a father and two sons to serve on active service in wartime and survive without injury beats all the odds. We know that God had other plans for our lives and that He does answer prayer.
William R. Weir, Issue #19, November, 2001

A Veteran Remembers

I am proud to say that I was one of more than one million Canadians who fought in the Second World War (1939-45).

In April of 1945, I was knocked out of my tank by an explosion and saw the war end while in a Belgium hospital. By the time the war was over, over 45,000 Canadians had given their lives.

For me, November 11 means remembering fallen comrades. They were strong, devoted, focused and afraid. They believed in their country and their duty and freedom. This November 11, I will again pray for peace and I will honour the fact that I was part of a very special nation that fought to preserve a way of life, the Canadian culture and the freedom we currently enjoy.
by Don Sharon, Issue #11, November 2000

After his convalescence, Don, who had worked at Windsor's CKLW radio as a Sound Effect Man and Transcription Officer prior to the war, served briefly as a Program Engineer with Canadian Forces Radio Service in London, England. One of his projects was to pipe the popular "Happy Gang from Canada" radio shows, which had aired coast to coast on the CBC network, into the reinforcement depots where soldiers waiting to return to Canada were based. Don was instructed to remove all the commercials and was able to bundle five shows into the space of one! In 1946, Don returned to Canada and resumed his career with CKLW (now CBET). He retired in 1985 as the Film Department Manager. A father of six, grandfather of 14 and great-grandfather of 10, Don has gathered with his wife Ruth and family to remember, on November 11.

Saviours of Ceylon

by Laryssa Landale, Issue #29, November 2002

At a formal dinner in Washington, D.C. in 1946, former British Prime Minister, Winston Churchill, declared that an "unknown airman, who lay deep in the waters of the Indian Ocean made one of the most important single contributions to the Allied victory." Lester Pearson promptly informed Churchill that the "unknown airman" was in fact Leonard J. Birchall, a Royal Canadian Air Force officer currently stationed just down the street from the British Embassy in Washington.

It was just after midnight on Saturday, April 4th, 1942, when "Birch" (a native of St. Catharines, Ontario) was roused and asked if his squadron would cover a 20-hour (or more) patrol flight over the Indian Ocean. The Dutch crew originally scheduled for the mission had unexpectedly withdrawn.

Birchall and eight other men (one RCAF and seven RAF) made up Royal Canadian Air Force's #413 Squadron, which had recently spent fourteen days travelling from their former base in the Shetland Islands, in the north of Scotland. They had arrived at their new post in Ceylon barely two days earlier. Nonetheless, Birchall agreed.

At Kogalla, in the southwest corner of the then-British colony of Ceylon (now Sri Lanka) the men were briefed for their patrol. The majority of these missions were uneventful. The orders were to sweep back and forth over the water to the south of Ceylon. Their objective: to spot enemy ships within range to reach the island under cover of night and carry out a surprise attack. Strategically, Ceylon was crucial to the war. Whoever controlled this island militarily would control the entire Indian Ocean – from Africa to Australia.

As they neared the end of their patrol, Warrant Officer G.C. Onyette (of Huntsville, Ontario), the seaplane's navigator, requested that Birchall embark on one more crossover so he could figure an accurate heading back to Kogalla. Onyette's calculations placed them farther south than the mission should have taken them, but it was not a concern since they had plenty of time and fuel to return to base. As the Catalina flying boat turned its nose for home, one of the crew spotted a speck on the horizon and Birchall adjusted course to investigate.

Aboard the relatively slow Catalina, the crew could make out the forms of what – as they would learn soon enough – was the same Japanese fleet, headed by Admiral Nagumo, that had devastated Pearl Harbour less than four months prior.

Since their flight briefing gave them no indication that a large Japanese presence was expected in the area, 413 Squadron initially assumed it was an Allied fleet operating out of a nearby naval base. There was no way to verify this assumption by radio, as their orders were strict radio silence unless reporting a sighting. Birch knew he needed to be certain of the ships' identities before returning to base, so they flew closer.

"The first Japanese Zero fighter plane we saw was coming right at us, firing," said Birchall. And thus began the attack. The seaplane was no match in speed or armament, but Birch was determined to get full details of the enemy fleet back to base. He began evasive maneuvers. But, it was only a matter of time before the seaplane would be

Above: A wartime photo of then-Squadron Leader Len Birchall in the cockpit of one of 413 Squadron's amphibious Catalina aircrafts.

down on the water and they would be at the mercy of the Japanese.

A message was being sent back to Ceylon by wireless air gunner, Sergeant F.C. Phillips (RAF) – to be repeated three times as per protocol – when the wireless radio was hit during the third transmission. Bullets from the Zero fighters strafed the Catalina, and cannon shells from the ships below began to wreak havoc on the plane's integrity. Birchall and his co-pilot fought to get the flying boat down on the water before she broke apart in mid-air. As the craft touched the water, her tail fell away.

Soon the crew found themselves hastening to get out of the slowly sinking aircraft. Sgt. Colarossi (RAF), whose left leg had been blown off at the knee by a cannon shell, was unable to get out and went down with the ship. The eight other men soon found themselves bobbing in the vastness of the Indian Ocean.

Suddenly, bullets rained down on them as the Japanese fighter planes began making passes overhead. Six of the men were able to dive beneath the surface to avoid the bombardment. Sadly, two soldiers who were badly wounded had been put into full life jackets, which in this case would doom them. They were unable to escape the enemy fire. The remaining men were taken aboard a Japanese destroyer and repeatedly beaten for information.

Birchall, stepping forward as commanding officer, was able to convince the Japanese that their wireless radio operator was killed by the Zeros' initial attack. Thus, nothing had been sent. The enemy seemed ready to accept this story until the request for a repeat message come over the wire from a naval base in Ceylon, destroying Birchall's credibility.

The enemy attack was launched as planned on April 5th, 1942 – Easter Sunday. Due to the timely warning, damage was limited and these nine men of 413 Squadron became known as "the Saviours of Ceylon."

The Squadron's six surviving members were on board Japanese ships during the battle, which spanned five days. Upon arrival in Japan, three badly wounded men were taken to a naval hospital. Birchall, his co-pilot, and navigator went directly to Ofuno prison camp for interrogation.

Birchall spent some 40 months in Japanese POW camps. His courageous conduct and devotion to his fellow prisoners during this time earned him great respect and many commendations. He endured unspeakable horrors, yet was unwaveringly valiant and honourable. The detailed diaries he kept during his imprisonment were crucial to the War Crimes Trials that ensued.

Now a retired Air Commodore, Leonard J. Birchall has served over 68 years in the Canadian Forces. In 1996 he became the first ever to qualify for the fifth bar to the Canadian Forces Decoration (the medal signifies 12 years service and each bar represents an additional 10 years) – an honour which only he, and the late Queen Mother have earned.

Birchall has been honoured with 17 medals (including the Order of Canada, Order of Ontario, Order of the British Empire for Gallantry, Distinguished Flying Cross, and the Legion of Merit U.S.A.), and the Vimy Award.

He has been a guest speaker for numerous military functions including one at the Military Institute of Windsor in September of 1999. He has other reasons to visit Windsor as his nephew, Captain Ellis Landale grandnephew, Len Landale (his namesake and godson) and wife, Beth, grandnieces Lani and Laryssa Landale, and great-grandniece, Caleigh, all live in the area.

Now 87 years old, Birch lives an active and fulfilling life. He and his wife, Kay, reside in Kingston, Ontario but travel extensively due to Len's speaking engagements and ceremonial obligations.

Above: A.C. Len Birchall in January 2000, at a street naming ceremony at the Norman Rogers Municipal Airport in Kingston. The new sign reads "Len Birchall Way." photo: The Kingston Whig-Standard

The Canadian Women's Army Corps

The Canadian Women's Army Corps was part of the Canadian Army's support system – working at home, and short distances behind the front-lines, as need arose – freeing fighting men for overseas action and for battle.

Pictured at left, are C.W.A.C's from across North America, including Windsor's Margaret (Tobin) Jobin at the far right. Margaret was president since 1983 of the CWAC Windsor Association, was stationed in Ottawa in the Department of Military Training as a secretary in the Russian section of Foreign Publications during the war. In 1995, she travelled with some other C.W.A.C.s to Holland for the 50th Anniversary of the Liberation.

This photo, originally a tiny worn snapshot in Margaret's war time album, was enlarged, restored and colourized by *The TIMES* graphic designer, Chuck Rees and used as the cover of Issue #29, November 2002 (see page 369 for the full color version).

Turning in My Tin Helmet

**from an interview with Dr. Tom Robson
(condensed by Laryssa Landale),
Issue #19, November 2001**

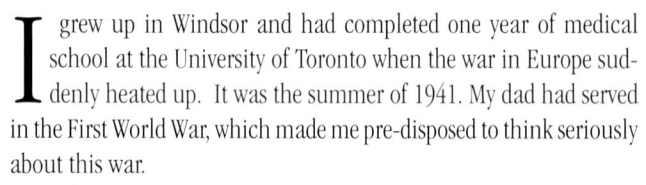

Tom Robson after war ended in 1945

I grew up in Windsor and had completed one year of medical school at the University of Toronto when the war in Europe suddenly heated up. It was the summer of 1941. My dad had served in the First World War, which made me pre-disposed to think seriously about this war.

In the army everyone starts out as a private. I chose to enlist in the Navy since they allowed qualified people to come in and be trained as officers. Also, the Navy seemed to offer more of a chance to travel and see the world. So, I went down to HMCS Hunter here in Windsor and enlisted. And travel I did.

In May of 1942, with my second year of medical school and a few months of training and drill at HMCS Hunter under my belt, I headed for Halifax as a probationary sub-lieutenant. The Navy had taken over King's College University as the officer's training school. In September of 1942 I graduated and was appointed to a corvette, *HMCS Quesnel*, and we went to sea for the first time.

The *Quesnel* was part of a local escort force, and we shepherded and convoyed merchant ships on what they called the "triangle run." It was sort of a Halifax, Newfie-John, and New York routine. We dropped an awful lot of depth charges, but we never saw a submarine. The greatest enemy we faced was the North Atlantic weather. The officers had to live in bunks on the ship, while the crew lived in hammocks. When the ships were rocking the hammocks were remarkably steady; the bunks, on the other hand, were difficult to keep ourselves in.

In May of 1943, I was appointed back to training school as a training divisional officer. Four months later I was appointed to the frigate *HMCS Cape Breton* as both watchkeeping officer and anti-submarine officer. It was on a run back from Murmansk, in north Russia, that the *Cape Breton* ran into some German submarines. We were part of the advance screen of a convoy and ended up with two good explosions from the hedgehog (an apparatus that fired anti-sub bombs off the bow.) We aboard ship knew we had hit a German submarine. Our ship got credit for a possible sinking when the sonar records were submitted. The captain also put my name in the dispatches, which earned me a certificate of recognition "by order of the King."

While we were off the coast of Wales waiting for the word, our captain let each officer have an hour during the night to read the overall plan for D-Day. I don't think too many people as far down the ladder as I was in command got a chance to see this ahead if time. It detailed what the various units were going to do. It was outstanding.

A while later, after D-Day, I got word that I had been accepted for a navigation course back at King's College. But, my ship was not due to go back. So, I got dropped off on a jetty in the Faeroe Islands, off Iceland. Then a Royal Navy trawler took me to Scotland. The Canadian Navy had a depot just outside Glasgow, in a former insane asylum in Greenock. It was a standing joke in the Navy over there that the Canadians were in the insane asylum. Finally, I got passage on the *Queen Mary* back to New York.

After the four-month course at King's College, I was reappointed as navigating officer of the *Cape Breton*. I was serving aboard her when we got the word about V-E Day. Around the end of August 1945, I was on a six-week leave back here in Windsor (which my new bride and myself used as our belated honeymoon.) I decided to get out and go back to medical school. I sent a telegram to the rear admiral in charge and received word that I was to report to HMCS Hunter, right here in Windsor, for discharge.

After the medical exam and forms were completed, they said, "You have to turn in your tin helmet." Well, I'd never been issued with a tin helmet; I never wore one; I had no idea what they were talking about. Still, they insisted they could not discharge me without the return of a tin helmet. So, I borrowed the $22 from my father-in-law who had driven me down there, bought a tin helmet from their supply and handed it back in. They signed my discharge papers and I was back in medical school for September classes in 1945.

Drastic Measures

He was born 50 years before me, in a place a thousand miles away. I am in his kitchen pouring him another drink. I regard him thoughtfully and notice how striking he looks as the sun sets behind him through the window. The grey of his hair contrasts vividly with the rosiness of his skin.

Soon we are joking, laughing and feeling pretty good. The alcohol has triggered a memory and he has something to tell me. I recognize that certain heaviness in his expression and brace myself for the words, which begin to spill out of his mouth like lead weights.

I am uneasy. I never know where to look when he starts on one of his stories; when to look away, to laugh or sigh, to intervene or close my mouth. And on this particular night he has a most horrible story to tell, which brings me close to tears, even now.

I lift my eyes back up to him as he lowers his drink, wipes his lips and begins. "Behind the trees, the tanks were running over the bodies," he says in a shrill voice. "They would burn them, throw them on the ground and run over them with tanks." He grips his glass tightly and shuffles from one foot to another.

I start falling into a trance while my mind races to come to grips with the horror he attempts to describe; I find it hard to follow him. His accent has hardly changed in 30 years and he leaves out details. I realize he's telling me about what he saw but not exactly about what he knew.

"I could smell something in the air," he says. "A very bad smell. I see what looks like coal smoke and I look around but there are no houses. You know what it is?" I shake my head. "Behind the trees, they were burning the bodies of Jews and Partisans."

A line from Winston Churchill pops into my head: "Drastic measures."

With the horror that is war, drastic measures meant nothing to this old man seated in front of me. He saw his own brother shot by a firing squad just feet away from him. He was forced to fight for an army he hated. And when it was over, he had no real home to return to.

I can't help thinking, where is the retribution for this man?

He continues to tell his story, but my mind is having a hard time processing what he is telling me. When his words falter, his eyes continue to tell the story; I can't get over his eyes. They are like rain – I can see right through them – right through him. Like a body living, with a heart that died long ago.

His voice grows louder and his adjectives get stronger; I find it hard to see the man I know.

"Come to bed," his wife yells from the bedroom. His eyes flicker, as if he were just jolted back into the present. He throws his hands up in the air and walks into the living and sits down.

"He doesn't talk about that stuff," his wife says to me. "He just wants to forget."

That's exactly what I see in him – a man trying to forget.

"He talks to very few people about what happened to him," his wife says. I look over at him and he is just sitting there in his chair, staring into space.

There aren't many times when we reach a point of total non-judgmental conversation.

He will not even let me use his name because he fears judgment. Someone may think he is a Nazi sympathizer because he fought for the Germans. Someone may think he is a traitor because he changed sides (forced at gunpoint) when the partisan group he was fighting with was defeated by the Germans.

Most of all, he is afraid no one will understand.

Christopher Shoust, Windsor, Issue #29, November 2002

Autograph Book of Long-Lost Heroes

Tucked away in a forget-me-not drawer, carefully blanketed in plastic, is a small autograph book that has withstood the test of time. Plastic wrap had not been invented when this little book was signed in 1941. My mother embossed its green faux leather cover with two flags, the Union Jack and the Stars and Stripes. This book represents a story which knows no end, for we never knew the fate of the boys whose names are inscribed on those pages.

A request for rooms to accommodate young men arriving daily from the U.S. to enlist in the R.C.A.F. had appeared in the Windsor Star. Housing with board was required for several days while these men awaited the processing of their papers and their enlistment acceptance. When papers were finalized they went off to Manning Depot in Toronto, possibly to Gimli, Manitoba for their very short training period. Then they were off across the Atlantic to join in the battle of Britain.

Pearl Harbour had as yet not brought the U.S into combat. These were eager boys, 19-21 years young and anxious for the adventure of flying into the wild blue yonder in dusty Air Force blue with a Canadian insignia on their shoulders.

My brother was in England serving with the Essex Scottish Regiment awaiting the invasion of Europe. His room stood as an empty shrine awaiting his return. My mother and father opened our home for those boys, who generally arrived in pairs. Each had a story to tell and left behind in this autograph book their name, address and their thanks for the Canadian hospitality.

These young boys from across the U.S. also left behind frivolous little verses, "I'll remember you 'til the Detroit River wears rubber pants to keep its bottom dry" or, "I've never met such nice people 'til I thumbed my way into Windsor." Short and sweet the messages, and perhaps, short and sweet their lives.

I wonder, where did their stories end? Where are they now? Some might be old men recalling past glories and perhaps, now and then, a fleeting recollection of a city called Windsor.

Ruth M. Smith, Windsor, Issue #29, November 2002

Walkerville Landmark Bombed!

by Currie Bednarick, Issue #19 November 2001

The Peabody Building, once located on the southwest corner of Riverside and Devonshire, was a Walkerville landmark for many years. Situated beside the Peabody bridge, the familiar complex was the home of many companies and associations over the years, despite the attack it endured during World War I close to a century ago.

The building first housed the Peabody Leather Label Overall Company, which produced the Peabody brand overalls, known by the shiny buckles on their shoulder straps. During World War I, the company manufactured uniforms for the British Army. The company had only been in business a few years when American-based German sympathizers tried to blow up the building at 3 a.m. on June 21st, 1915.

The sympathizers placed a bomb in a hole under the building, next to the old wooden Peabody Bridge. The framework on one side of the bridge was blown away, and the other side was twisted and bent; the concrete crumbled to powder. The force of the explosion also was strong enough to blow out every window in the building. Some of the window sashes also broke and a few sills snapped.

Repairs were made, and the building went on to live a long life, becoming the starting place for several companies. R.P. Scherer produced gelatin for pharmaceutical companies, occupied the building for several years, as well as Butcher Engineering Enterprises, Lorence Enterprises, Reid Industries, and the McCord Corporation. The building also provided space for Junior Achievement of Windsor.; it was demolished in 1985.

Above: German sympathizers bungled the job when they tried to blow up the Peabody Ltd. factory in 1915. The factory manufactured uniforms for the British Army. The explosion was strong enough to blow out most of the windows. Below: The bomb was placed in the hole under the boarding of the building.

12
Paintings & Postcards from the Past

Postcards from the past
Windsor & the Border Cities
Including Walkerville, Sandwich and Ford City
VOL. 1

1957 oil painting of riverfront in Walkerville by Bernie Riendeau.

Ford City Bathing Beach.

Ford City Town Hall, Riverside Drive at Drouillard Road.

Tecumseh Boat House, foot of Devonshire Road.

Walkerville Train Station, Devonshire Road near Riverside Drive.

All postcards from the David L. Newman Postcard Collection

Hiram Walker & Sons world headquarters, grainery and malt house.

Aerial view of Walkerville c. 1935 – note giant sign and steamships.

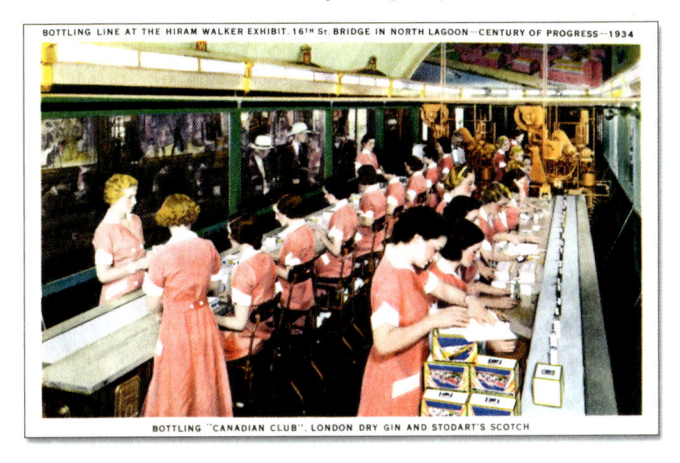

Production line at Hiram Walker & Sons.

Devonshire Road & Riverside Drive with "flat iron" building and streetcar.

The Home Bank, corner Wyandotte Street and Windermere Road.

King Edward School, built 1905 and designed by Albert Kahn.

Walkerville Ferry Landing at the foot of Devonshire Road, circa 1907.

Walkerville Golf and Country Club.

Artist rendering, Hiram Walker's original flour mill, 1859.
from Hiram Walker & Sons archives

the natural law

"We let a river shower its banks with a spirit that invades the people living there, and we protect that river, knowing without its blessing, the people have no source of soul. A river sings a holy song conveying the mysterious truth that we are a river, and if we are ignorant of this natural law, we are lost."

Thomas Moore

HMS Schooner Nancy off Moy Hall, Windsor
painting by Peter Rindlisbacher

372 • postcards and paintings from the past

Walkerville 1885 painted from a hot air balloon. Hiram Walker & Sons archives

best of the times • 373

Bird's Eye view of Factory District, Windsor.

Aerial view, armouries, riverfront c. 1905.

Aerial view of downtown Windsor and Detroit around 1925.

Pitt Street facing west, early 1900s.

Sandwich Street (Riverside Drive at Ouellette Avenue) facing east, late 1890s. All postcards from the David L. Newman Postcard Collection

Scenes from Main Street (Ouellette Avenue), Downtown Windsor

Ferry Hill, Ouellette Avenue at Sandwich Street (Riverside Drive), Windsor with views of Detroit skyline.

All postcards from the David L. Newman Postcard Collection

376 • postcards and paintings from the past

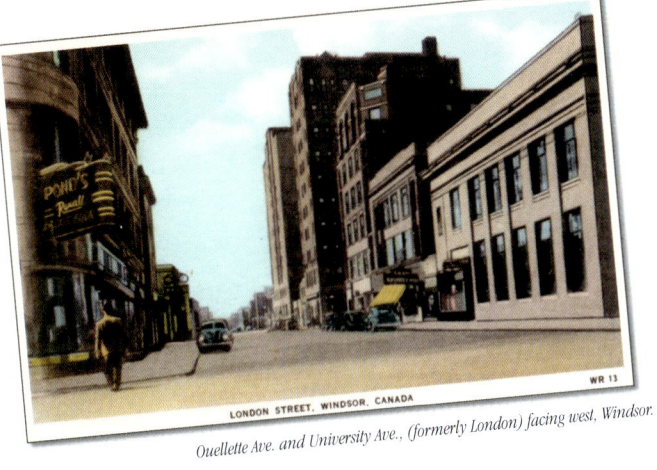

Windsor Railroad Station, foot of Goyeau Avenue at Riverside Drive.

Classic view of Ouellette Avenue looking north towards Detroit, MI.

Ouellette Ave. and University Ave., (formerly London) facing west, Windsor.

Windsor Factory District, the area bounded by Walker and Drouillard Roads, from the Detroit River to Tecumseh Rd.

Old firehall, Pitt Street at McDougall Street, Windsor.

The ferry docks of Windsor & Detroit.

All postcards from the David L. Newman Postcard Collection

378 • postcards and paintings from the past

Ferry Steamers on the Detroit River.

HARBOR, DETROIT, MICH.

best of the times • 379

Train ferry "Transfer"

Ill-fated Great Lakes luxury liner, The Noronic.

The original Fowler plan of proposed Detroit-Windsor bridge, 1924.
All postcards from the David L. Newman Postcard Collection

The "S.S. Marine Star," built in 1945 as a naval troop ship, then converted to a passenger cruise ship in 1955, and rechristened the "S.S. Aquarama."

The opening of the Ambassador Bridge and Windsor-Detroit auto and train tunnels signalled the end of the ferry steamers on the Detroit River.
All postcards from the David L. Newman Postcard Collection

Assumption Church and College, Windsor. David L. Newman Postcard Collection

Trolley line, Kingsville, Ontario. David L. Newman Postcard Collection

Old City Hall, Windsor David L. Newman Postcard Collection

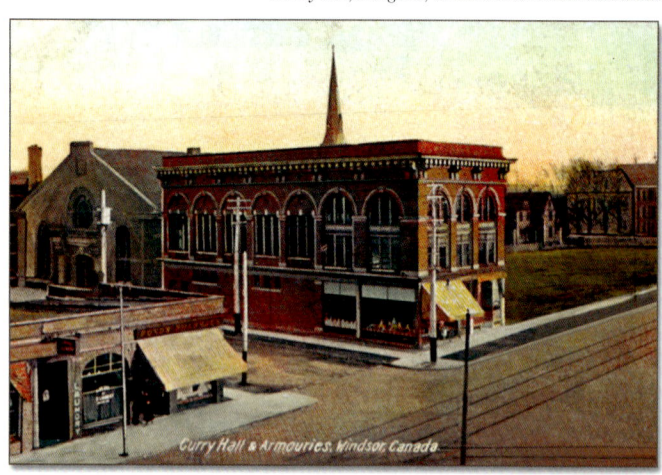

Curry Hall, Ouellette at University Avenues (formerly London Street), Windsor.
David L. Newman Postcard Collection

Remember the Chicken Court Restaurant on Pelissier in Windsor?
David L. Newman postcard Collection

Prohibition postcard
Courtesy Bill Marentette, Windsor

382 • postcards and paintings from the past

Walkerville, as painted by Nicholas Hornyansky — 1896-1965

Painter, engraver, print-maker, etcher. Born in Budapest, Hungary, Hornyansky studied portrait painting at the Academy of Fine Arts in Budapest and did postgraduate work in Paris, where he was trained in the art of the singlepull, multicolour aquatint. He came to Canada in 1929 and settled in Toronto. Hornyansky was commissioned by Hiram Walker & Sons to produce the following unique perspectives of Walkerville in the 1890s into the early twentieth century. The permanent collection of these paintings resides in a board room at the Canadian Club Brand Center in Walkerville.

All images courtesy Hiram Walker & Sons

The Gates of Willistead, 1908

The Walkerville Boat Club in winter, 1895

The Crown Inn, Devonshire Road near Riverside Drive, 1905

Race between the generations, Devonshire Road, 1895

*The Walkerville Ferry Docks
sketched from the roof of the Walker grain silos, 1900*

Lake Erie and Detroit Railroad Station, Walkerville, 1899

The Walker Farms, 1905

Walkerville Fire Station, Walker Road, 1902

Willistead Manor, 1908

13
Cover Story

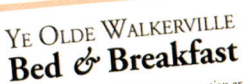

Birth of The Walkerville Times
March 1999

Issue #2
May/June 1999

Issue #3
July/August 1999

Issue #4
September/October 1999

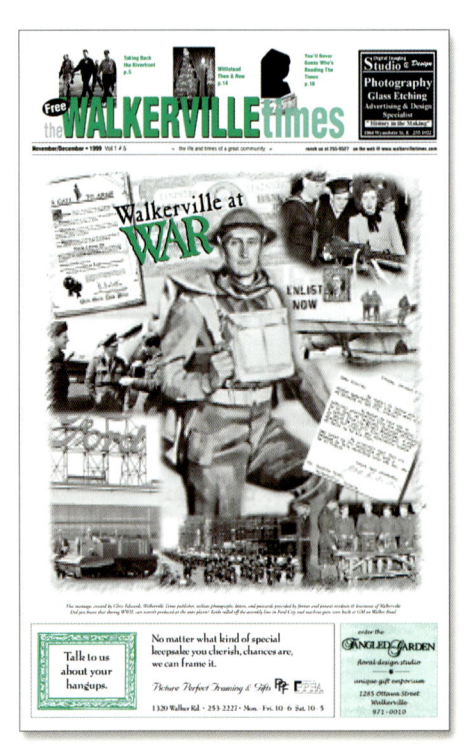

Issue #5
November 1999
(1st Remembrance Day Special)

Issue #6
Christmas 1999

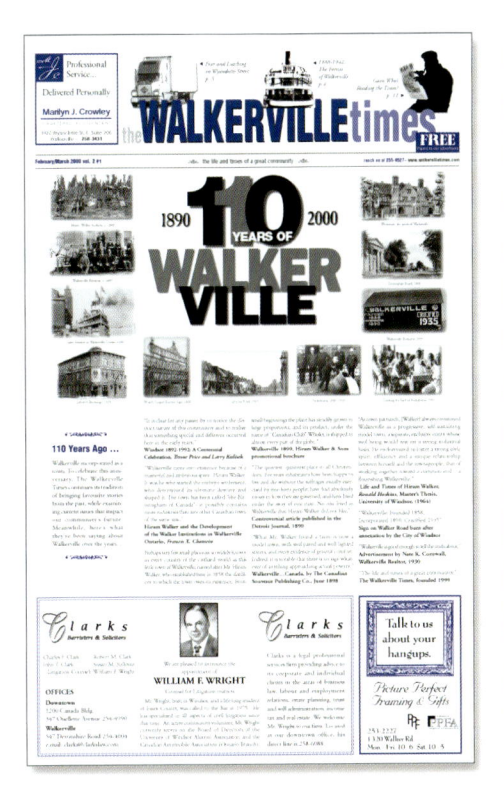

Issue #7
February/March 2000

Issue #8
April/May 2000

Issue #9
June/July 2000

Issue #10
September/October 2000

Issue #11
November 2000
(2nd Remembrance Day Special)

Issue #12
Christmas 2000
(1st full colour cover)

Issue #13
February 2001

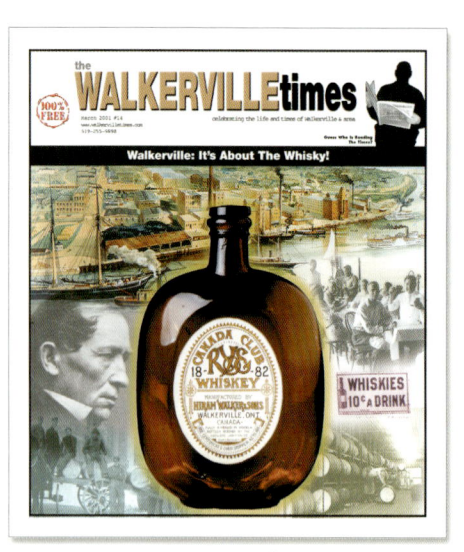

Issue #14
March 2001

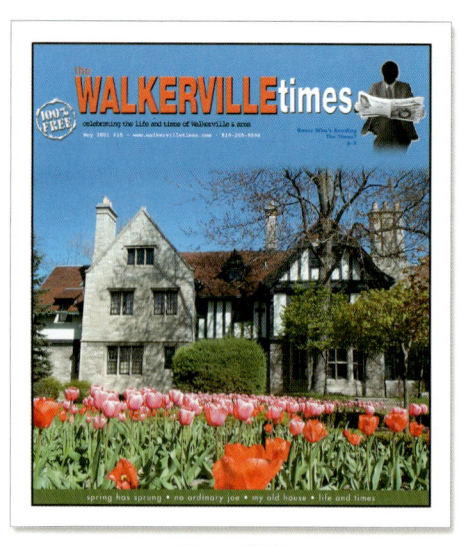

Issue #15
May 2001

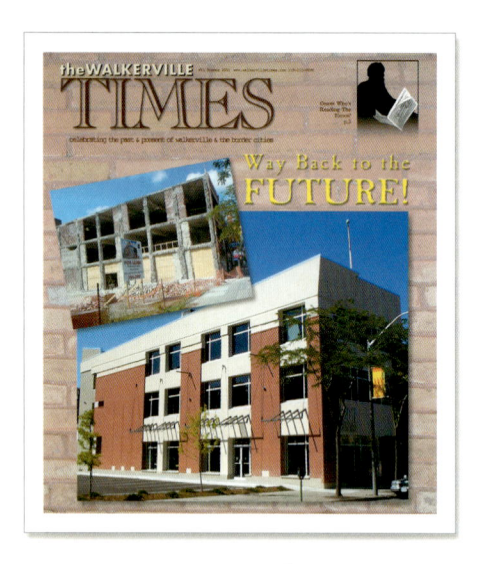

Issue #16
Summer 2001

Issue #17
September 2001

Issue #18
October 2001

Issue #19
November 2001
(3rd Remembrance Day Special)

Issue #20
Christmas 2001

Issue #21
February 2002

Issue #22
March 2002

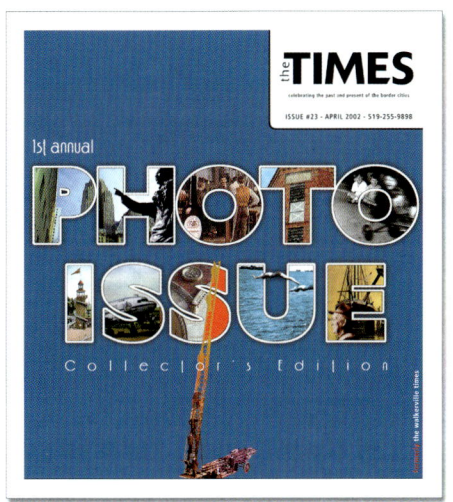

Issue #23
April 2002
(1st Annual Photo Issue)

Issue #24
May 2002

Issue #25
June 2002

Issue #26
Summer 2002

Issue #27
September 2002

Issue #28
October 2002

Issue #29
November 2002
(4th Remembrance Day Special)

Issue #30
Christmas 2002

Issue #31
February 2003

Issue #32
March 2003

Issue #33
April 2003

Issue #34
May 2003

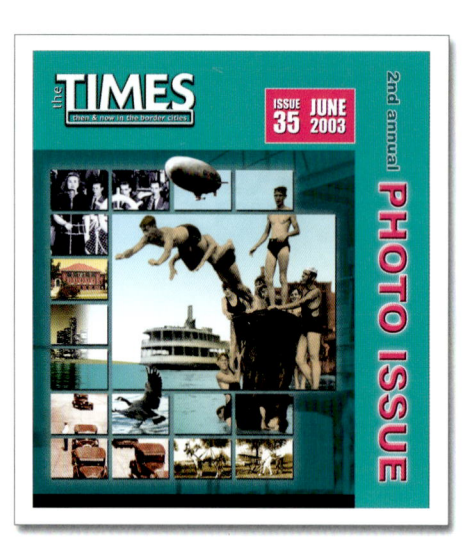

Issue #35
June 2003
(2nd Annual Photo Issue)

Issue #36
Summer 2003

Issue #37
September 2003

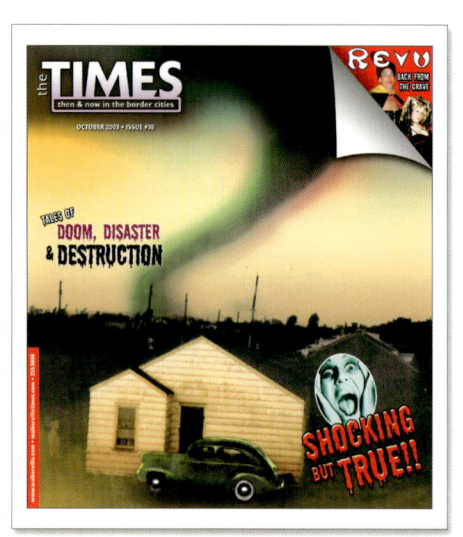

Issue #38
October 2003

Issue #39
November 2003
(5th Remembrance Day Special)

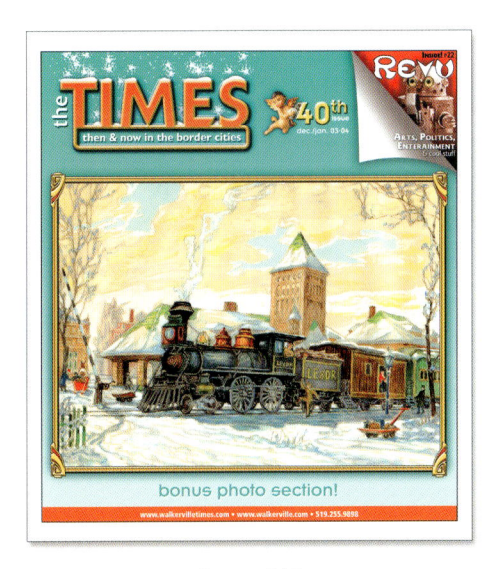

Issue #40
Christmas 2003

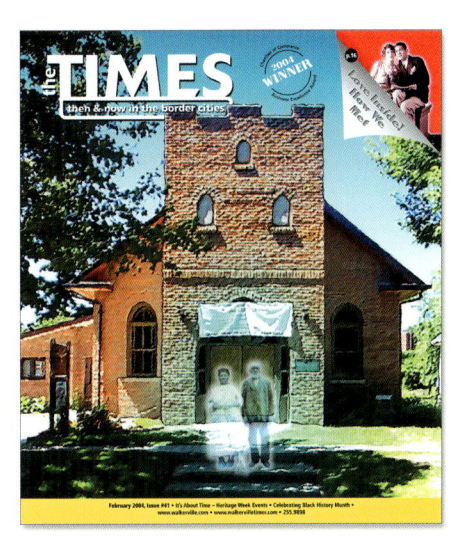

Issue #41
February 2004

Issue #42
March 2004

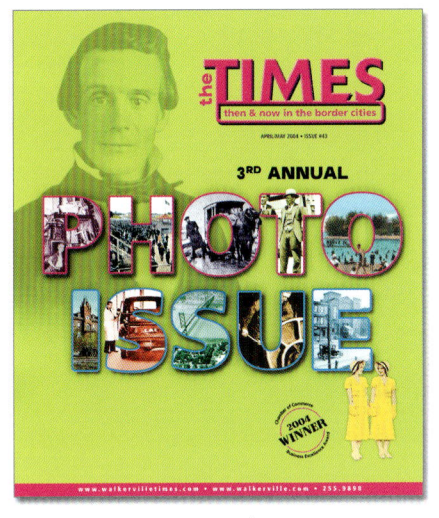

Issue #43
April/May 2004
(3th Annual Photo Issue)

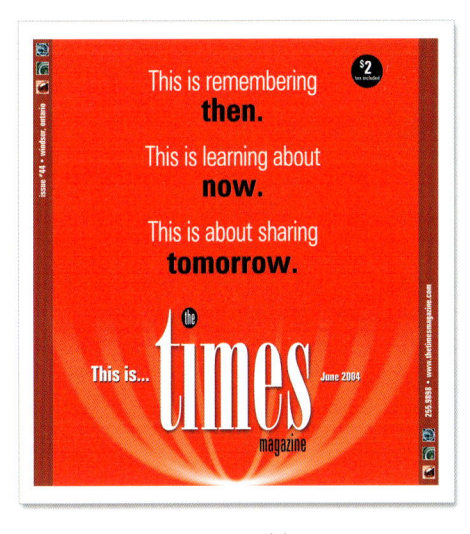

Issue #44
June 2004

Issue #45
July 2004

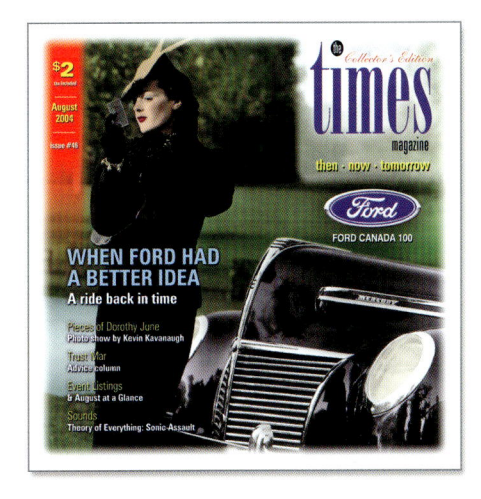

Issue #46
August 2004

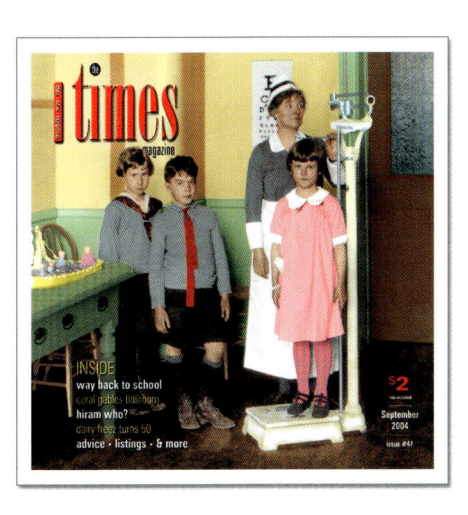

Issue #47
September 2004

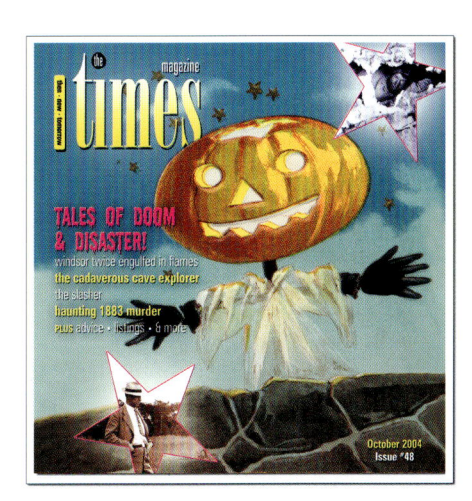

Issue #48
October 2004

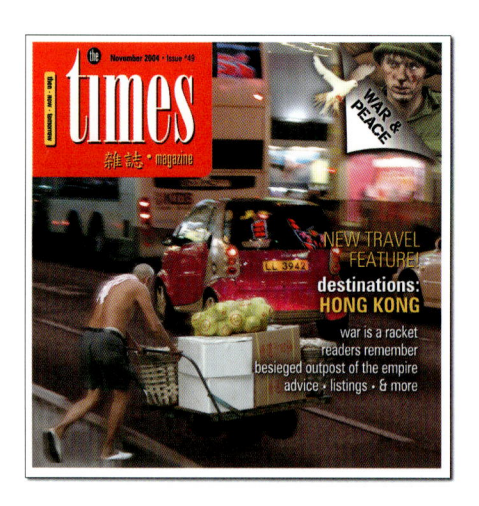

Issue #49
November 2004

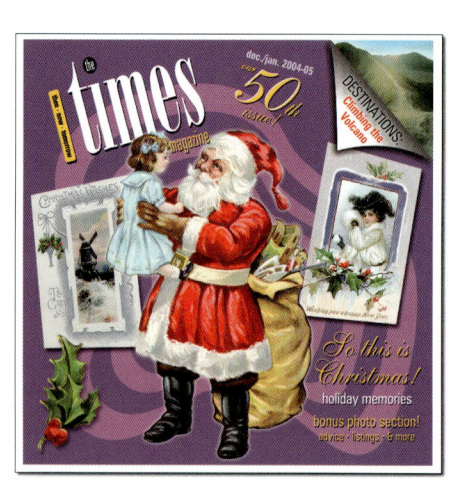

Issue #50
Christmas 2004

Issue #51
February 2005

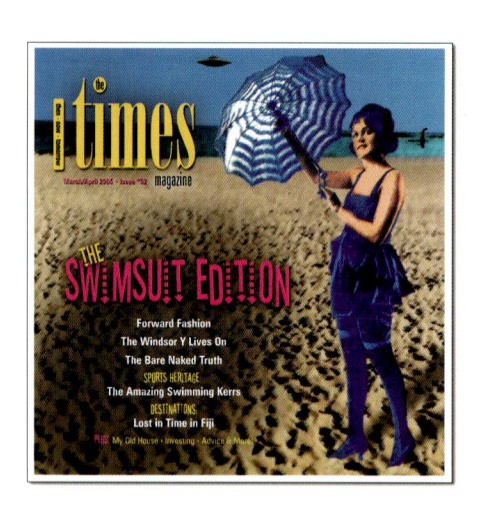

Issue #52
March/April 2005

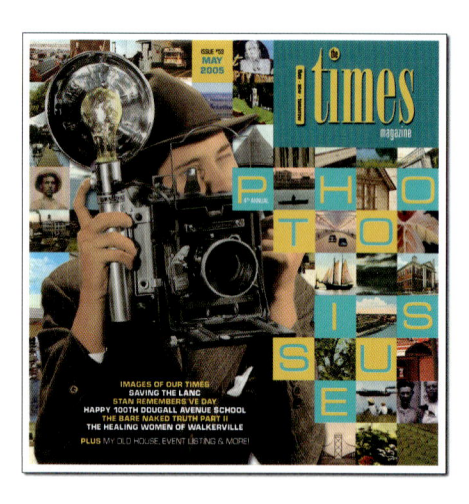

Issue #53
May/June 2005
(4th Annual Photo Issue)

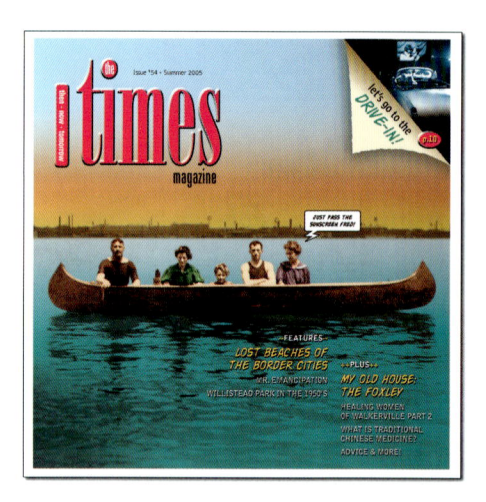

Issue #54
July/August 2005

Issue #55
September/October 2005

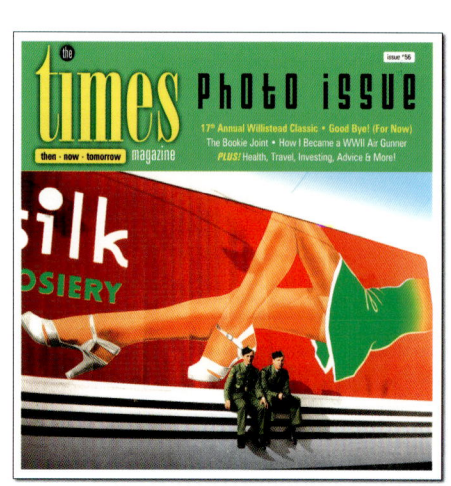

Issue #56
November/Christmas 2005

Need more to read?

Selected back issues of The TIMES are still available with more stories, readers' letters and photos!

For copies call 519-255-9898 or email elaine@walkerville.com

We're History!

Going down once, going down twice...

It was indeed an honour learning we had created something considered significant enough to be chosen to "go down in history." Twice over the seven years *The TIMES Magazine* was in print, several copies were meticulously sealed inside time capsules in the Windsor area for future generations to unearth.

Dan Tullio, Director – Brand Heritage, Hiram Walker's & Sons, and Tish Harcus, Assistant to the Director – Brand Heritage, Hiram Walker's & Sons, are seen at right placing two issues of *The TIMES Magazine* in a Canadian Club crate in September, 2002. The crate was then placed in a specially constructed steel time capsule and buried on the north lawn behind Hiram Walker's newly-christened Brand Heritage Centre in the company's Canadian Club Brand Centre on Riverside Drive. These two issues of *The TIMES* were chosen for inclusion in the capsule, as they contained informative articles about the history of the 148-year-old company, and its founder, Hiram Walker.

photo C. Edwards

Windsor Regional Cancer Centre Time Capsule Committee members Nancy Morton, Carol Webster, (head of the committee), Barb Ouellette, and Mary Hone stand with a time capsule buried in 2001 in the cornerstone of the new centre, attached to Windsor Regional Hospital - Metropolitan Campus, in South Walkerville. photo E. Weeks

A custom-made, stainless steel time capsule was buried at the new Windsor Regional Cancer Centre in November 2001. Inside was a message from CEO Dr. Ethan Laukkanen to Windsorites who would some day open the container, predictions of what life would be like 100 years hence by Hugh Beaton Elementary School students, and examples of current Canadian stamps and currency.

Times reader Carol Webster, Senior Health Records Technician at the Cancer Centre (second from left), was in charge of the Time Capsule Committee. She loved our magazine so much, she asked us if she could include copies in the capsule.

Two issues of *The Walkerville Times* from September and October 2001 (which includes a story about the 1927 time-capsule unearthed during construction of the Centre) were inserted into the capsule.

No other publication was chosen for this honour! (Since we produced a heritage-focused publication, what could have been more appropriate?)

Legacy Profiles

Legacy Profile

Anchor Lamina Inc.

In 1975, we bought a company doing only $400,000 a year in sales; it was losing money and would require a great deal of effort to move it forward. To stand in the shop as I did and promise everyone decent wages, good working conditions, paid benefits, and profit-sharing was very ambitious and optimistic. But it was also realistic; I knew we could do it. If everyone cooperated and worked together as a team, there was no limit to what we could achieve.

Clare E. Winterbottom

Creating the World's Largest Die Set Manufacturer

Anchor Lamina's rise from an obscure player to an international powerhouse in the die set industry has become the stuff of local legend around Windsor. What is lesser known is how the company achieved its success.

The die set industry was considered past its prime, with few prospects for growth, when in 1975, a group of investors, including myself, purchased troubled Anchor Machine and Manufacturing Ltd. in Mississauga, a company with an uncertain future.

But we knew better.

Anchor Lamina Inc. is truly a "Made in Windsor" success story. Built on the foundation of a money-losing plant in Mississauga, it eventually became the largest die set manufacturer in the world!

More than thirty years later, the question I am frequently asked is: "How did you do it, Clare?"

Hence, the idea for a book that would not only celebrate the 30th anniversary of the company's founding in 1975, but would also act as a "how to" guide of sorts for striving entrepreneurs and business students.

Within the pages of *"Made in Windsor – The Anchor Lamina Way"* is the true story of how a group of men rolled up their sleeves and built a company that became the world leader in die set supplies and manufacturing, with 14 factories in three countries, utilizing the most modern equipment and technologies in the industry, eventually employing almost 1,000 highly trained workers.

Along the way, there was plenty of hard work, but we also had a lot of fun, because we really enjoyed the work we did.

I recognized early on that we would need the support of all our workers to become successful. I believed then, as I do now, that everyone had to feel they were benefiting from the company's success, so I established a profit sharing program and encouraged all employees to buy stock in the company. While very much in fashion today, back in 1975, employee stock ownership and profit-sharing were considered radical concepts. And yet, these two innovative programs were crucial pillars that allowed us to deliver high-quality products at a fair price, in Canada, the United States and Europe.

As described in this book, we stuck to a pretty simple business formula, built on several key pillars: hire and maintain the best-trained work force, produce the highest quality products, seek out friendly acquisitions, and purchase the latest equipment with the largest capacity in the industry, regardless of the economic conditions. Everything revolved around three simple words: service, service, service. Anchor Lamina set a new standard for highly professional service in its industry.

I once told the men we had an excellent opportunity to become a major factor in the industry in Canada, since we knew what we were doing, and that it was simply a matter of working together as a team. This approach enabled us to tackle problems within our business, take full advantage of the strength of individual members, but also ensure their weaknesses did not interfere with important decisions, nor slow the momentum required to maintain our growth.

And the rest, as they say, is history.

Clare E. Winterbottom, August, 2006

(turn to page 406 for more information about "Made in Windsor– The Anchor Lamina Way," by Clare E. Winterbottom with Chris Edwards, produced by Walkerville Publishing)

Legacy Profile

City of Windsor

The first visitors to our area busied themselves establishing lines of trade between the fur-producing wilderness and the markets of old-world Europe. Upon this trade, and what economists today call its "trickle down" effects, a pair of prosperous communities began to grow along the banks of the Detroit River. The earliest settlers were of French extraction, a fact reflected in local place names and less obviously in the configurations of major roads, initially influenced by the long, narrow fields of the "seigneurial" system of farmland allotment.

In 1796, the now independent United States took control of Michigan from the British, and an international border was established mid-river. This geo-political boundary remains an essential determinant of the region's cultural identity and economic outlook.

Time plowed forward, and Windsor evolved from a huddle of farm fields across the way from Fort Pontchartrain (Detroit) into an independent frontier community. A thing called the Underground Railroad guided oppressed slaves from the south to the nearest and most welcoming border point. Schools, hospitals, fire halls and saloons went up. A church gradually evolved into a university. A man named Walker started making whisky. A thing called the Volstead Act launched Prohibition – described by one American wag as "better than no booze at all." The illicit cross-border trade was irresistibly profitable, albeit treacherous.

Meanwhile, a man named Ford had established one of his automotive manufactories here. It, along with those of other auto barons, was changing the landscape in big ways. People everywhere, infatuated with shiny cars and the mobility they afforded, pumped millions into the border communities, and shaped a skyline that echoed the car-makers' towering fortunes. While mass production made cars more affordable, workers' unions strove to make the production process more humane. Their success too, dramatically altered the economic landscape.

In time, the flow of international trade converging on our strategic location made Windsor a major checkpoint along the North American superhighway. Diversification in the form of increased tourism brought a measure of welcome stability to the auto plants' remorseless cycles, and the industry was bolstered by the opening of Casino Windsor.

And still the city grows. Today, people visit Windsor in numbers unimaginable by our forebears. It's a vibrant riverfront community that combines economic opportunity, exceptional lifestyle and a strategic location at the busiest Canadian-American border crossing. And the unmistakable feeling, throughout the community, is that the best is yet to come.

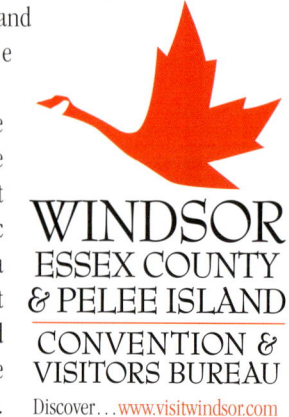

WINDSOR ESSEX COUNTY & PELEE ISLAND CONVENTION & VISITORS BUREAU

Discover... www.visitwindsor.com

Legacy Profile

R.J. Cyr Co.

"Conveyors of Ideas" since 1958

Born to French-Canadian prairie homesteaders in 1923, Raymond Joseph (R.J.) Cyr left the Saskatchewan farm at the age of 14. During the Great Depression he worked his way across the country on farms, lumber camps, construction of the St. Lawrence Seaway and eventually learned the conveyor business from C.H. McInnis.

Common to many young men of the day, Ray lied about his age and joined the navy. While at home convalescing from an appendectomy performed in the North Atlantic in 1943, he met "Jo," a Ukrainian nurse at the local hospital. Raymond and Josephine re-united after the war, married in Windsor and raised their family in Walkerville.

In 1958, the couple founded R.J. Cyr Co., in a converted bus garage at 1263 McDougall Street in Windsor's then industrial heartland.

current facility occupies 40,000 square feet

original R.J. Cyr location in a converted bus garage

Ray's no-nonsense, keep it simple ethic spoke for itself as the fledging firm steadily grew in diversity, customer base and reputation. By 1973, R. J. Cyr had out grown the neighbourhood and moved to its present location at Highway 401, Exit 14 on the outskirts of Windsor.

R.J. Cyr's current facility occupies over 40,000 square feet. We are a full-service material handling firm providing custom and standard design engineering, manufacturing and field installation services. Virtually every motor vehicle produced in North America contains a part that has already "had a ride" on one of our conveyors. From scrap metal to seats, tires to transmissions, R. J. Cyr conveys ideas.

The firm prides itself on the company (and the companies) it keeps. Proof of our commitment to products and services that meet and exceed expectations are the customers who have been with us since 1958. While we've changed too, our reasons for doing business together haven't. World-class manufacturing standards are maintained by a stable work force which is truly the firm's most valued asset. Quality, training, innovation, profit sharing, feedback – all spells good business. As it was in 1958, our reputation speaks for itself.

Until his death in 2001, Ray's other passion was hunting. A sportsman and conservationist, he traveled the world in its pursuit and acquired a collection of over 70 "trophy" species. He shot more buffalo than any man in recorded history and by reducing the adult male and predator population, saved the Wood Buffalo from near extinction in the early 1960s.

R.J. Cyr Co. has remained under family ownership and management now entrusted to Randall Jay (Randy). Since 1971 he has assumed every task in the enterprise as part of his personal "apprenticeship" and has taken an active roll in every major project and evolution the company has experienced.

Although its main focus is the material handling business, R.J. Cyr Co.'s main service has always been ideas. While its founders, Raymond and Josephine have passed on, their dream and spirit is alive and well in the R. J. Cyr family of dedicated employees who continue to define success in business as a journey, and not a destination.

Le plus on change, le plus en revient.

Ray Cyr was an avid sportsman and conservationist

Dillon Hall, built in 1927, is the campus' signature building, even today.

Legacy Profile

University of Windsor

The University of Windsor can trace its roots back almost 150 years, to the small college for boys that opened its doors in 1857. Its students have borne witness to its unique evolution from a religious college to a non-denominational university, prevailing in the face of challenges, naysayers and often, long odds.

Geographically and historically, it has close links with Assumption Parish, first established in 1748 as a mission to the Huron Indians. In 1767, it was raised to the official status of a parish – the oldest west of Montreal.

Under the direction of Father Pierre Point S.J., the parish priest of Assumption Church, the cornerstone of the college was laid in the spring of 1855, and blessed by the Bishop of Detroit. Assumption was originally 90 feet long, 50 feet wide and 43 feet high, spread among three storeys. The building cost $11,000.

Classes began on February 10, 1857 for 20 boarders and 60 day students. The first few years were difficult, with the rapid succession of presidents, including a Benedictine who unfortunately was misjudged on his ability to speak sufficient English and French. In 1870, the Basilians returned, and under the direction of a remarkable president, Father Denis O'Connor, achieved success. President of the college from 1870 to 1890, he undertook two major building renovations at a cost of $20,000 and $35,000 that are reflected in the gothic structure seen today.

In 1919, the College became affiliated with Western University (later the University of Western Ontario). The London institution was very proprietary and, in 1920, the Bishop of London proposed that the entire Assumption College and community move to London – a move that the Assumption Basilians appealed successfully to Rome to deny.

Between 1934 and 1962, an association with Holy Names College, administered by the Sisters of the Holy Names of Jesus and Mary, allowed Assumption to be co-educational. The link with Western was terminated in 1953, with Assumption then granted its own university powers by an act of the Ontario Legislature. Its president, Father E.C. LeBel, put the affairs of the university on a more solid financial basis by placing the Engineering, Commerce, Nursing and Science Departments under a separate organization, the non-denominational Essex College, which permitted public funding to go directly to these units. Essex College affiliated with Assumption University in 1954.

In 1957, Fr. LeBel carried through an extraordinary decision that caused astonishment in Rome, in England, and within the Canadian university community. Assumption, a Roman Catholic university, affiliated with Canterbury College, an Anglican institution! (In 1964 similar recognition was extended to Iona College, under the auspices of the United Church.)

In 1962, the University of Windsor was established by an act of the Ontario Legislature, and accepted Assumption University in federation. The University of Windsor assumed control of the campus in July 1963. New departments, schools and colleges developed as the university moved from its basic structure as a liberal arts college into that of a university.

In 1964 Dr. Francis Leddy became president of the University of Windsor, and presided over a period of explosive growth. From 1967-77, Windsor grew from approximately 1,500 to 8,000 students.

The 1980s and early 1990s continued this growth, particularly under the leadership of President Ron Ianni. Several buildings were erected during this time period, including the Odette Business Building and the CAW Student Centre.

Current president Dr. Ross Paul introduced his vision for the university, "The Best of Both Worlds," in 1999, building on the foundation of Windsor's broad range of programs and its personal touch. Enrolment reached record heights in fall 2003 as both OAC and Grade 12 students converged on Ontario campuses in a double cohort. The University of Windsor invested more than $50 million in a new student residence, the Anthony P. Toldo Health Education Centre, the Jackman Dramatic Art Centre, the Centre for Automotive Research Education, and in classroom and lab upgrades.

Dr. Paul's current strategic plan, "To Greater Heights," will take the university to 2009. It envisions a University of Windsor recognized for its three pinnacles – automotive, environmental and social justice – and most particularly, for the qualities of its graduates.

Today, the University of Windsor covers 51 hectares (125 acres) at the foot of the Ambassador Bridge. It offers more than 140 undergraduate and graduate programs across nine faculties for 15,000 full- and part-time students. It offers nine cooperative education programs for 1,100 students. More than 80,000 individuals around the world are proud to call the university their alma mater.

With a recent successful bond issue, and plans for a new engineering facility and a medical school, the University of Windsor is well-poised to capitalize on its strengths.

Almost 150 years since its humble beginnings, the University of Windsor remains committed to fulfilling a vision as a unique institution – proud of its past and ready for the future.

Ambassador Bridge, 1929
When walking on the University of Windsor campus, one of the most striking visuals is that of the Ambassador Bridge just west, and within a few hundred feet, of the university – a towering mass of steel and cables rising majestically to link two countries.

The two institutions stood side by side for more than seven decades. In 1994, the symbolic partnership was transformed into reality with the announcement that the university would hold a licence for a duty free shop on bridge property to be operated by the Canadian Transit Company (CTC). And, in 2001, the Ambassador Bridge Corporation announced a $1.1 million donation by the Ambassador Bridge Duty Free Store.

"We are blessed by the generosity of the Ambassador Bridge Corporation," says University of Windsor President Ross Paul. "Over the years, we have worked together on many initiatives. We are truly grateful to have such a unique opportunity for partnership with our neighbour."

photo courtesy Windsor's Community Museum P5488

Legacy Profile

Windsor Grove ~ Windsor Memorial Gardens

Honouring Lives Well Lived

Soon after the arrival of the Great Western Railway in 1854 hundreds of families from eastern cities, towns and farms traveled to the village of Windsor in search of a new life. Many put down roots and helped Windsor grow up into a proper city.

When Windsor Grove opened its gates in 1866 to provide burial services for the early inhabitants, Windsor had gained town status but still only comprised a few streets along the Detroit River. Almost a century and a half later, the city would be virtually unrecognizable to those long gone residents.

Windsor Grove's registry ledger, dating back to the Grove's inception, reveals many of these names that helped mold 21st century Windsor. Not surprisingly, the first mayor of Windsor (1858), Samuel Smith Macdonell, is buried in Windsor Grove. Samuel was also a successful land developer and businessman, and had been re-elected mayor when the cemetery opened.

F. S. Seagrave, originally of Columbus, Ohio, was a highly respected manufacturer of fire trucks (his factory still stands on Walker Road). His dome-shaped mausoleum serves as an intriguing monument to this American entrepreneur who chose to be interred in his adopted city in the early 1900s.

Perhaps one of the most famous and historical inhabitants of Windsor Grove is Gordon McGregor, who helped establish Ford Canada in Windsor in 1904. Shortly after McGregor's auspicious meeting with Henry Ford in a small Walkerville tavern to sign the deal the Canadian company was launched in an old wagon works on the waterfront.

400 • best of the times

This small but momentous event signaled the dawn of Windsor's massive and still thriving automotive industry. After McGregor's passing in March, 1922, his funeral cortege, one of the largest ever seen in Windsor, reached Windsor Grove before the last car had taken on mourners at his house on Victoria Avenue at Wyandotte Street.

Bailiffs, police magistrates, schoolmasters, barristers and builders also chose Windsor Grove as their final home. So did an interesting cross section of people who comprised the fabric that was Windsor in the late 1800s and early 1900s: laborers like blacksmiths, tinsmiths, livery workers, ferry men, farmers, plumbers, railway men, painters, boat builders and Hiram Walker workers can be found side by side with commercial and retail owners including shoemakers, barbers, grocers, ice dealers, confectioners, tailors, booksellers, bakers, hotel and store keepers. Even a pork packer by the name of William Ferguson was laid to rest here.

Due to the times, the women were given considerably less import: women like Mary Woods and Maggie Peters were identified merely as widow and servant while Miss Margaret Wallace will be known for all eternity as "spinster."

When Windsor Grove first opened, it was on the outskirts of town, but as Windsor grew, well-established residential and commercial districts soon surrounded its high wrought iron fence. It is now bounded by Giles Boulevard on the north, Howard Avenue on the east, Mercer Street to the west and Ellis Road to the south.

As Windsor Grove neared capacity, its sister cemetery, the spacious Windsor Memorial Gardens, opened in 1968 on Division Road south of Devonshire Mall near Cabana Road. With the recent unveiling of Windsor Memorial's elegant new mausoleum, which complements the original structure built shortly after the cemetery opened, even more burial options are available to Windsorites seeking a centrally located final resting spot.

Windsor Memorial welcomes all faiths and denominations and has allocated sections for ethnic groups, and includes a special area honouring our veterans. Cremations, which have become increasingly popular, can be performed on-site at the crematorium; a wide variety of niches are available for purchase.

While the funeral business has changed dramatically from 140 years ago when the dearly departed were laid out in the front parlour and then driven by horse and carriage to the graveyard, the tradition of providing personal and caring help at what can be a difficult time has been perpetuated by Windsor Memorial Gardens.

In keeping with its slogan, "Honouring Lives Well Lived" Windsor-owned and operated Windsor Memorial Gardens is proud to offer affordable burial and cremation options for all citizens of Windsor and area. Contrary to public belief, a select number of spots are still available in Windsor Grove that can accommodate those seeking an historical setting.

Whether choosing pre-planning packages or leaving it up to family to take care of the details, the staff of Windsor Memorial Gardens can be relied on to provide experienced and sensitive assistance in honouring and respecting the lives and memory of "lives well lived."

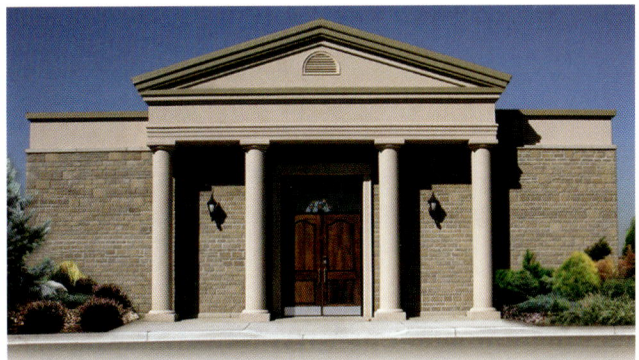

Left: Entrance to Windsor Memorial Gardens; F. S. Seagrave mausoleum in the Windsor Grove Cemetery

Right: Veterans area in Windsor Memorial; Windsor Memorial's new mausoleum. Since the time of Egyptian Pharaohs, above ground internment in a mausoleum has been the burial method of choice for those preferring something other than an earth burial. For centuries, mausoleums were only available to a few, but today the "burial of Kings" is an affordable option to anyone; A beautiful spot of tranquility within Windsor Memorial's spacious grounds

photo: E. Weeks

Legacy Profile

Bert Weeks 1917-1990 ~ Mayor, Humanitarian, Visionary

Born in Montreal in 1917, Bert Weeks moved with his wife Sheila and twin daughters to Windsor in 1946. Surprisingly, one of his main reasons for moving here was because, as he later put it, "Windsor looked like a town to become Mayor of."

A watchmaker by trade, Weeks set up a watch repair and jewelry business in downtown Windsor. He soon realized all was not well in his new city due to police indifference to widespread corruption. He decided he could do something to help.

Weeks organized what became known as the "Citizens Action Committee" and met secretly with OPP officers in Detroit, out of sight of Windsor police, to pass along information. He never tired of telling how, when invited to meet with some shady characters, he was offered a gun for protection. He decided to take a large screwdriver instead, reasoning that he could say, if questioned, he was on his way to fix a clock.

As a result of Weeks' evidence, a massive shakeup occurred in 1950; the Chief of Police, his deputy, two police commissioners and the Crown Attorney were all forced to resign. *(see Portrait of a Scandal, p. 198)*

With this impressive success under his belt, Weeks began his quest for the mayor's seat. He ran for a spot on city council but this would not prove to be as simple as risking his life to help clean up his adopted city. He lost in his first attempt but won an alderman's seat in 1954.

Weeks also tried his luck running for provincial and federal seats. Considered by some "a dangerous socialist" due to his affiliations with the CCF party (the predecessor to the New Democratic Party), his efforts were unsuccessful.

In 1965, after a couple of fruitless attempts to gain the coveted mayor's seat, he was again elected to Windsor council as an alderman. He never lost a municipal election again.

In 1975 Weeks was finally voted into the mayor's office and was easily elected for two more terms before retiring in 1982. To this day many people regard him as one of Windsor's finest mayors.

During his years in office, Weeks was a tireless city booster and was instrumental in several city-twinning efforts. He was dedicated to pursuing industrial investment in Windsor including General Motor's Transmission Plant, the Maple Leaf Monarch Oil-Processing Plant, Birla Industries and many others.

One of his most impressive accomplishments was ensuring the Ford Essex Engine Plant was built in Windsor rather than losing it to Lima, Ohio in the late 1970s. Weeks also convinced the government to kick in $65 million towards bringing the plant here.

Hardships suffered during his formative years in the Great Depression had a huge and profound affect on Weeks. As a result he developed both socialistic tendencies and a fiscal conservative outlook. When he discovered the city was losing out on transfer grant monies, Weeks pestered the province into finally passing along $20 million the city was entitled to. Upon retirement, he left the Mayor's office with a balanced budget.

Weeks continued to be extremely active in civic affairs. He served as Chair of the Windsor Utilities Commission, was a member of the Harbour Commission and was a founding member of the Greater Windsor Community Foundation. He also served for many years on the Windsor Housing Authority which is dedicated to building housing for low-income seniors and families. During his years with the Utilities Commission, Weeks led the way to converting city street lights to the more economical sodium luminaries, thus saving the city many thousands of dollars in energy costs annually.

Weeks also actively supported many global causes such as Unicef, the Children's Aid Society and Amnesty International. He organized local committees on behalf of refugees such as those from the 1956 Hungarian uprising, Hong Kong in 1960, and Czechoslovakia and Uganda in later years. And he was the first city mayor to organize assistance for the Vietnamese "boat people" in 1978.

Weeks loved parks, gardens and fountains. In his spare time, he indulged in his passion for gardening, then translated this devotion into greening the city. For 20 years he fought for the continued planning, acquisition and non-commercial development of riverfront lands. He spearheaded the acquisition of railway lands, a crucial step in his plan for an unbroken stretch of parkland along five kilometres of riverfront from the Ambassador Bridge to the Canadian Club distillery.

Weeks was also instrumental in the development of nine city parks including Ganatchio Park, Ganatchio Trail, Malden Park, Stop 26, Coventry Gardens, Lakeview Marina, Sandpoint Beach, Peche Island Landing, Goose Bay and Plaza Udine. Weeks guided the city in obtaining major parks in Windsor's west end including portions of Ojibway Prairie Complex, and set the foundation for the Windsor Trail – a walk/cycle trail that is expanding to encircle the city.

Bert Weeks' death in 1990 from cancer was a huge loss to Windsor. In 2005, he was commemorated with the opening of Bert Weeks Memorial Gardens (BWMG), a spectacular fountain and garden on a two-acre site along the city's eastern section of riverfront – on former railway land. A more fitting location could not have been imagined.

BWMG was designed by Windsor architect Michele R. Di Maio who envisioned it as representing various stages of Weeks' life. Its circular shape and futuristic looking noon mark in the the reflecting pond pay homage to Weeks' trade as a watchmaker. The bubbling font at the top of the park, the dramatic curved waterfall plunging into a reflecting pond, and the small waterfall flowing towards the river and over a plaque describing Weeks' life symbolize his birth, career and death.

Bert Weeks did not live to see his riverfront dream come true but his time in Windsor left the city with an indelible legacy. He is survived by his second wife Sheelagh, his children Carolyn Chedour, Barbara Moluchi, Howard Weeks, Brenda Weeks-Clarke, Elaine Weeks and Douglas Weeks, step children David Beneteau and Catherine Hay, eight grandchildren and four great grandchildren.

"I believe people want more green space, not commercial space along the river." Bert Weeks, Windsor mayor, 1975-1982

top left: Bert Weeks Memorial Gardens looking west, photo Elaine Weeks
top, this page: Bert Weeks early 1980s, photo Pat Sturn
left: a bird's eye view, photo George Mock

Legacy Profile

St-Leonard's Society

Nothing is known for certain of St. Leonard's history, as his early "life," written in the eleventh century, has no historical value whatever. So let's begin with the legend that recounts a sixth century French monk named Leonard who saved the lives of both the Queen and her newborn daughter, Bertoara.

A grateful King Clovis granted Leonard a huge tract of land, where he built a monastery christened Noblac. The King permitted Leonard to take prisoners under his care at Noblac, and then release them when they had proved themselves ready. St. Leonard became the patron saint of prisoners; his icon is generally represented holding broken chains in his hands.

In 1962, the first St. Leonard's half-way home in Canada opened its doors right here in Windsor, to welcome men who had spent time behind bars and needed a safe haven to make a clean start.

A practical and determined Anglican priest named Thomas Neil Libby and his supporters developed a vision of helping offenders to rehabilitate, in a social climate where ex-offenders were regarded as unfit and undeserving of any support.

Neil Libby pioneered the halfway house movement in Canada; today there are sixteen Society homes and affiliates across the country. Yet, when the first St. Leonard's House was proposed in Windsor, it was greeted with extraordinary resistance. Neighborhoods and local politicians rallied against the idea of housing "ex-cons." They waved fists in town meetings, screamed telephone threats to Board members and wrote angry letters to newspaper editors describing the dangers and risks to their wives and children, property values and business income.

All this, however, only strengthened the resolve of the founding members and convinced them of the importance of their mission.

Over 40 years later, St. Leonard's has earned this community's support. Situated in a non-descript, split-level building on Victoria Avenue in downtown Windsor, St. Leonard's Society has intentionally kept a low profile, to prevent residents from being singled out as they quietly rebuild their lives.

And yet, St. Leonard's is much more than the bricks and mortar of a building. A United Way supported agency since 1968, the society's services are designed to give back to the community that supports its work with ex-offenders.

St. Leonard's provides a place to live for those who have been in trouble with the law, and an opportunity to remove the stigma of being an ex-con through guidance, counseling, and understanding. St. Leonard's also advocates reforms to the social justice system, to ensure that those who leave prison do not return to the community less able to live crime-free than when they left it.

The Society has steadily grown and responded to the changing needs of subgroups such as probationers, young men and women in conflict with the law, and those dependent on alcohol and drugs. Programs have been expanded to include life skills and job placement training, intermittent programs, and Lifeline, which helps those who have received long-term sentences to readjust to "life on the outside."

Currently, there are sixteen Society homes and affiliates across the country. St. Leonard's Society continues to be active in Correctional Services and frequently makes presentations to parliament and other provincial government groups on issues that concern the incarcerated and released offender. They also organize seminars for the public, and develop position papers on the judicial system.

The strength and heart of the society's work rests on building genuine one-on-one friendships with the people they serve in a setting of support – a place where they are challenged to value themselves and to actively find meaning in their lives through education, employment and relationships within the community.

"Unless our society can redeem those who go astray, we can hardly call ourselves civilized; and, anyone doing the work being undertaken in St. Leonard's halfway houses deserves the support of all who believe in human dignity." Stanley Knowles, M.P.

The St. Leonard's Society of Canada continues its work in response to the changing social justice environment in Canada.

Neil Libby pioneered the halfway house movement in Canada right here in Windsor; today there are twenty Society homes and affiliates across the country.

"A non-descript, split-level building on Victoria Avenue in downtown Windsor"

About Walkerville Publishing

Established in 1998, Walkerville Publishing is a full-service traditional
and new media publishing house based in Windsor, Ontario.
Capabilities include graphic design, copy writing, editing, website development
and promotion, corporate marketing and communication strategies.

Owned and operated by Chris Edwards, M.A., and Elaine Weeks, B.A.,
Walkerville Publishing also assists authors interested in self-publishing
high-quality, professionally edited and designed soft and hardcover books.

For more information or to view our online portfolio,
please visit www.walkerville.com.

AWARDS
Windsor Chamber of Commerce Business Excellence Award
Windsor Tourist and Convention Bureau Ambassador Award
LaJeunesse Historical Preservation Award

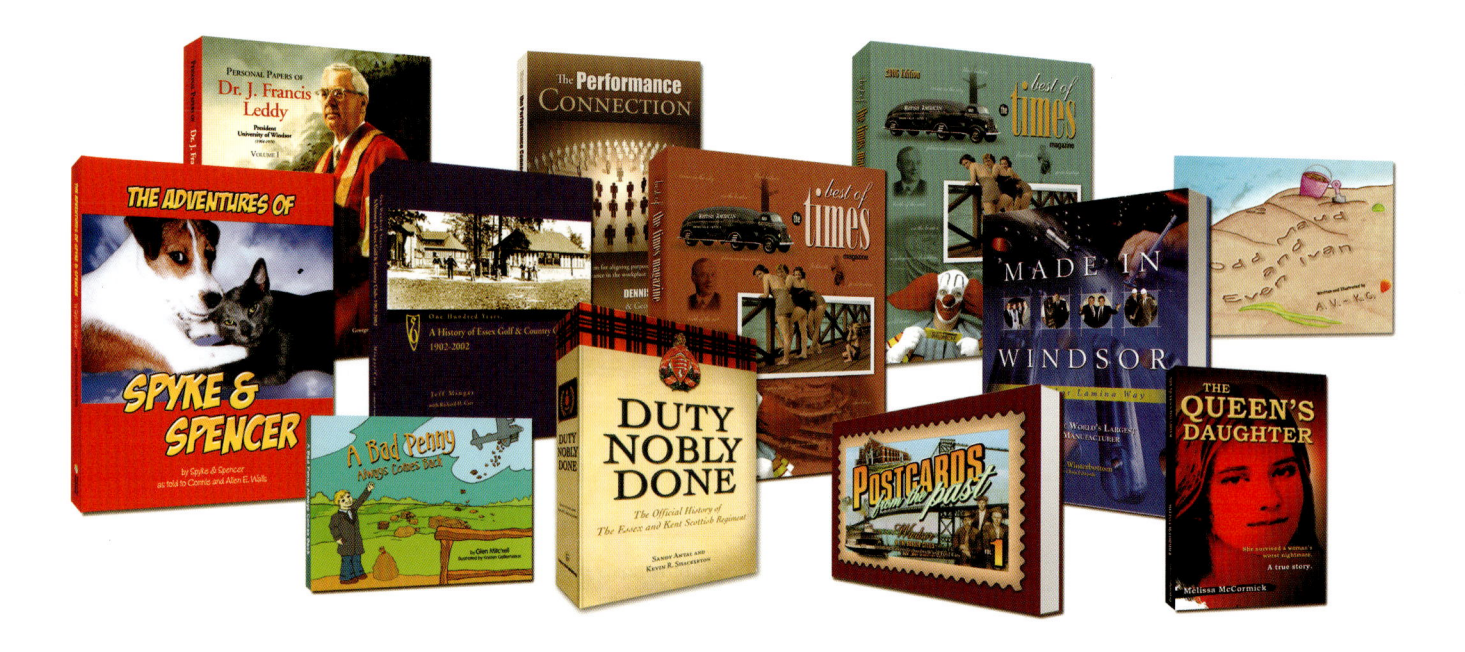

Books By Walkerville Publishing

www.walkerville.com

MADE IN WINDSOR – THE ANCHOR LAMINA WAY (2006)
By Clare Winterbottom with Chris Edwards
Few businesses have achieved the level of success as Windsor, Ontario-based Anchor Lamina Inc. The company's growth was meteoric – from sales of $400,000 to almost $200 million in less than 23 years, despite three major recessions. In 1997, 100% of Anchor Lamina Inc.'s stock was acquired by Harrowston Inc. for an all-time high of $8 per share; this translated into a sale price of over $250 million.

Made In Windsor is the true story of how a highly-motivated workforce grew a company that expanded to 14 factories in three countries, utilizing the most modern equipment and technologies in the industry, with almost 1,000 highly skilled workers.

In 1975, the die set industry was considered past its prime, with few prospects for growth. Undaunted, a group of investors led by Clare E. Winterbottom, purchased troubled Anchor Machine and Manufacturing Ltd. of Mississauga.

This group of entrepreneurs and risk-takers, led by a visionary armed with a dogged determination, succeeded in building the biggest and best die set manufacturer on the planet.
Hard cover with dust jacket, 148 pages, full colour, high quality archival paper

ONE HUNDRED YEARS – A HISTORY OF ESSEX GOLF AND COUNTRY CLUB: 1902-2002 (2002)
By Jeff Mingay with Richard H. Carr
The history of Essex Golf and Country Club reaches back to the early years of the last century. The story of Essex begins with an idea conceived by an intrepid group of Windsor businessmen, who were joined in the mid 1900s by a number of Detroit residents. Their idea was nurtured by founding members and became a reality in 1902. For the club's first 100 years, it was sustained by the tenacity and resolve of members who, even when times were most difficult, were determined their club would not only survive, but prosper.
Hard cover, black and white with full colour; hole by hole descriptions, 94 pages, over 120 photos

PERSONAL PAPERS OF DR. FRANCIS LEDDY (2005)
President of the University of Windsor (1964-1978), Volume 1
Edited by George A. McMahon, Sr.
For over 10 years George McMahon sorted through the personal papers of former University of Windsor President John Francis Leddy to create this intriguing first volume of letters. Dr. Leddy, recipient of 12 honorary doctorates as well as a Nobel Peace Prize nomination, was the first Catholic layman to be appointed president of a Canadian non-denominational university. Leddy presided over the University of Windsor's spectacular growth from 1964-1978.
Soft cover, 280 pages

THE QUEEN'S DAUGHTER (2004)
By Melissa McCormick
On February 12, 1967, six young and beautiful Windsor women prepared for a big night out in Detroit. One did not make it home that night. She was kidnapped and held for 12 hours against her will. This experience was so brutal and frightening she first begged her assailants to kill her, then tricked them into letting her go. 28 years later, Melissa McCormick was finally ready to tell about the night she became "The Queen's Daughter." A true story of hope and inspiration.
Soft cover, 120 pages

THE ADVENTURES OF SPYKE AND SPENCER (2006)
As told to Connie and Allan E. Walls

The first in a series, *The Adventures of Spyke and Spencer* features a real dog and cat who are "brothers." This amusing and endearing book teaches children values such as friendship, honesty, responsibility, compassion and loyalty. It features over 200 photographs of Spyke and Spencer, beginning with their arrival at the home of their "parents" Allen and Connie, their exploration of the world around them and the many friends they make along the way.

Hard cover, 76 pages, full colour

A BAD PENNY ALWAYS COMES BACK (2006)
By Glen Mitchell, Illustrated by Kristen Gallerneaux

This unusual children's book uses simple text and vibrant illustrations to describe the time near the end of World War II when the Royal Canadian Air Force helped feed the starving people of Holland by "bombing" them with food packages. Bad Penny was the first Lancaster bomber used in this dangerous mission dubbed "Operation Manna." Like the old espression, "A bad penny always come back" she always returned from each mission.

Soft cover, 32 pages, full colour

ODD MAUD AND EVAN IVAN (2004)
Written and Illustrated by A.V. – K.C.

Katherine Clark, a Windsor elementary school teacher, has written a series of under-the-sea educational adventures for children. In this lively adventure, the first of the series, a starfish named Maud and an octopus named Ivan take a journey together while teaching the concept of odd and even numbers.

Soft Cover, 24 pages, full-colour

DUTY NOBLY DONE – THE OFFICIAL HISTORY OF THE ESSEX AND KENT SCOTTISH REGIMENT (2006)
By Sandy Antal and Kevin R. Shackleton

This is the first comprehensive look at one of Canada's most storied militia units that spans three centuries. From their origins as the first militia organization in what is now Ontario to the present, the units of Essex and Kent counties have loomed large in the history of their province and nation.

This book goes beyond the "drums and bugles" events and considers the human cost, on and off the battlefield. *Duty Nobly Done* bespeaks the contributions and sacrifices of generations of citizen soldiers who did their duty and their part in forging this Canada.

Hard cover, 864 pages, over 300 photos, 16 full colour pull-out maps

THE PERFORMANCE CONNECTION (2006)
By Dennis DeWilde and Geoff Anderson

Why do some employees do just the right things – time after time? Why do some workers act, while others sit around, waiting for direction? According to authors Dennis DeWilde and Geoff Anderson the answers can be found in their relational connection to their jobs.

Written in a concise and easily understood manner, this how-to book outlines a structure that integrates three simple human needs – purpose, identity, and accountability – into organizational and leadership process. In an era of rapid change, *The Performance Connection* is the perfect book for leaders who face staffing challenges related to both performance and personal growth.

Soft cover, 232 pages

POSTCARDS FROM THE PAST:
Windsor & The Border Cities, including Walkerville, Sandwich, Ojibway and Ford City – featuring the collection of David L. Newman (2005)

It is estimated that by 1913, almost one billion postcards were mailed in the U.S. Cheap and reliable, these missives were often used to set up engagements for the same day.

Due to their compact size, postcards were easy to collect. For David L. Newman of Windsor, Ontario, saving old postcards became a passion. He devoted 23 years towards building a magnificent collection of his city's postcards. More than 290 of them are represented here and offer a fascinating glimpse into this region's rich and colourful history.

Within these pages is a mostly lost world. Pastoral settings, Victorian and Edwardian buildings, idyllic boulevards, ancient automobiles and outdated fashions harken back to "simpler" times. In fact, this book serves as a catalogue of sorts for many fine buildings that fell victim to the wrecker's ball over the last 100 years. "The Border Cities," once encompassing Windsor, Walkerville, Ford City (later East Windsor) and Sandwich, are well represented here.

Each card was researched and catalogued into ten chapters, including one for each Border City, as well as chapters highlighting important stages in Windsor's industrial, urban and cultural development: Downtown Windsor, Ferry Hill, Public Places, Lost Buildings, Crossing the Border, Faces in the Crowd, and Bird's Eye View.

Hard cover with dust jacket, 334 pages, full colour, archive quality paper featuring 291 digitally enhanced, high-quality postcard reproductions

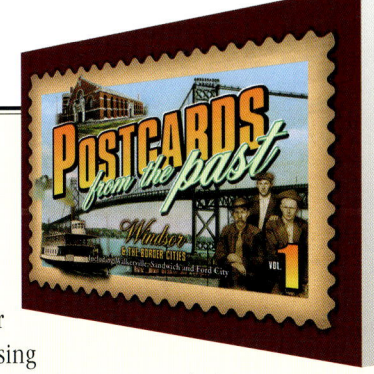

Windsor–Detroit skyline; this recent photo is by renowned local photographer Spike Bell, (PPA Certified, M. Photog., M.P.A.). Spike has won several national awards, including the Governor-General of Canada award, the 125th Anniversary Medal and the H.M. Queen Elizabeth II Golden Jubilee Medal (2003); eight of his pictures reside in the National Archives.

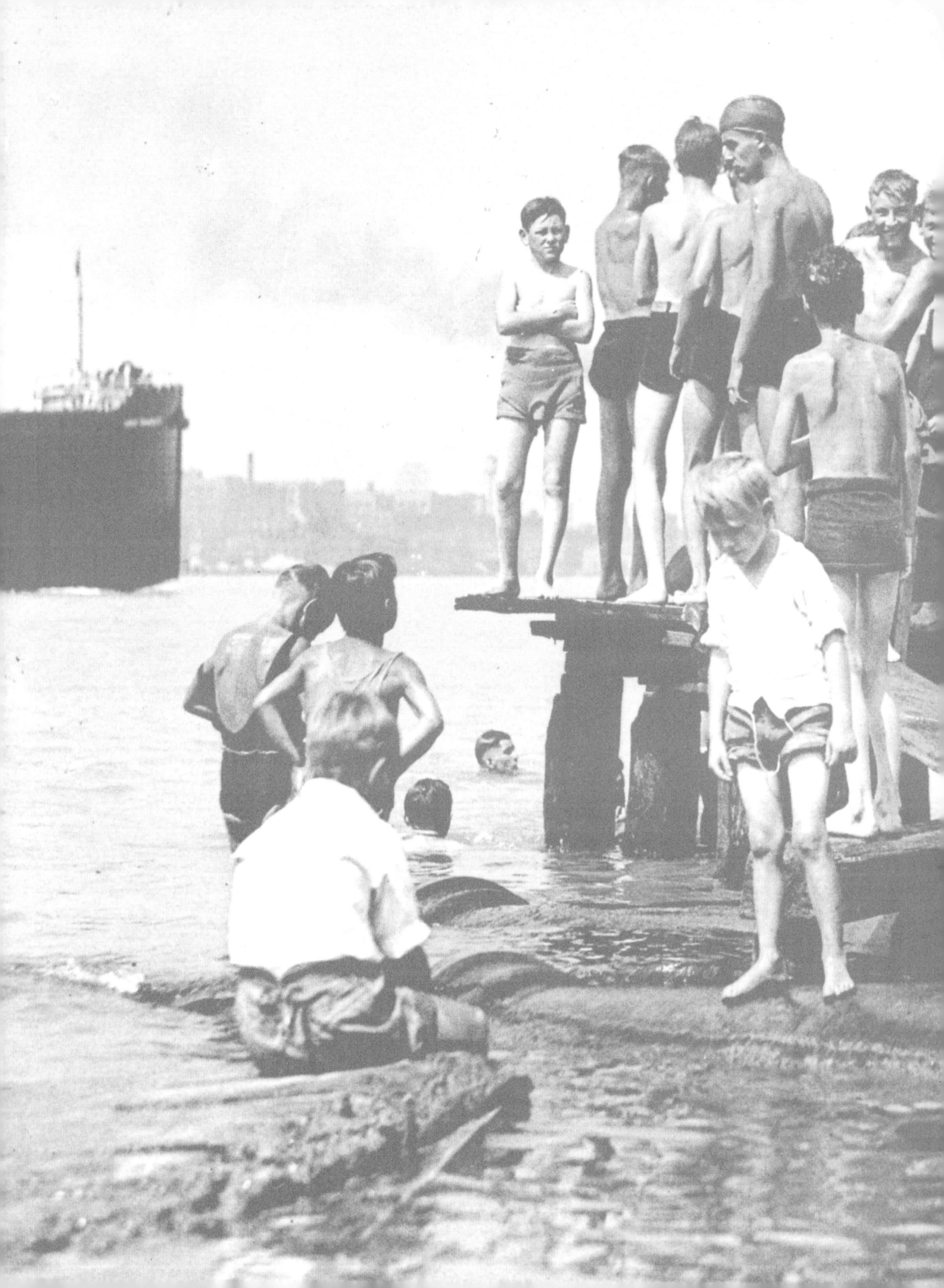